POLITICIANS AND PAMPHLETEERS

To Mum and Dad

Politicians and Pamphleteers

Propaganda During the English Civil Wars
and Interregnum

JASON PEACEY

ASHGATE

Published by
Ashgate Publishing Limited
Gower House
Croft Road
Aldershot
Hants GU11 3HR
England

Ashgate Publishing Company
Suite 420
101 Cherry Street
Burlington, VT 05401-4405
USA

Ashgate website: http://www.ashgate.com

British Library Cataloguing-in-Publication Data
Peacey, Jason
    Politicians and pamphleteers : propaganda during the English Civil Wars and interregnum
    1. Propaganda – England – History – 17th century 2. Pamphlets – England – History –
    17th century 3. Politics in literature – History – 17th century 4. Great Britain – History –
    Civil War, 1642–1649 – Pamphlets 5. Great Britain – History – Civil War, 1642–1649
    6. Great Britain – History – Commonwealth and Protectorate, 1649–1660 7. Great Britain –
    History – Civil War, 1642–1649 – Propaganda 8. Great Britain – Politics and government –
    1642–1660
    I. Title
    320'.014'0942'09032

Library of Congress Cataloging-in-Publication Data
Peacey, Jason.
    Politicians and pamphleteers: propaganda during the English civil wars and interregnum
/ Jason Peacey.
        p. cm.
    Includes bibliographical references and index.
    ISBN 0-7546-0684-8 (alk. paper)
    1. Great Britain – Politics and government – 1642–1660. 2. Politics and literature – Great Britain –
History – 17th century. 3. Pamphlets – Publishing – Great Britain – History – 17th century. 4.
Popular literature – Great Britain – History and criticism. 5. Pamphleteers – Great Britain – History –
17th century. 6. Pamphlets – Great Britain – History – 17th century. 7. Propaganda, British – History
– 17th century. I. Title.

DA406.P43 2003
942.06'28–dc 21   2003045335

ISBN 0 7546 0684 8

Printed on acid-free paper

Typeset in Times New Roman by Bournemouth Colour Press, Parkstone
Printed and bound in Great Britain by MPG Books Ltd, Bodmin, Cornwall.

Contents

Contents

Acknowledgements

This book has taken far too long to complete. I have come to liken the experience of writing it to that of taking a sauna: long, largely uncomfortable, but ultimately rewarding, if only for myself. In the course of its composition, I have accumulated substantial debts to a variety of institutions and organisations, and to a number of individuals. Expressions of thanks to academic libraries are perhaps more commonly uttered than heartfelt. But, as someone who has probably been a reader somewhat demanding of librarians' time, I have genuine grounds for thanking the staff of the rare books room and manuscripts room in the Cambridge University Library, as well as the staff of Duke Humphrey's Library in the Bodleian, and the British Library, as well as to the staff of the Institute of Historical Research, whose library, like so many national treasures, is criminally neglected. I would also like to express my thanks to the staff of the Beinecke Library at Yale, where I was able to spend an enjoyable and profitable month with the assistance of an Osborn fellowship. I must also thank those innumerable world libraries whose staff have helped with my many requests for information, and the British Academy, without whose financial support, in the shape of a postgraduate scholarship, this project could never have been started, let alone completed.

Academically, I have benefited greatly from the comments offered by those who have attended the seminar papers where some of my ideas were given trial outings, often in rather crude manifestations, at Oxford, Cambridge and London, and at conferences in London, New York, Pasadena and Baltimore. The encouragement offered by scholars such as Tom Cogswell, Peter Lake, Ian Gentles, Paul Hammer, Michael Graves, Peter Lindenbaum, Barry Coward, Derek Hirst and Tim Harris has regularly served to boost my enthusiasm at times when it was flagging. I must make special mention of the members of the Seventeenth Century British History seminar at the IHR, and particularly its convenors, Ian Roy, John Miller and Justin Champion. I have also received encouragement from the supervisor of the dissertation from which this work takes its origins, Richard Tuck, as well as from its examiners Austin Woolrych and John Morrill, the latter of whom has offered more assistance, at various stages of my career, than I can ever repay. I have also benefited immensely from the experience of working for the History of Parliament. Having up to fifteen early modernists in one building on a regular basis can only be described as a privilege. However, there are some upon whom I have leaned disproportionately, and who have every reason to be thoroughly bored by this book by now. The frequency with which I have exploited the expertise of, and received references from, Patrick Little, Andrew Barclay and Simon Healy, as well as my editors, John Adamson and Stephen Roberts, is reflected throughout this work, too much so to be spelt out. Special mention has to be made, however, to those many stimulating, heated and not always entirely sober discussions regarding the seventeenth century, on big issues as well as minor details, held with Ariel Hessayon, Elliot Vernon and Phil Baker, and particularly with Sean Kelsey, David Scott and Chris Kyle. Evenings spent with these three in London's pubs have proved far more fruitful than all my time in the famed Cambridge University Library tea room, which I cherish for reasons unconnected with history.

Beyond academia, I must thank those who have kept me sane over the last decade, not least by reminding me of more important things than this book. These include Martin, Paul, Andrew, Dave, Duncan, Trevor, Emma and Annette, as well as my brother, Nathan. Most especially, of course, I want to thank my parents, for unstinting moral, as well as financial, support, and it is to them that this book is dedicated.

Abbreviations

A&O	C. H. Firth & R. S. Rait, eds, *Acts and Ordinances of the Interregnum, 1642–1660* (3 vols, London, 1911)
Abbott, *Cromwell*	W. C. Abbott, *The Writings and Speeches of Oliver Cromwell* (4 vols, Oxford, 1988)
Add.	Additional Manuscript
AHR	*American Historical Review*
BIHR	*Bulletin of the Institute of Historical Research*
BJRL	*Bulletin of John Rylands Library*
BL	British Library, London
Bodl.	Bodleian Library, Oxford
CCSP	O. Ogle, W. H. Bliss, W. D. Macray, and F. J. Routledge, eds, *Calendar of the Clarendon State Papers* (5 vols, Oxford, 1872–1970)
CJ	*Journals of the House of Commons*
CJH	*Canadian Journal of History*
Clarendon State Papers	R. Scrope and T. Monkhouse, eds, *State Papers Collected by Edward, Earl of Clarendon* (3 vols, Oxford, 1767–86)
Clarendon, *History*	E. Hyde, Earl of Clarendon, *The History of the Rebellion and Civil Wars in England* (ed. W. D. Macray, 6 vols, Oxford, 1888)
Clarendon, *Life*	*The Life of Edward, Earl of Clarendon* (3 vols, Oxford, 1827)
CLRO	Corporation of London Record Office
CP	C. H. Firth, ed., *The Clarke Papers* (4 vols, Camden Society, 1891–1901)
CSPD	*Calendar of State Papers Domestic*
CSPI	*Calendar of State Papers Ireland*
CSPV	*Calendar of State Papers Venetian*
CUL	Cambridge University Library

D'Ewes Diary, ed. Coates	W. H. Coates, ed., *The Journal of Sir Simonds D'Ewes* (New Haven, 1942)
D'Ewes Diary, ed. Notestein	W. Notestein, ed., *The Journal of Sir Simonds D'Ewes* (New Haven, 1923)
EHR	*English Historical Review*
Gardiner, *Constitutional Documents*	S. R. Gardiner, ed., *Constitutional Documents of the Puritan Revolution, 1625–1660* (Oxford, 1979)
GCW	S. R. Gardiner, *History of the Great Civil War* (4 vols, Adlestrop, 1987)
GL	Guildhall Library, London
Hartlib Papers	Sheffield University Library, Hartlib Papers
IHS	*Irish Historical Studies*
HJ	*Historical Journal*
HLQ	*Huntington Library Quarterly*
HLRO	House of Lords Record Office
HMC	Historical Manuscripts Commission
HPT	*History of Political Thought*
HR	*Historical Research*
IHR	Institute of Historical Research
JBS	*Journal of British Studies*
JEH	*Journal of Ecclesiastical History*
JHI	*Journal of the History of Ideas*
JMH	*Journal of Modern History*
Laud, *Works*	J. H. Parker, ed., *The Works of … William Laud* (8 vols, Oxford, 1847–60)
Letters and Journals of Robert Baillie	D. Laing (ed.), *The Letters and Journals of Robert Baillie* (3 vols, Edinburgh, 1841–42)
LJ	*Journals of the House of Lords*
LPL	Lambeth Palace Library
Ludlow, *Memoirs*	C. H. Firth, ed., *Memoirs of Edmund Ludlow* (2 vols, Oxford, 1894)
Madan, *Oxford Books*	F. Madan, *Oxford Books* (3 vols, Oxford, 1895–1931)
N&S	C. Nelson and M. Seccombe, *British Newspapers and Periodicals 1641–1700* (New York, 1987)
Nalson, *Impartial Collection*	J. Nalson, *An Impartial Collection* (2 vols, London, 1682)
NP	G. F. Warner, ed., *The Nicholas Papers* (4 vols, Camden Society, 1886–1920)

OPH	*The Parliamentary or Constitutional History of England* (24 vols, London, 1761–63)
P&P	*Past and Present*
Peacey, 'Henry Parker'	J. T. Peacey, 'Henry Parker and parliamentary propaganda in the English civil wars' (Cambridge University PhD, 1994)
Pepys, *Diary*	R. Latham and W. Matthews, eds, *The Diary of Samuel Pepys* (11 vols, London, 1970–83)
PER	*Parliaments, Estates and Representation*
PH	*Parliamentary History*
PHE	*Cobbett's Parliamentary History of England* (36 vols, London, 1806–20)
PJ	W. C. Coates, A. S. Young and V. Snow, eds, *The Private Journals of the Long Parliament* (3 vols, New Haven, 1982–92)
PRO	Public Record Office, Kew
RO	Record Office
Rushworth, *Historical Collections*	J. Rushworth, ed., *Historical Collections of Private Passages of State* (8 vols, London, 1721)
SCH	*Studies in Church History*
SHR	*Scottish Historical Review*
SR	*A Transcript of the Registers of the Worshipful Company of Stationers* (3 vols, London, 1913)
State Trials	T. B. Howell, ed., *A Complete Collection of State Trials* (34 vols, London, 1809–26)
TRHS	*Transactions of the Royal Historical Society*
TSP	T. Birch, ed., *A Collection of the State Papers of John Thurloe* (7 vols, London, 1742)
Whitelocke, *Memorials*	B. Whitelocke, *Memorials of the English Affairs* (4 vols, Oxford, 1853)
Wood, *Athenae*	A. Wood, *Athenae Oxonienses* (ed. P. Bliss, 4 vols, London, 1813–20)

Introduction

The subject of this book is the political and polemical literature of the English civil wars and Interregnum. This material is, in many ways, familiar enough. Most scholars and students are now aware of the vast numbers and bewildering variety of tracts and pamphlets, of all sizes and shapes, which emerged from the presses between 1640 and 1660. The most important sources are now thoroughly and routinely explored, and the authors – whether poets, clerics, journalists, or political theorists – are well known. Where this work differs from other books on the literature of the 1640s and 1650s is in its approach to such tracts and pamphlets, and to their authors. It is as much concerned with *why* books were written as with *what* was contained within them, and it is as much concerned with the processes by which works were conceived and executed, as it is with the ideas and theories developed, or the historical evidence incorporated. Based upon a recognition that there are a number of contexts in which polemical literature can be situated, it seeks to explore one such context which has largely been neglected by scholars of the mid-seventeenth century. This involves recognising that many political tracts combined elements which were timebound as well as timeless, and that in order to gain a full understanding of their nature it is necessary to explore the events to which such works were intimately connected.[1] The approach of this book is to cultivate the hitherto barren ground between historical analyses of political events on the one hand, and literary and intellectual studies of prose in an era of political unrest and upheaval on the other, not least by introducing into the history of the period some of the approaches adopted by scholars of the 'history of the book'.[2]

However, the book is concerned not merely to demonstrate that works can be understood by examining the political context in which they were written, and the local political debates to which they contributed, but also to outline the political forces which operated on the world of publishing during the period, and the exploitation of print by politicians. What this work seeks to do, therefore, is to explore the political history of the book, in terms of the interaction between politics and print, and in order to bring the insights of the 'new bibliography' to bear on the

---

[1] D. Hirst and R. Strier, 'Introduction', in *Writing and Political Engagement in Seventeenth Century England* (Cambridge, 1999), pp. 1–2.

[2] R. Darnton, 'What is the history of books?', in K. E. Carpenter, ed., *Books and Society in History* (New York, 1983); J. Rose, 'The history of books: revised and enlarged', in H. T. Mason, ed., *The Darnton Debate* (Oxford, 1998).

study of the political life and political culture of early modern Britain.[3] The aim is to trace the processes by which propaganda came about; the means of detecting its existence; the ways in which it was produced, distributed and employed; and the nature of relationships between propagandists and politicians. More than merely being concerned to contextualise books, therefore, this work is concerned with propaganda in its strictest sense. This means not simply books produced with the intention of advocating, promulgating and propagating a political message to a public audience. This is what might be called political *polemic*. Rather, *propaganda* is taken to mean polemical works which appeared with the connivance of those political figures whose interests were best served by the existence of such books, tracts and pamphlets.[4] The term 'propaganda' is, of course, problematic, since it was not in general and widespread use during the early modern period. Nevertheless, the phenomenon is unmistakable. In the words of Bob Scribner, the 'extreme linguistic nominalism that asserts that we should not use words for historical phenomena that contemporaries of the time would not have used clearly founders on such an example'.[5] Furthermore, it is possible that the term 'propaganda' would not have confused contemporaries as much as we might assume. The OED dates the use of the word 'propagation' to 1588, the word 'propagating' to John Pory in 1600, and the verb 'to propagate', including beliefs and doctrine, to 1570. In some sense, the term propaganda itself was in circulation, and men such as William Prynne certainly interpreted the Catholic *Congregatio de Propaganda Fide*, founded in 1622 by Pope Gregory XV, as a body involved in propaganda as we would understand it.[6] Contemporaries also appear to have begun to develop the use of the term 'manifesto', or more commonly 'manifest', in the way which we would recognise, and which the OED defines as 'a public declaration or proclamation usually issued by or with the sanction of a sovereign prince or state, or by an individual or body of individuals whose proceedings are of public importance, for the purpose of making known past actions, or explaining the reasons or motives for actions announced as forthcoming'.[7] One prominent pamphleteer of the 1640s, Nathaniel Ward, noted, for example, that 'it were good if states would let people know so much before hand, by some safe-woven manifesto'.[8]

---

[3] For a recent study of political culture in the mid-seventeenth century, see: S. Kelsey, *Inventing a Republic* (Manchester, 1997).

[4] The term propaganda is often used to describe something which runs the two together: S. Murdoch, 'The search for Northern allies: Stuart and Cromwellian propagandists and protagonists in Scandinavia, 1649–60', in B. Taithe and T. Thornton, eds, *Propaganda* (Stroud, 1999); T. Harris, 'Propaganda and public opinion in seventeenth century England', in J. D. Popkin, ed., *Media and Revolution* (Lexington, 1995), p. 51; H. Rusche, 'Prophecies and propaganda, 1641 to 1651', *EHR* 84 (1969); L. B. Wright, 'Propaganda against James I's "appeasement" of Spain', *HLQ* 6 (1943).

[5] R. W. Sribner, *For the Sake of Simple Folk. Popular Propaganda for the German Reformation* (Oxford, 1994), p. 274.

[6] W. Prynne, *Canterburies Doom* (London, 1646), pp. 440–42.

[7] See: Rushworth, *Historical Collections*, i. 308.

[8] N. Ward, *The Simple Cobbler* (London, 1647).

No work has yet attempted to discuss the centrality of print to the political life of the central decades of the seventeenth century. There has yet to be a systematic study, in other words, of the role of the press and propaganda in the political life and political culture of the period. This is somewhat surprising, given the widespread recognition that the political and religious tensions in England in the decades after printing arrived with William Caxton ensured that printing quickly became employed for propaganda purposes, not least since insecure monarchs needed to project a favourable image. From that point on there are many well-known incidents of propaganda, and a significant amount of analysis has been undertaken concerning the extent to which subsequent regimes in the sixteenth century did, or did not, manipulate and exploit the press. Early modern governments were, to a greater or lesser extent, interested in the world of print, and historians have given recognition to the existence and importance of propaganda in England during the sixteenth and early seventeenth century.[9] Furthermore, recent studies of the late seventeenth and early eighteenth century indicate a growing awareness that print was central to political life and political processes.[10] Nevertheless, scholarly attention to early modern propaganda has tended to assume a position of only tangential importance in wider studies of high politics or political literature. Thus, while, historians are alive to the use made of print by politicians, there have been few studies of the processes and practices of propaganda in the seventeenth century. This is particularly true of the historiography of the civil wars and Interregnum. Recent scholars have noted the importance of pamphleteering to the political process, and the fact that books have

---

[9] N. Wheale, *Writing and Society. Literacy, Print and Politics in Britain, 1590–1660* (London, 1999); T. Thornton, 'Propaganda, political communication and the problem of English responses to the introduction of printing', in Taithe and Thornton, eds, *Propaganda*; below, pp. 32–4.

[10] T. Harris, *London Crowds in the Reign of Charles II* (Cambridge, 1987); M. Knights, *Politics and Opinion in Crisis, 1678–81* (Cambridge, 1994); T. Claydon, *William III and the Godly Revolution* (Cambridge, 1996), esp. pp. 64–89; P. Harth, *Pen for a Party. Dryden's Tory Propaganda in its Contexts* (Princeton, 1993); B. Harris, *Politics and the Rise of the Press* (London, 1996); J. A. Winn, *John Dryden and His World* (New Haven, 1987); M. Harris, 'Print and politics in the age of Walpole', in J. Black, ed., *Britain in the Age of Walpole* (Basingstoke, 1984); M. Harris, *London Newspapers in the Age of Walpole* (London, 1987); R. Harris, *A Patriot Press* (Oxford, 1993); T. O'Malley, 'Religion and the newspaper press, 1660–1685: a study of the *London Gazette*', in M. Harris and A. Lee, eds, *The Press in English Society from the Seventeenth to Nineteenth Centuries* (London, 1986); P. B. J. Hyland, 'Liberty and libel: government and the press during the succession crisis in Britain, 1712–1716', *EHR* 101 (1986); S. Targett, 'The premier scribbler himself: Sir Robert Walpole and the management of political opinion', *Studies in Newspaper and Periodical History* (1994); J. O. Richards, *Party Propaganda Under Queen Anne* (Athens, Ga, 1972); L. Schwoerer, 'Propaganda in the revolution of 1688–89', *AHR* 82 (1977); L. Schwoerer, *The Declaration of Rights, 1689* (London, 1981), chap. 5; L. Schwoerer, 'Liberty of the press and public opinion, 1660–1695', in J. R. Jones, ed., *Liberty Secured? Britain Before and After 1688* (Stanford, 1992); G. C. Gibbs, 'Press and public opinion: prospective', in Jones, ed., *Liberty Secured*; W. A. Speck, 'Politics and the press', in G. Holmes, ed., *After the Glorious Revolution* (London, 1969); R. B. Walker, 'The newspaper press in the reign of William III', *HJ* 17 (1974). For an exception, see: J. L. Malcolm, *Caesar's Due* (London, 1983).

both an intellectual and a historical context, and have also recognised instances of political manipulation of the press, but none has made the subject their prime concern.[11] It has, of course, become familiar to see preachers such as Stephen Marshall labelled as 'almost the official spokesman of the parliamentarians', and to recognise authors such as John Milton, Marchamont Nedham, William Prynne and Henry Parker as being parliamentarian propagandists.[12] Nevertheless, little attempt has been made to undertake a systematic study of the motives and methods of civil war propaganda, despite the fact that, as Tom Cogswell has argued, 'there is more than ample evidence to support such an investigation'. Cogswell has also suggested that 'there are few more alluring tracts of historiographical *terrae incognitae* than the role of public relations and propaganda in early Stuart politics', and that 'the dividends for exploration are potentially dazzling'.[13]

For the most important precedents in this area it is necessary to turn to the efforts of scholars of continental history, where much attention has focused upon France, and upon the role of Cardinal Richelieu in the development of propaganda. Jeffrey Sawyer has noted, therefore, that it was during the early seventeenth century that 'the manufacture and dissemination of royal propaganda in pamphlet form was becoming a routine government function'.[14] However, Sawyer is only one of a number of scholars of continental European history during the early modern period who have recognised the centrality of print and propaganda to political culture and the political system, and there are a number of other works which analyse the part which printing presses played in political life, and the processes by which politicians sought to gain control of, and exploit, the print media. Such works seek to identify authors and analyse their relations with politicians and patrons, and to understand how the political elite involved themselves in the mechanics of book production.[15] This book seeks to answer, with

---

[11] W. Lamont, 'Pamphleteering, the Protestant consensus and the English revolution', in R. C. Richardson and G. M. Ridden, eds, *Freedom and the English Revolution* (Manchester, 1986). For example: T. Barnard, 'Planters and policies in Cromwellian Ireland', *P&P* 61 (1973), p. 43; T. Barnard, 'Crises of identity among Irish Protestants, 1641–1685', *P&P* 127 (1990), pp. 51–2, 59–70; B. Worden, *The Rump Parliament* (Cambridge, 1974), pp. 345–63; A. Woolrych, *Commonwealth to Protectorate* (Oxford, 1982), pp. 110, 260; J. S. A. Adamson, 'The baronial context of the English civil wars', *TRHS*, 5th series 40 (1990), p. 108.

[12] C. Hill, *The Bible and the Seventeenth Century Revolution* (London, 1994), p. 303; W. Lamont, *Marginal Prynne, 1600–69* (London, 1963); M. Mendle, *Henry Parker and the English Civil War* (Cambridge, 1995).

[13] T. Cogswell, 'The politics of propaganda. Charles I and the people in the 1620s', *JBS* 29 (1990), pp. 190, 215.

[14] J. K. Sawyer, *Printed Poison. Pamphlet Propaganda, Faction Politics and the Public Sphere in Early Seventeenth Century France* (Berkeley, 1990), p. 25.

[15] H. J. Martin, *Print, Power, and People in 17th-Century France* (trans. D. Gerard, London, 1993); C. E. Harline, *Pamphlets, Printing, and Political Culture in the Early Dutch Republic* (Dordrecht, 1987); J. M. Hayden, 'The uses of political pamphlets: the example of 1614–15 in France', *CJH* 21 (1986); T. Kaiser, 'The Abbe de Saint-Pierre, public opinion, and the reconstitution of the French Monarchy', *JMH* 55 (1983); J. Klaits, *Printed Propaganda under Louis XIV: Absolute*

regard to political literature produced in England, the kind of questions posed by Craig Harline in his study of pamphleteering in the Dutch republic:

> Who wrote pamphlets and why? For whom were they intended? How and by whom were pamphlets brought to press and distributed, and what does this reveal? Why did their numbers increase so greatly? Who read them? How were pamphlets different from other media?[16]

It is in the hope of providing a study of English print and polemic in the seventeenth century with which to complement such work that this book is undertaken.

Before outlining the strategy adopted in the chapters which follow, however, it is necessary to discuss in more detail the historiographical traditions and trends from which this work seeks both to differ and to learn. Scholarship regarding books and authors in the early modern period can be shown to fall into six more or less distinct strands, all of which have their strengths and weaknesses, and all of which can be incorporated in some way into this project.

Early modern historiography regarding political and religious texts has traditionally been dominated by analyses of political thought, and of intellectual and religious history, in terms of the ideas and theories developed. Scholars have been interested, therefore, in both the sermons and the political texts of the civil wars and Interregnum, and in the most prominent exponents of each form.[17] Attention has obviously been caught by canonical authors – such

---

Monarchy and Public Opinion (Princeton, 1976); H. M. Solomon, *Public Welfare, Science and Propaganda in Seventeenth Century France* (Princeton, 1972); H. M. Solomon, 'The *Gazette* and Antistatist propaganda: the medium of print in the first half of the seventeenth century', *CJH* 9 (1974); J. R. Censer, *The French Press in the Age of Enlightenment* (London, 1994); C. Todd, *Political Bias, Censorship and the Dissolution of the 'Official' Press in Eighteenth Century France* (Lampeter, 1991); L. F. Parmelee, *Good Newes from Fraunce* (Rochester, NY, 1996); G. Ianziti, *Humanistic Historiography Under the Sforzas. Politics and Propaganda in Fifteenth Century Milan* (Oxford, 1988); N. Z. Davis, 'Printing and the people', in *Society and Culture in Early Modern France* (London, 1987); B. Richardson, *Printing, Writers, and Readers in Renaissance Italy* (Cambridge, 1999); D. B. Smith, 'Francois Hotman', *SHR* 13 (1916).

[16] Harline, *Pamphlets, Printing and Political Culture*, p. ix.

[17] J. W. Allen, *English Political Thought, 1603–1644* (London, 1967); J. P. Sommerville, *Politics and Ideology in England, 1603–1640* (London, 1986); C. C. Weston and J. R. Greenberg, *Subjects and Sovereigns* (Cambridge, 1981); D. Wootton, ed., *Divine Right and Democracy* (Harmondsworth, 1986); M. A. Judson, *The Crisis of the Constitution* (London, 1988); L. A. Ferrell and P. McCullough, eds, *The English Sermon Revised* (Manchester, 2000); P. Zagorin, *A History of Political Thought in the English Revolution* (New York, 1966); Z. Fink, *The Classical Republicans* (Chicago, 1962); W. H. Greenleaf, *Order, Empiricism and Politics* (Oxford, 1964); J. A. W. Gunn, *Politics and the Public Interest* (London, 1969); J. C. Davis, 'Radicalism in a traditional society: the evaluation of radical thought in the English commonwealth, 1649–1660', *HPT* 3 (1982); G. Schochet, 'The English revolution in the history of political thought', in B. Y. Kunze and D. D. Brautigam, eds, *Court, Country and Culture* (Rochester, NY, 1992); R. Eccleshall, *Order, Reason and Politics* (Oxford, 1978); G. Burgess, *Absolute Monarchy and the Stuart Constitution* (New Haven, 1996); G. Burgess, *The Politics of the Ancient Constitution* (Basingstoke, 1992); R. Tuck, *Natural Rights Theories* (Cambridge, 1979);

as Henry Parker, John Milton, Henry Ferne and Charles Herle, as well as
Thomas Hobbes and James Harrington – and by canonical texts such as the
Areopagitica and the *Eikon Basilike*.[18] However, it is also true that a number of
'lesser' figures have received scholarly treatment, most recently and most
notably Marchamont Nedham.[19] There is also a long tradition of exploring the

---

R. Tuck, *Philosophy and Government, 1572–1651* (Cambridge, 1993); B. Worden, 'Classical
republicanism and the Puritan revolution', in H. Lloyd Jones, V. Pearl and B. Worden, eds, *History and
Imagination* (London, 1981); R. Zaller, 'The figure of the tyrant in English revolutionary thought', *JHI*
54 (1993); J. M. Wallace, 'The Engagement controversy, 1649–1652', *Bulletin of the New York Public
Library* 68 (1964); M. Mendle, 'The Great Council of Parliament and the first ordinances: the
constitutional theory of the civil war', *JBS* 31 (1992); G. Burgess, 'Usurpation, obligation and
obedience in the thought of the Engagement controversy', *HJ* 29 (1986); J. P. Sommerville, 'History
and theory: the Norman Conquest in early Stuart political thought', *Political Studies* 34 (1986); J. H.
Burns and M. Goldie, eds, *The Cambridge History of Political Thought, 1450–1700* (Cambridge,
1991); N. Phillipson and Q. Skinner, eds, *Political Discourse in Early Modern Britain* (Cambridge,
1993).

[18] Mendle, *Henry Parker*; M. Mendle, 'The ship money case, *The Case of Shipmony*, and the
development of Henry Parker's parliamentary absolutism', *HJ* 32 (1989); L. B. Knight, 'Crucifixion
or apocalypse? Refiguring the *Eikon Basilike*', in D. B. Hamilton and R. Strier, eds, *Religion,
Literature and Politics in Post Reformation England, 1540–1688* (Cambridge, 1996); L. Potter,
'Royal actor as royal martyr: the *Eikon Basilike* and the literary scene in 1649', in G. J. Schochet,
ed., *Restoration, Ideology and Revolution* (Washington, 1990); J. Sanderson, 'The *Answer to the
Nineteen Propositions* revisited', *Political Studies* 32 (1984); M. Judson, 'Henry Parker and the
theory of parliamentary sovereignty', in *Essays in History and Political Theory in Honour of
Charles Howard McIlwain* (Cambridge, Mass., 1936); W. K. Jordan, *Men of Substance* (Chicago,
1942); R. Tuck, '"The ancient law of freedom": John Selden and the civil war', in J. Morrill, ed.,
Reactions to the English Civil War, 1642–1649 (Basingstoke, 1982); D. Armitage, A. Himy and Q.
Skinner, eds, *Milton and Republicanism* (Cambridge, 1995); J. P. Sommerville, *Thomas Hobbes:
Political Ideas in Historical Context* (Basingstoke, 1992); R. Tuck, *Hobbes* (Oxford, 1989); G.
Burgess, 'Contexts for the writing and publication of Hobbes's *Leviathan*', *HPT* 11 (1990); J. H.
Franklin, *John Locke and the Theory of Sovereignty* (Cambridge, 1981); B. Worden, 'Harrington's
'Oceana': origins and aftermath, 1651–1660', in D. Wootton, ed., *Republicanism, Liberty and
Commercial Society, 1649–1776* (Stanford, 1994); B. Worden, 'James Harrington and the
commonwealth of Oceana, 1656', in Wootton, ed., *Republicanism*; J. G. A. Pocock, 'James
Harrington and the good old cause: a study of the ideological context of his writings', *JBS* 10 (1970);
Q. Skinner, 'Conquest and consent: Thomas Hobbes and the Engagement controversy', in G. Aylmer,
ed., *The Interregnum* (Basingstoke, 1972); Q. Skinner, 'The ideological context of Hobbes's political
thought', *HJ* 9 (1966); J. P. Sommerville, 'John Selden, the law of nature, and the origins of
government', *HJ* 27 (1984).

[19] F. S. Allis, 'Nathaniel Ward: constitutional draftsman', *Essex Institute Historical Collections* 120
(1984); R. E. Mayers, '"Real and practicable, not imaginary and notional": Sir Henry Vane, *A Healing
Question* and the problems of the protectorate', *Albion* 27 (1995); N. von Maltzahn, 'Henry Neville and
the art of the possible: a republican *Letter Sent to General Monk* (1660)', *Seventeenth Century* 7
(1992); D. Nobbs, 'Philip Nye on church and state', *Cambridge Historical Journal* 5 (1935); R.
Greaves, 'William Sprigg and the Cromwellian revolution', *HLQ* 34 (1971); D. Woolf, 'Conscience,
constancy and ambition in the career and writings of James Howell', in J. Morrill, P. Slack and D.
Woolf, eds, *Public Duty and Private Conscience in Seventeenth Century England* (Oxford, 1993); J.
Raymond, 'John Streater and *The Grand Politick Informer*', *HJ* 41 (1998); N. Smith, 'Popular
republicanism in the 1650s: John Streater's "heroick mechanicks"', in Armitage, Himy and Skinner,
eds, *Milton and Republicanism*; D. Wootton, 'From rebellion to revolution: the crisis of the winter of

radical literature and thought of the seventeenth century, and the writings of those on the fringes of political and religious debates.[20] More recently, attention has begun to become focused upon civil war political rhetoric.[21] In recent decades, of course, scholarship relating to authors and authorship in the early modern period has been profoundly influenced by 'new historicism', and intellectual historians have become much more sensitive to 'context', 'authorial intention' and the importance of contemporary reception and perception for establishing 'meaning'. Texts of political theory are no longer studied simply in terms of the ideas which they contain, and such ideas are no longer examined as if propositions of timeless truths.[22] Nevertheless, the context explored has tended to be an intellectual, rather than a political one, and authors' aims are assumed to have been intellectual, philosophical and theoretical, rather than

---

1642/3 and the origins of civil war radicalism', *EHR* 105 (1990); B. Worden, 'Marchamont Nedham and the beginnings of English republicanism, 1649–1656', in Wootton, ed., *Republicanism*; B. Worden, 'Milton and Marchamont Nedham', in Armitage, Himy and Skinner, eds, *Milton and Republicanism*; B. Worden, '"Wit in a roundhead": the dilemma of Marchamont Nedham', in S. D. Amussen and M. A. Kishlansky, eds, *Political Culture and Cultural Politics in Early Modern England* (Manchester, 1995); M. P. Weinzierl, 'Parliament and the army in England, 1659: constitutional thought and the struggle for control', *PER* 2 (1982); J. Coffey, *Politics, Religion, and the British Revolutions: the Mind of Samuel Rutherford* (Cambridge, 1997); J. Coffey, 'Samuel Rutherford and the political thought of the Scottish covenanters', in J. R. Young, ed., *Celtic Dimensions of the British Civil Wars* (Edinburgh, 1997); J. D. Ford, 'Lex, rex iusto posita: Samuel Rutherford on the origins of government', in R. A. Mason, ed., *Scots and Britons* (Cambridge, 1994); Jordan, *Men of Substance*; J. Daly, 'John Bramhall and the theoretical problems of royalist moderation', *JBS* 11 (1971); W. Epstein, 'Judge David Jenkins and the great civil war', *Journal of Legal History* 3 (1982); M. Nutkiewicz, 'A rapporteur of the English civil war: the courtly politics of James Howell', *CJH* 25 (1990); J. Sanderson, 'Phillip Hunton's appeasement', *HPT* 3 (1982); J. Sanderson, 'Serpent Salve, 1643: the royalism of John Bramhall', *JEH* 25 (1974); I. M. Smart, 'An interim period in royalist political writing, 1647–8', *Durham University Journal* 76 (1983); J. F. Wilson, 'Another look at John Canne', *Church History* 33 (1964).

[20] F. D. Dow, *Radicalism in the English Revolution, 1640–1660* (Oxford, 1985); C. Hill, *The World Turned Upside Down. Radical Ideas During the English Revolution* (Harmondsworth, 1975); G. Aylmer, *The Levellers and the English Revolution* (London, 1975); H. Shaw, *The Levellers* (London, 1968); W. Haller, ed., *Tracts on Liberty in the Puritan Revolution, 1638–47* (2 vols, New York, 1965); J. F. McGregor and B. Reay, eds, *Radical Religion in the English Revolution* (Oxford, 1984); J. R. McMichael and B. Taft, eds, *The Writings of William Walwyn* (London, 1989); B. Capp, *The Fifth Monarchy Men* (London, 1972); W. K. Judson, *The Development of Religious Toleration in England, 1640–1660* (London, 1938); P. Zagorin, 'The authorship of *Mans Mortalitie*', *The Library*, 5th series 5 (1950); B. R. White, 'Henry Jessey in the great rebellion', in R. Buick Knox, ed., *Reformation, Conformity and Dissent* (London, 1977); A. L. Morton, *The World of the Ranters* (London, 1970); G. Aylmer, 'Collective mentalities in mid-seventeenth century England III: varities of radicalism', *TRHS*, 5th series 38 (1988); T. Sippell, 'The testimony of Joshua Sprigge', *The Journal of the Friends Historical Society* 38 (1946).

[21] E. Skerpan, *The Rhetoric of Politics in the English Revolution, 1642–1660* (London, 1992); B. Donagan, 'Casuistry and allegiance in the English civil war', in Hirst and Strier, eds, *Writing and Political Engagement*.

[22] J. G. A. Pocock, 'The history of political thought: a methodological enquiry', in P. Laslett and W. G. Runciman, eds, *Philosophy, Politics and Society*, 2nd series (Oxford, 1962); J. Tully, ed., *Meaning and Context. Quentin Skinner and his Critics* (Oxford, 1988).

polemical and propagandistic.[23] The personal and political lives of authors have tended to be studied in a fairly cursory manner, and few works have sought to interpret non-intellectual motivations for the composition and publication of books and pamphlets, or the interaction of political writers with the day-to-day political life of the times in which they lived.[24] Even studies of political writers which have recognised that their subject was heavily involved in political machinations as well as political thought have arguably concentrated on the latter at the expense of the former.[25] Part of the problem with assessing polemical literature along intellectual lines, and in terms of intellectual contexts, is that the skills of theorists and propagandists were very different, and it would be misleading either to assess the importance of polemic, or to judge the quality of propaganda, in terms of its ideas and expression, rather than in terms of its ability to fulfil particular political functions at specific moments.[26] This has arguably been a less serious problem for scholars of early modern sermons, who have clearly been alive to both the political content and implications of sermon texts when considered within political contexts, and who have also been alive to the need to address the circumstances surrounding the preaching of particular sermons, in terms of their sponsors, timing, and the location in which they were preached.[27]

Aside from intellectual historians, the study of political texts during the early modern period has been dominated by scholars of literature, and the most important literary historians have fundamentally re-evaluated the complexity of literary forms in the seventeenth century. Their historicist sensibilities and sensitivity to context are reflected in the desire to detect topicality, and to analyse political messages in literary works. Furthermore, while studies of civil war literature continue to be dominated by Andrew Marvell and John Milton, there is a long tradition of exploring other less well-known authors, and works of both an

---

[23] D. Norbook, 'Levelling poetry: George Wither and the English revolution, 1642–1649', *English Literary Renaissance* 21 (1991).

[24] R. Ashcraft, *Revolutionary Politics and John Locke's Two Treatises of Government* (Princeton, 1986); J. Scott, *Algernon Sidney and the English Republic, 1623–1677* (Cambridge, 1988); J. Scott, *Algernon Sidney and the Restoration Crisis, 1677–1683* (Cambridge, 1991); M. Goldie, 'John Locke's circle and James II', *HJ* 35 (1992).

[25] Mendle, *Henry Parker*; 'M. Mendle, 'Henry Parker: the public's privado', in G. J. Schochet, ed., *Religion, Resistance and Civil War* (Washington, 1990). But, see: J. Gurney, 'George Wither and Surrey politics, 1642–1649', *Southern History* 19 (1997).

[26] G. Aylmer, 'Collective mentalities in mid-seventeenth century England II: royalist attitudes', *TRHS*, 5th series 37 (1987), pp. 19–20; G. Bowler, 'Marian protestants and the idea of violent resistance to tyranny', in P. Lake and M. Dowling, eds, *Protestantism and the National Church in Sixteenth Century England* (London, 1987).

[27] G. Davies, 'English political sermons, 1603–1640', *HLQ* (1939); J. F. Wilson, *Pulpit in Parliament, Puritanism During the English Civil Wars 1640–1648* (Princeton, 1969); H. Trevor-Roper, 'The Fast sermons of the Long Parliament', in *Religion, the Reformation and Social Change* (London, 1973); Ferrell and McCullough, eds, *English Sermon Revised*; P. McCullough, *Sermons at Court: Politics and Religion in Elizabethan and Jacobean Preaching* (Cambridge, 1998).

ephemeral and a substantial nature.[28] As with intellectual historians, the textual studies of literary analysts are useful assistants in the process of attributing tracts to specific authors, and thus in enabling a better appreciation of their work, thought and careers.[29] Literary scholars have also proved more willing than most to unearth biographical information relating to their subjects, particularly figures such as George Wither and John Milton.[30] Furthermore, it is of unquestionable value to study the political status and functions of literature, given that, under conditions of heavy censorship, literature could be used to deliver coded messages.[31] However, as historians are only too willing to point out, literary scholars often have a rather inadequate understanding of the political contexts in

---

[28] D. Norbrook, *Poetry, Rhetoric and Politics, 1627–1660* (Cambridge, 1999); D. Norbrook, '*The Masque of Truth*: court entertainment and international Protestant politics in the early Stuart period', *Seventeenth Century* 1 (1986); N. Smith, *Literature and Revolution in England, 1640–1660* (New Haven, 1994); D. Norbrook, *Writing the English Republic* (Cambridge, 1999); M. Wilding, *Dragons Teeth. Literature in the English Revolution* (Oxford, 1987); S. Zwicker, *Lines of Authority. Politics and English Literary Culture, 1649–1689* (London, 1993); S. Wiseman, *Drama and Politics in the English Civil War* (Cambridge, 1998); K. Sharpe and S. Zwicker, eds, *Politics of Discourse. The Literature and History of Seventeenth Century England* (Berkeley, 1987); T. N. Corns, *Uncloistered Virtue. English Political Literature 1640–1660* (Oxford, 1992); R. Wilcher, *The Writing of Royalism, 1628–1660* (Cambridge, 2001); J. Raymond, 'Framing liberty: Marvell's *First Anniversary* and the Instrument of Government', *HLQ* 62 (1999); C. Condren, 'Andrew Marvell as polemicist: his account of the growth of popery and arbitrary government', in C. Condren and A. D. Cousins, eds, *The Political Identity of Andrew Marvell* (Aldershot, 1990); W. Lamont, 'The religion of Andrew Marvell', ibid.; D. Hirst, '"That sober liberty": Marvell's Cromwell in 1654', in J. M. Wallace, ed., *The Golden and the Brazen World* (Berkeley, Ca., 1985); J. M. Wallace, *Destiny His Choice* (Cambridge, 1980); T. Healy, '"Dark all without it knits": vision and authority in Marvell's *Upon Appleton House*', in T. Healy and J. Sawday, eds, *Literature and the English Civil War* (Cambridge, 1990); D. Norbrook, 'Marvell's 'Horatian Ode' and the politics of genre', ibid.; F. Barker, 'In the wars of truth: violence, true knowledge and power in Milton and Hobbes', ibid.; T. N. Corns, '"Some rousing motions": the plurality of Miltonic ideology', ibid.; N. H. Keeble, ed., *The Cambridge Companion to Writing of the English Revolution* (Cambridge, 2001); A. Pritchard, '*Abuses Stript and Whipt* and Wither's imprisonment', *Review of English Studies*, new series 14 (1963); A. Pritchard, 'George Wither: the poet as prophet', *Studies in Philology* 59 (1962); A. Pritchard, 'George Wither's quarrel with the Stationers: an anonymous reply to *The Schollers Purgatory*', *Studies in Philology* 16 (1963); D. Norbrook, 'Safest in storms: George Wither in the 1650s', in D. Margolies and M. Joannou, eds, *Heart of the Heartless World* (London, 1995). See also: J. Goldberg, *James I and the Politics of Literature* (London, 1983); V. J. Scattergood, *Politics and Poetry in the Fifteenth Century* (London, 1971); J. N. King, *English Reformation Literature* (Princeton, 1982); D. Bevington, *Tudor Drama and Politics* (Cambridge, Mass., 1968).

[29] L. H. Kendall, 'An unrecorded prose pamphlet by George Wither', *HLQ* 20 (1957); W. Lamont, 'Prynne, Burton and the Puritan triumph', *HLQ* 27 (1963–64); Mendle, *Henry Parker*. See: H. Love, *Attributing Authorship* (Cambridge, 2002).

[30] A. Pritchard, 'George Wither and the Somers Islands', *N&Q* 206 (1961); J. M. French, 'George Wither in prison', *Publications of the Modern Language Association* 45 (1930); C. S. Hensley, *The Later Career of George Wither* (The Hague, 1969); J. M. French, *Life Records of John Milton* (5 vols, New Brunswick, 1949–58).

[31] D. Hirst, 'The politics of literature in the English republic', *Seventeenth Century* 5 (1990), p. 133. See: K. Sharpe, 'The politics of literature in renaissance England', in *Politics and Ideas in Early Stuart England* (London, 1989).

which to place their chosen texts.[32] Indeed, what is lacking is not merely detailed knowledge of political contexts, but also information relating to the circumstances in which individual authors were operating, and in which their works appeared.[33] So long as tracts and pamphlets are read, cited and employed without being contextualised, scholars will only be able to tell part of the story. Thus, John Pocock's recent analysis of the famous *History* written by Thomas May can be considered to be constrained by a lack of contextual evidence relating to May's involvement in factional parliamentarian politics during the 1640s. A more detailed awareness of the archival evidence relating to May could have been used, in other words, in order to solve some of the issues left unresolved in Pocock's account.[34]

A third strand in the scholarship relating to early modern polemic concerns literary patronage, and many scholars are clearly aware that authors were implicated in immediate social relations, and that it is necessary to examine the connections between writers, publishers and patrons.[35] Patronage of high art and literature was intrinsic to the lives of men schooled in humanism, and to the late renaissance in general, and has received much attention as a result, whether in terms of monarchs (and their consorts), ministers, or leading peers.[36] Furthermore, such scholarship reveals that there were well-established precedents for literary humanists turning their skills to the benefit of their patrons, and doing so in a political manner.[37] Although such forms of patronage were probably in decline, at least some figures who were to become prominent writers and pamphleteers during the 1640s and 1650s had received what might be regarded as a traditional form of patronage, in which a wealthy and powerful grandee sought to assist a talented author, and in which authors looked to grand patrons for support.[38] Perhaps the pre-eminent example of the survival of

---

[32] K. Sharpe, 'Religion, rhetoric and revolution in seventeenth century England', *HLQ* 57 (1995), p. 277.

[33] see: G. H. Turnbull, 'John Hall's letters to Samuel Hartlib', *Review of English Studies*, new series 4 (1953).

[34] J. G. A. Pocock, 'Thomas May and the narrative of the civil war', in Hirst and Strier, eds, *Writing and Political Engagement*.

[35] A. F. Marotti, 'Patronage, poetry and print', in *Politics, Patronage and Literature in England, 1558–1658* (Yearbook of English Studies, 21, 1991) p. 1; P. Thomson, 'The literature of patronage, 1580–1630', *Essays in Criticism* 2 (1952), p. 277.

[36] H. S. Bennett, *English Books and Readers, 1603 to 1640* (Cambridge, 1970), pp. 23–39; E. Rosenberg, *Leicester: Patron of Letters* (New York, 1955); J. A. van Dorsten, *Poets, Patrons and Professors. Sir Philip Sidney, Daniel Rogers, and the Leiden Humanists* (London, 1962); J. K. McConica, *English Humanists and Reformation Politics* (Oxford, 1965), pp. 44–75, 200–234; J. A. van Dorsten, 'Sidney and Languet', *HLQ* 29 (1966); D. Howarth, ed., *Art and Patronage in the Caroline Courts* (Cambridge, 1993); Parmelee, *Good Newes from Fraunce*, pp. 43–4.

[37] D. R. Carlson, *English Humanist Books. Writers and Patrons, Manuscript and Print, 1475–1525* (Toronto, 1993), pp. 6–7.

[38] P. J. Voss, 'Books for sale: advertising and patronage in late Elizabethan England', *Sixteenth Century Journal* 29 (1998); A. Fox, 'The complaint of poetry for the death of liberality: the decline of literary patronage in the 1590s', in J. Guy, ed., *The Reign of Elizabeth I* (Cambridge, 1995); P. Lindenbaum, 'John Milton and the republican mode of literary production', *Yearbook of English Studies* 2 (1991).

literary patronage is provided by the poet, Thomas May, whose talents were nurtured under the care of the Earl of Dorset, whose favours May willingly acknowledged. May was a well-established writer by the time that Dorset recommended him to the Lord Mayor of London in 1637, as being an 'honest and deserving' candidate for the office of City chronicler.[39] Another leading member of the peerage, the Earl of Pembroke, has also been revealed as someone who was eager to advance his literary clients, by attempting to secure their appointment as Masters of the Revels.[40] The nature of 'patronage' in the early modern period is clearly essential to a study such as this, and it will obviously be necessary to analyse the nature of the relationships which existed between those individuals who became the pamphleteers of the civil wars and Interregnum, and those who acted as political leaders. It will be necessary to ascertain, in other words, whether they were 'clients' of 'patrons', and the basis on which patronage was given and received. It will be necessary to explore the social and cultural world of the author, and his/her connection with patrons and politicians.[41] It will also be necessary, however, to recognise that relationships were more complex than those of a 'patron' and his 'client'. Few individuals can neatly be categorised as being either a patron or a client, and most seem to have operated in a world in which individual relationships were only tiny parts of a wider nexus which incorporated networks based on family, friends and associates, and networks situated in local, national and international communities, and in the world of education, administration, government, the church and business. In order to understand the world of the polemical author in the seventeenth century, therefore, it is necessary to understand court culture and composition, gentry society, public administration, political life and the world of commerce. It is necessary to recognise that individuals were bound together by ties of mutual obligation, and that although there were many individual acts of patronage, such patronage was not always conferred upon an individual as part of a process in which they became a 'client', who subsequently served their 'patron'. Networks were based upon ideas of collegiality and reciprocity, mutual aid and mutual benefit.[42] Contextualising polemical authors, therefore, will require examination of their families, friendships and local communities, and acts of patronage from which they had benefited, as well as exploration of the arenas in which the operation of patronage networks can be detected, and in which contacts were forged, and relationships developed.[43]

---

[39] D. L. Smith, 'The political career of Edward Sackville, 4th Earl of Dorset' (Cambridge University PhD, 1990), pp. 169–70.

[40] R. Dutton, 'Patronage, politics, and the Master of the Revels, 1622–1640: The case of Sir John Astley', *English Literary Renaissance* 20 (1990).

[41] R. Darnton, *The Literary Underground of the Old Regime* (Cambridge, Mass., 1982), p. 2; E. H. Miller, *The Professional Writer in Elizabethan England* (Cambridge, Mass., 1959), pp. 1–26.

[42] L. L. Peck, 'Benefits, brokers and beneficiaries: the culture of exchange in seventeenth century England', in Kunze and Brautigam, eds, *Court, Country and Culture*; T. Webster, *Godly Clergy in Early Stuart England* (Cambridge, 1997); BL, Add. 70002, fos. 80, 223.

[43] I. Morgan, *Prince Charles' Puritan Chaplain* (London, 1957); M. Dever, 'Richard Sibbes'

The perils and the pitfalls of scholarship which seeks to understand literature in terms of both its political topicality and aristocratic patronage can be demonstrated through recent examinations of early Stuart theatre. Attempts have been made not merely to detect political messages, both courtly and oppositional, in familiar works by authors such as Thomas Middleton and Philip Massinger, but also to contextualise such works in terms of the positions of authors and their patrons, and in terms of the motives for, and timing of, performances. However, as a number of historians have sought to stress, such work provides a 'cautionary tale' about the need for far greater thoroughness, particularly in terms of historical contextualisation.[44] However, those in the best position to understand the political context of polemical literature are not always interested in such works. While recent historical studies have revolutionised our understanding of the political machinations of the period, scholars such as Kevin Sharpe have 'wondered if the entire notion of an early modern government engaging in propaganda is not anachronistic', and even those more sympathetic to the idea of analysing texts in this way, such as Cogswell, have reflected that 'this question has never seriously been considered in early Stuart history'.[45] Indeed, it is possible that the tendency to ignore pamphlets and pamphleteering represents a particular failure of 'revisionist' scholarship, which is only now coming to be rectified. Scholars are only just beginning to demonstrate awareness that, since a somewhat different picture of political and religious consensus and conflict emerges from contemporary pamphlet literature than from high political sources, it is of profound importance to understand the nature and culture of polemical print in the period.[46] Nevertheless, while the best historians now exploit contemporary pamphlets as a valuable source of evidence relating to political events, and as a

---

(Cambridge University PhD, 1993), pp. 42–86; M. J. Condick, 'The life and works of John Bastwick (1595–1654)' (University of London PhD, 1983); K. L. Sprunger, *The Learned Doctor William Ames* (Urbana, 1972).

[44] J. Limon, *Dangerous Matter. English Drama and Politics in 1623/24* (Cambridge, 1986); G. Parry, 'The politics of the Jacobean masque', in J. R. Mulryne and M. Shewring, eds, *Theatre and Government under the Early Stuarts* (Cambridge, 1993); M. Butler, 'Reform or reverence? The politics of the Caroline masque', ibid.; M. Heinemann, 'Drama and opinion in the 1620s: Middleton and Massinger', ibid.; M. Butler, 'Politics and the masque: *The Triumph of Peace*', *Seventeenth Century* 2 (1987); M. Butler, 'Politics and the masque: *Salmacida Spolia*', in Healy and Sawday, eds, *Literature and the English Civil War*; T. H. Howard-Hill, 'Political interpretations of Middleton's *Game at Chess* (1624)', *Yearbook of English Studies* 21 (1991); T. Cogswell, 'Thomas Middleton and the court, 1624: *A Game at Chess* in context', *HLQ* 47 (1984), p. 284. See also K. Sharpe, 'Court and communication', *HJ* 25 (1982), pp. 737–8, and the reviews of Heinemann by Robert Ashton and Christopher Haigh: *History* 65 (1980), p. 484; *EHR* 98 (1983), pp. 194–5.

[45] K. Sharpe, *Criticism and Compliment* (Cambridge, 1987), pp. 3–4; Cogswell, 'Politics of propaganda', pp. 190, 215.

[46] Harris, 'Propaganda and public opinion', p. 48; P. Lake, 'Constitutional consensus and Puritan opposition in the 1620s: Thomas Scott and the Spanish match', *HJ* 25 (1982); E. Shagan, 'Constructing discord: ideology, propaganda and English responses to the Irish rebellion of 1641', *JBS* 36 (1997); Wootton, 'From rebellion to revolution'.

guide to political attitudes, too few are sensitive to the circumstances surrounding their appearance, and the possibility of political involvement in their production. Like any historical source, tracts and pamphlets need to be submitted to rigorous and sceptical scrutiny in terms of their reliability, and their message needs to be understood in the light of the reasons for their existence.[47]

Such comments notwithstanding, there is clearly a growing recognition of the importance of print in the early modern period, and a growing interest in pamphleteering and print culture.[48] Indeed, recent scholarship betrays a heightened awareness of the existence and spread of print in the early modern period, and an appreciation of the emergence of a variety of forms of popular literature, as well as an exploration of different forms of literary, political and religious books, pamphlets and broadsides.[49] These include astrological tracts and providential pamphlets, as well as apprentice literature, and murder stories, all of which have

---

[47] For use of pamphlet evidence: K. Lindley, 'Impact of the 1641 rebellion upon England and Wales, 1641–5', *IHS* 18 (1972); I. Gentles, 'The struggle for London in the second civil war', *HJ* 26 (1983); R. Clifton, 'The popular fear of Catholics during the English revolution', in P. Slack, ed., *Rebellion, Popular Protest and the Social Order in Early Modern England* (Cambridge, 1984); Adamson, 'Baronial context'; J. S. A. Adamson, 'The English nobility and the projected settlement of 1647', *HJ* 30 (1987); S. Kelsey, 'Legal aspects of the trial of Charles I' (forthcoming); S. Kelsey, 'The trial of Charles I' (forthcoming); S. Kelsey, 'The death of Charles I' (forthcoming); C. Holmes, 'Colonel King and Lincolnshire politics, 1642–1646', *HJ* 16 (1973); C. Holmes, *The Eastern Association in the English Civil War* (Cambridge, 1974); D. Cressy, 'The protestation protested, 1641 and 1642', *HJ* 45 (2002); N. Carlin, 'Extreme or mainstream? The English Independents and the Cromwellian reconquest of Ireland, 1649–51', in B. Bradshaw, A. Hadfield and W. Maley, eds, *Representing Ireland* (Cambridge, 1993), pp. 211–12; A. Walsham, *Providence in Early Modern England* (Oxford, 1999); S. Barber, *Regicide and Republicanism* (Edinburgh, 1998). I am grateful to Sean Kelsey for showing me his forthcoming articles.

[48] D. Loades, 'Books and the English reformation prior to 1558', in J. F. Gilmont, ed., *The Reformation and the Book* (Aldershot, 1998); I. Green, *Print and Protestantism in Early Modern England* (Oxford, 2000); D. Freist, 'The world is ruled and governed by opinion. For formation of opinion and the communication network in London, 1637 to c.1645' (Cambridge University PhD, 1992), part 2.

[49] S. Clark, *The Elizabethan Pamphleteers. Popular Moralistic Pamphlets 1580–1640* (London, 1983); J. Barry, 'Literacy and literature in popular culture: reading and writing in historical perspective', in T. Harris, ed., *Popular Culture in England, c.1500–1850* (Basingstoke, 1995); T. Watt, *Cheap Print and Popular Piety, 1550–1640* (Cambridge, 1991); M. Spufford, *Small Books and Pleasant Histories: Popular Fiction and its Readership in Seventeenth Century England* (London, 1981); B. Capp, 'Popular literature', in B. Reay, ed., *Popular Culture in Seventeenth Century England* (London, 1985); A. Fox, 'Popular verses and their readership in the early seventeenth century', in J. Raven, N. Tadmor, and H. Small, eds, *The Practice and Representation of Reading in England* (Cambridge, 1996); A. Fox, 'Ballads, libels and popular ridicule in Jacobean England', *P&P* 145 (1994); P. Croft, 'The reputation of Robert Cecil: libels, political opinion and popular awareness in the early seventeenth century', *TRHS*, 6th series 1 (1991); A. Bellany, 'Rayling rymes and vaunting verse': libellous politics in early Stuart England, 1603–1628', in K. Sharpe and P. Lake, eds, *Culture and Politics in Early Stuart England* (Basingstoke, 1994); A. Bellany, 'Libels in action: ritual, subversion and the English literary underground, 1603–42', in T. Harris, ed., *The Politics of the Excluded, c.1500–1850* (Basingstoke, 2001); A. Bellany, *The Politics of Court Scandal in Early Modern England* (Cambridge, 2002); Friest, 'The world is ruled and governed by opinion', part 4.

been shown to have been susceptible to exploitation for political and religious ends.[50] As such, this fourth strand of scholarship on early modern literary forms – the popular and 'pulp' press – must also be subjected to scrutiny in the chapters which follow, albeit only tangentially, and only to the extent that such works formed part of the interests of the political elite.[51] More pressing will be the need to address a fifth strand in early modern scholarship relating to print culture, namely the growing interest in the 'news revolution' of the seventeenth century. Crucial to this study will be the task of addressing the extent to which politicians sought to exploit the growing public interest in political affairs, both nationally and locally, which has been detected in recent historiography.[52] Indeed, it will also be necessary to draw upon and develop recent interest in pamphleteering as a cultural phenomenon, and as an increasingly important part of religious

---

[50] H. Rusche, '*Merlini Anglici*: astrology and propaganda from 1644 to 1651', *EHR* 80 (1965); Rusche, 'Prophecies and propaganda'; B. Capp, *The World of John Taylor the Water Poet, 1578–1653* (Oxford, 1994); B. Capp, *Astrology and the Popular Press* (London, 1979); A. Walsham, '"The fatall vesper": providentialism and anti-popery in late Jacobean London', *P&P* 144 (1994); Walsham, *Providence*; B. Worden, 'Providence and politics in Cromwellian England', *P&P* 109 (1985); M. T. Burnett, 'Apprentice literature and the 'crisis' of the 1590s', in C. C. Brown, ed., *Patronage, Politics and Literary Traditions in England, 1558–1658* (Detroit, 1991); P. Lake, 'Puritanism, Arminianism and a Shropshire axe-murder', *Midland History* 15 (1990), esp. p. 55–6; P. Lake, 'Deeds against nature: cheap print, Protestantism and murder in early seventeenth century England', in Sharpe and Lake, eds, *Culture and Politics in Early Stuart England*; P. Lake and M. Questier, *The Antichrist's Lewd Hat* (New Haven, 2002).

[51] Watt, *Cheap Print*; J. Friedman, *Miracles and the Pulp Press During the English Revolution* (London, 1993).

[52] R. Cust, 'News and politics in early seventeenth century England', *P&P* 112 (1986); C. J. Sommerville, *The News Revolution in England* (Oxford, 1996); J. Raymond, *The Invention of the Newspaper*; A. Cotton, 'London newsbooks in the civil war: their political attitudes and sources of information' (Oxford University DPhil, 1971); J. Raymond, ed., *News, Newspapers and Society in Early Modern Britain* (London, 1999); J. Raymond, '*The Great Assises Holden in Parnassus*: the reputation and reality of seventeenth century newsbooks', *Studies in Newspaper and Periodical History* (1994); P. J. Voss, *Elizabethan News Pamphlets* (Pittsburgh, 2001); J. Frank, *The Beginnings of the English Newspaper, 1620–1660* (Cambridge, Mass., 1960); J. B. Williams, *The History of English Journalism* (London, 1908); M. Frearson, 'The distribution and readership of London corantos in the 1620s', in R. Myers and M. Harris, eds, *Serials and their Readers, 1620–1914* (Winchester, 1993); L. Hanson, 'English newsbooks, 1620–1641', *The Library*, 4th series 18 (1938); S. Lambert, 'Coranto printing in England: the first newsbooks', *Journal of Newspaper and Periodical History* 8 (1992); M. Frearson, 'London corantos in the 1620s', *Studies in Newspaper and Periodical History* (1993); F. Levy, 'How information spread among the gentry, 1550–1640', *JBS* 21 (1982); Wright, 'Propaganda against James I's 'appeasement' of Spain'; J. Raymond, '"A mercury with a winged conscience": Marchamont Nedham, monopoly and censorship', *Media History* 4 (1998); J. Raymond, 'The cracking of the republican spokes', *Prose Studies* 19 (1996); D. Underdown, '*The Man in the Moon*: loyalty and libel in popular politics, 1640–1660', in *A Freeborn People* (Oxford, 1996); D. Woolf, 'News, history and the construction of the present in early modern England', in B. Dooley and S. Baron eds, *The Politics of Information in Early Modern Europe* (London, 2001); M. Mendle, 'News and the pamphlet culture of mid-seventeenth century England', ibid.; G. J. McElligott, 'Propaganda and censorship: the underground royalist newsbooks, 1647–1650' (Cambridge University PhD, 2000).

controversy and of the political process, which reflects appreciation of the extent to which politics took place outside of Parliament.[53]

One of the results of this growing interest in popular literature has been an enhanced understanding of the need to explore the circumstances of the author. The sixth strand of scholarship on early modern literature, therefore, involves a developing awareness of the emergence of the 'professional' writer, albeit merely in terms of men and women who made their livelihood from their pens, rather than being employed in a professional capacity.[54] It is possible that there was little political involvement in such literature, and there has certainly been little consideration of the possibility of its exploitation by politicians in the historiography on this subject. To the extent that politicians and political forces are crucial to the publishing industry in the seventeenth century, this book is concerned with something different from early modern 'Grub Street', which has been explored to such startling effects by Robert Darnton. The phenomenon with which this book deals is only tangentially interested in professional hacks seeking to make a living from their pens; those 'poor devils' who 'could not afford to be consistent', but who 'put themselves up for hire and wrote whatever was ordered

---

[53] A. Walsham, '"Domme preachers": post-reformation English Catholicism and the culture of print', *P&P* 168 (2000); G. Mattingley, 'William Allen and Catholic propaganda in England', in *Aspects de la Propagande Religieuse* (Travaux d'Humanisme et Renaissance 28, 1957); T. Kilburn and A. Milton, 'The public context of the trial and execution of Strafford', in J. F. Merritt, ed., *The Political World of Thomas Wentworth, Earl of Strafford, 1621–1641* (Cambridge, 1996); Holmes, 'Colonel King'; C. Holmes, 'Drainers and fenmen: the problem of popular political consciousness in the seventeenth century', in A. Fletcher and J. Stevenson, eds, *Order and Disorder in Early Modern England* (Cambridge, 1985); M. K. Peters, 'Quaker pamphleteering and the development of the Quaker movement, 1652–1656' (Cambridge University PhD, 1996); K. Peters, 'The Quakers quaking: print and the spread of a movement', in S. Wabuda and C. Litzenberger, eds, *Belief and Practice in Reformation England* (Aldershot, 1998); Lindley, 'Impact of the 1641 rebellion'; K. Lindley, *Fenland Riots and the English Revolution* (London, 1982); Greaves, 'William Sprigg', p. 99; Shagan, 'Constructing discord'; S. Achinstein, 'The politics of Babel in the English revolution', in J. Holstun, ed., *Pamphlet Wars* (London, 1992); D. Scott, 'The Barwis affair: political allegiance and the Scots during the British civil wars', *EHR* 115 (2000); A. Hughes, 'Approaches to Presbyterian print culture. Thomas Edwards's *Gangraena* as source and text', in J. Andersen and E. Sauer, eds, *Books and Readers in Early Modern England* (Philadelphia, 2002); R. P. Stearns, 'The Weld-Peter mission to England', *Colonial Society of Massachusetts Publications* 32 (1937); W. L. Sachse, 'English pamphlet support for Charles I, November 1648–January 1649', in W. A. Aiken and B. D. Henning, eds, *Conflict in Stuart England* (London, 1960).

[54] C. Nicholl, *A Cup of News. The Life of Thomas Nashe* (London, 1984); Miller, *Professional Writer*; Capp, *World of John Taylor*; A. Halasz, 'Pamphlet surplus: John Taylor and subscription publication', in A. F. Marotti and M. D. Bristol, eds, *Print, Manuscript and Performance. The Changing Relations of the Media in Early Modern England* (Columbus, 2000); J. Loewenstein, 'Wither and professional work', ibid.; A. Walsham, '"A glose of godlines": Philip Stubbes, Elizabethan Grub Street and the invention of Puritanism', in Wabuda and Litzenberger, eds, *Belief and Practice*; V. F. Stern, *Gabriel Harvey* (Oxford, 1979); Lindenbaum, 'John Milton'; P. Lindenbaum, 'Authors and publishers in the late seventeenth century: new evidence on their relations', *The Library*, 6th series 17 (1995); P. Lindenbaum, 'Authors and publishers in the late seventeenth century, II: Brabazon Aylmer and the mysteries of the trade', *The Library*, 7th series 3 (2002).

by the highest bidder, when they were fortunate enough to sell themselves'.[55] The following analysis will deal with both professional writers and those whose vocations lay elsewhere; with men who could afford to be principled as well as those who were forced to be mercenary hacks; and with those who formed an integral part of the aristocratic and gentry world, as well as those who eked out a living on the margins of the social and political elite.

The aim of this work is to blend these six strands of scholarship and historiography relating to the political and religious literature of the early modern period. The intention is to produce neither an 'Annal-ist' history of the political book industry from below, nor high-political analysis. Rather, what follows is an exploration of the area where 'politicians' interacted with the 'people'.[56] The aim is also to recognise that there is no such thing as a single political message in any given work. The meaning of texts is not determined by authorial intention, and it is certainly not fixed, but rather is liable to change in different circumstances, and is highly dependent upon readership and reception.[57] It is necessary to explore the use to which texts were put, and the publishing – rather than merely textual – intention, and even their precise circulation within social networks. It is necessary to add material and political context to the 'Cambridge school' of political thought, and to new historicist literary scholarship.[58] Blending these six approaches, in order to understand message, author, medium, circumstances and audience, is essential in order to understand the politics of propaganda in the early modern period.

In part, this process has been undertaken by another important historiographical trend on which this project seeks to draw: the 'history of the book'. In order to achieve a greater understanding of the politics of print culture during the seventeenth century, it is essential to undertake analysis not just of authors and authorship, but also the nature of the publishing industry and book trade. There are a number of studies of the careers of individual printers and publishers, and their professional, political and confessional positions.[59] Recent work has also shown the

---

[55] Darnton, *Literary Underground*, p. 115. See also: R. Darnton, 'Trade in the taboo: the life of a clandestine book dealer in pre-revolutionary France', in Paul J. Korshin, ed., *The Widening Circle* (Pennsylvania, 1976).

[56] D. Hirst and S. Zwicker, 'High summer at Nun Appleton, 1651: Andrew Marvell and Lord Fairfax's occasions', *HJ* 36 (1993); Hirst, 'That sober liberty'; Hirst, 'Politics of literature', p. 136.

[57] C. A. Edie, 'Reading popular political pamphlets: a question of meanings', in Schochet, ed., *Restoration, Ideology and Revolution*.

[58] J. Raven, 'New reading histories, print culture and the identification of change: the case of eighteenth century England', *Social History* 23 (1998); Limon, *Dangerous Matter*, p. 14; M. Dzelzainis, 'Milton and the protectorate in 1658', in Armitage, Himy and Skinner, eds, *Milton and Republicanism*, p. 201.

[59] L. Rostenberg, 'The new world: John Bellamy, pilgrim publisher of London', in *Literary, Political Scientific, Religious and Legal Publishing, Printing, and Bookselling in England, 1551–1700* (2 vols, New York, 1965); L. Rostenberg, 'The regeneration of man and trade: Michael Sparke, Puritan crusader', ibid.; L. Rostenberg, 'Republican credo: William Dugard, pedagogue and political apostate',

potential for contextualising and interpreting the work of particular – and sometimes short-lived – printing presses or publishing ventures.[60] Furthermore, scholarship concerning the Puritan literary 'underground' of the period before 1640, and regarding radical political pressure groups thereafter, has entailed valuable research into techniques by which the press was exploited for political ends, and the methods by which historians can employ historical, biographical and bibliographical skills in order to detect evidence of political involvement, and of patronage of polemical literature.[61] For much of the twentieth century, of course, work on publishing and the history of the book concentrated upon developing general histories of the industry, and upon how it worked.[62] It developed in different ways, however, in England and France.[63] French scholars have tended to look to the social world of the book industry, and in France the history of the book has always been cultural and social. Continental historians' primary interest, therefore, has been a socio-economic analysis of 'the milieu of those who manufactured and sold books'.[64] As Roger Chartier has written: 'the historian's chief concern has been to measure the unequal presence of the book in the various groups that made up the society of the *ancien regime*'.[65] The English approach, on the other hand, has tended

---

ibid.; L. Rostenberg, 'Nathaniel Butter and Nicholas Bourne. First "masters of the staple"', *The Library*, 5th series 12 (1957); L. Rostenberg, 'William Dugard, pedagogue and printer to the commonwealth', *Papers of the Bibliographical Society of America* 52 (1958); M. H. Curtis, 'William Jones: Puritan printer and propagandist', *The Library*, 5th series 19 (1964); M. Mendle, 'Putney's pronouns: identity and indemnity in the great debate', in Mendle, ed., *The Putney Debates of 1647* (Cambridge, 2001); A. E. M. Kirwood, 'Richard Field, printer, 1589–1624', *The Library*, 4th series 12 (1931); L. Spencer, 'The politics of George Thomason', *The Library*, 5th series 14 (1959); L. Spencer, 'The professional and literary connexions of George Thomason', *The Library*, 5th series 13 (1958); K. Sprunger, *Dutch Puritanism* (Leiden, 1982); P. Lindenbaum, 'John Playford: music and politics in the Interregnum', *HLQ* 64 (2001); C. L. Oastler, *John Day, the Elizabethan Printer* (Oxford Bibliographical Society, occasional publications, 10, 1975).

   60 Mendle, 'Putney's pronouns'.

   61 S. Foster, *Notes from the Caroline Underground* (Hamden, Ct., 1978); D. Loades, 'Illicit presses and clandestine printing in England, 1520–1590', in A. C. Duke and C. A. Tamse, eds, *Too Might to be Free. Censorship and the Press in England and the Netherlands* (Zutphen, 1987); Condick, 'Bastwick'; Curtis, 'William Jones'; D. B. Woodfield, *Surreptitious Printing in England, 1550–1640* (New York, 1973); A. F. Johnson, 'The exiled English church at Amsterdam and its press', *The Library*, 5th series 5 (1951); A. F. Johnson, 'J. F. Stam, Amsterdam and English Bibles', *The Library*, 5th series 9 (1954); D. A. Kirby, 'The parish of St Stephen's, Coleman Street' (Oxford University Blitt, 1968), p. 118; K. L. Sprunger, *Trumpets from the Tower. English Puritan Printing in the Netherlands, 1600–1640* (Leiden, 1994).

   62 R. Hirsch, *Printing, Selling and Reading 1450–1550* (Wiesbaden, 1967); M. Plant, *The English Book Trade* (London, 1939); H. R. Plomer, *A Short History of English Printing, 1476–1900* (London, 1915); H. J. Martin, *Print, Power and People in 17th-Century France* (trans. D. Gerard, London, 1993).

   63 J. Feather, 'Cross-channel currents: historical bibliography and *l'histoire du livre*', *The Library*, 6th series 2 (1980).

   64 L. Febvre and H. J. Martin, *The Coming of the Book* (London, 1976); R. Chartier, *The Order of Books* (trans. Lydia G. Cochrane, Cambridge, 1992), p. 26.

   65 Chartier, *Order of Books*, p. 6; D. T. Pottinger, *The French Book Trade in the Ancien Regime 1500–1791* (Cambridge, Mass., 1958).

to be more technological. Its exponents have been concerned with printing costs, the logistics and mechanics of printing-house practices, and with the technical means of distinguishing between different editions of particular books, and between the work of different printing houses. This approach has been labelled 'scientific bibliography', and has been made possible by the survival of detailed documentary sources and large collections of early modern books and pamphlets.[66] Its approach is probably epitomised by the statement of Sir Walter Greg, who claimed that 'what the bibliographer is concerned with is pieces of paper or parchment covered with certain written or printed signs. With these signs he is concerned merely as arbitrary marks; their meaning is no business of his'.[67]

Both of these approaches to the history of the book have their limitations, as Michael Hunter has demonstrated:

> While bibliographers study the making of early books and can be accused ... of devoting insufficient time to reading them, historians and literary scholars who spend their lives perusing such volumes are often alarmingly ignorant of physical and technical considerations which might affect their judgment of a work's background and impact.[68]

Indeed, dissatisfaction with such methodologies, together with the advent of 'new historicism', has led to a number of important changes in historical practice. In one sense, those interested in the 'history of the book' today are more concerned with 'attempting to trace the impact of the printed word on society'.[69] This approach is probably best represented by Marshall McLuhan and Elizabeth Eisenstein, as well as by Robert Darnton's exploration of the 'biography of a book' (the *Encyclopédie*). Studies have been written, therefore, in order to understand print 'as a force in history', from the Reformation to the cultural revolution of the late eighteenth century.[70] Moreover, there is also growing interest in what has been called the 'sociology of texts', based upon the idea that the meaning of texts is linked to the form in which they appeared, and that it is important to understand the history of 'reading'.[71] Donald McKenzie set out his opposition to 'analytical'

---

[66] K. I. D. Maslen, 'Printing charges: inference and evidence', *Studies in Bibliography* 24 (1971); D. F. McKenzie, 'Printers of the mind: some notes on bibliographical theories and printing house practises', *Studies in Bibliography* 22 (1969).

[67] MacKenzie, 'Printers of the mind', p. 1.

[68] M. Hunter, 'The impact of print', *Book Collector* 28 (1979), p. 335.

[69] G. T. Tanselle, 'Printing history and other history', *Studies in Bibliography* 48 (1995), p. 272.

[70] M. McLuhan, *The Gutenberg Galaxy* (London, 1962); E. Eisenstein, *The Printing Revolution in Early Modern Europe* (Cambridge, 1983); R. Darnton, *The Business of Enlightenment. A Publishing History of the Encyclopédie, 1775–1800* (Cambridge, Mass., 1979); M. U. Edwards, *Printing, Propaganda and Martin Luther* (London, 1994); J. N. Wall, 'The reformation in England and the typographical revolution', in G. P. Tyson and S. S. Wagonheim, eds, *Print and Culture in the Renaissance* (New York, 1986); A. Pettegree, 'Printing and the reformation: the English exception', in P. Marshall and A. Ryrie, eds, *The Beginnings of English Protestantism* (Cambridge, 2002). See also: A. Johns, *The Nature of the Book* (Chicago, 1998).

[71] Chartier, *Order of Books*; R. Chartier, *The Cultural Uses of Print* (1987); R. Darnton, 'First steps toward a history of reading', *Australian Journal of French Studies* 23 (1986); R. Chartier, *Frenchness*

or 'physical' bibliography, and to the internal analysis of books, in favour of an approach which recognises that medium affects message. As such, he contended, 'bibliography cannot exclude from its own proper concerns the relation between form, function, and symbolic meaning'. As a result, McKenzie called for 'history' and 'cultural history' to be added to conventional bibliography. He suggested that:

> any history of the book which excluded study of the social, economic and political motivations of publishing, the reasons why texts were written and read as they were, why they were rewritten and redesigned, or allowed to die, would degenerate into a feebly digressive book list and never rise to a readable history.[72]

Writing on the new historians of the book, G. Thomas Tanselle has noted that:

> although their subject is, in one sense, the spread of ideas, their approach differs from the traditional study of intellectual history through their focus on the role of printed books in the process. To them, the geography of the printing industry, the economics of the publishing business, the systems of book distribution, the demographics of reading, and the effects of book design on the reading process, are primary elements in social and intellectual history.[73]

Nevertheless, historians of the book have arguably played insufficient attention to the interaction between the publishing industry and the politics of print, either in terms of the impact of politics on print culture, or the effects of print on political culture, although there are hints of growing sophistication in this area.[74] It is the need for a detailed, strenuous, or 'deep' contextualisation of civil war authors and their works, together with the McKenzian insight regarding the need to blend history, bibliography and book history, which are of most importance to this study.[75] This book is not concerned with offering an economic analysis of the publishing business, or the social status of writers. Neither is it concerned with assessing the impact of print and the reception of texts. Rather, it concentrates upon the interaction of an historical or sociological bibliography with political and cultural history. The crucial idea is that books ought to be understood in terms of the purposes, aims and intentions of those involved in setting them before the public. This is not necessarily limited to the 'authorial intention' behind the message of the text, but rather concerns the intention behind the publication of a work on the part of all of those who were involved. More than merely looking to 'authors', therefore, this work seeks to look at the interaction between authors, publishers and 'patrons'. Most importantly, it looks to the involvement of those patrons who were also politicians, whether as individuals, members of sectional interests, or participants in government and public administration. Polemical and

---

in the History of the Book: From the History of Publishing to the History of Reading (Worcester, Mass., American Antiquarian Society, 1988).

[72] D. F. McKenzie, Bibliography and the Sociology of Texts (London, 1986), pp. 2, 3, 5.

[73] Tanselle, 'Printing history', p. 272.

[74] Hunter, 'Impact of print', p. 351; Pettegree, 'Printing and the reformation'.

[75] R. D. Hume, 'Texts within contexts: notes towards a historical method', Philological Quarterly 71 (1992). The term 'deep' contextualisation is that of Hirst and Zwicker, 'High summer', p. 248.

pamphlet literature needs, in other words, to be placed in a local political context in order to tease out the political power embedded in books and pamphlets.[76]

In this sense, the purpose of the book chimes with the rise of interest in 'material culture', in terms of the 'the interrelations of thought and objects', and 'the material evidences of mental activity'. Indeed, one recent commentator has noted that 'there cannot be a history of ideas without a history of objects'.[77] My contention is that there cannot be a history of objects without a history of the influences, processes, and political forces behind their production. Books, therefore, are to be seen as a primary, rather than as a secondary source, and as embodying personal, social, cultural, and political relationships, and they can be used as a means of understanding those relationships.[78] Political texts ought to be regarded, in other words, as political events. This is true not just in the sense that books represent embodiments of contextual language and illocutionary force, nor even merely in terms of the importance of understanding them through their translation and reception by contemporary readers.[79] Texts were also 'events' in the sense of being encapsulations, expressions, and embodiments of political power. Pamphlets ought to be regarded 'not as repositories of historical facts but as a historical phenomenon in their own right'.[80] They need to be analysed in such a way as to reveal the forces at work behind their appearance, and to expose those political relationships. In essence, therefore, this book is concerned with exploring the political literature of the civil wars and Interregnum by means of an understanding of the conditions in which writers, journalists, and publishers operated.[81] As Nigel Smith has noted: 'at the centre of any attempt to understand the remarkable transformation of literary activity during the central years of the century must be the conditions of writing and the related issue of the nature of authorship'.[82] The 'conditions of writing' have generally been taken to mean the varieties of censorship which existed in the early modern period, and this remains a hotly debated area of study.[83] However, there are many more factors which need

---

[76] Hirst and Zwicker, 'High summer'.

[77] Tanselle, 'Printing history', p. 271.

[78] Tanselle, 'Printing history', p. 279.

[79] J. G. A. Pocock, 'Texts as events: reflections on the history of political thought', in Sharpe and Zwicker, eds, *Politics of Discourse*.

[80] Harline, *Pamphlets, Printing, and Political Culture*, p. ix; Davis, 'Printing and the people', p. 192.

[81] See: R. Silver, 'Financing the publication of early New England sermons', *Studies in Bibliography* 11 (1958).

[82] Smith, *Literature and Revolution*, p. 23.

[83] Hirsch, *Printing, Selling and Reading*, chap. 6; Pottinger, *French Book Trade*, I. iv; C. S. Clegg, *Press Censorship in Elizabethan England* (Cambridge, 1997); A. Patterson, *Censorship and Interpretation. The Conditions of Writing and Reading in Early Modern England* (Madison, 1984); D. Loades, 'The theory and practice of censorship in sixteenth century England', in *Censorship and the English Reformation* (London, 1991); D. Loades, 'The press under the early Tudors', *Transactions of the Cambridge Bibliographical Society* 4 (1964); Miller, *Professional Writer*, pp. 171–202; A. Milton, 'Licensing, censorship and religious orthodoxy in early Stuart England', *HJ* 41 (1998); B. Worden,

to be taken into consideration. In essence, these concern the positive, rather than negative influence which patrons, public authorities and governments could exercise on the world of printing and publication.[84] Although there have always been hints of a more sophisticated approach to the complicated reality of authorship and textual formation, and of the political context of important polemical tracts, analysis has thus far been fragmentary in nature.[85]

In its scope, it will be necessary for this study to examine the printed word in all its forms: from the official declaration to the political tract and broadside, the sermon to the newspaper, as well as to almanacks and astrological works, and even to ballads and fictive literature. As such, it will be necessary to look at the works of well-known authors, such as Henry Parker, William Prynne, John Milton and Marchamont Nedham, as well as Henry Ferne, Peter Heylyn and Griffith Williams. It will also be necessary, however, to examine a host of less well-known authors, such as Payne Fisher and Cuthbert Sydenham, Edward Symmons and Joseph Jane. In its aims, on the other hand, this book has clear limitations. No attempt will be made to consider either the 'truth' or the 'impact' of propaganda, in terms of the extent to which it was believed, changed attitudes and influenced behaviour. Fascinating though such subjects are, they nevertheless lie outside the scope of this book, and would require greater research into practices of reading, and the reception of texts, than has been undertaken hitherto. Furthermore, no attempt has been made to develop a rigorous comparative analysis of the place of the mid-seventeenth century in the history of relations between politics and the press in England. The aim is not necessarily to argue, in other words, that the 1640s and 1650s represented an entirely new world in terms of propaganda and the

---

'Literature and political censorship in early modern England', in Duke and Tamse, eds, *Too Mighty to be Free*; C. S. Clegg, *Press Censorship in Jacobean England* (Cambridge, 2001); S. Lambert, 'The printers and the government, 1604–1637', in R. Myers and M. Harris, eds, *Aspects of Printing From 1600* (Oxford, 1987); S. Lambert, 'State control of the press in theory and practice: the role of the Stationers' Company before 1640', in R. Myers and M. Harris, ed., *Censorship and the Control of Print in England and France, 1600–1910* (Winchester, 1992); S. Lambert, 'Richard Montague, Arminianism, and censorship', *P&P* 124 (1989); W. M. Clyde, *The Struggle for the Freedom of the Press from Caxton to Cromwell* (Oxford, 1934); F. S. Siebert, *Freedom of the Press in England, 1476–1776* (Urbana, 1952); G. D. Johnson, 'The Stationers versus the Drapers: control of the press in the late sixteenth century', *The Library*, 6th series 10 (1988); J. Clare, *Art Made Tongue-Tied by Authority* (Manchester 1990); M. Bland, '"Invisible dangers": censorship and the subversion of authority in early modern England', *Papers of the Bibliographical Society of America* 90 (1996); Friest, 'The world is ruled and governed by opinion', part 1.

[84] Frearson, 'London corantos in the 1620s', p. 3.

[85] A. Milton, 'The creation of Laudianism: a new approach', in T. Cogswell, R. Cust and P. Lake, eds, *Politics, Religion and Popularity in Early Stuart Britain* (Cambridge, 2002); J. Morrill and P. Baker, 'The case of the armie truly re-stated', in Mendle, ed., *Putney Debates*; D. H. Willson, 'James I and his literary assistants', *HLQ* 8 (1944–45); J. E. Farnell, 'The Navigation Act of 1651, the first Dutch war, and the London merchant community', *Journal of Economic History*, 2nd series 16 (1964), pp. 441–2.

press, nor to claim that the developments of the mid-seventeenth century proved to have permanent importance.

However, there are a number of general aims and themes which will become clear throughout the body of this work. The overriding goal is to understand why and how print came to be exploited by politicians; how propaganda was produced; how it was deployed; and the dynamic of propaganda over the course of the 1640s and 1650s. The first requirement, therefore, is to understand the 'motor' of propaganda, and to understand something about the motives leading politicians to engage in the production of polemic, and to consider not just why they sought to engage with the people, but also how they regarded the nature of the process of communicating with the public. The aim of the first section of the book, therefore, is to gain an understanding of the variety of reasons motivating politicians and writers to engage in propagandising, and of differing views regarding the purposes of propaganda. Chapter 1 explores the attitudes of political grandees, and seeks to demonstrate why politicians turned away from officially written, produced and distributed propaganda in order to employ the services and skills of authors. Chapter 2, meanwhile, examines the motives leading authors to place their pens at the disposal of political grandees, in order to engage in the production of political and religious polemic.[86]

In order to understand the way in which print propaganda was conceived by contemporaries, however, it is necessary to explore not just the overt comments of those responsible for its production, but also to examine the ways in which print was employed, and the methods by which it was deployed, and to question the extent to which different political groups, interests, and factions proved adept at developing their skills. A study of propaganda in the mid-seventeenth century requires, therefore, the development of a methodology for recovering the processes which lay behind the publication of tracts, pamphlets, and newspapers. Such a methodology requires some subtlety, given that those who were engaged in the production of propaganda obviously sought to cover their tracks, and to work in ways which were not always visible to contemporaries. Inevitably, such processes, like all political action, are beyond full recovery by the historian, not least given the possibility that certain moves were orchestrated verbally, and that certain written evidence was destroyed, either immediately or at the Restoration. Nevertheless, it is possible to 'decode' tracts and pamphlets, in order to reveal evidence of political collusion in the process of composition, production and publication. The second part of the book, therefore, examines the 'mechanics' of propaganda, in order to display the ways and means of official involvement in the production of polemic.

In seeking to determine which works were produced with official backing and political involvement, it will be necessary to recognise a sliding scale of

---

[86] R. E. Giesey, 'When and why Hotman wrote the Francogalia', *Biblioteque d'Humanisme et Renaissance* 29 (1967).

transparency, and a broad range of evidential sources. At one extreme will be those works still lost to historians, and at the other those works which would, should, or could have been immediately recognisable to contemporaries as having been officially inspired. Between these two extremes will be the bulk of the works with which this book will be concerned. Some will be shown to betray one or more from a variety of possible visible clues, some or all of which will have been obvious to readers. These would have been both biographical, in terms of the public fame of particular authors, as well as presentational, in terms of more or less coded messages contained on title pages and within texts, and in terms of bibliographical clues. Other works, however, will only be revealed to have been officially backed or inspired through historical detective work, with the benefit of hindsight, and via archival research. Ultimately, it will be necessary to develop a more subtle methodology for detecting propaganda than that which has been deployed hitherto. Historians such as Geoffrey Elton relied upon transparency, whether to the contemporary reader or later historian, and their analyses were restricted to works printed officially, and/or written by hired hands.[87] Elton's criteria cannot be ignored, and it will certainly be necessary to explore the work of official printers, and to look to the public and private archives of politicians and officials in order to seek evidence of the hiring of authors. However, it will also be necessary to take into consideration other evidence, and to examine the political literature of the mid-seventeenth century by a much more rigorous process of 'grubbing in archives'.[88]

Firstly, it will be necessary to take seriously the comments made by contemporaries, in both private and official correspondence, as well as in contemporary printed literature.[89] While contemporary perceptions on such a contentious topic as propaganda must be treated with great care, not least during a bitter struggle such as that witnessed in the civil wars and Interregnum, it is nevertheless possible to draw upon the notice taken of authors and their books, and of the connections between print and politics, in the words of the men with whom we will be interested, as well as of their friends and enemies. The part played by print in the civil wars was clearly recognised by contemporaries, whose ruminations upon, and allegations regarding, the nature of the publishing industry are too valuable, not to say colourful, to be ignored by the historian. Furthermore, a work of this sort, and this book in particular, must exploit the full potential of the remarkable Thomason Tracts in the British Library, which provide not just a more or less comprehensive collection of pamphlets from the 1640s and 1650s, but also a great deal of valuable contextual information from the hand of Thomason himself, above and beyond his invaluable method of recording the precise date on

---

[87] G. Elton, *Policy and Police: the Enforcement of the Reformation in the Age of Thomas Cromwell* (Cambridge, 1972), p. 173.

[88] Darnton, *Literary Underground*, p. 1.

[89] McCullough, *Sermons at Court*, pp. 210–12.

which he acquired individual works. Other evidence will be contextual in nature. In order to explore the political and propagandistic function of texts, therefore, it is necessary to reconstruct the historical and political background of particular works.[90] This means exploring the circumstances surrounding publication, in terms of political events, and the needs and concerns of political and religious grandees at specific moments. Contextual evidence will also involve biographical information regarding writers and politicians, and regarding the relationships between authors and patrons, including memoirs, biographies and autobiographies. There are important biographies of a few political authors of the early modern period, such as Thomas Hobbes, John Selden and John Owen, although there are arguably few thorough case studies of civil war propagandists to match those of Tudor poets such as John Skelton, or Restoration luminaries such as John Locke and Algernon Sidney.[91] Nevertheless, it will be possible to draw upon the example set by contemporary memorials and scholarly analysis of journalists such as John Dillingham and John Berkenhead, clerical activists such as Hugh Peter and Peter Heylyn, and writers such as John Dury, John Milton and William Prynne, from which much can be learnt regarding the politics of print and propaganda.[92]

Chapter 3 demonstrates how it is possible to 'decode' individual works, by examining biographical evidence linking authors to political patrons, and the ties which can be shown to have existed prior to, as well as at the time of, composition and publication of tracts and pamphlets. Decoding can also be undertaken by examining the way in which such polemical works can be shown to have been used to promulgate messages which bolstered the positions and policies of political grandees at key moments during the 1640s and 1650s. Furthermore, this chapter will also draw attention to possible evidence of authors being rewarded for their literary services, and will explore bibliographical clues linking specific works to favoured printing presses and publishing houses. Such contextual evidence will also include information pertinent to the relation between the moment of publication and political events, and to the congruence of a work's message with the ideas of its author's patrons. Chapter 4, meanwhile, explores the way in which press licensing functioned as more than merely a means of enforcing

---

[90] Limon, *Dangerous Matter*, p. 131.

[91] T. Hobbes, *The Correspondence*, ed. N. Malcolm (2 vols, Oxford, 1994); A. P. Martinich, *Hobbes, A Biography* (Cambridge, 1999); D. S. Berkovitz, *John Selden's Formative Years* (Washington, 1988); G. Walker, *John Skelton and the Politics of the 1520s* (Cambridge, 1988).

[92] A. N. B. Cotton, 'John Dillingham, journalist of the middle group', *EHR* 93 (1978); J. Frank, *Cromwell's Press Agent* (Lanham, 1980); P. W. Thomas, *Sir John Berkenhead* (London, 1969); R. P. Stearns, *The Strenuous Puritan: Hugh Peter, 1598–1660* (Urbana, 1954); W. R. Parker, *Milton: A Biography* (2 vols, Oxford, 1968); J. M. Batten, *John Dury* (Chicago, 1944); E. W. Kirby, *William Prynne* (Cambridge, Mass., 1931); G. Vernon, *The Life of the Learned and Reverend Dr Peter Heylyn* (London, 1682); E. C. Walker, *William Dell, Master Puritan* (Cambridge, 1970); P. J. Wallis, *William Crashawe. The Sheffield Puritan* (Transactions of the Hunter Archaeological Society, 8, 1960–63). See also M. Eccles, 'Thomas Gainsford, "Captain Pamphlet"', *HLQ* 45 (1982).

censorship, in order to provide another key element in the mechanism by which political pressure was brought to bear on the substantive content of the output of the printing industry. Chapter 5, on the other hand, analyses more concrete evidence regarding the interaction between authors and politicians, in terms of archival material relating to the submission of book proposals and completed texts; the commissioning of individual works; the payment of authors and printers; and ultimately the hiring of salaried propagandists. Beyond this, it will also be possible to examine concrete evidence of political patronage and pressure, from private and public, unofficial and official manuscript sources, both in terms of correspondence and financial accounts. Analysis of the mechanics of propaganda concludes with Chapter 6, which analyses the ways in which political grandees involved themselves in the composition of propaganda, both in terms of providing intelligence, information, and official paperwork, as well as in terms of participating in the writing process.

In addition to outlining the various means by which political literature appeared, and the methods by which it was influenced by politicians, the third part of the book serves to stress the importance of recognising the 'dynamics' of propaganda over the course of one of the most important and dramatic periods in British history. This means analysing the ways in which propaganda was used and deployed by those within royalist and parliamentarian ranks, as well as the potential of propaganda as a political tool, in terms of its tactical deployment with respect to specific goals and audiences (Chapter 7). It also means scrutinising the ways in which specific relationships between authors and politicians operated and evolved. In order to understand the nature of the propaganda processes of the civil wars and Interregnum, therefore, it is necessary to understand the way in which the relationships between politicians and patrons on the one hand, and authors on the other, were regarded by all participants. It is necessary to establish the foundations of such relations, and their nature over time, not least in terms of the strains placed upon them by political events and changing political situations, as well as by the characters and requirements of individuals (Chapter 8).

Needless to say, exploration of the propaganda practices of the central decades of the seventeenth century will involve comparing parliamentarian and royalist attitudes towards print and polemic, and exploring also the differing views within parliamentarian and royalist camps. It will become clear that the exploitation of print involved more than just the development of 'parliamentarian' and 'royalist' propaganda machines. During the 1640s and 1650s, political rivalries were not confined to those between Parliament and the king, between Westminster and Oxford, and between Cromwellian and exiled courts. Factions existed within both parliamentarian and royalist ranks, and bedevilled both the parliamentarian and royalist causes from the very earliest phase of the troubles. Factionalism in the early 1640s partly reflected personal allegiance to political grandees, and the policies which they sought to pursue, but also represented conflicting attitudes towards the extent to which the constitutional reforms of 1640–41 provided the terms for a lasting settlement.[93] From late 1642, meawhile, it is possible to detect clear divisions over strategies towards war and peace, the timing and terms of a negotiated settlement, and issues relating to the settlement of the church. Many of the seeds of disunity were sown by the involvement of the Scots, who were essential to enable the challenge to the king but who brought pressure for Presbyterianism, pressure for a negotiated settlement, and opposition to the army. It was the questions of Presbyterianism and Independency, of the involvement of the Scots, and of the role of the army, which would provide the issues underlying factionalism in the mid 1640s. Historians are still coming to terms with the nature of such factional divisions, however, and with mapping the changing fortunes of the various political groupings, and this study will be heavily reliant upon their analyses.[94] During the late 1640s, royalist divisions likewise centred upon the desirability of pursuing an alliance with the Scots, as opposed to forging a settlement with the political Independents and army grandees, and the political and religious concessions attendant upon either option.[95] Divisions over the best path towards confronting the commonwealth and Cromwellian regimes also caused bitter rivalries within the exiled royalist community in the 1650s.[96] Within England, meanwhile, the 1650s saw tension over 'republican' ideals, religious toleration and social reform, as well as over 'healing and settling' and religious comprehension, and the shape of the constitution. Eventually, this became manifest in proposals for the crowning of Cromwell and the reintroduction of an upper House of Parliament, and in the resurgence of both civilian and army republicans.[97]

A solid grasp of factional politics in the 1640s and 1650s is crucial to an understanding of propaganda in the period, since such factions came to recognise

---

[93] D. Smith, *Constitutional Royalism and the Search for Settlement, 1640–49* (Cambridge, 1994).

[94] See for example: D. Underdown, *Pride's Purge* (Oxford, 1971); D. Underdown, 'Party management in the recruiter elections, 1645–48', *EHR* 83 (1968); J. S. A. Adamson, 'The peerage in politics, 1645–9' (Cambridge University PhD, 1986); J. S. A. Adamson, 'Strafford's ghost: the British context of Viscount Lisle's lieutenancy of Ireland', in J. H. Ohlmeyer, ed., *Ireland from Independence to Occupation, 1641–1660* (Cambridge, 1995); Adamson, 'English nobility'; I. Gentles, *The New Model Army* (Oxford, 1992); D. Scott, 'The "Northern gentlemen", the parliamentary Independents and Anglo-Scottish relations in the Long Parliament', *HJ* 42 (1999); J. Adamson, 'The frighted junto: perceptions of Ireland, and the last attempts at settlement with Charles I', in J. Peacey, ed., *The Regicides and the Execution of Charles I* (Basingstoke, 2001); M. Kishlansky, *The Rise of the New Model Army* (Cambridge, 1979); L. Kaplan, *Politics and Religion During the English Revolution* (New York, 1976); V. Pearl, 'Oliver St John and the middle group in the Long Parliament', *EHR* 81 (1966); V. Pearl, 'The royal Independents', *TRHS*, 5th series 18 (1968); M. P. Mahoney, 'The Presbyterian party in the Long Parliament, 2 July 1644–3 June 1647' (Oxford University Dphil, 1973).

[95] Smith, *Constitutional Royalism*.

[96] D. Underdown, *Royalist Conspiracy in England, 1649–1660* (New Haven, 1960).

[97] Worden, *The Rump*; L. H. Carlson, 'A history of the Presbyterian party from Pride's Purge to the dissolution of the commonwealth', *Church History* 11 (1942); A. Woolrych, 'Introduction', in *The Complete Prose Works of John Milton VII* (New Haven, 1980); G. Davies, *The Restoration of Charles II, 1658–1660* (London, 1955).

the value of print for fighting internecine battles. The production of propaganda, in other words, was not necessarily about the struggle between royalists and parliamentarians, so much as about infighting on both sides. Propaganda of both parliamentarian and royalist hues needs to be understood in terms of being addressed to political enemies and factional rivals, and to the people who supported each. Moreover, factional politics will also prove vital in another sense, given that one of the central tasks of this book is to establish the ways in which attitudes towards the press, and the methods by which it was exploited, altered during the course of the two decades under consideration. What will emerge is that the 1640s and 1650s saw not just the print explosion with which we are all now so familiar, as well as a growing concern with the politics of the press and with manipulating opinion, but also the development and exploitation of sophisticated propaganda techniques, and the development of new kinds of relationships between authors and politicians, in terms of the movement away from aristocratic networks towards professionalisation and the emergence of a civil service. Throughout, it will be necessary not merely to observe such changes, but also to analyse the circumstances in which such developments occurred, and those who were responsible for them, and to consider the extent to which they were provoked and influenced by political and religious factionalism.

Such analysis will provide the foundation for the concluding chapter, which explores the importance of this book's findings, and the meaning of propaganda during the civil wars and Interregnum. The aim is to employ the conclusions regarding the attitudes towards print and propaganda, revealed through developments in its practical application over the course of this period, in order to obtain a better understanding of contemporary notions of the relationship between politicians and the public in the early modern period. As such, it seeks to contribute to a growing body of literature which seeks to break down barriers between scholarship on 'high' and 'low' politics, and between 'social' and 'political' history.[98] The purpose will be to set the findings relating to propaganda within the context of recent work on ideas of 'state formation' in the early modern period, and on the possible detection of the emergence of a Habermasian 'public sphere' in the seventeenth century, as well as to explore how the political print culture of the civil war period can be used in order to demonstrate conflicting notions relating to the way in which politicians engaged with the people, the legitimacy of public debate and rational discourse in a political press, and the role of the state in fulfilling such goals relating to communicative practice.

---

[98] A. Wood, *Riot, Rebellion and Popular Politics in Early Modern England* (Basingstoke, 2002), p. 8; P. Collinson, *Elizabethan Essays* (1994), p. 11.

PART ONE
THE MOTOR OF PROPAGANDA

CHAPTER 1

Politicians and the Propaganda Impulse

Writing during the death throes of the Interregnum, the royalist grandee Sir Edward Nicholas provided a revealing insight into the rationale which underpinned his enthusiasm for the exploitation of print propaganda, by telling the Marquess of Ormond that 'reputation is the interest of princes'. Over thirty years earlier, before the print explosion which this study seeks to explore, John Holles offered a more cynical observation, when he opined to the Bishop of Lincoln that 'princes love to befoole the people' through the printed word.[1] Such comments demonstrate that understanding early modern propaganda, which must begin with analysis of the factors which motivated political grandees to engage in the production of print in order to talk to the people, involves confronting highly charged rhetoric. This chapter seeks to demonstrate that politicians turned to political propaganda for reasons which were partly personal, partly factional, and partly governmental, and that print was understood to be a means of boosting individual reputations and creating more or less formal and distinct political groupings, and also a way of undermining rival grandees and rival claimants to political power. In order to do so, it explores the reality as well as the rhetoric of propaganda – the practice as well as the principles – and develops a methodology for assessing the seriousness with which politicians took the task of engaging with the public through the medium of print. The major focus of attention at this stage will be official statements – declarations and proclamations – in terms of the methods by which they were produced, and the ways in which they were printed and distributed. By examining such works, it will be possible both to compare the practices and attitudes of royalists and parliamentarians, and to explore the strengths and weaknesses of official propaganda, as well as the conceptual and practical problems with such works, which prompted political grandees of all persuasions to turn to outsiders for help in the polemical process, and to invent more subtle forms for publicising their ideas and opinions.

Propaganda in the early modern period was generally produced by, or on behalf of, the monarch, by leading churchmen and prominent ministers of state, as well as by members of clerical and aristocratic households. Indeed, 'regime propaganda'

---

[1] PRO, SP 77/32, fo. 328; *CSPD 1659–60*, p. 259; P. R. Seddon, ed., *Letters of John Holles 1587–1637* (3 vols, Thoroton Society Records Series, 1975–86), ii. 366.

existed long before the arrival of print.[2] Early modern monarchs and statesmen evidently recognised the need to 'talk to the people'. This reflected the growing importance of public opinion, the fact that the public was taking greater interest in politics and parliamentary affairs, and the reality that information regarding national politics was circulating increasingly widely.[3] Such trends encouraged a desire to influence public attitudes, not least because of concern regarding public disorder, resistance and rebellion.[4] Early modern monarchs used declarations in order to explain and justify policy decisions, not least foreign wars, and it became common to issue explanations of parliamentary dissolutions.[5] Nevertheless, the extent to which particular regimes sought to engage with the people through the medium of print remains a matter of debate. Reluctance to use the press was a persistent feature of the period, and was overcome to differing degrees by individual monarchs and ministers. The efficiency with which the press was exploited in the century preceding the civil war depended heavily upon the dynamism of individual ministers, as well as the willingness of particular monarchs to overcome reticence about engaging in, and fostering, public debate. While the potential of the press had been understood since the early sixteenth century, it was not always a power harnessed willingly.

There was no steady march towards the development of a sophisticated machinery of state propaganda. Nevertheless, intensive print campaigns may have been intrinsic to the Henrician 'revolution' in government and the break with Rome, as well as to the Edwardian reformation.[6] Nevertheless, the Marian regime arguably

---

[2] W. R. Jones, 'The English church and royal propaganda during the hundred years war', *JBS* 19 (1979), pp. 18–30; A. K. McHardy, 'Liturgy and propaganda in the diocese of Lincoln during the hundred years war', *SCH* 18 (1982), pp. 215–26; S. Gaunt, 'Visual propaganda in England in the later middle ages', in B. Taithe and T. Thornton, eds, *Propaganda* (Stroud, 1999); J. Loach, 'The function of ceremonial in the reign of Henry VIII', *P&P* 142 (1994); C. S. L. Davies, 'The Cromwellian decade: authority and consent', *TRHS*, 6th series 7 (1997), p. 181. See: S. Anglo, *Images of Tudor Kingship* (London, 1992).

[3] F. J. Levy, 'How information spread among the gentry, 1550–1640', *JBS* 21 (1982); R. Cust, 'News and politics in early seventeenth century England', *P&P* 112 (1986); I. Atherton, 'The itch grown a disease: manuscript transmission of news in the seventeenth century', in J. Raymond, ed., *News, Newspapers, and Society in Early Modern Britain* (London, 1999).

[4] Jones, 'English church and royal propaganda', p. 18; C. Ross, 'Rumour, propaganda and popular opinion during the Wars of the Roses', in R. A. Griffiths, ed., *Patronage, the Crown and the Provinces* (Gloucester, 1981), p. 15; Cust, 'News and politics', p. 73; T. Kilburn and A. Milton, 'The public context of the trial and execution of Strafford', in J. F. Merritt, ed., *The Political World of Thomas Wentworth, Earl of Strafford, 1621–1641* (Cambridge, 1996).

[5] *A Declaration, Conteynyng the Iust Causes of this Present Warre with the Scotts* (London, 1542); *A Declaration of the Iust Causes Moouing her Maiestie to Send a Nauie, and Armie to the Seas, and Toward Spaine* (London, 1597); *His Majesties Declaration* (London, 1628), pp. 9–45; T. Cogswell, 'The politics of propaganda: Charles I and the people in the 1620s', *JBS* 29 (1990), p. 197; E. S. Cope, 'The king's declaration concerning the dissolution of the Short Parliament of 1640: an unsuccessful attempt at public relations', *HLQ* 40 (1976–77), pp. 325–7.

[6] G. R. Elton, *Policy and Police. The Enforcement of the Reformation in the Age of Thomas Cromwell* (Cambridge, 1972), pp. 171–216, esp. pp. 206–7; V. M. Murphy, 'The debate over Henry

failed to exploit the potential of the press, although in this respect it appears to have been something of an exception in the sixteenth century.[7] Under Elizabeth, successive ministers developed sophisticated methods for producing propaganda in order to project a favourable public image of the queen, and to defend official policies and actions, expose plotters, counteract false reports and rumours, as well as to stir up public sympathy.[8] Reluctantly, men such as John Whitgift recognised the need to engage with critics, even though they risked fanning the flames of public debate.[9] Indeed, the difficulties of enforcing censorship may have encouraged the use of propaganda as the best means of countering opponents' influence.[10] The early Stuarts, however, have sometimes been portrayed as being more reticent about using print for fear of fostering public discussion. James I certainly encouraged authors to refute key texts by religious enemies, but scholarly disputation may have been one of the few areas in which he was prepared to encourage such activity.[11] More problematic is Charles I, whose apparent failure to exploit the press has been connected with a wider attempt to distance himself from his subjects. However, this picture of 'contemptuous indifference to public opinion' has been challenged by those who argue that the king and his ministers were sometimes adept at using the pulpits, press and stage for disseminating the royal line, and that Charles' reign demonstrates that 'concern for public relations had become standard operating procedure'.[12] However, if this is the case, Charles may have altered his view in the

---

VIII's first divorce. An analysis of the comptemorary treatises' (Cambridge University PhD, 1984); V. Murphy, 'The literature and propaganda of Henry VIII's first divorce', in D. MacCulloch, ed., *The Reign of Henry VIII* (Basingstoke, 1995); J. Black, 'Thomas Cromwell's patronage of preaching', *Sixteenth Century Journal* 8 (1977); J. N. King, 'Freedom of the press, Protestant propaganda and Protector Somerset', *HLQ* 40 (1976), p. 1.

[7] C. S. L. Davies, *Peace, Print and Protestantism* (London, 1977), p. 303; J. W. Martin, 'The Marian regime's failure to understand the importance of printing', *HLQ* 44 (1981); J. Loach, 'Pamphlets and politics 1553–9', *BIHR* 48 (1975); J. Loach, 'The Marian establishment and the printing press', *EHR* 101 (1986); E. J. Baskerville, *A Chronological Bibliography of Propaganda and Polemic Published in English Between 1553 and 1558* (Philadelphia, 1979). However, see: T. Freeman, 'Nicholas Harpsfield and the genesis of anti-martyrology' (paper delivered at the IHR, London, 7 Feb. 2000).

[8] M. A. R. Graves, *Thomas Norton* (Oxford, 1994); C. Read, 'William Cecil and Elizabethan public relations', in S. T. Bindoff, J. Hurstfield and C. H. Williams, eds, *Elizabethan Government and Society* (London, 1961), pp. 21–55; V. Sanders, 'The household of Archbishop Parker and the influencing of public opinion', *JEH* 34 (1983); V. Sanders, 'John Whitgift: primate, privy councillor and propagandist', *Anglican and Episcopal History* 56 (1987); Jones, 'English church and royal propaganda', p. 19; A. Hunt, 'Tuning the pulpits: the religious context of the Essex revolt', in L. A. Ferrell and P. McCullough, eds, *The English Sermon Revised* (Manchester, 2000), p. 97; L. F. Parmelee, *Good Newes from Fraunce* (Rochester, NY, 1996).

[9] Sanders, 'John Whitgift', pp. 392–3.

[10] F. J. Levy, 'Staging the news', in A. F. Marotti and M. D. Bristol, eds, *Print, Manuscript and Performance* (Columbus, 2000), pp. 272–3.

[11] F. Levy, 'The decorum of news', in Raymond, ed., *News, Newspapers, and Society*; D. H. Willson, 'James I and his literary assistants', *HLQ* 8 (1944).

[12] Cogswell, 'Politics of propaganda', pp. 190, 196, 197, 213; T. Cogswell, 'Thomas Middleton and the court, 1624: *A Game at Chess* in context', *HLQ* 47 (1984), p. 284; Cust, 'News and politics', p. 81.

late 1620s, as he increasingly 'found the simplicity of James's old rigid defence of the *arcana imperii* irresistible'.[13] Indeed, such reticence on the part of Charles to communicate with his subjects may represent an important stage in the souring of political relations in the 1630s, and may have proved harmful to the king.[14]

Engagement with the public was not merely a concern for monarchs and their ministers, however, and print had always been exploited by individual grandees to produce 'personal' propaganda; for self-promotion and self-defence, and for furthering personal goals and fighting personal battles. Aristocratic grandees had long employed the services of men with literary and scholarly talents, with 'think tanks' of advisers engaged in 'knowledge transactions' and 'scholarly services'. This did not necessarily involve the production of propaganda, but rather the employment of researchers, advisers and 'privados', but their tasks could be political, and they were certainly ideally placed to write and publish when their employers and patrons felt the need to bolster their personal standing and reputation, and to advance personal causes in a public arena.[15] For political malcontents, seeking 'popularity' provided an alternative to both futile rebellion and quietism.[16] However, it is not simply the

---

[13] Cogswell, 'Politics of propaganda', p. 213. See: *CSPD 1627–8*, pp. 269, 273, 278; *CSPD 1628–9*, p. 185.

[14] Cogswell, 'Politics of propaganda', p. 214; K. Sharpe, 'Crown, parliament and locality: government and communication in early Stuart England', *EHR* 101 (1986), p. 345; K. Sharpe, 'The king's writ: royal authors and royal authority in early modern England', in K. Sharpe and P. Lake, eds, *Culture and Politics in Early Stuart England* (Basingstoke, 1994), pp. 134–5; J. Richards, 'His nowe majestie and the English monarchy: the kingship of Charles I before 1640', *P&P* 113 (1986), p. 78; Cope, 'King's declaration', pp. 325–31.

[15] L. Jardine and W. Sherman, 'Pragmatic readers: knowledge transactions and scholarly services in late Elizabethan England', in A. Fletcher and P. Roberts, eds, *Religion, Culture and Society in Early Modern Britain* (Cambridge, 1994); W. Sherman, *John Dee: The Politics of Reading and Writing in the Renaissance* (Amherst, Mass., 1994); P. Collinson, 'The monarchical republic of Queen Elizabeth I', *BJRL* 69 (1986–87); P. Collinson, 'Puritans, men of business, and Elizabethan parliaments', *PH* 7 (1988); P. Hammer, 'The uses of scholarship: the secretariat of Robert Devereux, 2nd Earl of Essex, c.1585–1601', *EHR* 109 (1994), pp. 26–51; P. Hammer, 'The Earl of Essex, Fulke Greville, and the employment of scholars', *Studies in Philology* 91 (1994), pp. 167–80; L. L. Peck, *Northampton. Patronage and Policy at the Court of James I* (London, 1982), ch. 6; P. Hammer, 'Patronage at court, faction and the Earl of Essex', in J. Guy, ed., *The Reign of Elizabeth I. Court and Culture in the Last Decade* (Cambridge, 1985), p. 79; Hunt, 'Tuning the pulpits', p. 90; J. Guy, *Tudor England* (Oxford, 1988), pp. 447–9; F. J. Levy, 'Hayward, Daniel and the beginnings of politic history', *HLQ* 50 (1987); K. Fincham and P. Lake, 'Popularity, prelacy and puritanism in the 1630s: Joseph Hall explains himself', *EHR* 111 (1996), pp. 856–7, 860; K. Fincham, 'Prelacy and politics: Archbishop Abbot's defence of Protestant orthodoxy', *HR* 61 (1988), pp. 57–9; Croft, 'The reputation of Robert Cecil: libels, political opinion and popular awareness in the early seventeenth century', *TRHS*, 6th series 1 (1991), p. 63; M. Mendle, 'Henry Parker: the public's privado', in G. J. Schochet, ed., *Religion, Resistance and Civil War* (Washington, 1990), p. 156.

[16] T. Cogswell, 'The people's love: the Duke of Buckingham and popularity', in T. Cogswell, R. Cust and P. Lake, eds, *Politics, Religion and Popularity in Early Stuart Britain* (Cambridge, 2002); M. Heinemann, 'Rebel lords, popular playwrights and political culture: notes on the Jacobean patronage of the Earl of Southampton', in *Politics, Patronage and Literature in England, 1558–1685* (Yearbook of English Studies, 21, 1991), p. 67.

case that members of the gentry and aristocracy were concerned with 'lobbying' or self-promotion.[17] The use of print also reflected political and religious agendas, and 'personal' propaganda could extend to policies and personalities with which individual grandees were associated. Some revealed a concern for 'good works', not least the provision of printed sermons as a form of 'sound and spiritual food'.[18] Print was also used in association with the corporate interests with which grandees were involved, such as the Virginia Company.[19] Moreover, it was employed to advance political and religious interests during periods of domestic strife, when 'public' life revolved not merely around governments, but around rival claimaints to political authority. Pamphleteering was central to Catholic campaigning in England in the late sixteenth century, as well as to the opponents of Caroline policies in the mid-seventeenth century.[20] Certain grandees were remarkably consistent in their patronage of Puritan preachers, and were prepared to go to great lengths to procure sermons from, and to provide safe havens for, controversial ministers.[21] Being conscious of the need for skilled preachers, they patronised the most able controversialists and polemicists; the men who emerged as pamphleteers in the 1640s.[22] This understanding of the power of preaching explains their attempts to gain control of pulpits, not least through the Honourable Artillery Company and the Feoffees for the Purchase of Impropriation; bodies which their opponents considered to have been exploited for political purposes, and to have

---

17 J. Limon, *Dangerous Matter. English Drama and Politics in 1623/4* (Cambridge, 1986), p. 4.

18 Hammer, 'Patronage at court', p. 79; E. Rosenberg, *Leicester, Patron of Letters* (New York, 1955), p. 185. The analogy between printed sermons and food is Henry Newcombe's: J. Rigney, 'To lye upon a stationers stall, like a piece of coarse flesh in a shambles': the sermon, print and the English civil war', in Ferrell and McCullough, eds, *English Sermon Revised*, p. 188.

19 Limon, *Dangerous Matter*, 4; A. Fitzmaurice, 'Every man, that prints, adventures': the rhetoric of the Virginia Company sermons', in Ferrell and McCullough, eds, *English Sermon Revised*; P. J. Wallis, *William Crashawe, The Sheffield Puritan* (Transactions of the Hunter Archaeological Society, 8, 1960–63). The adventurers for the drainage of the fens engaged in print campaigns in the 1650s: Cambridgeshire RO, R.59.31.19a, pp. 7, 11.

20 J. Bossy, 'The character of Elizabethan Catholicism', in T. Aston, ed., *Crisis in Europe 1560–1660* (London, 1965); T. M. McCoog, 'The slightest suspicion of avarice: the finances of the English Jesuit mission', *Recusant History* 19 (1988), p. 103.

21 *CSPD 1625–49*, p. 175; A. Hughes, *Politics, Society and Civil War in Warwickshire, 1620–1660* (Cambridge, 1987); A. Hughes, 'Thomas Dugard and his circle in the 1630s', *HJ* 29 (1986); J. Preston, *The Golden Scepter* (London, 1638), sig. A4; K. L. Sprunger, 'The Dutch career of Thomas Hooker', *New England Quarterly* 46 (1973); F. Shuffleton, *Thomas Hooker* (Princeton, 1977); B. Donagan, 'The clerical patronage of Robert Rich, 2nd Earl of Warwick, 1619–1642', *Proceedings of the American Philosophical Society* 120 (1976), pp. 407–8.

22 A. Duffy, 'The godly and the multitude in Stuart England', *Seventeenth Century* 1 (1986), p. 35; Peacey, 'Henry Parker', pp. 8–9; Donagan, 'Clerical patronage', pp. 393, 397, 399. See the patronage of Lord Brooke: J. S. A. Adamson, 'The peerage in politics 1645–49' (Cambridge University PhD, 1986), pp. 88–97; Warwickshire RO, CR 1886, unfol.; J. Peacey, 'Led by the hand: manucaptors and patronage at Lincoln's Inn in the seventeenth century', *Journal of Legal History* 18 (1997), pp. 36–7; 'John Sadler' (History of Parliament biography); Hartlib Papers, 50H/46/9/36a; Hughes, 'Dugard', p. 776.

been turned into seminaries for preachers and writers.[23] Moreover, prominent Puritan grandees can be shown to have circulated controversial manuscripts, and to have supported and sponsored stage productions and printed polemics.[24]

In the decades before the civil war, therefore, the regimes of the early modern period, as well as individual political grandees, and the interest groups with which they were associated, had demonstrated their willingness to employ print media for political purposes. Their engagement with the public was, however, more or less episodic, and more or less reluctant. It was such voluntarism and hesitation which was swept away by England's troubles.

Understanding how this happened requires examination of why and how politicians contributed to the explosion of print of the early 1640s; why they promoted the emergence of literature which addressed sections of society previously ignored; and why they communicated with the public in novel ways. Civil tension and ultimately war was accompanied by the widespread production of propaganda, and both parliamentarians and royalists set about the task with zeal. The crisis of the Stuart monarchy helped to overcome doubts about the need to engage with the people, and reticence about public debate became a restraining factor of less power, because a politically aware mass reading public was a fact which could no longer be ignored.[25] Both royalists and parliamentarians recognised the need to exploit the press and to talk to the people, in order to justify their policies, and to try and counter the impact of their opponents' efforts. This ensured that during subsequent years hundreds of declarations were issued, printed and distributed throughout the country. Pamphleteering became an intrinsic aspect of political life; a factor contributing to, rather than merely commenting upon, the conflict. As early as the summer of 1642, indeed, Isaac Massey argued that there could be no peace without an end to 'writing and indighting'.[26]

---

[23] P. Collinson, 'Lectures by combination. Structures and characteristics of church life in 17th century England', in *Godly People* (London, 1983); P. Seaver, *The Puritan Lectureships* (Stanford, 1970); G. Davies, 'English political sermons, 1603–1640', *HLQ* (1939), p. 1; E. W. Kirby, 'The lay feoffees: a study in militant Puritanism', *JMH* 14 (1942); Peacey, 'Henry Parker', pp. 15–21; I. M. Calder, 'The St Antholin's lecturers', *Church Quarterly Review* 160 (1959); I. M. Calder, ed., *Activities of the Puritan Faction of the Church of England, 1625–33* (Church History Society, 1957); H. A. Parker, 'The feoffees of impropriations', *Publications of the Colonial Society of Massachusetts* (1906–7); J. Chestlin, *Persecutio Undecima* (Np, 1648), p. 56; Laud, *Works*, iii. 216–17.

[24] L. Rostenberg, *The Minority Press and the English Crown. A Study in Repression 1558–1625* (The Hague, 1971), pp. 170–86; R. Cust, *The Forced Loan and English Politics 1626–1628* (Oxford, 1987), pp. 170–71; T. Cogswell, *Home Divisions* (Manchester, 1998), p. 90; Heinemann, 'Rebel lords', pp. 67, 73; P. W. White, 'Patronage, Protestantism, and stage propaganda in early Elizabethan England', in *Politics, Patronage and Literature in England, 1558–1685*; Levy, 'Staging the news', p. 262; Limon, *Dangerous Matter*, p. 2; I. Morgan, *Prince Charles's Puritan Chaplain* (London, 1957), pp. 55–9.

[25] Graves, *Norton*, p. 113.

[26] T. Cogswell, 'Underground verse and the transformation of early Stuart political culture', in S. D. Amussen and M. Kishlansky, eds, *Political Culture and Cultural Politics in Early Modern England* (Manchester, 1995), p. 292.

The impetus for overcoming royal reticence regarding propaganda was provided by innovation on the part of the Long Parliament. Unlike royal proclamations, which constituted public ordinances with power to affect events, parliamentary declarations merely had polemical force. Unlike petitions and remonstrances, which were traditionally presented to the king in a supplicatory fashion, they were printed and widely circulated.[27] The 'grand remonstrance' of December 1641 not only helped to clarify the divisions between parliamentarians and royalists, but was addressed to the public, and was widely recognised as an appeal to the people.[28] As a rival claimant to governmental legitimacy, Parliament's subsequent communications with the king appeared concurrently in print in order to justify its demands and policies. A Parliament which was moving 'out of the normal sphere of political manoeuvre' needed to garner support and convince members of the public.[29] Parliamentarian propaganda was intrinsically aimed at forging a parliamentarian party, and securing allegiance. Such appeals to the people naturally provoked hostility from the emerging royalist party, and there was a furious reaction to the idea of printing and distributing the 'grand remonstrance', not least before it had been presented to, and answered by, the king.[30] Sir Edward Dering complained: 'I did not dream that we should remonstrate downward, tell stories to the people, and talk of the king as of a third person'.[31] Nevertheless, royalists could no longer avoid appealing to the people themselves, and as a result they too found themselves required to use printed propaganda, albeit in order to create and define a party which sought to deny Parliament's claims and to defend the king's authority.[32] It quickly became apparent that Charles 'keenly appreciated' the importance of propaganda, and the comments of leading royalist grandees reflect as much.[33] In January 1653, Sir Edward Nicholas wrote that a royalist polemic 'might do much good', and in the late 1650s some saw print as the best, and perhaps only, hope for the royal cause.[34]

Print was, therefore, intrinsic to political polarisation, and both sides needed to appeal to the people.[35] Both sides recognised that the people needed not just to

---

[27] J. F. Larkin and P. L. Hughes, eds, *Stuart Royal Proclamations* (2 vols, Oxford, 1973–83), i. viii.

[28] W. H. Coates, 'Some observations on the Grand Remonstrance', *JMH* 4 (1932), p. 3; Clarendon, *History*, i. 419; *CSPV 1642–3*, p. 72.

[29] Kilburn and Milton, 'Public context', p. 236.

[30] *CJ* ii. 344; *D'Ewes Diary*, ed. Coates, pp. 183–7, 295; Coates, 'Grand Remonstrance', pp. 7–8. For contemporary comment on these disputes, see: *CSPD 1641–3*, pp. 179, 180, 182, 203; Bodl. MS Clarendon 21, fo. 56; Clarendon, *History*, i. 419, ii. 64.

[31] Rushworth, *Collections*, iv. 425. Parliamentarians may later have shared this view, and Thomas Juxon recorded that Parliament resented the fact that the Scots 'should in a clandestine and seditious way go about to court the people': Dr Williams Library, MS 24.50, fos. 91v–92.

[32] *His Majesties Declaration to all his Loving Subjects* (London, 1641).

[33] J. L. Malcolm, *Caesar's Due. Loyalty and King Charles, 1642–1646* (London, 1983), p. 124.

[34] *NP* ii. 1–2; *CCSP* iv. 210.

[35] T. Harris, 'Propaganda and public opinion in seventeenth century England', in J. D. Popkin, ed., *Media and Revolution* (Lexington, 1995), p. 49.

be informed about the reasons for the decisions taken by their representatives and rulers, but also to be persuaded by them, and convinced of the righteousness of the cause of either king or Parliament. Print was a means of convincing people, not just about political 'ideas', but also about specific policies and actions. Such attempts at persuasion were vital in forming and defining parties. Indeed, this was as true of the army interest as it was of royalists and parliamentarians, and as the military rose to political prominence in 1647, some of its members recognised the value of print. Edward Sexby called for a 'press got into the army', or else 'we shall be at a loss', and Edmund Chillenden advised that 'if it be not thought on to have a press in the army we are undone'.[36] Moreover, print was also used to defend such parties from the criticism of opponents. Parliament felt obliged to respond to critics of their military leader, the Earl of Essex, and to vocal enemies such as John Lilburne.[37] Such opponents could also be factional, however. In April 1646, for example, as tensions emerged between parliamentary Independents and the Scots, Robert Baillie commented that 'the word was made to go far and near' that the Scots retarded a peace settlement because of 'many unreasonable desires', and as a result the Scots 'thought it necessary to have our papers printed' in order to counter such allegations.[38] Later, the Council of State explained the decision to respond to critics of its Irish campaign in terms of 'perpetuating a just and deserved infamy upon the Irish papists', as well as of the need to answer

> so many here in this nation [who] by their causeless cavils and queries … turn obstructers of their indended relief, whereby they weaken the hands of the well-affected in both nations and do in effect second the designs of the bloody rebels there to the manifest hazard of the ruin of the Protestant cause and English interest.[39]

Beyond responding to overt and explicit criticism, however, it also proved necessary to counteract opponents' propaganda. In January 1645, therefore, Parliament's ambassador in the Low Countries proposed issuing a response to Archbishop Laud's scaffold speech, to offset the possible damage that it would do on the Continent.[40] His thought process was expressed by a parliamentarian pamphlet of 1649, which said that 'if our adversaries write all … and we nothing at all, the conquering sword will be conquered by the pen'.[41] Propaganda was also crucial, of course, for securing revenue from taxation, and in convincing the public to part with its money, and it was essential to allegiance in a more direct sense, in terms of reconciling individuals to the need to take up arms.[42] Paolo Sarpi, while

---

[36] Worcester College, Oxford, Clarke MS XLI, fo. 103v; *CP* i. 86.

[37] *CJ* iii. 188–9, 191; *A Declaration of the Commons Against a Scandalous Book Entituled The Second Part of England's New Chains Discovered* (London, 1649).

[38] *Letters and Journals of Robert Baillie*, ii. 367.

[39] PRO, SP 25/62, pp. 279–80.

[40] BL, Add. 72435, fo. 57.

[41] *Rectifying Principles* (London, 1648), preface.

[42] Jones, 'English church and royal propaganda', p. 23; Heinemann, 'Rebel lords', p. 84; B. T.

acknowledging that books were made only of words, said that 'from those words are formed the opinions of the world that bring about parties, seditions, and eventually wars. Yes, they are words, but they are words that draw armies behind them'.[43]

In order to obtain a more detailed picture of the ways in which contemporaries understood the purpose and value of propaganda, and the role of print in political life, it is necessary to search deeper into the rhetoric with which they surrounded such works.[44] Both sides agreed that securing popular support involved 'educating' the people. Peter Heylyn explained the desire for discourses justifying altar policy in the 1630s by the need 'to bring them to a right understanding of the truth'.[45] Sir Edward Hyde reflected upon the royalist concern that parliamentarian suppression of royal statements meant that the people 'were not in truth generally informed of the matter of fact and the justice of the king's cause'.[46] In July 1642, a parliamentary committee was ordered to prepare a declaration to let the people know the 'matters of fact' in the dispute with the king, and in the folllowing December John Pym produced a declaration regarding the 'state of the kingdom'.[47] In August 1648 the Scottish Committee of Estates recognised the need to 'provide for the fittest way how the public condition of the affairs of the kingdom and of our army' could be 'represented to the kingdom'.[48] In 1651, the Scottish kirk considered 'the great prejudice rebounding to the public by want of a press ... whereby the people want information how to carry on the public business'.[49] In part, such comments reflected recognition that print could be used to correct misapprehensions, as well as mistaken or misleading ideas, errors and untruths, and it was considered necessary to undo the effects of false information which had appeared in the public domain. In June 1646, for example, parliamentarian authorities ordered the printing of the terms of the surrender of Oxford, because there were 'many short and imperfect copies abroad'.[50] It was also necessary to counteract statements which were deliberately intended to mislead, and to respond to allegations made by opponents. In 1639, the Scots sought to engage with the public 'in a printed sheet or two ... to clear ourselves of all slander, especially of that vile calumny of our intention to

---

Whitehead, *Brags and Boasts. Propaganda in the Year of the Armada* (Stroud, 1994), p. 195; J. Hale, 'War and public opinion in the 15th and 16th centuries', *P&P* 22 (1962), p. 24.

43 Sarpi quoted in M. Infelise, 'The war, the news and the curious', in B. Dooley and S. Baron, eds, *The Politics of Information in Early Modern Europe* (London, 2001), pp. 232–3.

44 Harris 'Propaganda and public opinion'; S. Achinstein, 'The uses of deception from Cromwell to Milton' in K. Z. Keller and G. J. Schiffhorst, eds, *The Witness of Time* (Pittsburgh, 1993).

45 P. Heylyn, *Cyprianus* Anglicus (London, 1671), p. 279.

46 Clarendon, *History*, ii. 432.

47 *CJ* ii. 655, 808, 810, 849.

48 D. Stevenson, 'Scotland's first newspaper, 1648', *The Bibliothek. A Scottish Journal of Bibliography and Allied Topics* 10 (1981), pp. 123–6.

49 D. Stevenson, 'A revolutionary regime and the press: the Scottish covenanters and their printers 1638–51', *The Library*, 6th series 7 (1985), p. 335.

50 *CSPD 1645–7*, p. 445.

invade England, or to cast off our dutiful obedience to our prince'.[51] The king was then advised to issue a reply; Robert Baillie recognising that this simply provided testimony of the effectiveness of the Scots' propaganda, since 'our adversaries, being extremely galled with our success, moved the king to make that pitiful declaration ... where we are, on the contrary to all reason and law, declared ... the foulest traitors and rebels that ever breathed'.[52] The royalist secretary of state, Sir Edward Nicholas, would later stress the need to counter the false reports circulating regarding the Catholicism of Charles Stuart.[53]

The rhetoric of education was often mixed with language which intimated that the people had been deceived and deluded.[54] The author of one royalist newspaper claimed that 'the members contrive all means and ways imaginable to dismay and delude the loyal citizens with the noise of victories against the royalists'.[55] The same author also said that 'it is deemed safest now and then to sing placebo to the people' regarding attitudes towards a personal treaty with the king.[56] Another royalist, Griffith Williams, claimed that books were used to 'seduce the people of God and to lead them headlong into perdition'.[57] However, all sides spoke of the need to 'undeceive', and to undo the harm done by opponents. The parliamentarian diplomat Walter Strickland spoke of the need for a 'speedy, full and clear declaration to justify the Parliament's proceedings', in order to 'wash off that dirt they cast in the Parliament's face'.[58] In January 1648, meanwhile, a committee was appointed to publish intercepted letters, 'for the clearing of all objections and undeceiving of the people', and for 'vindication of aspersions cast upon Parliament', and after the establishment of the republic and the imposition of the Engagement, a committee was established with the express purpose of finding ways of 'undeceiving' the people regarding the new oath.[59] Similarly, an army memorandum from May 1647 mentioned the need to 'keep a party of able pen men at Oxford and the army, where their presses be employed to satisfy and undeceive the people'.[60] In August 1648, the Scottish Committee of Estates bemoaned the

---

[51] *Letters and Journals of Robert Baillie*, i. 188–9.

[52] *CSPD 1639*, pp. 233–4; *Letters and Journals of Robert Baillie*, i. 188–9.

[53] *CSPD 1659–60*, pp. 259, 276. In June 1667 notice was taken of a book against the king which 'will do much harm if not well answered': *CCSP* v. 618. It is also evident, however, that it was necessary to alter the perception of the court and king as well as the public. After January 1649, for example, it became necessary for some, particularly the Scots who had proclaimed Charles II as king, to influence the perceptions of the exiled court, and in April 1649 Baillie, advocated a reply to John Bramhall's attack on Presbyterianism on the grounds that 'it does much ill to the king and all about him': *Letters and Journals of Robert Baillie*, iii. 87, 90.

[54] Achinstein, 'Uses of deception'.

[55] *Mercurius Elencticus* 33 (5–12 July 1648), p. 255.

[56] *Mercurius Elencticus* 34 (12–19 July 1648), p. 265. See also: J. Taylor, *A Letter Sent to London from a Spie at Oxford* (1643), p. 3.

[57] G. Williams, *The Discovery of Mysteries* (Oxford, 1643), pp. 48–9.

[58] BL, Add. 72435, fo. 74v.

[59] Rushworth, *Collections*, vii. 959; *CJ* vi. 312–14, 337.

[60] Worcester College, Clarke MS XLI, fo. 21; *CP* i. 22–3.

'many false scandals and reports that are vented and spread through this kingdom against the proceedings and success of our armies, to the disheartening ... and deceiving of His Majesty's good subjects from their duties in this great work'.[61]

However, the rhetoric with which such attempts to engage with the people were surrounded reveals contrasting attitudes to propaganda, not least regarding the notion of 'awakening' and 'stirring up' the people. In March 1640, Robert Baillie recognised that propaganda was 'very needful' to 'waken up the spirits of our own countrymen', and for 'the rousing up of our slippery neighbours of England'.[62] In March 1644, the Earl of Denbigh asked for papers to be circulated to Warwickshire ministers, 'to publish in their several churches, thereby the better to stir up the people to express their affection to the Parliament'.[63] During the Protectorate, President Henry Lawrence ordered George Monck to disperse copies of a narrative of the fleet's victory against the Spanish, and to ensure that it was read by all ministers in their churches, 'the better to stir up the hearts of the people to praise the Lord'.[64] Royalists, however, were more ambivalent. Some bemoaned the way in which pamphlets had been used to 'animate rebellion', and to 'poison the dutifull affections and the obliged loyalty', and their employment for 'stirring up the people'.[65] In July 1642, Lord Montagu regretted that 'so much printing hath stirred up too much heat'.[66] Not all royalists were so apprehensive, and Sir Edward Hyde wrote of the need to 'awaken' and 'inflame the people', not least to 'make them sensible of the destruction that attended them' as a result of Cromwell's decimation tax.[67] In December 1659, Sir Edward Nicholas advocated the use of propaganda 'to mind the people what an advantage and happiness the king's restoration would be to the nation, for though few can be ignorant of it, yet the frequent asserting of his just title would awake them, and make them think of their duty'.[68] Nevertheless, royalist texts generally reveal a much more vivid concern regarding the harmfulness of books. Hyde perceived parliamentarian sermons to be 'trumpets of war and incendiaries towards rebellion'.[69] Royalist orders explained the necessity of countering parliamentarian propaganda in terms of offering an 'antidote' to 'their poison'.[70] Hyde argued that the Grand Remonstrance had 'so much poisoned the hearts of the people', and that it had 'already done much harm, and would do much more if it were not answered'.[71] Charles sought to

---

[61] Scottish RO, PA.11/6, fos. 104–5v; Stevenson, 'Scotland's first newspaper', pp. 123–6.

[62] *Letters and Journals of Robert Baillie*, i. 242.

[63] Warwicks. RO, CR 2017/C9/60.

[64] *CSPD 1656–7*, pp. 126, 137.

[65] G. Williams, *Vindicaie Regum* (Oxford, 1643), sig. A2; *Sober Sadnes* (Oxford, 1643), p. 19.

[66] *HMC Buccleuch III*, p. 417.

[67] Clarendon, *Life*, i. 308.

[68] *CSPD 1659–60*, pp. 275–6.

[69] Clarendon, *History*, ii. 320–21.

[70] W. Phillips, ed., 'The Ottley papers relating to the civil war', *Transactions of the Shropshire Archeaological and Natural History Society*, 2nd series 7 (1895), pp. 344–5.

[71] Clarendon, *Life*, i. 98.

respond to Parliament's declaration of 26 May 1642 in order that 'the poison thereof might not work too long upon the minds of the people'.[72] Griffith Williams concluded that such declarations served to 'poison the love and loyalty of the king's subjects'.[73] During October 1641, as news spread of the 'Incident' – the royal attempt to arrest leading covenanters in Scotland – Nicholas recognised that 'it is most necessary that there be instantly sent hither a perfect relation of this business … to stop the mouths of disaffected persons', and 'to prevent and stop the false rumours here which are spread everywhere'.[74]

The politically charged and even contingent nature of such statements means that understanding contemporary attitudes to print requires scrutiny of the reality, as well as the rhetoric of propaganda; the practice as well as the theory. By exploring the way in which propaganda was produced it will be possible to reveal not just the extent to which both sides sought to communicate with the people, but also valuable evidence regarding their methodology for doing so. The most obvious way to engage with the public was by means of official statements, declarations, and 'manifestos', including printed royal speeches.[75] Whatever the reticence of the early Stuart monarchs regarding the use of propaganda, James I and Charles I both used official statements, such as the declaration issued following the dissolution of the 1629 Parliament, which contained not just the royal proclamation, and the king's speech at the dissolution, but also a lengthy declaration 'to all his loving subjects, of the causes which moved him' to make his decision.[76] Such works make up a high proportion of the polemical literature of the 1640s and 1650s, particulary during the 'paper war' of 1642, as each new declaration from either side provoked a response in a seemingly endless cycle of claim and counterclaim.[77] When the king received Parliament's declaration of 26 May 1642, for example, Charles

---

[72] Clarendon, *Life*, i. 138–9.

[73] Williams, *Discovery of Mysteries*, pp. 68–9.

[74] Surrey RO, G52/2/19/25, 28, 30; G85/5/2/17, 19, 20.

[75] A. Allan, 'Yorkist propaganda: pedigree, prophecy and the "British History" in the reign of Edward IV', in C. Ross, ed., *Patronage, Pedigree and Power in Later Medieval England* (Gloucester, 1979); A. Allan, 'Royal propaganda and the proclamations of Edward IV', *BIHR* 59 (1986); Ross, 'Rumour, propaganda and popular opinion', pp. 15–32; A. Gransden, 'Propaganda in Medieval English Historiography', *Journal of Medieval History* 1 (1975); J. A. Doig, 'Political propaganda and royal proclamations in late medieval England', *HR* 71 (1998); J. W. Mckenna, 'Piety and propaganda: the cult of King Henry VI', in B. Rowland, ed., *Chaucer and Middle English Studies* (London, 1974); J. W. McKenna, 'Henry VI of England and the dual monarchy: aspects of royal political propaganda 1422–1432', *Journal of the Warburg and Courtauld Institutes* 28 (1965); M. A. Shaaber, *Some Forerunners of the Newspaper in England, 1476–1622* (Philadelphia, 1929), chap. 3; L. S. Marcus, 'From oral delivery to print in the speeches of Elizabeth I', in Marotti and Bristol, eds, *Print, Manuscript and Performance*.

[76] *His Majesties Declaration* (London, 1628), pp. 9–45; Cust, 'News and politics'; E. R. Foster, 'Printing the Petition of Right', *HLQ* 38 (1974), pp. 81–3.

[77] S. Lambert, *Printing for Parliament 1641–1700* (London, 1984); S. Lambert, 'The beginning of printing for the House of Commons, 1640–42', *The Library*, 6th series 3 (1981).

'wished an answer should be prepared as soon as possible it might be'.[78] The following analysis explores the phenomena of official propaganda, to reveal the time and attention devoted not just to composing such statements, but also the energy and resources deployed in ensuring their publication and promulgation.

Since the sixteenth century there had developed a system of official royal printers, whose activities were funded from the Exchequer.[79] As tension mounted prior to the outbreak of civil war, the royal printing house provided a clear advantage for Charles, and one of the strengths of his propaganda machine.[80] There survives a note from 2 January 1642, for example, in which Sir Edward Nicholas instructed the royal printer regarding one of the king's proclamations, and regarding the need to use 'very good paper'.[81] The court's peripatetic existence after Charles's withdrawal from London obviously hindered the production of official propaganda, although royalist attempts to secure the services of printers and presses wherever they could be found made it evident to observers that the king intended to 'publish manifestos to justify the steps he has taken as well as his past proceedings, and to use pamphlets to stir up the people to promote his cause'.[82] The king's printer had been utilised at Newcastle-upon-Tyne during the first Bishops' War in 1639, and was still being employed in late March 1642.[83] Furthermore, Charles evidently managed to secure the use of a variety of other presses across the country, which received royal warrants for specific jobs.[84] They also received orders from the likes of Sir Edward Hyde, who sent several books to Sir Francis Ottley in January 1643, which were 'fit should be reprinted at Shrewsbury and spread abroad about the country'.[85] Once settled at Oxford, of course, Charles was able to co-opt the presses of Leonard Lichfield, printer to the university.[86] Thereafter, leading royalist grandees remained closely involved with printing official royal statements throughout the Interregnum. In January 1653, for

[78] Clarendon, *Life*, i. 138–9.

[79] Elton, *Policy and Police*, 173; King, 'Freedom of the press'; W. W. Greg, *A Companion to Arber* (Oxford, 1967), pp. 4–6; *CSPD 1611–18*, p. 67. See: H. R. Plomer, 'The king's printing house under the Stuarts', *The Library*, new series 2 (1901); BL, Add. 5756, fos. 134–8; J. C. Warner, *Henry VIII's Divorce. Literature and the Politics of the Printing Press* (Woodbridge, 1998), chap. 1.

[80] Malcolm, *Caesar's Due*, p. 125; BL, Add. 5756, fos. 141–5v.

[81] HLRO, Braye MS 7, fo. 22v.

[82] *CSPV 1642–3*, p. 25.

[83] J. Philipson, 'The king's printer in Newcastle-upon-Tyne in 1639', *The Library*, 6th series 11 (1989); BL, Add. 5756, fo. 147.

[84] W. K. Sessions, *The King's Printer at Newcastle upon Tyne in 1639, at Bristol in 1643–1645, at Exeter in 1645–1646* (York, 1982); W. K. Sessions, *The King's Printer at York in 1642, at Shrewsbury in 1642–3* (York, 1981); W. H. Allnutt, 'The king's printer at Shrewsbury, 1642–43', *The Library*, new series 1 (1900), pp. 355–64; *CSPD 1641–3*, p. 408.

[85] W. Phillips, ed., 'The Ottley papers relating to the civil war', *Transactions of the Shropshire Archaeological and Natural History Society*, 2nd series 6 (1894), pp. 55–6.

[86] *His Majesties Answer to a Printed Book Intituled A Remonstrance, or the Declaration of the Lords and Commons* (Oxford, 1642); *His Majesties Proclamation and Declaration* (Oxford, 1642); Madan, *Oxford Books*, ii. 160–61.

example, Hyde sent instructions regarding a 'manifest from the king', which was 'to be quickly published', and he added that care was to be taken that it should be 'handsomely printed, in quarto, in a fair letter'.[87]

Parliament, therefore, needed both to undermine the king's printers and to establish a printing regime of its own. As early as August 1641, a parliamentary committee examined printers who had been given instructions by Secretary Windebanke, and the king's departure from London appears to have provoked a struggle for the control of the king's printing house.[88] Attempts were also made to undermine the king's ability to exploit provincial presses, and concern regarding royalist propaganda emerges from the treatment of Roger Daniel, printer to the University of Cambridge, whose services were employed by the king in the late spring and summer of 1642, and who was summoned to appear before the Commons.[89] Parliament would eventually secure the services of both Daniel and Leonard Lichfield, but before such men were co-opted, Parliament developed its own network of reliable printers and publishers.[90] In doing so, they clearly learned from their Scottish friends. The convenanters had demonstrated how to take over and mobilise royal presses such as that of Evan Tyler, and how to exploit the power of the press to produce official propaganda.[91] Among others, Parliament secured the services of Joseph Hunscott and John Wright, who worked for the House of Lords, and Edward Husband and John Frank, who published for the Commons. It was Hunscott, the beadle of the Stationers' Company, who published the *Grand Remonstrance* in December 1641, while John Wright later worked particularly closely with the Committee of Revenue, which was dominated by his friends in the upper House.[92]

It was Husband, however, who became the pre-eminent official publisher during the 1640s, and the records of Parliament and its committees reveal the extent of his financial interest in the contracts granted by Westminster.[93] Husband was given encouragement to further publicise Parliament's work when he was granted

---

[87] Bodl. MS Clarendon 45, fo. 16; *CCSP* ii. 170. See also: *CCSP* ii. 174, 177, 188; *CCSP* iii. 233.

[88] *HMC House of Lords XI Addenda 1514–1714*, pp. 284–5; BL, Add. 18777, fo. 123.

[89] *CJ* ii. 733, 751; D. McKitterick, *A History of Cambridge University Press* (2 vols, Cambridge, 1992–8), i. 297.

[90] PRO, SP 28/140/2, fo. 52; McKitterick, *Cambridge University Press*, i. 300; S. Lambert, 'The beginning of printing'; *LJ* v. 554.

[91] Stevenson, 'Revolutionary regime', pp. 325, 329; Scottish RO, PA15/2 (Inventory of Worke done for the State by Evan Tyler).

[92] BL, Add. 5501, fos. 6–14; PRO, SP 46/108, fo. 307; PRO, SC6/Chas.1/1665 m.16d; SC6/Chas.1/1661 m.10r; SC6/Chas.1/1662 m.14r; SC6/Chas.1/1663 m.12r; SC6/Chas.1/1664 m.22r; SC6/Chas.1/1667 m.24; SC 6/Chas.1/1669 m.16; PRO, E 101/67/11b, fos. 129v–30v; PRO, SP 28/52, fo. 266; SP 28/54, fo. 761; SP 28/57, fo. 419; SP 28/59, fo. 470; SP 28/61, fo. 523; SP 28/66, fo. 254; BL, Add. 5501, fo. 11v; Lambert, 'Beginning', pp. 53–4, 56, 59; *Articles of Impeachment* (London, for John Frank, 1642); *His Majesties Letter to the Lord Keeper* (London, for John Frank, 1642).

[93] *CJ* iv. 78; PRO, SP 23/1a, pp. 66, 104; SP 28/33, fo. 210; SP 28/41, fo. 192; SP 28/57, fo. 386; SP 28/60, fo. 111; SP 28/64, fo. 226; SP 28/263, fos. 105, 107. For Husband: H. R. Plomer, *A Dictionary of the Booksellers … 1641–1667* (London, 1907), pp. 104–5.

copyright on the publication of a collection of official declarations in March 1643, which he was subsequently ordered to update in August 1644.[94] He retained this favoured position under the Rump, although he was joined as official parliamentary printer by John Field, by whom he was subsequently eclipsed.[95] The commonwealth also employed William Dugard and Henry Hills, the latter having previously been patronised by the army, and by Lieutenant General Fleetwood in particular.[96] Indeed, the emergence of Hills reflected the growing importance of the army, which had, like Parliament, developed an increasingly well-funded roster of printers during the 1640s. In addition to Hills, army accounts reveal payments to John Harris, overseer of printing at Oxford, Edmund Chillenden, for arranging printing at Cambridge, and the printers at York, Thomas Broad and Stephen Bulkley.[97] As the army became increasingly radical and assertive, however, the House of Lords appears to have attempted to exert a degree of control over army publications, by appointing Henry Walker and Matthew Simmons as printers of all army papers in September 1647.[98] After the establishment of the commonwealth, of course, the army press came under the sway of Cromwell, not least on his campaign to Scotland in 1650.[99] Moreover, during the Rump, the Council of State became the focal point for official printing, and it paid stationers such as Dugard from its substantial contingency fund.[100] In May 1653, furthermore, the Council ordered its secretary, John Thurloe, to consider the possible employment of Giles Calvert, Henry Hills and Thomas Brewster, and there is evidence that these three stationers worked together on official statements.[101] Under the Protectorate, meanwhile, it was Hills, Field and Dugard who survived as official Cromwellian printers, and all three received payments through the secretary of state, John Thurloe.[102] The recall of the Rump in 1659, however, prompted a split among the official printers. The

---

[94] *CJ* iii. 16, 580.

[95] Bodl. MS Rawl. A.246, fo. 29; *CJ* vi. 349; PRO, SP 28/19, fo. 125; SP 28/81, fo. 441; SP 28/84, fo. 431; SP 28/98, fo. 231; BL, Add. 32471, fos. 7v, 18; PRO, E 101/67/11b, fos. 129v–30v.

[96] Bodl. MS Rawl. A.328, p. 145; *CSPD 1653–4*, p. 4; Stationers' Company, Court Book C, fos. 265, 265v; *CSPD 1655*, p. 32; *The Life of H.H.* (London, 1688), p. 48.

[97] PRO, SC 6/1190, unfol.; Chequers, MS 782, fo. 43v, 44, 44v, 51, 52v, 54, 59. They also indicate the employment of John Twyne, Christopher Higgins, John Playford, John Partridge and George Whittington: Chequers, MS 782, fos. 4, 5v, 6, 7v, 14, 93, 99; Worcester College, Clarke MS XVII, unfol.; Clarke MS LXIX, fo. 20v. Whittington produced: *A Declaration from his Excellencie Sir Thomas Fairfax* (London, 1647); *The Heads of Proposals* (London, 1647).

[98] HLRO, MP 27/9/47; *LJ* ix. 450; *HMC 6th Report*, p. 197; Lambert, *Printing for Parliament*, p. 135; *Perfect Occurrences* 39 (24 Sept.–1 Oct. 1647), pp. 269, 271. Walker and Simmons produced: *A Declaration of the Engagements, Remonstrances, Representations ...from his Excellency Sir Thomas Fairfax* (London, 1647).

[99] Stevenson, 'Revolutionary regime', 334; J. D. Ogilvie, 'Papers from an army press, 1650', *Edinburgh Bibliographical Society Transactions* 2 (1938–45), pp. 420–23.

[100] *CSPD 1653–4*, p. 4.

[101] *CSPD 1652–3*, p. 320.

[102] Bodl. MS Rawl. A.14, fo. 1; BL, Add. 4184, fo. 48; Add. 32471, fos. 7v, 18; PRO, SP 18/71, fos. 91–98; *TSP* vi. 590–91.

re-emergence of the the army as a political force was accompanied by efforts to find a printed outlet through Hills, who was styled 'printer to the army', while Field continued to work for Parliament.[103] Dugard, meanwhile, returned to his work for the Council in September 1659, alongside Abel Roper and Thomas Collins.[104] After the second dissolution of the Rump in October 1659, the army reunited Hills and Field, who were able to ensure that the army could issue defences of its actions in print.[105] Finally, after the return of the Rump once again in December 1659, John Streater was employed as official printer, in partnership with John Macock, and he retained his post until 16 March 1660, when the Long Parliament was finally dissolved.[106]

Reconstructing the official print networks of the 1640s and 1650s, and identifying those stationers whose services were employed, is of more than antiquarian interest. The activities of such printers will need to be reconsidered in other contexts in later chapters, and mapping their involvement with royalist and parliamentarian regimes serves to highlight the seriousness with which contemporaries took the task of engaging with the public. Indeed, this is evident not just from the strenuous efforts to secure and retain the services of a significant number of printers, but also from the amount of money spent on official propaganda. Evidence for the royalists is necessarily limited, due to the paucity of surviving administrative records. Nevertheless, a payment of £40 is recorded for the 'king's declarations' in June 1642, and it is known that Lichfield received one payment of nearly £700 for work completed between October 1642 and February 1644, and that he was owed well over £1,000 by 1646.[107] Further evidence of the extent of financial commitment to printing official propaganda survives for the convenanters, who acknowledged a debt to Robert Bryson of nearly £900 (Scots) 'for the price of any number of books and declarations sent into England by public orders before the army went there in 1640'. They also acknowledged a debt of £166 (Scots) 'for his expense, service, and hazard in going in through England with the said books'.[108] When Evan Tyler presented his bill for work undertaken for the covenanters in the period from

---

[103] For Hills: *A Declaration of the Officers* (London 1659); *The Petition and Addresse of the Officers* (London, 1659); *The Representation and Petition of the Officers of the Army* (London, 1659); *The Army's Plea for their Present Practice* (London, 1659); *A Declaration of the General Council* (London, 1659). For Field: *A Declaration of Parliament* (London, 1659); *An Act for Appointing Judges* (London, 1659).

[104] *CSPD 1659–60*, pp. 223, 598.

[105] *By the Committee of Safety. A Proclamation* (London, 1659); *The Agreement of the General Council of Officers* (London, 1659); A. Woolrych, 'Introduction', *The Complete Prose Works of John Milton VII* (New Haven, 1980), pp. 124–6.

[106] *An Act for Further Continuation of the Customs* (London, 1659); *An Act for Taking the Accounts* (London, 1660). For payments to them, see: *CSPD 1659–60*, p. 596; PRO, SO 3/14, unfol.

[107] Madan, *Oxford Books*, ii. 161; *CSPD 1644*, p. 73; *CSPD 1661–2*, p. 135. See also: *A Narrative by John Ashburnham* (2 vols, London, 1830), ii. appendix, pp. xx, xxvi.

[108] Stevenson, 'Revolutionary regime', p. 325.

1642–47, he claimed to have printed over 130,000 sheets, for which he claimed over £13,000 (Scots).[109] Similarly, a wealth of information survives regarding the work undertaken by Edward Husband, and the payments which he received.[110] By the time that he presented a £12 bill for printing on 28 July 1642, Parliament already owed him £179.[111] When he petitioned for payment of his arrears in March 1648, he received £617, and in the following August the House of Commons agreed to pay an additional £500. Further calls for payments of similar size were made frequently during the last days of the Long Parliament, and in the early months of the Rump.[112] However, valuable though such information undoubtedly is for providing a sense of the scale of the operation to produce official propaganda in the 1640s, it offers little scope for comparing parliamentarian and royalist attitudes. This can be done, however, from evidence relating to the print-runs for official works, where the contrast between the king and Parliament is striking. Evidence from royalist papers suggests that declarations were printed in editions of 1,400, as was apparently traditional.[113] Parliament, on the other hand, regularly ordered the production of 6,000–12,000 copies of their statements.[114] In the high-stakes political contest of the 1640s, it was Parliament which demonstrated the clearest appreciation of the need to spread declarations to a broad audience.

Appreciation of politicians' zeal for engaging with the public through the medium of print, and of the sophistication of royalist and parliamentarian propaganda, can also be garnered by examining the ways in which official statements were distributed. In order to communicate with the people it was necessary both to draft propaganda and to ensure that ideas circulated beyond Westminster and Oxford, and in addition to producing manifestos, both sides sought to ensure that such works were 'published' in a wider sense. In part this meant exploiting the nation's pulpits, and Parliament clearly relied upon ministers to read declarations in their churches; despatching 'divers godly ministers' into the regions 'to possess the people with the truth and justice of the Parliament's cause in taking up of defensive arms'.[115] They also used army chaplains to ensure

---

[109] Stevenson, 'Revolutionary regime', pp. 325, 329; Scottish RO, PA15/2.

[110] *CJ* ii. 513, 698, 791, 922, 978; *CJ* iii. 16, 126, 181, 234, 394, 580, 606; *CSPD 1644–5*, p. 487.

[111] *HMC 5th Report*, p. 40; *CJ* ii. 698; HLRO, MP 28/7/42.

[112] *CJ* v. 216–18, 512, 639, 692; *CJ* vi. 49, 123, 221; PRO, SC6/Chas.1/1664 m.12d; SC6/Chas.1/1667 m.15; *LJ* ix. 280, 310; *LJ* x. 157, 181, 476, 532, 547; Bodl. MS Rawl. A.246, fo. 29; PRO, E 101/67/11b, fos. 129v–30v. Other printers had to wait just as long, if not longer, for their money. John Bartlett, for example, received £25 in July 1649, for printing work undertaken in May 1642: PRO, SC 6/Chas.1/1667, m.15.

[113] BL, Add. 5756, fos. 146–7. For precedents see: Foster, 'Printing the petition of right', pp. 81–3.

[114] *CJ* ii. 650, 698; *CJ* iii. 181; HLRO, MP 28/7/42; Lambert, 'Beginning', p. 58; PRO, SP 16/515ii, fos. 48, 71–2, 98–9v; *CSPD 1650*, p. 312; *CSPD 1651–2*, p. 65; *CJ* v. 692; PRO, SC6/Chas.1/1664 m.12d; PRO, E 101/67/11b, fos. 129v–30v; PRO, SP 23/1a, p. 66; SP 28/66, fo. 678; SP 28/68, fo. 243; SP 28/74, fo. 809; SP 16/516, fo. 20; SP 21/29, p. 39.

[115] *LJ* v. 533; *CJ* iii. 202. See: E. M. Furgol, 'The military and ministers as agents of Presbyterian

penetration of such material among the troops.[116] Parliamentarians and royalists both employed the services of diplomats, such as William Curtius, Sir Richard Browne and Walter Strickland, in order to disperse declarations on the Continent.[117] Successful distribution also required enlisting the services of local governors and gentry grandees, who had always been required to read and display official statements in public places.[118] On 25 February 1642, for example, the Lords ordered that the propositions for an Irish 'adventure' were to be printed and 'published' at the forthcoming assizes, and on 9 April 1642 another declaration was ordered to be printed and 'published' by sheriffs in all market towns.[119] Parliamentary control of London was hugely important in this regard, and on one occasion the sheriff's zeal is evident from the plea for 100 extra copies of a declaration, 'to paste upon the posts of the Exchange and other chief places of the City and suburbs'.[120] Royalist attempts to employ local governors and gentry can also be documented.[121] Between February and August 1642, therefore, the sheriff of Flintshire, David Pennant, received a series of orders from Charles and Viscount Falkland to 'publish and disperse in the towns, markets and other chief places' the royal contributions to the paper war.[122] In the first week of March 1642, furthermore, Charles sent orders to the sheriff of Berkshire to disperse royal statements regarding the militia, and in late March bundles of declarations were ordered to be made up for distribution around the country.[123] In late August, meanwhile, the royalist secretariat sent official papers to William Dugdale, to be passed to Sir Richard Leveson, with orders 'to disperse them so soon as is possible'.[124] However, surviving evidence suggests that royalist distribution networks were disrupted by parliamentarians such as John Feilder, high sheriff of Hampshire, who refused to obey royal orders in March 1642, and simply forwarded such works to Parliament.[125] Parliament also prosecuted ministers who

---

imperialism in England and Ireland, 1640–1648', in J. Dwyer, R. A. Mason, and A. Murdoch, eds, *New Perspectives on the Politics and Culture of Early Modern Scotland* (Edinburgh, 1982); J. Eales, 'Provincial preaching and allegiance in the first English civil war, 1640–6', in Cogswell, Cust and Lake, eds, *Politics, Religion and Popularity*; L. A. Ferrell, *Government by Polemic. James I, the King's Preachers and the Rhetoric of Conformity 1603–1625* (Stanford, 1998); M. McLure, *The Paul's Cross Sermons, 1534–1642* (Toronto, 1958); T. Claydon, 'The sermon, the 'public sphere' and the political culture of late seventeenth century England', in Ferrell and McCullough, eds, *English Sermon Revised*.

[116] R. P. Stearns, *The Strenuous Puritan: Hugh Peter (1598–1660)* (Urbana, 1954), pp. 220–70.

[117] BL, Add. 37047, fo. 145; BL, Evelyn Papers, RB2, vol. 5, unfol.: Sir Edward Nicholas to Sir Richard Browne, 13/23 Mar. 1648, 23/30 Mar. 1648, 6 Apr. 1648, 10/20 Apr. 1648, 4 May 1648; Bodl. MS Nalson IV, fos. 82–3.

[118] East Sussex RO, Rye 48/1.

[119] *LJ* iv. 613–14, 707; *CJ* iii. 202.

[120] BL, Add. 22546, fo. 81.

[121] BL, Sloane 1519, fo. 26v; *HMC Portland I*, p. 613.

[122] Flintshire RO, D/DE271, fos. 3–44. I am grateful to Dr Lloyd Bowen for drawing this document to my attention, and to Simon Healy for providing me with a detailed transcript.

[123] BL, Add. 71534, fo. 22; Add. 5756, fo. 147.

[124] Staffordshire RO, D868/5/1; *HMC 5th Report*, p. 175.

[125] HLRO, MP 31/3/42. See also: *PJ* ii. 91; *PJ* iii. 37.

sought to use their pulpits to read royal statements.[126] Royalists naturally faced difficulties, furthermore, in securing distribution in London, where orders to the lord mayor to publish royal proclamations were quickly countermanded by the House of Lords.[127] Nevertheless, despite such difficulties, there is evidence that royalists had some success in the capital, thanks to loyal and zealous individuals. Smuggling of books into London by boat is known to have taken place, not least from stories of their capture.[128] Furthermore, in December 1649, Lord Hatton reported success in publicising a declaration by Charles Stuart, saying that 'Mr Parker' had 'left his sick bed to see it pasted upon the Exchange and other places … and did take care by the posts and all the carriers of that week to send packets of those declarations into all parts of England'.[129] On other occasions, however, royalists faced dilatoriness on the part of their supporters. In January 1643, Hyde wrote to Sir Francis Ottley at Shrewsbury, saying that he had sent several books which 'tis very fit should be reprinted at Shrewsbury and spread abroad about the county, in which His Majesty desires your assistance upon all occasions'. In the following July, however, Ottley received another letter regarding 'a complaint … that your press is idle and doth the king no service', and imploring him to 'have an eye upon the press'. And in December 1643 the king himself wrote to Ottley regarding the failure to publish and proclaim declarations, and to order that 'you do immediately take effectual order for publishing and proclaiming the same in the market or other places, in that our town, most convenient for the purpose, and that thereupon the same be affixed against some posts or walls where it may be publicly seen'.[130]

Once again, the nature of surviving records permits parliamentarian distribution to be documented most fully. Hyde later commented that, by May 1642, Parliament's declarations were being 'dispersed throughout the kingdom' with 'care and dexterity', and this probably reflects the development of a new methodology for their dispersal, which is recorded in the official record of the Commons.[131] On 4 June 1642, a committee was appointed 'to consider of the best way of putting the public orders and votes of the House in execution, and of divulging, dispersing, and publishing the said orders, votes, and also the declarations of the House, through the kingdom'. Thomas Pury, the committee's chairman, presented a scheme for making up sets of the most important declarations, and on 17 June members were ordered to repair to the room next to the committee chamber, in order to receive copies of declarations which were to be dispersed. By the end of July 1642, indeed, there was a committee specifically

[126] Bodl. MS Nalson XIII, fo. 178; *HMC Portland I*, p. 42.

[127] HLRO, MP 23/6/42, 28/6/42; *HMC Portland I*, p. 41.

[128] Malcolm, *Caesar's Due*, pp. 126–7; *The True Informer* 26 (16–23 Mar. 1644), p. 186; *CJ* iii. 40.

[129] *NP* i. 158.

[130] Phillips, ed., 'Ottley papers' (1894), pp. 55–6; Phillips, ed., 'Ottley papers' (1895), pp. 344–5, 359.

[131] Clarendon, *History*, ii. 64.

concerned with the dispersal of such works.[132] A document from December 1647 records that Edward Husband delivered 9,600 copies of a printed order regarding the thanksgiving for a military victory, which recorded the number assigned to each county, and the name of the MP who received them, and the weight of official literature is evident from those gentry collections which contain multiple copies of parliamentary orders.[133] Furthermore, in addition to providing copies for MPs, the official printers also sent thousands of copies to dedicated agents and messengers.[134]

Official propaganda proved, therefore, to be of demonstrable concern to royalists and parliamentarians alike, but evidence relating to the employment of stationers to produce, and the money expended upon printing, official declarations, as well as that pertaining to print-runs and methods of distribution, indicates that Sir Marmaduke Langdale was correct to opine in November 1642, that 'the parliament is far too nimble for the king in printing'.[135] This superiority centred upon the growing bureaucratisation of the process of producing official propaganda, and must be regarded as having been founded upon a novel understanding of the dynamic of communicating with, and appealing to, the people.

In the absence of detailed expositions of contemporary philosophies of propaganda it is necessary to distil attitudes from practice, not merely regarding the mechanics of publishing and distributing official propaganda, but also relating to the construction of texts themselves. By observing the techniques adopted and developed for drafting official literature, it is possible to demonstrate further why, how and by whom traditional practices were modified, and ultimately why political grandees turned to pamphleteers and polemicists for the production of propaganda.

During much of the early modern period, declarations were produced by monarchs, ministers and administrators, rather than by proven authors. Some of the most important political and religious propaganda of the century before the civil wars was produced by Henry VIII and James I, by Burghley and Walsingham, and by Archbishops Parker and Whitgift.[136] During the late 1630s,

---

[132] *CJ* ii. 604, 609, 611, 616, 628, 630, 650, 662, 681, 698; Lambert, 'Beginning', p. 58. Simon Mayne MP got 30 copies of one declaration for distribution in his county: *CSPD 1651–2*, p. 146.

[133] PRO, SP 16/515ii, fos. 98–99v; Somerset RO, DD/HI/466. This contained five sheets each with two copies of the order of 29 February 1648 regarding the raising of troops for foreign states. In 1655, Sir John Barrington's accounts record receipt of 411 copies of a declaration for distribution: Essex RO, D/Dba/A5.

[134] Husband delivered to William Hulls 5,600 copies of the declaration regarding 'no further addresses', 3,500 of which were for MPs to distribute: *CSPD 1648–9*, p. 18; *CSPD 1645–7*, pp. 567, 572, 579.

[135] *HMC Portland I*, p. 70.

[136] R. Rex, 'The English campaign against Luther in the 1520s', *TRHS*, 5th series 39 (1989), p. 85; Read, 'William Cecil', pp. 21–55; P. Croft, 'Serving the archduke: Robert Cecil's management of the parliamentary session of 1606', *HR* 64 (1991), p. 297; Sanders, 'John Whitgift'; Peck, *Northampton*, p. 111.

declarations were penned by men such as Edward Nicholas, clerk of the privy council, Edward Norgate, signet clerk, and Sir Francis Windebanke, secretary of state.[137] This traditional method of producing royal messages persisted throughout the 1640s and 1650s. Royalists continued to rely upon the services of leading political figures such as Sir Edward Hyde, who began writing for the king as soon as he left Parliament in the spring of 1642, and who penned works as he travelled towards York. From Nostal he sent 'the answer that was prepared to the declaration of the 19 of May'. The following day the king sent to Hyde Parliament's declaration of 26 May, 'to which he wished an answer should be prepared as soon as possible it might be'.[138] Hyde's role was widely recognised, and one parliamentarian tract from 1642 noted that 'he is the man that draweth and correcteth all His Majesties declarations, proclamations, and protestations and what not, before they are published to the whole world'.[139] At Westminster during the early 1640s, meanwhile, the most common method of producing official propaganda was by small committees of the most prominent members of either House.[140] Indeed, the journals of the Lords and Commons reveal that a large proportion of declarations were drafted by a limited group of men.[141] Once composed, declarations were reported to Parliament in order to receive amendment and approval.[142] When the Scottish resolutioners sought to respond to protester literature in the late 1650s, they too worked through a committee.[143]

Declarations were not without their drawbacks, however, and by elucidating the problems inherent in the production of official propaganda, it is possible to understand the reasons for turning to the services of professional polemicists. Firstly, the conditions of civil war placed considerable demands upon politicians' time. Hyde was a reliable and capable propagandist for the king, but as Chancellor

---

[137] *CSPD 1639*, pp. 126, 144–6; *CSPD 1640*, pp. 20–21; *CSPD 1625–49*, p. 621.

[138] Clarendon, *Life*, i. 120, 124, 138–9, 154–6, 161–3, 244–5, 308; Bodl. MS Clarendon 21, fos. 124–33, 149r–v; Bodl. MS Clarendon 30, fo. 234; Bodl. MS Clarendon 56, fos. 365–8v; *CCSP* i. 234–5, 406; *CCSP* ii. 2; *CCSP* iv. 288; *CCSP* v. 447, 725–6; *His Majesties Declaration to Both Houses of Parliament... In Answer to that Presented to him at Newmarket the 9th of March 1641* (London, 1641). See: G. Roebuck, *Clarendon and Cultural Continuity* (London, 1981), p. 23; M. W. Brownly, *Clarendon and the Rhetoric of Historical Form* (Philadelphia, 1985). See also texts by the Earl of Bristol: *CCSP* i. 406; Bodl. MS Clarendon 30/2, fos. 236–42v.

[139] *Another Famous Victorie Obtained* (London, 1642), sig. [A4].

[140] *CJ* ii. 253, 975, 1002.

[141] Two of the most important draftsmen in the Commons were Pym and John Glynne: *CJ* ii. 762, 872, 881, 901, 903, 907–8, 909, 915, 928; Add. 31116, pp. 27, 95, 251; *LJ* v. 385. In the Lords those most often associated with such work included Viscount Saye: *LJ* iv. 708; *LJ* v. 42, 46, 154. Others involved in drafting declarations included Bulstrode Whitelocke, whose papers contain draft notes for such pieces from 1642, and Francis Rous, one of the great godly reformers of the early Stuart period, whose utility lay in his proven talents as an author: Longleat House, Whitelocke Papers VIII, fo. 292; *CJ* iii. 93, 100, 132, 173, 182, 394, 398.

[142] *CJ* ii. 478–9.

[143] W. Stephens, ed., *Registers of the Consultations of the Ministers of Edinburgh* (2 vols, Scottish Records Society, Edinburgh, 1921–30), ii. 141, 142, 143–7.

he could clearly not give his undivided attention to the task, while the demands upon individual members in a busy parliamentary session may have been sufficient to hinder the composition of such pieces, particularly as the Houses thinned during the war, through defections to Oxford, illness, and military and local service. There is at least one instance where the pressure of time fatally delayed consideration of official propaganda. In August 1644, the Commons resolved to publish a statement based upon intelligence from leading parliamentarians, but 'the committee neglecting it awhile', the matter was forgotten and the work was never printed.[144] Robert Baillie noted how a similar fate befell works composed during the Glasgow Assembly of 1638, which were resolved to be published, but 'the multitude of our public affairs that daily since has come thicker and thicker on our backs, has envied us that honour'.[145] In the spring of 1648, meanwhile, Sir Edward Nicholas expressed clear frustration at the delay in producing royalist declarations.[146]

Working within strict time constraints, and with a heavy workload, political figures ran the risk of producing works of an insufficiently high standard, and of working too slowly. Robert Baillie recorded how some covenanter literature produced hastily was deemed inadequate for the press.[147] Peter Heylyn, writing of the desire for a statement regarding altar policy in the 1630s, reflected that the 'burden' was 'held of too great weight for any one to undergo', particularly given the necessity of 'a quick despatch'.[148] Parliamentary statements, of course, were hampered by the need for discussion in committee, and approval by either or both Houses, before being sent to the printer and returned to Parliament in proof form for re-examination.[149] Furthermore, such risks were exacerbated by the growing polemicism of official declarations, which were intended to offer justifications and vindications of policies and actions, and narratives of plots, battles and campaigns, as much as to outline policy.[150] As such, 'manifestos' became less distinct from the pamphlets being written and published by parliamentarian and royalist authors.[151] Some of the most interesting of these broad statements were issued in the wake of the various peace treaties. Having commissioned a declaration concerning the Oxford treaty, for example, the Commons subsequently widened its scope in order to incorporate the causes of the war, the

[144] BL, Harl. 166, fo. 107a.

[145] *Letters and Journals of Robert Baillie*, i. 153.

[146] BL, Evelyn Papers, RB2, vol. 5, unfol.: Sir Edward Nicholas to Sir Richard Browne, 20/30 Mar. 1648.

[147] *Letters and Journals of Robert Baillie*, i. 189–90.

[148] Heylyn, *Cyprianus*, 279.

[149] HLRO, Braye MS 7: Declaration of Both Houses of 19 May 1642, with printer's annotations and signature marks; HLRO, MP 20/11/43: printed ordinance endorsed 'this print is perfect'.

[150] Lambert, 'Beginning', p. 58; BL, Harl. 165, fo. 112; *The Cleere Sense: Or, a Just Vindication of the Late Ordinance* (London, 1645).

[151] Perhaps the first occasion on which the term 'manifest' was used was for the planned declaration of 1627: *CSPD 1627–8*, p. 269.

distractions of the kingdom, and the state of Ireland.[152] This drift from declarations to manifestos is well illustrated by an incident in April 1643, when the Commons considered the Lords' answer to a message from the king. According to one diarist, 'it was thought fit by the House to forbear sending any answer to it, until we might have time to take the whole treaty into consideration', because 'we conceived the sending of an answer to that particular message might engage us in a new treaty'. What was needed, on the other hand, was 'to frame … some general manifest declaration'.[153]

Such general polemical statements were more difficult to compose, and inevitably took longer to draft. Part of the solution was the co-option of outsiders.[154] The shortcomings of official declarations, in other words, provided the motivation to employ more subtle means of expressing the attitudes and ideas of men within Westminster, and to exploit the talents and services of writers who were not themselves members of either House, in order to produce works which were official in both nature and appearance.[155] On some occasions, Parliament needed the expertise of lawyers. It was, of course, possible to draw upon the vast wealth of legal knowledge of members of both Houses, and the papers of John Selden reveal the lengths to which he was prepared to go to research and prepare official statements regarding the legal status of royalist Commissions of Array in 1642.[156] However, expert legal advice was also taken from outsiders, and when this same declaration was passed, on 28 June 1642, the Commons rewarded the assistance of Sir John Borough with an annuity of £50.[157] On other occasions, religious experts were seconded. In 1639, the Dean of Durham was involved in writing the so-called 'large declaration', and in July 1645, William Gouge was employed to draft a declaration in response to John Archer's *Comfort for Believers*.[158] Gouge's secondment demonstrates that the talents of proven pamphleteers were exploited by Parliament, and it is also possible that the selection of Henry Parker as secretary to the Committee of Safety, the powerful bi-cameral body established by Parliament in the summer of 1642, involved little more than the employment of an outsider to assist in drafting official declarations. Parker's hand can be detected not only on hundreds of warrants issued by the committee, but also on other official orders and diplomatic letters, although it cannot be determined with any degree of certainty whether he was the author of

---

[152] *CJ* iii. 58–9, 72–3, 86, 89, 91, 434–5.

[153] BL, Add. 31116, p. 91.

[154] Elton, *Policy and Police*, p. 200.

[155] *CSPD 1644*, p. 19. To some extent, politicians had long recognised the need to delegate in this fashion, not least given their limited polemical skills: Croft, 'Serving the archduke'; Graves, *Norton*, p. 113, 161.

[156] *LJ* v. 66; *CJ* ii. 795, 818; Bodl. MS Selden Supra.124, pp. 1–135; Bodl. MS Selden Supra 123, fos. 4–5, 7–15v, 63–74, 96–99v, 100–103, 118v–19, 120–51v, 160, 176–91v.

[157] *CJ* ii. 643, 657. Borough had written declarations for the king in June 1639: *CSPD 1639*, pp. 324, 351.

[158] *CSPD 1639*, pp. 264–5; *LJ* vii. 494, 505–6.

these, or merely their scribe.[159] The real interest in Parker's role lies, however, in the possibility that he was employed in drafting declarations. From July 1642 onwards, much of the responsibility for drafting declarations fell to the Committee of Safety, particularly those declarations or manifestos which were of a polemical nature. For example, on 6 July 1642, in the week when Parker's famous *Observations* appeared, the committee was ordered to prepare a declaration to let the people know 'matters of fact' in the dispute with the king, and the reasons for Parliament's decision to raise forces.[160] They were also ordered to prepare a preamble to a printed edition of an intercepted letter from Lord Digby, and were responsible for drafting the declaration of the 'state of the kingdom', presented to Parliament on 14 December 1642.[161] While Pym was undoubtedly the most prominent member of Parliament involved in the Committee of Safety's declaration work, the reliance upon the committee for declarations must also be considered as a way of employing the talents of polemicists such as Parker.[162]

By the time of the Uxbridge peace treaty in 1645, a more sophisticated and open approach was employed. The first call for a declaration responding to the talks was issued on 1 March 1645, and responsibility was initially given to the Uxbridge commissioners themselves.[163] Having failed to secure such a declaration, however, the Commons eventually opted for a much larger statement, setting forth the state of Parliament's cause, and the grounds and necessity of 'this unhappy and unnatural war'.[164] On 24 June, the House resolved that the section of the declaration concerning the church was to be completed by two prominent clerics, Stephen Marshall and Richard Vines, but the circumstances changed yet again with Parliament's success at the battle of Naseby, and the seizure of the king's letters.[165] On 26 June 1645, the Commons made a decision of great importance for the way in which parliamentary declarations were drafted, since two eminent pamphleteers, Henry Parker and John Sadler, were appointed special secretaries to Parliament, and ordered to prepare a declaration regarding the justice of Parliament's cause, and to complete the work begun by Marshall and Vines. On 30 June, furthermore, it was decided to pass the transcripts of the Naseby letters to the two writers, 'to make observations upon and make use of in a great declaration upon the breach of the treaty'.[166] When the Lords approved the observations made upon the Naseby

---

159 PRO, SP 28/261-264; Bodl. MS Nalson XIII, fos. 104r–v; HLRO, MP 26/7/42, 1/9/42, 28/7/42, 14/12/42; Bodl. MS Clarendon 22, fos. 128r–v.
160 *CJ* ii. 655, 659, 683, 805, 817, 849, 986; *CJ* iii. 176; *LJ* v. 398, 430–31, 444.
161 *CJ* ii. 700, 808, 810.
162 *CJ* ii. 808, 819, 832, 839, 882, 884, 988.
163 *CJ* iv. 65, 92.
164 *CJ* iv. 134, 146–7, 163.
165 *CJ* iv. 183.
166 *CJ* iv. 187, 189–90.

letters, the work was published within the week, as *The King's Cabinet Opened*.[167] Parliament's action over these declarations set something of a precedent. On 28 July, the papers taken at Pontefract Castle were sent to Parker and Sadler, and although Parker was made redundant in early 1646, Sadler and another pamphleteer, Thomas May, were confirmed as special secretaries, and charged with producing another vindication of Parliament, with salaries of £100 per annum. On 19 January 1646, furthermore, when the letters of Lord Digby were ordered to be printed, copies were delivered to Sadler and May for their ongoing work on the 'public declaration for vindicating to the world the honour of Parliament, in this great cause of religion and liberty'.[168] The use of such outsiders was also evident on occasions when it was considered necessary to reply to critics. On 29 January 1646, for example, a committee under the guidance of Nathaniel Fiennes was ordered to investigate the book called *Truth's Manifest*, written by the Scots' propagandist, David Buchanan, but on the same day it was ordered that Sadler and May should issue declarations in response to Buchanan's book, and other papers of the Scots which the Commons found scandalous.[169] Sadler may also have been responsible for the declaration in justification of the vote of 'no further addresses' in January 1648, and he subsequently remained involved in the production of such works after the establishment of the republic.[170]

However much early modern political grandees may have grown used to the need to communicate with the people, and however much the conditions of civil war encouraged the production of polemic in order to appeal to the wider political nation, the circumstances of the 1640s and 1650s placed pressures upon those traditionally involved in the preparation of official statements, whether royalist or parliamentarian. Surviving evidence indicates that it was parliamentarians who developed means of circumventing such problems. The most important way in which they did so involved co-opting the services of proven polemicists and experienced pamphleteers, at least some of whom were retained and salaried, and able to be exploited on demand.

The employment of outsiders solved the most obvious limitation of the process of producing official propaganda. However, the demand for polemics, and the need to overcome the problems of workload were not the only drawbacks with traditional methodology. A further problem lay in the process by which declarations were approved, since it was possible for objections to be raised to

---

[167] *CJ* iv. 194; BL, Add. 5880, fo. 35.

[168] *CJ* iv. 200, 222, 414, 416, 426, 439, 445, 448; *CSPD 1645–7*, p. 315; *CJ* iv. 410–11; PRO, SC6/Chas. 1/1663, m. 8d.

[169] *CJ* iv. 422, 507. The committee appointed on 29 January 1646 to investigate *Truth's Manifest* did not report until mid-April, when Buchanan was declared delinquent, and copies of the book were ordered to be burnt: *CJ* iv. 422, 505, 507.

[170] *CJ* vi. 108; *CSPD 1645–7*, p. 522; PRO, SP 16/515, fo. 30. During his spell as an MP, Sadler wrote declarations: *CSPD 1653–4*, p. 229.

portions of declarations which were perceived to be controversial, and such
objections could force delays as contested pieces were reconsidered, and could
ultimately cause the shelving of unfinished or unratified declarations.[171] Thus,
while the Caroline regime's concern to explain policies and decisions was evident
from the discussions in the Privy Council over the formulation of the 'manifest'
justifying the expedition to the Isle de Ré, this piece became sufficiently bogged
down in complex discussions that it was eventually abandoned.[172] Furthermore,
later royalist pieces – such as Hyde's declaration of March 1649, regarding the
death of Charles I – could be rejected as a result of such procedural
complications.[173] Parliament too faced serious problems of this kind. When a split
occurred in the Lords in September 1641 over church policy, the minority group
entered their dissent, and may have been responsible for ensuring that their views
were made public in print.[174] Prior to the outbreak of hostilities, of course, the
Lords contained many peers who would later become royalists, and who sought to
block the moves of those zealous for 'further reformation'. On 7 March 1642, for
example, the attempt to pass a declaration regarding 'fears and jealousies' led to a
protest by a group of fourteen members of the upper House.[175] Such tensions were
replicated in the Commons, and in December 1642 Sir Simonds D'Ewes recorded
his hostility to one declaration on the grounds of 'all the virulent and unsavoury
passages'.[176] Problems also arose from the divisions between the two Houses,
although in part these were couched in terms of disputes over the privileges of
different printers employed by either House.[177] Indeed, some of the most
controversial official statements, such as the 'grand remonstrance', provoked
divisions within and between both Houses.[178]

If such stumbling blocks in the passage of official declarations reflected
tensions between incipient royalist and parliamentarian groupings within
Parliament, during the later 1640s the problem became one of the competing
factions within parliamentarian ranks at Westminster. By the spring of 1646,
divisions between Presbyterians and Scots on the one hand, and Independents on

---

[171] The surviving draft of a controversial declaration from May 1647 reveals the extent to which
pieces were subject to revision: *CSPD 1645–7*, pp. 558–9; PRO, SP 16/515i, fos. 167–8v. See also:
Bodl. MS Nalson XXII, fos. 84–9v; *CJ* iv. 280, 326, 336; *HMC Portland I*, pp. 296–300; Beinecke
Library, Yale University, Osborn MS fb.155. And see: J. S. A. Adamson, 'Pym as draftsman: an
unpublished declaration of March 1643', *PH* 6 (1987), pp. 133–40.

[172] *CSPD 1627–8*, pp. 273, 278; Cogswell, 'Politics of propaganda', p. 213.

[173] *CCSP* ii. 2; Clarendon, *Life*, i. 120; Bodl. MS Clarendon 45, fo. 96.

[174] *After Debate About the Printing and Publishing of the Orders of the 16th of January Last*
([London, 1641]). This broadside, outlining which peers voted which way, was probably published in
mid-September 1641.

[175] *LJ* iv. 629–31.

[176] *D'Ewes*, ed. Coates, pp. 294–5.

[177] *CJ* ii. 728; *CJ* iii. 179–82, 184, 192; *LJ* vi. 133, 147, 151; BL, Add. 31116, p. 130; HLRO, MP
10/2/44, 24/2/44, 22/2/45.

[178] *CSPD 1641–3*, pp. 179, 180, 203.

the other, were very much in the open, and former reticence about attacking each other in print had evaporated. At times it was possible to issue declarations affirming that the English Parliament would not have 'any advice or consent from [the Scots] in the framing of any law or ordinance', and to issue a narrative of the Scots proceedings.[179] At other times, however, the factional balance within Westminster frustrated such methods. On 16 May 1646, factional wrangling clearly affected the passage of a declaration, when a committee was appointed to compose a work, directed to the Scots, vindicating the rights and privileges of Parliament. On 22 June 1646, a draft was reported by Nathaniel Fiennes, which revealed distinctly anti-Scottish sentiments, and five days later a division was forced over whether it should be read. Denzil Holles and Sir Philip Stapilton, leaders of the pro-Scottish faction in the Commons, acted as tellers for the opposition, while Sir Arthur Hesilrige and Henry Marten, both anti-Scottish Independents, were tellers in support of the declaration, and narrowly won.[180] This was not a unique incident, and there were a number of similar factional divisions over the wording of the declaration regarding the vote of 'no further addresses' in January 1648.[181] Moreover, this was the kind of problem hindering the passage of declarations which could not be solved by means of the employment of outsiders. When the House considered the declaration prepared by Sadler and May in response to the Scottish polemicist, David Buchanan, the Commons divided on what appears to have been factional lines over some of the clauses. Over one section, those whose votes were recorded by two Presbyterians, Denzil Holles and Sir Philip Stapilton, were defeated by those represented by two Independents, Sir John Evelyn of Wiltshire and Sir Arthur Hesilrige. Over another clause, two more Presbyterians, Sir Walter Erle and William Ashurst, were defeated by the same men. On this occasion, the factional balance in the Commons enabled the declaration by Sadler and May to be approved, and it was ordered to be printed.[182] However, it was obvious that the employment of proven pamphleteers to draft declarations represented no solution to the problem of factionalism, which could generate serious obstacles to the success of individual pieces of work.[183]

The employment of outsiders to draft official declarations was a response to the need to produce a steady stream of polemically sophisticated propaganda, at a time when Parliament had many other things to do, and fewer people to do them. Parliament's secondment of men with religious and legal expertise, and proven literary talents, however, could not solve all of the problems which hindered the production of official propaganda, not least the growing importance of factional divisions. It was this situation which encouraged moves to bypass the

---

[179] *CJ* iv. 539–40, 541, 544; BL, Add. 31116, pp. 536, 538, 546, 548.

[180] *CJ* iv. 548, 585, 590, 591. In December 1646 the Commons witnessed factional divisions over the text of *Jus Divinum Regiminis Ecclesiastici*: *CJ* v. 10–11.

[181] Bodl. MS Clarendon 30, fos. 292–4; *CJ* v. 461–2.

[182] *CJ* iv. 507, 513–14.

[183] *NP* ii. 349–50.

tiresome opposition from within Westminster, and the prospect of both debate and delay in the passage of declarations, by employing more subtle means of conveying a desired message. The fragmentation of both national and parliamentary politics, in other words, provided an important context for propaganda and pamphleteering.[184] Situations where it proved difficult to produce declarations because of the existence of factional divisions, or where such problems were anticipated, provided the motivation for supplementing conventional procedures, and for blurring the distinction between publications which were 'public' and those which were 'private'; between those evidently official and those apparently unofficial. It is to the subtle methods of employing the talents of men outside official circles, in order to side-step the problems of official declarations, that the remainder of this chapter is devoted.

One solution to the troublesome nature of the process of drafting official pronouncements was to create substitute forms, in the shape of tracts which performed the precise function of declarations, which may have been composed in tandem with the work of drafting committees, and which may have been more or less indistinguishable from parliamentary statements. An important example of this phenomenon is provided by Henry Parker's *A Question Answered*.[185] This broadside appeared on the day of the third reading of the militia bill (22 April 1642), and was probably instigated by politicians who felt uncertain about their ability to secure agreement for a bold statement of incipient parliamentarian theory at this crucial juncture.[186] That Parker's work was designed as a substitute for a declaration is evident from its resemblance to official statements of the period.[187] Indeed, this resemblance was sufficiently strong for Parker's work to be treated as official by contemporaries, including Edward Husband, who included it in his collection of official statements, as well as by later historians.[188] A more important example, although one whose visual appearance was more distinct from official statements, is provided by Parker's most famous tract, the *Observations*, which served as the declaration which some figures at Westminster sought as a contribution to the paper war in the months before the outbreak of hostilities. When the king replied to the 'Nineteen Propositions' in June 1642, one committee was appointed to prepare a point-by-point rejoinder, while another was charged

---

[184] C. E. Harline, *Pamphlets, Printing and Political Culture in the Early Dutch Republic* (Dordrecht, 1987), p. 13.

[185] [H. Parker], *A Question Answered* ([London, 1642]); See M. Mendle, *Dangerous Positions* (Alabama, 1984), pp. 187–8.

[186] *CJ* ii. 537.

[187] R. Steele, *Tudor and Stuart Proclamations 1485–1714* (2 vols, Oxford, 1910), i. 244; *Divers Questions Upon His Majesties Last Answer* (London, for Joseph Huscott, 1641[/2]).

[188] Rushworth, *Collections*, iv. 542–3; *An Exact Collection of all Remonstrances* (London, 1643), pp. 150–51; BL, Harl. 581, fo. 22v. Lilburne, who was greatly influenced by the piece, assumed it to be official: A. Sharp, 'John Lilburne and the Long Parliament's *Book of Declarations*: a radical's exploitation of the words of authorities', *HPT* 9 (1988). See also *PHE* ii. 1183–5; *OPH* x. 451–4; Steele, *Tudor and Stuart Proclamations*, i. 251.

with considering the preamble, and with preparing a powerful vindication of Parliament, 'to stir up the people'.[189] Nevertheless, progress was painfully slow, and the willingness of some members to compromise with the king, and to drop certain demands, clearly frustrated grandees such as John Pym and Viscount Saye. They appear to have turned to Parker to produce the response which they desired, but which they felt unlikely to secure through parliamentary means.[190] It is no coincidence that the Commons suspended consideration of their declaration on the day that Parker's work appeared, or that some contemporaries voiced suspicions about the circumstances surrounding Parker's work. When Nathaniel Fiennes eventually reported the general declaration on 23 July, Sir Simonds D'Ewes claimed to have been 'extremely provoked at their unjust violent proceeding', and he decried 'this long, impertinent and dangerous declaration'. He was 'very much afraid that a great part of this declaration is already printed in a pamphlet of observations', and it would 'be much to the dishonour of this House to put out that for their declaration which is already to be had in a published pamphlet, and so be taken out of a budget or a pocket'.[191]

Instances of substitute declarations are obviously hard to detect, but another case which can be uncovered centres once again upon Parker. In late April 1645, Parliament's diplomat in the Low Countries received word from London that he would receive a declaration concerning the Dutch diplomatic mission to England, which had been commissioned from the Committee of Both Kingdoms.[192] This piece was delivered to the Commons on 7 May, but was re-committed because of opposition to certain sections.[193] A new version was produced on the following day, with the intention that it should be sent abroad in English and French editions, and the Committee of Both Kingdoms was ordered to 'consider of the way and manner of sending and publishing it, and by whom'.[194] On 23 May, it was resolved that the declaration should be delivered by Sir John Temple, and on 6 June, a Latin letter to the Dutch was read in the Commons, 'together with our declaration made concerning the negotiation of their late ambassadors'.[195] On 13 June, Georg Weckherlin, the parliamentarian secretary, recorded in his diary having sent copies to Strickland in both English and French, and on 24 June, the committee ordered Weckherlin to translate it into Dutch, while Strickland was ordered to effect its printing.[196] The interest in such detail lies in the fact that no formal declaration was

---

[189] *CJ* ii. 635–48; *LJ* v. 153, 161–3.

[190] *HMC Buccleuch I*, p. 306; BL, Harl. 163, fo. 252v; *CJ* ii. 642.

[191] *CJ* ii. 687–9; BL, Harl. 163, fos. 291–2; *PJ* iii. 254-9; Peacey, 'Henry Parker', pp. 73–4.

[192] BL, Trumbull Papers, Weckherlin diary, unfol.; *CJ* iv. 106, 111, 119; *LJ* vii. 314, 323; *The Speech of Their Excellencies the Lords Ambassadors* (London, 1645); *CSPD 1644–5*, pp. 412, 414.

[193] BL, Add. 31116, p. 416; *CJ* iv. 134; *CSPD 1644–5*, p. 462.

[194] *CJ* iv. 134–5, 147; *LJ* vii. 359; *CSPD 1644–5*, p. 510. On 12 May Weckherlin was ordered to make the translation into French: *LJ* vii. 366.

[195] *CSPD 1644–5*, pp. 514–15; BL, Add. 31116, p. 427.

[196] BL, Trumbull Papers, Weckherlin Diary, unfol.

ever produced. Rather, there survives a manuscript by Parker entitled 'points of consideration', which was printed in Dutch, which relates the affair of the ambassadors, and which appears to contain the Commons' declaration.[197] Moreover, the Dutch ambassador complained of a 'feigned letter' which purported to have been directed by Parliament to the Dutch, which was printed in *Mercurius Civicus*, and which was identical to Parker's work.[198] Once again, the implication is that a group of leading parliamentarians, including Parker's cousin, Sir John Temple, fearing persistent wrangling over the text of a declaration, turned to Parker in order to provide a substitute, which was published in the Low Countries and leaked to the press in England.

Such cases demonstrate that certain problems inherent in the production of official declarations could be solved not just by the employment of outsiders, but also by the development of substitute forms of propaganda, which were produced outside official channels, but which resulted in documents which resembled official statements to a greater or lesser extent. There were other drawbacks with official declarations, however, which prompted the use of more radical forms. One such difficulty centred upon the 'reception' of texts which were self-evidently produced at Westminster, and which may have had little impact upon committed royalists. In some contexts, and with some readers, official declarations would have proved a blunt weapon. In June 1642, the attempt to read a proclamation regarding the militia provoked a public disturbance in Cheapside, and in December 1659, attempts by the serjeant at arms, protected by a squadron of cavalry, to read a declaration by the Committee of Safety, provoked a riot at the Exchange.[199] The public, in other words, may have been less inclined to pay attention to works which visibly emanated from Westminster, than to consume tracts and pamphlets which appeared to have been produced spontaneously by parliamentarian sympathisers acting independently of powerful interests. This may explain why the Puritan divine John Preston, who had been involved in the production of propaganda in the 1620s, recognised that 'when we ... have any great things to be accomplished, the best policy is to work by an engine which the world sees nothing of'.[200] Likewise, Joseph Jane recommended to royalist leaders that while it was important to foster a 'good understanding' with the people, a formal declaration might not prove profitable, 'for it will endanger more, and make the greater watchfulness in the villains'.[201] Such appreciation of the problem of reception may have underpinned the appearance of some rather strange official statements in the 1640s. On 10 September 1642, for example, a book called *A Safeguard from Shipwreak* was reported to the Commons, on the grounds that it

---

[197] [H. Parker], 'Points of Consideration' (BL, E286/16); [H. Parker], *Poincten van Consideration* (Rotterdam, 1645); *PHE* iii. 364–5.

[198] *Mercurius Civicus* 105 (22–29 May 1645), pp. 939–40; *CJ* iv. 164; *LJ* vii. 403, 406.

[199] HLRO, Braye 57, fo. 6; *LJ* v. 124; Woolrych, 'Introduction', pp. 144–6.

[200] Morgan, *Puritan Chaplain*, p. 69.

[201] *NP* iii. 22–3. See also: *NP* ii. 350; *CCSP* iv. 236.

gave reasons why Catholics might attend church and take the oaths of allegiance and supremacy. The book was referred to two MPs, Laurence Whitaker and Francis Rous, who were ordered to re-publish the work with a new preamble and marginal notes, and the task was completed with the assistance of the cleric, Daniel Featley. The result was a book entitled *Virtumnus Romanus*.[202] In 1644, furthermore, there appeared a work called *God Appearing for the Parliament*, which was the work of a Commons committee which had been charged with perusing various letters, and making a narrative to be printed.[203] Close readers would have recognised the official nature of both these works, but their appearance was designed to mask their origins.

Such evidence highlights one of the most profound dilemmas of the propagandist: the tension between the need to define a particular 'orthodoxy' on the one hand, and the desire for anonymity on the other. Political grandees of any persuasion needed to produce works which demonstrated what was, or what they sought to make, the 'party line', but they also needed to produce works which broadcast their message in ways which were not recognisably official, and which created the impression of being spontaneous manifestations of support. This tension, which will be apparent throughout the present study, exacerbated the problem with official declarations. Indeed, this dilemma was made more thorny by the fact that it was not always possible to rely upon works which were visually 'official' in order to establish orthodoxy, since private individuals could imitate parliamentary declarations; marketing themselves by designing title pages which mimicked those of official literature in order to attract the attention of book buyers. One broadside which appeared in March 1642, for example, bore typographical similarities to official productions, and was based upon *Some Passages that Happened the 9th of March between the King's Majestie and the Committee of Both Houses*. While readers may have believed this to be official, it was produced without parliamentary sanction, aroused anger at Westminster, and resulted in the arrest of the man responsible.[204] In March 1643, furthermore, Henry Walker was sent to the Fleet prison for producing a work which claimed to represent *The Remonstrance of the Commons of England*. Though the conceit was ultimately obvious from the text, Parliament felt impelled to take action by arresting Walker and by issuing a public response, for fear that some readers would not have perceived the truth of its origins.[205] Readers may also have been confused by a pamphlet which appeared in October 1648 entitled *The Answer of the Commons to a Petition in the Name of Thousands of Wel-Affected Persons*, since

---

[202] *CJ* ii. 760, 818; [D. Featley], *Virtumnus Romanus* (London, 1642); *SR* i. 53; *PJ* iii. 345; *DNB*. See also: *That Great Expedition for Ireland* (London, for Hunscott, 1642).

[203] *God Appearing for the Parliament in Sundry Late Victories* (London, for Husband, 1644).

[204] *Some Passages that Happened the 9th of March* (London, 1642); *LJ* iv. 652–3, 660. The work was ostensibly accurate, based on leaked information.

[205] *The Remonstrance of the Commons of England* (London, 1643); *LJ* v. 651; *A Disclaimer of the Commons of England* (London, 1643).

a reply was issued – though not by Parliament – in which it was claimed that the tract was the work of 'an imposter giving answer in their names'.[206]

What brought the propaganda dilemma into focus was not merely the problems associated with the process of composing declarations, their likely reception, and the difficulties of using them to pronounce orthodoxy. There were also tasks which official declarations could never hope to achieve. It may have been regarded as necessary to respond to critics in kind, to devise methods of reaching a wider audience than that to which official declarations could extend, and to convey particular messages repeatedly. In December 1659, therefore, Sir Edward Nicholas commented not only on the need to 'mind the people what an advantage and happiness the king's restoration would be to the nation', but also that such a message need to be repeated often, 'for though few can be ignorant of it yet the frequent asserting of his just title would awake them, and make them think of their duty'.[207] On other occasions, alternative media may have been sought because of the impossibility of issuing a declaration. In May 1647, for example, a declaration was drafted against one of the London petitions, but this became redundant when the House refused to accept the petition. However, while a formal reply was thus unnecessary, its message may have been considered relevant, and certain members may have sought to ensure that their ideas found an outlet in some other form.[208] Since official declarations could not achieve all of the aims of successful propaganda, those who needed to talk – or appeal – to the people, recognised the need not merely to engage the services of capable writers, but also to find alternative media, in the form of political tracts, pamphlets, and newspapers.

The impulse for engaging in the production of propaganda sprang from the need to 'talk to the people', whether for personal or official reasons. This had become progressively more pressing during the century preceding the civil wars, with the spread of print and with the growing public interest in the political affairs of the nation. It became acute in the conditions of the 1640s, as rival political groups claimed authority, and sought to secure public support. It became necessary to win hearts and minds, as well as wallets and purses, as never before. Royalists and parliamentarians, as well as factional and military interest groups, sought to engage in public debate in order to explain and justify policies, reply to critics, and 'undeceive' the people. By analysing the rhetoric with which such works were surrounded, it is possible not merely to understand the role which propaganda was perceived to play, but also to demonstrate that some royalists felt uneasy about the way in which propaganda served to 'stir up' the people. By scrutinising the ways in which official propaganda was produced, printed and distributed, it is possible

---

[206] *The Answer of the Commons to a Petition in the Name of Thousands of Wel-Affected Persons* (London, 1648); *A Reply to the House of Commons* (London, 1648). See: *CJ* vi. 18.

[207] *CSPD 1659–60*, pp. 275–6.

[208] *CSPD 1645–7*, pp. 558–9; PRO, SP 16/515, fos. 167–8v; *CJ* v. 162, 179.

not merely to demonstrate the seriousness with which contemporaries took the task of engaging with the public, but also to suggest that parliamentarians were more zealous than royalists about spreading their message to a wider audience. By examining the methodology by which official propaganda was produced, it is possible to explore the reasons for employing the talents of writers and pamphleteers, rather than relying simply upon their own resources, and for suggesting that parliamentarians proved more willing than royalists to transfer such duties to proven polemicists rather than political grandees. Furthermore, while allowance must be made for the differences between royalist and parliamentarian archives, and for the probability that the circumstances in which the royalists found themselves affected their ability to organise propaganda, it is also possible to demonstrate that during the 1640s, Parliament's efforts to enhance the efficiency with which propaganda was produced involved willingness to bureaucratise and professionalise their techniques, whether through formal procedures for distributing official literature, or by the creation of a salaried position of 'special secretary', which involved nothing other than the drafting of official literature. Finally, it is possible to demonstrate that the employment of writers with proven polemical talent represented more than merely an attempt to find a solution to the problems inherent in the production of official texts. It reflected the fact that the production of any kind of officially inspired literature involved negotiating the central conceptual dilemma of propaganda, and that while it was necessary to produce works which were transparently official, in order to establish orthodoxy, it was also important to inundate the market with books which could not easily be traced back to their official origins, in order to create the impression of spontaneous support for particular parties and positions.

CHAPTER 2

Authors and the Propaganda Impulse

When the cleric, Edward Boughen, published the text of a visitation sermon in 1620, he dedicated the book to John Howson, Bishop of Oxford, to whom he was chaplain, by saying that, 'having heretofore ... preached this sermon at your lordship's appointment, and since enlarged it (by your advice) with some necessary additions, I have now also, according to your directions, and by public authority, committed it to the press'.[1] Readers of Boughen's work were confronted, in other words, with a number of claims regarding both the author's status and the circumstances surrounding the composition and publication of his text. The aim of this chapter is to pay attention to, and unravel, such statements, for having explored the motivation for politicians producing propaganda, it is necessary to examine why authors were willing to engage with the public through the production of polemical tracts and pamphlets. The task is to assess from where the impetus to write, print and publish came, and to understand why authors put pen to paper, and then endeavoured to get their efforts into print. This chapter offers, therefore, an analysis of authorial intention, and the motivations for composition and publication. The aim is not to produce an overly stylised analysis, or to suggest that the overwhelming bulk of polemical literature of the mid-seventeenth century reflected political patronage, whether directly or indirectly.[2] It is necessary to be alive to the fact that authors had mixed and multiple motives for engaging in such work, and to the fact that the motives for writing and publishing may not have been the same, not least because the two events may have been separated in time. In seeking to gain an insight into the minds of seventeenth-century political writers and pamphleteers, it is obviously possible to consider the claims made by contemporaries, including hostile critics, as well as the comments made in memoirs and reminiscences. Given the problematic nature of the former, and the rarity of the latter, it is more important at this stage to observe those statements made by authors at the time of publication, and in their own works, and the explanations which they themselves provided for venturing into print.[3]

Authors felt the need to explain their motivation, and they tended to do so at the very outset; sometimes on the title page, but more commonly in prefatory

---

[1] E. Boughen, *A Sermon of Confirmation* (London, 1620), sig. A2.

[2] A. Fox, *Politics and Literature in the Reigns of Henry VII and Henry VIII* (Oxford, 1989), p. 11.

[3] B. Richardson, *Printing, Writers and Readers in Renaissance Italy* (Cambridge, 1999), pp. 77–80.

addresses and dedications. There was evidently a perception that publishing was not intrinsically worthy, and that the printing of works required justification. This has been described as the 'stigma of print', and although it may have been a phenomenon more gestured at than real, the fact that so many writers felt compelled to explain their projects is of at least some use to the historian.[4] Such claims clearly have limitations. They could be rhetorically hackneyed at best, and disingenuous at worst, and it is tempting to dismiss prefatory comments as mere 'sycophantic ephemera'.[5] It is certainly worth recognising that dedications and opening remarks were to some extent formulaic and 'ritualised'; that they cannot be trusted entirely; and that they have only varying degrees of credibility.[6] They may have been inspired by a range of motives other than truth, whether personal loyalty or political bias, just as the claims of enemies and opponents were often intended to defame, and possibly to libel, because of personal animus or political necessity. Problematic though such claims are, however, they cannot be ignored, because few authors left memoirs, or explained their motivations in correspondence, and because part of the aim of this study is to develop a picture of the evidence which contemporary readers would have had at their disposal, to assist in their own understanding of the way in which books appeared. Furthermore, the significance of such prefatory comments lies in demonstrating that authors were prepared to serve the interests of political patrons, and this in turn enables attention to be shifted towards less public evidence relating to the ways in which writers sought to attach themselves to, and represent the interests of, grandees, factions, public authorities and particular regimes.

Authors could clearly operate independently of politicians and patrons, and could engage in writing and publishing for their own reasons, and in order to express their own opinions. Many were motivated to publish by commercial and financial considerations, not least the editors of newspapers.[7] The financial incentive was probably a powerful factor in the world of print in the mid-seventeenth century, and it is certainly evident that the appearance of at least some counterfeit newspapers resulted from the lure of money to be made by capitalising upon a popular and well-respected journal. This appears most clearly in the rhetoric

---

4 J. W. Saunders, 'The stigma of print. A note on the social bases of Tudor poetry', *Essays in Criticism* 1 (1951); A. Halasz, *The Marketplace of Print: Pamphlets and the Public Sphere in Early Modern England* (Cambridge, 1997), p. 87. For criticism of this idea see: S. W. May, 'Tudor aristocrats and the mythical stigma of print', *Renaissance Papers* (1980), pp. 11–18.

5 M. Brennan, *Literary Patronage in the English Renaissance: the Pembroke Family* (London, 1988), p. 3.

6 H. S. Bennett, *English Books and Readers 1603–40* (Cambridge, 1970), p. 3.

7 A. Cotton, 'London newsbooks in the civil war: their political attitudes and sources of information' (Oxford University DPhil, 1971), p. 18; A. Bellany, *The Politics of Court Scandal in Early Modern England* (Cambridge, 2002), pp. 117, 127. See also: J. F. Merritt, 'The pastoral tight-rope: a Puritan pedagogue in Jacobean London', in T. Cogswell, R. Cust, and P. Lake, eds, *Politics, Religion and Popularity in Early Stuart Britain* (Cambridge, 2002), p. 159.

surrounding counterfeits, as authors traded insults and allegations.[8] In part, such professionalisation of authorship can be portrayed as having accompanied a decline in traditional forms of literary patronage, which forced authors to turn to their readers as patrons, and to develop marketing techniques. These could relate to genre, in terms of the emergence of cheap print; to visuals, in terms of crude notions of graphic design; and to literary devices, in terms of commendatory verses and prefaces. They could even involve primitive advertising.[9] Evidence of manuscripts, both large and small, being sold to publishers, and of the emergence of publishing contracts, has prompted recognition that the early modern period witnessed the emergence of the professional author, and realisation that such professionalism extended beyond the popular press of Thomas Nashe and Gabriel Harvey, and of John Taylor and Henry Walker.[10] The professional world of print in the early modern period embraced not merely those driven by money, but also those for whom writing was a vocation.

The vast majority of writers in the early modern period cannot be categorised in this fashion, publishing as they did without the promise of financial gain. That they were prepared to engage in publication indicates a degree of self motivation, and there is plentiful evidence of authors arranging for, and financing, the publication of works themselves, and of their also being involved in the distribution of such books.[11] Bishop Williams evidently paid for the printing of *Holy Table*, although he probably sought to distance himself from the transaction by working through the Cambridge don, Richard Holdsworth.[12] When Thomas Cheshire published an edition of a sermon which he had preached in 1642, the cover of the work said that it was 'published for the author'. Perhaps unkindly, the book collector George Thomason added that this was done 'because none else

---

[8] J. Peacey, '"The counterfeit silly curr": money, politics and the forging of royalist newspapers in the English civil war', *HLQ* (forthcoming).

[9] P. J. Voss, 'Books for sale: advertising and patronage in late Elizabethan England', *Sixteenth Century Journal* 29 (1998); A. Marotti, 'Patronage, poetry and print', in *Politics, Patronage and Literature in England 1558–1658* (Yearbook of English Studies, 21, 1991), p. 22.

[10] J. Raymond, *The Invention of the Newspaper. English Newsbooks, 1641–1649* (Oxford, 1996), p. 17; J. Rigney, 'To lye upon a stationers stall, like a piece of coarse flesh in a Shambles': the sermon, print and the English civil war', in L. A. Ferrell and P. McCullough, eds, *The English Sermon Revised* (Manchester, 2000), p. 191; J. Loach, 'The Marian establishment and the printing press', *EHR* 101 (1986), pp. 145–6; E. H. Miller, *The Professional Writer in Elizabethan England* (Cambridge, Mass., 1959), pp. 137–70; I. M. Green, *Print and Protestantism in Early Modern England* (Oxford, 2000), p. 22; P. Lindenbaum, 'John Milton and the republican mode of literary production', *Yearbook of English Studies* 21 (1991); P. Lindenbaum, 'Authors and publishers in the late seventeenth century II: Brabazon Aylmer and the mysteries of trade', *The Library*, 7th series 3 (2002); K. Lindley, 'London and popular freedom in the 1640s', in R. C. Richardson and G. M. Ridden, eds, *Freedom and the English Revolution* (Manchester, 1986), pp. 113–14. For Walker, see: E. Sirluck, 'To Your Tents, O Israel: a lost pamphlet', *HLQ* 19 (1956), pp. 301–5. For Taylor, see: B. S. Capp, *The World of John Taylor the Water Poet, 1578–1653* (Oxford, 1994).

[11] H. Oxinden, *Charls Triumphant* (London, 1660); H. Oxinden, *Eikon Basilike* (London, 1660); BL, Add. 28004, fos. 133, 155, 161, 173, 212, 236, 237, 277.

[12] *CSPD 1641–3*, p. 228; PRO, SP 16/487, fo. 115.

would'. It would appear that Cheshire felt sufficiently motivated to put his views into the public domain to face possible financial loss.[13] The desire to convey personally held convictions, or to display literary talents, may also have contributed to the appearance of many of the thousands of anonymous works which appeared during the mid-seventeenth century. The publisher of Sir William Sales' anonymous *Theophania* explained that the author 'rather chose to be glorious in obscurity than shine in popular applause'.[14] In 1658, Peter Heylyn wrote that he was 'none of those dogs which bark for company', and that he sought neither 'public fame', nor 'the credit of such petit chapmen'.[15] Such writers may have sought to satisfy not just a desire for self-expression, but also for self-defence, self-justification and self-promotion, and pamphlets could clearly be used to lobby for a personal cause, to defend a reputation from critics, and to undermine interlopers and counterfeiters.[16] Writing in 1637, the Bishop of Down and Conner, Henry Leslie, justified a treatise by saying that it was 'published upon occasion of a libel sent abroad in writing, wherein this sermon, and all his proceedings are most falsely traduced'.[17]

The rhetoric of authorship, however, indicates that print was also used to serve a particular vision of the 'public good', and explanations for publication often extended to the high-minded and disinterested pursuit of knowledge and understanding. Some authors who were ostensibly writing for themselves may be regarded as having been altruistic to the extent that they claimed to be concerned with the 'truth'.[18] This certainly applies to those clerics who published sermons and theological works in order to fulfil their pastoral duties, and to Daniel Featley, who professed in his will to having written in order to glorify God.[19] It also applied to the Quakers, for whom books were a valuable means of overcoming their limited number of preachers.[20] Later, in times of heightened political tension, writers turned such selflessness to the advantage of particular groups in society, whether sectional interest groups or political and religious causes, which they defended from the criticism of enemies, or from misapprehension and misrepresentation.[21] Members of Puritan networks certainly engaged in print as

---

[13] T. Cheshire, *A Sermon Preached at St Peters* (London, 1642, BL, E107/17).

[14] [Sir. W. Sales], *Theophania* (London, 1655), sig. A3v.

[15] BL, Add. 28104, fo.8.

[16] M. Elsky, *Authorizing Words* (London, 1989), p. 193; *The Lord George Digbies Apologie for Himselfe* (Oxford, 1642), p. 5.

[17] H. Leslie, *A Treatise of the Authority of the Church* (Dublin, 1637), title page.

[18] Saunders, 'Stigma of print', p. 6; Bennett, *English Books*, p. 8; C. E. Harline, *Pamphlets, Printing and Political Culture in the Early Dutch Republic* (Dordrecht, 1987), pp. 11–13.

[19] H. Love, 'Preacher and publisher: Oliver Heywood and Thomas Parkhurst', *Studies in Bibliography* 31 (1978); J. Taylor, *The Rule and Exercises of Holy Dying* (London, 1651), sigs. A3–A4; PRO, PROB 11/193, fo. 266v.

[20] M. K. Peters, 'Quaker pamphleteering and the development of the Quaker movement, 1652–1656' (Cambridge University PhD, 1996), pp. 36–8, 49.

[21] Bennett, *English Books*, pp. 13–18.

part of a process of closing ranks in the face of opposition, such as in order to counter anti-Puritan exploitation of a well-known murder story.[22] For the royalists, Edward Boughen claimed to have been motivated by a sense of 'faith and duty' to the king's cause, while John Maxwell explained that he had 'put pen to paper to right our gracious sovereign, [and] to undeceive his subjects'.[23] Peter Heylyn explained in some detail his motivation for writing and publishing his *Historie of Episcopacie* in 1642. Heylyn's justification was the persistence of the attacks by the church's opponents, though he admitted that:

> Tis true indeed, as long as the assault was only made by scurrilous and unlearned libels or empty and unworthy pamphlets, there was no better answer to be given than contempt and silence; as being neither considerable for the authors nor formidable for the dangers which might thence ensue.

Nevertheless, he felt the need to assist the work undertaken by Joseph Hall, in his debate with 'Smectymnuus', and to offer his 'poor endeavours to the public service'. He explained that:

> When that reverend pen grew wearied, not with the strength or number of his adversaries, but their importunity, who were resolved to have the last word ... I then conceived it might not be unfit to bethink myself what further course might be pursued for the church's peace.[24]

Meanwhile, addressing the prominent Presbyterian William Prynne, the tolerationist writer Henry Robinson explained his decision to enter into print in 1645 by the need to defend fellow religious Independents from scurrilous attacks.[25] Similarly, the Quaker Richard Farnworth wrote in 1653 that he was 'moved to write this ensuing treatise in the behalf of a harmless and innocent people', and Amon Wilbee, writing in the summer of 1647, noted that his work was 'printed and published for the information, advice and benefit of the poor, oppressed, betrayed and almost destroyed commons of England'.[26] The biographer of the parliamentarian journalist and author, John Hall, claimed that his subject, observing that the royalist cause had 'devolved from arms to pens', sought to respond to royalist literature and made his 'appearance for the state'.[27] Among parliamentarian clerics, it is possible that members of the Westminster Assembly of Divines, such as Thomas Bakewell, felt compelled to defend that body's work,

---

[22] P. Lake, 'Puritanism, Arminianism and a Shropshire axe-murder', *Midland History* 15 (1990), pp. 56–8.

[23] E. Boughen, *Mr Gerees Case of Conscience Sifted* (London, 1648), sig. A2; J. Maxwell, *Sacro-Sancta Regum Majestas* (Oxford, 1644), sig. A2.

[24] Theophilus Churchman [aka Peter Heylyn], *The Historie of Episcopacie* (London, 1642), sigs. A4–A4v, av, a2.

[25] H. Robinson, *The Falsehood of Mr William Pryn's Truth Triumphing* (London, 1645), sig. A2; N. Smith, *Literature and Revolution in England, 1640–1660* (New Haven, 1994), p. 27.

[26] R. Farnworth, *The Generall-Good to All People* (London, 1653), sig. A2; A. Wilbee, *Plain Truth Without Fear of Flattery* (London, 1647).

[27] J. Hall, *Hierocles Upon the Golden Verses* (ed. J. Davies, London, 1657), sig. b3v.

and a sense of collective responsibility clearly emerges from the literary and publishing activity undertaken by many of the leading Presbyterian ministers in the late 1640s, in terms of the collaborative production of controversial tracts and pamphlets.[28] Likewise, it is possible to demonstrate how a group of like-minded Presbyterian stationers worked together to defend their professional interests, political cause and religious beliefs, during the so-called 'beacon controversy' of the early 1650s.[29] What such examples attest to is an awareness of the fact that political and religious causes required vigorous defence and constant vigilance, and that political victory was insufficient without a propaganda triumph. Ultimately, at times of political and religious tension, writers were prepared to use their literary skills in order to advance controversial political and religious causes, and to take such controversies and arguments into the public domain.

Beyond engaging in the production of 'public texts', whether for selfish or selfless reasons, authors used books in order to make public their connections with individuals who might loosely be described as 'patrons', most commonly through dedications and prefatory comments.[30] Of course, such connections did not necessarily pre-date publication, and dedications may have been used to forge relationships with men with whom they sought to be associated, even if only to create such linkage in the mind of the reader. However, many authors made such comments and compliments in order to indicate to readers that such contacts were meaningful, and as such, dedicatory material can assist the study of the processes by which works appeared, and the ways in which printed texts could represent and embody personal and political relationships.

Many authors dedicated books to men with whom they had no personal connection, in the hope of either material or non-material benefits.[31] It was clearly common to dedicate works to 'patrons' in the hope of receiving monetary payments, and in order to 'extort some benevolences or gift'.[32] However, it was

---

[28] T. Bakewell, *The Ordinance of Excommunication Rightly Stated and Vindicated from Several False Opinions* (London, 1646); *A Vindication of the Presbyteriall Government and Ministry* (London, 1650), p. 175; *A Serious and Faithfull Representation of the Judgments of Ministers* (London, 1649), pp. 16–20; *A Testimony to the Truth of Jesus Christ and to our Solemn League and Covenant* (London, 1648).

[29] [L. Fawne] *A Beacon Set on Fire* (London, 1652); M. Sparke, *A Second Beacon Fired by Scintilla* (London, 1652); F. Cheynell, *The Beacon Flameing* (London, 1652). The first was co-authored with Samuel Gellibrand, Joshua Kirton, John Rothwell, Thomas Underhill, and Nathaniel Webb.

[30] F. B. Williams, *Index of Dedications and Commendatory Verses in English Books Before 1641* (London, 1962); Miller, *Professional Writer*, pp. 94–136; Marotti, 'Patronage, poetry and print', pp. 21–2; Green, *Print and Protestantism*, p. 9; J. N. King, 'Freedom of the press, Protestant propaganda and Protector Somerset', *HLQ* 40 (1976–77); P. J. Lucas, 'The growth and development of English literary patronage in the later Middle Ages and early Renaissance', *The Library*, 6th series 4 (1982). For examples, see: T. Fuller, *The Holy State* (3rd edn, London, 1652), p. 186; M. Dever, 'Richard Sibbes' (Cambridge University PhD, 1993), pp. 47, 57–8; A. Foster, 'The function of a bishop: the career of Richard Neile, 1562–1640', in R. O'Day and F. Heal, eds, *Continuity and Change. Personnel and Administration of the Church of England, 1500–1642* (Leicester, 1976), p. 42.

[31] Miller, *Professional Writer*, pp. 126–8; Marotti, 'Patronage, poetry and print', p. 2.

[32] Bennett, *English Books*, pp. 23–39; W. A. Jackson, *Records of the Court of the Stationers'*

also possible that authors could use books as earlier generations had used manuscripts; in order to flatter potential patrons with unsolicited dedications as a 'means of approach', and in order to 'buy patronage' by showcasing their talents in the hope of securing promotion and favour.[33] It had long been recognised that many authors were 'gaping for preferment', and some openly sought personal advancement, although it is often easier to detect the desire for reward than to establish the precise nature of authors' aims.[34] Likewise, it is rarely possible to establish the response which such dedications provoked, although it is evident that dedications were sometimes received unfavourably, and that they rarely prove dedicatee approval of a given work.[35] Indeed, there are certain instances where offence was taken, as when Sir Edward Hyde noted the less than enthusiastic reaction of George Monck to the appearance of his name at the head of a printed sermon by Dr John Griffith, in April 1660.[36] Since unsolicited dedications could be counterproductive, some authors who sought a 'patron' sought permission from the intended dedicatee.[37]

While some authors used dedications in order to achieve improvements in their fortunes, others sought to gain respectability and to secure protection from critics or the authorities. This prompted John Davies to comment that 'under Lords' wings metaphorical all authors creep'.[38] Patronage was synonymous with protection, and the manner in which writers published their work was sometimes influenced by the need to win support. A well-placed dedication could provide a means of securing 'favourable patronage and defence of their works by high dignity, and authority, against all malevolous cavillers and backbiters, whereof this

---

Company 1602–1640 (London, 1957), p. 250; P. Sheavyn, *The Literary Profession in the Elizabethan Age* (Manchester, 1967), pp. 17–25; Miller, *Professional Writer*, pp. 110–36; Richardson, *Printing, Writers and Readers*, pp. 49–57; Fox, *Politics and Literature*, p. 12; Harline, *Pamphlets, Printing and Political Culture*, p. 105; Marotti, 'Patronage, poetry and print', pp. 25–6; Green, *Print and Protestantism*, p. 10.

[33] Bennett, *English Books*, pp. 29–35; H. R. Woudhuysen, *Sir Philip Sidney and the Circulation of Manuscripts 1558–1640* (Oxford, 1996), pp. 88–103; D. R. Carlson, *English Humanist Books: Writers and Patrons, Manuscript and Print, 1475–1525* (Toronto, 1993), pp. 20–59; C. H. Clough, 'Erasmus and the pursuit of English royal patronage in 1517 and 1518', *Erasmus of Rotterdam Society Yearbook* 1 (1981), pp. 126–40; H. Love, *Scribal Publication in Seventeenth Century England* (Oxford, 1993), p. 179; Fox, *Politics and Literature*, p. 11; Saunders, 'Stigma of print', p. 13; T. J. McCann, 'The known style of a dedication is flattery': Anthony Browne, 2nd Viscount Montague of Cowdray and his Sussex flatterers', *Recusant History* 19 (1989), pp. 403–5.

[34] Quoted in Halasz, *Marketplace of Print*, p. 82; C. Gebert, *An Anthology of Elizabethan Dedications and Prefaces* (Philadelphia, 1933), p. 52.

[35] *CCSP* v. 628.

[36] *CCSP* iv. 638. See also: E. R. Foster, ed., *Proceedings in Parliament, 1610* (2 vols, New Haven, 1966), i. 18, 29, 188; L. Richardson, 'Tacitus, Sir John Hayward and the historiography of the 1590s' (paper delivered at the IHR, London, 5 June 2000); F. J. Levy, 'Hayward, Daniel and the beginning of politic history in England', *HLQ* 50 (1987), pp. 15–16.

[37] *TSP* vii. 595; BL, Add. 4165, fos. 23–4.

[38] Bennett, *English Books*, pp. 29–31; J. Davies, *A Scourge for Paper Persecutors* (London, 1625), sig. C2v.

wicked world is always full'.[39] Thus, 'protection' and 'shelter' were terms frequently used in authors' dedications.[40] Writing a dedication to the Earl of Pembroke in 1625, Cornelius Burges sought 'protection to preserve this fire from quench-coale. Shall you vouchsafe me the honour of your arms upon mine alter, I shall be confident that no man will dare to approach these harmless flames with spouts and pails'.[41] In 1647, Nathaniel Hardy dedicated the printed version of a sermon to the mayor of London by saying that he would have been 'well pleased to have kept this scarce plumed bird in my private cage, had not the noise of some virulent fowlers' shot forced her to fly abroad for refuge; where to build her nest better she knew not, than in the secure clefts of your favourable protection'.[42] In 1642, meanwhile, the royalist author, Robert Mossom, sought to secure 'protection' from Sir Thomas Glemham, while in 1657 he asked the Countess of Pembroke for 'patronage and protection', since 'I know well, what I publish in print, will find a critical comment, and censorious paraphrase'.[43] The utility of dedications lay not merely in affording protection, however, but also in the credibility and respectability which endorsement by a prominent public figure could bring, and even the possibility that this could enhance the chances of securing a favourable reception sufficiently to boost sales.[44] Dedicating a work to the widow of his patron Edward Ferrers, therefore, the royalist cleric Thomas Swadlin sought patronage for his devotions so that 'they may find entertainment and welcome abroad'.[45] It may even have been possible for writers such as James Howell to deploy dedications as part of the 'deliberate construction of a public image'.[46] Howell, who had been imprisoned by Parliament in the 1640s, certainly sought to curry favour with the commonwealth regime after 1649 by dedicating one of his books to Oliver Cromwell.[47] Ultimately such protection and respectability was most beneficial to those writing books which were politically sensitive.[48] This was doubtless why, before 1642, some Puritan writers were advised by their publishers to send works to patrons to seek permission for a

---

[39] G. Wither, *A View of the Marginal Notes* (London, 1588), sig. A2.

[40] Gebert, *Elizabethan Dedications*, p. 52; Lucas, 'English literary patronage', p. 238; J. Tillinghast, *Demetrius his Opposition to Reformation* (London, 1642), sig. A2.

[41] C. Burges, *The Fire of the Sanctuarie* (London, 1625), sig. A4v.

[42] N. Hardy, *Justice Triumphing, or the Spoylers Spoyled* (London, 1647), sig. A2.

[43] R. Mossom (trans.), *Anti-Paraeus* (York, 1642), sig. A3; R. Mossom, *The Preacher's Tripartite* (London, 1657), sig. [A3v].

[44] Marotti, 'Patronage, poetry and print', pp. 2, 25; Lucas, 'English literary patronage', p. 238; Bennett, *English Books*, pp. 29–31.

[45] T. Swadlin, *A Manuall of Devotions* (London, 1643), sig. [A4].

[46] D. Woolf, 'Conscience, consistency and ambition in the career and writings of James Howell', in J. Morrill, P. Slack and D. Woolf, eds, *Public Duty and Private Conscience in Seventeenth Century England* (Oxford, 1993), p. 257; Marotti, 'Patronage, poetry and print', pp. 25–6.

[47] J. Howell, *Som Sober Inspections* (London, 1655), sig. A2.

[48] This is implied by the comment of Hamon L'Estrange, in dedicating a work to Parliament in 1641, that 'I invoke not your aid to boulster out mischievous doctrine (the main scope of too many late dedications)': H. L'Estrange, *Gods Sabbath* (Cambridge, 1641), sig. A2v.

dedication. In 1634, the stationer Philemon Stephens offered just such advice to the minister Christopher Harvey, whose book had been refused a licence. Stephens proposed that a dedication to the Puritan grandee, Sir Robert Harley, would prove beneficial, and his advice was accepted.[49]

Harvey's example demonstrates that dedications could indicate fellow feeling between author and dedicatee, and shared religious and political sympathies, even if only in the mind of the author.[50] The diarist Walter Yonge certainly used dedications in order to interpret the beliefs of dedicatees; compiling 'observations of the inclinations of several noble personages out of the dedications of some good books'.[51] The importance of Yonge's analysis lies not in the accuracy of his assessments, but in the fact that he, and other readers, made such connections. Public perception was crucial to the deployment of dedications in books which engaged with controversial topics, and which adopted controversial positions on religious and political issues, and authors were probably consciously seeking to foster, in the minds of readers, a connection between themselves, their message, and the 'patron' to whom the work was dedicated. 'Public texts', produced by authors intent on personal advantage and on conveying a personal message, could be linked in a deliberate fashion to the reputations of prominent patrons, and to the political and religious causes with which they were associated.

In addition to carrying political overtones, and indicating to readers a degree of sympathy between author and 'patron', dedications could be used to demonstrate the existence and strength of relationships of a more personal and meaningful nature.[52] Moreover, rather than merely reflecting hierarchical and unilinear patronage relationships, authors could demonstrate the complexity of patronage networks, and works were dedicated to friends, long-term associates, and prominent members of local communities. John Ley, for example, dedicated works to a number of prominent gentry and clerical figures from the north west of England, including grandees such as Sir Robert Harley, William Brereton and Viscount Kilmurrey, as well as friends from the clerical community, such as Charles Herle.[53] In 1643, Francis Cheynell dedicated his *Rise and Growth of Socinianism* to Viscount Saye, a neighbour in the Banbury area during the early 1630s.[54] Others used dedications to commemorate 'old friendship and familiarity',

---

[49] BL, Add. 70002, fo. 82; T. Pierson, *The Cure of Hurtfull Cares and Feares* (London, by R. B. for P. Stephens and C. Meredith, 1636), sigs. A3, A5v, A6v.

[50] P. Thomson, 'The literature of patronage, 1580–1630', *Essays in Criticism* 2 (1952), p. 277; Bennett, *English Books*, p. 31.

[51] G. Roberts, ed., *The Diary of Walter Yonge* (Camden Society, 41, 1847), p. 118.

[52] Lindenbaum, 'John Milton', pp. 121–2.

[53] J. Ley, *A Comparison of the Parliamentary Protestation* (London, 1641), sig. A2; *A Case of Conscience* (London, 1641), sig. a2; *Defensive Doubts* (London, 1641), sig. a2; *A Letter Against the Erection of an Altar* (London, 1641), sig. a2.

[54] F. Cheynell, *The Rise, Growth and Danger of Socinianism* (London, 1643), sig. A2.

and 'old long continued love'.[55] In dedicating posthumous works by John Preston to Puritan grandees such as the Earl of Warwick and Richard Knightly, Preston's literary executors were fulfilling his desire for works to be dedicated to 'special friends'.[56] Likewise, published funeral sermons tended to be dedicated to friends of both the author and the deceased.[57] Moreover, dedications were commonly used in order to express gratitude to a 'patron', or loyalty to a family, and to demonstrate a sense of obligation which could clearly extend over long periods.[58] In dedicating his major work of royalist theory to the Marquess of Montrose in 1644, John Maxwell referred to 'so many ties by personal favours received above my desert', while the royalist cleric William Stampe thanked the Earl of Cleveland for 'the ample experience I have had of your favour and benignity both at home and abroad', and Thomas Fuller expressed his 'particular gratitude' to patrons such as Sir John Danvers.[59] Edward Reynolds, meanwhile, mentioned favours received from three generations of the Yelverton family.[60] In dedicating their works to patrons, of course, authors also made such contacts visible to readers. The patron was revealed as a benefactor, and the author revealed himself to be well-connected. It seems certain that Jeremiah Burroughes was eager for the public to know that when his dedicatee, the Earl of Warwick, had been ill some three years earlier, 'I was then for some time daily with your lordship'. Burroughes clearly felt that he and his work could benefit from making known to the world the strength of his personal friendship with one of the most important political figures of the 1640s.[61]

In many cases, the nature of the patronage which was being acknowledged in dedications remained unclear. Authors often expressed thanks merely for 'manifold', 'noble' and 'unmerited' favours, or for 'protection'.[62] However, some

---

[55] Wither, *A View*, sig. A2.

[56] J. Preston, *The Breast-Plate of Faith and Love* (ed. R. Sibbes and J. Davenport, London, 1630), sig. ¶2; J. Preston, *The Goden Scepter* (ed. T. Ball and T. Goodwin, London, 1638), sig. A4; J. Preston, *Sermons Preached Before His Majestie* (ed. T. Ball and T. Goodwin, London, 1634), sigs. A2–A2v.

[57] J. Owen, *The Labouring Saints Dismission to Rest* (London, 1652), sig. A2.

[58] I. M. Calder, ed., *Letters of John Davenport* (London, 1937), pp. 190–94; Bennett, *English Books*, pp. 35–9.

[59] Maxwell, *Sacro-Sancta*, sig. ¶3v; W. Stampe, *A Treatise of Spiritual Infatuation* (Hague, 1653), sig. A2; T. Fuller, *A Sermon of Assurance* (London, 1647), sig. A2. See also: T. Fuller, *The Cause and Cure of a Wounded Conscience* (London, 1647), sigs. A3, A4.

[60] E. Reynolds, *A Sermon Touching the Use of Humane Learning* (London, 1658), sig. A2; E. Reynolds, *Animalis Homo* (London, 1650), sig. A2. See also: J. Despagne, *New Observations upon the Decalogue* (London, 1652), sig. A3; J. Trapp, *A Brief Commentary or Exposition Upon the Gospel According to St John* (London, 1646), sig. A2; Ley, *A Comparison*, sigs. A2–A2v; R. Sibbes, *The Complete Works* (ed. A. B. Grosart, 6 vols, Edinburgh, 1862–64), i. 35–7.

[61] J. Burroughes, *Moses his Choice* (London, 1641), sig. A4v. See also: J. Burroughes, *A Vindication* (London, 1646), pp. 16–21.

[62] A. Rosse, *Leviathan Drawn Out with a Hook* (London, 1653), sig. A6; L. Owen, *The Running Register* (London, 1626), sig. A2v; J. Vicars, *A Looking Glass for Malignants* (London, 1643), sigs. A3–A3v; W. Dell, *Power from on High* (London, 1645), sig. A4; W. Pinke, *The Tryall* (Oxford, 1631), sig. A2; McCann, 'The known style of a dedication', pp. 406–7.

such favours were clearly pecuniary in nature. Peter Bulkley dedicated an edition of his sermons to Oliver St John as thanks for the latter's generosity; 'his liberality having been a great help and support unto me in these my latter times, and many straits'.[63] Sir Richard Baker, writing from prison in 1640, dedicated his treatise on the psalms to Lord Craven, out of gratitude for 'the remission of a great debt'.[64] Thomas Swadlin mentioned having received from Edward Ferrers 'the best part' of his livelihood, 'and in gratitude gives this public remonstrance of it', although in the same year he dedicated another work to Lord Craven, 'as a perpetual acknowledgement of your munificence and a lasting testimony of my gratitude'.[65] Thomas Fuller wrote of the 'strong obligations' which resulted from the 'bounty' of Sir John Danvers, Lord George Berkeley and Edward, Lord Montagu.[66] In this case, the bounty in question may have been transparent, since Fuller was writing from within the households of such men, as was Peter du Moulin when he dedicated a work to his patron, the Earl of Cork.[67] Furthermore, authors specifically offered thanks for clerical appointments and household chaplaincies.[68] William Stampe intimated that the favours for which he thanked the Earl of Cleveland included nomination to the living at Stepney, while John Robotham dedicated a work to two prominent Sussex parliamentarians, Anthony Stapley and William Cawley, by styling them 'benefactores mei', for having secured him a clerical position in the region, and John Beadle thanked the man who secured his clerical living in Essex, the Earl of Warwick.[69] John Gumbleden, on the other hand, dedicated a work to his employer, the Earl of Leicester, to whom he was chaplain, and Samuel Clarke dedicated a work to his employer, the Earl of Warwick, saying 'it is now above twenty years since I was chosen lecturer in Warwick, at which time meeting with some opposition, your lordship was pleased so far to own me, as to make me your chaplain, and to write your letter in my behalf'.[70] Furthermore, the 'patronage' for which thanks was given could be institutional as well as personal. Samuel Torshell, for example, thanked the Haberdashers' Company, who had been responsible for finding him a clerical position, and the parliamentarian controversialist John Vicars dedicated his early works to the governors of Christ's

---

[63] P. Bulkley, *The Gospel Covenant* (London, 1646), sig. A2–A3v.

[64] Sir R. Baker, *Meditations and Disquisitions* (London, 1640), sigs. A3–A4.

[65] Swadlin, *Manuall of Devotions*, sig. A3; T. Swadlin, *The Scriptures Vindicated* (np, 1643), sig. [A2].

[66] Fuller, *Sermon of Assurance*, sig. A2v; Fuller, *Cause and Cure*, sig. A3; T. Fuller, *The Appeal of Iniured Innocence* (London, 1659), sig. [A2].

[67] Fuller, *Cause and Cure*, sig. A4; Fuller, *The Appeal*, sig. [A2]; P. du Moulin, *Of Peace and Contentment of Minde* (London, 1657), sigs. A3r–v.

[68] Bennett, *English Books*, pp. 37–8.

[69] Stampe, *Treatise of Spirituall Infatuation*, sig. A2v; J. Robotham, *The Preciousness of Christ* (London, 1647), sigs. A2–4; J. Beadle, *The Journal or Diary of a Thankful Christian* (London, 1656), sig. A3. See also: J. Church, *The Divine Warrant of Infant Baptism* (London, 1648), sig. A3.

[70] J. Gumbleden, *Christ Tempted* (London, 1657), sig. A2; S. Clarke, *The Second Part of the Marrow of Ecclesiastical History* (London, 1650), sig. Aaa2.

Hospital, where he was a tutor.[71] Most importantly, authors thanked patrons for the 'encouragement' offered to academic or literary studies. William Dillingham, for example, dedicated a work to Sir Horatio Townshend by informing readers that it was his 'by purchase', having 'freely contributed' to help defray the costs of publication.[72] Robert Mossom, meanwhile, thanked Frances, Marchioness of Hertford, for having encouraged his scholarly endeavours.[73] Others were encouraged to publish, and while Richard Sibbes resisted the pressure to publish from the Puritan patriarch John Dod, others were more forthcoming.[74] Thomas Swadlin, for example, informed the dedicatees of his *Manuall of Devotions* that, 'for some of you most of these devotions and meditations were undertaken'.[75]

The most obvious literary form to be produced upon request was the sermon, particularly those delivered in prestigious pulpits, before auspicious audiences, and on special occasions. Such high-profile sermons include those preached for Christ's Hospital, those delivered before the Inns of Court, and those preached before the mayor and civic authorities in London.[76] Nathaniel Holmes's sermon before the mayor of London in 1650 was published 'in answer to desires', and his sermon before another mayor, Thomas Foote, was dedicated to the latter with the comment that 'according to your desires, I have printed this sermon'.[77] Simeon Ashe's sermon at St Paul's in November 1654 was printed with a dedication to the lord mayor which stated that the 'acceptance which this sermon found, when preached, did incline you to order that I should make it more public than it was in the pulpit'.[78] Likewise, Peter Vinke's 1658 sermon was dedicated to the mayor, who was told that 'it comes forth only at your honour's call'.[79] Such prominent sermons also include addresses preached before London's Honourable Artillery Company, by the likes of John Davenport, William Gouge, Calybute Downing and Samuel Kem.[80] Beyond these 'institutional' orations were those sermons preached

---

[71] S. Torshell, *The Saints Humiliation* (London, 1633), sig. ¶2; S. Torshell, *The Three Questions* (London, 1632), sig. A4; J. Vicars, *A Prospective Glasse* (London, 1618), sig. A2; J. Vicars, *Englands Hallelu-jah* (London, 1631), sig. A2; F. Herring, *Mischeefes Mysterie* (trans. J. Vicars, London, 1617), sig. A2; J. Vicars, *November the 5. 1605* (London, 1641), sig. A4.

[72] *The Commentaries of Sir Francis Vere* (ed. W. Dillingham, Cambridge, 1657), sig. A3. In April 1656, Dillingham had written to Townshend asking for £30 for this purpose: Folger Shakespeare Library, L.d.259.

[73] Mossom, *Preacher's Tripartite*, book II, sig. A2.

[74] Sibbes, *Works*, ii. 3–4.

[75] Swadlin, *Manuall of Devotions*, sig. A3.

[76] GL, MS 12806/5, pp. 246, 269; J. Ridley, *A Sermon of Humbly Walking with God* (London, 1649); J. Cranford, *Haereseo-Machia* (London, 1646); R. Vines, *Obedience to Magistrates* (London, 1656).

[77] N. Holmes, *A Sermon Preached Before Thomas Andrews* (London, 1650), sig. A2; N. Holmes, *A Sermon Preached Before the Right Honourable Thomas Foote* (London, 1650), sig. A.

[78] S. Ashe, *The Doctrine of Zeal* (London, 1655), sig. A3. See also: S. Ashe, *Religious Covenants Directed* (London, 1646), sig. A2.

[79] P. Vinke, *The Reason of Faith* (London, 1659), sig. A2.

[80] C. Downing, *A Sermon Preached to the Renowned Company of the Artillery* (London, 1641); S. Kem, *The New Fort of True Honour* (London, 1640); Peacey, 'Henry Parker', pp. 15–21.

and printed at the request of individuals, including prominent political figures.[81] Some clerics merely admitted to having been asked by their congregations to make their texts more widely available. The royalist minister Robert Mossom, for example, claimed that 'what many of mine auditory have importuned me for in a transcript, I here present them with advantage by an impression', and when Thomas Drayton published sermons which had been delivered at Wilton House in 1657, he commented that they appeared in print 'at the request of the parishioners and auditors then present'.[82] Others were more specific. John Shaw, for example, both preached and printed in response to the requests of the prominent parliamentarian MP, Francis Thorpe, while John Bramhall informed his dedicatee, the Marquess of Newcastle, that 'this sermon is yours in right of the author, being first preached, then published by your special command', and by saying that 'it flyes thither most justly for protection, from whence it had a being'.[83]

Many such sermons were preached at the funerals of gentry and aristocratic figures. When John Bryan published his funeral sermon for Cicely Puckering, he dedicated it to her father, Sir Thomas Puckering, with the words: 'it being yours by all manner of right, and the best present I am able to present'.[84] Edward Boteler, in publishing the Earl of Mulgrave's funeral sermon, said that,

> the press and I have hitherto been strangers, nor did I ever intend my pen should scrape acquaintance with it but the desires of some (which carry the force of commands) and the importunity of other friends, calling for more copies than I had list or leisure to transcribe, have overruled these thoughts.[85]

When Thomas Gataker published his funeral sermon for the prominent merchant John Parker, he told Parker's widow that,

> having been, with much importunity and renewed requests incessantly solicited by divers who either had themselves heard or from others heard of, what was delivered at the interment of your late worthy consort ... to make that more public, that was then uttered in the audience but of a few to speak of, and by reason of the lowness and feebleness of my voice, of the fewer, I was at length over-wrought (though having formerly no such purpose) to condescend thereunto.[86]

As well as being solicited from personal friends, funeral sermons also served to reflect the solidarity of Puritan networks, and with the funerals of some public figures the request to publish evidently came from within the political

---

[81] N. Hardy, *Thankfulness in Grain* (London, 1654), sig. A2.

[82] Mossom, *Preachers' Tripartite*, sig. A3v; R. Mossom, *Sion's Prospect in its First View* (London, 1651), sig. *4; T. Drayton, T*he Proviso or Condition of the Promises* (London, 1657), title page.

[83] J. Shaw, *Britannia Rediviva* (London, 1649), pp. 3–7; 'The Life of Master John Shaw', in *Yorkshire Diaries and Autobiographies* (Surtees Society, 65, 1875), p. 393; J. Bramhall, *A Sermon Preached in the Cathedrall Church of York* (York, 1643), sig. A3.

[84] J. Bryan, *The Virtuous Daughter* (London, 1636), sig. A2; J. Brockett, *God's Statute for General Judgment* (London, 1642); Reynolds, *Sermon Touching the Use of Humane Learning*.

[85] E. Boteler, *The Worthy of Ephratah* (London, 1659), sig. a3.

[86] T. Gataker, *The Decease of Lazarus* (London, 1640), sig. A2.

hierarchy.[87] When the Dean of Cork, Edward Worth, published the sermon delivered at the funeral of the Lord Chief Justice of the Upper Bench, Richard Pepys, in 1659, it was dedicated to the Cromwellian secretary of state, John Thurloe, and readers were informed that 'this sermon was a child of obedience to his excellency's and the council's order'.[88] Similarly, Richard Vines preached the funeral sermon of his erstwhile patron, the Earl of Essex, at the request of the parliamentary authorities in 1646.[89]

In addition to publishing sermons at the request of those who had commissioned their delivery, or who had heard them preached, many other works were published upon request, having initially been composed for some other purpose.[90] In many cases, authors failed to identify those who had encouraged them into print with any meaningful degree of specificity, such as Nathaniel Hardy, who published a work in 1654 with the comment that he did so at the request of an unnamed patron.[91] The royalist cleric Edward Symmons told readers he was 'quickened' in his work 'by a noble gentleman of great faithfulness and loyality', and that he was 'solicited by some friends' to publish what had previously been laid aside.[92] It is obviously possible that such comments represented a mere rhetorical device, and provided a means of both acknowledging and negotiating the 'stigma of print'. John Tillinghast came close to admitting as much, for while he claimed to have published his work because of the 'importunity of friends', he added that this was 'that stale and common apology which by many is made for their appearing in stationary view'.[93] Many authors, however, were willing to identify their sponsors, and in doing so may be presumed to have been doing more than merely providing an excuse for publication.[94] Thomas Bedford claimed to have published his *Treatise of the Sacraments* in 1639 because he was encouraged to do so by the Bishop of Exeter.[95] When William Dell dedicated a work to his patroness, the Countess of Bolingbroke, he commented that it was published in response to 'your desire', and when Christopher Harvey dedicated his edition of a work by Thomas Pierson to Sir Robert Harley, he commented: '[that] I presume to present this little treatise unto you, is not my respect only but your right: your interest in all, the author, the work, and publication, doth more than require

[87] A. Hughes, 'Thomas Dugard and his circle in the 1630s', *HJ* 29 (1986), p. 775; Dever, 'Richard Sibbes', pp. 55–8.

[88] E. Worth, *The Servant Doing and the Lord Blessing* (Dublin, 1659), sig. A3; T. Barnard, 'Planters and policies in Cromwellian Ireland', *P&P* 61 (1973), pp. 49–53; BL, Lans. 823, f. 79.

[89] R. Vines, *The Hearse of the Renowned, the Right Honourable the Earle of Essex* (London, 1646); V. Snow, *Essex the Rebel* (Lincoln, Nebraska, 1970), pp. 413, 490–93.

[90] Saunders, 'Stigma of print', pp. 139–64.

[91] Hardy, *Thankfulness in Grain*, sig. A2; Bennett, *English Books*, p. 4.

[92] E. Symmons, *A Vindication of King Charles* (London, 1648), sigs. A2–B4.

[93] Tillinghast, *Demetrius*, sig. A3.

[94] Bennett, *English Books*, pp. 4–6.

[95] T. Bedford, *A Treatise of the Sacraments* (London, 1639), epistle.

it'.[96] Thomas Fuller explained to Sir John Danvers that one of his books, 'as it is small, so it desired to be secret, and intended no appearance in public ... but seeing such was your importunity to have it printed'.[97] Ephraim Huit, meanwhile, dedicated a work to Lady Brooke because her late husband had approved of it, according to the preface written by Simeon Ashe and Samuel Clarke.[98] In 1646, the Presbyterian minister, Anthony Burgess, claimed that one of his works was published at the request of another prominent London minister, Arthur Jackson, together with members of Sion College.[99]

Evidence from dedications and prefatory remarks, however, indicates more than that clerics and pamphleteers were encouraged to print works which had already been preached and composed, and that they were assisted in this process. In certain cases authors were willing to admit that they had been encouraged to compose individual pieces. Once again, some such claims were general in nature. The prominent Presbyterian minister, John Geree, claimed that he had been encouraged to compose his highly charged political tracts of the 1640s.[100] Some authors claimed that the demand for books had been popular rather than particular, and the royalist Robert Mossom informed his readers that 'if any demand a reason of the author's composing this treatise, this answer will be satisfactory ... that the public behoof did put him upon it'.[101] John Maxwell informed readers of *Sacro-Sancta Regum Majestas* that 'this is an extemporary piece, which was extorted by the importunity of friends, who prevailed so far with me, that I chused [sic] rather to expose my weakness and it to the censure of the world, than uncourteously refuse them'.[102] Hugh Peter was hardly more specific when he explained on one of his title pages that the work had been 'occasioned by the importunity of a friend'.[103] The royalist controversialist Edward Boughen noted that he was 'entreated by a very good friend to take Mr Gerees *Case of Conscience* into consideration', and Alex Rosse explained that he undertook to compose one of his works 'being animated by some lovers of the truth', and 'being desired by some of my friends a while ago to peruse Mr Hobbes his *Leviathan*'.[104]

On other occasions, authors were prepared to identify those responsible for instigating individual works. Sometimes such admissions were made years after

[96] W. Dell, *Power from on High* (London, 1645), sigs. A2, A4; Pierson, *Cure of Hurtfull Cares*, sigs. A3–A3v.

[97] T. Fuller, *A Sermon of Contentment* (London, 1648), sigs. A2v–A3.

[98] E. Huit, *The Whole Prophecie of Daniel* (London, 1644), sigs. A2–A2v.

[99] A. Burgess, *Vindiciae Legis* (London, 1646), title page.

[100] J. Geree, *The Down Fall of Antichrist* (London, 1641), sig. A3; J. Geree, *The Red Horse* (London, 1648), pp. 26, 28.

[101] Mossom, *Sion's Prospect*, sig. [*4].

[102] Maxwell, *Sacro-Sancta*, sig. [¶4].

[103] H. Peter, *Mr Peters Last Report of the English Wars Occasioned by the Importunity of a Friend Pressing an Answer to Seven Queries* (London, 1646).

[104] E. Boughen, *Mr Geree's Case of Conscience Sifted* (London, 1648), sig. A2v; Rosse, *Leviathan Drawn Out*, sig. A3, preface.

the event, in autobiographical asides and reminiscences, or in biographical sketches.[105] When they published Richard Sibbes' *Fountain Sealed*, Thomas Goodwin and Philip Nye dedicated it to Lady Elizabeth Brooke, and indicated that she and her late husband, Sir Robert Brooke, had played an important part in the initial composition:

> besides that deserved interest your ladyship held in the affections and esteem of this worthy man, more than any friend alive, which might entitle you to all that may call him author, this small piece of his acknowledgeth a more special propriety unto your ladyship. For though his tongue was as the 'pen of a ready writer' in the hand of Christ who guided him, yet your ladyship's hand and pen was in this his scribe and amanuensis whilst he dictated a first draft of it in private, with intention for the public.

They went on to say that they were returning the work to Lady Brooke, 'unto whom it owes even its first birth'.[106] However, there were many authors who felt little compunction about informing readers of their own 'patrons', and who felt no need to delay such admissions regarding the identity of those responsible for sponsoring their efforts. John Geree admitted being asked by two fellow ministers, William Gouge and Cornelius Burges, to preach and publish *The Red Horse*, while another controversial minister, John Reading, implied that his *Antidote Against Anabaptism* was written at the request of Sir William and Lady Anne Brockman.[107] Similarly, John Ley admitted writing at the request of his friend Philip Mainwaring, and the Sussex minister Thomas Barton said that one of his works was written at the request of Walter Dobell, a prominent local gentleman, in order to respond to another minister from the area, Mascall Giles.[108] In 1656, Christopher Fowler, minister of St Mary's Reading, was involved in the prosecution of the Ranter, John Pordage, before the commissioners for scandalous ministers, and when he produced the second instalment of his account of the affair, he informed readers that his works had been written at the request of the commissioners.[109] It is also possible to demonstrate instances where writers were prepared to admit in print that they were writing on behalf of their employers. Henry Parker, who was employed as a secretary to the Merchant Adventurers in Hamburg during the late 1640s, wrote a tract called *Of a Free Trade* (1648) as an explicit defence of the company against those Leveller-inspired critics who sought to revoke the company's charter. While readers would have been unaware that it was produced by the company secretary, few would have failed to realise that the work was inspired by the company. It was dedicated to John Kenrick, governor of the Merchant Adventurers in London, and to Isaac Lee, deputy of the company in

---

[105] J. Barwick, *ΙΕΡΟΝΚΗΣ, or the Fight, Victory and Triumph of St Paul* (London, 1660), p. 132.

[106] Sibbes, *Works*, v. 410.

[107] Geree, *Red Horse*, pp. 26, 28; J. Reading, *An Antidote* (London, 1654), sig. A3v.

[108] Ley, *Case of Conscience*, sig. a2; T. Barton, *ΑΠΟΔΕΙΞΙΣ … or, a Tryall of the Counterscarfe* (London, 1643), sig. A2. Barton said 'what you desired is done'.

[109] C. Fowler, *Daemonium Meridianum, Satan at Noon. The Second Part* (London, 1656), p. 2.

Hamburg, and Parker described himself as the company's 'advocate' and 'servant', and dated his preface from Hamburg.[110]

The most important examples of such authorial admissions regarding the impetus behind the composition of books and pamphlets concern cases where the request came from members of the political elite, and where the work in question was designed for a political or religious cause. Such examples bring us within the realm of political propaganda; produced on behalf of another individual or organisation, or on behalf of a shared cause, and written by 'clients', and those connected to powerful patrons and political figures. In spite of the stigma attached to a 'pen for hire', therefore, certain authors were prepared to admit that they were writing for a 'political' figure. Obviously some such admissions were more controversial than others, and the stigma attached to men writing for a recognisably legitimate public authority may have been minimal. In 1611, for example, few eyebrows would have been raised at the admission made by George Carleton that he had been put upon *Tithes Examined* by the request of the Archbishop of Canterbury, and likewise John Favour probably had little reason to fear admitting that he wrote *Antiquities Triumphing over Noveltie* (1619) because of 'the commanding entreaty' of the Archbishop of York.[111] Amid the political tension of the late 1630s, Peter Heylyn apparently felt little reticence about admitting that one of his polemical works, in which he responded to the Puritan martyr Henry Burton, had been written at the request of Archbishop William Laud.[112] Likewise, Joseph Hall freely admitted having been 'invited' to complete his defence of the divine right of episcopacy by the Caroline authorities, having tendered to the king 'some few short propositions concerning church government'.[113] Even during the civil wars, royalist authors such as Isaac Basire evinced little anxiety in admitting that, 'but that, in obedience to your royal command, [that] I must now practice as well as preach allegiance, this present argument ... had never presumed further than your royal ear'.[114] Jeremy Taylor admitted that one of his books had been perused at an early stage by the king.[115] Parliamentarians, on the other hand, were rarely so open during the 1640s, although William Prynne admitted that his *Popish Royal Favourite* was 'collected and published by authority'; that his *Sovereign Power of Parliaments* was compiled by the 'encouragement' of the Long Parliament; and that *Hidden Workes of Darkenes* was 'importuned by divers members of both Houses'.[116] However,

---

[110] H. Parker, *Of a Free Trade* (London, 1648), sigs. A2–A2v; Peacey, 'Henry Parker', pp. 126–9.

[111] Elsky, *Authorizing Words*, p. 184; Bennett, *English Books*, p. 6.

[112] P. Heylyn, *A Brief and Moderate Answer to the Seditious and Scandalous Challenges of Henry Burton* (London, 1637), sigs. dv–d2. See also: P. Heylyn, *Cyprianus Anglicus* (London, 1671), p. 312.

[113] J. Hall, *Episcopacie by Divine Right Asserted* (London, 1640), sig. A3.

[114] I. Basire, *Deo et Ecclesiae Sacrum* (Oxford, 1646), sig. A2.

[115] J. Taylor, *An Apology for Authorised and Set Forms of Liturgie* (London, 1649), sig. A3.

[116] W. Prynne, *The Popish Royall Favourite* (London, 1643); W. Prynne, *The Soveraigne Power of Parliaments* (London, 1643), sig. A2; W. Prynne, *Hidden Workes of Darkenes* (London, 1645), sig. (a).

matters were different after 1649. In 1651, John Salmon, a former prisoner, admitted taking up his pen after discussions with the parliamentarian grandee, William Purefoy, and after 'engaging to his honour and the rest that I would with all convenient speed declare myself in print against those things which I was then charged withall'.[117] Peter English admitted writing his treatise against Salmasius at the request of John Lambert and Robert Lilburne, two leading figures in the Cromwellian campaign in Scotland.[118] And when the New England preacher, Thomas Cobbet, dedicated a book on church government to Oliver Cromwell in 1653, he said: 'it seemeth, according to our best intelligence here, that the subject of this discourse beginning to grow the great controversial business of these polemic times, your honour with some other of the Lord's worthies in England, have expressed some desire of yours that something might be spoken thereunto'.[119]

Far more sensitive were cases where authors were prepared to admit writing for an individual political figure who did not represent a recognised 'authority'. Although writers rarely named their patron, they were often prepared to offer an explicit defence of an individual grandee in such a way as to betray to readers that they were motivated by personal loyalty, if not by pecuniary reward. Authors who admitted being prompted into print by political patrons included Thomas May, and the anonymous author (Sir Robert Cotton) of a 1640 work called *A Briefe Discourse Concerning the Power of the Peeres and Commons of Parliament in Point of Judicature*, although both declined to identify the individual in question.[120] Other works, however, explicitly defended named political figures. When the astrologer, William Lilly, defended a group of prominent parliamentarians from claims of financial impropriety in 1648, he sought to 'profess sincerity', and to stress that he was not engaged in flattery, and that he wrote 'impartial truths'. Nevertheless, he admitted that two of his subjects, Robert Reynolds and Bulstrode Whitelocke, were men to whom he was personally 'obliged'.[121] One of the controversial works by George Wither in the mid-1640s, meanwhile, printed a letter from the parliamentarian MP, John Maynard, encouraging him to publish, probably as part of factional political battles in Surrey.[122] More interesting are works which defended another parliamentarian grandee, Viscount Saye. The author of one 1643 tract made clear that the work was an overt attempt to rebut accusations made against Saye, and mentioned their long personal acquaintance,

---

[117] J. Salmon, *Heights in Depths* (London, 1651).

[118] P. English, *The Survey of Policy* (Leith, 1653), sig. a.

[119] T. Cobbet, *The Civil Magistrates Power in Matters of Religion* (London, 1653), sig. A2.

[120] [T. May], *A Discourse Concerning the Successe of Former Parliaments* (London, 1642), p. 1; [T. May], *Observations Upon the Effects of Former Parliaments* ([London, 1642]), p. 1; [Sir R. Cotton], *A Briefe Discourse Concerning the Power of the Peeres and Commons of Parliament in Point of Judicature* (London, 1640), title page.

[121] W. Lilly, *An Astrologicall Prediction* (London, 1648), p. 60.

[122] G. Wither, *Se Defendendo* (London, 1643), p. 3; J. Gurney, 'George Wither and Surrey politics, 1642–1649', *Southern History* 19 (1997), pp. 78–9.

which dated back over twenty years.[123] Another author who explicitly defended Saye against his critics was his nephew, Henry Parker. In *A Discourse Concerning Puritans* of 1641, Saye was named in a number of places as being 'known to me', while in another work from the same year Parker described himself as Saye's 'allies man'.[124] Saye was also explicitly defended in a work published by one of the family's chaplains, Robert Bacon, who dedicated his work to Saye in remembrance of 'your taking notice of me', and in commemoration of 'some dependance on you'. Moreover, in his observations upon the bilious Presbyterian, Thomas Edwards, Bacon was concerned to defend both himself and Saye, since Edwards had accused Bacon of being 'entertained' and encouraged to print by the parliamentarian peer.[125] Such defences of Saye are of particular interest because of the willingness on the part of their authors to make plain to readers that they were concerned to take up the cudgels on behalf of the peer because of ties of friendship, employment, and mutual political interests. Such openness regarding authorial motivation for engaging in controversial political pamphleteering is rare, but it is echoed in a work written in 1659 by Henry Stubbe, who engaged in one of the most explicit defences of a personal patron when he sought to use his pen to support the reputation of Sir Henry Vane junior, even if he stopped short of admitting that his book had been written at Vane's behest. Stubbe's *Essay in Defence of the Good Old Cause* included 'a vindication of the honourable Sir Henry Vane from the false aspersions of Mr [Richard] Baxter', author of *Holy Commonwealth*, whom Stubbe suspected of being 'instigated by the [Cromwellian] courtiers'. In the prefatory remarks, Stubbe denied that he himself served 'any party or designs', but admitted that he was 'engaged out of a sense of the truths, and apprehension of those favours I had received from Sir Henry Vane, to vindicate his repute from the calumnies of this whistler in theology'.[126]

The comments of Lilly and May, Parker and Bacon, as well as those by Henry Stubbe, would have ensured that contemporary readers of polemical literature were aware not merely that authors were connected to powerful patrons, to whom they sought to express gratitude, and not merely that they were sometimes encouraged to print and even compose religious and political texts. Readers were aware that such men could also be involved in determined attempts to defend specific political patrons and grandees, and the political interests with which they were associated.

---

[123] *A Copy of a Letter Written to a Private Friend to Give Him Satisfaction in Some Things Touching the Lord Say* (London, 1643), pp. 1–2.

[124] H. Parker, *A Discourse Concerning Puritans* (London, 1641), pp. 10, 52–3; H. Parker, *The Altar Dispute* (London, 1641), epistle.

[125] R. Bacon, *The Spirit of Prelacie Yet Working* (London, 1646), sigs. A3, A3v, pp. 31–2. See also: R. Bacon, *Christ Mighty in Himself and Members* (London, 1646), sigs. A4–A4v; J. S. A. Adamson, 'The Peerage in Politics, 1645–49' (Cambridge University PhD, 1986), p. 99.

[126] H. Stubbe, *An Essay in Defence of the Good Old Cause* (London, 1659), sigs. *2v–3, ***3. See also: H. Stubbe, *Malice Rebuked* (London, 1659).

In addition to more or less explicit statements regarding authorial intention and motivation, it is possible to explore less public evidence of attempts by writers to forge connections with political patrons, and to draw attention to ways in which authors approached politicians with a view to publishing specific books, tracts and pamphlets. In the first instance it is possible to highlight occasions where authors approached political grandees and patrons with ideas for books, and with proposals to issue works which would serve their interests.[127] Such proposals are particularly evident during the 1650s, both from supporters of the regime in London and their opponents. In November 1653, an unspecified author wrote to Cromwell and John Thurloe offering, rather cryptically, to defend Cromwell in print.[128] In June 1655, one of Thurloe's agents in Cadiz, Henry Daubne, reported having a contact who had offered to the regime a political discourse he had written, 'in order to the past, present, and future government of England, which he thinks may be somewhat seasonable for the satisfaction of some, if speedily published'. The author wished to know whether he should send a copy in advance of his impending visit to England.[129] Other such offers came via the good offices of Samuel Hartlib, who passed to Thurloe in September 1659 news of a proposal by one Dr Hornius, professor of history at Leiden, regarding a biography of Cromwell.[130] It is also possible to draw attention to James Howell's proposal, submitted to the Council of State, for a new version, in French and English, of Selden's treatise on the sovereignty of the seas. Howell said that it was 'expedient' for 'a new treatise' to be compiled 'for the vindication and continuance of this right', and that 'if the state be pleased to impose so honourable a command upon the subscriber, he will employ his best abilities to perform it'.[131] Sir Balthazar Gerbier, meanwhile, proposed visual propaganda, saying that 'it hath been practised in most parts of the world to propose such subjects unto the people's view, whereby the memorable acts of their general welfare, or those of their deliverances from some eminent danger may be extant'.[132]

The royalists too received offers from scholars and authors.[133] Salmasius' famous defence of the royalist cause in the aftermath of the regicide may have emerged as a result of his having offered his services in June 1649, and in February 1653, Abbot Castiglione in Turin wrote to Charles II with a proposal to write a history of his fortunes, having already written a history of Charles I.[134] In March 1660, meanwhile, Hyde was informed that Clement Spelman proposed writing

---

[127] This was hardly a new phenomenon: Wither, *A View*, sig. A4v; G. R. Elton, *Policy and Police. The Enforcement of the Reformation in the Age of Thomas Cromwell* (Cambridge, 1972), p. 185.

[128] *TSP* i. 591–2.

[129] *TSP* iii. 399–400.

[130] Bodl. MS Rawl. A.67, fos. 56–7.

[131] BL, Add. 32093, fo. 370.

[132] BL, Stowe 184, fo. 283.

[133] G. Vernon, *The Life of … Dr Peter Heylyn* (London, 1682), p. 54.

[134] Bodl. MS Carte 130, fo. 56; *CCSP* ii. 175; Bodl. MS Clarendon 45, fo. 62.

'observations' upon 'all printed papers that came forth about the time of the king's death ... and if you think they may be useful for his Majesty's service at this time, he will send them to you'.[135] Furthermore, the letter by which Sir Edward Walker, former secretary of the council of war, offered a tract to Hyde in January 1653, provides fascinating insight into authorial motivation. Upon reading William Lilly's *Monarchy or No Monarchy*, Walker had:

> so much indignation to find that so contemptible a creature as he should dare to asperse His Majesty as that I held myself bound in duty to discover his falsehood and ridiculous malice and to make it appear how traiterous, barbarous and untrue all his suggestions were, and though it may be truly said he is a person below the thoughts of a gentleman or loyal person, yet you know how much his pen hath prevailed with the credulous multitude, so I undertook to answer him and with so much ardour as in ten days and nights I had prepared it.

Walker was initially reticent about publishing the work, but eventually offered to send it to Hyde, saying that he 'must rely on the judgement you shall please to give of it and accordingly as it may be for His Majesty's service I may either publish or lay it by as an effect of my zeal, though below the right so many abler pens have paid to the exemplary virtue and goodness of that most excellent king'.[136]

The royalist figure who appears to have been among the most zealous for the use of print, however, was Joseph Jane. In April 1654, Jane sought to secure the translation of his book against Milton, indicating that 'if it were printed in French and dispersed ... it might do some good, especially now that Mr Milton's is printed in French in England', and that it would 'both sell well and do much good in the rectifying of many persons of the scandalous errors Milton hath laid down in his published book'. However, in September 1655, Jane complained that the work had still not been commissioned, even though 'there is much industry used in venting the translation of Milton'.[137] In October 1654, Jane wrote to Sir Edward Nicholas regarding 'a book lately written to declare the justice of Cromwell's new government, a translation into Latin, the original being English, which, if I could get it, should have an answer, if it were thought seasonable'. Having secured a copy of the work by December, Jane informed Nicholas that he intended 'to answer it, which being done it may be translated into Latin and printed here ... I have written to Mr Chancellor about it, and if he think it fit, shall proceed'. He also proposed a relation of:

> the business of the Duke of Gloucester ... and the people here are much pleased with it. I have been moved that the story of it might be composed from the beginning with the king's proceedings thereon, and it will be here turned into French and Dutch and printed. I think it will be of use and desire your directions in it, if it be approved.[138]

---

[135] *TSP* vii. 870.
[136] BL, Add. 33223, fo. 96.
[137] Bodl. MS Clarendon 48, fos. 135–6, 200–201; *NP* iii. 42–3.
[138] *NP* ii. 108–9, 146.

He added that, 'it will be fit the king's despatches were inserted, or such of them as are most to the advantage of the business'.[139] In August 1655, Jane proposed a printed account of Penruddock's trial, and said that 'if it were in French it would sell very well, and it were good that some such things should appear for us, that they may see there are some spirits left in England for the king, which they scarce believe'. At the same time, he proposed publishing the letters written between the separatists and Franciscus Junius during the reign of Elizabeth I, expressing his belief that 'they would be more observed at this time and might have good use ... if it be thought worthy, I shall endeavour to get them printed'.[140] In November 1655, Jane proposed a book to challenge Cromwell's case against Spain over the West Indies, and in June 1658 he advised Nicholas that Charles II 'should publish some large remonstrance of his case, which might be translated into several languages, and might be fit for all the Christian princes to see, and that I would have done with great candour and clearness'.[141]

Beyond such proposals of ideas for books, or the proposed submission of works, it is also possible to find surviving examples of more detailed plans and proposals. These sometimes survive among official papers, although they are not always possible to distinguish from position papers for policy discussions, or lobbying documents.[142] The same applies to items within the private papers of prominent political figures, such as the parliamentarian grandee, Sir Arthur Hesilrige.[143] It is also to private archives that attention needs to be turned in order to find examples of such proposals from royalist authors, and Hyde's papers contain a note from William Rumbold in January 1659, in which he sent rough heads for a declaration proposed by an unnamed friend.[144] Furthermore, it is also possible to draw attention to evidence of complete manuscripts being sent to political figures during this period, for consideration and possible publication. On a number of occasions, the practice of submitting manuscript tracts can be deduced from surviving examples in official and political archives.[145] The mere presence of such items in the papers of men such as Viscount Saye need say nothing about their provenance, and it is not always possible to contextualise works such as the lengthy treatise entitled 'eldership the greatest lordship', which advocated an Erastian church settlement, and which is extant in the papers of the parliamentarian solicitor general, Oliver St John.[146] The papers of the

---

[139] *NP* ii. 145.

[140] *NP* iii. 24–5, 26–8.

[141] *NP* iii. 140–41; *NP* iv. 53.

[142] *CSPD 1649–50*, pp. 43, 44, 243; *TSP* vii. 647–51.

[143] Leicestershire RO, DG21/286: 'The case stated between Sweden and Denmark in relation to England' (1659).

[144] *CCSP* iv. 137.

[145] J. Black, 'Fresh light on ministerial patronage of eighteenth century pamphlets', *Publishing History* 19 (1986); P. Seaward, 'A restoration publicist: James Howell and the Earl of Clarendon, 1661–6', *HR* 61 (1988), p. 127; PRO, SP 29/52, fos. 262–72.

[146] Bodl. MS Tanner 88*, fos. 115r–v; BL, Add. 25278, fos. 119–59v.

parliamentarian grandee, Sir Arthur Hesilrige, contain an undated tract by Anthony Norwood, aimed at convincing royalists after 1649, and based upon the idea of demonstrating that authority lay with the heads of families rather than the king, and asserting that a council of representatives of these independent heads of families was the most just form of government.[147] For royalists, meanwhile, Sir Edward Hyde's archive contains a treatise by Lionel Gatford regarding the Protestation from the mid-1640s, and a 1647 paper, apparently by Dr Joseph Henshaw, which sought to prove the illegality of taking up arms against the king, as well as a treatise by Sir William Morton entitled 'Jus Monarchiae Anglicanae', and a 1653 attack upon Cromwell entitled 'The Complete Hypocrite'.[148] John Clayton, meanwhile, sent Hyde a tract entitled 'state colours and complections in which are reasons against the proceeding to try the king', which he had earlier 'delivered to [Henry] Ireton about a fortnight before the king's trial', in a vain attempt to dissuade a potential regicide.[149] Furthermore, it is probably fair to suppose that manuscripts contained within official archives had been submitted for approval.[150] The state papers contain, for example, a short manuscript called the 'state of the difference between king and the two houses of Parliament and the directing of conscience from matter of fact and from the doctrine of the Church of England and Scotland', probably from 1641 or 1642.[151] On some occasions, however, such items appear to have gone astray or been intercepted, and the commonwealth state papers contain a seven-page manuscript tract entitled 'reasons and motives against [the States of Holland] acknowledging the present power in England', which had been sent to Sir Edward Nicholas by Sir William Macdowal in January 1651.[152] On rare occasions, readers of printed tracts learned something of the ways in which authors approached grandees with draft works. William Ball, therefore, admitted having presented a manuscript to the parliamentarian commander, Philip Skippon, in May 1644, 'wherein was contained the heads and chief points of that subject', and it is possible that he secured some degree of official approval, upon which he 'promised to give further

---

[147] Leics. RO, DG21/275b, pp. 3–6 (Norwood's 'Modest Proposals for all ingenuous Protestants of the late king's party to a just, peaceable and lasting settlement'). Norwood's other works: *New Errors Made Palpable by an Old Light* (London, 1652) and *A Clear Optick Discovering to the Eye of Reason* (London, 1654).

[148] Bodl. MS Clarendon 25, fos. 46–65v; *CCSP* v. 726; Bodl. MS Clarendon 92, fos. 14–16; Bodl. MS Clarendon 132; Bodl. MS Clarendon 138.

[149] *CCSP* i. 504; Bodl. MS Clarendon 36, fos. 115–20. See also: Northamptonshire RO, FH 61: 'Short animadversions upon the remonstrance of the 19th of May 1642'; Bodl. MS Clarendon 21, fos. 143v–92v: H. W., 'A treatise or argument in law upon the late orders and ordinances made ... without the king's consent' (1643); Bodl. MS Carte 77, fos. 484–90: 'Arguments and considerations upon questions whether or not the king may impose taxes without assent of Parliament'.

[150] Seaward, 'Restoration publicist', p. 127.

[151] *CSPD 1641–3*, p. 348; PRO, SP 16/491, fos. 127–29v. For other manuscript pamphlets see: *CSPD 1641–3*, p. 426, 428; PRO, SP 16/493, fos. 124–6v, 153–65.

[152] *CSPD 1651*, p. 31; PRO, SP 18/15, fos. 6–10v.

satisfaction', and which resulted in the work which was printed as his *Tractatus* in 1645.[153]

On other occasions greater evidence survives with which to contextualise such manuscripts, and to understand the processes by which they were submitted. Some works were mentioned in correspondence, while others survive in full in either official or private archives, although it is rarely possible to assess which were expected by their recipients and which were unforseen and unsolicited.[154] Peter Heylyn appears to have sought to ingratiate himself with William Laud by presenting him with a copy of his provocative sermon against the Feoffees for the Purchase of Impropriations in 1630, and may also have sought to secure its publication.[155] In January 1641, Heylyn alluded to his having enclosed a 'paper friend' in a letter to Endymion Porter.[156] In the following month, John Clayton's letter to John Pym implied the submission of a manuscript:

> Considering these tottering times, both of law and otherwise, I thought it my duty, when I thought of some things, to put them down, if perhaps I might bring any props or stays thereunto. And no man I thought better able to judge ... than yourself, which makes me thus bold to present you with my observations, when your leisure, if any be, will permit you to peruse them, if any are worthy; as for those of the law I know they are, you may put them to some committee of lawyers to consider upon, and I shall wait upon them if required.[157]

In March 1640, the Scottish minister Robert Baillie sent Archibald Johnston of Wariston a nearly complete book along with a recommendation,

> that a treatise of this kind were very needful at this time to be published, both to show to the churches abroad the true state of our controversies, and to waken up the spirits of our own countrymen ... also for the rousing up of our slippery neighbours of England, who readily, if God have not given them over for their own destruction to a spirit of sopor, cannot fail at this time to press more earnestly the king than ever for justice on those our oppressors.

Baillie affirmed that he had undertaken the task 'only at your desire', and informed Johnston that he should 'make use of it [as] you think good'.[158] At the end of May 1642, Baillie mentioned to Robert Blair his having drawn up 'four or five

---

[153] W. Ball, *Tractatus de Jure Regnandi et Regni* (London, 1645), sig. A2.

[154] There was evidently a long tradition of submitting works in the hope of gaining official approval for their publication: *CSPD 1611–18*, p. 22; PRO, SP 14/9, fos. 81–113; SP 16/98, fos. 46–52v; *CSPD 1631–3*, p. 275–6; PRO, SP 16/211, fos. 107–9, 119; *CSPD 1637–8*, p. 330; PRO, SP 16/386, fo. 112; *CSPD 1637–8*, pp. 37–8; PRO, SP 16/374, fo. 85; Elton, *Policy and Police*, p. 172; C. Russell, 'The Anglo-Scottish union, 1603–1643: a success?', in A. Fletcher and P. Roberts, eds, *Religion, Culture and Society in Early Modern Britain* (Cambridge, 1994), p. 248; Foster, 'Function of a bishop', p. 42.

[155] Magdalen College, Oxford, MS 312; G. E. Gorman, 'A Laudian attempt to 'tune the pulpit': Peter Heylyn and his sermon against the Feoffees for the Purchase of Impropriations', *Journal of Religious History* 8 (1975).

[156] *CSPD 1640–1*, p. 440; PRO, SP 16/476, fo. 215.

[157] *CSPD 1640–1*, p. 462; PRO, SP 16/477, fo. 56.

[158] *Letters and Journals of Robert Baillie*, i. 242–3.

sheets' against the Brownists, which he had shown to Alexander Henderson and David Dickson, and which he now referred to Blair for approval.[159] The papers of the royalist agent, John Barwick, contain a short manuscript of eight folios, probably from the summer of 1653, which represented a planned royalist work called 'The bond of love and loyalty'. This was endorsed with the comment that it was 'humbly desired His Majesty would please to pass something of the nature of what is specified within this paper for the just and full satisfaction of all his subjects of each interest in all his dominions'.[160] During the 1640s, there is also evidence that works were submitted to prominent individual politicians for consideration by potential backers and employers. In September 1655, Bulstrode Whitelocke recorded in his diary having received a work by James Howell 'for his judgement of it before its printing'.[161] In the 1650s, the Cromwellian regime appears to have established a system whereby such works were submitted to the secretary of state, John Thurloe, or referred to him by the Council of State, as in January 1653, when he was instructed to inspect a book tendered for publication by one Mr White.[162] For royalists, meanwhile, works were evidently still being submitted to the highest possible powers, and in March 1653 Edward Massey wrote to Charles II in order to lobby on behalf of a work which had been presented to him for consideration, and which sought to vindicate the king from the charge of popery.[163]

Occasionally, it is possible to demonstrate that certain authors offered not merely individual works to potential or actual patrons, but also their polemical skills and services as pamphleteers. In 1621, therefore, John Pory sought a patent to be overseer of newsbooks, with leave to print gazettes of his own, and he submitted a proposal with the aim of devising 'means to raise the spirits of the people and to guide their conceits and understandings', and 'to establish a ready and easy way whereby to disperse into all the veins of the whole body of the state such matter as may be ... most agreeable to the disposition of the head and the principal members', and to ensure obedience on the part of the 'vulgar', 'by spreading amongst them such reports'.[164] The desire to secure employment as polemicists and propagandists, furthermore, may have underlain the way in which certain authors employed their pens to advertise their services and skills. Certain men used writing and publication as a means of advertising their talents and

---

[159] *Letters and Journals of Robert Baillie*, ii. 27.

[160] Gloucestershire RO, D678, Barwick MSS, no. 29; *Calendar of Sherborne Muniments* (1900), p. 143.

[161] R. Spalding, ed., *The Diary of Bulstrode Whitelocke 1605–1675* (Oxford, 1990), p. 413; Woolf, 'Conscience, consistency and ambition', p. 273. This work was: Howell, *Som Sober Inspections*.

[162] *CSPD 1652–3*, p. 103.

[163] *CCSP* ii. 187; Bodl. MS Clarendon 45, fos. 187r–v.

[164] PRO, SP 14/124, fos. 230r–v. See A. Mousley, 'Self, state and seventeenth century news', *Seventeenth Century* 6 (1991), pp. 159–60; F. Levy, 'The decorum of news', in J. Raymond, ed., *News, Newspapers and Society in Early Modern Britain* (London, 1999), p. 28.

ingratiating themselves with those in a position to act as patrons. Peter Heylyn contrived, with Laud's assistance, to present copies of his book on the history of St George to the king, and also presented 'several copies of it fairly bound to all such knights of the order and men of eminence as were about the town'. Heylyn later recalled that his work 'was used by all of them with great respect, save only by Archbishop Abbot and the Earl of Exeter, the first of which disliked the argument, and the other snapped me up for a begging scholar'.[165] During the 1640s, Andrewes Burrell used his book, already in print, to secure the attention of the Commons, who appointed a committee to consider his proposals for the good of the navy.[166] While Heylyn may have sought to become a favoured author, Burrell probably sought to become a specialist adviser, or to secure administrative employment. For prisoners, meanwhile, writing and publishing was a useful means, and perhaps the only avenue available, to draw attention to themselves, and for the royalist, James Howell, writing was probably perceived to be a means of securing release from prison. In 1648, therefore, he wrote *Bella Scot Anglica*, an attack upon Hamiltonian Scots during the second civil war, and he subsequently offered his services as a writer to the commonwealth. Released from prison in 1650, he wrote *SPQV* in 1651, and published *Finetti Philoxenis* in 1656 in order to encourage Cromwell to take the crown.[167]

In certain cases, the use of print to seek administrative employment may have meant that authors considered such posts to be a means of working as writers. Thomas May had a particular post in mind when he drew attention to himself through the print medium, petitioning in early 1645 for the office of remembrancer of the first fruits, having reminded the world of his literary talents, and parliamentarian credentials, in *The Character of a Right Malignant*.[168] The royalist author of *Mercurius Elencticus* alleged that John Hall used his newspaper, *Mercurius Britanicus*, as a means of offering his services as a hack to Parliament. He claimed, with regard to one of the early issues of the paper, that 'there was but 200 in all printed for his own use, which he run a begging with amongst the members to let them see what a brave fellow he was, and what faithful services he could do them, if they would but condescend to a weekly allowance for him'.[169] The case of Michael Hawke indicates that some such men saw themselves as writers. In January 1656, Hawke, a Middle Temple lawyer,

---

[165] P. Heylyn, *Memorial of Bishop Waynflete* (ed. J. R. Bloxam, London, 1851), pp. x, xx; Vernon, *Peter Heylyn*, pp. 37–8.

[166] *CJ* v. 47; A. Burrell, *The Humble Remonstrance of Andrewes Burrell … for a Reformation of England's Navie* (London, 1646); G. Aylmer, *The State's Servants* (London, 1973), p. 292.

[167] Woolf, 'Conscience, consistency and ambition', pp. 257, 268, 273; *CSPD 1649–50*, p. 178; J. Howell, *Bella Scot Anglica* (London, 1648); J. Howell, *SPQV. A Survay of the Signorie of Venice* (London, 1651), sig. B; *Finetti Philoxenis* (London, 1656).

[168] T. May, *The Character of a Right Malignant* (London, 1645); *LJ* vii. 401; *CJ* iv. 158. May was appointed to join John Sadler and Henry Parker as special secretary to Parliament: *CJ* iv. 200.

[169] *Mercurius Elencticus* 29 (7–14 June 1648), sig. Ff2v.

published *The Right of Dominion and Property of Liberty*, which advocated a monarchical constitution, and which suggested 'the necessity of his highness' acceptation of the empire' by the 'law of arms'. Cromwell was described as 'our prince, a Caesar for valour, Augustus for fortune, and for prowess and prudence second to neither'.[170] After publication, Hawke issued a petition, in May 1656, seeking an unspecified position, or nomination as sheriff of a county, and drew attention not only to his loyalty, but also to his writings, and the effectiveness of the latter in convincing royalists to support the protectorate.[171] Although it is not known what such efforts achieved, Hawke's subsequent book, an attack upon *Killing Noe Murder*, intimated that 'some great personages' were at least aware of his efforts.[172] Indeed, it seems clear that Andrew Marvell considered the post of Latin Secretary in this way, and that he sought this position in order to become 'verse-propagandist'. It is clear also that this was why he supported his application with his account of the 'character of Holland'.[173] John Dury, meanwhile, sought to enlist the support of his friend Francis Rous in order to secure a fellowship at Eton, a post which would have enabled him to engage in literary work. Dury admitted that he 'did represent to the Parliament his condition, and the ways wherein he could be serviceable to the public'. Having already claimed that he had suffered a financial loss of £200 per annum upon leaving Rotterdam to join the Westminster Assembly, Dury was effectively putting a price on his services as an author.[174]

However, perhaps the most stark examples are provided by individuals who sought employment as writers without the 'cover' of a sinecure. The papers of John Jones, for example, reveal how he offered his services to the likes of John Pym in 1641, and how he was effectively interviewed by Pym and the Earls of Essex and Northumberland in August 1642. Jones was no more successful in securing employment from these leading parliamentarians than he had been in attracting the attention of the king, to whom he wrote in April 1642, offering to inform him of 'the art of government and the great mystery in the right governing of a Christian commonwealth', as well as how to secure a reconcilement with Parliament.[175] Nevertheless, the willingness of leading parliamentarian grandees to meet Jones proves revealing about their attitude to the possibility of securing the services of such men. A more serious candidate for employment, however, was the journalist Marchamont Nedham, who offered to serve the commonwealth in 1649, partly in order to secure release from prison. As an established polemicist,

---

[170] M. Hawke, *The Right of Dominion* (London, 1655), pp. 41, 86.

[171] *CSPD 1655–6*, p. 388; PRO, SP 18/127, fo. 96; *TSP* iv. 445.

[172] M. Hawke, *Killing is Murder* (London, 1657), sig. A3. See: *CCSP* iii. 397–8.

[173] H. Kelliher, *Andrew Marvell, Poet and Politician, 1621–78* (London, 1978), pp. 55–8.

[174] BL, Add. 24863, fo. 80.

[175] BL, Add. 33374, fos. 2–5, 15–20; J. S. A. Adamson, 'Parliamentary management, men of business, and the House of Lords, 1640–49', in C. Jones, ed., *A Pillar of the Constitution* (London, 1989); p. 30.

Nedham did not need to make explicit the type of work intended.[176] Later in the year, following a brief escape from prison, Nedham petitioned the lord president of the Council of State, John Bradshaw, and wrote to Thomas Scot to say: 'my ruin can no way advantage the commonwealth, but my preservation may, wherein if you will be so noble as to assist me, I dare be valiant and active, or remain innocent and silent, in prosecuting my own particular, under your protection'.[177] Later, in May 1659, John Canne wrote a tract entitled *A Seasonable Word to the Parliament Men*, in what appears to have been an attempt to remind the restored Rump of his literary and polemical talents, with a view to being hired as a writer.[178]

While it is important to recognise that authors could operate independently of patrons and political grandees, and that they could be motivated by anything from money to a public-spirited desire for the expression of truth and the representation of a cause, or a combination thereof, it is also necessary to consider evidence of alternative methodologies and motivations. Royalists and parliamentarians can be demonstrated, therefore, to have been eager to use their pens in order to establish and affirm connections with patrons and politicians, and to use the medium of print in order to commemorate their friendships and ties to patronage networks; to demonstrate the nature of their social and professional circles; and to express thanks to their 'patrons'. In doing so, however, it was also possible to offer readers an insight into the nature of specific relationships, and the nature of the ties which existed between authors and their associates, and the services which members of patronage networks could perform for each other. Dedications were used to establish and demonstrate connections which were based upon shared political and religious outlooks, and a shared interest in literary activity. Furthermore, they affirm that such relationships could be based upon the patronage of authors *as* authors, and that authors sometimes appeared in print as a result of the importunity or encouragement of others, whether family and friends, or patrons and political associates. Moreover, they were also willing to connect themselves with politicians out of the public eye, and to offer their services to political causes by proposing and submitting works to individual grandees and political regimes, and by offering their services as writers of polemical literature. In a time of civil war, however, such offers by authors, and the composition of books as a result of the encouragement of friends, colleagues and political grandees, may not have been considered a sufficiently reliable method of securing the production of polemical literature. In the spring of 1648, Sir Edward Nicholas certainly complained that royalist pen-men were not sufficiently forthcoming in the cause, and he told Sir Richard Browne that 'it's a shame that (there being so many good pens of the kings party) none do use more

---

[176] PRO, SP 46/95, fo. 151.
[177] PRO, SP 46/95, fo. 190.
[178] J. Canne, *A Seasonable Word to the Parliament Men* (London, 1659).

diligence to vindicate his honour'.[179] Nicholas's frustration suggests that at least some political leaders recognised the need to be more proactive in securing the publication of books, tracts and pamphlets. Demonstrating the mechanisms which they developed in order to achieve this, and the individuals to whom they turned, forms the next section of this book. The chapters which follow will display how such men were used to produce works which were more or less 'official' in nature and appearance, as well as to create works which betrayed little evidence of the involvement of either royalist or parliamentarian hierarchies. They contain a more detailed exploration of the methods of identifying propaganda, and they assess both the ways in which it was produced, and the uses to which it was put.

---

[179] BL, Evelyn Papers, RB2, vol. 5, unfol.: Sir Edward Nicholas to Sir Richard Browne, 20/30 Mar. 1648.

PART TWO
THE MECHANICS OF PROPAGANDA

CHAPTER 3

Decoding Pamphlets

In a bitter attack upon parliamentarian policies, personalities and practices, Bishop Griffith Williams not only recognised the importance placed upon propaganda, but also claimed to have identified those responsible. Naming the likes of William Prynne, Cornelius Burges and Stephen Marshall, Williams also professed to understand that parliamentarian polemic relied upon 'trencher chaplains and parasitical preachers', as well as upon 'some busy lawyers, and pettyfoggers'.[1] Williams was not alone in recognising the career trajectories of political and religious pamphleteers. In seeking to understand the nature of parliamentarian propaganda in the 1640s, a number of royalist authors pieced together evidence with which to contextualise particular authors. They certainly seem to have had the measure, for example, of Henry Parker. Contemporary commentators, as well as individual readers, recognised Parker's role in a number of anonymous tracts, and they also appear to have been familiar with his personal history. Sir Edward Nicholas recognised him to be an intimate friend of Viscount Saye, and to have been involved in the latter's political schemes, while the author of *Sober Sadnes* not only pieced together portions of Parker's *oeuvre*, but also recognised that he was one of Parliament's 'great clerks'. Another author provided readers with a detailed account of Parker's role as secretary to the Committee of Safety, and his tribulations therein.[2] Such analysis ought to be standard practice for scholarly treatment of civil war literature.

The aim of the preceding chapters was to assess why politicians were motivated to engage with the public, and why they felt the need to turn to the services of authors, as well as to demonstrate the willingness on the part of authors to identify themselves with political grandees and their causes, and even to offer their services as polemicists. The purpose of this section is to move beyond theory into practice, and to develop a methodology with which to establish which polemical works of a non-official nature were produced with at least some degree of official involvement, and which can, as a result, be considered as propaganda, even in the

---

[1] Williams named William Prynne, John Goodwin, Cornelius Burges, Stephen Marshall and Obadiah Sedgwick and other 'emissaries of wickedness': G. Williams, *The Discovery of Mysteries* ([Oxford], 1643), pp. 69, 77.

[2] *CSPD 1645–7*, p. 99; *Sober Sadnes* (London, 1643), pp. 22, 38–9, 42; *A Discourse Discovering Some Mysteries of Our New State* (Oxford, 1645), p. 28. See also: C. Walker, *Anarchia Anglicana* (London, 1649), p. 199; *Mercurius Elencticus* 13 (16–23 Feb. 1648), p. 93; J. Lilburne, *Innoncency and Truth* ([London], 1645), p. 57.

absence of direct admission or evidence that a work's composition and publication was inspired by political grandees. The foundation of this process of 'decoding' individual works involves four different approaches: biographical, contextual, visual and consequential. The first involves examining authors' patronage networks, and requires establishing individuals' personal circumstances and career trajectories, in terms of their backgrounds, the public figures whom they knew, and with whom they worked, and their activity at the time of writing and publishing. The second approach involves building upon such analysis in order to contextualise individual works by well-connected writers, and in order to examine the timing of their appearance, the congruity between their message and that of plausible or potential patrons, and potential reasons for books' appearance. Particularly valuable in this regard is information recorded by George Thomason, pertaining to the precise timing of works' appearance. The third approach explores the possibility of deducing official involvement from visual evidence relating to the identity of printers and publishers, while the fourth explores the response which individual writers, and their works, elicited from those in authority.[3] Ultimately, of course, such methods are neither precise nor scientific, and at times it will only be possible to offer circumstantial associations and suggestive conclusions regarding the background to individual tracts and pamphlets. Nevertheless, the cumulative impact will prove valuable for particular authors and specific works, and as a result it will be possible to progress beyond the educated guesswork with which some scholars have characterised the process of understanding early modern propaganda.[4]

The most basic way of decoding polemical literature is by contextualising authors in terms of their background and contacts. Such prosopography, and the location of individuals within patronage networks, has been undertaken for Stuart administration, but rarely for seventeenth-century authors.[5] The most obvious, though least persuasive way of connecting works of political literature with political grandees is by tracing connections between authors and patrons, politicians and grandees, whether through kinship and friendship, or education and employment, and to explore how individuals secured patronage and preferment, and the contacts that they made.[6] Thoughts of propaganda almost certainly played no part in most acts of patronage which benefited the men who became writers during the civil wars and Interregnum, and it is unlikely that theoreticians, clerics

---

[3] J. Loach, 'The Marian establishment and the printing press', *EHR* 101 (1986).

[4] V. Sanders, 'John Whitgift: primate, privy councillor and propagandist', *Anglican and Episcopal History* 56 (1987), p. 395.

[5] But see: H. Trevor-Roper, 'The Fast sermons of the Long Parliament', in *Religion, the Reformation and Social Change* (London, 1972); J. F. Wilson, *Pulpit in Parliament* (Princeton, 1979). See also: J. E. Phillips, 'George Buchanan and the Sidney circle', *HLQ* 12 (1948).

[6] P. Croft, 'The reputation of Robert Cecil: libels, political opinion and popular awareness in the early seventeenth century', *TRHS*, 6th series 1 (1991), pp. 64, 66–7.

and journalists were nurtured as propagandists. Rather than 'patrons' and 'clients' being brought together by the need for the production of political tracts and pamphlets, contacts were made, allegiances forged and debts incurred in the decades prior to 1640s; future writers became part of patronage networks, and became known to political figures whose interests they later represented in print.[7] As a result, demonstrating historical connections between authors and political grandees offers a valuable means of illustrating possible reasons for writing, and plausible motivations for publishing and printing political works.[8] Moreover, particular attention must be paid to the activity of writers at the time of the appearance of specific tracts, and to pamphleteers who were employed by political figures and institutions at the time that they engaged in composition or publication.

The most obvious place to look is a writer's family network and circle of friends. Merit was only one of a number of factors underlying a successful career, and the most useful adjunct to talent was genetics, and the possession of a propitious pedigree. Civil war writers such as Sir John Spelman and Thomas May can be shown, therefore, to have emerged from prominent public families.[9] Furthermore, in an age where marriages could reflect personal, political and dynastic strategies, it is important to draw attention to marital connections, particularly those of men such as Cuthbert Sydenham and Philip Nye, which reflected shared religious and political outlooks.[10] This means following the example of contemporaries by recognising extended, rather than merely immediate family networks, as well as the importance of godparents in understanding the careers of authors such as Henry Parker and William Chillingworth.[11] However, there was more to patronage networks than blood and marriage, and it is possible to show that authors such as John Owen, Peter Heylyn and Marchamont Nedham became integrated into local gentry communities.[12]

---

[7] This is akin to clients emerging as tools of parliamentary management: M. A. R. Graves, 'The common lawyers and the Privy Council's parliamentary men of business, 1584–1601', *PH* 8 (1989); J. S. A. Adamson, 'Parliamentary management, men of business and the House of Lords, 1640–49', in C. Jones, ed., *A Pillar of the Constitution* (London, 1989); M. A. R. Graves, 'Thomas Norton the parliament man: an Elizabethan MP, 1559–1581', *HJ* 23 (1980); M. A. R. Graves, 'The management of the Elizabethan House of Commons: the Council's 'men of business'', *PH* 2 (1983); M. A. R. Graves, 'Patrons and clients: their role in sixteenth century parliamentary politicking and legislation', *The Turnbull Library Record* 18 (1985).

[8] L. F. Parmelee, 'Printers, patrons, readers and spies: importation of French propaganda in late Elizabethan England', *Sixteenth Century Journal* 25 (1994).

[9] *DNB*; A. G. Chester, *Thomas May, Man of Letters, 1595–1650* (Philadelphia, 1932), pp. 11–29; East Sussex RO, SAS/M/691; East Sussex RO, AMS 1503; BL, Add. 39477, fos. 92–3; PRO, WARD 9/162, fo. 275v.

[10] *DNB*; PRO, PROB 11/245, fo. 376v; F. Peck, *Desiderata Curiosa* (2 vols, London, 1732), ii. 496. For Nye, see: *The Winthrop Papers III* (Massachusetts Historical Society Collections, 5th series 1, 1871), p. 210; D. Nobbs, 'Philip Nye on church and state', *Cambridge Historical Journal* 5 (1935).

[11] *CSPD 1645–7*, p. 99; P. des Maizeaux, *The Life of William Chillingworth* (London, 1683), p. 1.

[12] P. Toon, ed. *The Correspondence of John Owen (1616–1683)* (London, 1970), p. 8; P. Heylyn, *Memorials of Bishop Waynflete* (ed. J. R. Bloxam, London, 1851), p. xii; R. H. Gretton, *The Burford*

Some writers, such as John Wilkins and Joshua Sprigge, had grown up in the households of prominent political and religious figures, while others, such as Henry Killigrew and Francis Quarles, had grown up at court.[13] Looking beyond family and locality, it is possible to explore the circles of friends of which authors such as Thomas Morton, Jeremy Taylor, James Howell and Edward Bowles formed a part, and from which they could benefit.[14] Most important are those networks of friends and associates who shared interests and outlooks, as well as a concern with literary, political and religious endeavours. These include the group of academics, clerics, and scientists – as well as pamphleteers – who surrounded the politically well-connected reformer Samuel Hartlib, including John Sadler, John Hall, John Dury, Peter Sterry, Walter Frost, Benjamin Worsley, Hezekiah Woodward, Henry Robinson and William Potter.[15] They also include informal networks of Puritan activists on the radical Protestant fringe, such as the men around Henry Burton, John Bastwick and William Prynne, who were deeply involved in the advancement and propagation of particular religious visions, and explicitly concerned with spreading their message through the medium of print and through 'conspiratorial' publications. This circle included John Lilburne, Samuel Richardson, Edmund Chillenden and John Vicars.[16] Many civil war writers can also be located within prominent literary circles centred around public figures, whether in terms of close-knit groups such as that which met at Great Tew in Oxfordshire, from which emerged royalist authors such as Dudley Digges, or in terms of looser groups of literary acquaintances such as Digges, Thomas May, James Howell, John Hall, Marchamont Nedham, Sir John Berkenhead and Andrew Marvell.[17] That such networks are not mere scholarly reconstructions is

---

Records (Oxford, 1920), pp. 62, 129, 352; Oxfordshire RO, Burford parish register; Wood, *Athenae*, iii. 1180–90. For the importance of understanding Heylyn's background, see: A. Milton, 'The creation of Laudianism: a new approach', in T. Cogswell, R. Cust and P. Lake, eds, *Politics, Religion and Popularity in Early Stuart Britain* (Cambridge, 2002), p. 167.

[13] For Wilkins, Killigrew and Quarles: *DNB*. For Sprigge, whose father was a longstanding estate steward to the Fiennes family: Oxfordshire RO, Dash v/ii/13, Hyde I/iii/2, Hyde I/iv/1–2, Hyde I/xvi/1, Hyde II/v/1, Hyde II/vi/1, Saye I/i/2; Wil/ii/27; PRO, C 54/2814/15, C 54/2817/9, C 54/2818/19, C 54/2894/34, C 54/2977/4, C 54/3070/5, C 54/3035/7, C 54/3292/27-8, PRO, SP 28/10, fo. 197, SP 28/252i, fos. 67v, 337, SP 28/252ii, fo. 54v.

[14] *DNB*; D. Woolf, 'Conscience, consistency and ambition in the career and writings of James Howell', in J. Morrill, P. Slack and D. Woolf, eds, *Public Duty and Private Conscience in Seventeenth Century England* (Oxford, 1993); 'The Life of Master John Shaw', in *Yorkshire Diaries and Autobiographies* (Surtees Society, 65, 1875), pp. 157, 413–14, 439–40.

[15] *LJ* ix. 119–20; BL, Add. 32471, fos. 13v, 22; Hartlib Papers, 50H/39/4/2A–B, 50H/30/4/70A, 50H/23/12/1A–8B, 50H/23/11/4A, 50H/23/10A–B, 50H/46/9/22A–B, 36A, 50H/7/31/1A–2B, 50H/4/1/24A–B, 50H/10/11/1A–8B, 50H/3/3/13A–B, 50H/47/9/34A–35B, 50H/63/7/1A–B, 10A–13B; BL, Add. 44846, fo. 55; Hull RO, Hull Corporation Letterbook, L633–4: two letters from Robinson to Hull corporation, 1658.

[16] F. Condick, 'The Life and Works of Dr John Bastwick' (London University PhD, 1982), p. 92; S. Foster, *Notes from the Caroline Underground* (Hamden, Ct., 1978).

[17] K. Weber, *Lucius Cary, Second Viscount Falkland* (New York, 1940), chaps. 4–5; H. Trevor-Roper, 'The Great Tew circle', in *Catholics, Anglicans and Puritans* (London, 1989); *Ionsonus Virbius,*

evident from the tendency for contemporary authors to draw attention to close personal relationships between writers and grandees. Royalists highlighted the links between the parliamentarian journalist, John Dillingham, and leading political figures such as Viscount Saye, Lord Wharton and Oliver Cromwell, to whose meetings he reportedly played host.[18] Later, on the eve of the Restoration, observers drew attention to the similarly close relationship between the journalist and polemicist, Marchamont Nedham, and republican grandees such as Sir Henry Mildmay and Thomas Scot.[19]

Patronage networks commonly proved beneficial to those writers with whom this study is concerned through the assistance which they could offer in securing admission to schools and universities, and to inns of court and chancery. The entry requirements of such institutions generated a complex, interlocking and reciprocal system of patronage exchange, which can be shown to have worked to the advantage of at least two prominent pamphleteers of the 1640s: Henry Parker and John Sadler.[20] The education of men as different as Robert Mossom, John Saltmarsh and Henry Stubbe was sponsored by specific individuals, and once at university young men such as Saltmarsh could clearly be introduced to the world of letters.[21] Moreover, students such as John Collings, William Jenkyn and John Wilkins, as well as Selden and Hobbes, forged strong bonds with their tutors, who may have been able to secure employment for their charges.[22] That student–tutor

---

or, the memorie of Ben: Johnson (London, 1638), pp. 1–10, 21–4, 32; R. Brome, ed., *Lachrymae Musarum* (London, 1650), pp. 43–8, 81–5; J. Hall, *Catch that Catch Can* (London, 1652); R. Brome, *Joviall Crew* (London, 1652), sig. A3; J. Shirley, *The Cardinall* (London, 1652); R. Lovelace, *Lucasta* (London, 1649); J. Hall, *Hierocles upon the Golden Verses* (London, 1657), sigg. A4r–v; P. W. Thomas, *Sir John Berkenhead, 1617–1679* (Oxford, 1969), pp. 140–44; J. M. Osborn, 'Thomas Stanley's lost "register of friends"' *Yale University Library Gazette* 32 (1958), pp. 133–5; T. Stanley, *Poems* (London, 1651), p. 76; T. Stanley (trans.), *Aurora Ismenia* (London, 1650).

[18] *Mercurius Pragmaticus* 17 (18–25 July 1648), sig. R4v; *Mercurius Pragmaticus* 18 (25 July–1 Aug. 1648), sig. S2v; *Royall Diurnall* 1 (25–31 July 1648), sig. A2v. Army accounts clearly reveal that Dillingham was receiving money for Cromwell in this period: PRO, SP 28/56, fo. 430r–v. More than one contemporary drew attention to a connection between Cromwell and Dillingham, and to the fact that Cromwell had a chamber at Dillingham's house: J. Lilburne, *Jonah's Cry* ([London, 1647]), p. 9; *Mercurius Bellicus* 19 (30 May–6 June 1648), p. 7; J. S. A. Adamson, 'Oliver Cromwell and the Long Parliament', in J. Morrill, ed., *Oliver Cromwell and the English Revolution* (London, 1990), p. 57.

[19] Staffordshire RO, D868/3/30.

[20] J. Peacey, 'Led by the hand: manucaptors and patronage at Lincoln's Inn in the seventeenth century', *Journal of Legal History* 18 (1997), pp. 36–40; M. Dever, 'Richard Sibbes' (Cambridge University PhD, 1993), pp. 57–61; M. Burrows, ed., *The Register of the Visitors of the University of Oxford* (Camden Society, new series, 29, 1881), pp. 239, 242, 477, 531–5; G. D. Squibb, *Founders' Kin* (Oxford, 1972).

[21] R. Mossom, *The Preachers Tripartite* (London, 1657), Book II, sig. A2; *DNB*; Peacey, 'Henry Parker', p. 12; J. R. Jacob, *Henry Stubbe* (Cambridge, 1983), p. 18; N. Malcolm, ed., *The Correspondence of Thomas Hobbes* (2 vols, Oxford, 1994), ii. 899–902; J. Russell, *The Two Famous Pitch Battels of Lypsich and Lutzen* (Cambridge 1634), epistle and pp. 78–9; G. Du Gre, *Breveet Accuratum Grammaticiae* (Cambridge, 1636), preface.

[22] *DNB*; B. J. Shapiro, *John Wilkins, 1614–1672* (Berkeley, Ca.,1969), pp. 14–17; A. P. Martinich, *Hobbes, A Biography* (Cambridge, 1999), pp. 1–18; D. S. Berkowitz, *John Selden's Formative Years* (Washington, 1988), pp. 14–15.

relations impacted upon literary activity is evident from John Milton's involvement in the 'Smectymnuus' debate alongside his former tutor, Thomas Young.[23] Furthermore, civil war authors such as John Sadler and John Vicars had themselves been teachers and college fellows, wherein they may have established contacts with important gentry and aristocratic families.[24] For a great many pamphleteers, therefore, educational establishments, and particularly college fellowships, provided career stepping stones, from which bright scholars could be plucked in order to secure professional employment. In this context, it is important to recognise that certain institutions developed associations with particular religious persuasions. This meant that choices of educational establishment could be conditioned not merely by regional trends, family traditions, and the presence of friends and patrons, but also by 'ideological' factors, and it also meant that prominent patrons probably made certain colleges their first port of call when seeking new chaplains and household staff. Thus, while Emmanuel College, Cambridge, was considered a bastion of the godly, study at Christ Church, Oxford, appears to have provided a fast-track to preferment and promotion in the early Stuart court and church, for the likes of Edward Boughen and Griffith Williams.[25]

Turning from education to employment, therefore, authors can be contextualised within a variety of career patronage networks. The most obvious is the world of commerce, whether as part of monopolistic ventures, or mercantile companies.[26] The latter, of course, permitted involvement in civic government, and some bodies, such as the Stationers, were obviously involved in the world of print. Thus, individuals such as John Bellamy became prominent in both civil war literature and local government.[27] The same can also be said of the colonial companies, with which civil war writers such as John White, Nathaniel Ward and Hugh Peter had been connected, since such bodies tended to be concerned with proselytising literature, whether of a commercial or religious nature.[28] More

---

[23] *The Works of John Milton* (19 vols, New York, 1931–3), xii. 4–7, 12–15; J. Milton, *Animadversions upon the Remonstrants Defence Against Smectymnuus* (London, 1641).

[24] J. Crossley, ed., *The Diary and Correspondence of Dr John Worthington* (2 vols, Chetham Society, 1847), i. 7, 12–14; BL, Add. 5851, fo. 5; BL, Add. 33145, fos. 129v, 135v, 139v; PRO, SP 16/414, fo. 26; GL, MS 12806/3, fos. 132, 193v, and pp. 251, 491–4, 507, 526; GL, MS 12806/4, pp. 25, 54–5, 250, 392–4; PRO, SP 16/141/34; *CSPD 1631–3*, p. 20; *CSPD 1639–40*, p. 267; *CSPD 1640*, pp. 401, 405, 416, 421, 425, 430; *CSPD 1640–1*, p. 384.

[25] Peacey, 'Henry Parker', p. 20; *DNB*.

[26] For example, Thomas Violet: BL, Add. 5755, fos. 76–7, 90–91; *CSPD 1635–6*, p. 169; *CSPD 1636–7*, pp. 267, 402; *CSPD 1637*, p. 312; *CSPD 1637–8*, p. 153; PRO, C 66/2824/11.

[27] L. Rostenberg, 'The new world: John Bellamy, 'pilgrim' publisher of London', in *Literary, Scientific, Religious and Legal Publishing, Printing and Bookselling in England 1551–1700* (2 vols, New York, 1965), i. 97–129; M. Mahoney, 'Presbyterianism in the City of London, 1645–1647', *HJ* 22 (1979).

[28] Peacey, 'Henry Parker', p. 20; F. S. Allis, 'Nathaniel Ward: constitutional draftsman', *Essex Institute Historical Collections* 120 (1984), pp. 243–5; R. P. Stearns, *The Strenuous Puritan. Hugh Peter, 1598–1660* (Urbana, 1954), pp. 30–1, 39–40, 44, 88, 93–6, 106, 124, 153, 157, 159–61; R. P. Stearns, 'The Weld-Peter mission to England', *Publications of the Colonial Society of Massachusetts*

commonly, however, authors can be contextualised in terms of aristocratic or gentry households, and some can be shown to have been attached to the retinues and 'interests' of political grandees while being engaged in writing polemical literature.[29] Many had served as domestic chaplains, such as John Doughtie, Thomas Morton and John Wilkins.[30] Others had been nominated to clerical livings, such as Henry Hammond, John Tombes, William Dell and Samuel Torshell.[31] Parish studies demonstrate the extent to which prominent pulpits brought ministers such as John Goodwin of Coleman Street into an elite social and political world.[32] Furthermore, Goodwin was not alone among ministers and chaplains in supplementing preaching with writing. Other examples include John Sadler, who assisted the literary projects of Lord Brooke, to whom he was chaplain in the early 1640s.[33] Indeed, Sadler retained this position long after Brooke's death, and was living at Brooke House in Holborn as late as August 1645, shortly after he published *The Ancient Bounds*, and shortly before the publication of his reply to John Bastwick in *Flagellum Flagelli*.[34] The royalist cleric, Richard Watson, meanwhile, penned his 'second faire warning' (1651), against the Scottish Presbyterian, Robert Baillie, from a position as chaplain to the royalist grandee, Lord Hopton.[35] The careers of a number of other writers involved employment as household tutors, including Thomas Gataker, Charles Herle and Peter du Moulin, not to mention Thomas Hobbes.[36] Others served as stewards, secretaries and 'men of business', including Francis Quarles and Abraham Cowley, Samuel Sheppard

---

32 (1937). For their interest in prose see: S. M. Kingsbury, ed., *The Records of the Virginia Company* (4 vols, Washington, 1906–35), i. 286, 369, 444, 451–2; *A Declaration of the State of the Colonie and Affaires in Virginia* (London, 1620); J. Peacey, 'Seasonable treatises: a godly project of the 1630s', *EHR* 113 (1998); A. P. Newton, *The Colonising Activities of the English Puritans* (New Haven, 1944), pp. 22–3.

29 J. N. King, *English Reformation Literature* (Princeton, 1982), chap. 2.

30 B. Donagan, 'The clerical patronage of Robert Rich, second Earl of Warwick, 1619–1642', *Proceedings of the American Philosophical Society* 120 (1976); *DNB*; Shapiro, *John Wilkins*, p. 17.

31 *DNB*; E. C. Walker, *William Dell. Master Puritan* (Cambridge, 1970), pp. 22–3; R. C. Richardson, *Puritanism in North West England* (Manchester, 1972), pp. 33, 129–30.

32 D. A. Kirby, 'The parish of St Stephen's, Coleman Street' (Oxford University BLitt, 1968).

33 Hartlib Papers, 50H/46/9/27: Sadler to Hartlib, 11 Sept. 1640; J. Sadler, *Masquarade du Ciel* (London, 1640, by the 'chaplain to the Lord Brooke': BL, E238/3); R. Greville, Lord Brooke, *The Nature of Truth* (London, 1641), sig. A4; J. Wallis, *Truth Tried* (London, 1643), p. 7. See: J. Merritt, 'The pastoral tightrope: a Puritan pedagogue in Jacobean London', in Cogswell, Cust and Lake, eds, *Politics, Religion and Popularity*.

34 PRO, SP 28/252i, fo. 137v; J. S., *The Ancient Bounds* (London, 1645); J. Sadler, *Flagellum Flagelli* (London, 1645). For the authorship of these works, see: B. Kiefer, 'The authorship of *Ancient Bounds*', *Church History* 22 (1953); *SR* i. 167, 188.

35 *CCSP* ii. 90.

36 *DNB*; B. Coward, *The Stanleys, Lords Stanley and Earls of Derby 1385–1672* (Chetham Society, 1989), p. 168; Richardson, *Puritanism in North West England*, pp. 68, 119, 151; Chatsworth, Lismore MS 29, unfol.; P. du Moulin, *Of Peace and Contentment of Minde* (London, 1657), sigs. A3, A3v; Martinich, *Hobbes*, pp. 19–120. I am grateful to Dr Patrick Little for providing references from the Chatsworth material. See also: David R. Carlson, 'Royal tutors in the reign of Henry VII', *Sixteenth Century Journal* 22 (1991).

and John Brinsley.[37] Writers such as John Cook, meanwhile, had become close to legal clients among the political elite, and pamphleteers and journalists such as Henry Robinson and Samuel Kem, Thomas Audley and John Dillingham, had been employed as newswriters and intelligencers for aristocratic grandees.[38]

Aside from newswriters, household employees had not necessarily been hired as writers. Nevertheless, it is possible that such positions were considered ideal by those who harboured literary ambitions.[39] Furthermore, it would be a mistake to adopt an overly functionalist analysis of their roles, and it is necessary to consider the possibility that at least some household positions were conceived in broad, rather than narrow terms. Indeed, there was a tendency for the activity of such employees to extend beyond the strict terms of their employment, and men such as Thomas Hobbes and Peter Sterry entered into the wider social world of the political elite; serving as conduits, facilitators, and points of contact, and becoming involved in matters unconnected to their formal duties.[40] Indeed, the households of certain prominent political and clerical figures tended to be semi-public in nature, and were staffed with men known to be useful for political purposes.[41] Moreover,

---

[37] *DNB*; *NP* i. 219; *Three Great Victories Obtained by the Parliament Forces* (London, 1644), which was 'printed by a true copy of the early of Manchester's secretary's letter'. See: P. Hammer, 'The uses of scholarship: the secretariat of Robert Devereux, 2nd Earl of Essex, c.1585–1601', *EHR* 109 (1994); P. Hammer, 'The Earl of Essex, Fulke Greville and the employment of scholars', *Studies in Philology* 91 (1994); Graves, 'Common lawyers'; Graves, 'Management'; Graves, 'Thomas Norton'; Graves, 'Patrons and clients'.

[38] *LJ* x. 324–5; J. S. A. Adamson, 'The peerage in politics, 1645–49' (Cambridge University PhD, 1986), p. 200; For Robinson: Warwickshire RO, CR2017/C100/1–4; PRO, SP 16/485, fo. 152. For Kem: Warwicks. RO, CR2017/C10/95, 104, 105, 129–32, CR2017/C8, fos. 26–7. For Audley: *CSPD 1640*, p. 27. For Dillingham: E. S. Cope, *The Life of a Public Man. Edward, First Baron Montagu* (Philadelphia, 1981), pp. 157–8, 168–9, 184–5, 197; *CSPD 1637–8*, p. 591; *HMC Montagu*, pp. 118–67; *HMC Buccleuch I*, pp. 280–89; *HMC Buccleuch III*, p. 382; Warwicks. RO, CR 1886, vol. 1, unfol.; A. Cotton, 'London newsbooks in the civil war: their political attitudes and sources of information' (Oxford University DPhil, 1971), pp. 82–3.

[39] H. R. Woudhuysen, *Sir Philip Sidney and the Circulation of Manuscripts 1558–1640* (Oxford, 1996), p. 77.

[40] PRO, PROB 11/180, fo. 4. For Hobbes: R. Tuck, *Hobbes* (Oxford, 1989), p. 4; F. Toennies, 'Contributions a l'histoire de la pensee de Hobbes', *Archives de Philosophie* 12 (1936), pp. 81–6; J. P. Sommerville, *Thomas Hobbes: Political Ideas in Historical Context* (London, 1992), p. 11; Malcolm, ed., *Correspondence of Thomas Hobbes*, esp. i. 1–4, 7–8. For Sterry: Warwicks. RO, CR 1886, vol. 1, unfol. See also: M. Brennan, *Literary Patronage in the English Renaissance: the Pembroke Family* (London, 1988), p. 185; A. Hughes, 'Thomas Dugard and his circle in the 1630s', *HJ* 29 (1986), pp. 777, 781; W. Gibson, *A Social History of the Domestic Chaplain, 1530–1840* (London, 1997), pp. 88–102.

[41] M. L. Robertson, 'Thomas Cromwell's servants: the ministerial household in early Tudor government and society' (UCLA PhD, 1975), pp. 284–98; V. Sanders, 'The household of Archbishop Parker and the influencing of public opinion', *JEH* 34 (1983), pp. 534–47; D. S. Berkowitz, *Humanist Scholarship and Public Order. Two Tracts Against the Pilgrimage of Grace by Sir Richard Morison* (Washington, 1984), pp. 9–71; J. K. McConica, *English Humanists and Reformation Politics* (Oxford, 1965), pp. 150–99; W. G. Zeeveld, 'Richard Morison, official apologist for Henry VIII', *Publications of the Modern Language Association* 55 (1940), pp. 406–25; A. J. Slavin, 'Profitable studies: humanists and government in early Tudor England', *Viator* 1 (1970), pp. 307–25.

the conscious attempts by grandees to seek out talent meant that the patronage nexus could be highly dynamic.[42] Thus, the commonwealth legal reformer, William Sheppard, moved from a gentry network into central administration, while clerical pamphleteers such as Henry Ferne, Alex Ross and Isaac Basire progressed from household employment into royal chaplaincies.[43] Many more moved between households on the basis of patron recommendation, whether royalists such as Peter Heylyn and Robert Mossom, or parliamentarians such as John Wilkins, Arthur Wilson and Lazarus Seaman.[44] Moreover, that individuals such as Calybute Downing and John Ley secured employment from, and became associated with, a succession of like-minded individuals, suggests that patrons were interested in securing the services of men with whom they shared political and religious outlooks.[45] This probably reflects the desire on the part of public figures and political grandees for employees who were capable of acting as advisers, and it is occasionally possible to identify the employment of 'scholars', such as Edward Bowles, who were politically aware, and who could serve political purposes.[46] Such 'scholarly services' and 'knowledge transactions' included political research and advice, even if they rarely involved propaganda.[47] Nevertheless, it is interesting to observe that Henry Stubbe, whose education was sponsored by the parliamentarian grandee, Sir Henry Vane junior, was recognised as being Vane's adviser by at least one reader of his contributions to republican literature in 1659.[48] And whatever the motivation behind specific household

---

[42] J. Eales, *Puritans and Roundheads. The Harleys of Brampton Bryan* (Cambridge, 1990), p. 65; BL, Add. 70002, fos. 70, 80; *CSPD 1627–8*, p. 242; PRO, SP 16/70, fos. 38r–v; *NP* ii. 19–20; *Clarendon State Papers*, iii. 186; *TSP* v. 13, 522–3; *TSP* vii. 162.

[43] N. L. Matthews, *William Sheppard, Cromwell's Law Reformer* (Cambridge, 1984), pp. 9–14, 22, 31; *DNB*; W. N. Darnell, ed., *The Correspondence of Isaac Basire* (London, 1831), pp. 4, 39; PRO, LC 5/135, p. 12.

[44] LPL, MS 3516, fos. 203–4; Bodl. MS Tanner 68, fo. 248; G. Vernon, *The Life of the Learned and Reverend Dr Peter Heylyn* (London, 1682), pp. 9, 13–14, 35–6; Shapiro, *John Wilkins*, pp. 16–17; R. Mossom, *Sion's Prospect in its First View* (London, 1651), sigs. *2r–v; CUL, Add 33; Peck, *Desiderata*, ii. 460–83; PRO, SP 28/3, fo. 67.

[45] *DNB*; V. Pearl, *London and the Outbreak of the Puritan Revolution* (Oxford, 1961), pp. 41–2, 168; J. Morrill, *Cheshire 1630–1660* (Oxford, 1974), pp. 20, 165–6; Hughes, 'Thomas Dugard', p. 786; A. Hughes, *Politics, Society and Civil War in Warwickshire, 1620–1660* (Cambridge, 1987); BL, Add. 70002, fo. 368; Eales, *Puritans and Roundheads*, chap. 3.

[46] A. Woolrych, 'Yorkshire and the Restoration', *Yorkshire Archeaological Journal* 39 (1958), pp. 487–8; J. Price, *The Mystery and Method* (1680), in F. Maseres, *Select Tracts* (2 vols, London, 1815), ii. 751–2; A. Grafton and L. Jardine, 'Studied for action: how Gabriel Harvey read his Livy', *P&P* 129 (1990), pp. 33–4.

[47] L. Jardine and W. Sherman, 'Pragmatic readers: knowledge transactions and scholarly services in late Elizabethan England', in A. Fletcher and P. Roberts, eds, *Religion, Culture and Society in Early Modern Britain* (Cambridge, 1994); W. Sherman, *John Dee: The Politics of Reading and Writing in the Renaissance* (Amherst, Mass., 1994); P. Collinson, 'The monarchical republic of Queen Elizabeth I', *BJRL* 69 (1986–87); P. Collinson, 'Puritans, men of business, and Elizabethan Parliaments', *PH* 7 (1988); Hammer, 'The uses of scholarship'; Hammer, 'Employment of scholars'.

[48] H. Stubbe, *A Letter to an Officer* (London, 1659, BL, E1001/8). See also: H. Stubbe, *Malice*

appointments, it is clear that employees' relationships with patrons and grandees tended to be transformed as tension mounted in the late 1630s and early 1640s.[49]

In addition to aristocratic and gentry households, and the clerical positions within their grasp, many men who contributed to civil war pamphleteering had secured appointments to, and preferment through, central administration.[50] Some, such as Sir John Berkenhead, had worked within the central administration of the church.[51] Others, such as Clement Walker, William Ball and Henry Parker, had been employed within the courts at Westminster.[52] And during the civil wars, many authors can be found among the order books, accounts and warrants of royalist and parliamentarian administration. Henry Parker served as secretary to the Committee of Safety from the summer of 1642, which meant almost daily attendance at Westminster in the months which followed.[53] In addition to signing hundreds of warrants, Parker drafted the instructions for Hugh Peter's mission to the Low Countries; deputised for Robert Coytmor as secretary to the Earl of Warwick (Lord Admiral); and effectively headed the committee's secretariat, as contemporaries recognised.[54] Moreover, it was during these busy months that Parker wrote a number of key parliamentarian tracts, as well as a stream of minor pamphlets.[55] Meanwhile, the journalist and pamphleteer, Theodore Jennings, spent

---

Rebuked (London, 1659), p. 60; H. Vane, A Light Shining Out of Darknes (2nd edn, London, 1659); H. Stubbe, The Common-Wealth of Oceana Put Into the Ballance, and Found too Light (London, 1660); Jacob, Stubbe, pp. 25–40; Malcolm, ed., Correspondence of Thomas Hobbes, ii. 899–902.

[49] E. C. Vernon, 'The Sion College conclave and London Presbyterianism during the English Revolution (Cambridge University PhD, 1999), chap. 1; V. Sanders, 'The household of Archbishop Parker and the influencing of public opinion', JEH 34 (1983).

[50] Peacey, 'Henry Parker', pp. 21–2; G. Aylmer, The King's Servants (London, 1961), pp. 69–143; H. E. Bell, An Introduction to the History and Records of the Court of Wards (Cambridge, 1953), pp. 16–45; C. W. Brook, Pettyfoggers and Vipers of the Commonwealth (Cambridge, 1986).

[51] Thomas, Sir John Berkenhead, pp. 3, 12, 15–18, 21–4.

[52] For Walker, chief usher of the Exchequer: PRO, E 403/1716, 1722, 1725, 1728, 1751, 1753; PRO, E 159/445 Hil. rec. 492, E159/452 Easter rec. 139, E 159/501 Trin. rec. 52; Somerset RO, DD/WHb/140–42; Somerset RO, DD/GB/148, p. 57. For Ball: PRO, SP 16/488, fo. 205v; For Parker: PRO, C 66/2593/25; PRO, SO 3/10, unfol.; PRO, T 56/1, fo. 13v, T 56/2, fo. 5v, T 56/3, p. 3; PRO, PC 2/49, fo. 194v.

[53] PRO, SP 28/261, fos. 3–436, SP 16/491, fo. 233, SP 16/539, fo. 186, SP 28/1C, fo. 266; BL, Add. 32426, fo. 7v; PRO, SP 28/2a, fo. 86, SP 28/47, fo. 286, SP 16/492, fos. 92, 197, SP 28/262, fos. 2–474, SP 28/3, fos. 4, 53, 78, 96, 132, 331, 389, 479, 489, SP 28/4, fo. 201, SP 16/493, fos. 4, 20, SP 28/263, fos. 1–210, 222–68, SP 28/64, fos. 673–4, SP 28/264, fo. 305.

[54] Bodl. MS Clarendon 22, fos. 128r–v; PRO, SP 28/2a, fos. 6, 8, SP 28/3, fo. 95, SP 16/503ii, fo. 28, SP 28/262, fo. 446; CJ iii. 53; PRO, SP 28/261, fo. 168, SP 28/263, fo. 254–5, SP 28/264, fos. 62, 384; Discourse Discovering Some Mysteries, p. 28.

[55] J. Peacey, 'Print detection and political propaganda: a radical press in 1642' (paper delivered at IHR, 2002); A Short Discourse Tending to the Pacification of all Unhappy Differences ([London, 1642]); An Appeale to the World in These Times of Extreame Danger ([London, 1642]); A Petition or Declaration (London, 1642); The Danger to England Observed (London, 1642); Reasons Why This Kingdome Ought to Adhere to the Parliament ([London, 1642]). Parker may also have been responsible for The Case of the Commission of Array Stated ([London, 1642]) and Some Considerations Tending to the Undeceiving ([London, 1642]).

much of the 1640s as an employee of the Committee of Both Kingdoms and the Derby House Committee.[56] Another key member of the secretariat who combined administrative duties with literary activity was Walter Frost, who served as secretary to the Council of State until his death in 1652, and who edited the *Brief Relation* from October 1649 to October 1650.[57] Less prominent, but no less interesting, is George Wither, who was a commissioner for the sale of royal property during the period when he wrote works such as *British Appeals*, to commemorate military victories, and *Republica Anglicana*, in order to reply to Clement Walker.[58] Similarly, the protectorate civil service contained men such as John Rushworth, who served as one of the registrars in the Court of Admiralty while writing his famous *Historical Collections*, and Samuel Morland, who was employed as Clerk of the Signet while he wrote the history of the Protestants in Piedmont.[59] The official archives also reveal the extent to which the pamphleteering of Hartlib's acolytes was undertaken from within the republic's civil service. Henry Robinson, for example, was made a commissioner of accounts, and comptroller for the sale of crown lands in 1649, and became secretary to the excise commissioners, and comptroller of receipts for the sale of fee farm rents, in 1650.[60] This provides the context for considering his consultations with the authorities over economic reform, as well as for scrutiny of his writings, whether works of political theory such as *A Short Discourse Between Monarchical and Aristocratical Government*, or works regarding economic and legal reform.[61] Another of Hartlib's associates, William Potter, was acting as

---

[56] T. Jennings, *Truth's Return* (London, 1646); T. Jennings, *The Right Way to Peace* (London, 1647); *Perfect Summary* (1649, N&S pp. 457–8); *CJ* ii. 823–4; *CJ* v. 150; *CJ* vi. 573; PRO, SP 28/252i, fo. 263; *CSPD 1644–1650*, passim; Warwicks. RO, CR2017/C10/32.

[57] *Briefe Relation* (1649–50, N&S pp. 22–3); *CJ* vi. 143, 364, 533; *CJ* vii. 45; G. Aylmer, *The State's Servants* (London, 1973), pp. 254–6.

[58] PRO, SP 28/104, unbound; A. Pritchard, 'George Wither and the sale of the estate of Charles I', *Modern Philology* 77 (1980); G. Wither, *British Appeals* (London, 1651); G. Wither, *Republica Anglicana* (London, 1650).

[59] Rushworth was appointed in 1654: BL, Add. 4184, fo. 24. Morland was in position by June 1656: BL, Stowe 497; BL, Add. 4184, fo. 106.

[60] *CJ* vi. 306, 426; Bodl. MS Rawl. A.246, fos. 37v, 167; Aylmer, *State's Servants*, p. 225; *A&O*, ii. 180, 277, 362; For the work with the committee of accounts see: PRO, SP 28/14, fo. 142, SP 28/89, fos. 152–3, SP 28/81, fo. 1126, SP 28/258, SP 28/260; *CSPD 1652–3*, p. 157; *CSPD 1654*, p. 287; PRO, SP 28/42, fo. 1027. For Robinson as comptroller for the sale of fee farm rents, see: Bodl. MS Rawl. A.246, fos. 37v, 167; *CSPD 1655–6*, p. 126; PRO, SP 26/8, p. 91.

[61] Hartlib Papers, 50H/28/1/9, 26; *CSPD 1649–50*, pp. 44, 475; *CSPD 1650*, pp. 120, 182–3; PRO, SP 18/9, fos. 103–6; *CSPD 1653–4*, pp. 364, 366; H. Robinson, *A Short Discourse* (London, 1649); H. Robinson, *Certain Considerations* (London, 1651); H. Robinson, *Certain Proposals* (London, 1652); H. Robinson, *Briefe Considerations Concerning the Advancement of Trade and Navigation* (London, 1649); H. Robinson, *Certain Considerations* (London, 1651). Throughout this period, Robinson was seeking to gain control of the post office: *CSPD 1650*, p. 478; *CSPD 1651*, p. 467; *CSPD 1651–2*, pp. 15, 390, 444; *CSPD 1652–3*, pp. 109, 366–8, 450–51; *CSPD 1653–4*, p. 373; *CSPD 1654*, pp. 21–2, 26–7. See: P. Gaunt, 'Interregnum governments and the reform of the post office, 1649–59', *HR* 60 (1987).

registrar of debentures at the time of his publication of *The Key of Wealth* and *The Tradesman's Jewel* in 1650.[62] Lastly, Benjamin Worsley was acting as secretary to the Council of Trade when he published his defence of the Navigation Act in *The Advocate*, and his advocacy of trade reforms in *Free Ports*.[63]

Other writers held less formal positions, such as the parliamentarian journalist, John Dillingham, who was one of Oliver St John's attendants to the peace negotiations at Uxbridge in 1645.[64] Philip Nye, who supported the Solemn League and Covenant in a number of pamphlets in 1643–44, was likewise involved in the negotiations which led to its agreement with the Scots.[65] One of the commonwealth's most important advocates, Anthony Ascham, emerged into print after working as tutor to the royal children under the control of the Earl of Northumberland.[66] Furthermore, many lawyer-pamphleteers were employed as counsel by Parliament and the commonwealth. The most prolific polemicist of the period, William Prynne, produced a series of works relating to the 'state' trials of Nathaniel Fiennes, Connor Macguire and William Laud, from the position of chief prosecuting counsel.[67] Less well known, perhaps, is the fact that his famous pamphlet defences of the Presbyterians MPs who were impeached by the army in 1647, were written while he was the officially appointed counsel to assist their defence.[68] In later years, other state lawyers turned their skills towards the printing press, including John Cook, the solicitor general during the trial of Charles I, who subsequently became Chief Justice of Munster, and who penned *Monarchy no*

---

[62] Bodl. MS Rawl. A.246, fos. 70v, 79, 104, 123, 136, 155, 171, 179v; W. Potter, *The Key of Wealth* (London, 1650), *The Tradesman's Jewel* (London, 1650). For Potter and Hartlib see: Hartlib Papers, 50H/28/1/68, 50H/33/1/33–71, 50H/30/3/1–12, 50H/7/81/1–16.

[63] *CJ* vi. 383; B. Worsley, *The Advocate* (London, 1650); B. Worsley, *Free Ports* (London, 1652). For Worsley, see: C. Webster, 'Benjamin Worsley: engineering for universal reform from the invisible college to the Navigation Act', in M. Greengrass, M. Leslie, T. Raylor, eds, *Samuel Hartlib and Universal Reformation* (Cambridge, 1994); Aylmer, *State's Servants*, pp. 270–71; Bodl. MS Clarendon 75, fo. 300. Worsley's connections with parliamentarian grandees can be tracked earlier: *CJ* v. 247; *LJ* viii. 573–4; *LJ* ix. 337; *CSPI 1633–47*, pp. 776, 780, 787; *CJ* vi. 383; C. M. Andrews, *British Committees, Commissions, and Councils of Trade and Plantations 1622–1675* (Baltimore, 1908), pp. 24–34; C. Wilson, *Profit and Power* (London, 1957), pp. 25–58; B. Worden, *The Rump Parliament, 1648–53* (Cambridge, 1974), pp. 254–60.

[64] *TSP* i. 59.

[65] P. Nye, *An Exhortation* (London, 1644); P. Nye, *The Excellency and Lawfulness* (London, 1646); P. Nye, *The Covenant* (London, 1643); *The True Copy of the Letter Which Was Sent from Divers Ministers* (London, 1643).

[66] Folger Shakespeare Library, X.d.154; *CJ* vi. 216; *CCAM* ii. 595; *LJ* viii. 446; *CSPD 1649–50*, p. 483; PRO, SC 6/Chas.1/1667 m.11; A. Ascham, *A Discourse Wherein is Examined What is Particularly Lawful During the Confusions and Revolutions of Government* (London, 1648); *SR* i. 294; A. Ascham, *A Combat Between Two Seconds* (London, 1649); A. Ascham, *The Bounds and Bonds of Publique Obedience* (London, 1649); A. Ascham, *Of the Confusions and Revolutions of Governments* (London, 1649); *SR* i. 294. For Ascham, see: J. Peacey, 'Order and disorder in Europe: parliamentary agents and royalist thugs 1649–1650', *HJ* 40 (1997), pp. 966–75.

[67] Peacey, 'Henry Parker', pp. 176–81.

[68] *CJ* v. 243, 250; Peacey, 'Henry Parker', pp. 183–4.

Creature of Gods Making.[69] William Sheppard, meanwhile, produced a series of important legal tracts during his time as a leading lawyer at the Cromwellian court.[70]

Such examples reveal the prevalence of authors within the parliamentarian civil service in the 1640s, particularly after the establishment of the republic. Although the lack of official paperwork means that we know a great deal less about the structures and characters of the royalist court and administration, whether in Oxford or in exile, it is nevertheless apparent that far fewer royalist authors were employed in comparable positions. It is possible to find evidence of authors who held royal chaplaincies, not least Henry Ferne, one of the most important royalist theorists of the early 1640s.[71] Nevertheless, the evidence suggests that Richard Steward, who was clerk of the closet to Charles I at the time he wrote *An Answer to a Letter Written at Oxford*, and Joseph Jane, who was clerk of the royalist council at the time he published *Eikon Aklastos* in 1651, were exceptions rather than the norm.[72] Although it is possible that some of those authors who joined the king at Oxford during the civil wars, such as John Taylor, Dudley Digges, and Sir John Spelman, joined the royalist administration, there is little firm evidence of their having done so.[73]

However, attention ought not be restricted to formal and salaried employment, and it is important not to discount those writers in positions secured through official intervention. These include Lewis Du Moulin, who was controversially installed by Parliament as professor of history at Oxford University, and who occupied that chair when he published *The Power of the Christian Magistrate* during the Engagement controversy.[74] Meanwhile, Andrew Marvell, who sought the position as assistant Latin Secretary after leaving his tutorial role in the household of Sir Thomas Fairfax, with the help and recommendation of John

---

[69] J. Cook, *Monarchy no Creature of Gods Making* (London, 1652); *CSPD 1649–50*, pp. 121, 130, 154; *CJ* vi. 246, 258; *CSPD 1650*, p. 481; T. C. Barnard, *Cromwellian Ireland* (Oxford, 1975), pp. 149, 255–81.

[70] Matthews, *William Sheppard*, pp. 31, 52; PRO, SP 25/76, fos. 531–2, 547, 552, 562, SP 25/77, fo. 150, 175, 216.

[71] PRO, LC 5/135, p. 12; J. Taylor, *The Great Exemplar* (London, 1649).

[72] [R. Steward], *An Answer to a Letter Written at Oxford* ([London], 1647); *CCSP* ii. 63; J. Jane, *Eikon Aklastos* (Np, 1651). Sir Edward Walker, Garter King at Arms, and secretary to the royalist council of war in the 1640s, drafted but did not publish historical accounts of royalist military campaigns, as well as a response to William Lilly's life of Charles I: Bodl. MS Clarendon 136; BL, Add. 33224, fos. 1–50.

[73] B. S. Capp, *The World of John Taylor the Water Poet, 1578–1653* (Oxford, 1994), p. 152; *DNB*. Spelman only arrived in Oxford in the spring of 1643, shortly before his death in July: R. W. Ketton-Cremer, *Norfolk in the Civil War* (London, 1969), pp. 166–9, 176. Thus, he was not in Oxford when he published: *A Protestant's Account* (Cambridge, 1642), *Certain Considerations* (Oxford, 1642), *The Case of our Affaires* (Oxford, 1643), and *A View of a Printed Book* (Oxford, 1642). See: J. De Groot, 'Space, patronage, procedure: the court at Oxford, 1642–46', *EHR* 117 (2002).

[74] *LJ* viii. 450; *CJ* v. 334, 342; *CJ* vii. 436, 438–9, 465, 474; Burrows, ed., *Register of the Visitors*, pp. 185–6.

Milton, was appointed as governor to Cromwell's protégé, William Dutton, in June 1653.[75] It was while working in this capacity that Marvell wrote the 'first anniversary of the government under his highness the lord protector'.[76] Furthermore, it is also necessary to consider the printed works by men who, without being formally employed, nevertheless enjoyed a degree of access to, and involvement with, politicians. These included men involved in policy formation and reform in the 1650s, such as Thomas Violet, whose ideas regarding trade and the transport of gold led to consultations with the council and the drafting of legislation, as well as to a series of tracts.[77]

During the 1640s and 1650s, an increasingly important realm to which attention needs to be drawn in order to contextualise polemical literature centred on rival armies and their secretariats. Numerous tracts emerged, of course, from the pens of parliamentarian army chaplains, not least *The Souldiers Catechisme* by Robert Ram, as well as the battlefield sermons of Christopher Love, John Saltmarsh and William Dell.[78] Royalist chaplains likewise printed sermons delivered before troops in the field, such as Edward Symmons, who was chaplain to the lifeguard of the Prince of Wales, and who published a sermon preached before Prince Rupert's army at Shrewsbury in May 1644. Indeeed, chaplains such as Symmons and Lionel Gatford also wrote more substantial works.[79] Moreover, being positioned on the front line gave chaplains access to up-to-the-minute military news, and many became involved in the provision of intelligence. Pre-eminent among these were the parliamentarian chaplains, Simeon Ashe and William Goode, who produced a series of printed newsletters during 1644–45, and who served as agents for their regimental commander, the Earl of

---

[75] H. Kelliher, *Andrew Marvell, Poet and Politician, 1621–78* (London, 1978), pp. 55–8; PRO, SP 18/33, fo. 152; *CSPD 1652–3*, p. 176; J. Nickolls, ed., *Original Letters and Papers of State* (London, 1743), pp. 98–9. For Marvell in the Fairfax household see: D. Hirst and S. Zwicker, 'High summer at Nun Appleton, 1651: Andrew Marvell and Lord Fairfax's occasions', *HJ* 36 (1993).

[76] Kelliher, *Andrew Marvell*, p. 60.

[77] BL, Harl. 6034, fos. 1v–23v; *CSPD 1649–50*, pp. 178–83, 281, 431, 455, 473, 480; *CSPD 1650*, pp. 178–82, 292, 431, 454–5, 473, 480; *CSPD 1651*, pp. 231–4, 460–62; *CSPD 1651–2*, pp. 23–5, 156, 441; *CSPD 1652–3*, pp. 15, 23, 47, 75, 233, 241, 398; *CSPD 1653–4*, pp. 123, 152, 162, 178, 199, 412; *CSPD 1654*, pp. 55, 356; *CSPD 1655*, pp. 292–3, 360; *CSPD 1655–6*, pp. 117, 129, 235; *CSPD 1658–9*, p. 394; T. Violet, *The Advancement of Merchandize* (London, 1651); T. Violet, *A True Discoverie* (London, 1651); T. Violet, *Mysteries and Secrets* (London, 1653); T. Violet, *The Answer of the Corporation of Moniers* (London, 1653); T. Violet, *A True Narrative of Some Remarkable Procedings* (London, 1653); T. Violet, *Proposals Humbly Presented* (London, 1656).

[78] R. Ram, *The Souldier's Catechisme* (London, 1644); J. Saltmarsh, *A Solemn Discourse* (London, 1643); W. Dell, *The Building of the Truly Christian and Spiritual Church* (London, 1646); C. Love, *Englands Distemper* (London, 1645); A. Laurence, *Parliamentary Army Chaplains, 1642–1651* (Woodbridge, 1990), pp. 120–21, 149–50, 168, 170.

[79] E. Symmons, *A Military Sermon* (Oxford, 1644). See also: W. C., *A Manuall of Prayers Collected for the Use of Sir Ralph Hopton's Regiment* (Oxford, 1643). For extended treatises: E. Symmons, *A Vindication of King Charles* (London, 1648). Gatford, chaplain to the royalists in the West, and later on Jersey, wrote a powerful treatise regarding the compatibility of royalism with the 1641 Protestation: Bodl. MS Clarendon 25, fos. 46–65v; *CCSP* i. 305.

Manchester.[80] It was not just army chaplains who turned their attention to literary warfare, however, and tracts were produced by men from within the army administration as well as soldiers of a wide variety of ranks and social backgrounds. Records reveal, therefore, that John Sadler was employed as commissary-general of the parliamentarian forces in Staffordshire and Warwickshire while he published polemics such as *Malignancy Un-masked*.[81] Thomas May, meanwhile, was attached to the retinue of the parliamentarian commander, Sir Thomas Fairfax, when he published an account of the defence of Hull in 1643.[82] And Henry Parker's tracts during the period 1649-51 need to be understood in the light of his role as secretary to the forces under Oliver Cromwell.[83] Among military figures, on the other hand, a wide variety of tracts and pamphlets were produced by individuals as diverse as Payne Fisher (gentleman lifeguard to George Monck in November 1655), Josiah Ricraft (scoutmaster of the London militia), and Richard Lawrence (Marshall General).[84]

---

[80] *A Particular Relation of the Several Removes* (London, 1644), *A Particular Relation of the Most Remarkable Occurrences* (London, 1644), *A Continuation of the True Intelligence* (London, 1644), *A True Relation of the Most Chief Occurrences* (London, 1644); Laurence, *Chaplains*, pp. 92–3, 129–30. For their pay and work as agents for Manchester, see: PRO, SP 28/1A, fo. 280, SP 28/2, fo. 300, SP 28/3, fo. 330, SP 28/28, fo. 137, SP 28/72, fo. 441.

[81] PRO, SP 28/253B, unfol.; J. S[adler], *Malignancy Un-masked* (London, 1642). Sadler was almost certainly the author of: J. S., *A True Relation of the Lord Brooke's Setling of the Militia in Warwickshire* (London, 1642).

[82] *A True Relation from Hull* (London, 1643).

[83] H. P[arker], *A Letter of Due Censure* (London, 1650); H. Parker, *Scotland's Holy War* (London, 1650); H. Parker, *The Cheif Affairs of Ireland* (London, 1651). Parker was evidently in position from mid-May 1649: BL, Add. 21417, fos. 134r–v. By late June he was styled secretary to the council of war, and was planning his journey to Ireland: PRO, SP 28/77, fo. 20; Claydon House, Verney Papers, reel 10, unfol.: William Denton to Wiliam Roades, 28 June 1649. By 6 July he was styled secretary to Cromwell, and thereafter is present among the records until November 1649: PRO, SP 28/61, fos. 348–96, SP 28/62, fos. 3, 8, 21, 31, 38a, 55, 419, 451, 453a, 457, SP 28/63, fos. 1–57, SP 28/64, fos. 5–34; Bodl. MS Tanner 56, fos. 91–2v; Abbott, *Cromwell*, ii. 122; BL, Add. 63788A, fo. 4; *CSPD 1649–50*, p. 364. Thereafter, Parker was forced to withdraw from active secretarial duties due to illness, and evidently returned to England in December 1649. Parker's clerk received money in his name until February 1650, when Parker was formally replaced: PRO, SP 28/64, fos. 12, 312; Claydon House, Verney Papers, reel 10, unfol.: William Denton to Ralph Verney, 27 Dec. 1649. Nevertheless, he retained some form of position within the secretariat. On 2 May 1651, Cromwell signed a warrant for payment of £136, a year's pay for Parker, although Parker received only £71 of this, since the work had been undertaken by deputies: PRO, SP 28/77, fos. 20r–v. Copies of letters from Ireland survive in Parker's hand from the spring and early summer of 1651: Bodl. MS Tanner 54, fos. 50–51, 74–5, 81–2; BL, Add. 63788B, fos. 81, 101. Indeed, that Parker was buried at Kensington in 1652 probably indicates that he was living at, and employed by, army headquarters in Holland House until his death: F. N. Macnamara and A. Story-Maskelyne, eds, *The Parish Register of Kensington* (London, 1890), p. 122.

[84] For Fisher: PRO, SP 28/108, fos. 442–3; P. Fisher, *Miscellania* (London, 1655). For Ricraft: PRO, SP 28/237, unfol.; Mahoney, 'Presbyterianism in London', p. 108; J. Ricraft, *A Survey of England's Champions* (London, 1647); J. Ricraft, *A Perfect List of the Many Victories* (London, 1646). For Lawrence: *The Wolf Stript of his Sheeps Clothing* (London, 1647); PRO, SP 28/39, fo. 41, SP 28/54, fo. 117, SP 28/58, fos. 692, 694.

They could be penned by soldiers of various ranks, including John Spittlehouse, John Streater, George Wither and Philip Skippon, the latter of whom published a series of tracts for the troops during the first civil war.[85] They could also be published by Edmund Chillenden, William Goffe and George Joyce, the latter of whose writings are less well known than his role in removing the king from Holmby.[86] Once again, surviving evidence suggests that this was an area where parliamentarian attitudes and abilities differed from those of royalists, and members of the king's army appear rarely to have engaged in print in the same way.[87]

Biographical information alone can neither explain authorial motivation, nor indicate that those political patrons and institutions with which authors can be linked played any part in instigating, organising or arranging specific publications. Nevertheless, such prosopographical analysis provides a methodological foundation for a more subtle examination of potential links between the work of writers and political grandees, and demonstrates one core method of understanding the appearance of particular works. It certainly enables a contextualisation of authors' motives for promoting the interests of patrons, defending the reputations of employers, and representing the political views of regimes in which they held a personal and professional stake. When civil war broke out, individuals associated with colonial ventures, such as Edward Winslow, sometime governor of Plymouth in New England, could use their experience to contribute to English religious debates.[88] Furthermore, 'men of business', as well as lawyers, tutors, advisers and chaplains, could display their allegiance, and repay their debts, with propaganda for their employers, whether on an individual level or for the factions and parties they formed. Chaplains who had been lecturing in the family chapel or local parish could stir electors, soldiers, and the mob to support their benefactors. Thus, John Geree, a preacher at Tewkesbury in Gloucestershire who was well-connected with prominent local Puritans, undertook electioneering for his friends in 1640, and began writing controversial pamphlets such as *The Downfall of Antichrist*.[89] Lawyers and advisers who had been working on personal business, such as Henry

---

[85] J. Spittlehouse, *The Army Vindicated* (London, 1653); [J. Streater], *The Grand Informer* (Np, 1647); G. Wither, *Campo Musae* (London, 1643); G. Wither, *Se Defedendo* (London, 1643); G. Wither, *Vox Pacifica* (London, 1645); P. Skippon, *A Salve for every sore ... the Christian Centurion's Infallible Ground of Confidence* (London, 1643); P. Skippon, *The Christian Centurians Observations, Advices and Resolutions* (London, 1645); P. Skippon, *True Treasure; or Thirtie Holy Vowes* (London, 1644).

[86] E. Chillenden, *Preaching Without Ordination* (London, 1647); W. G[offe], *A Just Apologie for an Abused Armie* (London, 1646); G. Joyce, *A True Impartiall Narration* ([London], 1647); G. Joyce, *A Vindication of His Majesty and the Army* (London, 1647).

[87] M. Lluelin, *Men Miracles* (Oxford, by Hall, 1646).

[88] Warwicks. RO, CR 2017/C10/128; Aylmer, *State's Servants*, pp. 218–19; W. Sterry-Cooper, *Edward Winslow* (Birmingham, 1953); C. M. Andrew, *The Colonial Period of American History* (New Haven, 1934); E. Winslow, *Hypocrisie Unmasked* (London, 1646), *New England's Salamander* (London, 1647), *The Danger of Tolerating Levellers* (London, 1649).

[89] *CSPD 1639–40*, pp. 580–83; J. Geree, *The Downfall of Antichrist* (London, 1641).

Parker and John Cook, formulated the ideology behind political actions. Agents who had provided personal news services, such as John Dillingham, joined the burgeoning newspapers business. Moreover, such biographical information means that it is essential to consider the possibility that the works of individuals who were employed within the central administration and the military appeared with the knowledge, approval and involvement of employers, commanders and paymasters.

In order to substantiate such suggestive possibilities, it is necessary to explore the congruity between the message of particular works and the ideas and interests of those in a position to influence their composition or appearance, and to demonstrate such congruity between authors and grandees for whom personal connections can be shown to have existed. It is possible to detect, in other words, the existence of pamphlets which appear to represent the interests, if not necessarily the involvement, of politicians.[90] That prose and print were used to demonstrate loyalty to former employers is evident from the posthumous works written about the Earl of Essex by former chaplains, such as Daniel Evans, and former secretaries, such as Henry Parker.[91] It is also possible to observe authors representing the interests of men to whom they were connected, as with the parliamentarian journalist, John Dillingham.[92] Naturally, the many pitfalls facing those who seek to demonstrate how texts served the political and religious interests of patrons mean that the contextualisation of individual works needs to be undertaken with great care.[93] Rarely will there be evidence from private correspondence, like that of Robert Baillie, which expressed unequivocal proof of congruity between grandees and authors such as David Buchanan.[94] Analysing the ways in which works represented the interests of men to whom contact can be demonstrated requires a close reading of texts alongside a detailed understanding of grandee politics and the political and religious positions of patrons, as well as an appreciation of the timing of the appearance of particular works, and plausible reasons for their appearance.[95] This is clearly undertaken more easily for

---

[90] B. Galloway, *The Union of England and Scotland* (Edinburgh, 1986), p. 48; P. Seaward, 'A restoration publicist: James Howell and the Earl of Clarendon, 1661–6', *HR* 61 (1988), pp. 125–6.

[91] J. S. A. Adamson, 'The baronial context of the English civil wars', *TRHS*, 5th series 40 (1990), p. 107; R. Vines, *The Hearse of the Renowned … Earle of Essex* (London, 1646); [H. Parker], 'An elegie upon the death of my most noble lord' (BL, E358/1). See also: Edward Walsingham's eulogy for Sir John Smith, to whom he had been secretary, and who died at Cheriton in March 1644: E. Walsingham, *Britanicae Virtutis Imago* (Oxford, 1644).

[92] A. N. B. Cotton, 'John Dillingham, journalist of the middle group', *EHR* 93 (1978); Cotton, 'London newsbooks', pp. 86–90.

[93] T. A. Dunn, *Philip Massinger* (London, 1957); S. R. Gardiner, 'The political element in Massinger', *The Contemporary Review* 28 (1876); R. Gill, 'Necessitie of State: Massinger's *Believe as You List*', *English Studies* 46 (1965); A. Gross, 'Contemporary politics in Massinger', *Studies in English Literature* 6 (1966). See above, pp. 8–10, 12–13.

[94] *Letters and Journals of Robert Baillie*, ii. 367.

[95] Seaward, 'Restoration publicist', pp. 125–6.

parliamentarians than royalists, given the paucity of detailed information on the decision-making process at Oxford, and the roles played by individual grandees.

Such contextualisation of polemical literature by means of biographical information, congruity of authorial message and the interests of political grandees, as well as opportune timing, can serve, firstly, to demonstrate how pamphlets were used to overcome the difficulties with the drafting of, and securing approval for, official declarations. Pamphlets could be used not merely to produce substitutes for such statements, as demonstrated above, but also to produce works which were almost impossible for contemporaries to identify as having been officially inspired, even if they appear to have been so with the benefit of hindsight. It is possible, in other words, to identify texts which served the purposes of controversial declarations, which were carefully timed, and which were composed by men who were connected with the politicians whose interest they served. An early attempt to produce just such an alternative to a declaration occurred in August 1641, following an investigation into the appearance of a printed paper which purported to contain the votes of the Commons concerning the 'protestation': the test of loyalty imposed in the aftermath of the 'Army Plot'. The Lords were partly motivated by a desire to ascertain whether this work had been printed by order of the Commons, which the latter duly admitted, but the implication was that the Lords were unhappy about the justifications which were being used.[96] As a result, those eager to deploy certain arguments apparently decided to side-step such opposition, not by means of a pseudo-declaration, but rather through a work which bore no resemblance to an official statement, and every resemblance to an independently inspired tract. The fact that such a pamphlet was produced by John Ley, who was connected to prominent MPs such as Sir Robert Harley (to whom the book was dedicated) and godly peers such as Lord Brooke, suggests that the Commons, or members thereof, sought to avoid further confrontation with the Lords by seeking Ley's services, rather than trying to persevere with the apparently fruitless task of producing further declarations.[97] Ley's contribution, if officially inspired, represented an attempt to produce an alternative to a declaration, rather than a clever imitation, and there are grounds for at least suspicion that it was produced in collusion with parliamentary grandees. Similar conclusions emerge from an anonymous work in justification of the 'parliamentary covenant', imposed in the summer of 1643, when it is possible to link calls made by the House for official declarations with non-official pamphlets.[98]

On another occasion, in 1646, an attempt appears to have been made to supplement official pronouncements with a much more substantial and forceful polemic. This reflected the concern on the part of the political Independents at

---

[96] *CJ* ii. 232; *LJ* iv. 337–9.

[97] J. Ley, *A Comparison* (London, 1641); *SR* i. 34.

[98] *CJ* iii. 173, 182; *The Harmony of Our Oaths* (London, 1643).

Westminster to undermine the propaganda emanating from the Scottish Presbyterians, particularly David Buchanan's *Truth its Manifest*, which the Commons investigated in April 1646, and which they felt required a response in the form of a 'manifest'.[99] Viscount Saye himself intended to answer Buchanan, but would not do so for another eight years.[100] The speedy response which Saye and his friends so badly needed emerged in early July 1646, in the form of *Manifest Truths* by Edward Bowles, a well-connected minister whose father, Oliver, had been John Preston's tutor and Sir Henry Vane senior's chaplain.[101] Bowles's activity as an army chaplain had made him familiar with the Scots and their military activities in the North.[102] Moreover, he explained the rationale behind his book by arguing that, 'whereas it may be said that this labour might have been spared, in regard of the censure adjudged by Parliament to *Truth's Manifest*', nevertheless, 'there is as much difference betwixt a censure and an answer, as betwixt the offence in writing the book, and the hurt done by spreading it'. Parliament had, he continued,

> taken just notice of the fault, but have not thereby prevented the mischief, for since the author was called in question, the book hath been studiously dispersed, and (as I believe) reprinted, and hath found some readers so confident, as to say, that the book was censured, because it could not be answered, the contrary of which doth now appear.[103]

Once again, the congruity between Bowles's work and the interests of men at Westminster with whom he was probably personally familiar, conspire to suggest that his book appeared with the knowledge, and support, of key parliamentarian grandees.

Such contextualisation of particular pamphlets need not merely explore works which appeared as alternatives for, or supplements to, official declarations. One of the most interesting examples of an author whose work reflected the interests of a political figure with whom he is known to have been associated is Henry Parker, a 'privado' who turned to print in the interests of his patron and kinsman.[104] Parker's polemics of the late 1630s and early 1640s, though not his views, may have been prompted by a desire to repay those kinsmen who had earlier advanced his education. As a younger son of a gentry family, Parker had needed to make his way in the world, and he had exploited his kinship ties with his uncle, Viscount

---

[99] *CJ* iv. 505, 507; *Perfect Occurrences* 16 (17 Apr. 1646), sig. Q3v; BL, Add. 10114, fo. 12v.

[100] W. Fiennes, *Vindiciae Veritatis* (London, 1654); Adamson, 'Peerage in politics', p. 24; J. S. A. Adamson, 'The *Vindicaie Veritatis* and the political creed of Viscount Saye and Sele', *HR* 60 (1987).

[101] E. Bowles, *Manifest Truths* (London, 1646); J. E. B. Mayor, *Autobiography of Matthew Robinson* (Cambridge, 1856), pp. 128–30; *CSPD 1631–3*, pp. 394, 468; A. Everitt, *The Community of Kent in the Great Rebellion* (Leicester, 1973), pp. 71, 118, 180, 324.

[102] Laurence, *Chaplains*, pp. 101–2.

[103] E. Bowles, *Manifest Truths* (London, 1646), p. 75; *SR* i. 235.

[104] M. Mendle, 'Henry Parker: the public's privado', in G. J. Schochet, ed., *Religion, Resistance and Civil War* (Washington, 1990), pp. 157–8.

Saye, in order to secure admission to Winchester School, just as he later benefited from Saye's patronage network in securing admission to Lincoln's Inn.[105] Moreover, it is possible to contextualise Parker's early writings in the context of Saye's views during the period before the opening of the Long Parliament, and to interpret them as being intended as responses to Saye's critics, as well-timed works in support of specific political policies, and as important defences of the Anglo-Scottish Puritan alliance. *Divine and Publike Observations*, which was published in the Low Countries in 1638, as a response to Laud's speech at the trial of Burton, Bastwick and Prynne, accurately reflected Saye's attitude to Laudian church policies and innovations.[106] *The Case of Shipmony* dealt with a case in which Saye was deeply involved, and was published upon the opening of the Long Parliament to coincide with the political campaign against those responsible for the policy.[107] *A Discourse Concerning Puritans* explicitly defended Saye and his covenanter allies from enemies such as Henry Leslie, Bishop of Down and Conner, and though drafted sometime before its publication in January 1641, was published at a time when Saye faced bitter criticism at Westminster, reflected the debates during the opening weeks of Parliament, and echoed speeches by the likes of Sir Benjamin Rudyerd.[108] Parker's analysis of *The Altar Dispute* was similarly composed during the debate of the late 1630s, but was published as an explicit defence of Saye at a time when innovations were being damned by petitions to, and policies emanating from, Parliament, and when the cases of men such as John Williams, who had suffered for their attack on altar policy, were being raised.[109] Another two works by Parker, *The Question Concerning the Divine Right of Episcopacy* and the *True Grounds*, reflected the Erastian line taken by Saye and his friends during the debates on the London petition in early 1641, and later during the debates on the 'grand remonstrance'.[110] Parker's reply to Lord Digby, meanwhile, was an aptly timed riposte to one of the most important obstacles to the prosecution of the Earl of Strafford, and whose speech against the attainder had been surreptitiously printed, and was soon the 'talk of the nation'. It was also a means of protecting Saye, who faced accusations from Strafford for his complicity with the Scots.[111]

---

[105] Peacey, 'Henry Parker', pp. 44–5; Peacey, 'Led by the hand', pp. 37–40.

[106] [H. Parker], *Divine and Publike Observations* (Amsterdam, 1638); M. Mendle, 'The Great Council of Parliament and the first ordinances: the constitutional theory of the civil war', *JBS* 31 (1992), p. 139; M. Mendle, *Henry Parker and the English Civil War* (Cambridge, 1995), pp. 7–10; Peacey, 'Henry Parker', p. 50.

[107] [H. Parker], *The Case of Shipmony* ([London], 1640); Peacey, 'Henry Parker', pp. 51–3.

[108] [H. Parker], *A Discourse Concerning Puritans* (London, 1641); H. Leslie, *A Speech Delivered at the Visitation* (London, 1639); Peacey, 'Henry Parker', pp. 53–6.

[109] H. P[arker], *The Altar Dispute* (London, 1641); Peacey, 'Henry Parker', pp. 58–60.

[110] H. Parker, *The Question Concerning the Divine Right of Episcopacy* (London, 1641); [H. Parker], *The True Grounds of Ecclesiastical Regiment* (London, 1641); Peacey, 'Henry Parker', pp. 56–7.

[111] [H. Parker], *An Answer to the Lord Digbies Speech* ([London], 1641); Peacey, 'Henry Parker',

Pamphleteers like Parker can be contextualised, therefore, by examining the parallels between their works and the beliefs of leading political figures with whom they are known to have been connected. This often reveals that such authors came to represent factional grandees during the 1640s, as Parker did the Earl of Essex, to whom he was secretary from the summer of 1642.[112] Parker's status within the Lord General's retinue is evident from the inventory of Essex House, which refers to 'Mr Parker's lodgings', and was reflected in the support which Parker lent to Essex's authority.[113] In early 1643, therefore, Parker advocated enhancing Essex's authority; arguing that 'till I see him looked upon, and served as a temporary dictator ... I shall never think the Parliament's safety sufficiently provided for'.[114] It rapidly became clear that Parker was working for the faction around Essex, whom he styled 'my master', and the figure in whom lay his 'chiefest worldly hopes'.[115] Parker drafted a controversial defence of Essex in August 1643, and as parliamentarians became divided over the question of peace proposals, and the terms of a projected settlement, he served as the spokesman for the dove-ish tendencies of his employer.[116] Bolstered by victories at Gloucester and Newbury in September 1643, Essex renewed pressure for peace in October which he had instigated in July, and Parker followed his lead with *The Oath of Pacification*, which argued that 'if a faire way of accommodation were now tendered by the Parliament, it would bee held as honourable, [and] as seasonable', and he concluded that 'it seems not impossible to propose such termes of pacification'.[117] While Parker was working closely with Essex in the autumn of 1643, other pamphleteers represented, and probably colluded with, different political interests. It is possible, therefore, to link the appearance of John Saltmarsh's reply to Parker, entitled *A Peace But No Pacification*, to the group of radical opponents of peace within Parliament, and to Henry Marten in particular. Saltmarsh's opposition to a hasty accommodation with the royalists, and his views

---

pp. 60–62; see T. Kilburn and A. Milton, 'The public context of the trial and execution of Strafford', in J. F. Merritt, ed., *The Political World of Thomas Wentworth, Earl of Strafford 1621–1641* (Cambridge, 1996), pp. 240–41.

[112] E. Peacock, *Army Lists* (London, 1874), p. 21; PRO, SP 28/1a, fos. 2–301, SP 28/2a, fos. 50–210, 238, SP 28/3, fos. 214, 413, 482, SP 28/4, fo. 278, SP 28/261, fos. 231–44, SP 28/262, fos. 6–7, 23, SP 16/539 part 1, fo. 186.

[113] BL, Add. 46189, fo. 160v.

[114] [H. Parker], *The Contrareplicant* ([London, 1643]), p. 19; Adamson, 'Baronial context', pp. 100, 108, 111n; *CSPV 1642–3*, pp. 154, 276.

[115] Parker, 'An Elegie'.

[116] [H. Parker], *A Remonstrance to Vindicate His Excellencie* (London, 1643); Adamson, 'Peerage in politics', p. 381.

[117] *The Earle of Essex his Letter to Master Speaker* (Oxford, 1643), p. 3; *LJ* vi. 127; BL, Harl. 165, fos. 122–5; *Mercurius Aulicus* 28 (9–15 July 1643), p. 368; *CSPV 1642–3*, p. 297; *Mercurius Aulicus* 32 (6–12 Aug. 1643), p. 427; *CJ* iii. 144, 278; *LJ* vi. 127; *PHE* iii. 156–60; Rushworth, *Collections*, v. 290–91; *CSPV 1643–7*, p. 29; *HMC Hastings II*, p.105; [H. Parker], *The Oath of Pacification* (London, 1643), p. 2; Peacey, 'Henry Parker', pp. 92–3; Mendle, *Henry Parker*, pp. 121–3; Adamson, 'Baronial context', p. 111; Clarendon, *History*, vii. 138–43.

on the trustworthiness of the king, reflected the views of Marten, who had defended him in the House in August 1643, upon the discovery of a paper in which Saltmarsh 'speculated on what might be done to settle the kingdom if the king and his Parliament could not agree', and in which he had concluded that it might be necessary to 'root him out, and the royal line'. Marten's defence of Saltmarsh – in which he said that 'it were better one family should be destroyed than many' – resulted in his being ejected from the Commons.[118] Gratitude regarding Marten's assistance may have helped to motivate Saltmarsh's provocative and incriminating pamphlet, and the silencing of Marten may have prompted the two men to collude in order to find a means of expressing such views.

It was not only over peace that writers were willing to serve friends, allies and employers. Joshua Sprigge provides another example of an author who was close to Saye, and whose writings reflected Saye's Independent interests in the later 1640s. Sprigge's father was a long-serving steward to the Fiennes family, and contemporaries such as Clement Walker and Marchamont Nedham, who both understood the importance of this connection, mused that Sprigge's account of the civil wars in *Anglia Rediviva* (1647) reflected the political interests of the Fiennes family.[119] The reason for reaching such a conclusion was the attention which Sprigge paid to vindicating Saye's son, Nathaniel Fiennes, over his alleged culpability in the fall of Bristol to the royalists in 1643, which received greater attention even than the battle of Naseby.[120] Sprigge's willingness to reflect the political interest of the man with whom his family had such profound associations probably explains why Saye expressed a clear preference for his work over Thomas May's account of the wars.[121] Moreover, the possibility of contextualising authors in terms of representing the political interest of grandees such as Saye is also evident from the works of Marchamont Nedham and John Cook in the period 1646–47. Nedham, the former author of *Mercurius Britanicus*, had been imprisoned for his loose words in May 1646, but had quickly issued a petition to Lord Denbigh, who was able to effect his release, on condition that he should refrain from publishing anything without prior permission.[122] This Independent-led manoeuvre provides the context for understanding the appearance of Nedham's *Independencie No Schisme*; an attack upon two leading Presbyterian polemicists,

---

[118] [J. Saltmarsh], *A Peace But No Pacification* (London, 1643), pp. 4, 12; C. M. Williams, 'Extremist tactics in the Long Parliament, 1642–1643', *Historical Studies* 57 (1971), p. 149; *GCW* i. 202; *Mercurius Aulicus* 16 (16–22 Apr. 1643), p. 195; *Mercurius Aulicus* 33 (13–19 Aug. 1643), p. 452; BL, Harl. 165, fo. 180v. For Saltmarsh see: L. F. Solt, 'John Saltmarsh, New Model Army chaplain', *JEH* 2 (1951).

[119] C. Walker and W. Prynne, *A True and Full Relation* (London, 1644), p. 2; C. Walker, *Relations and Observations* ([London], 1648), p. 34; *Mercurius Pragmaticus* 19 (18–25 Jan. 1648), sig. T4v.

[120] J. Sprigge, *Anglia Rediviva* (London, 1647, reprinted Oxford, 1854), pp. 129–31.

[121] Fiennes, *Vindicaie Veritatis*, p. 109. Sprigge later married the widow of James Fiennes in 1673: J. L. Chester and G. J. Armitage, *Allegations for Marriage Licences* (Harleian Society, 23, 1886), p. 238; PRO, SP 9/26, fos. 139r–v.

[122] Warwicks. RO, CR 2017/C10/115; *LJ* viii. 341, 355; *HMC 4th Report*, p. 273.

John Vicars and Thomas Edwards.[123] It also serves to contextualise his tracts from the summer of 1647. In *The Case of the Kingdom Stated* (June 1647), Nedham expressed the views of those Independents who sought to re-open negotiations with the king, and demonstrated the logical superiority of the king reaching an agreement with the Independents, rather than with the Presbyterians.[124] Weeks later, Nedham replied to the Presbyterian propagandist, William Prynne, in a work which defended the army in the period leading up to the presentation of the 'heads of the proposals' for settlement with the king, and in early August 1647 he published *A Paralell of Governments*, which reinforced the message regarding the need for settlement, and which affirmed the superiority of monarchy to a republic realised by armed force.[125] Cook, meanwhile, who was employed as a lawyer by army grandees and leading Independents, developed similar themes in the summer of 1647, in *Redintegratio Amoris*, while *What the Independents Would Have*, published in September 1647, offered another timely promotion of the 'heads of the proposals'.[126]

Evidence which demonstrates the integration of writers within powerful patronage networks can be supplemented, therefore, by careful analysis of the timing of political tracts and pamphlets from the civil wars, which indicates that when grandees felt the need for polemical literature of a subtle and non-official nature, they turned to men with whom they were intimately familiar, and that authors defended the causes, interests and reputations of those grandees to whom they were connected, and by whom they were employed.

The process of decoding polemical and political literature of the civil war period requires, however, more than merely the contextualisation of authors, and scrutiny of the congruity of their message with the interests of political grandees. A third approach involves interpretation of the visual clues presented to readers, which may or may not assist in identifying the publishers and printers by whom such works were produced. This involves demonstrating the strong personal connections between individual printers and politicians; observing the way in which 'official' printers engaged in the production of 'non-official' literature; and using bibliographical techniques in order to establish how politicians worked surreptitiously in order to produce works which were ostensibly anonymous in terms of their print provenance.

---

[123] M. Nedham, *Independencie* (London, 1646).

[124] [M. Nedham], *The Case of the Kingdom Stated* (London, 1647).

[125] [M. Nedham], *The Lawyer of Lincolnes-Inn* ([London], 1647); [M. Nedham], *A Paralell of Governments* (London, 1647).

[126] J. Cook, *Redintegratio Amoris* (London, 1647); J. Cook, *What the Independents Would Have* (London, 1647). For Cook as lawyer: J. S. A. Adamson, 'The English nobility and the projected settlement of 1647', *HJ* 30 (1987), p. 589; Worcester College, Clarke XLI, fo. 65v; Chequers, MS 782, fo. 43. See also: J. Cook, *Vindication of the Professors and Profession of the Law* (London, 1646); J. Cook, *Unum Necessarium* (London, 1648).

Scholars have long been alive to the possibility that early modern politicians worked with printers in order to manipulate the presses, and that stationers can be connected to the households of individual public figures in the same way as writers, lawyers and administrators.[127] Since at least the late sixteenth century, therefore, individual grandees had favoured particular printing houses and publishers, who could be subsidised, and brought into employment, even within private households.[128] Episcopal leaders such as Bancroft and Parker used favoured printers to work in subtle ways, and William Laud was accused of having employed Richard Hodgkinson in order to produce works such as Peter Heylyn's *Moderate Answer* to Henry Burton.[129] The same phenomenon can clearly be found in later years, with connections evident between Viscount Saye and Richard Whitaker, and between Sir Henry Vane junior and both Gregory Dexter and Thomas Brewster.[130] A more important instance is provided by John Thomas, who appears to have worked closely with John Pym during the autumn of 1641.[131] Likewise, there is much to be learnt about commonwealth propaganda by studying the works produced by Thomas Newcomb.[132] In April 1660, meanwhile, the army grandee John Disbrowe revealed the special relationship which had developed between himself and Livewell Chapman, upon whom he relied to spread news,

---

[127] R. N. Kingdon, 'Patronage, piety and printing in sixteenth century Europe', in D. H. Pinkney and T. Ropp, eds, *A Festschrift for Frederick B. Artz* (Durham, NC, 1964), p. 21; J. N. King, 'John Day, master printer of the English revolution', in P. Marshall and A. Ryrie, eds, *The Beginnings of English Protestantism* (Cambridge, 2002), pp. 186–9; I. M. Green, *Print and Protestantism in Early Modern England* (Oxford, 2000), p. 20; M. Knights, *Politics and Opinion in Crisis, 1678–81* (Cambridge, 1994), p. 160.

[128] P. Blayney, 'William Cecil and the Stationers', in R. Myers and M. Harris, eds, *The Stationers' Company and the Book Trade, 1500–1900* (Winchester, 1997); Kingdon, 'Patronage, piety and printing'; D. B. Woodfield, *Surreptitious Printing in England, 1550–1640* (New York, 1973), pp. 24–33; Parmelee, 'Printers, patrons, readers and spies', pp. 858–60; B. T. Whitehead, *Brags and Boasts. Propaganda in the Year of the Armada* (Stroud, 1994), p. 141.

[129] G. Jenkins, 'The Archpriest controversy and the printers, 1601–1603', *The Library*, 5th series 2 (1947–48), pp. 180–86; J. Bruce and T. T. Perowne, eds, *The Correspondence of Matthew Parker* (Parker Society, Cambridge, 1853), pp. 411–12; S. Lambert, 'The Printers and the government, 1604–1637', in R. Myers and M. Harris, eds, *Aspects of Printing from 1600* (Oxford, 1987), p. 11; P. McCullough, 'Making dead men speak: Laudianism, print, and the works of Lancelot Andrewes, 1626–1642', *HJ* 41 (1998), pp. 405–8.

[130] V. Malvezzi, *Discourses Upon Cornelius Tacitus* (London, 1642), sig. A2; Adamson, 'Baronial context', p. 95; Mendle, '*De facto* freedom, *de facto* authority: press and Parliament, 1640–1643', *HJ* 38 (1995), p. 320; G. W. LaFantasie, ed., *The Correspondence of Roger Williams. Volume I, 1629–53* (London, 1988), p. 366; H. S[tubbe], *The Commonwealth of Israel* (London, for T. Brewster, 1659).

[131] S. Lambert, 'The beginning of printing for the House of Commons, 1640–42', *The Library*, 6th series 3 (1981), p. 53; *The Heads of Severall Petitions* (London, for Thomas, 1641); *The True Copy of a Letter Sent from Thomas, Earle of Arundel* (London, for Thomas, 1641); *The Discovery of a Late and Bloody Conspiracie* (London, for Thomas, 1641); *The Copy of a Letter Sent by the Lords and Commons* (London, for Thomas, 1641).

[132] J. Peacey, 'Cromwellian England: a propaganda state?' (forthcoming); S. Baron, 'Licensing readers, licensing authorities in seventeenth century England', in J. Andersen and E. Sauer, eds, *Books and Readers in Early Modern England* (Philadelphia, 2002), p. 228.

both verbally and in print, and to publish books such as *Plain English*.[133] Much less is known about the strength of the links between royalist grandees and those printers who more or less consistently reflected their interests, but who were not involved in printing official statements. During the first civil war, the Oxford press of Henry Hall produced a huge quantity of royalist literature, but his relationship with the leadership is hard to fathom, although he certainly complained in later life about never having been paid for the printing of *Mercurius Aulicus*.[134] After the fall of Oxford, the royalists relied upon support within London's publishing industry, and upon men such as Richard Royston, and although the latter was probably instructed to print the *Eikon Basilike* in late 1648, the extent of official involvement in his press is similarly unclear.[135] The same applies to the press operated by Samuel Browne in the Hague after 1649, which produced a range of royalist books, including some drawn from the works of Charles I, and others commemorating his martyrdom.[136] Browne also produced works which contained material which could only have come from royalist sources, and which were written by men intimately associated with the exiled court, such as the preachers William Stampe and Richard Watson, including sermons delivered before Charles II's exiled court.[137] A printer whose links with royalist grandees can be demonstrated, however, is William Dugard, who was induced to produce key pieces of propaganda during 1649. Dugard was responsible for producing the *Eikon Basilike*, and the fact that he was approached by Sir Edward Nicholas in April 1649 to print Ετρατοστηλιτευτικον, provides important contextual background for his other publishing ventures at this time, such as Salmasius' *Defensio Regia*, as well as *Apopthegmata Aurea Regia Carolina*, and George Bate's *Elenchus Motuum*.[138]

The advantage of developing such ties with individual stationers lay in the opportunity which they afforded for producing a variety of forms of political literature in a surreptitious fashion, and in ways which would have been less obvious to contemporaries than employing the presses of men known to have been in the pay of particular political authorities. In January 1646, for example, Robert Baillie complained that the Independents at Westminster sought to effect the

---

[133] *CSPD 1659–60*, pp. 409–11.

[134] Bodl. MS Ballard 49, fo. 250; Madan, *Oxford Books*, ii. passim.

[135] L. Potter, *Secret Rites and Secret Writing. Royalist Literature, 1641–1660* (Cambridge, 1989), pp. 7–12; F. F. Madan, *A New Bibliography of the Eikon Basilike* (Oxford Bibliographical Society Publications, new series 3, 1949), pp. 131, 153, 164. Royston liased with Edward Symmons.

[136] *Traytors Deciphered* (Hague, Samuel Brown, [1650]); *Reliquae Sacrae Carolinae* (Hague, Samuel Browne, 1650); *An Anniversary Ode upon the Kings Birthday* (Hague, for Samuel Browne, 1654); *To Xeiphos Ton Marytron* (Hague, by Samuel Brown, 1651); *Stipendariae Lacrymae* (Hague, for Samuel Browne, 1654).

[137] *A Letter from Sr Lewis Dyve to the Lord Marquis of Newcastle* (Hague, Browne, 1650); W. Stampe, *A Treatise of Spiritual Infatuation* (Hague, Browne, 1650). R. Watson, *Regicidium Judaicum* (Hague, Browne, 1649); H. Leslie, *The Martyrdome of King Charles* (Hague, Browne, 1649).

[138] *CSPD 1661–2*, p. 132; F. Madan, 'Milton, Salmasius and Dugard', *The Library* 4 (1923).

'underhand' printing of a 'libel of invectives' against the Scots.[139] During the 1640s, however, it was Baillie and his allies among the Scottish commissioners in London who proved particularly adept at forging ties with non-official printers in order to produce propaganda. One of their most important allies in the trade was Robert Bostock, whose proximity to the commissioners became evident under the scrutiny of the Scots' rivals at Westminster. When Bostock was questioned by a committee in November 1645 and April 1646, regarding the publication of the Scots' papers, he revealed that such books had been divided between different printing houses, to ensure both speedy completion and strict secrecy, and that before the papers were published he was summoned to meetings at St Paul's, where he was encouraged to 'make haste' and sworn to silence regarding the operation. Bostock, who revealed that such works had been written by David Buchanan and John Cheislie (secretary to the Scottish commissioners), sent the proofs to Buchanan before publication. Furthermore, in April 1646, he informed a parliamentary committee that on his way to his examination at Westminster that very day, 'he met Mr Baillie's man at Ludgate Hill, who told him the Scots commissioners sent for him to come to speak with them'. When he explained to the commissioners at Worcester House that he had been summoned to appear before a committee, they 'demanded of him how he would answer this business', to ensure that he would not incriminate them in the affair. Bostock went so far as to write a note to his wife to get their stories straight in case she too was examined by the committee.[140] Such evidence of political intrigue and secret assignations revealed the sophistication of the propaganda machine created by the Scots in the mid-1640s.[141]

It is not clear precisely how readers of civil war literature interpreted the evidence provided by the identity of such publishers, in seeking to understand the provenance of tracts and pamphlets. Moreover, bibliographical evidence which confronted and possibly confused readers also involved cases in which identifiably official printers and publishers produced works which were not apparently official in nature. Scholars have obviously been interested in such activity, in the hope of detecting official backing for works such as St German's *Doctor and Student*, but they have also shown awareness that this is an interpretative minefield, and that the presence of a particular printer's colophon need not necessarily enable a specific work to be traced back to authority.[142] On occasions, documentary

---

[139] *Letters and Journals of Robert Baillie*, ii. 344.

[140] Bodl. MS Nalson XIX, fo. 299; HLRO, MP 15/4/46; *CJ* iv. 348; *HMC 6th Report*, pp. 111–12; *Perfect Diurnall* 142 (13–20 Apr. 1646), pp. 1137–8; *Perfect Occurrences* 16 (17 Apr. 1646), sigs. Q2v, Q3v. As late as July 1646 Parliament was still seeking Buchanan: *CJ* iv. 628.

[141] For evidence of the Scots' printing press see: *The Moderate Intelligencer* 88 (5–12 Nov. 1646), sig. Ffff2.

[142] D. Hirst, 'That sober liberty: Marvell's Cromwell in 1654', in J. M. Wallace, ed., *The Golden and the Brazen World* (Berkeley, Ca, 1985), p. 18; R. Rex, 'The English campaign against Luther in the 1520s', *TRHS*, 5th series 39 (1989), p. 96; T. F. T. Plucknett and J. L. Barton, eds, *St German's*

evidence probably permits confident statements of official involvement in the supplementary work of a royal printer such as John Bill, and contextual evidence indicates that other publications received official sanction, such as the keynote sermon delivered by Thomas Morton at Durham in May 1639, which was published by the king's printer at Newcastle.[143] However, during the 1640s and 1650s, a number of printers and publishers who worked on official parliamentarian and commonwealth literature can be shown to have produced pamphlets of a more or less substantial nature. In the months prior to the outbreak of war in 1642, for example, Joseph Hunscott published news from Ireland and attacks upon Jesuits.[144] During the same year, John Frank was reponsible for the appearance of letters relating the campaign against the Irish rebels which probably came from official sources, or particular political grandees.[145] John Wright, meanwhile, was responsible for producing one of the leading parliamentarian newspapers, *Mercurius Civicus*.[146] During the summer of 1647, furthermore, the army's press at Oxford, under the guidance of John Harris and Henry Hills, produced a range of radical polemical pieces.[147]

Although some such works appear to have originated in official material, their provenance remains uncertain, and too little is known about the extent to which official printers were able to retain independent interests, and to operate private practices. Nevertheless, non-official works by official printers during the commonwealth often informed readers that their publishers, whether William Dugard, or the consortium of Henry Hills, Giles Calvert and Thomas Brewster, were 'printers to the Council of State'. Dugard's often bore the coat of arms of the commonwealth.[148] Later, Hills and John Field styled themselves 'printers to his

---

Doctor and Student (Selden Society, 91, 1974), p. xii; G. W. Bernard, 'Politics and government in Tudor England', *HJ* 31 (1988), p. 173; J. C. Warner, *Henry VIII's Divorce. Literature and the Politics of the Printing Press* (Woodbridge, 1998), chap. 4.

[143] *CSPD 1629–31*, pp. 271–2; PRO, SP 16/167, fo. 86. For Morton, see: J. Philipson, 'The king's printer in Newcastle-upon-Tyne in 1639', *The Library*, 6th series 11 (1989), pp. 1–9.

[144] *That Great Expedition for Ireland* (London, for Joseph Hunscott, 1642); W. Castle, *The Jesuit's Undermining of Parliaments and Protestants* (London, Hunscott, 1642).

[145] *Joyfull Newes from Ireland* (London, for Frank, 1642).

[146] H. R. Plomer, 'An analysis of the civil war newspaper *Mercurius Civicus*', *The Library*, new series 6 (1905).

[147] *The Life of H. H.* (London, 1688), p. 48; M. Mendle, 'Putney's pronouns: identity and indemnity in the great debate', in M. Mendle, ed., *The Putney Debates of 1647* (Cambridge, 2001), pp. 126–33; Peacey, 'Henry Parker', p. 244.

[148] *A Brief Narrative of the Great Victory* (London, by Dugard, by the appointment of the Council of State, 1650), with arms; *A Short Plea for the Commonwealth* (London, by Dugard, printer to the Council of State, 1651), with arms; *The King of Scotlands Negotiations* (London, by Dugard, 1650); *A True Confutation* (London, by Dugard, 1650); *The Troubles of Amsterdam* (London, by Dugard, printer to the Council of State, 1650), with arms; *Dominium Maris, or the Dominion of the Sea* (London, by William Du Gard, 1652); *True Relation of the Progress of the Parliamentary Force in Scotland* (London, by Dugard, by appointment of the Council of State, 1651); *A True Relation of the Last Great Fight at Sea* (London, by Calvert, Hills and Brewster, printers to the Council of State, 1653); *Severall Informations and Examinations* (London, by Hills, Calvert and Brewster, 1653). See also: L.

highness' on the title page of a 1657 reply to the Quaker, Richard Farnworth, which was also dedicated to Cromwell.[149] And when John Streater and John Macock printed letters written by various army officers in late 1659 and early 1660, they sometimes informed readers that they were 'printers to the Parliament'.[150] In the absence of such visual clues, however, establishing the provenance of works by such publishers is hampered by the fact that they retained independent publishing interests.[151] This may not have applied, however, to the leading parliamentary publisher of the 1640s, Edward Husband, who appears to have published little besides official work. Readers may always have assumed, therefore, that his more unusual, and apparently unofficial, pamphlets received official backing. These included items of news, probably from official sources, on which Husband sometimes informed readers that he was 'printer to the Honourable House of Commons'.[152] Nevertheless, his publication of *The Great Assizes Holden in Parnassus*, an exposé of parliamentarian newspapers, clearly confused contemporaries, who did not expect him to produce anything which did not obviously have official backing.[153]

In addition to these anonymous pamphlets, however, official publishers produced works by identifiable authors who can, moreover, be contextualised in ways which suggest the possibility of official involvement. These included Puritans who had suffered during the personal rule, such as Peter Smart, who was being rehabilitated by prominent grandees in the Long Parliament at the time that one of his books against Laudian innovations was published by Joseph Hunscott in 1642.[154] A work by another former sufferer, John Bastwick, who had been imprisoned with William Prynne and Henry Burton in 1637, was published by John Wright shortly after Bastwick was arrested by royalists, while employed in Parliament's service in putting the Militia Ordinance into execution.[155] Husband,

---

Rostenberg, 'Republican credo: William Dugard, pedagogue and political apostate', in *Literary, Scientific, Religious and Legal Publishing*, ii. 130–60.

[149] J. Stalham, *The Reviler Rebuked: Or, A Re-inforcement of the Charge Against the Quakers* (London, by H. Hills and J. Field, printers to his highness, 1657), sig. (a2).

[150] *A Letter Sent from Col. William Lockhart* (London, 1660); *A Letter Sent from Col. John Disbrowe* (London, 1659); *A Letter Sent from Ireland* (London, 1659); *A Letter from a Captain of the Army* (London, 1660); *A Letter Sent from General Monck* (London, 1660).

[151] It seems particularly clear that works produced by either one or two members of the consortium of Hills, Calvert and Brewster, were probably independent in origin: *A Faithfull Discovery of a Treacherous Design* (London by Hills for Brewster, 1653), sigs. A2–3; M. Cary, *The Resurrection of the Witnesses* (London, by Hills for Brewster, 1653), sig. A2; G. Wither, *The Modern States-man* (London, by Hills, 1654).

[152] *A Letter Written by Sir Richard Grenvile … Concerning the Affairs of the West* (London, 1646). Husband also published: *Verses on the Siege of Glocester* (London, 1644).

[153] *The Great Assizes Holden in Parnassus* (London, for Edward Husband, 1645); *Mercurius Britanicus* 70 (10–17 Feb. 1645), sigs. Bbbb3v–4. See also: *Perfect Passages* 17 (12–19 Feb. 1645), pp. 130–31; *Scotish Dove* 70 (14–21 Feb. 1645), p. 547.

[154] P. Smart, *A Catalogue of Superstitious Innovations* (London, Hunscott, 1642); Peacey, 'Henry Parker', pp. 29–30.

[155] J. Bastwick, *A Learned, Useful, and Seasonable Discourse* (London, 1643). Bastwick was arrested at York while working for Parliament in August 1642: *LJ* v. 282, 283.

meanwhile, published works by yet another sufferer, William Fenwick, which were dedicated to the Earl of Northumberland.[156] John Wright published a book by Lord Brooke's chaplain and literary assistant, John Sadler, as well as polemical works by the parliamentarian army chaplain, Robert Ram.[157] The reliability of Wright's name on tracts is undermined, however, by the fact that it was hijacked by the king's supporters. On one occasion, therefore, the royalist cleric, Thomas Swadlin, produced a doctored version of Ram's catechism for parliamentarian soldiers, apparently under Wright's imprint.[158] Husband meanwhile, published Daniel Evans's funeral elegy for his old employee, the Earl of Essex.[159] Later, the fact that Sir Thomas Fairfax's financial accounts reveal payments to Richard Whittington may support the suggestion that the latter was sanctioned to print *Preaching Without Ordination* by Lieutenant Edmund Chillenden, who was, moreover, involved in mobilising the army press and in organising its activity in Cambridge.[160] During the early period of the commonwealth, meanwhile, Husband and Dugard both published works by those members of Hartlib's circle who were in the employment of the republican civil service, and by other men close to the regime, including Thomas Violet and Hugh Peter.[161] Hartlib himself had a work published by Dugard in 1650, which was dedicated to the Council of State in thanks for the fact that he had 'found unexpectedly from your honours some peculiar expression of favour towards myself'.[162]

For royalists, on the other hand, it is possible to examine the work of provincial presses which came under Charles's power in the early 1640s. Evidence that the Cambridge press of Roger Daniel was co-opted for the production of official royalist literature during the second half of 1642, therefore, makes it possible to draw attention to other works for which he was responsible, such as Henry Ferne's *Resolving of Conscience*, and Lionel Gatford's *Harmonie of the Doctrine of the Reformed Churches*, both of which greatly perturbed Parliament.[163] Daniel's

---

[156] W. Fenwick, *An Exact Enquiry after Ancient Truths* (London, for Husband, 1643), sig. A2; W. Fenwick, *Zion's Rights* (London, for Husband, 1642), sig. A2.

[157] J. S[adler], *Malignancy Unmasked* (London, Wright, 1643); R. Ram, *Paedobaptisme* (London, for Wright, 1645); R. Ram, *A Sermon Preached at Balderton* (London, for Wright, 1646).

[158] Swadlin took the title, imprint, preface and questions from a book by Robert Ram, but changed the answers so that the parliamentarian soldier was made to look foolish. Not until the end of the work was the deceit acknowledged: Madan, *Oxford Books*, ii. 397. Wright complained to the House of Lords, leading to the arrest of Richard Royston, the printer most likely to have been responsible: *HMC 6th Report*, pp. 71, 74; HLRO, MP 31/7/45.

[159] D. Evans, *Justa Honoraria* (London, 1646).

[160] Worcester College, Clarke LXIX, fos. 19; Chillenden, *Preaching Without Ordination*; Peacey, 'Henry Parker', pp. 244–5.

[161] W. Potter, *The Tradesman's Jewel* (London, Husband and Field, 1650); B. Worsley, *The Advocate* (London, Dugard, 1652); Thomas Violet, *Mysteries and Secrets of Trade and Mint-Affairs* (London, Dugard, 1653; Hugh Peter, *Good Work for a Good Magistrate* (London, by Dugard, printer to the Council of State, 1651).

[162] S. Hartlib, *A Discours of Husbandrie* (London, by Du-Gard, 1650), sigs. A2r–v.

[163] H. Ferne, *Resolving of Conscience* (Cambridge, 1642); L. Gatford, *An Exhortation to Peace*

official duties for the king during this period may also enable recontextualisation of works by Sir Henry Spelman, Richard Watson and Thomas Fuller, all of whom were well connected in royalist circles.[164] More important is consideration of the work of the Oxford presses of Leonard Lichfield during the first civil war. These were clearly employed by the king and his ministers for official statements and speeches, but the degree to which their other activity was controlled is more often assumed than demonstrated. It is possible that many of the vast number of royalist sermons and tracts which appeared from Lichfield's press during the period from 1642 to 1646 were officially approved in some way, if not officially inspired. They were certainly written by prominent royalists such as Henry Ferne, Peter Heylyn, Joseph Hall and Brian Duppa.[165] Some bore the royal arms on their title pages.[166] Furthermore, Lichfield was reported to have been personally close to Charles and his inner circle.[167] However, there seems little way of proving beyond reasonable doubt that Lichfield did not operate with some degree of independence. He was consistently styled 'printer to the university of Oxford', rather than being credited as a royal printer, and his imprint was widely 'forged' by royalist sympathisers in London who sought to avoid the unwelcome attention of Parliament.[168]

In addition to observing the non-official printers with whom political grandees are known to have associated, and examining the works produced by official publishers, it is also possible to demonstrate how politicians used printers to operate much more secretively. Illicit presses and printers had been used by 'oppositional' figures since the mid-sixteenth century, in order to evade arrest and prosecution, not least by denuding works of the bibliographical clues by which printers could be identified, such as woodcut initials and colophons, as well as by employing common types and ornaments.[169] However, such methods could also be

---

(London, 1643), sigs. Av–A2; *CJ* ii. 900, 951; D. McKitterick, *A History of Cambridge University Press* (2 vols, Cambridge, 1992–98), i. 297, 299. Gatford claimed that copies of his work were seized from the press on 26 January 1643 by Oliver Cromwell and his troops.

[164] Sir H. Spelman, *A Protestants Account* (Cambridge, 1642); R. Watson, *A Sermon Touching Schism* (Cambridge, 1642); T. Fuller, *The Holy State* (Cambridge, 1642).

[165] H. Ferne, *Conscience Satisfied* (Oxford, by Lichfield, 1643); H. Ferne, *The Camp at Gilgal* (Oxford, 1643); H. Ferne, *A Reply unto Several Treatises* (Oxford, by Lichfield, 1643); P. Heylyn, *The Rebells Catechisme* (Oxford, by Lichfield, 1644); J. Hall, *The Lawfulnes and Unlawfulnes of an Oath or Covenant* (Oxford, by Lichfield, 1643); B. Duppa, *A Collection of Prayers* (Oxford, by Lichfield, 1643); D. Whitby, *The Vindication of a True Protestant* (Oxford, Lichfield, 1644).

[166] [F. Quarles], *A Plea for the King* (Oxford, for Lichfield, 1642).

[167] Cotton, 'London newsbooks', pp. 34–5.

[168] Madan, *Oxford Books*, ii. passim. See for example: E. Dobson, *XIV Articles of Treason* (Oxford, by Lichfield for Dobson, 1643). For Dobson, see: *CJ* iv. 22. See also: *Insigma Civicas* (Oxford, by Lichfield, 1643, E251/5), which Thomason recognised to be a forgery. See also: W. Prynne, *The Falsities and Forgeries* (London, 1644), which exposed the true printing location of *The Fallacies of Mr William Prynne* (Oxford [London], by Lichfield, 1644).

[169] C. L. Oastler, *John Day, the Elizabethan Printer* (Oxford Bibliographical Society Occasional Publications 10, 1975), pp. 9, 39–64; King, 'John Day, master printer', pp. 198–9. See: M. A. Shaaber, 'The meaning of the imprint in early printed books', *The Library*, new series 24 (1943), pp. 120–41.

adopted by those in positions of authority, in order to respond to critics in their own style, and to remove as much evidence as possible of official involvement.[170] Furthermore, attention to such bibliographical detail by scholars sometimes permits identification of publishers of works of uncertain provenance, and certainly seems to assist in identifying a group of works during the second half of 1642, probably produced by the presses of George Bishop and Robert White, which conveyed the ideas of a group of parliamentarians within Westminster. These anonymous tracts, which included works by Henry Parker, such as the famous *Observations*, as well as a string of less substantial works, can be contextualised in terms of the policies being pursued by those most zealous for reform and for the vigorous pursuit of the war effort, who could not necessarily command a majority at Westminster, and who appear to have recognised the need to express their message frequently and forcefully.[171] Charles I clearly believed that works such as the *Observations* were 'published by their direction, at least under their countenance'.[172]

Methodological problems notwithstanding, therefore, visual clues and bibliographical evidence can be shown to have been interpreted by contemporaries, and need to be examined by those who seek to understand the ways in which politicians involved themselves in the production of polemical literature. Tracts and their authors can fruitfully be contextualised, therefore, in the light of evidence of meaningful relationships between political grandees and particular stationers, whether of a personal or official nature, as well as evidence which indicates official donation of material to writers and printers, and which suggests that even anonymous works of obscure print provenance may have been orchestrated from within political circles in order to convey particular messages in an extremely subtle and inconspicuous way.

Having sought to demonstrate how civil war literature can be 'decoded' by means of bibliographical, contextual and visual evidence, a fourth approach involves the possibility of deducing official sanction and approval of polemical works through evidence that authors' efforts were subsequently rewarded, either by political patrons or public administrations. Such 'consequential' analysis is obviously fraught with danger, since it is difficult to establish with certainty *why* individuals received promotion and preferment. Nevertheless, it is pertinent to draw attention to examples of authors receiving positions and pensions after having published works for which those in a position to dispense patronage might have had cause to be grateful.[173] Although this does not necessarily indicate anything about the nature

---

[170] J. Black, 'The rhetoric of reaction: the Martin Marprelate tracts (1588–89), anti-Martinism, and the uses of print in early modern England', *Sixteenth Century Journal* 28 (1994), p. 712.

[171] M. Curtis, 'William Jones: Puritan printer and propagandist', *The Library*, 5th series 19 (1964); Peacey, 'Print detection and political propaganda'; Peacey, 'Henry Parker', appendix.

[172] *An Exact Collection of all Remonstrances* (London, 1643), p. 558.

[173] Rex, 'English campaign against Luther', p. 99; T. S. Nowak, 'Propaganda and the pulpit.

of a specific book, and the conditions of its appearance, such evidence nevertheless assists in the process of contextualising the careers of individual writers, and offers potentially revealing insights into the relationships between authors and politicians.

It is possible to analyse, firstly, contemporary perceptions. That rewards were considered as something which could be expected for literary services may be concluded from statements made by Henry Parker in the mid-1640s. Parker had certainly been paid for his services as one of the secretaries to Parliament during 1645, if not for his services as secretary to Essex and to the Committee of Safety, and so his comments about being 'driven' to leave the country for employment abroad by financial 'necessity', and his claim to have been 'disappointed … of divers hopeful preferments' and to have undergone the 'torture of Sisyphus' for seven years, implied that he expected rewards for his literary efforts.[174] In May 1648, the royalist author of *Mercurius Elencticus* alleged that the parliamentarian journalist and astrologer, William Lilly, sought to secure a reward from Parliament for the literary efforts of his assistant on *Mercurius Britanicus*, John Hall, and that he 'promised Bulstrode Whitelocke's assistance to procure … a weekly stipend from the rebels'.[175] Later, in March 1660, when Clement Spelman approached Sir Edward Hyde with an offer to write 'observations' upon 'all printed papers that came forth about the time of the king's death', he implied that the *quid pro quo* was his appointment as Clerk of the Pells under a restored Stuart monarch.[176] After that Restoration, a number of royalists sought reward for their literary efforts on behalf of the king during the wars. The civil lawyer, Sir Edmund Peirce, supported his petition for a place as Master of Requests by demonstrating that, despite his sufferings, he 'yet wrote and published, at much danger and expense, many things very serviceable to king and church'. Peirce listed twelve works which he had printed and published privately.[177] Similarly, George Wharton petitioned for a place as Gentleman Porter of the Tower of London, by saying that he had employed both pen and person in the royal cause, and that he had suffered imprisonment as a result.[178] Nathaniel Butter, meanwhile, petitioned for a place in Sutton Hospital by outlining his services as printer for the royal cause, for which he claimed to have risked his life.[179]

That the writing of books could be rewarded by members of the political elite

Robert Cecil, William Barlow and the Essex and Gunpowder plots', in K. Z. Keller and G. J. Schiffhorst, eds, *The Witness of Times* (Pittsburgh, 1992), p. 48; D. H. Willson, 'James I and his literary assistants', *HLQ* 8 (1944–45), p. 50.

[174] H. Parker, *Memoriall* ([London], 1647); [H. Parker], *Reformation in Courts* ([London, 1650]), p. 9.

[175] *Mercurius Elencticus* 27 (24–31 May 1648), p. 206.

[176] *TSP* vii. 870.

[177] *CSPD 1660–1*, pp. 11–12, 106; PRO, SP 29/1, fos. 192–3; SP 29/6, fos. 239–40.

[178] *CSPD 1660–1*, p. 104; PRO, SP 29/6, fo. 221. Wharton got power to control publications of almanacks: *CSPD 1660–1*, p. 274.

[179] *CSPD 1660–1*, p. 168.

had always been clear.[180] It was also commented upon in contemporary popular literature. In July 1649, for example, royalists alleged that Henry Parker's appointment as secretary to Cromwell's Council of War was a reward 'for his nonsense against Reverend Judge Jenkins', a reference to his pamphlet debate with the famous royalist controversialist two years earlier.[181] Sir Edward Hyde, having engaged his pen for the service of the king in the spring of 1642, recorded in his memoirs the occasion when he arrived in York, by noting that Charles spoke of 'the service he had done him, and of the great benefit he had received from it, even to the turning the hearts of the whole nation towards him again, and of his gracious resolution of rewarding him with the first opportunity'.[182] Parliament's decision to grant William Laud's library to Hugh Peter seems unlikely to have represented a reward for his services as an army chaplain, for which he was a salaried servant of Parliament, but probably reflected instead gratitude for his battlefield news reports.[183] In other cases it is yet more transparent that rewards were granted, or at least recommended, for literary services, as when Walter Strickland was ordered to help one John Gueul for displaying his affection to the parliamentarian cause in his writings.[184] In June 1652, meanwhile, it was reported that Charles II 'hath seen Joseph Jane's book, and you may assure him hath a singular good esteem of the work and of the workman, and will express it when he is able'.[185] Samuel Richardson's petition in May 1656, for payment for his service in a public place for three years without allowance, appears straightforward, given that he had earlier secured office on the committee regarding the Savoy and Ely House.[186] However, there is another context to Richardson's claims, in the shape of a letter from Major General William Goffe to John Thurloe in January 1656, which recommended assistance for Richardson in regard of the utility of one of his books.[187] Likewise, in June 1660, Dr George Morley wrote to Hyde in connection with the possible grant of a fellowship for John Doughty, as a reward for his earlier literary efforts.[188] Such comments were made in private, if official correspondence,

---

[180] *CSPD 1611–18*, pp. 417, 423, 432, 443, 474, 476, 479, 488, 526.

[181] *Mercurius Elencticus* 11 (2–9 July 1649), sig. L4v. Parker's appointment to the Prerogative Court of Canterbury in 1649 was noted in the press, but no connection was made with his writings: *The Kingdomes Weekly Intelligencer* 321 (17–24 July 1649), p. 1429; *The Moderate* 54 (17–24 July 1649), sig. Hhhv; Walker, *Anarchia Anglicana*, p. 199.

[182] Clarendon, *Life*, i. 146.

[183] *CJ* iii. 543–4. It is evident that such news reports could be rewarded from the payment of £40 to Gilbert Mabbott in August 1648 for bringing news of the surrender of Colchester: *CJ* v. 695.

[184] *CSPD 1645–7*, p. 165. Gueul appears to have been employed by Northumberland and/or the Dutch ambassador on admiralty matters in June 1641: *CSPD 1641–3*, pp. 10–11.

[185] Bodl. MS Clarendon 43, fo. 139v. What this meant is not clear, and Jane was clearly turned down for preferment within the exiled court in June 1654: Bodl. MS Clarendon 48, fo. 251.

[186] Aylmer, *State's Servants*, p. 122; *CSPD 1652–3*, p. 525; *CSPD 1653–4*, p. 40.

[187] *TSP* iv. 444–5. Richardson had written many works, including: *An Apology for the Present Government* (London, 1654), and *Plain Dealing* (London, 1656), and would write *Of the Torments of Hell* (London, 1657). Goffe was probably referring to *Plain Dealing*, written against Vavasor Powell.

[188] *CCSP* v. 41.

but on other occasions literary services were rewarded more openly. On 2 July 1649, therefore, the House of Commons, 'being informed of some good services lately done by Dr Ussher, Bishop of Armagh, and of an excellent piece written by him (and very large) now in the press (shortly to be published etc), it was ordered that the £400 a year formerly allowed him out of the revenue should be continued for six months'.[189]

Although it is possible on occasions to demonstrate overt connections between literary effort and politically inspired reward, whether financial or otherwise, it is also necessary to recognise that reticence about publicising such rewards meant that forms of recompense and demonstrations of gratitude could sometimes be more subtle. They could take the form of preferment as well as financial gifts, and it is thus important to observe the proximity of a book's appearance to an act of preferment, and to be aware of coded messages which hint at the reasons for rewards being made.[190] A number of authors who wrote controversial and inflammatory books, therefore, were appointed to clerical livings during the reign of Charles I. Richard Montague and Roger Mainwaring appear to have been rewarded for controversial sermons and tracts in the late 1620s with clerical appointments.[191] John Pocklington's appointment to a prebends place at Windsor in December 1639 may have represented a reward for his contributions to debates on altar policy and sabbatarianism in preceding years.[192] Likewise, William Chillingworth's literary efforts may have been rewarded with the appointment as Chancellor of Salisbury in 1638, and Peter Heylyn's clerical appointments in the early 1630s appear to have reflected his utility as a polemicist.[193] The same almost certainly applies to Henry Ferne's appointment as a royal chaplain in December 1643, after the publication of one of his key royalist texts.[194] Among parliamentarians, on the other hand, it is possible to draw attention to the appointment of John Dury as keeper of the library at St James' in October 1650, after the appearance of his contributions to the Engagement controversy.[195] It is also possible to consider the possibility that the appointment of John Sadler as

---

[189] *CJ* vi. 247; *Perfect Occurrences* 131 (29 June–6 July 1649), p. 1152.

[190] Slavin, 'Profitable studies', p. 319; D. T. Pottinger, *The French Book Trade in the Ancien Regime* (Cambridge, Ma., 1958), pp. 85–94.

[191] R. Cust, *The Forced Loan and English Politics, 1626–1628* (Oxford, 1987), pp. 62–3. Montague was made Bishop of Winchester, and Mainwaring was made rector of St Giles in the Fields: *CSPD 1628–9*, pp. 193, 196, 211, 217, 235.

[192] PRO, SO 3/12, unfol.; J. Pocklington, *Altare Christianum* (London, 1637); J. Pocklington, *Sunday No Sabbath* (London, 1636).

[193] Maizeaux, *William Chillingworth*, pp. 265–6; PRO, SO 3/10, unfol.; Vernon, *Heylyn*, p. 51; Milton, 'Creation of Laudianism', pp. 164, 171, 174.

[194] PRO, LC5/135, p. 12. Ferne's works were: *Resolving of Conscience; Conscience Satisfied* (Oxford, 1643); *A Reply unto Severall Treatises* (Oxford, 1643). After the Restoration, Ferne was further rewarded by being made master of Trinity College (1660), Dean of Ely (1661) and Bishop of Chester (1662): PRO, SO 3/13, unfol., SO 3/14, unfol., SO 3/15, p. 4.

[195] *CSPD 1650*, pp. 401, 403.

town clerk of London, and as Master of Magdalene College, Cambridge, not to mention Cromwell's offer to make him Chief Justice of Munster, reflected gratitude for his defence of the commonwealth in *Rights of the Kingdom*, published in June 1649.[196] George Wither's appointment as clerk of the recognizances in November 1655 followed shortly after the publication of poetical works honouring Cromwell.[197] Finally, William Sheppard's legal writings during the protectorate may have encouraged his appointment as Sergeant at Law at the end of October 1656, and may also help explain why, when he 'retired' as a special lawyer for the Council in 1657, he was awarded £3,000, and recommended for a pension of £100.[198]

In other cases, it is necessary to consider that services with the pen and the printing press provided the justification for 'extraordinary' rewards. Many payments made by the parliamentarian administration during the civil wars, therefore, were for unspecified 'services'. William Dell received extraordinary payments from John Rushworth in November 1646, 'for good service in the army', and in August 1648 Rushworth was himself awarded £50 'for good service'.[199] Payments for 'good service' or 'public service' made to authors such as Henry Parker and Payne Fisher may also have related to their literary activities, rather than to their formal duties as secretaries and chaplains.[200] This probably represented, indeed, a way of accounting for money which had been used for a range of activities which it was thought necessary not to specify, whether in terms of intelligence, espionage and 'secret service', or in terms of propaganda. Likewise, when the royalist journalist, Sir John Berkenhead, was appointed as reader in moral philosophy at Oxford in April 1643, he was commended for his 'discretion and abilities', and his many 'acceptable services'.[201] At times, however, such coded statements are less cryptic. When the royalist cleric, Robert Mossom, was promoted to the deanery of Christchurch, Dublin, the citation mentioned his 'piety, learning and integrity'.[202] This is also apparent from the support offered by the Earl of Essex to his secretary, and propagandist, Henry Parker, in the autumn of 1643. Parker, who sought appointment as registrar of the Prerogative Court of

---

[196] *CJ* vi. 183; CLRO, JOR 41X, fos. 1v, 2v; PRO, SP 28/255, unfol., SP 28/258i, fos. 198, 220v, 406; SP 28/259, fo. 339v; PRO, E 101/67/11b, m. 7; W. Kennett, *A Register and Chronicle* (London, 1728), p. 222; Abbott, *Cromwell*, ii. 186–7; 'John Sadler' (History of Parliament biography).

[197] PRO, C 66/2914/38; *CSPD 1655–6*, p. 149; G. Wither, *The Protector* (London, 1655); *Vaticinium Causuale, A Rapture Occasioned by the Late Miraculous Deliverance of his Highnesse the Lord Protector* (London, 1655 [actually 1654]); C. S. Hensley, *The Later Career of George Wither* (Hague, 1969); D. Norbrook, 'Safest in storms: George Wither in the 1650s', in D. Margolis and M. Joannou, eds, *Heart of the Heartless World* (London, 1995), pp. 19–32.

[198] Matthews, *William Sheppard*, pp. 59, 62–3, 68.

[199] PRO, SP 28/140/2, fo. 51; *CJ* v. 695. Rushworth's job involved organising propaganda, and paying printers: PRO, SP 28/140/2, fo. 52.

[200] PRO, SP 28/264, fo. 62; *CSPD 1651–2*, p. 591.

[201] Thomas, *Sir John Berkenhead*, pp. 33–4.

[202] BL, Eg. 2542, fo. 438.

Canterbury, wrote of his 'extraordinary offices ... to the whole state, which have not been altogether unacceptable, and which I hope, were in part pointed in the Houses' order', and Essex's letter offered 'a good testimony of his faithful and acceptable service to the state, and to myself, ever since the first forming of the army; and his parts and abilities, I presume, are not unknown to the House'. In another letter a year later, Essex affirmed that Parker had been 'active and passive in this cause, and though he be made obnoxious to the other side by his service to the Committee of Safety and myself, and by his ingenious endeavours otherwise, yet he hath hitherto received no satisfaction at all, either as gratuitous, or as due'. When the diarist, Sir Simonds D'Ewes, recorded the presentation of Parker's petition, he noted that Parker had written many scandalous pamphlets, and he implied that he considered that such a grant would effectively represent a reward for his polemical services.[203]

The process of identifying civil war propaganda must begin with a decoding methodology which explores biographical evidence of connections between authors and political grandees, whether grounded in kinship, friendship or employment, and which contextualises the work of such authors in terms of message, timing and the reason for publication. This contextual approach must also involve decoding more or less explicit bibliographical clues relating to the printers and publishers who were responsible for particular works, as well as evidence which indicates that political grandees were prepared to reward literary endeavour in a more or less overt fashion. Being an imprecise science, 'decoding' offers something less than direct evidence of official involvement in the production of polemical literature during this period. Demonstrating that a particular author was well-connected, and that he was employed within political and adminstrative structures at the time of publication, demonstrates nothing automatically about the provenance of particular works. Demonstrating congruity between specific books and the views of political grandees need not imply the involvement of the latter in the appearance of the former, even when publication of tracts and pamphlets appears to have been carefully timed. There are also many reasons for doubting whether appearance under the imprint of stationers who were favoured, or even employed, by public figures, indicates official sanction, as well as for being careful about concluding that clerical and administrative preferment and promotion, and even financial gifts, reflected a desire to reward authors for their efforts. Nevertheless, such contextual devices need always to be considered by readers of civil war literature, and can sometimes prove fruitful, particularly when deployed in combination. The pamphleteering of royalist authors such as Peter Heylyn and Henry Ferne, but more particularly parliamentarians such as

---

[203] Parker, *Memoriall*; BL, Add. 18779, fo. 6; *CJ* iii. 687–8; BL, Harl. 165, fo. 210v. Essex must have known about Parker's tract writing, and owned copies of his books: V. Snow, 'An inventory of the Lord General's library, 1646', *The Library*, 5th series 21 (1966).

John Sadler and Henry Parker, can be contextualised thoroughly by recognising their personal connections with political grandees, their employment at the time of their writing and publishing, the sympathy between their message and the views of their patrons and employers, the involvement of favoured and official printers in the publication of their works, and the evidence that they were considered worthy of some form of recompense for their efforts.

Such analysis reveals a number of important conclusions about the way in which polemical literature was produced, and some apparent differences between parliamentarians and royalists. It is clear that, as might be expected, a great many civil war authors emerged from patronage networks which incorporated key public figures, and that they can be shown to have benefited from, and worked for, a variety of grandees. Royalists and parliamentarians alike can be shown to have had contacts with aristocratic and gentry patrons and households, but while this remained true of those who engaged for the king in the 1640s and 1650s, it became increasingly common for parliamentarian authors, even those who had connections with aristocratic and gentry grandees, to be employed within the civil service and the military. It is also evident that, while parliamentarians and royalists alike sought to exploit the services of printers in order to publish non-official polemical literature, the parliamentarians tended to be more open about the fact that some such printers and publishers were official employees. Although this became more obvious after 1649, when a settled regime felt more at ease about such public affirmations regarding such individuals, as the crown had to some extent been before 1642, it is nevertheless evident that parliamentarians had begun to adopt this practice long before the establishment of the commonwealth. Thirdly, while parliamentarians and royalists both recognised the need to reward polemicists for their unpaid literary efforts, and while all sides made grants of offices, whether clerical or administrative, when and as they had such positions at their disposal, parliamentarian grandees appear to have been more willing to reward authors with sinecures, and even financial grants. Such conclusions attest to the fact that parliamentarian propaganda was, to a far greater extent than that produced by royalists, increasingly professional in nature. The extent to which this conclusion can be substantiated will become clear in the chapters that follow.

CHAPTER 4

Licensing and Propaganda

The bedrock of political involvement in the press in the 1640s and 1650s was the system of licensing, by which books were required to secure the approval of some publicly appointed authority – whether clerical, legal or political – at manuscript stage. This was a fundamental necessity for preventing the appearance of seditious and scandalous literature, and represented a form of pre-publication censorship. However, licensing represented an attempt to exert positive as well as negative influence on the press. Press censorship was intimately associated with political propaganda, and an exploration of licensing practices provides a way of demonstrating that the two were part of the same process. Although largely constrained by the nature of the surviving evidence to analysis of parliamentarian rather than royalist licensing, it is nevertheless possible to indicate general trends common to both sides in the civil wars. These concern the ways in which content could be altered by licensers, by adding and removing key passages, and the ways in which systematic bias could be used in the selection of works to be approved. They also concern the way in which authorities worked with grandees of the publishing industry, in the form of the Stationers' Company; the extent to which contemporaries were made aware of the approved status of individual books and pamphlets; and the ways in which the licensing process became factionalised in the 1640s. Exploration of press licensing serves, therefore, as a means of shedding light upon important themes with which this book is concerned. It demonstrates the extent to which propaganda was a priority for politicians during the civil wars and Interregnum; the means by which such propaganda could be organised; and the strengths and weaknesses of such mechanisms. More importantly, scrutiny of the way in which licensing worked and developed during this period serves to draw attention to the dynamic nature of propaganda, and the way in which it was transformed by political developments at Westminster and Oxford, not least the factionalism which bedevilled both Parliament and the royalist court. The systems established to enforce press control and exploit propaganda mirror political developments, and they reflect the very nature of governmental authority during the course of the upheavals.

Press 'licensing' was integral to a public–private partnership which existed in the world of publishing in early modern Britain, a partnership based upon an interest in opposing unfettered 'liberty of the press' which was shared by those who governed the company of stationers and those who governed the country.[1] The entry of 'licensed' books into the Stationers' register served as a means of enforcing copyright and of protecting publishers (rather than authors), by securing them against interlopers. In addition, the licensing of publications prior to their appearance was a fundamental part of the process of controlling and censoring the press. The act of granting or refusing a 'licence' to a particular work was a means of ensuring pre-publication censorship, and in the period before 1640 the system of licensing was introduced, reformed and strengthened at moments when governing authorities felt most need to suppress scandalous literature, and when the Stationers felt most threatened by counterfeiters. Much of the framework for the licensing of printed books was designed, not alongside the introduction of printing into England, but in order to regulate an industry which boomed, and threatened to get out of control, during periods of controversy.

The first royal declaration on censorship dated from 1538, and it was followed by a string of proclamations against seditious pamphlets. Such measures reveal the nature of the partnership which existed between the Stationers' Company and the government, in order to enforce press control, record which books had been licensed, and search for seditious literature. It also reveals the way in which governments 'out-sourced' the job of reading manuscripts and granting licences. Ordinances in 1559 and 1566 granted such powers to the Stationers' Company, members of the Privy Council, the archbishops and the university chancellors, in addition to which the government employed a roster of searchers to hunt for illicit works. In the wake of the Catholic threat in the 1580s, moreover, new measures were implemented, and trials for printing libels began to take place. It was the Star Chamber decree of 1586, however, which represented the first rigorous attempt at censorship, restricting printing to certain towns and stationers, and imposing a system of licensers centred upon the prelatical authorities.[2] Other clampdowns

---

[1] S. Lambert, 'State control of the press in theory and practice: the role of the Stationers' Company before 1640', in R. Myers and M. Harris, eds, *Censorship and the Control of Print in England and France 1600–1900* (Winchester, 1992). For the internal politics of the Stationers' Company during this period, see: C. Blagden, *The Stationers Company* (London, 1960), pp. 130–52; C. Blagden, 'The Stationers' Company in the civil war period', *The Library*, 5th series 13 (1958).

[2] H. W. Winger, 'Regulations relating to the book trade in London from 1357–1586' (Illinois University PhD, 1953); E. Arber, *A Transcript of the Registers of the Company of Stationers of London 1554–1640* (4 vols, London, 1877), iv. 528–36; W. W. Greg, *A Companion to Arber* (Oxford, 1967); F. S. Siebert, *Freedom of the Press in England 1476–1776* (Urbana, 1965), pp. 88–104; P. Sheavyn, *The Literary Profession in the Elizabethan Age* (Manchester, 1967), pp. 39–63; H. S. Bennett, *English Books and Readers 1603 to 1640* (Cambridge, 1970), pp. 40–58; W. M. Clyde, *The Struggle for the Freedom of the Press* (St Andrews, 1934), pp. 1–20; D. Loades, 'The theory and practice of censorship in sixteenth century England', in *Politics, Censorship and the English Reformation* (London, 1991); D. Loades, 'The press under the early Tudors', *Transactions of the Cambridge Bibliographical Society* 4 (1964); D. Loades, 'Illicit presses and clandestine printing in England, 1520–1590', in A. C. Duke and C. A. Tamse, eds, *Too Mighty to be Free. Censorship and the Press in Britain and the Netherlands* (Zutphen, 1987); P. M. Took, 'Government and the printing trade, 1540–1560' (London University PhD, 1979), pp. 1–86; A. W. Pollard, 'The regulation of the book trade in the sixteenth century', *The Library*, 3rd series 7 (1916); R. Dutton, *Mastering the Revels. The Regulation and Censorship of English Renaissance Drama* (Iowa City, 1990).

followed, however, once it became clear that the licensing system could be circumvented by altering works between examination and publication.[3] Later, William Laud tightened the system after succeeding to the archbishopric of Canterbury in 1633, in an attempt to secure greater control of presses which had been fuelling disputes over the direction in which the church was being pushed. He arguably did little to alter the fundamental methods by which licensing and press control were enforced, although new licensers were appointed from among the episcopal chaplains and university professors. Sir John Lambe, meanwhile, was appointed to prepare another Star Chamber press decree in 1637, in accordance with the wishes of the Stationers' Company. Before 1640, the partnership between the government and the industry remained intact.[4]

In order to understand the significance of licensing, however, it is necessary to recognise that mechanisms which enabled control over the press, and the suppression of scandalous literature, also enabled the approval of works which were deemed worthy. The ability to exert a positive impact on the press was profoundly important, not least given the difficulty of enforcing censorship, and it is important to understand how such power was employed.[5] The power to suppress undesirable books meant, of course, that *failure* to suppress works was a form of official support and sanction, and it also enabled the granting of publishing monopolies.[6] More significantly, licensing powers enabled public authorities to

---

[3] *CSPD 1598–1601*, pp. 450–51; E. Kuhl, 'The Stationers' Company and censorship, 1599–1601', *The Library*, 4th series 9 (1929), pp. 388–94.

[4] F. B. Williams, 'The Laudian imprimatur', *The Library*, 5th series 15 (1960); W. W. Greg, *Licensers for the Press, &c to 1640* (Oxford, 1962); *CSPD 1637*, p. 476; PRO, SP 16/369, fos. 226–7; *CSPD 1635–6*, pp. 39, 75; *CSPD 1636–7*, p. 266; *CSPD 1637*, pp. 344, 573; Clyde, *Struggle*, pp. 40–43; *CSPD 1640*, p. 352; S. Lambert, 'The printers and the government, 1604–1637', in R. Myers and M. Harris, eds, *Aspects of Printing from 1600* (Oxford, 1987); *The Court and Times of Charles the First* (2 vols, London, 1848), ii. 186, 188; H. R. Plomer, 'Some petitions for appointment as master printers called forth by the Star Chamber decree of 1637', *The Library*, 3rd series 10 (1919); *CSPD 1625–49*, pp. 567–8. See: B. Worden, 'Literature and political censorship', in Duke and Tamse, eds, *Too Mighty to be Free*; A. B. Thompson, 'Licensing the press: the career of G. R. Weckherlin during the personal rule of Charles I', *HJ* 41 (1998); S. A. Baron, 'Licensing readers, licensing authorities in seventeenth century England', in J. Andersen and E. Sauer, eds, *Books and Readers in Early Modern England* (Philadephia, 2002).

[5] P. McCullough, 'Making dead men speak: Laudianism, print, and the works of Lancelot Andrewes, 1626–1642', *HJ* 41 (1998), p. 423; J. Klaits, *Printed Propaganda Under Louis XIV* (Princeton, 1976), p. 7; F. J. Levy, 'Staging the news', in A. F. Marotti and M. D. Bristol, eds, *Print, Manuscript and Performance* (Columbus, 2000), pp. 272–3.

[6] T. Edwards, *Gangraena* (London, 1646), ii. 155, 185; Nalson, *Impartial Collection*, i. 795. Monopolies were granted for publication of the psalms, newspapers, and biblical annotations: *CSPD 1629–31*, pp. 514, 557; PRO, SP 16/185, fo. 42; *CSPD 1631–3*, p. 294; *CSPD 1633–4*, p. 222; *CSPD 1638–9*, p. 182; PRO, SO 3/12, fo. 8v; PRO, SO 1/3, fo. 110; Greg, *Companion to Arber*, p. 62; L. Hanson, 'English newsbooks, 1620–41', *The Library*, 4th series 18 (1938); L. Rostenberg, 'Nathaniel Butter and Nicholas Bourne, first Masters of the Staple', *The Library*, 5th series 12 (1957); *CSPD 1638–9*, p. 182; A. Hunt, 'Book trade patents, 1603–1640', in A. Hunt, G. Mandelbrote, and A. Shell, eds, *The Book Trade and its Customers 1450–1900* (Winchester, 1997); C. S. Clegg, *Press Censorship in Elizabethan England* (Cambridge, 1997), pp. 6–13; I. M. Green, *Print and Protestantism in Early Modern England* (Oxford, 2000), p. 15.

exert a positive influence over the press by means of biased approval of new books. Thus, while recent scholarship has sought to deny the existence of a rigorous system of press censorship during the early seventeenth century, or an intention to suppress all criticism, it is necessary to analyse possible proscription of certain forms of religious literature alongside scrutiny of patterns of press licensing. Only in this way is it possible to assess the extent to which the presses were closed to Calvinist authors at the same time as they were opened to Arminians. While it is advisable to strip away a 300-year layer of propaganda regarding the nature of press control under the early Stuarts, which survives through the work of men such as William Prynne, it is also necessary to treat cautiously the rhetoric employed by William Laud.[7] If Prynne exaggerated the extent of both religious innovation and press restraint, then Laud may be guilty of overplaying his moderation. Calvinist books were not outlawed entirely during the 1620s and 1630s, but it is crucial to examine the trials of authors such as Prynne, and the way in which the fear of repression prompted authors to print their works abroad.[8] It is also essential to recognise that Laud's licensers began to approve books of an extremely controversial nature, including works by Peter Heylyn, Richard Montague, Christopher Dow and John Pocklington, and a book by Richard Sibthorpe which had been rejected by Archbishop Abbot.[9] Whatever the patterns of censorship, there appears to have been a clear bias in the texts which received official approval.[10]

In addition to such bias, it is necessary to recognise the extent to which an instrinsic part of the licensing process involved detailed comment and revision of the substance of individual books.[11] This could be a consensual process, and correspondence survives between Joseph Hall (Bishop of Exeter) and Thomas Turner, one of the licensers employed by William Laud (as Bishop of London), regarding Hall's *Reconciler* (1629), which suggests that Hall was happy to consent to the removal of certain passages regarding Arminianism.[12] The same seems to emerge from Roger Widdrington's correspondence with another licenser, William

---

[7] P. White, *Predestination, Policy, and Polemic* (Cambridge, 1992), pp. 287–99; Lambert, 'Printers and the government'; S. Lambert, 'State control of the press'; S. Lambert, 'Richard Montague, Arminianism, and censorship', *P&P* 124 (1989); C. S. Clegg, *Press Censorship in Jacobean England* (Cambridge, 2001).

[8] S. Foster, *Notes from the Caroline Underground* (Hamden, Ct, 1978); K. L. Sprunger, *Trumpets from the Tower. English Puritan Printing in the Netherlands, 1600–1640* (Leiden, 1994); A. Milton, 'The Laudians and the Church of Rome, c.1625–1640' (Cambridge University PhD, 1989), pp. 128, 142.

[9] Arber, *Transcript*, iv. 321, 324, 329, 335, 348, 358, 359, 360, 362; P. Heylyn, *Cyprianus Anglicus* (London, 1671), p. 159; P. A. Welsby, *George Abbot. The Unwanted Bishop, 1562–1633* (London, 1962), pp. 126–8.

[10] A. Milton, 'Licensing, censorship and religious orthodoxy in early Stuart England', *HJ* 41 (1998).

[11] Clegg, *Press Censorship in Elizabethan England*, pp. 138–69.

[12] *CSPD 1628–9*, p. 484; PRO, SP 16/136, fos. 139–40. For Turner: Greg, *Licensers*, p. 91.

Haywood, in 1634, regarding his answer to the Jesuit, Edward Courtenay.[13] However, such power over the substance of texts could clearly be used in controversial ways, in order to introduce or remove sensitive religious and political passages. Laud instructed his licensers to excise passages which referred to the Pope as Antichrist, and Puritans became highly critical of the insertions and cuts relating to Catholicism made by his officials, and the brutal treatment of texts by godly authors.[14] Plentiful examples survive of the detailed alterations made to specific texts, and some would prove to be politically explosive in the early 1640s.[15]

It is the perceptions of the 'godly' regarding the Laudian press which are crucial to an understanding of the policies and actions of the Long Parliament.[16] Parliamentary reformers were derided by contemporary opponents for having brought about press freedom in 1641, and royalists frequently argued that the licensing system was taken away deliberately; that their opponents tolerated the appearance of seditious literature; and that 'some of the members of the House of Commons were heard to say the work would not be done without them'.[17] Robert Atkyns, writing the history of printing in England in 1664, suggested that one of the undesirable effects of Parliament's policies in 1640 and 1641 was liberty of the press.[18] Such comments have helped to ensure the persistence of confusion and misunderstanding regarding the extent to which the press became 'free' as a result of the deconstruction of the Caroline government in the 1640s. Despite Atkyns' recognition that, eventually, Parliament 'totally possesst the press', subsequent historians have arguably paid more attention to the very obvious removal of the means by which the press was controlled, and the explosion in political and religious pamphlets which resulted, than to the ways in which Parliament subsequently exerted influence over the press.[19]

Those who gathered at Westminster in October 1640, and who were intent to seek redress for grievances, clearly sought to take action regarding the press. Within a week of the opening of the Long Parliament the Commons displayed

[13] *CCSP* i. 67; Bodl. MS Clarendon 7, fos. 45–7v; *Clarendon State Papers*, i. 303, 305; W. Howard (pseud. Roger Widdrington), *A Pattern of Christian Loyaltie* (London, 1634).

[14] Heylyn, *Cyprianus*, pp. 392–3; *CSPD 1636–7*, p. 251; *CSPD 1625–49*, p. 758; PRO, SP 16/540iv, fos. 200–203v; N. W. Bawcutt, 'A crisis of Laudian censorship: Nicholas and John Okes and the publication of Sales's *An Introduction to a Devout Life* in 1637', *The Library*, 7th series 1 (2000).

[15] *CSPD 1634–5*, p. 412; PRO, SP 16/280, fos. 107–8v; *CSPD 1625–49*, p. 758; PRO, SP 16/540iv, fos. 200–203v.

[16] See: M. Mendle, 'Grub Street and Parliament at the beginning of the English revolution', in J. D. Popkin, ed., *Media and Revolution* (Lexington, 1995); M. Mendle, 'De facto freedom, de facto authority: press and parliament 1640–1643', *HJ* 38 (1995).

[17] Nalson, *Impartial Collection*, ii. 660, 806–9; *King Charles the First, No Man of Blood But a Martyr for his People* (London, 1649), p. 4.

[18] R. Atkyns, *Original and Growth of Printing* (London, 1664), sig. B2.

[19] Atkyns, *Original and Growth of Printing*, sig. B2. However, see: Mendle, 'De facto freedom'; K. Lindley, 'London and popular freedom in the 1640s', in R. C. Richardson and G. M. Ridden, eds, *Freedom and the English Revolution* (Manchester, 1986), pp. 112–13.

their resolve to investigate the printing industry, and the attack upon Laud's system saw the appointment of committees to investigate printing.[20] That Parliament abolished the High Commission and Star Chamber, and presided over an unprecedented explosion in political and religious literature, has led some commentators to conclude that the reformers 'had determined that the press should henceforth be free'.[21] However, closer examination of the actions and motivations of the reformers in the Long Parliament reveals opposition not to the use of licensing as a means of controlling the press, but rather to the way in which it had been used by Laud. The impression that the Long Parliament favoured a free press is erroneous, and it is important to distinguish between attacks made upon the system employed by Laud and Charles, and opposition to press restraint *per se*. The early 1640s witnessed a campaign against Laud's press, the release from prison of its victims, and the impeachment of Laud, Lambe and the licensers, but the grounds for so doing involved the *substance* rather than the *form* of Laud's control.[22] What prompted reform was the appearance of undesirable books, and the suppression of those which were thought valuable.[23] Licensers like Bray were forced to make public recantation for their role in approving works such as Pocklington's *Altare Christianum* and *Sunday No Sabbath*, while the charges levelled against Laud centred upon the way in which licensing had been exploited, rather than the fact that it had been exploited.[24] The Laudian system was opposed because it had authorised popish tenets and seditious opinions, rather than because it had been used in a biased and political way. Pym derided Laud's employment of chaplains 'notoriously disaffected to the form of religion' and bemoaned their licensing power, 'by which means divers false and superstitious books have been published, to the great scandal of religion, and to the seducing of many of his Majesties subjects'. Sir Edward Dering compared Laud's *imprimatur* to the *Index Expurgatorius*: 'so handled, that truth is suppressed, and Popish pamphlets fly abroad, *cum privilegio*'.[25] An anonymous set of notes from the early months of the Long Parliament, meanwhile, commented that the power of the bishops in the realm of licensing might prove 'a good means in a short time to introduce whatsoever religion they please'.[26] Events would soon demonstrate that, rather than seeking to introduce a free press, Parliament sought to seize the power to introduce 'whatsoever religion' they themselves pleased.

[20] *CJ* ii. 26, 29, 84, 108, 139, 167, 198; BL, Add. 42081, fo. 44; BL, Add. 36913, fo. 53; *CSPD 1640–1*, p. 455; Rushworth, *Collections*, iii. 1148; *LJ* iv. 138, 140, 160–61, 168.

[21] Clyde, *Struggle*, pp. 48–54; D. Friest, 'The formation of opinion and the communication network in London 1637–1645' (Cambridge University PhD, 1992), pp. 34–70.

[22] *CSPD 1640–1*, p. 479.

[23] *CJ* ii. 26, 79. See also: H. F. Snapp, 'The impeachment of Roger Maynwaring', *HLQ* 30 (1967).

[24] *HMC 4th Report*, p. 57; Rushworth, *Collections*, iv. 188, 207; *LJ* iv. 140, 160–61, 168, 180, 183, 208, 219; *CSPD 1641–3*, p. 553; PRO, SP 16/499, fos. 260–64v; *LJ* vi. 468–9. For Laud's trial, see *HMC House of Lords XI*, pp. 368–70, 427–8, 432–8, 440, 442.

[25] Rushworth, *Collections*, iii. 1366–7; Rushworth, *Collections*, iv. 55; *CSPD 1640–1*, pp. 333–4.

[26] PRO, SP 16/474, fo. 29.

The reformers in the Long Parliament were opposed to the substance rather than the form of licensing, and having overturned the administration of the personal rule in the opening months of the 1640s, and having swept away the props upon which the Laudian system rested, they soon displayed determination to reclaim power over the press, which had been lost as a result of their iconoclasm. They attempted almost immediately to reimpose strict controls on what could be printed, and to employ traditional methods.[27] In addition to the vendetta against the books of the 1630s with which they were in disagreement, Parliament began to persecute contemporary works appearing without licence, and to reimpose control over the presses, and eventually over royalist propaganda. There was a determination to make an example of malefactors, 'for a terror to the rest', and public book-burnings, undertaken symbolically by the hangman, were soon common occurrences in London.[28] Moreover, the community of interests between the Stationers and the authorities persisted, and Parliament continued to work closely with the company.[29] Petitions from within the industry for 'regulating their mystery' were gratefully received, and helped justify planned legislation in late 1641 and early 1642. The Stationers were also encouraged to tighten the procedures by which they recorded the names of those who brought books to be licensed.[30] Parliament was moved to press for renewed control in order to address the unauthorised printing of official documents and parliamentary speeches, while the Stationers and a group of well-connected Puritan ministers expressed their concern to protect copyright, and the interests of both writers and printers.[31]

Furthermore, press control under the Long Parliament continued to involve more than merely the suppression of scandalous books and unauthorised editions, as part of a public–private partnership with the Stationers' Company. Parliament quickly

[27] W. M. Clyde, 'Parliament and the press, 1643–7', *The Library*, 4th series 13 (1933); W. M. Clyde, 'Parliament and the press II', *The Library*, 4th series 14 (1933); Mendle, 'De facto freedom', pp. 307–32.

[28] Nalson, *Impartial Collection*, ii. 660, 723; *CJ* ii. 146, 148, 159, 166, 168, 190, 205, 221, 268–9, 404, 408, 421, 472, 482, 496, 499, 501-3, 506-7, 510, 512–14, 516, 525, 549, 625, 630, 631, 636, 646, 651, 652, 653, 658, 660, 663-4, 669, 679, 681–2, 684, 689, 691–2, 695–6, 712, 719, 722, 724, 728, 733, 829, 835, 839, 856–7, 864, 902, 905–6, 915, 919, 924, 974, 976, 983, 992; *LJ* iv. 175, 180, 182, 183, 204–5, 210–11, 237, 457, 704; *PJ* i. 96, 165–6, 216, 326, 416; *PJ* ii. 91, 139, 144, 248; *PJ* iii. 37, 77; *CSPD 1641–3*, p. 147; *HMC 4th Report*, p. 111; HLRO, MP 23/6/42, 28/6/42; Stationers Company, Liber A, fo. 136; *LJ* v. 345, 385, 386, *LJ* vi. 32; *CJ* iii. 585; BL, Harl. 163, fo. 194; Harl. 164, fos. 52, 76v; Harl. 479, fo. 86.

[29] Stationers Company, Liber A, fos. 130–30v; *LJ* iv. 232; *CJ* ii. 116, 168, 268; *HMC 4th Report*, p. 102; HLRO, MP 21/10/41.

[30] Rushworth, *Collections*, iv. 282, 357; *CSPD 1641–3*, p. 129; *D'Ewes Diary* (ed. Coates), pp. 164, 191–2, 229; *PJ* i. 120, 222; *PJ* ii. 97–8; BL, Harl. 163, fo. 409; *CJ* ii. 220.

[31] Rushworth, *Collections*, iv. 170; A. D. T. Cromartie, 'The printing of parliamentary speeches November 1640–June 1642', *HJ* 33 (1990); *D'Ewes Diary* (ed. Notestein), p. 332; BL, Harl. 163, fos. 9a, 28a, 119, 136, 228, 270; Harl. 164, fos. 47v, 52; *CJ* ii. 116, 139, 146, 148, 159, 190, 220; Stationers Company, Liber A, fos. 129v, 130v–32; *PJ* ii. 100; *LJ* iv. 576; *CSPD 1641–3*, pp. 97–8; N. F. Nash, 'English licenses to print and grants of copyright in the 1640s', *The Library*, 6th series 4 (1982).

displayed a determination to use licensing as a means of exerting a positive influence over the press in their own interests, and the attack upon Laud's system was quickly followed by plans for new licensing laws in 1641.[32] Seeking a means of securing the publication of certain types of work, Parliament turned to the licensing system as one of the most important foundations of literary warfare. However, rather than merely delegating licensing to external powers, Parliament sought to bring such tasks under its purview, in the form of the committee chaired by Sir Edward Dering and John White. This represented an explicit indication of the intention to use licensing in the interests of 'further reformation'. Dering was a zealous supporter of religious reform, thought not an uncomplicated figure, while White had long formed an integral part of prominent godly networks.[33] Their work would be guided by a distinct political and religious agenda, and demonstrated the extent to which Parliament was intent on substituting Laud's bias with one of its own.

Part of the role of the licensing committee was the consideration of complaints made against Laudian licensers who had denied approval to, or altered, works by 'godly' authors.[34] They soon found themselves inundated by such complaints, in the face of which they ordered that, 'if any manuscript be refused the press by the usual licensers, the refuser shall be sent for, to show cause unto this committee' (5 January 1641).[35] As early as 25 November 1640, Henry Bell pleaded that his edition of Luther's 'last divine discourses' had deliberately been delayed by Laud and one of the licensers, William Bray. Bell was ordered to present his translation, while Bray was called to appear before the committee.[36] Similarly, the printer Thomas Payne complained that Laud had issued orders preventing him from publishing an edition of Lancelot Andrewes' *Catechistical Doctrine*.[37] It was alleged that approval had been witheld from John Vicars' works against idolatry, on the grounds that 'the image of Christ was in churches as yet, and until they were pulled down there, he would not license it'.[38] It was also claimed that licensers had 'inserted new sense' into works by men such as Richard Sibbes, and that a book by the Jesuit, Sancta Clara, had been allowed while a work in which Bishop Thomas Morton had refuted it 'in a leafe' had been 'dispunged' by Bray.[39] Later,

---

[32] *CJ* ii. 108, 139; BL, Harl. 163, fo. 149; *CSPD 1641–3*, p. 129; Rushworth, *Collections*, iv. 292.

[33] For Dering: D. Hirst, 'The defection of Sir Edward Dering, 1640–1641', *HJ* 15 (1972). For White: I. M. Calder, ed., *Activities of the Puritan Faction of the Church of England, 1625–33* (Church History Society, 1957), pp. xii, xxiv, 26; A. Searle, ed., *Barrington Family Letters, 1628–1632* (Camden Society, 1983), pp. 179–80; *Winthrop Papers* (5 vols, Massachusetts Historical Society, 1929–47), ii. 82, 97, 103, 170; C. M. Andrews, *The Colonial Period of American History* (4 vols, New Haven, 1934–38), i. 345, 365, 366, 369.

[34] *CJ* ii. 84; *LJ* iv. 457; J. Bruce, ed., *Proceedings, Principally in the County of Kent* (Camden Society, 1862), pp. 80–95.

[35] Bruce, *Proceedings*, p. 94.

[36] Bruce, *Proceedings*, pp. 81–2, 83.

[37] Bruce, *Proceedings*, pp. 82–3.

[38] Bruce, *Proceedings*, pp. 84–95.

[39] Bruce, *Proceedings*, pp. 84–5, 95.

at Laud's trial, Daniel Featley would claim that Bray had 'expunged seventeen whole sheets' from a work of his which attacked popery.[40] Detailed notes were submitted regarding passages cut from the sermons of one Dr Clerke, while Dering discovered that one licenser 'disguised some parts and defaced others' in works by Dr William Jones. According to Dering, this work was 'so dashed and altered both in the words and sense of the author, by additions and by subtractions in several places', that it was made 'unvendible, as having the life, the vigour ... picked out'.[41] Dering asked to see manuscript copies of the works by some of these men, including Richard Carpenter, who had complained about being required not to deliver a sermon at St Paul's against the Church of Rome, 'because now the church of Rome and we were in a fair and quiet way and it was not fit to multiply controversies'.[42]

The interest in such cases lay not merely in a desire for retribution and recompense. In addition to investigating complaints made against Laud's licensers, Dering and White also had the power to influence which books could be published. Richard Ward, having issued a complaint regarding his treatment at the hands of the licensers, was called upon to produce a copy of his *Theological Questions*, in order to show which passages had been censored. Ward claimed that 'our licensers liberty in the licensing of books is most licentious', and that 'popery and pelagianism were too much favoured and befriended by them', and he illustrated how passages had been deleted in such a way as to alter the meaning of some sections, and to render others completely nonsensical.[43] Having submitted his work to Dering's committee, Ward issued a petition asking for a licence to publish, stating that 'your religious assembly and honourable court' could 'turn to anything they please' the works he had submitted.[44] In another instance, Dering examined a manuscript by Thomas Hearding, and ordered that it was to be printed, unless one of the licensers 'show good cause to the contrary in writing'.[45] Works submitted to, and approved by, Dering's committee could be entered into the Stationers' register and published, with the printed edition bearing some indication that it had received the '*imprimatur*' of the committee for printing, or one of its members.[46]

In this lies the real significance of the activity of the committee for printing. Dering and White were able to decide which books to call for consideration, and

---

[40] *HMC House of Lords XI*, pp. 433–5.

[41] Bruce, *Proceedings*, p. 86; *CSPD 1636–7*, p. 261; PRO, SP 16/339, fos. 136–47; LPL, MS 943, pp. 735–7.

[42] BL, Add. 26785, fo. 30; Bruce, *Proceedings*, pp. 85–6; Centre for Kentish Studies, U350/Q5: Richard Carpenter to Sir Edward Dering, 4 Mar. 1641.

[43] Bruce, *Proceedings*, pp. 82–3; R. Ward, *Theological Questions* (London, 1640); PRO, SP 16/540/4, fos. 201–203v.

[44] *CSPD 1640–41*, pp. 530–31.

[45] BL, Stowe 107, fo. 3v; Stowe 184, fos. 37, 41–2.

[46] H. L'Estrange, *Gods Sabbath* (Cambridge, 1641), sig. Av.

which books to request for publication. What resulted was the approval of a remarkable corpus of tracts.[47] Attention was concentrated upon works and writers abused by Laudian licensers, and the committee attempted to rectify this bias with a new bias of its own. Richard Ward's works began to appear with official sanction, as did those of men like John Ley, Peter Smart, Richard More, William Prynne, William Gouge and John Vicars. Indeed, the careers of such men reveal the way in which the licensed press came to be dominated not only by men who had suffered during the 1630s, but also by those with long-standing connections – as friends, colleagues and clients – with the political leaders in Parliament. The rehabilitation of such writers, and the appearance of their books, represented a conscious snub to Laud and Charles; an expression of the bonds of obligation uniting members of a godly network; and an exercise in propaganda. Ley, therefore, was a friend of Sir Robert Harley and Lord Brooke who had suffered for his beliefs, and during the opening months of the Long Parliament he worked closely with Dering's committee, which approved his many pamphlet contributions to religious debates.[48] Smart too had a notable Puritan record, having served as prebend of Durham Cathedral until his imprisonment for a sermon against the innovations of John Cosins. He was rehabilitated with the assistance of Francis Rous and Sir Robert Harley, and his willingness to express his views in print made him a perfect conduit for propaganda in the early 1640s.[49] Furthermore, the printing committee was useful for more than simply granting approval to works which had been censured and censored during the 1630s. It also helped arrange the publication of books issued in response to those scandalous tracts to which its attention was drawn by the House. In July 1641, for example, the Commons ordered an investigation into Henry Burton's *Protestation Protested*, which opposed the test of allegiance imposed in the aftermath of the Army Plot, and within weeks there appeared a response in the form of *Vindiciae Voti*, which was 'published by authority of the House of Commons'. Its author was John Geree, another well-connected Puritan minister to whom attention has already

---

[47] Stationers Company, Liber A, fo. 132.

[48] J. Morrill, *Cheshire 1630–1660* (Oxford, 1974), pp. 20, 165–6; A. Hughes, 'Thomas Dugard and his circle in the 1630s', *HJ* 29 (1986), p. 786; M. A. Groombridge, 'Calendar of Chester city council minutes 1603–42', *Lancashire and Cheshire Record Society* 106 (1956), pp. xxiii, 160; A. Hughes, *Politics, Society and Civil War in Warwickshire, 1620–1660* (Cambridge, 1987), p. 78; R. C. Richardson, *Puritanism in North West England* (Manchester, 1972), pp. 31, 35, 36, 50, 68–9, 82, 112, 133–5, 141, 187; BL, Add. 70002, fo. 368; *Historical Sketches of Nonconformity in the County Palatine of Chester* (London, 1864), p. 399; J. Ley, *A Comparison* (London, 1641); J. Ley, *A Case of Conscience* (London, 1641); J. Ley, *A Letter (Against the Erection of an Altar)* (London, 1641); J. Ley, *Sunday a Sabbath* (London, 1641); *SR* i. 33. One of Ley's pamphlets survives in the state papers: *CSPD 1641–3*, p. 230; PRO, SP 16/487, fos. 171–77v: J. L[ey], *England's Doxologie*.

[49] Peacey, 'Henry Parker', pp. 29–30; P. Smart, *A Catalogue* (London, 1642), pp. 9–12, 27–32; P. Smart, *A Short Treatise* (London, 1643), sigs. *v, *2v, pp. 3, 4, 11, 16; P. Smart, *Canterburies Crueltie* (London, 1643). For Smart's continued petitioning, see: *HMC 6th Report*, pp. 51, 140, 152, 156, 158, 164, 352.

been drawn.[50] It may have been John White who sought Geree's help, for when the latter subsequently led the literary charge against the 'popish plot', he dedicated a book to White, and claimed that it was a labour which he had been 'encouraged to consummate'.[51]

The zeal with which Dering and White investigated Laudian licensing, rehabilitated Puritan sufferers from the 1620s and 1630s, and secured the publication of a corpus of godly tracts and pamphlets, reflects Parliament's determination to use press control as part of a plan to exert a profound influence on the kind of works which reached the bookstalls. The case of Geree's reply to Burton, moreover, indicates that the licensing system could form part of a concerted effort to ensure the composition of works which were deemed politically necessary in the tense political situation in which England found itself in the early 1640s. After the iconoclasm of the opening months of the Long Parliament, therefore, the reformers displayed a commitment to regaining control over the press, in order to protect the interests of the Stationers' Company, their own secrecy, and their ability to control the flow of information emanating from Westminster, as well as in order to punish Arminian authors, and new works of a seditious or scandalous nature. In addition, they sought to employ licensing to 'tune' the press in a more positive way, and to ensure the appearance of books by godly authors, whether victims of Laudian censure or advocates of further reformation. While they continued to work alongside the Stationers, licensing was brought under the direction of a parliamentary committee, in what represented a novel, direct and proactive approach to the press.

Such advances were brought to an abrupt halt within months, however, as the rudimentary licensing system which Parliament constructed in 1641 collapsed almost entirely during 1642. As growing numbers of tracts appeared in the months before and after the outbreak of war, fewer and fewer received official sanction, or secured entry into the Stationers' register, and the number of complaints regarding scandalous pamphlets rose dramatically. The early months of 1642 witnessed a resurgence in claims about false editions of parliamentary speeches and orders, unauthorised accounts of parliamentary proceedings, and scandals offered to the Scots, to courtiers, and to the crown, as well as complaints about the spread of scandalous English books in Europe.[52] This collapse resulted from the inability of

---

[50] BL, Add. 26785, fo. 43; *CJ* ii. 206; *LJ* iv. 345; BL, Harl. 163, fos. 391v–92; Harl. 164, fo. 56; Rushworth, *Collections*, iv. 348; J. Geree, *Vindiciae Voti* (London, 1641), sig. D2; *SR* i. 30. For Geree: G. Soden, *Godfrey Goodman, Bishop of Gloucester, 1583–1656* (London, 1953), pp. 178, 192–4, 229, 271; *CSPD 1639–40*, pp. 580–83; S. R. Gardiner, *Reports of Cases in Star Chamber* (Camden Society, 1886), pp. 244, 269; J. S. Burn, *The Star Chamber* (London, 1870), p. 166; J. Geree, *A Catechisme* (Oxford, 1629).

[51] J. Geree, *Judah's Joy* (London, 1641), sigs. C2, D3, D3v; J. Geree, *The Downfall of Antichrist* (London, 1641), sig. A3; *A Discovery to the Praises of God … of a Late Intended Plot* ([London], 1641); *The Papists Conspiracie* ([London], 1641).

[52] *CJ* ii. 387, 402, 408, 441, 500, 501, 510, 514, 624, 625; *PJ* i. 96, 165–6, 230, 304, 311, 326; *PJ*

Dering's committee, whose members had other pressing concerns, to cope with the vast increase in printed literature which accompanied the souring of relations between king and Parliament.[53] Dering was himself questioned for printing his speeches, and was eventually removed from the House, and his 'defection' only exacerbated the difficulties in enforcing press control.[54] Parliament was itself blameworthy, however, having proved lax in removing Laud's licensers, and the result was a situation, in September 1642, in which one contemporary noted that 'here are divers dangerous books come, printed at London; I wonder no more care is taken, some of them are enough to put the world into a combustion'.[55]

By this stage, however, Parliament had begun the process of regaining control of the presses for a second time. The Commons began planning new legislation in March 1642, by ordering that all pamphlets should bear the author's name, and in April the committee dealing with scandalous pamphlets implored the gentleman usher to redouble his efforts to apprehend offenders. The new ordinance was eventually passed at the end of August 1642.[56] Such measures appear to have brought forth a clampdown on unwanted tracts, pamphlets and newspapers, but Parliament was still unable to control the press.[57] It became clear, for example, that the *imprimatur* of Parliament's clerk was being used fraudulently by pamphleteers who sought to lend their works legitimacy and respectability. Greater zeal was required, and in October 1642 the Commons ordered the committee for printing to sit daily, while the House of Lords also became more active in enforcing press control. Moreover, John White and his associates too became more active in the last months of the year.[58] Once again, White appears to have coordinated licensing with parliamentary activity, and in late December 1642 and early 1643 he licensed books against the most powerful royalist propagandist, Henry Ferne, at a time when Parliament had called the

---

ii. 55, 97, 100; *PJ* iii. 53, 78; *Diurnall Occurrences* 6 (7–14 Feb. 1642), sigs. A2, A3v; *LJ* iv. 462, 468–9, 653, 660, 674, 680–81, 699, 708, 721–2; *A True Diurnal of the Passages* (14–21 Mar. 1642), p. 15.

[53] For evidence of Oliver St John licensing a pamphlet against Lord Keeper Finch, see: PRO, SP 16/487, fos. 34r–v.

[54] *PJ* i. 261–3, 268, 283; *Diurnall Occurrences* 6, sig. A3; Hirst, 'Sir Edward Dering'.

[55] Wykes survived until November 1642; Hansley and Samuel Baker until May 1643: Greg, *Licensers*, pp. 40–41, 101–6; *SR* i. 1–53; *HMC 5th Report*, p. 86; *A Continuation of Our Weekly Intelligence* ([London], 1642), p. 5.

[56] *CJ* ii. 501, 611, 624, 734, 736, 739; *LJ* iv. 652, 700; *HMC 5th Report*, p. 16; *A Continuation of the True Diurnall* 11 (21–28 Mar. 1642), p. 82; HLRO, MP 5/4/42; *A Declaration of the Lords and Commons... Concerning Irregular Printing and for the Suppressing of all False and Scandalous Pamphlets* (London, 1642); *PJ* iii. 314.

[57] *A Perfect Diurnall* 15 (19–26 Sept. 1642), sig. Q3v. See also Thomason's comments on his copies of *England's Memorable Accidents* 49 (17–24 Oct. 1642, BL, E240/45) ('all other diurnalls now prohibited'), and *Proquiritatio* (London, 1642, BL, E240/1) ('this was scattered up and down London the 14 and 15 Sept. 1642 and suppressed by an order 16 September').

[58] *LJ* v. 156, 214, 321, 512, 529, 512, 529, 531, 545, 547, 554, 570–71, 593, 596-8, 614, 632; BL, Add. 18777, fos. 31a, 48b.

latter to account.[59] In March 1643, as pamphleteers such as the notorious Henry Walker fell foul of the Lords' attention, the Committee of Examinations appointed searchers to demolish illicit presses and to send their owners to prison, to seize copies of books from bookshops and book stalls, and to seek the assistance of JPs, militia officers and constables, while the Committee of Sequestrations was empowered to seize the estates of delinquent printers. Nevertheless, the backbone of the system remained the Stationers' Company, and as ever more printers filled London's prisons, it was men such as Joseph Hunscott, the company's beadle, who were most active in their pursuit.[60]

The Stationers' Company also welcomed the most serious attempt to rectify the weakness of the system, when Parliament heralded a more sophisticated licensing machinery by passing an ordinance for regulating printing in June 1643. The Stationers' Company had lobbied for the legislation with a printed remonstrance in April 1643, although it seems likely that the impetus for this petition came in part from within Parliament, and that it demonstrates the way in which Parliament and industry coordinated their efforts in order to pursue shared goals.[61] The work of the licensing committee had always been supported by petitions calling for control of the press, and one of these, from a group of London ministers (12 March 1641) had suggested a way of relieving the burden on the members of Dering's committee. The ministers asked for the power to license books to be granted to 'orthodox' and 'godly' men, to prevent 'diverse unsound and dangerous doctrines, tending to the maintaining of popery and Arminianism, superstition and prophaness'.[62] Their suggestion was not adopted in 1641, but probably influenced the 1643 ordinance. In June 1643, more than a dozen men were appointed to replace the remains of Laud's licensers, and to peruse books and enter them into the Stationers' register. John White continued to act as an occasional licenser, as did the Stationers' clerk, Henry Walley, who licensed newsbooks, but the lion's share of the work was undertaken by eminent and well-connected divines such as Calybute Downing, Edmund Calamy, Joseph Caryl, Charles Herle and Obadiah Sedgwick, as well as by less well-known figures like John Downham, John Bachelor and James Cranford.[63] Parliament backed this ordinance with an order in

---

[59] J. Burroughes, *The Glorious Name of God* (London, 1643); W. Bridge, *The Wounded Conscience Cured* (London, 1642); *CJ* ii. 900.

[60] *LJ* v. 647, 651; *LJ* vi. 16, 42; Stationers Company, Liber A, fos. 147, 151–2.

[61] Peacey, 'Henry Parker', pp. 98–9.

[62] *HMC 4th Report*, p. 57; *LJ* iv. 182; HLRO, MP 12/3/41.

[63] *LJ* vi. 96; *CJ* iii. 123, 129, 131, 138, 139; *A&O* i. 184–7; Stationers Company, Liber A, fo. 138. The complete list is as follows: *Divinity*; Thomas Gataker, John Downham, Calybute Downing, Thomas Temple, Joseph Caryl, Edmund Calamy, John Carter, Charles Herle, James Cranford, Obadiah Sedgwick, John Bachelor, John Ellis, *Law*; John Bramston, Henry Rolle, Peter Pheasant, Philip Jermyn, *Civil and Canon Law*; Nathaniel Brent, *Philosophy, History, Poetry, Morality, and Arts*; Nathaniel Brent, John Langley, Giles Farnaby, and *Mathematics/Almanacs*; John Booker. For Walley: Stationers' Company, Court Book C, fos. 109, 111v. For evidence of White's continued licensing, see: BL, Harl. 165, fo. 136v; *CJ* iii. 194; *The Kingdomes Case* (London, for Wright, 1643).

November 1643 which enabled the sequestration of the estates of those selling or publishing libels.[64]

The measures taken in 1642 and 1643 demonstrate that Parliament remained wedded to the notion of delegating the task of licensing to academics and ministers, and to a reliance upon the assistance of the Stationers' Company. This was despite the fact that the licensers often proved unreliable, and the reality that the Stationers may always have been a weak arm of government, who were increasingly opposed for their 'tyranny' over the industry.[65] However, the circumstances of war were perhaps not the time to experiment in the area of press control, and Parliament's reliance upon traditional methods mirrored that of their opponents in Oxford. Although evidence relating to royalist licensers is scarce, and while they could not work closely with the Stationers' Company, they nevertheless relied upon semi-independent licensers who included Sir John Berkenhead, as well as the Chancellor and Vice-Chancellor of the university, and three prominent academics: Dr Robert Sanderson (regius professor of divinity); Dr Thomas Clayton (regius professor of medicine); and Dr Richard Zouche (professor of civil law), most of whom were appointed in February 1644.[66] Evidence of their work is scant, although Berkenhead's licensing copy of John Taylor's *The Causes of Diseases* survives. Berkenhead's role as licenser evidently extended to making additions and amendments to such works, and many royalist works appear to have been subjected to stylistic editing by licensers.[67] This is clear from the testimony of the anonymous author of a response to Nathaniel Fiennes' attack upon episcopacy, complaining that his work had been hijacked by its licenser, William Bray, who apparently claimed it as his own when he forwarded it to Sir Edward Nicholas. In the course of his complaint, our anonymous plaintiff provided telling insight into the treatment of his text, affirming that Bray 'did nothing but altered and transposed some things' before delivering it to 'the clerk of the closet and secretary Nicholas as his own by which means it was afterward printed'.[68]

Where royalists and parliamentarians appear to have differed, however, was over the transparency of their licensing. There is no evidence of any royalist works informing readers regarding official licences, even for those few works which are known to have been approved. Officially approved parliamentarian works, on the other hand, frequently informed readers of the fact that they had been 'published by authority', or by 'special authority', or that they were published 'according to order', and some of these were produced by official printers and publishers. Such

[64] *CJ* iii. 315; BL, Add. 18779, fo. 7b.

[65] *PJ* iii. 314.

[66] Madan, *Oxford Books*, ii. 313–14.

[67] Bodl. MS Add. C.209, fos. 2–4v. This was the copy marked up for the press. See: B. Capp, *The World of John Taylor the Water Poet, 1578–1653* (Oxford, 1994), p. 153.

[68] BL, Add. 34312, fo. 14v; *A Briefe Answer to a Late Pamphlett Entituled Unparralleld Reasons for Abolishing Episcopacy* (Oxford, 1644).

phrases referred to the fact that they had been licensed, and they generally appeared prominently on the cover, although occasionally on the final page.[69] On other occasions, readers were informed of the identity of licensers. With works licensed by the committee for printing, readers were sometimes informed that books had been 'ordered to be printed' by White's committee, not least works by Prynne, which readers had been informed were officially inspired.[70] Works published with the approval of licensers appointed from 1643 onwards could merely display the licenser's name, or else print their *imprimatur* entire, including their words of justification, either on the cover of or inside the book.[71] Not all such works betrayed their status as licensed and approved works, however, and it is not clear what importance to attach to the decision to display or disguise official approval.[72] It is possible that such decisions were made by stationers rather than authors, in order to assure readers of the legitimacy of texts which they might otherwise have been reticent about purchasing. However, it is also possible that those involved in polemical literature were once again negotiating the problem which arose out of the impossibility of both establishing orthodoxy and avoiding statements which betrayed political involvement. Indeed, it is also conceivable that, particularly during the 1640s, parliamentarians and religious radicals, whose views were less familiar, and less readily regarded as having been orthodox, needed to expend greater effort in displaying their orthodoxy than did royalists.

Measures taken in Oxford and London undoubtedly helped to tighten press

---

[69] Sample: H. Parker, *Jus Populi* (London, 1644); J. Goodwin, *Innocency and Truth* (London, 1644); *The Archbishop of Canterburys Speech* (London, 1644); J. Goodwin, *Calumny Arraigned* (London, 1645); H. Woodward, *The Life and Death of William Lawd* (London, 1645), p. 42; J. Cotton, *Way of the Churches* (London, 1645); R. Ram, *Paedobaptism* (London, 1645); J. Saltmarsh, *The Opening of Master Prynnes New Book* (London, 1645); G. G., *A Reply to a Namelesse Pamphlet, Intituled an Answer to a Speech Without Doors* (London, 1646); *The Several Speeches of Duke Hamilton* (London, 1649); *SR* i. 133, 141, 143, 145, 151, 157, 199, 254, 313. See also: William Bridge's annotated edition of Francis Quarles, *The Loyall Convert* (London, Husbands, 1644, 'published by authority'); *Prerogative Anatomised* (London, Wright, 1644, 'published by authority'); *The Great Assizes Holden in Parnassus* (London, for Edward Husband, 1645), p. 44. *Mercurius Britanicus* picked up on this last work, saying 'we have careful licensers to send things abroad so prejudicial and dishonourable to the Parliament': *Mercurius Britanicus* 70 (10–17 Feb. 1645), sigs. Bbbb3v–4.

[70] W. Bridge, *The Wounded Conscience Cured* (London, 1642); H. Palmer, *Scripture and Reason Pleaded* (London, 1643); W. Prynne, *The Doome of Cowardize and Treachery* (London, 1643); *SR* i. 56, 81. J. Tombes, *Fermentum Pharisaeorum* (London, 1643); W. Prynne, *The Popish Royall Favourite* (London, 1643), sig. ¶v; W. Prynne, *The Soveraigne Power of Parliaments* (London, 1643); W. Prynne, *Hidden Workes of Darkenes* (London, 1645).

[71] S. Torshell, *Case of Conscience* (London, 1643); *The Path Way to Peace* (London, 1643); H. Woodward, *A Solemn Covenant* (London, 1643); S. Bolton, *A Tossed Ship* (London, 1644), sig. [B4v]; J. Goodwin, *Grand Imprudence* (London, 1644); R. Bacon, *The Spirit of Prelacy* (London, 1646); J. Geree, *Touching the Subject of Supremacy* (London, 1647); *The Kings Last Farewell to the World* (London, 1649); *SR* i. 67, 73, 78, 96, 132, 226, 274, 309.

[72] *Powers to be Resisted* (London, 1643); *The Great Mysterie of God* (London, 1645); *Independency to be Abandoned* (London, 1647); G. Palmer, *Sectaries Unmasked* (London, 1647); J. Goodwin, *Sion-Colledg Visited* (London, 1648); *SR* i. 88, 153, 268, 273, 287.

'control', but arguably did more to assist in the creation of propaganda than to ensure suppression of scandalous and seditious books and pamphlets. Zealous licensing ensured, for example, the appearance of a range of works in the summer and autumn of 1643 in defence of the national covenant and the Solemn League and Covenant. Once again, it is possible to link calls made by the House for official declarations with non-official pamphlets. In July 1643, therefore, a committee was ordered to produce a vindication of the covenant, and within weeks one member of the committee, John White, in his capacity as chairman of the licensing committee, entered into the Stationers' register a work called *The Harmony of Our Oaths*.[73] Later in the year, the Solemn League and Covenant, which sealed the Anglo-Scottish treaty, was advocated in print by a range of licensed works, and by men such as Philip Nye, Hezekiah Woodward and Richard Ward.[74] Furthermore, it is evident that licensing continued to involve alteration of texts. The parliamentarian astrologer and pamphleteer, William Lilly, accused the licenser, John Booker, of having made 'impertinent obliterations' to one of his works in 1644.[75] However, it quickly became clear, at least in London, that the 1643 ordinance could not prevent the appearance of ever more radical and disturbing books.[76] Those Stationers, such as Joseph Hunscott, who were employed to trace and seize illicit presses, faced the problem that their actions provoked law suits, which forced them to issue repeated pleas for protection from Parliament.[77] It also became apparent that the *imprimatur* could be forged by those who sought to lend spurious authority and credibility to particular works, and to cover their tracks, and even to discredit individual licensers, to the extent that it was seriously devalued as a device with which to legitimate books, and to offer a reliable guide to official attitudes.[78]

The persistence of problems with press control would tax successive regimes throughout the 1640s and 1650s, and would help prompt a series of further legislative initiatives and administrative experiments, which shed important light upon the nature of governmental rule, and the structure of the state in the mid-seventeenth century. In order to assess such developments properly, however, it is

---

[73] *CJ* iii. 173, 182; *The Harmony of Our Oaths* (London, 1643); *SR* i. 65. See also: R. Ward, *The Analysis, Explication and Application of the Sacred Vow and Covenant* (London, 1643); *The Undeceiver* (London, 1643) and *A Vindication of the Late Vow and Covenant* ([London, 1643]); *SR* i. 61, 68, 71. The latter was also licensed by White.

[74] P. Nye, *An Exhortation* (London, 1644); H. Woodward, *The Solemn League and Covenant of the Three Kingdoms* (London, 1643); G. Smith, *The Three Kingdoms Healing Plaster* (London, 1643); R. Ward, *The Analysis, Explication and Application of the Sacred and Solemn League and Covenant* (London, 1643); *SR* i. 78–9, 99.

[75] C. Burman, ed., *The Lives of Those Eminent Antiquaries* (London, 1774), p. 64. The work in question was: W. Lilly, *Merlinus Anglicus Junior* (London, 1644).

[76] *CJ* iii. 202, 549; Clyde, 'Parliament and the press'.

[77] Stationers Company, Court Book C, fos. 121v, 153, 177v, 201v, 214; *LJ* vi. 42; HLRO, MP 21/10/41; *HMC 4th Report*, p. 102; *LJ* viii. 684; HLRO, MP 23/1/47; *HMC 6th Report*, p. 154.

[78] Peacey, 'Henry Parker', pp. 252–3; Clyde, *Struggle*, pp. 26, 64.

necessary to explore other factors which provided a stimulus for change, and which centred upon the way in which the ability to exploit licensing in order to produce political propanganda succumbed to political factionalism.

Licensing, like all aspects of the political process in the 1640s, became dominated by factions.[79] This was probably true at Oxford, although it is difficult to establish with precision whether the king's licensers contributed to the undermining of the 'constitutional royalists'.[80] It is certainly true at Westminster, where factionalism within parliamentarian ranks came to be replicated in the press, as different factions sought to enlist print in order to serve factional goals, as much as to fight royalists. Factions exploited Parliament, for example, in order to secure publishing monopolies for favoured authors.[81] More importantly, after the tightening of licensing in 1643, the system fell prey to the bias of the licensers, and the political aims of the politicians with whom they associated. This reflected the nature of the licensers appointed in June 1643, and the fact that licensing involved more than mere censorship. Factions regarded control of the mechanisms of licensing as a means of controlling what was published with official sanction, and as a result the 1640s witnessed a battle for control of the power to license books, pamphlets and newspapers. Such tensions over licensing, however, enable the examination of one of the central aspects of the propaganda dynamic during the 1640s and 1650s, since political developments which took place in response to the factionalisation of licensing led to power becoming increasingly concentrated within Westminster and Whitehall, and within the Council rather than the Commons. Perhaps unwittingly, the battle over licensing in the 1640s contributed to the centralisation of power, and the growth of the state.

The power of the press, which had been tapped by Parliament between 1640 and 1643, was hijacked thereafter by the Presbyterian faction, who used it to attack not just the king and his supporters, but also rivals at Westminster. What must have worried the Independents was the way in which the Earl of Essex used his friends in London's publishing community to support his political tactics. In particular, they must have worried at the way in which the press was managed to promote the cause of a negotiated settlement with the king, thereby accentuating the deficiency which already existed in a licensing system which approved works of known royalists such as Kenelme Digby, Thomas Fuller, James Howell and Meric Casaubon.[82] Since the majority of licensers were Presbyterians, what resulted was

---

[79] This had arguably always been the case: Clegg, *Press Censorship in Jacobean England*, pp. 66–7, and chap. 6.

[80] J. L. Malcolm, *Caesar's Due. Loyalty and King Charles, 1642–1646* (London, 1983), p. 138. For constitutional royalist works before the civil war, see: *A Vindication of the King* (London, 1642).

[81] HLRO, MP 6/8/46; *LJ* viii. 456; *HMC 6th Report*, p. 130.

[82] J. Howell, *Dodonas Grove* (Cambridge, 1645), and *Epistolae Ho Elianae* (London, 1645); M. Casaubon, *The Original Cause* (London, 1645); T. Fuller, *Good Thoughts in Bad Times* (Exeter, 1645); Sir K. Digby, *Two Treatises* (Paris, 1644, reprinted London, 1645); *SR* i. 140, 147, 171, 177, 188, 195.

the preponderance of Presbyterian works among those appearing with official sanction. Presbyterian dominance among the licensers brought selectivity to the licensing of pamphlets by parliamentarian writers. This is illustrated by an incident in late 1644, concerning the Independent author, Hezekiah Woodward. When questioned over the appearance of *Inquiries into the Causes of our Miseries*, Woodward explained that he had published it even after Joseph Caryl had refused to grant it a license, on the grounds that it had been approved by another licenser, John Bachelor.[83] Moreover, after the fall of Oxford, the Presbyterians at Westminster may have been able to control the appointment of the divines who were sent to preach in the city in September 1646, and who were given licensing power there.[84] More significantly, licensers also became closely linked with particular politicians, and worked alongside them in order to further mutual aims.

Among the Presbyterian licensers, James Cranford was probably the most prominent, and certainly the most controversial. In part, the animus towards him was bred by the suspicion that he, like so many before him, was slapdash in the approval of inappropriate works.[85] More commonly, however, it was Cranford's bias, rather than his carelessness, which gave offence. Authors with whom Cranford disagreed faced deliberate obstruction, while those whose writings were directed against Independents felt able to rely upon his help.[86] When John Dury told Samuel Hartlib of his plans to publish a response to two Independent pamphleteers, John Saltmarsh and Henry Robinson, he indicated that he had 'no doubt but Mr Cranford will license it'.[87] Furthermore, when Presbyterians in the Westminster Assembly sought to publish attacks upon the antinomians in the autumn of 1643, but faced difficulties in the Commons, it was Cranford who licensed tracts which served their purposes.[88] However, the Presbyterian power over the press, which was epitomised by Cranford, provided the impetus for a struggle for control of the licensing system. While licensers such as John Bachelor were inclined to support Independents like Woodward and John Goodwin, he and

---

For Howell's career see: M. Nutkiewicz, 'A rapporteur of the English civil war: the courtly politics of James Howell', *CJH* 25 (1990). The common denominator uniting these works was Nathaniel Brent, their licenser, and a former member of the court.

[83] *HMC 6th Report*, p. 39. In a subsequent work, Woodward explained why he had published without a licence; claiming that he disagreed with licensing which was based upon 'prejudice': H. Woodward, *Soft Answers Unto Hard Censures* (London, 1645), p. 3.

[84] *CJ* iv. 692; *LJ* viii. 486. The preachers in question were: Robert Harris, Edward Reynolds, Henry Wilkinson, Francis Cheynell, Edward Corbett, Henry Cornish and Henry Langley. For these men, see: W. A. Shaw, *A History of the English Church During the Civil Wars and Under the Commonwealth* (2 vols, London, 1900), ii. 301, 402–3; A. G. Matthews, *Calamy Revised* (Oxford, 1934), pp. 137–8, 314, 530; *CJ* iv. 258, 496, 634; *LJ* vii. 557, 564, 670; *LJ* viii. 224; *DNB*.

[85] Stationers Company, Court Book C, fos. 213r–v.

[86] BL, Add. 32093, fos. 243.

[87] Hartlib Papers, 50H/3/3/13A–B.

[88] R. S. Paul, *The Assembly of the Lord* (Edinburgh, 1985), pp. 83–4, 177–81; *CJ* iii. 237, 252, 271–2, 280, 288; T. Bakewell, *A Short View of the Antinomian Errours* (London, 1643); *The Second Part of the Undeceiver* (London, 1643), p. 24; *SR* i. 72.

his friends were unable to compete with the Presbyterian licensers. In a microcosm of the wider political struggle evident throughout this period, factions tried to drag the licensed press in conflicting directions. The determination to gain control over licensing, and the political intrigue with which it was accompanied, attests to its political importance. Moreover, licensers were not merely advancing such causes in isolation. Viscount Saye, who argued that Cranford was an emissary of the 'juggling' Scots, and that he was prompted by the Earl of Essex, recognised that licensing had become a crucial link in a 'propaganda chain' joining authors, politicians, and printers, with licensers acting as go-betweens and organisers.[89] In the period before 1647, Bachelor and the Independents lacked not just the number of licensers upon which Presbyterians could rely, but also their organisation at a more important level. What they faced was a powerful alliance which emerged between Presbyterian politicians such as Robert Baillie, licensers such as Cranford, writers such as Thomas Edwards and David Buchanan, and printers such as Robert Bostock.[90] It was such cooperation, and such integration of the elements involved in a successful propaganda campaign, which undermined the Independents most significantly. Edwards' *Gangraena*, therefore, bore not merely Cranford's *imprimatur*, but also his written preface.[91] Such instances demonstrate that Cranford was prepared to assist the Presbyterian cause in ways which supplemented his licensing, and on another occasion he played an active role in spreading accusations against the Independent grandee, Viscount Saye, regarding negotiations with Oxford during the summer of 1645, at the behest of Baillie.[92] Although punished for such behaviour, Cranford caused further frustration by granting licences to two highly controversial works by the Scottish writer, David Buchanan, which had probably been published with Baillie's approval.[93]

---

[89] W. Fiennes, *Vindiciae Veritatis* (London, 1654), pp. 163–4.

[90] Bodl. MS Nalson XIX, fo. 299; HLRO, MP 15/4/46. Bostock admitted that the Scots amended texts after they had been licensed by Cranford. See also: A. Hughes, 'Approaches to Presbyterian print culture: Thomas Edwards's *Gangraena* as source and text', in Andersen and Sauer, eds, *Books and Readers*.

[91] T. Edwards, *Antapologia* (London, 1644); *SR* i. 113; *Letters and Journals of Robert Baillie*, ii. 278–9; Edwards, *Gangraena*, ii. 138–9; Edwards, *Gangraena*, iii. 102–105. Calamy provided a preface for a book against John Tombes that he had licensed: T. Blake, *Mr Blake's Answer to Mr Tombes* (London, 1646).

[92] M. Mahoney, 'The Savile affair and the politics of the Long Parliament', *PH* 7 (1988); V. Pearl, 'London Puritans and Scotch fifth columnists: a mid-seventeenth century phenomenon', in A. Hollaender and W. Kellaway, eds, *Studies in London History* (London, 1969); Fiennes, *Vindiciae Veritatis*, pp. 137–40, 163–4; HLRO, MP 10/6/45, MP 13/6/45, MP 11/6/45, MP 17/6/45; Longleat House, Whitelocke Papers IX, fos. 41v, 45–45v; BL, Add. 31116, pp. 428, 442; *CJ* iv. 172–3, 174–5, 208, 211, 212–13, 216, 233, 245; *Letters and Journals of Robert Baillie*, ii. 278–86, 311–13, 316, 333, iii. 309–10; Tai Liu, *Puritan London* (London, 1986), pp. 79–80, 109.

[93] *CJ* iv. 342, 348, 422; [D. Buchanan], *A Short and True Relation* (London, 1645); *SR* i. 193; Paul, *Assembly of the Lord*, pp. 245, 380, 385; *Letters and Journals of Robert Baillie*, ii. 179, 252–4, 366; BL, Add. 10114, fo. 12v; *CSPD 1645–7*, pp. 327, 330, 343; CUL, Mm.I.46, p. 162; *HMC 13th Report I*, p. 360; [D. Buchanan], *L'Histoire Veritable de ces Derniers Troubles* (np, nd, BL, E547/1).

The second half of the 1640s saw two developments in the realm of licensing: the attempt by Independents to undermine Presbyterian licensers; and the growing centralisation of 'state' authority. To a great extent these processes went hand in hand. They can be demonstrated, moreover, through the way in which licensing, and the interaction between licensers, authors and political interest groups, impacted upon newspapers such as *Mercurius Britanicus*. Parliament's flagship journal underwent a number of changes of licenser, and such licensers were able to influence its political content and editorial comment. In its earliest phase, during late 1643 and early 1644, *Britanicus* reflected the political interests of those most zealous in pursuit of the war effort, particularly members of the Fiennes political dynasty, but this changed when the Earl of Essex assumed its licensing in late February 1644. At a time when Essex saw his political power being undermined, he evidently sought to secure a voice in the press which he lacked in Parliament. By mid-June 1644, however, Essex's power was waning, and his rivals sought to ensure that he lost control over *Britanicus*, the licensing of which passed to John Rushworth.[94] Rushworth, a Commons clerk, had been appointed licenser of newsbooks on 11 April 1644, as a replacement for Henry Walley, who was employed by the Stationers' Company rather than Parliament. The appointment of Rushworth reflected the growing importance of news, and the necessity of having an accountable agent in control of the nation's licensed journals.[95] It may also have reflected the desire to employ as licensers men with literary talents.[96] Under Rushworth's control, moreover, *Britanicus* soon obtained a new editor in October 1644, in the form of Marchamont Nedham, under whom the paper became much more clearly opposed to Essex.[97] Nedham's editorship brought marked praise for Viscount Saye; support for the new modelling of the army; virulent calls for Laud's execution; and scepticism regarding the likely success of peace talks. All of this revealed the distance between his views and those of Essex.[98] Essex was not a spent political force, however, and Nedham's editorial bias – particularly his

---

[94] M. Nedham, *A Check* (London, 1644); *SR* i. 103, 105, 108, 113, 115. See: A. Cotton, 'London newsbooks in the civil war: their political attitudes and sources of information' (Oxford University DPhil, 1971), pp. 30, 74–5.

[95] *CJ* iii. 457; J. B. Williams, *A History of English Journalism* (London, 1908), p. 59. Rushworth first appeared in the Stationers' Register on 12 April 1644: *SR* i. 111.

[96] John Rushworth subsequently edited a series of papers during the mid-1640s, including the *Country Foot Post, the Kingdoms Weekly Post*, and the *London Post*: N&S, pp. 45, 143, 182–3.

[97] For an extended analysis of what follows, see: J. Peacey, 'The struggle for *Mercurius Britanicus*: factional politics and the parliamentarian press, 1643–6' (forthcoming). See also: B. Worden, 'Wit in a Roundhead': the dilemma of Marchamont Nedham', in S. D. Amussen and M. Kishlansky, eds, *Political Culture and Cultural Politics in Early Modern England* (Manchester, 1995).

[98] *Mercurius Britanicus* 58 (11–18 Nov. 1644), pp. 459, 462; *Mercurius Britanicus* 59 (18–25 Nov. 1644), p. 470; *Mercurius Britanicus* 60 (2–9 Dec. 1644), pp. 472, 478; *Mercurius Britanicus* 61 (9–16 Dec. 1644), pp. 479, 481–3; *Mercurius Britanicus* 62 (16–23 Dec. 1644), pp. 493–4; *Mercurius Britanicus* 63 (23–30 Dec. 1644), pp. 500–502; *Mercurius Britanicus* 65 (6–13 Jan. 1645), p. 514; *Mercurius Britanicus* 66 (13–20 Jan. 1645), pp. 520–5; *Mercurius Britanicus* 67 (20–27 Jan. 1645), sig. Yyy4v.

opposition to peace negotiations – prompted a further takeover bid by the Lord General, who once more assumed responsibility for licensing *Britanicus* at the beginning of February 1645. This resulted not merely in glowing accounts of Essex, but also the espousal of pro-Scottish sentiments at precisely the moment when the weakened Essex turned to the covenanters for strategic support. Essex's takeover also resulted in a *volte face* on peace talks, which was probably the primary aim.[99] By May 1645, however, Essex had been usurped once again, after which the paper grew markedly more hostile to the king, and became a powerful voice of the Independents at Westminster.[100] Later, Essex and his friends sought to orchestrate Nedham's arrest in November 1645, but their lack of success left *Britanicus* able to criticise talk of a personal treaty, and to attack both the Scots and the Presbyterianism which they espoused.[101]

Independent inroads into licensing are evident not merely from the story of *Britanicus*, but also from the emergence of one of Rushworth's clients, Gilbert Mabbott, as deputy licenser in March 1646.[102] This appointment ensured that when Thomas Edwards published *Gangraena*, it was Mabbott (alongside John Bachelor) who licensed a series of works attacking the Presbyterians' darling propagandist. During 1646–47, indeed, the organisation and numerical superiority of the Presbyterians was matched by the zeal of a relatively small group of Independent licensers.[103] Bachelor, pre-eminent among these, recognised and responded to Presbyterian criticism of his licensing policy, in terms redolent of Milton's defence of a free press, and he came to be identified as a powerful ally of toleration.[104] Edwards claimed that Bachelor not only licensed works by Independents, but also assisted in the formulation of their texts, and Baillie saw this as part of a more concerted attempt by the Independents to undermine Scottish propaganda, which also involved issuing declarations against them, and ordering certain works to be

---

[99] *SR* i. 146; *Mercurius Britanicus* 68 (27 Jan.–3 Feb. 1645), pp. 539–40; *Mercurius Britanicus* 69 (3–10 Feb. 1645), sig. Aaaa4v; *Mercurius Britanicus* 70 (10–17 Feb. 1645), sig. Bbbb4; *Mercurius Britanicus* 80 (21–28 Apr. 1645), p. 733.

[100] *Mercurius Britanicus* 81 (28 Apr.–5 May 1645), pp. 737–9, 743–4; *Mercurius Britanicus* 84 (19–26 May 1645), p. 763; *Mercurius Britanicus* 85 (26 May–2 June 1645), pp. 769–70; *Mercurius Britanicus* 88 (23–30 June 1645), p. 793.

[101] *LJ* vii. 657; *Mercurius Britanicus* 112 (29 Dec.–5 Jan. 1646), p. 992; *Mercurius Britanicus* 116 (26 Jan.–2 Feb. 1646), pp. 1023–4; *Mercurius Britanicus* 119 (16–23 Feb. 1646), p. 1042.

[102] For the importance of Mabbott, and the controversy surrounding him, see: Cotton, 'London newsbooks', chap. 8.

[103] *CSPD 1641–3*, p. 417; PRO, SP 16/493, fos. 20r–v; Williams, *History*, pp. 66–7. George Thomason, a Presbyterian, added a telling comment on one work to which Mabbott's *imprimatur* had been granted. Thomason transformed the 'G. M.' *imprimatur* to 'G. Madman': *The Desires and Propositions of the Lord Inchiquin* (London, 1648, BL, E441/2), p. 6. The Independents may also have found allies in Thomas Temple and Charles Herle, who licensed *Ormonds Curtain Drawn* on 1 September 1646, and entered it into the Stationers' register on 21 September: BL, Add. 4819, fo. 332v; *SR* i. 246.

[104] J. Goodwin, *Twelve Considerable Serious Cautions* (London, 1646); Edwards, *Gangraena*, i. 97; Edwards, *Gangraena*, ii. 43; Edwards, *Gangraena*, iii. 102–5.

burnt by the hangman.[105] Nevertheless, advances by the Independents were only as secure as their strength in Parliament, and the ebb and flow of factional politics at Westminster was mirrored in the fate of the licensers. The growing influence of the Independents in the press provoked a backlash when Presbyterian forces re-grouped and assumed a dominant position in Parliament in early 1647. Independent tracts were targeted for investigation, and their licensers were victimised. Rushworth, who had been in the pay of the army since at least February 1646, was dismissed as a licenser by the Commons (9 March 1647), and Mabbott was likewise ejected from power.[106] However, in May 1647, the Independents were able to undermine Presbyterian attempts to grant Thomas May copyright protection for his history of the civil wars, forcing the House into a division along clear factional lines, which the Independents won on the Speaker's casting vote.[107] More importantly, when the army used the threat of force to re-enter London in August 1647, following the Presbyterians' 'forcing of the Houses', Mabbott returned to office at the request of Sir Thomas Fairfax.[108] Mabbott quickly resumed active service on behalf of the Independents. When Henry Walker sought authority for himself and Samuel Pecke to publish a newspaper, therefore, he asked that the Lords should appoint someone 'to peruse the notes before they be published'. His proposal – that 'some who know the proceedings of the Houses may license the diurnal and the occurrences weekly' – was evidently approved, and the power was granted to Mabbott on 30 September 1647.[109]

Furthermore, once the army had secured Independent power at Westminster in the autumn of 1647, new press control was regarded as an urgent requirement, as more and more scandalous attacks upon Parliament and the army grandees began to appear.[110] Investigation into the press revealed the frequency with which the *imprimatur* was forged, and the possibility that fictitious Acts of Parliament could appear with a false licence.[111] The tightening of control, which was sought by both

---

[105] Edwards, *Gangraena*, ii. 138–9; *Letters and Journals of Robert Baillie*, ii. 367; *CJ* iv. 505, 507–11, 516–17, 539–41, 544; *LJ* viii. 272, 274, 276, 277, 281; BL, Add. 31116, pp. 528, 536, 538, 546, 548; HLRO, MP 15/4/46.

[106] *CJ* v. 109; *SR* i. 267–76; *LJ* ix. 70, 152, 156; Clyde, 'Parliament and the press II', p. 57. For army payments to Rushworth, see: PRO, SP 28/36, fos. 119–21, 566–9; SP 28/37, fos. 253–8, 551–63; SP 28/38, fos. 52–5, 363–7; SP 28/39, fos. 15–23, 280–82, 361; SP 28/40, fos. 203–9, 268–70; SP 28/41, fos. 272–5, 322, 567–75, 624; SP 28/48, fo. 13; SP 28/57, fo. 441.

[107] *CJ* v. 175. In June 1647, Sir Ralph Verney recognised that May's book represented the history of the Earl of Essex, rather than Parliament: Claydon House, Verney Papers, Reel 7, unfol.

[108] *LJ* ix. 441, 456; *HMC 6th Report*, p. 198; *A Perfect Summary* 10 (20–27 Sept. 1647), p. 76; Clyde, 'Parliament and the press II', p. 57.

[109] HLRO, MP 27/9/47; *LJ* ix. 450; *Perfect Summary* 11 (29 Sept.–6 Oct. 1647), p. 85. Another licenser friendly to the Independents, John Bachelor, was rewarded with a fellowship at Eton: *LJ* ix. 413, 428.

[110] Claydon House, Verney Papers, Reel 8, unfol.: Dr. William Denton to Sir Ralph Verney, 28 Sept. 1647.

[111] *Perfect Diurnall* 226 (22–29 Nov. 1647), p. 1820; Rushworth, *Collections*, vi. 490, vii. 914–15; *A Declaration of his Excellency Sir Thomas Fairfax Disclaiming a Pamphlet* (London, 1647).

Mabbott and his employers, provided the basis for the press ordinance passed on 30 September 1647, which instituted a series of punishments for writers, printers and booksellers.[112] Part of the novelty of this measure lay in the fact that the Westminster militia was empowered to suppress seditious and unlicensed pamphlets, although only after it had been purged of the Presbyterians who had made it such a potent symbol of the 'counter-revolution', and who were replaced by more reliable characters such as John Brown (clerk of Parliament), the pamphleteer John Hall, faithful servants of the parliamentarian administration such as Walter Frost and Theodore Jennings, and William Ball, the MP who designed the new press legislation. Moreover, this ordinance represented a significant infringement of the power traditionally vested in the Stationers' Company, and the first indication that Parliament was prepared to sever the alliance between government and mercantile interest, upon which press control traditionally rested.[113] In the aftermath of the 1647 legislation, scandalous works – both radical and royalist – were pursued zealously and with financial backing, with rewards of up to £100 being offered for information leading to the discovery of seditious works.[114] The Lords also granted Henry Walker and Matthew Simmons a monopoly on the printing of army papers.[115] Furthermore, the Commons maintained their vigilance by ordering the committee for unlicensed pamphlets to sit continuously from January 1648, and made moves towards yet more effective legislation, not least by placing pressure on the presses at Oxford.[116]

Nevertheless, Mabbott's rise to prominence after 1646 was as much a reflection of the growing importance of the army as it was a sign of the strength of the Independents in Parliament. As well as serving Rushworth and Westminster, Mabbott acted as the agent for Sir Thomas Fairfax, and in his quest for power in 1647 had suggested that the licenser should be privy not just to the proceedings of the two Houses, but also to the actions of the army.[117] Of course, during 1647 and

---

[112] *A&O* i. 1021–23; *CJ* v. 290, 292, 305, 309, 319; Whitelocke, *Memorials*, ii. 204; Rushworth, *Collections*, vii. 818, 823, 824–5; *LJ* ix. 457–8; *Perfect Occurrences* 36 (3–10 Sept. 1647), p. 243; *Perfect Occurrences* 38 (17–24 Sept. 1647), p. 261; *Perfect Diurnall* 218 (27 Sept.–4 Oct. 1647), pp. 1751–2.

[113] *Mercurius Pragmaticus* 3 (28 Sept.–6 Oct. 1647), pp. 17–18; *LJ* ix. 432; *LJ* x. 7; *CJ* v. 290, 311, 316; *Perfect Diurnall* 215 (6–13 Sept. 1647), pp. 1730–31.

[114] *CJ* v. 420, 471; *LJ* ix. 472; *Perfect Diurnall* 217 (20–28 Sept. 1647), p. 1748; *Perfect Diurnall* 226 (22–29 Nov. 1647), p. 1820; *Perfect Occurrences* 53 (31 Dec. 1647–7 Jan. 1648), p. 370; *Perfect Occurrences* 42 (15–22 Oct. 1647), pp. 291, 295; *Perfect Occurrences* 36 (3–10 Sept. 1647), p. 247; *The Kingdomes Weekly Post* 8 (16–22 Feb. 1648), p. 62; *Perfect Occurrences* 60 (18–25 Feb. 1648), p. 421; Rushworth, *Collections*, vi. 635; Rushworth, *Collections*, vii. 887, 914–15, 944, 1002, 1006; *LJ* x. 14, 64.

[115] *LJ* ix. 450.

[116] *The Kingdomes Weekly Intelligencer* 248 (15–22 Feb. 1648), p. 847; Rushworth, *Collections*, vii. 920, 958; *CJ* v. 395, 424, 427; *LJ* ix. 541; HLRO, MP 22/3/48; *LJ* x. 111, 130; M. Burrows, ed., *The Register of the Visitors of the University of Oxford* (Camden Society, 1881), p. 34.

[117] HLRO, MP 30/9/47; Worcester College, Oxford, Clarke CX, fos. 167, 253; Clarke CXIV, fos. 4, 16, 51, 152-3; Clarke LXIX, fo. 3; National Library of Scotland, Adv.MS 35.5.11. fos. 17, 22,

1648, Mabbott's position offers testimony to the close links which existed between the army grandees and the leaders of the Independents at Westminster, and both political and military machines worked together in the interests of a press policy which could respond to the common enemy, whether Presbyterian, Scottish, or royalist. Increasingly, however, the radical elements amongst the army were straining this friendship, and just as radical political and military figures became more prominent at Westminster, so the press, and the agents of press control, shifted towards the radical position. The clearest indication of this was the growing radicalism of Mabbott, who extended his power by refusing to limit his licensing work to newspapers, and who granted his seal of approval to an ever larger number of provocative pamphlets. As he and the army grew more extreme, the power over the press was turned against Parliament, and the licensing system began to be undermined through what amounted to a deliberate toleration of a free press, and the approval of sectarian and politically unacceptable tracts.[118] One royalist commented that 'the paper kites that fly up and down the city with Gilbert Mabbott hanging at their arses, mount very high, squirting out lies by authority as fast as if they had eaten purging comfits'.[119] In August 1648, furthermore, Mabbott submitted proposals for yet tighter press control, in an attempt to extend his personal power even further.[120] He certainly sought to undermine the voice of more moderate Independents, by refusing a licence for John Dillingham's *Moderate Intelligencer* in June 1648. He also provoked complaints from another journalist, Henry Walker, who claimed that Mabbott, 'through covetousness, hath brought printing to such disorder, and offered such contempt against this honourable house'.[121]

The breakdown of the 'Independent alliance' in the late 1640s heralded, therefore, a new struggle for control of licensing, as the radical army faction and more moderate Independents both sought power over the press as well as Parliament. One effect was the progressive eclipse of the Stationers' Company as a partner in the process of press control. One royalist commentator claimed that the Stationers had refused to agree to a proposal to spend up to £1,000 per year on the suppression of seditious literature, since they would not 'foul their fingers in so unworthy and ridiculous an employment'.[122] In reality, the Stationers joined the struggle for the control of the press, and sought to secure the appointment of new

---

50–50v; Chequers, MS 782, fos. 43, 45, 58v, 60, 62, 94, 94v; PRO, SP 28/57, fo. 411; R. Bell, ed., *Memorials of the Civil War* (2 vols, London, 1849), ii. 28; *CJ* v. 695; *CJ* vi. 19; *LJ* x. 499, 501; *LJ* viii. 439, 441; *HMC 6th Report*, p. 127; *HMC 7th Report*, p. 52; *CP* i. 1–5, 218, ii. 11, 226; *HMC 10th Report VI*, p. 172; BL, Add. 21417, fos. 59, 65.

118 J. Tombes, *Two Treatises* (London, 1645); *The Anabaptists Catechisme* ([London], 1645); *SR* i. 191, 201. For statements by Bachelor regarding a free press, see W. Haller, ed., *Tracts on Liberty in the Puritan Revolution* (2 vols, New York, 1962), i. 138.

119 *Mercurius Melancholicus* 53 (21–28 Aug. 1648), p. 156.

120 Rushworth, *Collections*, vii. 1243.

121 HLRO, MP 23/6/48; *LJ* x. 345, 354, 442, 494, 508; HLRO, MP 8/9/48, 23/9/48.

122 *Mercurius Pragmaticus* 24 (5–12 Sept. 1648), sig. Ggv.

licensers in December 1648, in order to offset the power of the Independents. For perhaps the first time, the Stationers emerge as but one interest group lobbying for influence, rather than being an integral part of the governing process. Though not yet excluded from a role in official press policy, they had to work increasingly hard to maintain their position, and became as much petitioners as partners of Parliament. On this occasion, their attempt to retain influence in the selection of licensers proved to be in vain, and the two new men appointed in January 1649 probably did not meet with their approval.[123] Theodore Jennings was a servant of the Committee of Both Kingdoms and the Derby House Committee, whose appointment represented an attempt by the Independent grandees to offset Mabbott's radicalism, not least by someone with proven literary talents. Henry Whalley, on the other hand, was Advocate General of the army, whose appointment reflected the influence of the army hierarchy.[124] The army extended its grip on the system yet further in the first week of January 1649, as responsibility for the enforcement of press control was given to its marshall-general, Richard Lawrence. This order, less than a month before the execution of the king, both undermined the Stationers' Company, and made the licensers responsible to the Lord General's secretariat.[125] On 16 January, furthermore, a group of leading army officers supported Henry Walker's petition seeking authority to publish *Perfect Occurrences*.[126] By January 1649, therefore, the licensing system, which had begun as a stronghold for the Presbyterians, had become a bastion of army power, and it had been transformed in time for the press campaign which coincided with the trial of the king.

Despite the concentration of press power in the hands of the army, the execution of the king prompted a backlash from the Presbyterians. The weeks and months after the trial represented the last stand of some of those licensers appointed in 1643, whose activity suggests that they sought to inflict the maximum amount of damage before their removal from office, which must have seemed inevitable. Nevertheless, while the proliferation of unwelcome books and pamphlets during the early weeks of 1649 provided the catalyst for orders against preaching and printing in opposition to the king's trial, the new commonwealth initially allowed Cranford and his allies to survive in their posts.[127] They duly

---

[123] *Perfect Occurrences* 108 (18–25 Jan. 1649), p. 804; *HMC 7th Report*, p. 67; HLRO, MP 20/12/48.

[124] *LJ* x. 646. For Jennings' earlier career see: PRO, SP 28/252 part 1, fo. 263; SP 28/262, fos. 108, 330; *CJ* ii. 823–4; *CJ* v. 150; *CJ* vi. 573; above, pp. 104–5. He would later be likened to John Bachelor for his tolerance of Independent ideas: *Church Levellers* (London, 1649), sig. Av. For Whalley as Judge Advocate, see: Abbott, *Cromwell*, i. 585n; PRO, SP 28/54, fo. 144; SP 28/57, fos. 442, 489; SP 28/58, fo. 46. He is not to be confused with Henry Walley of the Stationers' Company.

[125] *A Warrant of the Lord General* (London, 1649); Rushworth, *Collections*, vii. 1384; *HMC Leyborne*, pp. 16–17. For Lawrence: PRO, SP 28/39, fo. 41; SP 28/54, fo. 117; SP 28/58, fos. 692, 694; R. Lawrence, *The Wolf Stript of his Sheeps Clothing* (London, 1647).

[126] J. Peacey, 'Reporting a revolution: a failed propaganda campaign', in Peacey, ed., *The Regicides and the Execution of Charles I* (Basingstoke, 2001); HLRO, MP 16/1/49; *LJ* x. 645.

[127] *CJ* vi. 131; *CSPD 1649–50*, p. 18.

exploited this opportunity by licensing a stream of works hostile to the new regime, including attacks upon the army, defences of the Solemn League and Covenant, and a series of protests by ministers from across the country, which they had also helped to draft.[128] While James Cranford and Edmund Calamy tested the degree to which they could use their power to benefit the opponents of the new regime, it was Joseph Caryl and John Downham who made the most extraordinary licensing decision, by approving *Eikon Basilike*, the touchstone for disgruntled Englishmen. That this was not a mere oversight is clear from the fact that seven months later, when the importance of this book was patently obvious, Downham licensed *Apophthegmata Aurea*, which was nothing more than extracts from the *Eikon*. It was the appearance of works such as these which led the Independent minister, John Price, to bemoan 'that bountiful and liberal imprimatur, donor to any lying, scurrilous and scandalous pamphlets against the Parliament and army'.[129] Given these decisions, it is no surprise that moves were made against at least some licensers, and that Cranford was removed on 16 March 1649.[130]

Such activity on the part of the Presbyterians obviously aroused the indignation of the Commons and Council of State, but as the latter began to play a more prominent role in supervising the press, it was not just the Presbyterian licensers who were targeted. Mabbott too was removed from office. His judgement had been called into question as early as December 1647, since when he had become an increasingly maverick figure, licensing the Levellers' *Agreement of the People*, and writing the Leveller-influenced *Moderate* newspaper. Given the threats to the new regime, both at home and from abroad, Mabbott posed too serious a threat to the unity of the army, and he was sacked on 22 May.[131] His valedictory statement, while it sought to stress that he had resigned, and that he had been undermined by systematic and deliberate forgery of his *imprimatur*, effectively justified his

---

[128] Rr, *The Armies Remembrancer* (London, 1649); *SR* i. 305; *The Testimony of the Truth of Jesus Christ* (London, 1648); *SR* i. 286; *A Serious and Faithful Representation* (London, 1649); [C. Burges], *A Vindication* (London, 1648); *SR* i. 307–8; *Humble Representation of the Committee ... Leicester* (London, 1648); *The Essex Watchman's Watchword* (London, 1649); [C. Love], *A Modest and Clear Vindication of the Serious Representation and Late Vindication of the Ministers of London* (London, 1649); *A Vindication of the Presbyteriall Government and Ministry* (London, 1650); *SR* i. 312, 313, 330; Peacey, 'Henry Parker', pp. 249–51.

[129] *CSPD 1649–50*, pp. 42, 45, 59, 63; *Eikon Basilike* (London, 1649); *Apophthegmata Aurea* (London, 1649); *SR* i. 314, 319; J. Price, *Clerico Classicum* (London, 1649), p. 4. The *Eikon* was erased from the Stationers' register on 6 August 1651.

[130] *CJ* vi. 166. Cranford was in trouble in August 1649 for licensing works after his removal from office in the previous March: *CJ* vi. 275; *Perfect Occurrences* 116 (16–23 Mar. 1649), p. 906. Caryl and Downham, however, somehow managed to survive in their posts during the early 1650s, and licensed some unwelcome books: D. Cawdry, *The Inconsistencie* (London, 1651); *SR* i. 362; *DNB*; [T. Tany], *Theauraujohn* ([London], 1651); *SR* i. 361; H. Ferne, *Of the Division* (London, 1652); *SR* i. 399; W. Sancroft, *Modern Policies* (London, 1652); *SR* i. 397; Sir R. Filmer, *Observations* (London, 1652); *SR* i. 397.

[131] *CJ* v. 395; *CJ* vi. 214; *CSPD 1649–50*, p. 127; *The Man in the Moon* 7 (21–30 May 1649), p. 60; E. Harrison, *Plain Dealing* (London, 1649).

removal, since he expressed his opposition to licensing and press control.[132] Furthermore, by June 1649, most newsbooks were being licensed by the civil servant, Jennings, rather than the army employee, Whalley.[133] Indeed, contemporaries clearly perceived that Jennings came under the sway of authors such as Henry Walker, as well as the Lord President, John Bradshaw, and that he was prevailed upon to refuse licences to particular newspapers.[134] Although the army briefly sought to reassert its authority in the first week of October 1649, when Richard Hatter licensed two copies of the *Perfect Diurnall* and *Perfect Occurrences*, this may merely have represented an attempt to suppress details of the Drogheda massacre, and Hatter quickly disappeared from the Stationers' register.[135]

The most obvious attempt to tighten the licensing system, however, was John Bradshaw's press act, passed on 20 September 1649. Bradshaw had been given control over the press in March, when he began preparing new legislation, as well as emerging as a licenser.[136] Although Whalley and Jennings appear to have consulted with the Stationers, it seems unlikely that they envisaged allowing the company extensive powers. The Stationers were granted searchers to inspect all carrier packs, and to inspect imported books, but the greatest enforcement power was given to the marshall of London. Not only did the legislation confirm the Stationers as junior partners in press policy, but it also ensured that licences for the press were to be issued either by the clerk of Parliament, the secretary of the army, or any other Council appointee.[137] The aim appears to have been for the Council to employ licensers on an *ad hoc* basis, which reveals that, having broken the partnership with the Stationers' Company, the Rump had also put an end to the practice of appointing semi-independent licensers.[138] Although Caryl and Calamy continued to act as licensers, and to enter works into the Stationers' register, until December 1655, they did so increasingly infrequently.[139] When Caryl, together with John Owen and Peter Sterry, licensed *Resurrection Revealed* in 1653, it was as a result of being delegated by the Council to take the work into consideration,

---

[132] Peacey, 'Henry Parker', p. 254; *Perfect Diurnall* 304 (21–28 May 1649), pp. 2530–31.

[133] *SR* i. 319–26.

[134] *The Kingdomes Faithfull and Impartiall Scout* 22 (22–29 June 1649), pp. 169–71.

[135] *SR* i. 326.

[136] *SR* i. 318, 328.

[137] *CSPD 1649–50*, pp. 43, 137, 188, 199, 259, 260, 263, 328, 344–5, 385–6, 386, 397, 400, 411, 449, 522–4; *CSPD 1650*, pp. 2, 516–19; *CJ* vi. 166, 214, 267, 275, 276, 296; *Mercurius Pragmaticus* 18 (14–21 Aug. 1649), sig. S2v; *Modest Narrative* 9 (26 May-2 June 1649), p. 71; *Mercurius Britanicus* 7 (29 May–5 June 1649), p. 46; *Mercurius Militaris* 1 (22–29 May 1649), p. 8; *A&O* ii. 245–54.

[138] *CSPD 1652–3*, pp. 73–4; *CSPD 1653–4*, p. 225. The *ad hoc* employment of licensers had begun as early as the spring of 1648, when the Lords ordered two Independent divines, Thomas Goodwin and Jeremiah Whitaker, to peruse works by the dissenting brethren: A. Byfield, *The Reasons Presented by the Dissenting Brethren* (London, 1648), sigs. A2v–3.

[139] *SR* i. 320–488, ii. 22. For Caryl as licenser of William Aspinwall's *Speculum Chronologicum* in 1652: Bodl. MS Rawlinson B.156, p. 1.

after its submission by Nathaniel Holmes.[140] Furthermore, while royalists predictably pledged defiance to the new legislation, the ensuing clampdown appears to have been rigorous, assisted as it was by searchers and financial incentives, often paid by Thomas Scot, controller of the intelligence system, or Walter Frost, clerk of the Council.[141] Alongside the new legislation, the regime exerted yet greater pressure upon the press by placing three key civil servants as licensers. Frost licensed the *Brief Relation*, while Henry Scobell (clerk of Parliament) oversaw *Several Proceedings*, and John Rushworth (secretary to the army) managed the *Perfect Diurnall*. This division of labour probably reflected the pervasive force of factionalism within the Rump, although much more work needs to be done on the differences between these newspapers.[142] Later, in March 1651, the Council extended its influence further by appointing the Latin Secretary, John Milton, as licenser of *Mercurius Politicus*.[143] As men like Hugh Peter had recommended, the Rump had taken steps to subordinate the Stationers, and to increase the power of the Council.[144]

Peter had based his recommendation upon fear over the prominence of Presbyterians within the Stationers' company, and this was given credence by the emergence of suspicion regarding the complicity of leading stationers, including former licensers such as Cranford, in Presbyterian plots against the government.[145] It was also suspected that Presbyterians colluded not only in the forging of the licenser's *imprimatur*, but also in securing the entry of such forgeries into the Stationers' register.[146] Such fears were compounded by the 'Beacon' controversy, in which a number of Presbyterian printers sought to reassert the authority of the Stationers' Company, and which prompted a group of army leaders, under the guidance of Thomas Pride, to respond with the accusation that the Stationers, printers and licensers were undertaking a 'Machiavellian design' against the Rump.[147] In its attempts to neuter this threat, and to tighten press control yet further, the Rump was willing to consult with the Stationers, but it was not

---

[140] *CSPD 1653–4*, pp. 189, 276; N. Holmes, *The Resurrection Revealed* (London, 1653).

[141] *Mercurius Elencticus* 14 (23–30 July 1649), p. 111; *The Man in the Moon* 23 (19–26 Sept. 1649), p. 188; *CSPD 1649–50*, pp. 340, 385, 400, 401, 438, 527, 529, 552-3, 568; *CSPD 1650*, p. 16; *CSPD 1651–2*, pp. 39, 41, 164, 287.

[142] *SR* i. 328, 331.

[143] *SR* i. 362; B. Worden, 'Milton and Marchamont Nedham', in D. Armitage, A. Himy and Q. Skinner, eds, *Milton and Republicanism* (Cambridge, 1998); H. S. Anthony, '*Mercurius Politicus* under Milton', *JHI* 27 (1966); J. M. French, 'Milton, Needham and *Mercurius Politicus*', *Studies in Philology* 33 (1936); E. A. Beller, 'Milton and *Mercurius Politicus*', *HLQ* 5 (1951–2), p. 479. See also: Baron, 'Licensing readers, licensing authorities', pp. 219, 234–5.

[144] H. Peter, *Good Work for a Good Magistrate* (London, 1651), postscript. See also: W. Ball, *A Briefe Treatise* (London, 1651).

[145] Peter, *Good Work*, postscript; *CSPD 1651*, p. 247.

[146] *SR* i. 400; Clyde, *Struggle*, pp. 231–2.

[147] [F. Cheynell], *The Beacon Flameing* (London, 1652), p. 2; L. Fawne et al., *A Beacon Set on Fire* (London, 1652); [M. Sparke], *A Second Beacon Fired* (London, 1652); T. Pride et al., *The Beacons Quenched* (London, 1652).

prepared to restore the company's authority. The process of drafting new legislation was eventually completed in January 1653, when it was concluded that Bradshaw's press act was 'a good and profitable law', but that it had proved insufficient in its enforcement, and that this had created an opening for 'the artifice and subtlety of restless spirits, unwilling to be confined within the limits of orderly government'. The changes made to the act were such that 'the government and regulation of the said mystery of printing and printers shall from henceforth be and remain in the Council of State for the time being'. The act also replaced the secretary of the army with the Council's own 'agent', to license works concerning their affairs, although the man chosen was the old army client, Gilbert Mabbott, who had remained part of the secretariat since his dismissal as licenser in 1649, and who had been chosen by Cromwell as his parliamentary agent and intelligencer.[148] He was joined as licenser by John Thurloe, secretary to the Council of State, who took control of *Mercurius Politicus*.[149] Such legislative reform and administrative appointments reinforced the centralisation of power, and the sidelining of the Stationers, and clearly frustrated radical supporters of the republic such as Roger Williams, who complained that 'at this present the Devil rageth and clamours in petitions and remonstrances from the stationers and others to the Parliament, and all cry "shut up the press"'.[150]

Moreover, subsequent years saw yet greater attempts to exert Council control. Such plans were supported by the Stationers, but though the company employed lobbyists who were close to the regime, such as Marchamont Nedham, their impact is unclear.[151] From the summer of 1654, the pre-eminent licensers were Cromwell's secretary, William Malyn (who licensed *Perfect Occurrences* and *Several Proceedings*), as well as Gilbert Mabbott (who licensed the *Perfect Diurnall*) and John Thurloe (who was responsible for *Politicus*).[152] During the late summer and autumn of 1655, new orders were issued for 'speedy and due execution' of laws relating to unlicensed and scandalous books, and the Council sanctioned the suppression of all newspapers except those allowed by Cromwell

---

[148] *CSPD 1651*, pp. 278–9, 438, 439, 481; *CSPD 1651–2*, pp. 48, 169, 204, 238, 239, 322, 444, 455; *CJ* vii. 145, 153, 183, 231, 236, 239, 244–5; *Mercurius Politicus* 120 (16–23 Sept. 1652), p. 1896; *A&O* ii. 696–9; C. Blagden, *The Stationers Company: A History, 1403–1959* (London, 1960), p. 147. For Mabbott: Worcester College, Clarke LXIX, fos. 8v, 14v, 16v, 17; Clarke MS XXV, fos. 61, 63v, 64, 68, 69; Chequers, MS 782, fos. 8v, 10, 94v, 292v; *CSPD 1650*, p. 236; *CSPD 1652–3*, p. 376; *CSPD 1653–4*, p. 82; A. Woolrych, *Commonwealth to Protectorate* (Oxford, 1982), pp. 62, 116–17, 134–36; *HMC Leyborne*, pp. 76, 103–5. For Cromwell's commission to Mabbott, see: Folger Shakespeare Library, X.d.483.

[149] *SR* i. 406.

[150] G. W. LaFantasie, ed., *The Correspondence of Roger Williams. Volume I. 1629–53* (London, 1988), p. 366; Williams, *Struggle*, pp. 235–6. The Stationers' role does not appear to have been restored after 1660: H. Weber, *Paper Bullets. Print and Kingship under Charles I* (Lexington, 1996), pp. 152, 154.

[151] Stationers Company, Court Book C, fos. 278, 278v, 280, 292, 294; Stationers Company, Court Book D, fo. 15; *CSPD 1653–4*, p. 199.

[152] *SR* i. 451, 455, 467, 488.

and the Council, 'which', it was predicted by Mabbott, 'will be few or none at all'.[153] The two papers which survived were both licensed by Thurloe.[154] In part this renewed zeal reflected the need to respond to the threat posed by the likes of the Quakers, whose presses produced a flood of works which were scattered around the country, 'whereby many simple ignorant people are seduced by them'.[155] Signs of growing discontent with the government during the second half of 1658 prompted the Council to tighten the controls over the press once again, and although the regime was fighting a losing battle, as the number of tracts and pamphlets increased dramatically, Cromwellian control would survive until the recall of the Rump in 1659, and the centralisation of licensing power would be retained until the final dissolution of the (restored) Long Parliament in 1660.[156]

Licensing was one of the central aspects of the propaganda machinery developed during the 1640s and 1650s. The practice of licensing, and the attempt to enforce authors to submit their works for approval prior to publication, represented an attempt to do more than just prevent the appearance of undesirable books, and to censor passages where authors erred or transgressed. Licensing was a means of encouraging the appearance of works with whose message public authorities were in agreement. The story of the opening months of the Long Parliament is one in which the means of ensuring press control were removed, but what followed was a concerted effort to reassert authority and regain control over the appearance of scandalous and seditious literature. Moreover, licensing became a way of rectifying past wrongs and rehabilitating authors whose works had been savaged or suppressed by Laudian licensers, and who had faced harsh penal measures for expressing views which were deemed erroneous. The Long Parliament used licensing in order to secure the publication of a significant corpus of Puritan works, as well as books which supported policies and reforms adopted by politicians in the early 1640s. The exploration of licensing practices reveals, therefore, one of the key themes of this book, namely the importance of propaganda in the minds of politicians during the political upheavals of the seventeenth century. It was probably no coincidence that the majority of the parliamentarian licensers in the 1640s and early 1650s had proven literary, journalistic and editorial skills. Of course, licensing generally, though not necessarily, proved most useful in serving the need to produce propaganda which helped to promulgate versions of political and religious orthodoxy, rather than subtle propaganda which concealed the involvement of the political authorities.

As with all other areas of propaganda, however, licensing was a tool fought

---

[153] *Orders of his Highness the Lord Protector ... for Putting in Speedy and Due Execution* (London, 1655); *CP* iii. 53.

[154] *SR* ii. 70–225. The two papers were *Mercurius Politicus* and the *Publick Intelligencer*.

[155] *Perfect Proceedings of State Affaires* 306 (2–9 Aug. 1655), p. 4854.

[156] *CSPD* 1658–9, pp. 71, 374; W. G. Mason, 'The annual output of Wing-listed titles, 1649–1684', *The Library*, 5th series 29 (1978), pp. 219–20; *SR* ii. 254–7.

over by factions within Parliament. The propaganda value of the licensing system was made clear by the protracted and convoluted struggle over its control, which lasted until the early 1650s. Having initially been dominated by Presbyterians, it later became coveted by the Independents, who sought to overhaul the personnel undertaking licensing. Furthermore, as tensions emerged within the Independent coalition, both the radical army interest and the Independent grandees sought to exert influence over licensers and licensing, in order to ensure that the press spoke their respective languages. However, the developments which took place in response to the factionalisation of licensing involved, and led to, such power becoming increasingly closely associated with a centralised state apparatus, as semi-independent ministers and members of the Stationers' Company were removed from positions of influence over the press, in favour of men employed by, and more directly responsible to, Parliament and the Council of State. The story of press licensing in the 1640s and 1650s is crucial, therefore, to an understanding of propaganda and state-building in the mid-seventeenth century.

CHAPTER 5

Politicians and the Press

If the licensing system, and its exploitation, was the bedrock of civil war and Interregnum propaganda, then the superstructure was provided by much closer cooperation between political grandees and individual authors. Licensing reflected approval of particular works, but in seeking to understand the nature of civil war literature it is necessary to understand more than just the ways in which tracts and treatises received official sanction. It is also important to analyse the processes by which works were written, printed and published, and thus to explore evidence of political involvement in the commissioning and composition of polemical works, and evidence that political forces provided not merely the impetus to write and publish, but also logistical and financial assistance. The aim of this chapter is to analyse the ways in which politicians adopted a proactive approach to a range of literary forms, and moved beyond relying upon works which had been submitted to publicly appointed authorities in order to secure an official seal of approval. It demonstrates how efforts were made to exploit publishing opportunities which presented themselves, to encourage and support the publication of particular tracts and pamphlets, and to commission new works from authors with whom grandees were more or less intimately associated. This chapter is concerned, in other words, with the highest level of political involvement in the business of engaging with the public through the medium of print, and with works that most clearly conform to the strictly defined notion of propaganda with which this book is concerned. As with the licenser's *imprimatur*, which was sometimes very prominently displayed, official support and sanction could be made explicit, and readers could be informed that books had been 'ordered to be printed', or published by 'special command'. However, in the same way that understanding official licensing required more than simply analysing which books wore their seal of approval publicly, consideration of political involvement in composition and publication requires recognising the possibility that such support may have been hidden from public view. While visual signals help to conceptualise the methodology of political involvement in the press, it is necessary to delve much deeper into the archives in order to unearth evidence of the more or less surreptitious methods and mechanisms by which the appearance of polemical literature was inspired.

Crucial to any consideration of propaganda at this level are questions relating to the identity of the writers whose works were supported by public political authorities and individual grandees; the nature of the relationships which they forged; the mechanisms by which particular pieces were solicited, produced and published; and the extent to which official resources, most notably financial, were deployed. The answers to these questions will permit further comparison between royalists and parliamentarians, as well as more detailed evaluation of the impact of political factionalism at Westminster and Oxford, as well as at Whitehall and in the exiled royalist court. They will also allow further consideration of the extent to which the decades of England's troubles witnessed innovation in the sphere of public political print culture, and identification of those who were responsible for such impulses. Ultimately, detailed analysis of the ways in which political figures of the mid-seventeenth century dirtied their hands in the controversial business of orchestrating and organising propaganda will help inform discussions of changing styles of government, and administrative innovation, in the early modern period.

The place to commence analysis of surreptitious political support for favoured authors centres on attempts to offer shelter and protection. The language of patronage, as displayed in authorial statements and printed dedications, and as discussed above, resonated with notions of 'protection', and the gratitude which such protection provoked. Though to some extent formulaic, there is evidence that such statements were far from hollow. Protection from enterpreneurial and counterfeiting publishers was intrinsic to the process by which books were entered into the Stationers' register, and an official *imprimatur* served as a talisman against suggestions of political or religious incorrectitude. For conspiratorial and confrontational authors before the civil wars, protection was occasionally literal rather than merely metaphorical, and provided a means of evading the beagles of High Court and Star Chamber.[1] Physical protection remained relevant during the 1640s, as authors such as Paul Amiraut sought, and received, security from the dangers inherent in having displayed allegiance to one particular party, and the threats which inevitably resulted.[2] However, political tension, together with concern at the growing prevalence of scandalous literature, also ensured that political exchanges of the 1640s and 1650s were filled with allegations regarding the protection of pamphleteers and polemicists. Writing in 1649, one royalist reflected that when the king complained about specific works 'publicly printed, against his person and government', 'so little care was taken to redress it ... and complaints being made against pamphlets and seditious books, some of the members of the House of Commons were heard to say the work would not be done without them'.[3] In 1641, Sir Edward Nicholas grumbled that Parliament would only 'make semblance' of punishing the printers of the Earl of Holland's private

---

[1] M. Dowling, 'The gospel and court: reformation under Henry VIII', in P. Lake and M. Dowling, eds, *Protestantism and the National Church in Sixteenth Century England* (London, 1987), pp. 51–5; F. J. Levy, 'Staging the news', in A. F. Marotti and M. D. Bristol, eds, *Print, Manuscript and Performance* (Columbus, 2000), p. 262; P. W. Hasler, *The House of Commons 1558–1603* (3 vols, London, 1981), ii. 405–6.

[2] PRO, SP 24/1, fos. 84v, 113, 116v.

[3] *King Charles the First, No Man of Blood* ([London], 1649), p. 4.

letters, and in 1647, royalists complained about the tolerance shown towards works which explicitly advocated the execution of Charles I.[4]

Such claims are difficult to substantiate, but there are occasions when evidence from official records lends credence to accusations of favouritism and protection. Royalist attacks upon individual tracts were legion, and attempts were frequently made to force Parliament to investigate their appearance and trace their authors, and to issue complaints when such investigations were carried out less than wholeheartedly. When Sir Thomas Aston complained in April 1641 about the way in which the notorious pamphleteer, Henry Walker, had printed spurious petitions against episcopacy, the Lords launched an inquiry, but took no action. This prompted claims that Walker received merely a 'gentle rebuke', which was 'a slender punishment for so notorious a piece of forgery'.[5] Another occasion for which documentary evidence survives concerns Henry Parker's *A Question Answered*, about which Charles complained in a message which reached London on 25 April 1642. Despite Charles's demand that its author be found, and the fact that one Norton offered to identify the man responsible, Parliament took no action.[6] In 1651, furthermore, the Dutch ambassadors sought punishment for the publisher who had revived old stories of atrocities committed by Dutch colonial adventurers, 'but the Parliament … thinking it a seasonable service done [to] the public, took no notice of the proposal'.[7]

During the second half of the 1640s, protection became centred on factional tensions within Parliament, and part of the complex manoeuvres which also involved attempts to arrest, intimidate and prosecute both writers and printers who served rival political interests.[8] Writing in 1646, Thomas Edwards claimed that his fellow Presbyterians had been subjected to numerous pamphlet attacks by sectarians, which had gone unpunished, and whose authors had been sheltered, protected, and befriended, and even preferred to places of trust and honour.[9] Complaints were also made about works attacking the Scots, and about the blind eye being turned to scandalous pamphlets circulating within the army.[10] In 1648, Presbyterians issued more specific complaints regarding the protection offered by Independent politicians to sectarian authors. The stationer, Thomas Underhill, for example, complained about the lenient treatment of John Goodwin's *Hagio-*

---

[4] Surrey RO, G52/2/19/10; Bodl. MS Clarendon 29, fo. 67r–v. See also: Clarendon, *History*, ii. 438.

[5] *LJ* iv. 182, 186, 204–5, 210–11; Nalson, *Impartial Collection*, i. 795.

[6] *PHE* ii. 1183–5; *CJ* ii. 537; *His Majesties Message to the House of Peers, April 22 1642* (London, 1642); Rushworth, *Collections*, iv. 542–3; *OPH* x. 451–4; *An Exact Collection* (London, for Husband, 1643), pp. 150–51; *LJ* v. 14–15, 17; *PJ* ii. 228; PRO, SP 16/490, fos. 22–5; *CSPD 1641–3*, pp. 308–10.

[7] J. Davies, 'An account of the author', in J. Hall, *Hierocles Upon the Golden Verses* (London, 1657), sig. b4v. The work in question was: [J. Hall], *A True Relation* (London, 1651).

[8] *CJ* iv. 692–6; BL, Add. 31116, p. 571.

[9] T. Edwards, *Gangraena* (London, 1646), ii. 155, 185; J. G. Fotheringham, ed., *The Diplomatic Correspondence of Jean de Montereul* (2 vols, Edinburgh, 1898), i. 280.

[10] *CJ* v. 109; *LJ* ix. 70, 152, 156.

Mastix, by claiming that 'such props have these irreligious and rotten builders procured in Parliament'.[11] That factional politics underlay the treatment of controversial authors is also clear from the case of William Dell, whose 1646 military sermon resulted in a Presbyterian inspired summons to appear before the House of Lords. That Dell was protected by friends at Westminster appears evident from the fact that he was quickly able to evade the charges brought against him.[12] However, protection was not a racket controlled by the Independents. In April 1646, when the soldier and radical polemicist, George Wither, produced a work attacking his bitter enemy, Sir Richard Onslow, who was a Presbyterian member of the Commons, the Presbyterians narrowly defeated an Independent attempt to block the order for the book to be burnt, and for Wither to pay compensation of £500.[13] Furthermore, the prominent Presbyterian author, Josiah Ricraft, was granted a protection order by the Committee of Both Kingdoms, having claimed to have received threatening letters as a result of his opposition to the Independent minister, John Goodwin.[14]

Perhaps the most intriguing evidence of protection concerns the astrologer and pamphleteer, William Lilly. Lilly later recalled that when complaints were made to the Committee of Examinations regarding his *Starry Messenger* in 1645, he received promises of assistance from a group of prominent MPs – Sir Philip Stapliton, Sir Christopher Wray, Denzil Holles and Robert Reynolds – who were evidently close friends, and who promised 'to be at the committee time enough to do the business'. Reynolds apparently even took the chair to oversee Lilly's case.[15] Lilly also claimed to have received advice from John Selden on how to deal with a committee hearing upon another complaint.[16] Most intriguing, however, is the evidence from 1652, when *Merlinus Anglicus* was referred to the Committee for Plundered Ministers, and when William Lenthall advised Lilly of the passages against which objections had been raised. This enabled Lilly to print six copies of a revised version, which he was able to present to the committee in order to deny responsibility for the offending version. Although sent to prison, Lilly was released after another committee hearing arranged by his friends.[17]

Thus, while there is little evidence on which to base a comparison of royalist

---

[11] J. Vicars, *Coleman-Street Conclave Visited* (London, 1648), p. 27.

[12] *LJ* viii. 397, 401, 403, 407, 417–18, 422, 433–4, 436; W. Dell, *The Building and Glory of the Truely Christian and Spiritual Church* (London, 1646).

[13] *CJ* iv. 505, 639–40; BL, Add. 31116, pp. 528, 559. The book in question was: G. Wither, *Justitiarius Justificatus* (London, 1646).

[14] *CSPD 1644–5*, p. 484. For Ricraft and the Presbyterians, see J. S. A. Adamson, 'The peerage in politics, 1645–49' (Cambridge University PhD, 1986), p. 164.

[15] C. Burman, ed., *The Lives of Those Eminent Antiquaries* (London, 1774), pp. 68–71.

[16] Burman, ed., *Eminent Antiquaries*, pp. 71–2, 81.

[17] Burman, ed., *Eminent Antiquaries*, pp. 102–6; *CJ* vii. 195; H. Rusche, '*Merlini Anglici*: astrology and propaganda from 1644 to 1651', *EHR* 80 (1965), pp. 331–2. Whitelocke, a friend of Lilly, admitted that he 'did him service' in this committee: R. Spalding, ed., *The Diary of Bulstrode Whitelocke, 1606–1675* (Oxford, 1990), pp. 280, 499.

and parliamentarian attitudes towards protection of authors, it seems clear that certain pamphleteers were spared the investigation, interrogation and censure which their works had provoked demand for from some quarters, and that certain parliamentarians were prepared to go to extraordinary lengths, to the point of manipulating the parliamentary process and perverting the course of justice, in order to shelter favoured authors. Given the strength of the connections which can be shown to have existed between some of these authors and the individuals and institutions by whom they were protected, as well as the significance of the contextual evidence regarding the circumstances of the appearance of such works, it is possible to conclude that these instances of protection indicate not merely that such books and tracts were considered useful, but also that their appearance may have been encouraged in some way. Protection may have been offered most readily, in other words, to those authors who were working most closely with members of the political elite.

In order to test such a theory, it is necessary to extend our analysis beyond evidence of personal protection, in order to demonstrate how political grandees could play a more constructive role in the appearance of polemical texts, by offering practical and substantive assistance to authors, as well as by ordering the publication of a variety of forms of tracts and pamphlets.

At the most basic level this meant assisting the distribution process. The early Stuart guide to political obedience, Mocket's *God and the King*, was spread on the basis of royal injunctions and proclamations which created a legal obligation to own copies, and during the 1640s some works informed readers that they were 'commanded to be published in all churches and chapels throughout the kingdom', not least at public fasts and days of humiliation. However, official involvement in spreading polemical literature was rarely so obvious.[18] Godly grandees were involved in circulating Scottish propaganda during the late 1630s and early 1640s, exploiting networks of friends and family, clients and agents for spreading news, albeit in surreptitious ways, given that such activity was politically unacceptable.[19] The 1640s and 1650s witnessed greater sophistication and official involvement in

[18] *A Proclamation for the Confirmation of all Authorised Orders* (London, 1615); W. W. Greg, *A Companion to Arber* (Oxford, 1967), pp. 157–61; *The Moderator* (London, 1646); *A Miraculous Victory* (London, 1643).

[19] *CSPD 1638–9*, pp. 473, 507, 517, 518, 595; *CSPD 1639*, pp. 152, 159, 398, 401–3; *CSPD 1639–40*, p. 594; *CSPD 1640*, pp. 27, 622, 634–5, 638, 647–8; *CSPD 1640–1*, p. 40; PRO, SP 16/429, fos. 69–70v; A. Hughes, 'Thomas Dugard and his circle in the 1630s', *HJ* 29 (1986), p. 788; P. Donald, *An Uncounselled King* (Cambridge, 1990), pp. 28n, 189, 191, 230; J. Eales, *Puritans and Roundheads. The Harleys of Brampton Bryan and the Outbreak of the English Civil War* (Cambridge, 1990), p. 91; T. Rymer, *Foedera* (Hague, 1744), ix, part iii, pp. 4–5; Rushworth, *Collections*, iii. 1094–5; See also: T. Harris, 'Propaganda and public opinion in seventeenth century England', in J. D. Popkin, ed., *Media and Revolution* (Lexington, 1995), p. 51; F. J. Levy, 'How information spread among the gentry, 1550–1640', *JBS* 21 (1982); G. R. Elton, *Policy and Police. The Enforcement of the Reformation in the Age of Thomas Cromwell* (Cambridge, 1972), p. 187.

such activities, if not greater transparency. Contemporary commentators clearly perceived official involvement in the circulation of pamphlets from the outset of hostilities.[20] That such perceptions were valid is evident from the fact that Secretary of State Nicholas dispersed copies of royalist tracts, including *Mercurius Aulicus*, which managed to find their way to London and the localities.[21] During the Rump, Walter Frost was ordered to distribute such works, while the Council of State assisted in spreading books by John Milton by allowing them to be exported customs-free.[22] John Thurloe likewise masterminded the distribution of favoured books, and in January 1656, Major General William Goffe encourage him to assist a book by Samuel Richardson, which he hoped 'could but follow the pamphlets that have been of late very much spread among the churches'.[23]

Such activity was not made public, however, just as logistical assistance which extended to the printing process tended to be undertaken out of the public eye. This might mean guiding particular books through the press, but it is also evident that it could involve much more, not least since political and religious propaganda had always been organised cooperatively, and by means of collaboration and public contribution, as with the organised attempts to raise money and organise printing by members of godly communities, for whom 'seasonable treatises' were integral to both spreading the gospel and undermining the Laudian church.[24] Writers could be provided with the 'garrets' in which they wrote, and Thomas Edwards was provided with a weekly lecture by 100 London ministers, in order to provide him with the opportunity to concentrate on controversial issues, and London's godly also organised a collaborative press in 1640.[25] Moreover, such assistance could clearly extend into the realm of finance, and there had long been evidence of political and public figures financing scholars, not to mention allegations that specific works had been financed by individuals in order to further their political interests and ambitions.[26] A more public manifestation of such collaboration, however, involved the posthumous publication of works by

---

[20] R. E., *A Letter Written Out of the Country to Mr John Pym* (Oxford, 1642), p. 1.

[21] *CSPD 1644*, p. 64; *CJ* ii. 1003; *The True Informer* 26 (16–23 Mar. 1644), p. 186; *London Post* 28 (11–18 Mar. 1645), p. 8; P. W. Thomas, *Sir John Berkenhead, 1617–1679* (Oxford, 1969), pp. 53, 56 58–9.

[22] *CSPD 1649–50*, p. 273; *CSPD 1652–3*, p. 250; *CCSP* ii. 32.

[23] *TSP* iv. 414, 445–6, 545.

[24] J. Barwick, *ΙΕΡΟΝΚΗΣ, Or the Fight, Victory and Triumph of St Paul* (London, 1660), p. 137; BL, Add. 34164, fo. 100; T. M. McCoog, 'The slightest suspicion of avarice: the finances of the English Jesuit mission', *Recusant History* 19 (1988), p. 103; J. Bossy, 'The English Catholic community, 1603–1625', in A. G. R. Smith, ed., *The Reign of James VI and I* (Basingstoke, 1973), pp. 99–100; Peacey, 'Henry Parker', p. 19; J. T. Peacey, 'Seasonable treatises: a godly project of the 1630s', *EHR* 113 (1998).

[25] J. Bruce and T. T. Penrose, eds, *Correspondence of Matthew Parker* (Parker Society, Cambridge, 1853), pp. 411–12; *Letters and Journals of Robert Baillie*, ii. 215; *CSPD 1640–1*, p. 40; PRO, SP 16/467, fo. 16.

[26] M. Greengrass, 'The financing of a seventeenth century intellectual: contributions for Comenius, 1637–1641', *Acta Comeniana* 11 (1995), pp. 77–8; *CSPD 1631–3*, p. 274.

celebrated divines, undertaken by friends, acolytes and fellow ministers, as well as the 'marketing' provided by the contribution of epistles, whereby books received approbation, by means of a short introduction, from prominent public figures, whether political, literary or clerical.[27]

In addition to offering logistical assistance, members of the political elite also provided the impetus to print particular treatises and tracts.[28] Court sermons cannot necessarily be regarded as having been officially commissioned, given that it is not obvious by whom preachers were selected, and since they may have sought to influence, rather than merely represent, official views. Nevertheless, those sermons which appeared in print certainly reflected official approval, and official requests for publication. Such encouragement was generally made explicit, and is certainly confirmed by authorial recollections, and readers may always have assumed that it took place.[29] Later, many sermons before the Oxford Parliament were published 'by their order', 'by command of authority', or 'by the allowance of authority'.[30] Furthermore, while *Mercurius Aulicus* denied that the king ordered court sermons to be published, his testimony is contradicted by numerous examples of sermons which were printed 'by special command'.[31] Likewise, many

---

[27] For posthumous publication: C. Love, *Heaven's Glory* (London, 1653); C. Love, *A Treatise of Effectual Calling and Election* (London, 1653); BL, Add. 23146, fos. 51v, 70, 92, 94v–95; Hughes, 'Dugard', p. 775, 790–91; M. Dever, 'Richard Sibbes' (Cambridge University PhD, 1993), pp. 54–9, 202–8. For marketing devices: A. Milton, 'Licensing, censorship, and religious orthodoxy in early Stuart England', *HJ* 41 (1998), p. 631; J. Trapp, *A Commentary* (London, 1647), sig. av; J. Trapp, *A Brief Commentary* (London, 1646), sig. A4; J. Church, *The Divine Warrant of Infant Baptism* (London, 1648), sig. A2; *A Faithful Discovery of a Treacherous Design of Mystical Antichrist* (London, 1653); J. Keymor, *A Cleare and Evident Way for Enriching the Nations of England and Ireland* (London, 1650), sig. A2; T. Blake, *Mr Blake's Answer to Mr Tombes* (London, 1646).

[28] *CSPD 1611–18*, p. 417; *CSPD 1627–8*, pp. 585, 589; PRO, SP 16/94, fos. 78, 101.

[29] LPL, MS 943, p. 567; T. Birch, *The Court and Times of Charles the First* (2 vols, London, 1848), i. 214–15; A. Hunt, 'Tuning the pulpits: the religious context of the Essex revolt', in L. A. Ferrell and P. McCullough, eds, *The English Sermon Revised* (Manchester, 2000), p. 87; P. McCullough, *Sermons at Court* (Cambridge, 1998), pp. 5, 138–40; L. A. Ferrell, *Government by Polemic. James I, the King's Preachers and the Rhetoric of Conformity 1603–1625* (Stanford, 1998); M. McLure, *The Paul's Cross Sermons, 1534–1642* (Toronto, 1958); T. Claydon, 'The sermon, the 'public sphere' and the political culture of late seventeenth century England', in Ferrell and McCullough, eds, *English Sermon Revised*; G. Davies, 'English political sermons, 1603–1640', *HLQ* (1939), pp. 8, 16.

[30] H. Vaughan, *A Sermon* (Oxford, by Lichfield, 1644); H. Leslie, *The Blessing of Judah* (Oxford, by Lichfield, 1644); H. Ferne, *A Sermon* (Oxford, by Lichfield, 1644); W. Strode, *A Sermon* (Oxford, by Lichfield, 1644); N. Bernard, *A Looking-Glasse for Rebellion* (Oxford, by Lichfield, 1644); P. Gosnold, *A Sermon* (Oxford, by Hall, 1644). Richard Harwood noted, in his dedication to a sermon preached before MPs in the Oxford Parliament in 1645, that 'authority, that hath called me forth, must be my apologie': R. Harwood, *The Loyall Subject's Retiring Room* (Oxford, 1645), sig. *2.

[31] *Mercurius Aulicus* 14 (2–9 Apr. 1643), p. 180; J. Bramhall, *A Sermon Preached in York Minster* (York, 1643); W. Stampe, *A Sermon Preached Before His Maiestie* (Oxford, 1643), sig. A2; T. Fuller, *Jacobs Vow* (Oxford, by Lichfield, 1644); W. Strode, *A Sermon* (Oxford, by Lichfield, 1644); J. Birkenhead, *A Sermon* (Oxford, 1644); W. Chillingworth, *A Sermon Preached at the Publike Fast* (Oxford, 1644); I. Basire, *Deo et Ecclesiae Sacrum. Sacriledge Arraigned* (Oxford, by Lichfield, 1646). The dedication of the latter to the king added: 'but that, in obedience to your royal command, [wherein] I must now practice as well as preach allegiance, this present argument ... had never presumed further than your royal ear' (sig. A2).

sermons delivered at parliamentarian fasts and days of humiliation were printed with official sanction – 'by order' of the House – although this actually meant official *request* rather than *order*, and some preachers felt able to keep their texts out of the public domain.[32] Of course, factional politics probably also lay behind both the selection of ministers to preach on official occasions, as well as decisions regarding which sermons to print.[33]

Beyond official sermons, other works betrayed official backing, as *God and the King* had done, by informing readers that they were printed by the king's 'special privilege and command'.[34] During the 1640s, for example, there are many instances of the political exploitation of papers which were presented to the authorities, through explicit orders for their printing and publication. This was particularly true of petitions to Parliament or the king, which need not all be assumed to have been printed by those with whom they originated in order to garner public support or lobby authority, but may sometimes have been published by those who sought to capitalise upon the popular support which they demonstrated. Parliamentarian examples include a petition from the civic authorities in London in March 1642, a petition from prisoners at Oxford in February 1643, and petitions from Irish Protestants who had been coldly received at Oxford.[35] Royalists likewise exploited local expressions of support in the early phase of the war, and produced a substantial collection of such pieces, which was 'published by his Majesties special command' in May 1642.[36] Once hostilities

---

[32] Sample: S. Marshall, *A Sermon* (London, 1641); *CJ* ii. 30; C. Burgess, *Another Sermon* (London, 1641); *CJ* ii. 306. Calybute Downing evidently declined the request to publish his sermon of August 1642; *CJ* ii. 746–7. See also: R. Jeffs, ed., *Fast Sermons to Parliament* (34 vols, London, 1970–71); H. Trevor-Roper, 'The Fast sermons of the Long Parliament', in *Religion, the Reformation and Social Change* (London, 1973); J. F. Wilson, *Pulpit in Parliament* (Princeton, 1979).

[33] Not all preachers were asked to publish their sermons: *LJ* vii. 627; *CJ* iv. 290. Subtle factional politicking appears, for example, to have surrounded the selection of preachers for a fast concerning the growth of heresy in March 1647: *CJ* v. 66, 69, 86, 109; *LJ* viii. 706–7; Trevor-Roper, 'Fast sermons', p. 322.

[34] *God and the King* (London, 1615); *A Proclamation for the Confirmation of all Authorised Orders* (London, 1615); Greg, *Companion to Arber*, pp. 157–61.

[35] *LJ* iv. 651–2; *A True Copy of the Relation of the Lord Major* ('ordered to be printed and published', London, for Frank, 1642); *CJ* ii. 965; BL, Add. 18777, fo. 155a; *The Humble Petition of Divers Poor Prisoners* (imp. Elsyng, London, for Husbands, 1642); BL, Add. 31116, p. 282; *CJ* iii. 513–14; T. Morley, *A Remonstrance of the Cruelties Committed by the Irish Rebels Against the Protestants in Ireland* ('published by special command, London, 1644); *A Full Relation of the Late Expedition of Lord Monroe in Ulster* ('published by authority, London, for Wright, 1644); BL, Add. 31116, p. 306; *A Declaration of the Lords and Gentry... of Lemster and Munster* ('published according to order', London, 1644); *A Manifestation Directed to the Honourable Houses of Parliament... from the Lord Inchequin* (imp. Brown, London, for Wright, 1644). See also *The Humble Petition of the County of Southampton* (London, for Hunscott, 1641). For the importance of petitions, see: D. Zaret, *Origins of Democratic Culture* (Princeton, 2000), chap. 8.

[36] *A Collection of Sundry Petitions* (np, 1642); *The Humble Petition of the Major, Aldermen and Commons of the Citty of London* (Oxford, 1642); *The Humble Petition of the Inhabitants of the County of Hertford* (Oxford, by Lichfield, 1642); *The Humble Petition of the Inhabitants of the County of Essex* (Oxford by Lichfield, 1642). The king also ordered the publication of at least one London petition which had been presented to him, in January 1643: BL, Add. 18777, fo. 123a.

commenced, furthermore, both sides eagerly capitalised upon news of military victories which was sent in letters to prominent grandees.[37] Such works often advertised their origins by being produced by official printers; by having obviously been read in Parliament or royal council; and by the prominent place accorded to official orders and warrants for publication, including those of the parliamentary clerks at Oxford and Westminster.[38] Important parliamentarian examples include: Audley Mervyn's relation concerning the Irish rebellion; the letters of Stephen Marshall and Philip Nye from the negotiations with the Scots over the Solemn League and Covenant; and news of a victory over Ormond in the summer of 1649.[39] The process of ascertaining the official nature of certain news tracts and intercepted letters, furthermore, can be assisted by matching printed works with manuscripts in official archives.[40] Moreover, such attempts to exploit military news were also employed by individual grandees in order to enhance their reputation, and on one occasion, in October 1643, the Earl of Essex secured an order for the publication of a relation of his victory at the Battle of Newbury.[41]

It was not merely valuable news and petitions which received such treatment,

---

[37] BL, Add. 18777, fos. 74a; BL, Add. 31116, pp. 225, 519; Bodl. MS Nalson XIII, fo. 386.

[38] *A Most True and Exact Relation of Both the Battels* ('commanded to be printed', London, for Hunscott, 1642); *An Exact and True Relation* (imp. Elsyng, London, for Husband and Frank, 1642); *Magnalia Dei* ('published by authority and entered according to order, London, 1644); *A True Relation Concerning the Late Fight at Torrington* ('ordered to be printed', London, for Husband, 1645); *A Miraculous Victory* (imp. Elsyng, London, for Husband, 1643); *The Good and Prosperous Success* (London, for Wright, 1642, imp. Browne); *A Perfect Relation of the Taking of ... Preston* (imp. Elsyng, London, for Husband, 1642); *Good Newes from Sea, Being a True Relation of the Late Sea-Fight* (imp. Elsyng, London, 1643); J. Ashe, *A Second Letter* (imp. Elsyng, London, Husband and Frank, 1642); J. Ashe, *A Perfect Relation* (imp. Brown, London, Hunscott and Wright, 1642); *Some Notable Observations Upon the Late Summons by the Earl of Newcastle* ('appointed to be printed', London, Husband, 1643); *Worse and Worse Newes from Ireland, Being the Coppy of a Letter Read in the House of Parliament, the 14. of this Instant Moneth of December, 1641* (London, for N. Butter, 1641); *A Most Exact Relation of a Great Victory* ('ordered to be printed', London, for Hunscott, 1642); *The Kings Cabinet Opened* ('published by special order of the Parliament', London, 1645). See also: *Two Letters Sent from Amsterdam* (London, for Hunscott and Wright, 1642). For royalists: *A True Relation of a Late Victory Obtained by Sir Ralph Hopton* (Printed by His Majesties Special Command, Oxford, 1642).

[39] *CJ* ii. 607; *PJ* iii. 20; A. Mervyn, *An Exact Relation* ('published by order of the House of Commons', London, 1642); BL, Harl. 165, of. 159; *A Letter from Mr Marshall and Mr Nye* ('published by order of the House of Commons', London, 1643); *CSPD 1649–50*, p. 273; *Lieut. General Jones's Letter to the Council of State* (imp. Frost, London for Husband, 1649).

[40] Bodl. MS Nalson XIII, fos. 424–27v; *HMC Portland I*, p. 177; *A True Relation of the Proceedings of Colonell Langharne* ('printed according to order', London, 1644); Bodl. MS Nalson XVIII, fos. 336–7, 366–8; *The Answer of the Parliament of the Commonwealth of England, to Three Papers Delivered into the Councel of State* (London, by Field, 'printer to the Parliament of England', 1652); Bodl. MS Nalson II, fos. 47, 49; Bodl. MS Nalson XII, fo. 83; *CJ* ii. 647.

[41] *CJ* iii. 265; *A True Relation of the Late Expedition* (imp. Elsyng, London, 1643). The same motives may explain the existence of two brief works, which appear to survive only in manuscript, which relate the military achievements of the Earl of Denbigh, and which survive among his papers: Warwickshire RO, CR 2017/R7–8: 'A true relation of the right hon. the Earl of Denbigh ... His Marches and Martial Actions' (1644), and 'A True Relation of the Earl of Denbigh his Proceedings' (1644).

but also more substantial treatises. Many royalist works produced by official printers were said to have been 'published by special command' or by 'His Majesties command', and these include: collections of official papers relating to peace treaties; reflections upon such negotiations by the likes of Sir William Dugdale; and important works by the likes of Dudley Digges, and by the astrologer George Wharton.[42] Other evidence, however, indicates that royalist aspirations to organise propaganda proved unsuccessful. During 1643, for example, Hyde was concerned to see that royalist tracts were reprinted at Shrewsbury, but having sent copies of such works, he subsequently expressed concern that the press was idle, and that Parliament was getting the upper hand.[43] This is not the only evidence that royalists found difficulty in getting tracts printed and distributed, and local royalist sympathisers appear to have been forced to circulate works in manuscript form.[44] Moreover, such difficulties became harder to overcome after the fall of Oxford in 1646. In 1650, the royalist ambassador in Paris was instructed to 'divulge and publish' the French translation of the proceedings at the king's trial, but it is not possible to verify his success, nor that of Hyde's attempts to locate unpublished works by Salmasius, or to publish the Levellers' address to Charles II, as he was instructed to do in January 1657.[45]

Parliamentarians, on the other hand, appear to have been far better able to secure the printing of works which they sought to publish. Members ordered the publication of keynote speeches from the trial of Strafford, as well as the sermon which had caused the suspension of Henry Wilkinson in 1640, and which readers were informed had been 'printed by order from the House of Commons'.[46] In early

---

[42] BL, Harl. 6802, fo. 19 [second foliation]; *The Collection of all the Particular Papers* (Oxford, by Lichfield, 1643); *A Full Relation of the Passages Concerning the Late Treaty* (Oxford, by Lichfield, 1645); [Sir W. Dugdale], *Considerations Touching the Late Treaty* (Oxford, by Lichfield, 1645); D. Digges, *An Answer to a Printed Book* (Oxford, 1642); *Christus Dei* (Oxford, by Hall, 1643); D. Digges, *A Review of the Observations* (York, 1643); J. Barwick, *Certain Disquisitions* (Oxford, by Lichfield, 1644); M. Pricket, *An Appeale to the Reverend and Learned Synod of Divines* (Oxford, Lichfield, 1644); G. Wharton, *Wharton 1645. An Almanack* (Oxford, by Hall, 1645); G. Wharton, *Naworth 1644. A New Almanack* (Oxford, by Hall, 1644); J. Taylor, *Of the Sacred Order and Offices of Episcopacy* (Oxford, Lichfield, 1642).

[43] W. Phillips, ed., 'The Ottley papers relating to the civil war', *Transactions of the Shropshire Archaeological and Natural History Society*, 2nd series 6 (1894), pp. 55–6; W. Phillips, 'The Ottley papers', *Transactions of the Shropshire Archaeological and Natural History Society*, 2nd series 7 (1895), pp. 344–5.

[44] In January 1644, for example, George Edgely, rector of Nuthurst in Sussex, mentioned having circulated manuscript copies of *A Plaine Case*: PRO, PRO 30/5/6, pp. 330–31; *A Plaine Case* ([Oxford], 1643).

[45] BL, Eg. 2547, fo. 13; J. Peacey, 'Reporting a revolution: a failed propaganda campaign', in Peacey, ed., *The Regicides and the Execution of Charles I* (Basingstoke, 2001), p. 173; *CCSP* ii. 233, 255; Bodl. MS Clarendon 46, fo. 262.

[46] Stationers Company, Liber A, fo. 131; O. St John, *An Argument of Law* ('published by order of the Commons', London, 1641); J. Pym, *The Declaration of John Pym* ('by order of the Commons House', London, 1641); H. Wilkinson, *A Sermon Against Lukwarmenesse in Religion* (London, 1641), sig. A3; *CJ* ii. 57. Wilkinson was granted liberty to print, rather than being ordered to do so.

1644, the House ordered the publication of the 'exhortation' in support of the Solemn League and Covenant, which had been penned by Philip Nye, and which appeared with the *imprimatur* of the Clerk of the Commons.[47] Other works professed to have been 'ordered to be printed according to an order of the House of Commons', although such claims must be treated with scepticism in the absence of supporting evidence.[48] After the outbreak of the Dutch war in the 1650s, the Council of State ordered the republication of Selden's *Mare Clausum*, which was undertaken by the official printer.[49] Moreover, Parliament also sought to exploit the potential offered by works with which it had been presented. In the spring of 1642, the Commons ordered the publication of the remonstrance which Dr Henry Jones had presented regarding the Irish rebellion, just as in the spring of 1649 the Council approved the publication of a work by Sir William Parsons, in order to assert the English interest in Ireland, although the latter does not appear to have borne fruit.[50] During the 1650s, Thurloe was ordered to arrange the publication of works such as *Curia Politica*, which betrayed official involvement on its final page.[51] Of course, the impetus to print, and official orders for publication, could also reflect factional interests, and it was probably the Independent peers who ordered the scribe of the Westminster Assembly to publish a book by the dissenting brethren in January 1648, which again revealed official involvement on its inside pages.[52]

Nevertheless, the authorities were only sometimes willing to make their influence publicly known. The official origin of particular petitions and relations is not always transparent, and certain works which betray little evidence of official instigation can be shown to have emerged as a result of official orders, and from official sources.[53] Moreover, political grandees and public authorities sometimes refrained from demonstrating their orchestration of more substantial works whose appearance can nevertheless be ascribed to them. Griffith Williams

---

[47] Stationers Company, Liber A, fo. 131; P. Nye, *An Exhortation* (London, 1644); *CJ* iii. 394; Rushworth, *Collections*, v. 475–7; BL, Add. 31116, pp. 158, 229. This work subsequently appeared as an appendix to the official account of the covenant, copies of which were ordered to be sent throughout the kingdom in February 1644: *The Covenant … Also Two Speeches … the One by Mr Nye* (London, 1643); *An Ordinance of the Lords and Commons … With Instructions for Taking of the League and Covenant … With an Exhortation for the Taking of the Covenant* (London, 1643).

[48] *The Justification of a Safe and Wel-Grounded Answer to the Scottish Paper* (London, 1646).

[49] *CSPD 1651–2*, p. 303.

[50] *CJ* ii. 480, 490; H. Jones, *A Remonstrance of Divers Remarkable Passages* (London, 1642); *CSPD 1649–50*, pp. 53, 131–2; PRO, SP 25/62, pp. 118, 279-80. Parsons was late Lord Justice of Ireland.

[51] *CSPD 1653–4*, p. 287; *Curia Politiae* (trans. E. Wolley, London, 1654), p. 191.

[52] *LJ* ix. 676; *The Reasons Presented by the Dissenting Brethren* (London, 1648), sig. A2v.

[53] Accounts of victory of Chudleigh over Hopton, which was ordered to be printed, do not betray their origins: BL, Add. 31116, p. 93; *Exploits Discovered* (London, 1643); *A Most Miraculous and Happy Victory* ([London], 1643); *A Full Relation of the Great Defeat* (London, 1643). Other pamphlets can be traced to manuscripts in the official archives: HLRO, MP 5/9/42; *A True Relation of the Late Proceedings of the London Dragonners Sent to Oxford under Sir John Seaton* (London, 1642).

recalled that the publication of his *Discovery of Mysteries* was sanctioned by the king, albeit only after an attempt by Viscount Falkland to suppress it on account of a passage regarding episcopacy.[54] Sir Edward Hyde claimed that his answer to the 'grand remonstrance' was published by royal command, although only after Lord Digby had happened to mention its existence to the king.[55] The evidence provided by Williams and Hyde indicates that official involvement was not necessarily made apparent to readers. One means of detecting such involvement is by examining the treatment of works which had been submitted to politicians on a more or less speculative basis. Many such works did not find their way into print, such as William Chillingworth's many outlines and drafts which remain among Laud's papers, and Sir Edward Walker's response to Lilly, which Hyde does not appear to have favoured.[56] Some works clearly received an unfavourable reception and critical comments, such as those expressed by Hyde in January 1653 regarding a book by Joseph Jane, which he doubted was 'sharp enough, and weighty enough, to get much credit'.[57] Some proved entirely unacceptable, such as the account of Montrose's military proceedings during the civil war, which the Prince of Wales rejected in 1647 on the grounds that certain 'persons of honour' were seriously impugned by the author; or the book by Robert Sheringham, which faced hostility from certain royalists because of its Presbyterianism.[58] It was not only personal and factional differences which affected the success of such submissions, however, and it was clearly possible for more mundane factors to come into play. Some proposals were rejected on grounds of timing rather than content, and others failed because political grandees lacked the time or inclination to consider them closely.[59]

Nevertheless, some books elicited a more favourable reception. Charles II evidently approved a number of books, including one submitted by Joseph Jane in 1652, and another written by a Benedictine monk in Rome.[60] Other works which were submitted for approval may be presumed to have been received warmly because of their subsequent publication, albeit some can be shown to have

---

[54] G. Williams, *The Persecution and Oppression* (London, 1664), p. 7.

[55] Clarendon, *Life*, i. 97–100.

[56] LPL, MS 943, pp. 855–937; P. Des Maizeaux, *The Life of William Chillingworth* (London, 1863), pp. 296, 301–2; BL, Add. 33223, fo. 96. Walker's work remains in manuscript form: BL, Add. 33224.

[57] Bodl. MS Clarendon 45, fo. 18v. See also: *CSPD 1611–18*, p. 231.

[58] BL, Stowe 184, fo. 213v; *CCSP* ii. 206, 243; *NP* ii. 13–14. Profound differences of opinion existed over the desirability of a particular French edition of the proceedings at the trial of Charles I by Marsys. Some courtiers clearly found this unacceptable: BL, Eg. 2547, fos. 5–10v. For more favourable comments, see: Beinecke Library, Yale, Osborn Files: Abraham Cowley to Robert Long, 21 Dec. 1649. See: Peacey, 'Reporting a revolution', p. 173.

[59] *Letters and Journals of Robert Baillie*, ii. 1. Similarly, Laud told Samuel Brooke that his work on predestination was acceptable in its own right, but the king did not want controversies stirred up: Laud, *Works*, vi. 292; PRO, SP 16/176, fo. 75; SP 16/177, fos. 8r–v; *CCSP* ii. 143.

[60] Bodl. MS Clarendon 43, fo. 139v; *CCSP* ii. 261, 230; Bodl. MS Clarendon 46, fo. 307.

appeared in slightly amended forms.[61] Parliamentarians too sought to keep their influence hidden on occasions, although it is evident that they were able to acquire manuscripts of old works which were considered beneficial to current arguments. These included the legalism of Sir Edward Coke, the second part of whose 'institutes' the Commons encouraged into print, and the baronialism of papers which are known to have come from collections in the possession of powerful grandees.[62] Other parliamentarian works which betray little visible evidence of their origins may be considered to have appeared with official backing from the existence of copies in the official archives.[63] Private correspondence reveals that it was the parliamentarian soldier and regicide, Sir Hardress Waller, who decided to print Robert Bennet's powerful defence of the trial of Charles I, which had been sent to him as a 'worthy present'.[64] The Rump's Council of State, moreover, ordered the publication of a number of works which are not obviously identifiable, including a treatise justifying invasion of Scotland, and 500 copies of a treatise on exchange.[65] Robert Baillie's papers, meanwhile, indicate the role of the Scottish commissioners in promoting a factional agenda, by encouraging the publication of Thomas Edwards' massive tirade against the Independents in 1646.[66]

Official involvement in the appearance of tracts and pamphlets was acknowledged on some occasions, but concealed on many others. Financial backing, on the other hand, was handled with much greater care, and strenuous efforts were made to ensure secrecy. Nevertheless, evidence indicates a growing tendency for official involvement to include financial assistance from the second half of the 1640s, although this too was an area where royalists proved less willing, or less able, than their parliamentarian rivals. In one of the few instances where royalists are known to have attempted to finance publication, regarding a book prepared by one Davis, they were forced to rely upon voluntary contributions from royalist courtiers.[67] Among parliamentarians, meanwhile, the army provided

---

[61] *CSPD 1657–8*, pp. 142–3; Bodl. MS Clarendon 21, fos. 173v–192v (H. W., 'A copy of a letter sent to a friend at Oxford together with his argument', dated London 12 Jan. 1642/3); *CCSP* i. 236.

[62] *PJ* ii. 262; *D'Ewes Diary*, ed. Notestein, pp. 108, 118, 174, 358; BL, Harl. 164, fo. 211; *CJ* ii. 45–6, 144, 470; Sir. E. Coke, *The Second Part of the Institutes* (London, 1642); *Certain Observations Touching the Two Great Offices of the Seneshalsey or High Stewardship and High Constableship of England* (London, 1642); BL, Cotton MS Titus C.I, fos. 25–30v; J. S. A. Adamson, 'The baronial context of the English civil war', *TRHS*, 5th series 40 (1990), pp. 98–9.

[63] J. Ley, *Englands Doxologie* (London, 1641); *CSPD 1641–3*, p. 230; PRO, SP 16/487, fos. 171–77v; *Arguments Proving that We Ought Not to Part with the Militia* (London, 1646); *CSPD 1645–7*, p. 451; PRO, SP 16/514, fo. 64.

[64] Folger Shakespeare Library, X.d.483/37: Sir Hardress Waller to Robert Bennet, 8 May 1649. Waller explained that 'as I cannot but highly acknowledge and value' the volume, 'so I could not ingross it to myself, it being a fit present for others, which the press will make way for'. The published version printed Bennet's letter with which he sent the book to Waller, on 23 April 1649: R. Bennet, *King Charle's Triall Justified* (London, 1649), p. 16.

[65] *CSPD 1650*, pp. 281, 448; *CSPD 1653–4*, p. 287; *Curia Politiae*, p. 191.

[66] *Letters and Journals of Robert Baillie*, ii. 278–9.

[67] BL, Add. 37047, fo. 209.

secretive financial support for the printing of books such as Joshua Sprigge's *Anglia Rediviva* (1647), while commonwealth regimes were able to devote significant sums of money to a number of projects, without making readers aware of the depth of their involvement.[68] In addition to financing an unspecified tract regarding the Engagement in June 1652, the Council of State provided £20 to Thomas Paine and Matthew Simmons for the cost of printing a sermon which Henry Walker had delivered before Cromwell's departure for Scotland in 1650, and also gave £50 to Nathaniel Holmes to print *Resurrection Revealed*.[69] The extent of their financial commitment to such works is evident from the willingess of the Protectorate Council to finance 2,000 copies of Samuel Morland's hefty history of the sufferings of the Protestants in Piedmont, to the tune of £700.[70] Moreover, such payments could also be paid retrospectively, for works which had appeared independently, but which were considered to have been useful, such as Thomas White's life of Charles I, for which they made a secret payment of £50.[71] Indeed, money could clearly be used to encourage the likes of Dr Goodwin, to whom Thurloe planned to pay £150 per annum as an incentive to concentrate on literary tasks rather than administrative duties at Cambridge.[72]

The close reader of civil war literature is made aware, therefore, that the publication of certain works was officially inspired, because political grandees and public authorities were prepared not merely to issue orders instigating printing and distribution, but also to make such orders in the public domain. Although the veracity of such public statements needs to be tested with reference to official archives and papers, they are clearly invaluable in conceptualising the politics of print culture in the early modern period, and the nature of the forces which underpinned the appearance of polemical literature. Moreover, examination of such evidence reveals many examples of works which concealed official orders, not to mention official financial backing, and suggests that parliamentarians proved more adept at both sponsoring political tracts and providing logistical support. Such conclusions cannot fail to influence profoundly our understanding of civil war polemic and propaganda.

Given such willingness on the part of royalists and parliamentarians to support, more or less publicly, the appearance of works which were perceived to be

---

[68] Chequers, MS 782, fo. 42v; E. Kitson and E. K. Clarke, 'Some civil war accounts, 1647–50', *Publications of the Thoresby Society* 11 (1904), p. 140; J. Sprigge, *Anglia Rediviva* (London, 1647).

[69] *CSPD 1651–2*, p. 303; *CSPD 1650*, p. 345; H. Walker, *The Creation of the World* (London, 1650); *CSPD 1653–4*, p. 225. For the engagement tract in question, see: A. Norwood, *New Errors* (London, 1652).

[70] R. Vaughan, *The Protectorate of Oliver Cromwell* (2 vols, London, 1839), ii. 97; *TSP* vi. 590; BL, Add. 32471, fo. 8; *CSPD 1656–7*, pp. 342, 367; *CSPD 1655*, p. 607.

[71] *CSPD 1651*, pp. 480, 497; *The Life and Reign of King Charls* (London, 1651). White later received £20 for another book 'on behalf of the public': *CSPD 1652–3*, p. 487.

[72] *TSP* vi. 539, 558.

beneficial to their respective causes, it was natural that political influence extended to commissioning and payments for the composition of particular tracts and pamphlets.[73] Seeking to demonstrate the existence of political and religious works whose formulation was inspired in this way requires exploring contemporary perceptions and authorial reflections and recollections, as well as concrete evidence from contemporary records, and it requires, moreover, sensitivity to questions of publicity, and the ability of readers to discern official involvement in textual formation.

Contemporaries clearly perceived that works were written in this way, although many accusations to this effect were rather vague, like the author who asked: 'what vile doctrines and cursed uses do their pamphleteers and their pulpiteers ... press upon the people?'[74] Pym was accused of supporting polemicists, and of having recognised their value to the cause, while Oliver St John was said to operate by 'unknown quils or conduits underground'.[75] Charles claimed that parliamentarian works were published 'by their direction, at least under their countenance', while Griffith Williams suggested that books were 'sent out of the bottomless pit to seduce the people of God and to lead them headlong into perdition', and 'with apparent lies, palpable slanders and abominable accusations, invented, printed and scattered over all parts of this kingdom by their trencher chaplains and parasitical preachers, and other pamphleteers, some busy lawyers and pettyfoggers'.[76] Parliamentarians likewise sought to discredit their opponents with allegations regarding the commissioning of royalist books. One writer claimed that the king's cause 'devolved from arms to pens', and that 'the wits of the ruined party had their secret clubs, [which] hatched mercuries, satires, and pasquinadoes, that travelled up and down the streets with so much impunity'.[77]

Beyond such generalities, however, were claims regarding specific authors and specific books. Bemoaning the influence of Laud over the press, therefore, Pym claimed that the archbishop had 'for the better accomplishment of his traiterous design, advised and procured sermons, and other discourses, to be preached, printed, and published, in which the authority of Parliaments, and the force of the laws of this kingdom, have been denied'. He concluded that the archbishop had 'been a great protector, favourer and promoter of the publishers of such false and

---

[73] M. H. Curtis, 'The Hampton Court conference and its aftermath', *History* 46 (1961); P. Croft, 'The reputation of Robert Cecil: libels, political opinion and popular awareness in the early seventeenth century', *TRHS*, 6th series 1 (1991), p. 65; R. Rex, 'The English campaign against Luther in the 1520s', *TRHS*, 5th series 39 (1989), pp. 89, 97, 101; D. H. Willson, 'James I and his literary assistants', *HLQ* 8 (1944–5), pp. 44–5, 52.

[74] T. Woodnote, *Hermes Theologus* (London, 1649), sig. A3.

[75] *King Charles the First, No Man of Blood*, p. 4; *Mercurius Elencticus* 10 (26 Jan.–2 Feb. 1648), p. 71.

[76] *Exact Collection*, p. 558; G. Williams, *The Discovery of Mysteries* ([Oxford], 1643), pp. 48–9, 69, 77.

[77] Quoted in D. Hirst, 'The politics of literature in the English republic', *Seventeenth Century* 5 (1990), pp. 139–40.

pernicious opinions'.[78] In August 1642, Charles claimed that Parker's *Observations* had been orchestrated by his parliamentarian critics.[79] Later, Griffith Williams named John Goodwin, Cornelius Burges, Stephen Marshall, Obadiah Sedgwick and William Prynne among those parliamentarian 'emissaries of wickedness' who were suffered to 'publish such treasons and blasphemies and abominable aphorisms'.[80] John Taylor, meanwhile, accused Henry Walker of being the 'tongue of [Viscount] Saye', while another royalist claimed that he was 'hired' by Cromwell 'with £30', to reprint Robert Parsons' notorious monarchomach treatise, copies of which were 'cunningly conveyed into the hands of Bradshaw and the regicides as a catechism to instruct them'.[81] Among parliamentarians, Francis Cheynell dedicated his attack upon William Chillingworth to a number of the latter's 'patrons and encouragers', who were 'the licensers of his subtle atheism'.[82] John Milton claimed that Salmasius was 'hired ... and at a large price' to write for the royalists; adding that 'you were unwilling to defend Charles the father, best of kings in your judgement ... without some royal recompense'. He went on to suggest that *Defensio Regia* was 'bought indeed for a hundred sovereigns, a fat reward from a starving king', and he claimed to know 'who brought the coins to your house, who carried that beaded purse, I know who saw you stretch forth your greedy hands, pretending to embrace the king's chaplain, who had been sent with your gift, but actually embracing the gift itself'.[83]

The problematic nature of contemporary claims, which may, after all, have been inspired by political necessity rather than historical veracity, requires that such statements be supplemented by authorial comments. Obviously, authors only rarely admitted in print that they wrote at the request of politicians, not least because part of the purpose of being a propagandist was to conceal the mechanisms by which works appeared, and because of contemporary hostility towards the idea of the 'hired pen', and the opprobrium heaped upon men whose services were deemed to have been 'bought' in this way. Nevertheless, authors were occasionally prepared to admit that they were serving the interests of patrons and politicians, and dedications provide important evidence regarding

---

[78] Rushworth, *Collections*, iii. 1367. Such accusations proved to be an important plank of the charge against Laud at his trial: *HMC House of Lords XI*, p. 369.

[79] *Exact Collection*, p. 558.

[80] Williams, *Discovery of Mysteries*, pp. 48–9, 69, 77. Prynne, indeed, was commonly regarded as having offered his services to political grandees since being set to work by figures such as John Preston in the 1620s: P. Heylyn, *Cyprianus Anglicus* (London, 1671), p. 149.

[81] J. Taylor, *A Reply as True as Steele* (London, 1641), p. 6; *The Man in the Moon* 12 (27 June–4 July 1649), sig. Mv.

[82] F. Cheynell, *Chillingworthi Novissima* (London, 1644), sig. A. The men in question were Sir John Culpeper, John Prideaux, Dr John Fell, Dr Thomas Bayly, Dr Gilbert Sheldon, Dr Christopher Potter and Dr George Morley.

[83] *The Complete Prose Works of John Milton IV* (New Haven, 1966), pp. 308–9; J. M. French, 'Some notes on Milton', *N&Q* 188 (1945), pp. 52–55. For Salmasius' denial of such charges: *Claudii Salmasii Ad Johannem Miltonum Responsio, Opus Posthumum* (London, 1660), pp. 21, 207.

commissioned polemics.[84] Such evidence can be supplemented, however, by comments such as that written in the late 1650s by the Cambridge academic, Ralph Cudworth, who informed John Thurloe that he was 'persuaded by friends to publish some discourses … that will be of a polemical nature'.[85] Such comments generally survive in recollections, memoirs, autobiographies, and biographies. At Laud's trial, therefore, William Prynne recalled that he wrote his 1628 reply to John Cosins because he was 'desired by some Parliament men to answer it', while in 1659 William Mewe informed Richard Baxter that he had been asked to reply to Milton's divorce tracts whilst a member of the Westminster Assembly of Divines.[86] The will of Daniel Featley, meanwhile, mentioned a book which had been commissioned by Lord Craven, and which was 'perfect for the press', though never printed.[87] Furthermore, Peter Heylyn's autobiographical account – together with Laud's papers and Heylyn's first biography – reveal not just that he was commissioned to write polemical works by Charles and Laud in the 1630s, but also that he was commissioned by Sir John Berkenhead to write 'a little book called *The Rebells Catechism*' in 1643.[88] Hyde's memoirs, meanwhile, indicate that he was often called upon 'for a speech, or a letter, which he very often provided upon several occasions, and the king always commanded them to be printed', as well as that he was commanded to 'write some discourse' in reply to Cromwell's 1655 declaration justifying decimation, in order to 'awaken the people … which he did by way of a letter to a friend'.[89]

Of course, the most valuable evidence is of a contemporary nature, although the hostility to the idea of political orchestration of polemical literature may mean that commissions and payments tended to be surreptitious or elliptic in nature.[90] Some

---

[84] above, pp. 78–82.

[85] *TSP* vii. 595. See also: BL, Add. 70001, fos. 49–50.

[86] *HMC House of Lords XI*, p. 429; W. Prynne, *A Briefe Survey and Censure of Mr Cozens His Couzening Devotious* (London, 1628); N. H. Keeble and G. F. Nuttall, eds, *Calendar of the Correspondence of Richard Baxter* (2 vols, Oxford, 1991), i. 406.

[87] PRO, PROB 11/193, fo. 266v.

[88] LPL, MS 731, pp. 1–159; P. Heylyn, *Memorial of Bishop Waynflete*, ed. J. R. Bloxam (London, 1851), p. xxiii; G. Vernon, *The Life of … Dr Peter Heylyn* (London, 1682), pp. 38, 87–8, 89–91, 95–6, 123, 128; Heylyn, *Cyprianus*, pp. 198–200, 279, 295, 312; J. Davies, *The Caroline Captivity of the Church* (Oxford, 1992), pp. 33–4; A. Milton, 'The Laudians and the church of Rome, c.1625–1640' (Cambridge University PhD, 1989), p. 148n; A. Milton, 'The creation of Laudianism: a new approach', in T. Cogswell, R. Cust and P. Lake, eds, *Politics, Religion and Popularity in Early Stuart Britain* (Cambridge, 2002), pp. 170–71.

[89] Clarendon, *Life*, i. 162, 308. Hyde's archive reveals him to have been responsible for anonymous books such as *Transcendent and Multiplied Rebellion* in 1645: Bodl. MS Clarendon 26, fos. 173–78v; *Transcendent and Multiplied Rebellion* ([Oxford], 1645). He also wrote fake pamphlets: *CCSP* iii. 79; below, pp. 256–7.

[90] M. A. R. Graves, *Thomas Norton* (Oxford, 1994), pp. 75–6, 113, 123, 275, 277–8; C. Read, 'William Cecil and Elizabethan public relations', in S. T. Bindoff, J. Hurstfield and C. H. Williams, eds, *Elizabethan Government and Society* (London, 1961), p. 36, 38, 41, 46; J. Loach, 'The Marian establishment and the printing press', *EHR* 101 (1986), p. 142; J. Guy, *Tudor England* (Oxford, 1988), p. 65; D. Hay, *Polydore Vergil. Renaissance Historian and Man of Letters* (Oxford, 1952); Curtis,

commissions may have resulted from favourable responses to book proposals submitted by authors. Sir Edward Nicholas responded favourably to the 'pious intention' underlying a proposal from Isaac Basire in 1647, which he promised to forward to the king, and Charles II approved of Joseph Jane's proposal to respond to one of Cromwell's declarations in 1655, as well as the 'heads' for a book forwarded by Hyde in January 1659.[91] In January 1653, Nicholas expressed his approval of a proposed 'treatise or discourse' justifying the overthrow of the republic, so long as 'a good pen would undertake it'.[92] It is also possible to examine manuscripts in political collections which can be connected to printed works. The papers of the parliamentarian Speaker, William Lenthall, contain an undated outline of a planned publication entitled 'Good English', subtitled 'reasons drawn from the interests of the royalists, Independents, Presbyterians, City of London, Scots', and which proposed a union between the king and the Independents, and for the City of London to abandon the Presbyterian interest. It seems likely that this was a prospectus for Nedham's *Case of the Kingdom*, and it is possible that Nedham was commissioned to write the work on the basis of official approval of this outline.[93]

Though plausible, such connections cannot be demonstrated definitively. There are, however, more concrete instances of works by men such as William Chillingworth and Peter Heylyn being commissioned by monarchs, ministers and clerics.[94] Specific orders to write polemical tracts are relatively scarce during England's troubles, given the danger of being seen to be prompting the publication of such works. While royalists probably needed to have fewer qualms about drawing upon the services of writers, they have not left much evidence of having done so. One notable example, however, is provided by Joseph Hall's defence of divine right episcopacy, for although Hall came up with the idea for such a work, his correspondence with Laud indicates that it was the archbishop who first suggested that Hall should be the one to complete the task. Only then did Hall send an outline proposal for such a work.[95] In December

---

'Hampton Court', pp. 1–3; Ferrell, *Government by Polemic*; B. Galloway, *The Union of England and Scotland, 1603–1608* (Edinburgh, 1986), p. 48; V. Sanders, 'The household of Archbishop Parker and the influencing of public opinion', *JEH* 34 (1983), pp. 534–47; Bruce and Penrose, eds, *Correspondence of Matthew Parker*, pp. 409–10.

[91] W. N. Darnell, ed., *The Correspondence of Isaac Basire* (London, 1831), pp. 63–4; Bodl. MS Clarendon 43, fo. 139v; *CCSP* iv. 137, 154, 238, 243, 285; *Clarendon State Papers*, iii. 128.

[92] *NP* ii. 1–2.

[93] Bodl. MS Nalson II, fos. 371r–v; M. Nedham, *Case of the Kingdom* (London, 1647). Nedham later wrote a work called *Good English* ([London], 1648). See B. Worden, 'Wit in a Roundhead': the dilemma of Marchamont Nedham', in S. D. Amussen and M. Kishlansky, eds, *Political Culture and Cultural Politics in Early Modern England* (Manchester, 1995), p. 334. Care needs to be taken, of course, since some manuscripts were merely copies taken from works already printed: BL, Add. 36913, fos. 163–70 ('A letter written out of the country to a Parliament man').

[94] LPL, MS 943, p. 69; Vernon, *Heylyn*, pp. 50–51; *CSPD 1637*, p. 429; P. McCullough, 'Making dead men speak: Laudianism, print, and the works of Lancelot Andrewes, 1626–1642', *HJ* 41 (1998); Milton, 'Licensing'.

[95] Laud, *Works*, vi. 572–8; *CSPD 1639–40*, pp. 30–31; PRO, SP 16/431, fos. 5–6v; *CSPD 1639–40*, pp. 138–9; PRO, SP 16/433, fos. 218–19.

1647, Hyde wrote to Lord Hopton regarding the possibility of commissioning one Harman to write a reply to Sir Richard Grenville, but the outcome remains unclear.[96] Charles I evidently commanded the clerk of the royalist Council of War, Sir Edward Walker, to produce a narrative history of the conflict, but although such a work was begun, it would not be published until the early eighteenth century.[97] Furthermore, the complexities of unravelling the nature of requests and commands for books, and the methods by which they were financed, are revealed through the case of Salmasius. The Dutchman was clearly requested to write a defence of the royal cause, and Sir William Boswell said that the king,

> m'a donne commandment expres de vous prier de sa part de vouloir prendre la peine et mettre la main a la plume pour deduire en forme de manifeste ce qui sera a propos de faire connaistre a tous les roys et princes et estate de la Chrestiente touchant la mort du feu roy et l'avancement de sa majestie d'a present aux couronnes d'Angleterre, d'Escosse et d'Ireland.[98]

Salmasius thanked Charles II for the honour of such a request, in June 1649, but the matter of its finance is more problematic.[99] Boswell informed Salmasius that his efforts would be 'recognised', and that he himself was willing to contribute towards the advancement of the project, to the author's 'contentment'. Discussing the necessity for anonymity in November 1649, Boswell said that Salmasius 'may own it hereafter, upon occasion of some advantage', and added that the work was to bear the royal arms on the title page, and the words which expressed that it was published 'nomine et sumptibus regis edita'. Whatever the implication for the remuneration of Salmasius, it is clear that Boswell paid for the work's printing.[100] That this was not an isolated instance, however, is clear from Hyde's having engaged the talents of Robert Creighton in 1658, and his having sought to commission a refutation of Buchanan's dialogues, while Sir Edward Nicholas advocated the production, in December 1659, of 'some handsome pamphlets' to advocate the restoration of Charles II.[101]

Attention can likewise be drawn to a range of works whose composition was orchestrated by Parliament and its grandees. In the spring of 1641, Parliament forced the Laudian licenser, William Bray, to produce a recantation, which was quickly ordered to be printed, and Prynne was commissioned to publish the official account of Laud's trial, and proudly displayed the order to his readers.[102]

---

[96] Bodl. MS Clarendon 30, fo. 214–15.

[97] Bodl. MS Clarendon 136 ('His Majesties happy progresse and successe', by Sir Edward Walker), pp. ix, xi; I. Roy, 'The royalist council of war, 1642–6', *BIHR* 35 (1962), p. 151. This lengthy account eventually appeared as part of: Sir E. Walker, *Historical Discourses* (London, 1705).

[98] W. McNeil, 'Milton and Salmasius, 1649', *EHR* 80 (1965), pp. 107–8.

[99] Bodl. MS Carte 130, fo. 56.

[100] Bodl. MS Carte 130, fo. 100; McNeil, 'Milton and Salmasius', pp. 107–8.

[101] *CCSP* iv. 85, 267; *CCSP* v. 68; *CSPD 1659–60*, pp. 275–6.

[102] Stationers Company, Liber A, fo. 131; W. Bray, *A Sermon of the Blessed Sacrament* ('published by command', London, 1641); W. Prynne, *Canterburies Doom* (London, 1645); *CJ* iv. 16, 48, 68.

Other works were less obviously commissioned, however. In January 1648, Walter Frost was charged with producing the exposé of Leveller activities, and a response to their declarations, but readers were able to establish merely that his work was published 'by authority' – or licensed – for the 'undeceiving of those that are misled by these deceivers'.[103] Other works are known to have been commissioned only fortuitously. The bookseller, George Thomason, recorded that Henry Parker's *Generall Junto* was commissioned, and paid for, by Sir John Danvers, although it is more likely to have been requested by the 'fiery spirits' with whom Parker was so familiar.[104] During the 1640s, it is difficult to document financial assistance for such projects, and if Parliament appears to have been reticent about making such support overt, it is possible that payments were made from aristocratic pocket books. Nevertheless, payments to parliamentarian authors can occasionally be found, albeit indirectly. In October 1642, the Committee of Safety issued a warrant to pay £100 to John Pym, 'to be disposed of as he shall in his discretion think fit'. Pym duly signed the receipt for his money, adding that it had been paid to the journalist, John Dillingham, whose signature also appeared on the receipt.[105] Payments, therefore, may have been sheltered and indirect, or they may have been made on a personal basis between individual politicians and authors. Subsequent evidence certainly suggests that payments for the composition of propaganda were offered with utmost discretion. Meric Casaubon, who had been deprived of his clerical living by Parliament for royalism in 1644, was approached by Cromwell to write an official history of the civil wars, albeit only through the offices of a lawyer called Greaves. When Casaubon turned down the offer, on the grounds that 'he would be forced to make such reflections as would be ungrateful, if not injurious to his leadership', Cromwell ordered that £300–400 should be delivered to Casaubon by a London bookseller 'without acknowledging the benefactor'.[106]

Such commissions, and the financial payments by which they were supported, became more frequent, however, as propaganda techniques improved, and as administration became more centralised after the establishment of the commonwealth. A series of orders exists, for example, by which the Council of State solicited published translations of key works, from declarations justifying invasion of Scotland, to diplomatic papers relating to the murdered diplomat, Anthony Ascham, and key works to be employed in relations with the Dutch.[107] Moreover, there is plentiful evidence relating to the commissioning of specific books. In May 1649, for example, Thomas Waring was ordered to publish 'with

---

[103] *CSPD 1648–9*, pp. 5, 14; W. Frost, *A Declaration of Some Proceedings* (London, 1648).

[104] Peacey, 'Henry Parker', pp. 65–9; J. Peacey, 'Junto practices: printing and publishing and the meaning of texts in the English civil war' (paper delivered at SHARP conference, London, 2002).

[105] PRO, SP 28/261, fo. 418r–v.

[106] Abbott, *Cromwell*, ii. 2; Wood, *Athenae Oxonienses*, iii. 935.

[107] *CSPD 1650*, p. 228; *CSPD 1651–2*, pp. 358, 483; P. R. Barnett, *Theodore Haak* (The Hague, 1962), pp. 91, 95. See: P. Seaward, 'A restoration publicist: James Howell and the Earl of Clarendon, 1661–6', *HR* 61 (1988), p. 124.

all convenient speed' papers relating to the sufferings of Protestants during the Irish Rebellion, the Council explaining that this was necessary because there were,

> so many here in this nation [who] by their causeless cavils and queries ... turn obstructors of their intended relief ... [and] weaken the hands of the well affected in both nations and do in effect second the designs of the bloody rebels there to the manifest hazard of the ruin of the Protestant cause and English interest.[108]

In January 1650, furthermore, Waring was paid £100 for his book, which Milton was ordered to oversee through the press.[109] Peter English's somewhat cryptic claim to have been commissioned by John Lambert and Robert Lilburne to produce his response to Salmasius is supported by the existence of a warrant, dated 3 May 1653, to pay him £20 for printing the book, which had apparently been 'reviewed by the commissioners at Dalkeith'.[110] The protectorate Council, meanwhile, ordered John Owen to respond to John Biddle's *Two-Fold Catechism* in March 1654, and prompted Samuel Morland to produce his account of the sufferings of the Piedmontese Protestants.[111] Later, Dr Thomas Clarges acted as propaganda agent for George Monck in late 1659. On 26 December he wrote of having become 'a great printer' since his arrival in London, and explained his role in organising the appearance of *A Letter ... From an Eminent Officer in the Army at Edinburgh* – which was orchestrated from Nottingham – and a work called *Hypocrites Unmasked*.[112]

Evidence relating to commissions and payments is also to be found outside the records of court and Parliament, and their leading protagonists. As is so often the case, Scottish evidence, and the papers of Robert Baillie, prove revealing. Baillie recorded that the task of explaining the lawfulness of defensive arms in 1639 was

---

[108] *CSPD 1649–50*, pp. 131–2; PRO, SP 25/62, pp. 118, 279–80. Waring had been clerk to the commission appointed to investigate the sufferings of Irish Protestants: N. Carlin, 'Extreme or mainstream?: the English Independents and the Cromwellian reconquest of Ireland', in B. Bradshaw, A. Hadfield, and W. Maley, eds, *Representing Ireland* (Cambridge, 1993), pp. 213, 220.

[109] *CSPD 1649–50*, pp. 474, 597; T. W[aring], *A Brief Narrative of the Plotting, Beginning and Carrying on of that Execrable Rebellion and Butcherie in Ireland* ('published by special authority, London, 1650); [T. Waring], *An Answer to Certain Seditious and Jesuitical Queries* (London, by Dugard, 1651); BL, Add. 4777, fos. 2–44 (Thomas Waring, 'Answer to certain seditious and scandalous and Jesuitical queries); PRO, SP 21/29, p. 191.

[110] Worcester College, Clarke MS XLIV, p. 1; P. English, *The Survey of Policy* (Leith, 1653). I am grateful to Patrick Little for this reference.

[111] *CSPD 1654*, p. 3; J. Owen, *Vindiciae Evangelicae* (Oxford, 1655); *CSPD 1656–7*, pp. 236, 254–5. For Owen, see: P. Toon, ed., *The Correspondence of John Owen* (London, 1970); P. Toon, *God's Statesman* (Exeter, 1971). Owen apparently delegated the task of writing on church government in 1657 to one of his own clients, Henry Stubbe: H. Stubbe, *Clamor, Rixa, Joci, Medacia* (London, 1657); N. Malcolm, ed., *The Correspondence of Thomas Hobbes* (2 vols, Oxford, 1994), i. 311–12; J. R. Jacob, *Henry Stubbe* (Cambridge, 1983), pp. 18–19.

[112] *HMC Leyborne-Popham*, p. 137; *A Letter ... From an Eminent Officer in the Army at Edenburgh* (np, 1659); *Hypocrites Unmasked, or, the Hypocrisie of the New Usurpers* (London, 1659). The former, hostile to the Wallingford House party, was apparently undertaken for Clarges by one Ethelbert Morgan.

'laid on Mr Henderson, our best penman, to draw up something for the common view'.[113] Writing to Johnston of Wariston on the eve of the Short Parliament, meanwhile, Baillie explained his reasons for writing *Landensium*; saying that 'your frequent and very pressing letters, together with the approaching of the English Parliament, has made me use all the speed I was able, in the midst of my very frequent and necessary distractions'. He added that 'only at your desire, have I undergone this labour'.[114] After the assembly of the Long Parliament, Baillie noted that the task of 'first moulding' books against Laud and Strafford was 'laid on me', while Henderson was importuned to advocate the abolition of episcopacy by 'the English ministers' and by the Scots commissioners to Westminster.[115] Reflecting on events in 1643, Baillie wrote that he was 'put to the labour of frequent writing' by the Scots commissioners, and that he was 'directed to write' his many works in defence of Presbyterianism.[116] The impetus for such works could also come from the Scottish Parliament, who issued orders to both himself and Henderson in the summer of 1642.[117] Furthermore, in noting how the General Assembly sought to encourage David Calderwood and Andrew Kerr to complete their history of the kirk in July 1648, Baillie recorded that the former was awarded a salary of £800, and the latter a salary of £1,000, 'with a gratuity of five thousand marks for bygones'.[118] Moreover, Baillie's letters also reveal his own role, as a commissioner from the Scots in London in the mid-1640s, in encouraging other writers, through the offices of the Presbyterian minister and licenser, James Cranford. In June 1645, Baillie asked 'what encouragement is there for [John] Bastwick? And how can [Thomas] Edwards be hastened to print [Jeremiah] Burroughes' sermons, and his own tractates?'[119] Baillie's testimony demonstrates the necessity of looking beyond the records of the central administration, and it is also possible to demonstrate that the organisational impetus for propaganda occasionally came from within local parliamentarian administration. During March 1644, therefore, a string of letters between the Kent county committee and Sir Edward Dering reveal the pressure placed upon the latter for a public declaration of his allegiance, in the wake of his 'defection' to the royalists.[120]

However publicly seventeenth-century politicians were prepared to acknowledge their role in instigating the publication of particular books and tracts, they were notably less willing to reveal their involvement in commissioning the composition of such works. This probably reflected fear of exposure as

---

113 *Letters and Journals of Robert Baillie*, i. 189–90.

114 *Letters and Journals of Robert Baillie*, i. 242.

115 *Letters and Journals of Robert Baillie*, i. 280, 289, 303, 305.

116 *Letters and Journals of Robert Baillie*, ii. 39.

117 *Letters and Journals of Robert Baillie*, ii. 47, 384.

118 *Letters and Journals of Robert Baillie*, iii. 60.

119 *Letters and Journals of Robert Baillie*, ii. 279.

120 BL, Stowe 184, fos. 69, 71, 73, 75–7; E. Dering, *A Declaration by Sir Edward Dering* (London, 1644).

Machiavellian manipulators, as well as a subtle understanding of the art of propaganda, and the fact that successful manipulation of public opinion relied to a great extent upon readers being prevented from observing, or perceiving, the mechanisms behind the appearance of specific works. That works were commissioned, however, can be extrapolated from contemporary comments, and the location of manuscripts of works which subsequently appeared in print, but also from official papers, which reveal the extent to which, among parliamentarians at least, efforts were made to address particular needs, and to support particular policies, by arranging for the composition of tracts whose authors were handsomely rewarded, and whose publications were extensively funded.

The most significant way in which politicians secured the services of authors and printers, as contemporaries recognised, was by retaining them, paying them pensions, and making them official and professional propagandists. Before the civil war, such professionalism generally involved either household employment, the payment of retainers or perhaps small pensions, and survival by means of *ad hoc* payments from patrons and friends.[121] Later, however, Parliament was thought to rely upon 'impudent agents and emissaries, and the allowed scribblers and news printers, the very pests of the age', and to have retained a 'scattered heard of scribbling villains'. John Taylor quipped: 'penniless pamphleteers they do maintain, whose only religion is stipendiary gain'.[122] Parliamentarians such as Henry Parker made similar accusations regarding the king's 'regiments' of 'pen and inkhorn men'.[123] Moreover such accusations also flew between factional rivals. The Scot, David Buchanan, claimed that the Independents 'gained the most part of the scribbling pamphleteers about the city to set forth lies and tales for them', while the army responded to critics in July 1647 by saying that it 'never went about to make a monopoly to themselves of the presses, as those who sought to destroy them did. The army give not pensions to 80 or 100 clerks to help them, they give not annuities to mercenary scribes, to spoil ink and paper, to abuse the kingdom'.[124] Once again,

---

[121] Elton, *Policy and Police*, p. 173; R. N. Kingdon, 'Patronage, piety and printing in sixteenth century Europe', in D. H. Pinkney and T. Ropp, eds, *A Festschrift for Frederick B. Artz* (Durham, NC, 1964), pp. 22–3; D. R. Carlson, *English Humanist Books* (London, 1993), p. 16; D. R. Carlson, 'Royal tutors in the reign of Henry VII', *Sixteenth Century Journal* 22 (1991); G. Walker, *John Skelton and the Politics of the 1520s* (Cambridge, 1988); V. Sanders, 'John Whitgift: primate, privy councillor and propagandist', *Anglican and Episcopal History* 56 (1987), p. 393; B. Dooley, 'News and doubt in early modern culture', in B. Dooley and S. Baron, eds, *The Politics of Information in Early Modern Europe* (London, 2001); E. H. Miller, *The Professional Writer in Elizabethan England* (Cambridge, Mass., 1959), chap. 4; F. W. Galpin, 'The household expenses of Sir Thomas Barrington', *Transations of the Essex Archaeological Society* 12 (1913), p. 224.

[122] Nalson, *Impartial Collection*, ii. vi; J. Taylor, *John Taylor ... to John Booker* ([Oxford], 1644), p. 4; J. Taylor, *A New Diurnall of Passages* (Oxford, 1643), sig. A3.

[123] [H. Parker], *The Contra-replicant* ([London, 1643]), p. 3.

[124] D. Buchanan, *Truth Its Manifest* (London, 1646), p. 127; *Animadversions Upon a Declaration of the Proceedings Against the XI Members* (Cambridge, 1647), p. 5.

however, such claims need to be contextualised in terms of more reliable evidence, in order to trace the development of this phenomenon, its publicity, and the extent to which it was a practice adopted by both royalists and parliamentarians.

Prior to the civil wars, political grandees appear to have been reticent about retaining the services of writers in a professional capacity, if not as clients. It is certainly possible to demonstrate occasions when they declined to employ writers on a regular basis, not least by failing to take up the offer of propagandistic services from John Jones in the summer of 1642.[125] By the mid-1640s, however, there is evidence that political figures could regret having dismissed the potential which writers offered. In September 1646, for example, Lord Inchiquin reflected on his having been introduced to 'one of the intelligence writers' at London, to whom Dr Worth 'advised me to speak kindly and give something, which I much disdained, but I perceive my error, for now I see he would have made me a brave servitor in one kingdom, though I remained whoring and playing the knave in another'.[126] Furthermore, it is possible to demonstrate the gradual movement towards salaried propagandists, from the payment of extraordinary salaries to preachers in strategic locations during the Bishops' Wars, to the apparently deliberate recruitment of administrative officials who possessed polemical skills.[127] From the earliest phase of the civil war, therefore, some appointments and positions were probably devised in terms of securing the services of talented authors, without having to pay them as writers. This may explain the selection of Henry Parker as secretary to the Committee of Safety in the summer of 1642, who demonstrates the utility of having proven writers working on official declarations, and of employing men who worked on official and non-official propaganda simultaneously. Later, of course, Parliament employed extraordinary secretaries in the summer of 1645, whose task was to write special, and especially polemical, declarations and official statements, with salaries of £200.[128] John Sadler and Thomas May were, therefore, little more than house writers, and they remained in position until the dissolution of the Rump.[129] That they composed political and religious works over and above official declarations during this time suggests that their salaries may have been intended to compensate them for more than just their declarations.[130] When May published his famous history in 1647, he admitted: 'my residence hath been, during these

---

[125] BL, Add. 33374, fos. 2–5, 15–20.

[126] *HMC Egmont I*, p. 317. I am grateful to Patrick Little for this reference.

[127] PRO, T56/5, fo. 37v.

[128] *CJ* iv. 410–11, 414, 416.

[129] PRO, SC6/Chas.1/1667, m.14; SC 6/Chas.1/1668, m. 10d; SC 6/Chas.1/1669, m. 10d; PRO, SP 18/38, fo. 140v. In July 1650, the declaration justifying the march of Cromwell's army into Scotland was ordered to be translated into Latin by Thomas May, to be sent to foreign parts: *CSPD 1650*, p. 228.

[130] J. S[adler], *The Ancient Bounds* (London, 1645); J. S[adler], *Flagellum Flagelli* (London, 1645); *SR* i. 167, 188. Interestingly, the former has sometimes been attributed to the MP Francis Rous: B. Kiefer, 'The authorship of Ancient Bounds', *Church History* 22 (1953).

wars, in the quarters and under the protection of Parliament'.[131] Little wonder, therefore, that Marvell styled him a 'servile wit and mercenary pen', or that an army memorandum from May 1647 mentioned the need for 'a party of able pen men ... to satisfy and undeceive the people'.[132]

One of the most significant ways in which writers came to be hired and paid was as editors of newspapers, the regularity and longevity of which obviously required writers who could work on more than a part-time or *ad hoc* basis.[133] Prior to the civil war, there appears to have been little inclination to retain the services of journalists – as Pory had proposed – although in 1639 Henry De Vic proposed responding to the Scots by means of a 'gazette', along the French model.[134] The growing importance of news during the civil wars, however, provided the impetus for greater exploitation of newspapers, and of journalists. During the 1640s it was alleged that such writers were employed or retained by individual grandees, as well as by factions and political parties. Lucy Hutchinson claimed that Sir John Gell 'kept the diurnall makers in pension, so that whatever was done in any of the neighbouring counties against the enemies was ascribed to him, and he hath indirectly purchased himself a name in story which he never merited, who was a very bad man'.[135] John Dillingham was accused of being a 'pensioner' of the Earl of Manchester, and of serving his personal interests.[136] John Taylor claimed that parliamentarian journalists were set to work by the 'incitement and spirit of damnable infusion' of the grandees, who did not 'fail to pay them their wages'.[137] By 1646, Thomas Edwards felt able to suggest that newspaper editors were the 'pensioners' of political parties, and after Pride's Purge Henry Walker was accused of being in the hire of Lord President John Bradshaw. It was alleged that Walker 'takes upon him the impudence to carry on his design with the Lord President and Council of State, under this notion or shadow, that this sheet takes its derivator from the sinews of malignancy'.[138]

From the outbreak of hostilities, Parliament exploited army chaplains' news reports, and proved willing to reward providers of intelligence. The chaplain and

---

[131] T. May, *History of the Parliament of England* (London, 1647); *CJ* iv. 410–11. For May's salary, see: PRO, E 404/235, unfol.

[132] H. M. Margoliouth, ed., *The Poems and Letters of Andrew Marvell* (2 vols, Oxford, 1971), i. 91; Worcester College, Clarke MS XLI, fo. 21.

[133] Dooley, 'News and doubt', p. 279.

[134] R. Cust, 'News and politics in early seventeenth century England', *P&P* 112 (1986); *CSPD 1639*, pp. 233–4. See: T. Cogswell, 'The people's love: the Duke of Buckingham and popularity', in Cogswell, Cust and Lake, eds, *Politics, Religion and Popularity*, pp. 224–5.

[135] L. Hutchinson, *Memoirs of the Life of Colonel Hutchinson* (ed. J. Sutherland, London, 1973), p. 68. The results can apparently be detected in the press: A. Cotton, 'London newsbooks in the civil war: their political attitudes and sources of information' (Oxford University DPhil, 1971), pp. 228–9.

[136] *Mercurius Aulicus* 23 (2–8 June 1644), p. 1009; *Mercurius Bellicus* 19 (30 May–6 June 1648), p. 7; C. Holmes, 'Colonel King and Lincolnshire politics, 1642–6', *HJ* 16 (1973), p. 455n.

[137] J. Taylor, *Mercurius Infernalis* ([Oxford], 1644), p. 6.

[138] Edwards, *Gangraena*, i. 110; Edwards, *Gangraena*, ii. 73, 208–9; *Kingdomes Faithfull and Impartiall Scout* 22 (22–29 June 1649), pp. 169–71.

pamphleteer Edward Bowles was evidently despatched to the Scots in May 1644, in order to provide news reports which were printed in London, and he was paid £100.[139] The payment made to him upon bringing news of the victory at Naseby in July 1645 may also have been a reward for his journalistic efforts in the summer of 1645, in the form of seven editions of a newsletter called *The Proceedings of the Army*, which were published 'according to order'.[140] This growing concern for the control and exploitation of news is also apparent from evidence regarding the invention of the newspaper north of the Tweed in 1648, as tension grew between the Engagers – those moderate royalists and covenanters who had reached agreement with Charles I, and who dominated the Parliament and Committee of Estates – and the hardline covenanters in the General Assembly of the kirk. The Engagers, fearing that they were losing the propaganda war, appointed the Earl of Lanark to head a sub-committee to 'consider and provide for the fittest way how the public condition of the affairs of the kingdom and of our army may be weekly represented to the kingdom'. The committee wrote to the Marquess of Hamilton (Lanark's elder brother), expressing the desire 'to send out in print an weekly information to the kingdom of the proceedings of our armies and of the public condition of affairs both at home and abroad', and asking Hamilton to appoint a news agent to provide material which was 'fit to be communicated, to arrive by Saturday night to appear on Mondays'. The paper was successfully established in August 1648, although the project collapsed almost immediately, following the Engagers' defeat at Preston.[141] That all sides came to recognise the importance of the new medium is evident from Sir Edward Nicholas's comment, in December 1659, that 'some handsome pamphlets should be weekly published, to mind the people what an advantage and happiness the king's restoration would be to the nation, for though few can be ignorant of it, yet the frequent asserting of his just title would awake them, and make them think of their duty'.[142]

Aside from the evidence of rewards granted to Bowles, however, the emergence of regular newspapers during the 1640s does not necessarily imply anything about

[139] *CJ* iii. 476; *CSPD 1625–49*, p. 660; PRO, SP 23/1a, p. 24; *A Faithful Relation* (London, 1644); *The Late Proceedings of the Scottish Army* (London, 1644); *Intelligence from the Scottish Army* (London, 1644); *Extracts of Letters* (London, 1644); *Intelligence from the South Borders* (London, 1644). For Bowles see: A. Laurence, *Parliamentary Army Chaplains, 1642–1651* (Woodbridge, 1990), pp. 101–2; PRO, SP 28/3, fo. 441; SP 28/6, fo. 95; SP 28/7, fo. 345.

[140] PRO, SC6/Chas.1/1663 m.9r; *HMC Portland I*, p. 212; *CJ* iv. 175; *LJ* vii. 433; *The Proceedings of the Army* 1 (1–6 July 1645); *An Exact and Perfect Relation of the Proceedings of the Army* 2 (6–11 July 1645); *A Continuation of the Proceedings* 3 (11–19 July 1645); *A Continuation of the Proceedings* 4 (19–23 July 1645); *The Proceedings of the Army* 5 (24–31 July 1645); *The Proceedings of the Army* 6 (1–7 Aug. 1645); *The Proceedings of the Army* 7 (8–15 Aug. 1645). Such payments were separate from payments as chaplain during this period: PRO, SP 28/29, fo. 49; SP 28/30, fos. 171, 224, 477, 587, 588; SP 28/31, fos. 116, 207, 208; SP 28/32, fo. 192; SP 28/33, fo. 111.

[141] Scottish RO, PA.11/6, fo. 104–5, 121; D. Stevenson, 'Scotland's first newspaper, 1648', *The Bibliothek* 10 (1981), pp. 123–6.

[142] *CSPD 1659–60*, pp. 275–6.

the nature of their editors' employment. It is sometimes difficult to distinguish between personal loyalty to a particular grandee, and to the political interest or faction with which they were associated. Some editors, such as John Dillingham, may have written out of a long-standing allegiance to a particular patron, but may also be regarded as spokesmen for a distinct parliamentarian faction.[143] Later, in December 1659, Henry Muddiman was employed by George Monck and Thomas Clarges to write the *Parliamentary Intelligencer*, and later *Mercurius Publicus*, Clarges writing that the former was 'a book published by my directions'. Muddiman later explained that the aim was to defend their political interest, rather than merely Monck himself, claiming that he was 'entreated' to provide 'a just vindication of his excellency and the army, to give faithful intelligence of their transactions, which were so basely and falsely represented by the pamphleteers then in being'. Muddiman served the interests of those who sought a return to civilian rule, and as a powerful weapon against the army and 'the seditious calumnies of their scribbling pamphleteers'.[144] Whatever the nature of the connections between editors and particular grandees, journalists such as Dillingham and Muddiman were becoming dedicated and professional, and they served political factions and parties as much as individual patrons.

Establishing a more thorough understanding of journalists' terms of employment in the 1640s requires turning attention to one of the most important early newspapers. The royalist *Mercurius Aulicus* was widely recognised as having been officially sponsored, and to have been written by Sir John Berkenhead, although it ought more properly be regarded as a vehicle for the Laudian faction at court, which ignored the views of moderate royalists.[145] The paper's quality was reflected in the response which it provoked from parliamentarians. One critic claimed: 'there is a deep excise put upon all brains that pretend in the least wise to wit, and that the returns of all jests, half jests, quarter-jests, and quibbles, happening within the limits of the camp, court, or the taverns, that may any ways twitch the roundheads, are once a week made upon just account, into Berkenhead's office, towards the maintenance of this same *Aulicus*'.[146] Its arch-rival, *Mercurius Britanicus*, informed

---

[143] A. N. B. Cotton, 'John Dillingham, journalist of the middle group', *EHR* 93 (1978).

[144] *HMC Leyborne-Popham*, p. 137; *The Parliamentary Intelligencer* 27 (25 June–2 July 1660), p. 430; J. B. Williams, 'The newsbooks and letters of news of the Restoration', *EHR* 23 (1908), pp. 255–6; *The Parliamentary Intelligencer* 2 (26 Dec. 1659–2 Jan. 1660), p. 10. In the first issue, Muddiman styled Monck 'the restorer of the liberties of this nation': *The Parliamentary Intelligencer* 1 (19–26 Dec. 1659), p. 7. Muddiman may also have written another shortlived paper in December 1659: *The Faithfull Intelligencer* (29 Nov.–3 Dec. 1659); *Mercurius Britanicus* 2 (8–15 Dec. 1659); *Mercurius Britanicus* 3 (15–20 Dec. 1659); *Mercurius Britanicus* 4 (20–23 Dec. 1659); *Mercurius Britanicus* 5 (23 Dec.–4 Jan. 1660); *Mercurius Britanicus* 6 (4–6 Jan. 1660); A. Woolrych, 'Introduction', *The Complete Prose Works of John Milton VII* (New Haven, 1980), p. 135; G. Davies, *The Restoration of Charles II, 1658–1660* (London, 1955), p. 170. Nedham noticed the arrival of Scottish pamphlets attacking his papers: *Mercurius Politicus* 598 (8–15 Dec. 1659), pp. 951–2, 955.

[145] *CSPV 1642–3*, pp. 306–7; Thomas, *Sir John Berkenhead*, pp. 74–6, 78, 86–7.

[146] *The Recantation of Mercurius Aulicus, or Berkinheads Complaint* ([Oxford], 1644), pp. 1–2.

readers that *Aulicus* was 'rewarded with a place at court, he is one of the new patentees, and hath a commission to lie for his life, for the better advancement of His Majesties service', and its editor stressed that his rival was 'a pensioner to belie, slander and delude as many as he can'.[147] One opponent went so far as to suggest that Berkenhead was paid a stipend of £30 by Sir Edward Nicholas.[148] Although such stories are hard to substantiate, Peter Heylyn's biographer noted that he was instructed to 'take directions for some special and important service' from Nicholas, 'which was at last signified to Dr Heylyn under the king's own hand, viz. to write the weekly occurrences'.[149]

The existence of *Aulicus* prompted attempts not merely to suppress the royalist press in the summer of 1643, but also to create a rival newspaper, *Mercurius Britanicus*, which was almost certainly officially inspired, and which was explicitly aimed at responding to *Aulicus*.[150] John Taylor claimed that *Britanicus* was ordered by the House to be 'receiver general of all quibbles, crops, clinches, puns, half-jests, jests, fine sentences, witty sayings, rare-truths', and he referred to it as Parliament's 'learned conduit pipe', who 'railes, and reviles, sheetly, weekly, and most wickedly, *cum privilegio*'.[151] *Britanicus* was assumed to represent the sense of the House, or at least the Committee of Safety, which reportedly held 'most of their secret meetings (like witches) in the night, which will beget another weekly pamphlet, which Master Rushworth will call the Nocturnal of the Close Committee'. *Mercurius Anti-Britanicus* saw in its opponent 'an illegitimate creature, to whose birth the House of Commons was the father'.[152] Another opponent claimed that Nedham received £3 per week for his efforts.[153] Few would probably have believed the paper's later claim not to have been prompted by Parliament.[154] In reality, however, *Britanicus* was, like *Aulicus*, probably the official journal of a faction. It was a parliamentarian author, Daniel Featley, who claimed that *Britanicus* had 'a patent to lie', and claims were made that the paper was in the pay of the Fiennes family, and that it was enlisted as press agent and personal adviser before the trial of Nathaniel Fiennes. William Prynne, who had prosecuted Fiennes, claimed that the pages of *Britanicus* were used to engage in

[147] *Mercurius Britanicus* 3 (5–12 Sept. 1643), p. 17; *Mercurius Britanicus* 53 (7–14 Oct. 1644), pp. 416–17. Britanicus alleged that 'Her Majesty intends to summon all poets and scholars of any competency of wit, from the age of 16 to 60, to be aiding and assisting to the next diurnall': *Mercurius Britanicus* 6 (26 Sept.–3 Oct. 1643), p. 41.

[148] *The Kingdomes Weekly Intelligencer* 83 (26 Nov.–3 Dec. 1644), p. 666.

[149] Vernon, *Heylyn*, p. 123.

[150] *LJ* vi. 233; J. Peacey, 'The struggle for *Mercurius Britanicus*: factional politics and the parliamentarian press, 1643–6' (forthcoming).

[151] J. Taylor, *Mercurius Aquaticus* ([Oxford], 1643), sig. A2; J. Taylor, *General Complaint* ([Oxford], 1644), p. 5.

[152] Thomas, *Sir John Berkenhead*, p. 48; *Mercurius Aulicus* 13, pp. 166–7, *Mercurius Aulicus* 35 (27 Aug.–2 Sept. 1643), p. 485; *Mercurius Anti-Britanicus* 1 (4 Aug. 1643), pp. 3–4.

[153] *Mercurius Academicus* 6 (19 Jan. 1646), p. 56.

[154] *Mercurius Britanicus* 85 (26 Jun.–2 Jul. 1645), p. 771.

'palpable flattery' of his paymaster, and he alleged that *Britanicus* had been, 'bribed by the defendent or his partisans', in order to 'trumpet forth his unknown eminent deserts and public virtues'.[155]

With *Aulicus* and *Britanicus*, however, it is possible merely to demonstrate their official (if factional) nature, and to record the allegations regarding their editors' status, and the money which they were reported to have been paid. The precise terms of their employment are impossible to fathom, and it is possible that such authors were not actually paid by the authorities, given that they may have been able to survive on the profitability of their journals. Evidence from other editors indicates the sums of money which may have been involved in newspapers which were run along commercial lines. John Hall, the young Cambridge scholar and Gray's Inn lawyer who wrote for the newspapers run by William Lilly in the late 1640s, was reputed to have received £6 per annum 'to quit his charges for pen, ink and paper', but in terms of his salary, 'I leave that to Lilly and Booker ... whose hireling he is, and who allow him money, for tobacco and beer, besides a Sunday dinner, of beef and pudding, to rail against *Elencticus* and the Scots'.[156] George Wharton, however, claimed that Hall was hired for 'five pound per week, to write anew those forgeries'.[157] It is also possible that the editors of 'official' newspapers were paid by results, and that their income was profit-related. The army agent, Gilbert Mabbott, who supplemented his licensing of the press with journalism, was alleged to have made in excess of £100 per annum from *The Moderate*.[158] Clement Walker, however, alleged that Mabbott – one of the 'railing pen-men of the faction' – received 'a large share of the £500 or £600 a year allowed to these pamphleteers for divulging state lies and slanders amongst the people'.[159]

Some editors, however, can be demonstrated to have been salaried in other capacities within the parliamentarian administration, and to have supplemented official duties with journalism, rather than being formally employed as writers. This was evident from official newspapers established by the Rump. Walter Frost, as secretary to the Council of State, was authorised to publish weekly news, and produced *A Briefe Relation*. John Rushworth (secretary to the army) produced the *Perfect Diurnall*, while Theodore Jennings (licenser and factotum of the Council) produced *A Perfect Summary*, and Henry Scobell (clerk of the Commons) produced *Several Proceedings in Parliament*.[160] Contemporaries clearly perceived

---

155 D. Featley, *Sacra Nemesis* (Oxford, Lichfield, 1644), p. 8; [W. Prynne], *A Checke to Brittanicus* (London, 1644), p. 3; Bodl. MS Tanner 62, fo. 363; *State Trials*, iv. 186–315; C. Walker and W. Prynne, *A True and Full Relation of the Prosecution, Arraignment, Tryall, and Condemnation of Nathaniel Fiennes* (London, 1644), pp. 2–4, 114. *Britanicus* replied by alleging that Prynne had been bribed by the court to launch this attack: *A Check to the Checker of Britannicus* (London, 1644), sig. E2.

156 *The Last Will and Testament of Tom Fairfax* (Np, 1648), p. 3.

157 Mercurius Elencticus, *The Anatomy of Westminster Juncto* (np, 1648), p. 6.

158 HLRO, MP 16/8/48; *HMC 7th Report*, p. 45; *LJ* ix. 441–2, 456.

159 C. Walker, *Anarchia Anglicana* (London, 1649), p. 24.

160 *CSPD 1649–50*, p. 316; *SR* i. 328, 331; *N&S*, pp. 22, 432, 457, 529. For references to 'Mr Frost's Gazette', see: *HMC De L'isle VI*, pp. 461, 464.

that such papers were 'run' by politicians. Frost, therefore, was styled 'secretary to the Council of Coxcombs, according to the direction of the regicides, that so the people may be abused for the future *cum privilegio*, suitable to the mind of Bradshaw and Scot, who sway all'. He was also called Lenthall's 'newshound', and he and his journalist, Henry Walker, were called 'the state news gablers'.[161] But though official, such men were not paid for their work. Their journals were available for public sale, and the journalists with whom they worked, such as Walker and Samuel Pecke, may have been paid, like Mabbott, from the proceeds, rather than by the Rump.

A brief exploration of the newspapers of the civil war period reveals the extent to which the services of capable polemicists were retained, sometimes over the course of a number of years, even if the nature of surviving evidence does not permit verification of contemporary claims regarding the way in which such individuals were financially rewarded for their efforts. The remainder of this chapter, however, serves to demonstrate the extent to which commitment to polemical activity on the part of political grandees involved payment of pensions and salaries.

Surviving evidence indicates that it was the Rump which proved innovative in the retention and employment of the pens of polemical writers. Though certain authors continued to work as propagandists without being given the job description, they differed from their predecessors by benefiting from the new regime's financial commitment to the press. More important are those writers who reveal a willingness to make much more obvious connections between job titles and the production of propaganda.

John Canne provides an example of an author who proved to be a loyal servant of the Rump in terms of the production of propaganda, but who did not work within Whitehall or Westminster, and whose services, though paid by the regime, were not recorded for accounting purposes. In the summer of 1649, Canne undertook the task of responding to the Levellers, as the Council desired, with two books which were 'published by authority', and for which Walter Frost was ordered to reimburse the printer, Matthew Simmons.[162] Immediately after their appearance, Canne's talents were endorsed by a group of leading Independent ministers, and from senior army officers such as John Okey, Edward Whalley and

---

[161] *Mercurius Elencticus* 25 (15–22 Oct. 1649), pp. 193–4; *The Man in the Moon* 26 (17–24 Oct. 1649), pp. 217–18; *Mercurius Pragmaticus (For King Charls II)* 12 (3–10 July 1649), sig. M4; *Mercurius Pragmaticus (For King Charls II)* 30 (20–27 Nov. 1649), sig. Ggv, Gg3v; *Mercurius Pragmaticus (For King Charls II)* 45 (5–12 Mar. 1650), sig. Yy4v; *Mercurius Pragmaticus (For King Charls II)* 51 (23–30 Apr. 1650), sig. Ee3; *Mercurius Pragmaticus (For King Charls II)* 53 (7–14 May 1650), sig. Ggg2; *The Man in the Moon* 43 (13–20 Feb. 1650), pp. 338–41; *Mercurius Aulicus* 4 (21–28 Apr. 1648), p. 29; *Mercurius Elencticus* 27 (29 Oct.–5 Nov. 1649), pp. 201, 210.

[162] J. Canne, *The Discoverer* (London, 1649); J. Canne, *The Discoverer … the Second Part* (London, 1649); *CSPD 1649–50*, p. 298.

William Goffe, who commented upon his propagandistic efforts on behalf of the new regime, and who recommended that 'he may be encouraged and enabled to do further service for the commonwealth'.[163] Contemporaries recognised that Canne was 'personating the Council of State', and it is certainly possible that ensuing works which were published by Simmons were produced under official scrutiny.[164] His reflections upon the victory in Ireland, published in August 1649, and upon the battle of Dunbar, published in October 1650, were also 'published by authority', and readers of *A Voice from the Temple*, published in June 1653, were informed that the work had been 'encouraged' by Cromwell.[165] Nevertheless, Canne was not a salaried author, but rather a preacher at Hull during this period, although his salary seems to have been paid directly by Whitehall.[166] Within Whitehall, other salaried administrators may have been chosen because of proven literary records, or with propaganda roles in mind. Leading council secretaries, such as Walter Frost and John Thurloe, were involved not merely in organising propaganda, but also in preparing texts. In September 1651, Frost was ordered to compile a narrative of relations between England and Scotland from the beginning of the wars, and in August 1653, Thurloe was commanded to prepare a work recounting the case of the notorious 'false Jew', although he may have deputed the task to others.[167] Furthermore, court preachers, such as Peter Sterry, who received salaries of £200, supplemented their official duties by acting as propaganda factotums. Sterry, therefore, sent news reports from the Scottish campaigns, and preached keynote political sermons.[168] He and another preacher, Joseph Caryl, were also involved in organising printing and propaganda for the Council.[169]

Whether the post of 'court preacher' was regarded as little more than a sinecure for a salaried hack is unclear, but the title given to a far more important propagandist went some way towards reflecting literary duties. Having proved his talents with *The Tenure of Kings and Magistrates*, which appeared on 13 February 1649, John Milton was installed as 'secretary of foreign tongues', or Latin secretary, a month later.[170] This clearly involved formal duties in relation to

---

[163] PRO, SP 46/95, fos. 155–6.

[164] *The Same Hand Again Against the Present Council of State's Bad Friends* (London, 1649), sig. Av; *The Perfect Weekly Account* (30 May–6 June 1649), p. 533.

[165] J. Canne, *The Improvement of Mercy* (London, 1649); J. Canne, *Emanuel* (London, 1650); J. Canne, *A Voice from the Temple* (London, 1653).

[166] *CSPD 1651–2*, pp. 100, 123, 211.

[167] *CSPD 1651*, p. 411; *CSPD 1653–4*, pp. 73, 101, 428; *Remarkable Observations of Gods Mercies Towards England* (London, 1651); *A False Jew* (Newcastle, 1653). The latter was based upon information from Cuthbert Sydenham and others in Newcastle.

[168] J. Nickolls, *Original Letters and Papers of State* (London, 1743), pp. 18-19; P. Sterry, *England's Deliverance from the Northern Presbytery* (London, 1652). The latter, delivered at St Margaret's Westminster, named Sterry as a preacher to the Council.

[169] *CSPD 1653–4*, pp. 189, 225, 459; *CSPD 1654*, pp. 45, 369, 370, 373, 447, 456; *CSPD 1655*, pp. 21, 50, 69, 182, 197, 256, 295, 317, 446, 601, 604; *CSPD 1655–6*, pp. 16, 52, 100, 134, 218, 279, 288, 370, 389, 500, 585, 587, 588; *CSPD 1656–7*, pp. 158, 199, 239, 280, 285, 512, 589, 590, 592, 593.

[170] *CSPD 1649–50*, pp. 37, 40; *CSPD 1650*, pp. 2, 10; *CSPD 1651–2*, p. 81.

diplomatic correspondence, but the sense that he was picked to undertake polemical tasks, and that the post itself was intended to involve propaganda, is evident not just from the books which he wrote, but from the commissions to which he responded in so doing.[171] On 26 March, therefore, Milton was ordered to respond to *The Second Part of England's New Chains*, and two days later was ordered to make 'observations' upon the articles of peace concluded with the Irish rebels.[172] In May he was ordered to respond to the most important royalist tract of the times, *Eikon Basilike*, which led to the official publication of *Eikonoklastes* in the following October.[173] Milton was also given the task of replying to Salmasius, author of *Defensio Regia*, in early January 1650, and having been ordered to print his *Pro Populo Anglicano Defensio* in the following December, the task was undertaken by the council's printer, Dugard, who displayed the arms of the commonwealth on the cover.[174] Milton was also encouraged to respond to John Rowland's *Pro Rege*, and when Pierre du Moulin published *Regii Sanguinis Clamor* in 1652, Milton was told that he was, 'expected to do a duty zealously for the commonwealth, namely to shut the mouth of this importunate crier'.[175] Milton's activities ensured contemporary notoriety as the Rump's 'goos-quill champion', and the intrinsic connection between the post of Latin Secretary and literary activity is evident from the fact that Milton was succeeded, in September 1657, by Andrew Marvell, whose tenure coincided with his authorship of 'a poem upon the death of Oliver Cromwell'.[176]

The importance of Milton and Marvell notwithstanding, it was with the appointment of Marchamont Nedham that the hiring and payment of authors as propagandists became clear for the first time. Nedham also provides the finest

---

[171] *CSPD 1650*, p. 216; R. T. Fallon, 'Filling the gaps: new perspectives on Mr Secretary Milton', *Milton Studies* 12 (1978), pp. 165–95; R. T. Fallon, *Milton in Government* (Pennsylvania, 1993); L. Miller, *John Milton's Writings in the Anglo-Dutch Negotiations, 1651–1654* (Pittsburgh, 1992).

[172] *CSPD 1649–50*, pp. 52, 57; D. Masson, *The Life of John Milton* (7 vols, London, 1871–80), iv. 99–104; W. R. Parker, *Milton: A Biography* (2 vols, Oxford, 1968), i. 356; T. N. Corns, 'Milton's *Observations Upon the Articles of Peace*: Ireland under English eyes', in D. Lowenstein and J. G. Turner, eds, *Politics, Poetics, and Hermeneutics in Milton's Prose* (Cambridge, 1990). See: *Articles of Peace Made and Concluded with the Irish Rebels and Papists by James Earle of Ormond* ('published by authority', London, by Simmons, 1649).

[173] J. Milton *Eikonoklastes* (London, by Dugard, 1652); Masson, *Milton*, iv. 132–45; Parker, *Milton*, i. 360–61.

[174] *CSPD 1649–50*, p. 474; *CSPD 1650*, p. 479; Masson, *Milton*, iv. 151, 230; Parker, *Milton*, i. 369, 378; L. Miller, 'Before Milton was famous: January 8, 1649/50', *Milton Quarterly* 21 (1987), pp. 1–6; C. Hill, *Milton and the English Revolution* (New York, 1977), pp. 165–204; J. Milton, *Pro Populo Defensio* (London, Dugard, 1651).

[175] Milton's *Defensio Secundo*, however, would not make its appearance for two years: Masson, *Milton*, iv. 453–65, 467–8, 470–74, 580–616; J. M. French, *The Life Records of John Milton* (5 vols, New Brunswick, 1949–58), iii. 245–6, 287; *Joannis Philippi Angli Responsio* (London, 1652).

[176] *The Character of the Rump* (London, 1660), p. 2; *Mercurius Pragmaticus* 30 (20–27 Nov. 1649), sig. Gg3v; H. Kelliher, *Andrew Marvell, Poet and Politician, 1621–78* (London, 1978), pp. 67, 70, 74, 77; *TSP* vi. 743, 747, 769, 770; *TSP* vii. 69, 487; *CSPD 1658–9*, p. 131; Margoliouth, *Poems and Letters*, i. 123–31.

example of a writer who was hired after proposing his services as a propagandist, although he was probably pushing at an open door when he issued the prospectus for a new pro-commonwealth newspaper in the spring of 1650. In it, he said that:

> the design of this pamphlet being to undeceive the people, it must be written in a jocular way, or else it will never be cried up: for those truths which the multitude regard not in a serious dress, being represented in pleasing popular airs, make music to the common sense, and charm the fancy, which ever sways the sceptre in vulgar judgment, much more than reason.

Nedham also indicated the day on which he sought to be published – arguing that Tuesday was most convenient for dispersing the work through the nation – and he concluded that 'it shall be my care to sail in a middle way between the Scylla and Charybdis of scurrility and profanes'.[177] Within days of his offer to write for the regime, Nedham was released from prison – Bradshaw's 'favour' having 'once more turn'd the wheel of my fortune' – and the first issue of *Mercurius Politicus* appeared on 13 June 1650.[178] In May 1650, Nedham was granted a pension of £100, with a probationary year, and an award of £50 for services already performed.[179] He became known as the 'lying court pamphleteer', while *Politicus* was 'the paper militia, a diurnall offensive and defensive: the only pamphlet in pay, and a libel of the establishment among the standing forces of the commonwealth'. It was also described as 'the storke of the commonwealth, strutting before Whitehall, and feeding upon the garbidge of the weekly intelligence'.[180] Nedham's journalism was considered so valuable that his pension was supplemented by a grant of half of the profits from *Politicus*. That this was lucrative is evident from subsequent allegations that, between May 1656 and August 1658, the profits amounted to £1,280.[181]

Nedham supplemented his journalism, however, with other polemical activity on behalf of the regime, and was something of an all-purpose propagandist, who could turn his talents to both journalism and prose, and to tasks both big and small.[182] Another such utility author was Cuthbert Sydenham, who likewise

---

177 PRO, SP 46/94, fos. 281–2.

178 D. Gardiner, ed., *The Oxinden and Peyton Letters, 1642–1670* (London, 1937), p. 161; BL, Add. 28002, fo. 172; PRO, SP 46/95, fo. 190; *Mercurius Politicus* 1 (6–13 June 1650).

179 *CSPD 1650*, p. 174. For payments to Nedham: *TSP* vi. 594; *TSP* vii. 481–2; *CSPD 1656–7*, pp. 591–2; *CSPD 1654*, pp. 447, 455, 458.

180 *A Second Narrative of the Late Parliament (So Called)* (np, 1659), p. 37; *The Character of Mercurius Politicus* (London, 1650), p. 1; *The Second Character of Mercurius Politicus* (London, 1650), p. 6. See also J. Webster, *The Picture of Mercurius Politicus* (London, 1653).

181 Bodl. MS Rawl. A.60, fo. 474; *TSP* vii. 470–71. See: J. Raymond, 'A mercury with a winged conscience: Marchamont Nedham, monopoly and censorship', *Media History* 4 (1998), p. 15. One opponent claimed that Politicus was paid £505 'to make good several sums of money by him lost in bowling greens and at the comb-maker's ordinary': *An Exact Accompt of the Receipts and Disbursements Expended by the Committee of Safety* (London, 1660), p. 8.

182 [M. Nedham], *A Cat May Look at a King* (London, 1652). He was also involved in an attempt to secure a recantation by the Ranter, Abiezzer Coppe, who was a prisoner in Newgate, and subsequently informed his readers about the recantation which Coppe had written: N. Smith, ed., *A*

became a salaried servant of the Rump. A highly regarded theologian, Sydenham spent most of his working life in Newcastle, but he was intimate with leading Independent ministers in London, and at some stage in the early 1650s moved to London, and began to involve himself in polemical activity.[183] The first evidence of Sydenham's special status emerged shortly after the trial of John Lilburne in October 1649, when he attacked the Leveller leader in a work dedicated to the Commons, and bearing a preface by Parliament's special secretary, Thomas May. Following its appearance, Sydenham was paid £50 for 'good services in writing several tracts upon various subjects'.[184] Sydenham supported Cromwell's military campaign in Scotland with *An English Translation of the Scottish Declaration*, as well as a more significant tract, entitled *The False Brother*, in which he justified the English invasion by tracing relations between the two nations back to 1643. The Council was clearly instrumental in securing the publication of this work, which readers were informed was 'humbly presented to the Council of State', and for his 'good service in writing on behalf of the commonwealth' Sydenham was rewarded with a further payment of £100 in February 1651, as well as a salary of the same sum 'during the council's pleasure'.[185] The regime supported the appearance of Sydenham's most important work, *The True Portraiture of the Kings of England*, by including a preface written by Henry Parker, and by financial support.[186]

The commonwealth did not merely hire, pay and give precise instructions to a series of writers, some of whom were employed specifically and exclusively for their polemical skills. They also ensured that certain writers were hired for specific purposes. The recruitment of Milton, for example, may have been intended to secure propaganda for an overseas market. His books were written in Latin, while *Pro Populo Anglicano* was translated into Dutch at the Council's command, and *Eikonoklastes* was ordered to be published in a French edition. Indeed, the council also took pains to ensure that such works could circulate on the Continent.[187] In this

---

Collection of Ranter Writings (London, 1983), pp. 156–7; *Mercurius Politicus* 58 (10–17 July 1651), sig. Aaaaaa4v.

[183] Peacey, 'Henry Parker', p. 207.

[184] [C. Sydenham], *An Anatomy of Lieut. Col. John Lilburns Spirit and Pamphlets* (London, 1649); *SR* i. 328; *CSPD 1649–50*, p. 476. The other works to which this order refers are unknown.

[185] These payments continued until November 1653, shortly before Sydenham's death: [C. Sydenham], *An English Translation* (London, 1650); C. Sydenham, *The False Brother* (London, 1651); *CSPD 1650*, p. 448, *CSPD 1651*, p. 42, *CSPD 1651–2*, p. 370, *CSPD 1653–4*, p. 456.

[186] [C. Sydenham] and H. Parker, *The True Portraiture* (London, 1650); Peacey, 'Henry Parker', pp. 137–8, 208–9; *CSPD 1650*, p. 275. The council's financial role may merely have been to purchase 300 copies on the day of publication. Nedham drew upon it in his editorials for *Mercurius Politicus* during 1651: *Mercurius Politicus* 53 (5–12 June 1651), sigs. Nnnnn-Nnnnn2; *Mercurius Politicus* 64 (21–28 Aug. 1651), pp. 1013–16; *Mercurius Politicus* 65 (28 Aug.–4 Sept. 1651), pp. 1029–32. See also: C. Sydenham, *A Christian, Sober, and Plain Exercitation* (London, 1653); C. Sydenham et al., *A False Jew* (Newcastle, 1653); C. Sydenham, *The Greatness and the Mystery of Godlines* (London, 1654); C. Sydenham, *Hypocrisie Discovered* (London, 1654).

[187] J. Milton, *Eikonoklastes, ou Response au Livre* (London, 1652); J. Milton, *Pro Populo*

context, it is intriguing that Milton was made licenser of *Mercurius Politicus*, the purpose of which may have been diplomatic as much as propagandistic.[188] Nedham, after all, was involved in writing and translating on the murder of the commonwealth's diplomat, Anthony Ascham, as well as in translating Selden's *Mare Clausum* (for which he was paid £200), and in defending the Rump's foreign policies.[189] More obvious specialist positions included the newly formalised post of official historian. Lewis Du Moulin, who had been controversially installed as professor of history at Oxford by Parliament in the late 1640s, received a pension from the Council in the 1650s.[190] Furthermore, upon the death of Thomas May, who had effectively carved out the role of official historian during the late 1640s, the council considered his replacement in such a role, and this was perhaps the task which Payne Fisher was intended to perform. He conspicuously failed to fulfil such hopes, however, and might more accurately be described as the regime's poet laureate.[191] Fisher was later accused of having used his pen in order to 'ingratiate himself with the great men then in power' during the early 1650s, doubtless with his many dedicatory verses to great men and, having drawn attention to his talents with *Marston Moor*, a Council committee was appointed in December 1651 to consider means of encouraging his activities.[192] Fisher reminded the Council of his talents with the publication of *Veni, Vidi, Vici*, and within weeks of its appearance in February 1652 they rewarded his good service with £50, and considered his employment.[193] The Council probably envisaged such employment as being related to the need to chronicle Cromwell's military campaigns, and having petitioned for assistance to help finish an unspecified treatise in August 1652, Fisher was awarded £100 and a pass to travel to Scotland, although he made only slight progress on a projected account of Dunbar.[194] Nevertheless, he published *Pro*

Anglicano (London, 1652); *CSPD 1651*, pp. 70, 208, 259; *CSPD 1651–2*, p. 492; *CSPD 1652–3*, pp. 144, 486. When the Council considered rewarding the translator of *Eikonoklastes*, they felt it warranted £200. For circulation: French, *Life Records*, ii. 291–2; *CSPD 1649–50*, p. 481; *CSPD 1652–3*, p. 250.

[188] *CSPD 1649–50*, pp. 204, 534, 541, 550. Milton served as licenser from January 1651 to January 1652: *SR* i. 362–89.

[189] *CSPD 1650*, p. 387; *CSPD 1651–2*, pp. 303, 358, 483; *CSPD 1652–3*, p. 486; J. Selden, *Of the Dominion, or Ownership of the Sea* (trans. M. Nedham, London, 1652); PRO, SP 18/33, fo. 29; [M. Nedham], *The Case Stated Between England and the United Provinces* (London, by Newcomb, 1652).

[190] *LJ* viii. 450; *CJ* v. 334, 342; *CJ* vii. 436, 438–9, 465, 474; M. Burrows, ed., *The Register of the Visitors of the University of Oxford* (Camden Society, 1881), pp. 185–6; *CSPD 1654*, p. 392; *CSPD 1657–8*, p. 365. He was author of *The Power of the Christian Magistrate* (London, 1650), dedicated to John Lisle and Bulstrode Whitelocke.

[191] *CSPD 1650*, p. 432; *CSPD 1651*, p. 1.

[192] Wood, *Athenae*, iv. 377; P. Fisher, *Inauguratio Olivariana* (London, by Newcomb, 1654); P. Fisher, *Marston Moor* (London, by Newcomb, 1650); *CSPD 1651–2*, p. 81.

[193] P. Fisher, *Veni, Vidi, Vici* (London, 1652); *CSPD 1651–2*, pp. 152, 591. Fisher then published *Irenodia Gratulatoria*, which included a verse by Nedham: P. Fisher, *Irenodia Gratulatoria* (London, by Newcomb, 1652), sigs. a–a2.

[194] *CSPD 1651–2*, pp. 366–7, 573; C. H. Firth, 'The battle of Dunbar', *TRHS*, new series 14 (1900).

Navali Anglorum in 1653, and Fisher's verses in honour of Cromwell in 1654 effectively signalled that the payments he continued to receive were for his poetry rather than for his historical scholarship.[195] Thereafter, he produced poems on state occasions, and to commemorate notable events both at court and in the country. These were published by official printers, and were supported by epistles by the likes of Nedham, and Fisher styled himself 'ab historiis et satellitio domini protectoris'.[196]

The commonwealth's employment of specialist propagandists is also evident during the Engagement controversy, in which government involvement has figured little in recent scholarship.[197] The concerted literary effort undertaken to secure support for the new oath is evident not merely from the number of licensed tracts which appeared on the subject, but also from the employment of John Dury, the roving irenicist who had returned to England in 1645 to join the Westminster Assembly, and to serve as chaplain to the imprisoned Duke of York.[198] In early 1649, Dury sought to obtain a fellowship at Eton College through the good offices of the provost and MP, Francis Rous, and it may have been the latter, interested in literary defences of the new regime, who persuaded Dury to serve the commonwealth. Dury certainly informed Parliament of 'his condition, and the ways wherein he could be serviceable to the public', and having claimed to have suffered a financial loss of £200 per annum upon leaving Rotterdam, where he had been minister to the English merchant community, he intimated that his services could be bought for a similar fee.[199] Dury had already published a tract against clerics meddling in state affairs, mirroring legislation which was passing

---

[195] P. Fisher, *Pro Navali Anglorum* (London, 1653); P. Fisher, *Panegyrici Cromwello* (np, 1654); Fisher, *Inauguratio Olivariana*; *CSPD 1654*, pp. 396, 457.

[196] P. Fisher, *Oratio Anniversaria in Diem Inaugurationis Serenissimi Nostri Principis Olivari* (London, 1655); P. Fisher, *Apobaterion* (London, by Newcomb, 1655). Fisher's successor during the Restoration was James Howell: Seaward, 'Restoration publicist', p. 124; PRO, E 403/2525, fos. 102v–103. Another official historian was John Dryden: R. G. Ham, 'Dryden as historiographer-royal: the authorship of *His Majesties Declaration Defended*, 1681', *Review of English Studies* 11 (1935); E. L. Saslow, 'Dryden as historiographer royal, and the authorship of *His Majesties Declaration Defended*', *Modern Philology* 75 (1978); P. Harth, *Pen for a Party. Dryden's Tory Propaganda in its Contexts* (Princeton, 1993).

[197] J. Wallace, 'The Engagement controversy 1649–1652', *Bulletin of the New York Public Library* 68 (1964); G. Burgess, 'Usurpation, obligation and obedience in the thought of the Engagement controversy', *HJ* 29 (1986).

[198] *Some Considerations About the Nature of an Oath* (London, 1649); *Discourse Concerning the Engagement* (London, 1650); *The Grand Case of Conscience* (London, 1650); *A Logical Demonstration* (London, 1650); T. B., *The Engagement Vindicated* (London, 1650); *SR* i. 326, 334–36. For Dury: *LJ* x. 280–81; J. M. Batten, *John Dury* (Chicago, 1944), p. 113; A. Milton, 'The unchanged peacemaker, John Dury, and the politics of irenicism in England, 1628–1643', in M. Greengrass, M. Leslie, and T. Raylor, eds, *Samuel Hartlib and Universal Reformation* (Cambridge, 1994); G. H. Turnbull, *Hartlib, Dury and Comenius* (London, 1947); H. R. Trevor-Roper, 'Three foreigners: the philosophers of the Puritan revolution', in *Religion, Reformation, and Social Change*; BL, Add. 34253, fo. 28: John Dury to Earl of Manchester, 3 Dec. 1643.

[199] Turnbull, *Hartlib, Dury, and Comenius*, p. 259; BL, Add. 24863, fo. 80.

through the Commons, and he may have been drafted in by a parliamentary committee to defend the new regime in further books and pamphlets.[200] His friend Rous certainly served on the committee for 'undeceiving' the people regarding the Engagement, and when the Council commissioned a declaration in December 1649 they also ordered that Dury be 'remembered', noting that his writings could be 'of great use for better carrying on the test'. It seems clear that Dury's *Considerations Concerning the Present Engagement* and the declaration of Rous's committee were one and the same, and that Dury was the official apologist for the government on this subject. When the declaration was presented to Parliament, Dury was awarded £200 per annum for life.[201] Moreover, Dury justified his pension by writing a raft of further Engagement tracts, and by assisting the production of others by the likes of Ephraim Elcock, and although none of the later works added anything of significance to the debate, they nevertheless reflected the importance of keeping the issue alive, as well as of replying to critics.[202]

Pre-eminent among the specialist propagandists, however, was John Hall, who was employed on 14 May 1649, on a salary of £100 per annum, with the task of answering pamphlets against the commonwealth.[203] His first duty was to respond to William Prynne, and in the following October the Council ordered, and paid for, the printing of 500 copies of his *Serious Epistle*.[204] When not required to answer specific critics, however, Hall was employed on other projects. He accompanied Cromwell to Scotland in September 1650, having been ordered to 'make such observations on affairs there', and during the ensuing nine months received £7 per month from the army, as well as £20 for 'extraordinary service'. He was clearly

---

[200] J. Dury, *A Case of Conscience* (London, 1649); J. Dury, *A Case of Conscience Concerning Ministers* (London, 1650); *CJ* vi. 175, 178, 183, 199.

[201] *CJ* vi. 312–14, 337, 474; *CSPD 1649–50*, p. 448; J. D[ury], *Considerations Concerning the Present Engagement* (London, 1649); *SR* i. 335. Rous himself produced a defence of the regime: F. Rous, *The Lawfulness of Obeying the Present Government* (London, 1649).

[202] J. Dury, *Just Reproposals* (London, 1650), *A Disengag'd Survey* (London, 1650), *The Unchanged, Constant and Single Hearted Peacemaker* (London, 1650), *Objections Against the Taking of the Engagment Answered* (London, 1650), *Two Treatises Concerning the Matter of the Engagement* (London, 1650), *A Second Parcel of Objections Against the Taking of the Engagement Answered* (London, 1650), *Conscience Eased* (London, nd). In addition to his own works, Dury assisted in the publication of the work of others, most notably Ephraim Elcock's *Animadversions on a Book Called A Plea for Non-Subscribers*, another defence of the Engagement, written against William Prynne: E. Elcock, *Animadversions* (London, 1651), sig. A2v. Dury was clearly intimate with the leadership at Westminster; becoming keeper of the library at St James's Palace, and travelling with John Lisle on his diplomatic mission to Sweden: Turnbull, *Hartlib, Dury and Comenius*, p. 269; L. Miller, *John Milton and the Oldenburg Safeguard* (New York, 1985); *CJ* vi. 337, 416, 474; *CSPD 1650*, pp. 272, 401, 403, 418, 436, 556; *CSPD 1651*, pp. 208, 468; *CSPD 1651–2*, pp. 173, 490, 492; *CSPD 1653–4*, p. 164; Longleat House, Whitelocke Papers, XIII, fos. 234–36v, XIV, fo. 96, XV, fo. 3.

[203] *CSPD 1649–50*, p. 139; Davies, 'Account', sigs. b3v–b4. Hall was provided with an advance of £30. For evidence of payments, see: *CSPD 1649–50*, p. 451; *TSP* vi. 593.

[204] J. Hall, *A Serious Epistle to Mr William Prynne* (London, 1649); *CSPD 1649–50*, p. 345; Davies, 'Account', sig. b4.

taken both as tract writer and 'war correspondent' for *Mercurius Politicus*.[205] Hall produced three pamphlets in Scotland; attacking monarchy, Charles II's Scottish ancestry, and warning against admitting into England a northern army which would bring with it 'an ignoble and ignominious vassalage under a Scottish usurpation'.[206] Thereafter, however, he returned to his primary task with an attack upon Christopher Love, who had been executed for his part in a Presbyterian plot against the Rump, and around whom a media circus had developed.[207] In November 1651, Hall republished an old account of the Amboyna 'massacre' by the Dutch, which was timed to coincide with the arrival of the Dutch ambassadors in London, and which was perceived to be a deliberate attempt to 'retard the peace', and he subsequently defended Cromwell's dissolution of the Rump in May 1653, in a work which royalists recognised had been written 'at Cromwell's order'.[208] Hall subsequently issued a reply to a key republican critic of the regime, John Streater, whose works had attracted the attention of the authorities, and whose activities formed part of the investigation undertaken by Henry Hills, who would publish Hall's response.[209] Hall also penned an attack upon John Lilburne, in response to the *Charge of High Treason* levelled against Cromwell, which had attracted the attention of the Council, who doubtless set Hall to work. Both works were guided through the press by the council's official printer.[210]

Royalist reticence about engaging with the public through the medium of print,

---

[205] *CSPD 1650*, p. 325; Chequers, MS 782, fos. 6, 6v, 7v, 8v, 10, 13v; Davies, 'Account', sigs. b4–b4v; Abbott, *Cromwell*, ii. 584–85; *Mercurius Politicus* 17 (26 Sept.–3 Oct. 1650), pp. 288–90; *The Declaration and Speech of Colonel Massey Concerning the Inthroning of the King of Scots* (London, 1650), pp. 1–3.

[206] [J. Hall], *The Nonesuch Charles his Character* (London, 1651); [J. Hall], *The Honour of the English Soldiery* (London, by Newcomb, 1651), p. 23; *Mercurius Politicus* 60 (24–31 July 1651), sig. Eeeeee4v; J. H[all], *The Grounds and Reasons of Monarchy Considered* (Edinburgh, 1650); Davies, 'Account', sigs. b4–b4v.

[207] J. H[all], *A Gagg to Love's Advocate* (London, by Dugard, printer to the Council of State, 1652); Davies, 'Account', sig. b4v.

[208] [J. Hall], *A True Relation* (London, 1651); *SR* i. 424; *TSP* i. 267, 607; *Mercurius Politicus* 77 (20–27 Nov. 1651), p. 1236; Davies, 'Account', sig. b4v; [Joh]N [Ha]ll, *A Letter Written to a Gentleman* (London, 1653); *SR* i. 417; *CCSP* ii. 212; Bodl. MS Clarendon 45, fo. 438v. This last work was originally attributed, by means of a rather bizarre argument, to Milton: H. C. H. Candy, 'Milton, N.LL, and Sir Thomas Urquhart', *The Library*, 4th series 14 (1934), pp. 470–76. For payments: *CSPD 1653–4*, p. 173.

[209] [J. Hall], *A Stop to the Mad Multitude* (London, Hills, 1653). This appeared sometime after 13 September, when it was entered into the Stationers' register. For my identification of this tract see: Peacey, 'Henry Parker', pp. 200–201. For Streater's works, see: [J. Streater], 'Ten Queries by a Friend of the New Dissolved Parliament' (MS in Thomason Collection, BL, E693/5); *A Glimpse of that Jewel* (London, 1653); *A Further Continuance of the Grand Politick Informer* (np, nd); *CSPD 1653–4*, pp. 106, 143, 243, 261, 268, 435, 457; *CJ* vii. 353; PRO, SP 46/97, fo. 64; *Clavis as Aperiendum ... the Case of Mr John Streater* (London, 1654); N. Smith, 'Popular republicanism in the 1650s: John Streater's 'heroick mechanicks', in D. Armitage, A. Himy, Q. Skinner, eds, *Milton and Republicanism* (Cambridge, 1998).

[210] *CSPD 1653–4*, pp. 151, 180, 187, 200; *CJ* vii. 333; J. Hall, *Sedition Scourg'd* (London, 1653).

which affected some cavalier grandees more than others, withered in the conditions of civil tension and domestic conflict. Royalists, like their parliamentarian rivals, were clearly prepared to protect their favoured writers, and to assist in the process of exploiting print to the extent of assisting in the distribution of works which their supporters had written and published. Moreover, there is evidence that grandees on all sides in the 1640s proved willing to encourage publication to the extent of exploiting publishing opportunities provided by petitions, letters of news from the battlefield, and even those substantial polemical treatises which were presented to them, and to do so in ways which demonstrated their involvement to the reading public. Royalists may have been hampered, after the end of the first civil war, by the logistical and financial conditions of exile, which evidently exacerbated problems which they had always faced at this organisational level. Nevertheless, their straightened circumstances probably cannot explain entirely the difference in approach between themselves and their parliamentarian rivals, for whom evidence suggests not merely a consistent desire to orchestrate the appearance of newsletters, tracts and sermons, but also a growing willingness to offer financial support to such ventures from central coffers.

Further differences emerge from consideration of the ways in which grandees involved themselves in the commissioning of polemical literature during this period. Royalists were certainly willing to commission writers, and although they appear to have relied fairly heavily on grandees such as Hyde as much as upon proven polemicists such as Heylyn, they can be shown on at least one occasion to have sought out the services of one of Europe's leading scholars, in the shape of Salmasius. Parliamentarians, meanwhile, though they too relied upon old friends and colleagues for commissioned literature, increasingly drew upon the services of men who were working within the administrative system at Westminster and Whitehall, and such activities became focused upon the Council of State, which assumed a position of great power in instigating, orchestrating and financing such projects. The centrality of the Council, the frequency with which it involved itself in a range of literary projects, and the openness with which it devoted significant sums of money to the production of propaganda, represented a significant innovation. This became most obvious in relation to the most important new medium of the period, the weekly newspapers. Journalism was an area in which royalists demonstrated their willingness to innovate, by instigating one of the most important early papers of the 1640s, the nature and longevity of which ensured that its commissioned editors operated in close proximity to the political process and leaders at Oxford. However, with this paper, as with early parliamentarian efforts, it is difficult to assess the precise nature of the relationship between author and grandee, and the nature of the financial backing which journalism received, or indeed needed to receive. It is certainly possible that some journalists during the 1640s – on both sides – were motivated by a sense of allegiance to individual grandees and patrons, whose political and personal interests they strove to serve.

For parliamentarians, however, there gradually emerged evidence that journalism, like other forms of commissioned literature, came under the sway of the Council and its functionaries; that it was closely managed; and that at least some editors were financially rewarded from governmental sources, as well as from sales receipts. Indeed, this growing sophistication in the production of propaganda became clear not merely from the parliamentarian newspaper industry, but also from the nature and number of other writers whose services were retained by the Rump and the Protectorate. While not all of these were officially recognised as hired hands, and were paid on an *ad hoc* or surreptitious basis, others were propagandists in all but name, and a few were explicitly employed as official writers. Such writers, whether generalists or specialists, were handsomely rewarded with substantial salaries, and were expected to work to a brief, and on occasions a defined timetable. Such evidence indicates the extent to which propaganda had become professionalised.

CHAPTER 6

Politicians and the Writing Process

Writing with the benefit of hindsight, and with the intention of demonising leading parliamentarian figures of the 1640s, the author of *Vox Veritatis* claimed in 1650 that the *Apologetical Narration* (1643) of the dissenting brethren, one of the key texts of the early civil war period, was written 'by the secret advice of the Lord Saye, Lord Wharton, Sir Henry Vane junior and Mr [Oliver] St John'.[1] Such phraseology may have been chosen carefully, in order to indicate not merely that Saye and his allies had instigated the work, but that they had also played a constructive part in its composition. Whatever the truth of this allegation, and whatever the accuser's precise meaning, understanding political influence over polemical publication clearly requires that analysis be extended beyond examination of the impetus behind specific tracts and pamphlets, in order to establish the depth of political involvement in particular texts. To the extent that political grandees were concerned to instigate the appearance of texts for specific purposes and at particular moments, they were naturally concerned with the content of such works, and the aim of this chapter is to explore the ways in which such concern was manifested, and the degree to which the substance of political texts was managed and manipulated. For texts to be subjected to substantive influence required collaboration between authors and political grandees before works reached the bookstalls. This naturally meant seeking to exert control during the composition process, which could involve interference in planning and progress, and scrutiny of substantive content and literary style, and which pertained to a variety of polemical forms, from the sermon to the newspaper, the substantial political treatise, and work of historical scholarship. Study of such processes will inform our understanding not merely of the commitment to the polemical process on the part of political grandees, but also of the role and status of propagandists, and the nature of their relationships with patrons and employers.

The most obvious stage at which to become involved in the construction of texts was before pen met paper. It seems logical to suggest that certain keynote sermons before Parliament were discussed beforehand, even if only to the extent that those who commissioned a sermon such as Stephen Marshall's *Meroz Cursed* of February 1642 knew in advance the fiery tone which he would take, although there

---

[1] *Vox Veritatis* (Hague, 1650), p. 5.

is little way of substantiating such possibilities.[2] Politicians clearly involved themselves in the planning process for projected volumes, by perusing plans and outlines submitted by authors. Of course, such plans may not have been committed to paper, but rather could be discussed informally between writers and politicians. In January 1657, therefore, Sir Edward Hyde discussed with Edward Sexby the content of his forthcoming work, *Killing No Murder*.[3] John Jones issued somewhat vague proposals to the parliamentarian grandees in the summer of 1642 – perhaps reflecting the vagueness of his thought – and prominent members of both Houses consented to meet him for discussions, although nothing appears to have emerged.[4] Other authors provided plans of a more detailed nature, such as the 'method' of Morland's history of the Piedmontese Protestants, which was submitted to John Thurloe in April 1656, and which found official favour.[5]

Other such plans do not appear to have been approved so easily. Having been set to work on what became *Landensium*, Robert Baillie became involved in detailed planning discussions with the covenanter leader, Archibald Johnston of Wariston, in terms not just of the general methodological approach, but also of length, chapter structure, and marginalia.[6] A 1648 manuscript, containing 'some heads of an answer' to Parliament's declaration of 'no further addresses', was subjected to correction by Edward Nicholas, although his comments were a great deal less rigorous than those provided by William Laud regarding Joseph Hall's planned defence of the divine right of episcopacy.[7] Hall sent Laud the outline of his book in late October 1639, and within two weeks Laud returned comments upon 'the whole plan of your intended work', which had been yielded up to his 'censure and better advice'. Laud offered detailed suggestions on both specific points and overall tone. Hall was apparently happy with this process, and claimed that Laud's 'animadversions' were 'so just that I had amended divers of those passages voluntarily 'ere I received this gracious admonition, for I only sent you the rude draft of what I meant to polish in the expression'.[8] On other occasions, however, such processes could become sufficiently protracted that works became

---

[2] S. Marshall, *Meroz Cursed* (London, 1642); H. Trevor-Roper, 'The Fast sermons of the Long Parliament', in *Religion, the Reformation and Social Change* (London, 1973); J. F. Wilson, *Pulpit in Parliament* (Princeton, 1979).

[3] *CCSP* iii. 229, 297; Bodleian MS Clarendon 53, fo. 189; Bodl. MS Clarendon 54, fo. 278; V. Sanders, 'The household of Archbishop Parker and the influencing of public opinion', *JEH* 34 (1983), pp. 540, 542; J. Bruce and T. T. Perowne, eds, *Correspondence of Matthew Parker* (Parker Society, Cambridge, 1853), pp. 409–15, 474–7.

[4] Above, p. 90; J. S. A. Adamson, 'Parliamentary management, men of business, and the House of Lords, 1640–49', in C. Jones, ed., *A Pillar of the Constitution* (London, 1989), p. 30.

[5] R. Vaughan, *The Protectorate of Oliver Cromwell* (2 vols, London, 1839), i. 380; *TSP* iv. 724; *OPH* xxiii, appendix, pp. 232–42.

[6] *Letters and Journals of Robert Baillie*, i. 242.

[7] *CCSP* i. 416–17; Bodl. MS Clarendon 31, fos. 33–35v.

[8] *CSPD 1639–40*, pp. 54–6, 87–8, 100; PRO, SP 16/431, fos. 122–3v; SP 16/432, fos. 82–3, 132r–v; P. Heylyn, *Cyprianus Anglicus* (London, 1671), pp. 374–7.

lost or forgotten. In 1644, Peter Heylyn presented to the king 'heads' for a discourse called 'The Stumbling Block of Disobedience', which were perused by royalist grandees such as Lord Hatton, the Bishop of Salisbury, Sir Orlando Bridgeman, and Dr Richard Steward, but although the proposal was approved by the king, the stumbling block of the project proved to be the decision to submit the plan to Lord Digby, 'in whose hands it did for a long time rest, neither was it made public till about ten years after the war was ended'.[9]

More significant is evidence that politicians could set the parameters for planned volumes, and issue instructions which ranged from brief remits to draft documents which merely required literary polish.[10] In September 1651, when Walter Frost was ordered to compile 'a narrative and history of the proceedings betwixt England and Scotland, from the beginning of the late troubles', he was requested to 'make such observations thereupon as may arise upon consideration of the nature of the fact and dealings of the Scottish nation and of their agents here; and for the better information of such as desire to know the truth of those proceedings'.[11] On other occasions, however, instructions were more detailed. It had long proved possible to exert influence over the texts of sermons by diocesan ministers and St Paul's Cross preachers, to the point of issuing sermon outlines, and during the early 1640s *Mercurius Aulicus* sought to expose the nature of parliamentarian 'fast' sermons by alleging that MPs were 'both auditors and composers, not only giving them their texts, but most of their sermons'.[12] Furthermore, such more or less detailed remits were also issued to authors of polemical treatises.[13] As one of the Scottish commissioners in London, Robert Baillie appears to have provided David Dickson with outline points for a work to be prepared in the summer of 1645, and Sir Edward Hyde's papers contain 'heads' for a work which were sent to one Major Wood as guidance for an unspecified

---

[9] G. Vernon, *The Life of the Learned and Reverend Dr Peter Heylyn* (London, 1682), pp. 130–31.

[10] G. R. Elton, *Policy and Police. The Enforcement of the Reformation in the Age of Thomas Cromwell* (Cambridge, 1972), pp. 185, 196; M. A. R. Graves, *Thomas Norton* (Oxford, 1994), pp. 75–6, 113, 123, 275, 277–8; C. Read, 'William Cecil and Elizabethan public relations', in S. T. Bindoff, J. Hurstfield and C. H. Williams, eds, *Elizabethan Government and Society* (London, 1961), pp. 36, 38, 41, 46; P. Hammer, 'The uses of scholarship: the secretariat of Robert Devereux, 2nd Earl of Essex, c.1585–1601', *EHR* 109 (1994), p. 38; D. H. Willson, 'James I and his literary assistants, *HLQ* 8 (1944), pp. 40, 51–2.

[11] PRO, SP 25/22, pp. 30–31; *CSPD 1651*, p. 411.

[12] A. Hunt, 'Tuning the pulpits: the religious context of the Essex revolt', in L. A. Ferrell and P. McCullough, eds, *The English Sermon Revised* (Manchester, 2000), pp. 91, 97, 100; G. Davies, 'English political sermons, 1603–1640', *HLQ* (1939), p. 7; T. S. Nowack, 'Propaganda and the pulpit. Robert Cecil, William Barlow and the Essex and Gunpowder plots', in K. Z. Keller and G. J. Schiffhorst, eds, *The Witness of Times* (Pittsburgh, 1992), p. 37; *Mercurius Aulicus* 14 (2–9 Apr. 1643), p. 180. *Aulicus* claimed that Isaac Pennington told ministers what to preach: *Mercurius Aulicus* 16 (16–22 April 1643), p. 203.

[13] Sanders, 'Household of Archbishop Parker', pp. 541–2; J. Strype, *Annals of the Reformation* (4 vols, Oxford, 1824), II. i. 275; J. Strype, *The Life and Acts of Matthew Parker* (3 vols, Oxford, 1821), ii. 253–4, iii. 207–8.

piece regarding the claims and promises of Charles II in the late 1650s.[14] During the early 1650s, as factional differences among the Scots spilled over into the press, Baillie encouraged James Wood, minister of St Andrews, to respond to a book called *The Nullity of the Pretended Assembly at St Andrews*, by stressing the need for 'a solid, succinct, handsome, modest taking answer', and by setting out his requirement that the task be undertaken 'with five or six sheets, or at most within ten, of animadversions, setting down the points whereto their controversie is now drawn, especially the heads of the Western Remonstrance'.[15]

The most intriguing instances of politicians setting down guidelines regarding required tracts, as well as providing detailed outlines, concern works which can be traced in printed form. The first example centres on the demand for an apologetical tract from the pen of Sir Edward Dering in the spring of 1644. The parliamentarian committee in Kent informed Dering that 'we expect your promise of your declaration', and outlined the nature of the work which was required:

> we desire no volume but an epitome, in which you may declare ... that Oxford produceth no other fruit than the effects of tyranny and popery. This, sir, may be done in a little pamphlet, which will better sink into the common people's brain than any long volume.[16]

In another letter the committee stressed that they wanted 'a pamphlet, which will satisfy the vulgar better than any elaborate piece of work, these being the men you have misled ... the better sort are so well satisfied as they shall not need any declaration'.[17] Dering, in no place to argue, replied by saying: 'the pamphlet you command shall go out sudden and un-polished', and that it would be 'a piece of a penny, fit (as you write) for the vulgar', although when he sent the work to the committee for printing he complained about being forced to pen such a piece.[18] Dering's work appeared in April 1644 as *A Declaration by Sir Edward Dering*, with John White's *imprimatur*, and contained his profession of loyalty to Parliament, and his fear regarding the drift of royalists towards arbitrary government and popery.[19] Perhaps the most intriguing instance of political involvement in the planning of polemical literature, however, is provided by evidence taken after the arrest of the Westminster scrivener, Alexander Aspinwall, in July 1659. Aspinwall, who claimed to have been a poor man with nothing but his pen upon which to subsist, informed his examiners that he had received 'heads' for a pamphlet from John Dunch, brother-in-law of the recently deposed protector, Richard Cromwell, together with 20s., for which he produced a short tract entitled

---

[14] *Letters and Journals of Robert Baillie*, ii. 277; *CCSP* iii. 408; Bodl. MS Clarendon 56, fos. 370–71v.

[15] *Letters and Journals of Robert Baillie*, iii. 213–14.

[16] BL, Stowe 184, fos. 69, 71.

[17] BL, Stowe 184, fos. 73, 76.

[18] BL, Stowe 184, fos. 75, 77.

[19] E. Dering, *A Declaration by Sir Edward Dering* (London, 1644). Earlier there had appeared *A Declaration Wherein is Full Satisfaction Given Concerning Sir Edward Dering* (London, 1644).

Timely Advice. This process was repeated the following week, when Aspinwall was promised 40s. for a work called *The Souldiers Alarum Bell*.[20] The two tracts had duly appeared, purporting to have been written by army officers disgruntled with the restored Rump, and arguing for the restoration of the Cromwellian protectorate, and rallying the troops for a forcible overthrow of the 'pseudo-Parliament'.[21]

While astute contemporary readers might have surmised that Dering's text was forced from his pen by retributive parliamentarians, they had little grounds to suspect the precise nature of the process by which his pamphlet was constructed. Unless they had grown entirely sceptical about the tracts which poured from the presses, however, Aspinwall's readers had little reason to suspect political involvement, and little way of establishing the true nature of the works for which he was discovered to have been responsible. However, though conceptually very different, the works by Dering and Aspinwall both reflect the lengths to which political grandees involved themselves not merely in instigating polemical literature, and in assisting in the logistical aspects of its production, but also in discussing projected volumes at a strategic level, and in offering constructive advice and instruction regarding style, length and content. They both reveal, in other words, the extent to which propaganda was orchestrated in a hands-on fashion.

Political involvement in propaganda did not stop, however, once the writing process began. Grandee participation was also reflected in the way in which favoured authors and official projects were granted access to material from governmental records and private archives.[22] Of course, like Jean D'Espaigne and George Carleton in the early part of the century, many writers probably argued that the greatest assistance which they could be offered was financial, but material assistance was clearly welcome, and was perhaps more readily available.[23]

To some extent, information was provided from within patronage networks and circulated within groups of like-minded individuals. During the 1630s, the Scottish covenanter, George Gillespie, was assisted in the production of works such as *A Dispute Against the English Popish Ceremonies* (1637) by English Puritan allies, whom Baillie called 'the chief of that side'.[24] On other occasions, of course, Scottish writers were able to look closer to home for their material, and during the summer of 1646, Robert Baillie relied upon the 'collections' of the kirk

---

[20] *CCSP* iv. 271–2, 282; Bodl. MS Clarendon 62, fos. 76, 141–2. Aspinwall was arrested on 9 July 1659: *CSPD 1659–60*, p. 14.

[21] *Timely Advice From the Major Part of the Ould Souldiers in the Army to All the Rest of Our Fellow Souldiers* (np, 1659); B.C., *The Souldiers Alarum Bell* (np, 1659).

[22] L. L. Peck, *Northampton. Patronage and Policy at the Court of James I* (London, 1982), pp. 111–12; Bruce and Perowne, eds, *Correspondence of Matthew Parker*, pp. 413–15.

[23] *CSPD 1625–49*, p. 392; PRO, SP 16/531, fo. 165; *CSPD 1611–18*, p. 77.

[24] *Letters and Journals of Robert Baillie*, i. 90.

historian, David Calderwood, in order to prepare a book against John Maxwell, and commented that such papers did 'good service'.[25] Nevertheless, the most important sources of material were clearly the court and Parliament. That politicians were willing to go to some lengths to provide such material is apparent from the work of Peter Heylyn, who was assisted in completing commissioned works in the 1630s by being granted access to royal records at Windsor, as well as to the collections of Sir Robert Cotton, from which he apparently borrowed items on security of £200 apiece.[26] Naturally, the provenance of many works produced on the basis of material from official archives would have been glaringly obvious to contemporary readers. Papers are known to have been provided to two of the official publishers, Joseph Hunscott and John Wright, for the production of an account of the 1641 Army Plot, which they undertook 'to return fair and safely within eight days', but the work which they produced was self-evidently official.[27] The official origins of John White's famous *First Century*, which outlined the cases of 100 scandalous ministers who had been sequestered by Parliament, would have been apparent not merely from the official *imprimatur* (of White's own committee for printing), but also from the fact that it was based upon material gleaned by the parliamentary committee which he chaired.[28]

This same transparency tended to apply to works relating to the Long Parliament's show trials of the 1640s. The provision of information from official archives was clearly vital to the process of producing accounts of such proceedings, and can be well-documented. In November 1643, William Prynne was ordered to receive records from the Tower which were relevant to the trial of Nathaniel Fiennes, and this evidently assisted not just the prosecution – which he led – but also his publications in relation to the case.[29] Prynne was also responsible for seizing the papers of William Laud; entering the archbishop's chamber in the Tower on 31 May 1643, accompanied by ten musketeers, and with a search warrant from the Committee of Safety.[30] Once again, the twenty-one bundles of papers removed from the Tower proved valuable not only for the legal proceedings, but also for a stream of books. The first fruit of Prynne's plunder was the appearance, in early August, of *Romes Masterpeece*, which uncovered details of the 'grand conspiracy of the Pope and his jesuited instruments, to extirpate the protestant religion ... by kindling a civil war in Scotland'. As if the official nature

---

[25] *Letters and Journals of Robert Baillie*, ii. 373, 377, 384.

[26] Vernon, *Heylyn*, pp. 38, 95.

[27] HLRO, Braye 57, fos. 5r–v; *CJ* ii. 573; *The Declaration or Remonstrance of the Lords and Commons ... with Divers Depositions and Letters* (imp. Brown, London, for Hunscott and Wright, 1642).

[28] J. White, *The First Century of Scandalous Malignant Priests* (London, 1643).

[29] *CJ* iii. 320. Such papers may have been too late to assist in the production of *The Doome of Cowardize* (London, 1643). But they were certainly useful for *A True and Full Relation of the Prosecution, Arraignment, Tryall and Condemnation of Nathaniel Fiennes* (London, 1644).

[30] *CSPD 1641–3*, p. 463; BL, Sloane 2035b, fo. 12; W. Laud, *The History of the Troubles and Tryal* (London, 1695), pp. 205–6; *Mercurius Aulicus* [101] (5–12 Jan. 1644[/5]), pp. 1332–3.

of his sources was not self-evident, Prynne informed readers, in the preface to the second edition, of 'the first publishing in print of the ensuing plot and letters by authority and directions from the House of Commons, which employed me in this service', and he added: 'I found all these ensuing letters ... when I was unexpectedly employed by the close committee'.[31] In time for the scheduled opening of Laud's trial, Prynne published his second instalment of Laud's papers in *The Popish Royal Favourite*, which contained letters ('collected and published by authority') between Charles and various recusants, priests and Jesuits, as well as his correspondence with the Pope from 1623.[32] When Prynne was subsequently required to print and publish an account of the legal proceedings against Laud, which appeared as *Canterburies Doome*, he was once again given authority to send for writings and papers relating to the case.[33] In such instances, the provenance of individual books, as well as the information which they contained, was transparently official.

On other occasions, however, this is much less clear. In December 1645, the Committee of Both Kingdoms issued a warrant to Prynne and Gabriel Beck to search prisoners in the Tower, probably for evidence relating to Connor, Lord Macguire, ringleader of the Irish rebellion.[34] Prynne published an account of Macguire's trial which was, once again, obviously official, and may also have had a hand in the appearance of the rebels' scaffold speeches.[35] More subtle was the way in which Beck, one of the trial's managers, donated the text of Macguire's confession to his old friend, Henry Parker, who intended to publish it in his account of the *Irish Massacre*. The planned publication of this work was evidently known to the Anglo-Irish parliamentarian grandee, Sir John Temple, although it appears to have been aborted in the press.[36] Furthermore, in later years, the public nature of such trials, and growing awareness on the part of the persecuted that published trial proceedings could prove valuable to the defence as well as the prosecution, ensured that it became far less easy to establish whether or not such works were official.[37] Moreover, there are a number of other occasions where

---

[31] W. Prynne, *Romes Masterpeece* (London, 1644), sig. A; *SR*, i. 67.

[32] W. Prynne, *The Popish Royal Favourite* (London, 1643).

[33] *CJ* iv. 68; W. Prynne, *Canterburies Doome* (London, 1646).

[34] *CSPD 1645–7*, p. 253.

[35] W. Prynne, *The Whole Triall of Connor Lord Macquire* (London, 1645); *SR* i. 150; *State Trials*, iv. 653–754; W. Lamont, *Marginal Prynne, 1600–69* (London, 1963), p. 129; *The Last Speeches and Confession* (London, nd); *SR* i. 150. Prynne would publish further details of his arguments at the trial in *The Subjection of all Traytors* (London, 1658).

[36] *LJ* v. 487; *CJ* iii. 653–4; *CSPD 1644–5*, p. 50; [H. Parker], *The Irish Massacre* ([London, 1646]), p. 4; Sir J. Temple, *The Irish Rebellion* (London, 1646), pp. 69–72. Beck's papers pertaining to the case survive, in the form of a copy of Macguire's confession, as well as a brief piece in Beck's hands entitled 'Philo-Britannus, or historical animadversions upon the constitution of the kingdom of Ireland and the management of the war there, 1641 and 1642': Bodl. MS Carte 64, fos. 5–29.

[37] The early accounts of proceedings at the king's trial were clearly official, but not those produced after the summer of 1649, and the accounts of the trials of Christopher Love, John Lilburne, and James Nayler were not official, and may have been recognisable as such, although the account of Miles

official provision of information to authors would have been difficult to detect. After the assembly of the Long Parliament, members of the Commons were sufficiently eager to see the publication of works by men who suffered during the Personal Rule to offer material assistance to published accounts of their troubles. In the spring of 1641, therefore, the MP Alexander Rigby delivered to Prynne thirty-seven parcels of writings concerning the proceedings against the three Puritan martyrs, which were to be returned in due course, and which enabled Prynne to produce *A New Discovery of the Prelates Tyranny*.[38] Adam Meredith, meanwhile, relied upon information provided by Sir John Temple for his attack upon the Marquess of Ormond, which was projected to appear as *Ormonds Curtain Drawn* in 1646, but which was, like Parker's work, aborted in the press.[39] And in January 1648, Walter Frost was provided with information by the Derby House Committee with which to complete the task of producing an exposé of Leveller activities, and a response to their declarations, but the resulting volume betrayed no more evidence of official involvement than an indication that it had been licensed.[40]

Such absence of evidence with which to connect material in books and pamphlets to official sources also applies to historical scholarship during the civil wars, for which access to information was obviously vital. There is evidence from July 1648, therefore, to indicate that the Scottish General Assembly, in preparing a projected history of the 'troubles', drew up a list of names of men to gather information in every province of Scotland.[41] In 1650, meanwhile, the publisher Michael Sparke sought material from the Council of State with which to complete his history of James I, which was published in 1651.[42] Whether or not Sparke received such assistance remains uncertain, but the commonwealth regime was clearly willing to make sources of information available to approved projects, and when Walter Frost was instructed to produce a narrative of relations between England and Scotland in September 1651, he was granted,

---

Sindercombe's trial was probably official: J. Peacey, 'Reporting a revolution: a failed propaganda campaign', in Peacey, ed., *The Regicides and the Execution of Charles I* (Basingstoke, 2001); *The Whole Triall of Mr Love* ([London], 1651); [C. Walker], *The Triall of Lieut. Collonell John Lilburne* (London, 1649); *The Triall of Mr John Lilburn* (London, 1653); *The Tryall of Leiutenant Colonell John Lilburn* (London, 1653); *A True Narrative of the Examination, Tryall and Sufferings of James Nayler* (London, 1657); *The Whole Business of Sindercome* (London, by Newcomb, 1657).

[38] *CSPD 1640–1*, p. 556; PRO, SP 16/479, fo. 131; W. Prynne, *A New Discovery of the Prelates Tyranny* (London, 1641).

[39] *HMC Egmont I*, pp. 353–4, 356, 426; BL, Add. 46931b, fo. 99v; *Ormond's Curtain Drawn* ([London, 1646], BL, E513/14); J. S. A. Adamson, 'Strafforde's ghost: the British context of Viscount Lisle's lieutenancy of Ireland', in J. H. Ohlmeyer, ed., *Ireland From Independence to Occupation, 1641–1660* (Cambridge, 1995), p. 140. Manuscript copies of Meredith's tract evidently circulated after its publication was abandoned: BL, Add. 4819, fos. 320–44.

[40] *CSPD 1648–9*, pp. 5, 14. Frost produced *A Declaration of Some Proceedings* (London, 1648).

[41] *Letters and Journals of Robert Baillie*, iii. 60.

[42] *CSPD 1650*, p. 492; PRO, SP 18/11, fo. 188; M. Sparke, *The Narrative History of King James* (London, 1651).

liberty to peruse, transcribe and make use of any records, letters, dispatches, or memorials within the custody or disposal of this council, relating to the matter whereof he is to treat. And it is desired that such of the members of Parliament or this Council whom Mr Frost may have occasion to consult touching this business will be pleased to afford him their best assistance therein, the service being of good consequence for the honour and advantage of this commonwealth.[43]

Other historians during the 1650s also received material assistance. John Thurloe appears to have provided information for Samuel Morland's history of the sufferings of the Protestants in Piedmont, following a plea from the author in January 1656 regarding his need 'to procure all the papers and letters, which have been written upon this subject, and which may in any manner contribute to the completing of an history'.[44] Having reassembled on the state's behalf the dipersed records of the Privy Council – 'with much enquiry, pains and charge' – John Rushworth was granted liberty, in September 1658, 'to resort unto the said books from time to time, as he shall see cause, for his making of collections out of them, in reference to the public work he hath now in hand'.[45]

Historical scholarship naturally only flourished after the end of the first civil war, and this inevitably meant that parliamentarians held an advantage over royalists who were dispersed and exiled, and who were separated from personal and official papers, many of which had anyway been destroyed. In the autumn of 1649, the Scottish Catholic, Robert Menteith, who was in the service of Cardinal de Retz, and who was engaged on producing the *Histoire des Troubles de la Grand Bretagne*, sought to secure historical material from Sir Richard Browne, the royalist ambassador in Paris, as well as copies of royalist books and pamphlets.[46] The response to this request is unclear, but that royalist historians faced difficulties is evident from Sir Edward Hyde's history of the rebellion. In November 1647, his shortage of material prompted Hyde to profess his regret at having begun such a project, and to bemoan the lack of assistance which he had been offered. Hyde told the king that his departure from Hampton Court had hindered his ability to obtain material, adding that he depended upon his 'ill memory' and a 'few pamphlets and diurnals'. Nevertheless, Hyde was able to consult with Dr John Earles regarding the battle of Newbury, and his memoirs reveal that Charles provided him with two manuscripts 'fairly written, containing all matters of importance that had passed from the time that the Prince of Wales went from His Majesty into the West [March 1645], to the very time that His Majesty himself went from Oxford to the

---

[43] PRO, SP 25/22, pp. 30–31; *CSPD 1651*, p. 411.

[44] *TSP* iv. 417; Vaughan, *Protectorate*, ii. 38.

[45] PRO, PRO 31/17/33, pp. 55–6; *CSPD 1658–9*, p. 142. Rushworth also drew upon material from civil war newspapers: F. Henderson, 'Posterity to judge – John Rushworth and his *Historical Collections*', *Bodleian Library Record* 15 (1996). Rushworth would continue to receive such assistance after the Restoration: PRO, PC 2/54, fo. 33v; *HMC 4th Report*, p. 231; R. MacGillivray, *Restoration Historians and the English Civil War* (The Hague, 1974), p. 13; Longleat, Coventry Papers XII, fo. 45.

[46] BL, Evelyn Papers, RB 2, vol. 11, unfol.; R. Menteith of Salmonet, *Histoire des Troubles de la Grand Bretagne* (Paris, 1649).

Scottish army [April 1646]'.[47] Hyde also secured assistance from Joseph Jane, in the form of an account of Cornwall during the civil wars, and probably had access to Sir Edward Walker's narrative of the royal campaigns of 1644.[48]

The willingness of political grandees to open official archives to researchers engaged in the production of political texts, and to those commissioned to produce propaganda, indicates the seriousness with which such tasks were regarded, as well as the subtlety with which they were sometimes conceptualised, and the extent to which royalist propaganda was hampered by logistical difficulties, if not by a reluctance to offer practical assistance to authors. It proved necessary on occasion to make plain the official nature and origins of material which was included in such literature, in order to demonstrate 'authenticity', while on other occasions it was impossible to disguise the official nature of the material upon which authors worked. However, in the interests of propagandistic sophistication, it was both necessary and possible for information to be provided to authors in less transparent ways, not least in order to assist historical projects which appeared to be the product of independent, if partisan, scholarship.

Political involvement in the writing process, however, involved a great deal more than the provision of information. Grandees who were interested in promoting the appearance of polemical and historical literature were naturally interested in the progress of their authors, and texts with which they were involved – including those which had been requested and commissioned – could be subjected to scrutiny at various levels, by various kinds of people, and to various degrees. Assessment of such scrutiny has generally focused upon the question of the extent to which sermons delivered from prominent pulpits and on official occasions were read prior to delivery. Evidence suggests that this rarely took place before the civil war, and that sermons, like that of Bishop Thomas Morton on the eve of the First Bishops' War, were scrutinised only in preparation for publication. Nevertheless, evidence also indicates that on at least one occasion, in 1629, Laud demanded to see the text of a sermon which was to be preached at St Paul's Cross.[49] Furthermore, certain kinds of sermon were more likely to be vetted than others, such as the recantation sermon preached by Richard Carpenter, the content of which Laud apparently tried to influence.[50] Another preacher, Thomas Case, claimed to have been interrupted by the parliamentarian peer, Lord Wharton,

---

[47] *CCSP* i. 246, 328, 342, 353, 355–7, 360, 382, 398, 400, 402-3, 419, 462, 503; Bodl. MS Clarendon 30, fos. 192, 208, 212v; Clarendon, *Life*, i. 243. For Hyde's reliance upon newspapers, see: R. Hutton, 'Clarendon's *History of the Rebellion*', *EHR* 97 (1982), p. 73.

[48] A. C. Miller, 'Joseph Jane's account of Cornwall during the civil war', *EHR* 90 (1975); Bodl. MS Clarendon 26, fos. 163–6. Walker's account (above, p. 181) survives in Hyde's papers: Bodl. MS Clarendon 136.

[49] *CSPD 1639–40*, pp. 212–13; PRO, SP 16/437, fos. 87–8; P. E. McCullough, *Sermons at Court. Politics and Religion in Elizabethan and Jacobean Preaching* (Cambridge, 1998), pp. 59, 141–2.

[50] BL, Stowe 743, fos. 163–4.

during the delivery of a sermon on 26 October 1642, albeit only in order that he could make a dramatic announcement about the news of Edgehill.[51]

Nevertheless, evidence relating to sermons needs to be supplemented by material relating to other forms of literature, which reveals the detailed ways in which texts could be monitored, as well as the extent to which participation in such processes extended to the highest political echelons.[52] On some occasions, therefore, and at some points in the supervision process, works could be considered by heads of state, whether Charles I or Oliver Cromwell. Charles appears to have involved himself in scrutiny not merely of works which were submitted by authors speculatively, but also of works which had been commissioned, such as Peter Heylyn's *A Coale from the Altar*, and after the outbreak of civil war he was actively involved in monitoring the declarations which appeared under his name.[53] Indeed, the king's interest extended beyond official statements to other works which appeared from the Oxford press, such as the response to Parliament's publication of his cabinet of letters, taken at Naseby in 1645.[54] Cromwell too was involved in considering potential pamphlets, even to the extent of holding private meetings with their authors. George Wither recalled that after the establishment of the protectorate he approached Cromwell, and 'signified unto him ... how he might settle a righteous government (as I believed) with safety and honour, if he would engage himself to the people, by publishing a remonstrance to that effect for their satisfaction'. Wither explained that 'this overture being made at a time wherein his fears and hazards were very great, though that discourse was very large, he with much seeming contentment, heard me read it over to the last word, and then protested, according to his usual manner, that it answered to his heart ... and pretended he would publish that declaration, and act accordingly'.[55]

Whatever the involvement of heads of state, such tracts and pamphlets were generally supervised by leading courtiers, ministers and grandees, both singly and in committee, as well as by administrative functionaries. Before the 1640s, the crown relied upon leading churchmen such as Laud and Juxon, to whom works such as Heylyn's *Coale from the Altar* were referred by the king, and by whom works could be amended before re-publication.[56] During the 1640s and 1650s, meanwhile, royalist polemical literature could be referred to a range of eminent grandees. Bishop John Bramhall's answer to Henry Parker's *Observations* seems to have been sent to Sir George Radcliffe in the spring of 1643, prior to its publication, while Lord Hopton was involved in scrutinising *Defensio Regia*,

---

[51] T. Case, *God's Rising* (London, 1644), p. 49; Wilson, *Pulpit in Parliament*, p. 66.

[52] Willson, 'James I and his literary assistants', pp. 53–4.

[53] Vernon, *Heylyn*, pp. 89–90; Clarendon, *Life*, i. 145.

[54] BL, Add. 32093, fo. 243.

[55] G. Wither, *A Cordial Confection* (London, 1659), p. 7; C. H. Firth, 'George Wither', *Review of English Studies* 2 (1926), pp. 457–9.

[56] Vernon, *Heylyn*, pp. 89–90; Laud, *Works*, vi. 326.

which had been commissioned from the pen of Salmasius, and in June 1653 Ormond assisted the king in the process of amending and altering a work submitted by Edward Massey.[57] In the period after the execution of Charles I, however, it was to Hyde that the task most often fell of considering in detail works which had been approved in principle. Hyde was evidently supposed to hold a meeting with Robert Menteith to discuss the latter's *Histoire* in the autumn of 1649, which he had read and which 'pleased him well', and he was delegated to consider in detail the book written by the Benedictine monk, Richard Clement, which the king could not 'tie himself to read' in detail, as well as the discourse written by Joseph Jane in 1652.[58] Likewise, Parliament relied upon a number of grandees for such tasks. In October 1648, for example, the upper House gave to Lord North the task of considering possible amendments to Lord Herbert of Cherbury's history of the reign of Henry VIII.[59] Less verifiable is the claim, made in a spurious printed speech of 1648, that the 'many learned, polite, and prolix treatises' written by William Prynne and Henry Parker were scrutinised by the solicitor general, Oliver St John.[60]

As often as not, however, detailed scrutiny of polemical literature was delegated to committees of more or less prominent individuals, whether in the Privy Council or the Council of State. The royalist Council in exile, therefore, considered 'a large discourse of the whole carriage of the Scots in answer to the declaration they sent to the Queen of Sweden' in 1649, and apparently became involved in making changes to texts by Hamon L'Estrange and Jeremy Taylor.[61] In August 1651, meanwhile, the Council of State in Whitehall referred to a small subcommittee a work prepared to be sent out in answer to the book by the royalist agent in the Low Countries, Sir William MacDowal, which appeared as *Anglia Liberata*.[62] Likewise, in Scotland during the late 1650s, the council of ministers in Edinburgh appointed a committee to consider a work written in response to *Protesters No Subverters*.[63] Moreover, the detailed scrutiny of texts was also delegated to specialists, particularly leading clerics such as Dr John Prideaux and Archbishop James Ussher, who were charged by Laud with considering works which had been commissioned from the pen of William Chillingworth in the

---

[57] E. Berwick, ed., *The Rawdon Papers* (London, 1819), pp. 93–4; Bodl. MS Clarendon 43, fos. 237r–v; Gloucestershire RO, D678, Barwick Papers, No. 25; *Calendar of Sherborne Muniments* (np, 1900), pp. 135–6.

[58] BL, Evelyn Papers, RB 2, vol. 11, unfol.; *CCSP* ii. 162, 261; Bodl. MS Clarendon 46, fo. 307; *Clarendon State Papers*, iii. 126.

[59] *Mercurius Elencticus* 48 (18–25 Oct. 1648), p. 391; *LJ* x. 552; Edward, Baron Herbert of Cherbury, *The Life and Reign of King Henry the Eighth* (London, 1649).

[60] *The Grave and Learned Speech of Serjeant Wilde* (London, 1648), p. 4.

[61] *CCSP* ii. 23; Bodl. MS Clarendon 38, fos. 31, 37–40v; *TSP* iii. 592; Bodl. MS Rawl. A.27, p. 757; *Anglia Liberata* (London, by Newcomb, 1651).

[62] *CSPD 1651*, p. 389.

[63] W. Stephens, ed., *Registers of the Consultations of the Ministers of Edinburgh* (2 vols, Scottish Records Society, Edinburgh, 1921–30), ii. 141, 142.

1630s.[64] Herbert of Cherbury's history was alleged to have been considered not merely by Lord North, but also by his 'crop-eared chaplain', and in 1653 Robert Baillie's long-delayed *Disswasive from the Errors of the Time* was submitted for detailed consideration and comment to a group of English divines.[65] More importantly, evidence from the commonwealth period reveals the extent to which the task of considering texts was undertaken by functionaries such as Secretary of State John Thurloe. It was Thurloe who oversaw the composition of Morland's account of the Piedmontese Protestants, and who was given the task of holding follow-up meetings with George Wither after the latter's audience with the protector regarding a proposed 'remonstrance' or 'declaration', Cromwell having declared that such a piece would be published 'as soon as he, with one in whose discretion he much confided, had considered what alteration it might need'.[66]

Examination of the processes by which works were scrutinised by the political authorities during the mid-seventeenth century reveals, therefore, the involvement of those at the very highest levels, as well as the delegation of such tasks to political grandees and those with specialist knowledge. The major difference between royalists and parliamentarians, however, was the extent to which the latter gradually focused such responsibilities upon administrators and functionaries, rather than upon grandees, or committees thereof. Although it is important to recognise that this may have been a matter of necessity and circumstance as much as design, it may nevertheless have had important ramifications for the efficiency with which the supervision of texts was undertaken.

Understanding political involvement in the writing process requires more than observing the methods by which commissioned and non-commissioned works were submitted to detailed scrutiny, and the individuals by whom such tasks were undertaken. Such analysis needs to be supplemented by evidence relating to the nature of the comments which such processes of consideration and consultation produced, in order to establish the purpose of official oversight, and the depth of political involvement in the composition process.

To the extent that works were submitted to friends and acquaintances, comments were likely to be brief, and perhaps also uncritical. Responding to Bramhall's *Serpent-Salve* in March 1643, therefore, Sir George Radcliffe commented: 'in your answer to the Observator there is enough said to vindicate the king's right and show the Observator's folly, and yet with as much moderation as any that I have seen on the argument'.[67] And to the extent that Charles was shown works as a matter of form and courtesy, for a final seal of approval, it was

---

[64] P. des Maizeaux, *The Life of William Chillingworth* (London, 1683), pp. 148–9, 297–8.

[65] *Mercurius Elencticus* 48 (18–25 Oct. 1648), p. 391; *Letters and Journals of Robert Baillie*, iii. 227.

[66] *TSP* iv. 724; Wither, *Cordial Confection*, p. 7; Firth, 'George Wither', pp. 457–9.

[67] Berwick, ed., *Rawdon Papers*, pp. 93–4.

to be expected that his comments too would be brief, as when he informed Sir Edward Nicholas of his gratitude for those works produced in response to publication of his letters in *The King's Cabinet Opened*. Charles said that he was 'glad to find that you there make so fair ... an interpretation of them, and particularly that you have so great a confidence in my consistency to my just cause'.[68] However, there are also many instances of works being approved or rejected with brief comments from those by whom they were submitted for more serious scrutiny.[69] Laud rejected re-publication of a book by Christopher Potter because he had given 'as much power to the Parliament as to the church in church affairs', and he criticised Richard Carpenter's recantation sermon for having failed to praise 'the orders and ceremonies, newly begun in the Church of England'.[70] In 1647, the Prince of Wales ordered the suppression of a book relating Montrose's proceedings in Scotland on the basis of a close reading of the text, and his concern that 'some persons of honour are by the author charged with many crimes, and so cannot in justice afford patronage to accusations to render persons of honour infamous'.[71] Equally brief comments and suggestions were made upon works which found approval, such as the book by Joseph Jane, which Hyde approved in December 1652, though he considered that the author might more clearly have shown the impossibility of the Dutch reaching an agreement with a commonwealth regime whose government might change every six months.[72] Among parliamentarians, the regicide and Rump councillor, John Jones, responded to a book by the Fifth Monarchist, Morgan Llwyd, by saying that he had found 'some expressions in it, especially in the paragraph at the top of the first page, and in the parenthesis of that paragraph, that I cannot possibly understand as yet, in any sound or safe sense, and that hath made me to pause upon those intentions of mine, until I receive a little more light from you therein'.[73]

On many other occasions, however, evidence suggests that critical and favourable comments alike were much more detailed. In part this probably reflected a concern to monitor and influence texts to a far greater degree. This certainly appears to have been true of a number of major projects, where the protracted nature of the composition process led not merely to frequent consultation over progress, but also close inspection of texts. With a few substantial commissioned works, indeed, grandees such as Hyde and functionaries such as Thurloe evidently demanded regular progress reports from their authors.[74] Naturally enough, such progress reports often involved authors making unrealistic

---

[68] BL, Add. 32093, fo. 243.

[69] V. Sanders, 'John Whitgift: primate, privy councillor and propagandist', *Anglican and Episcopal History* 56 (1987), p. 395; *CSPD 1611–18*, p. 231.

[70] Laud, *Works*, vi. 326; BL, Stowe 743, fos. 163–4.

[71] BL, Stowe 184, fo. 213v.

[72] *CCSP* ii. 162; *Clarendon State Papers*, iii. 126.

[73] National Library of Wales, Plas Yolyn MS 11440d, fos. 137–9.

[74] W. N. Darnell, ed., *The Correspondence of Isaac Basire* (London, 1831), pp. 63–4.

promises regarding likely completion dates, as well as attempts to excuse the fact that their projects had grown in size. In April 1656, for example, Samuel Morland explained to Thurloe that 'the work I find will swell into a great folio, and by consequence take up much time; however, I should not doubt to finish it within a month, and to the full satisfaction of the curious reader'.[75] The example of Dr Robert Creighton sheds further light on the protracted nature of such composition processes. Creighton was evidently set to work by Hyde in transcribing and translating a history of the Council of Florence, sometime before September 1658, when Hyde was informed that the transcription was almost complete. Creighton evidently completed this stage by the following month, although he explained that the translation would prove more difficult, and that he required more money.[76] Creighton provided updates during the spring of 1659, by April of which year Hyde felt confident that labours were nearing an end, and that the work would be ready to be sent to the press at Leiden within weeks.[77] Whether or not Hyde's hopes were realised, the process of publication dragged on for many more months. Between August 1659 and May 1660, Creighton wrote to Hyde on a number of occasions regarding the printing of his book, and his complaints with the way in which it was being undertaken, as well as regarding the delays of the printers, the painful process of making corrections, and his need for money.[78]

Such delays in completing large-scale projects led to the development of tactics to speed up the publishing process. Not the least of these was the delivery of portions of manuscripts as they were completed. Facing pressure from Archibald Johnston of Wariston for the completion of *Landensium* in March 1640, Robert Baillie sent sections of his work during its composition, and promised to send the finished draft in instalments.[79] Similarly, Laud asked to receive Joseph Hall's work on episcopacy on a chapter-by-chapter basis, rather than waiting for the finished book, in order to assist in the speedy completion of the project.[80] Such tactics suggest, however, that considerable time and attention was deemed necessary to the scrutiny of texts, and that consultations during the process of composition were aimed at making detailed comments on specific aspects of books and treatises. This also emerges from Hyde's recollection regarding the process of formulating official royalist declarations in the early 1640s. Hyde noted that upon joining the king in York in 1642, he discovered that Charles played an active role in the formulation of official statements during the 'paper war', and that upon his very

---

[75] *TSP* iv. 724.

[76] *Sylvester Sgouropoulos, Vera Historia Unionis ... sive Concilii Florentini* (ed. R. Creighton, Hague, 1660); *CCSP* iv. 85, 101; Bodl. MS Clarendon 59, fos. 2–3; MS Clarendon 56, fo. 127.

[77] *CCSP* iv. 130, 180, 188; Bodl. MS Clarendon 59, fos. 387–8; MS Clarendon 60, fos. 359–60.

[78] *CCSP* iv. 321, 391, 414, 424, 439, 464–5; *CCSP* v. 1; Bodl. MS Clarendon 63, fos. 194–5; MS Clarendon 65, fos. 84–5, 251–2; MS Clarendon 66, fos. 69–70, 216–17; MS Clarendon 67, fos. 103–4; MS Clarendon 72, fos. 105–6.

[79] *Letters and Journals of Robert Baillie*, i. 242.

[80] *CSPD 1639–40*, pp. 87–8, 100; PRO, SP 16/432, fos. 82–3, 132r–v.

arrival from London he found that 'the king was at Council upon the publishing his answer to the declaration of the 26 of May, which though it contained eight or nine sheets, he brought to the board in his own handwriting, having kept the promise he had made at Greenwich ... in writing out all the papers himself, which had been sent to him'.[81]

Such evidence of close scrutiny of texts does not, by itself, indicate the precise nature of the comments which political grandees sought to make, nor the influence they sought to exert. However, the supervisory process clearly involved stylistic editing. This was evidently part of the role of Secretary of State Sir Edward Nicholas in amending a draft 1648 treatise expressing the illegality of Parliament's proceedings against Charles I.[82] On other occasions, however, detailed comments and criticisms extended to matters substantive rather than merely stylistic. The protracted process of completing Creighton's book, therefore, reveals Hyde's concerns relating to the work's content, even if only the tone of the prefatory remarks regarding Charles II. Hyde called Creighton's attention to the king's dislike of being over-commended, although he urged that the author could not say too much of his justice and gentleness, or of his zeal for the Protestant religion.[83] Laud's interest in Joseph Hall's treatise on the divine right of episcopacy, however, evidently extended to its theological correctitude, and his piecemeal scrutiny of the text in late 1639 led to suggestions on matters of theology as well as style. Hall explained to Laud that, in response to the archbishop's critique, he had 'put a drop or two of vinegar more into my ink in two several places'.[84] Heylyn's account, moreover, reveals how Laud's 'care and diligence' impacted upon the substance of Hall's argument.[85] A similarly detailed process appears to have been undertaken for a sermon by Bishop Thomas Morton in 1639, as well as for works by Jeremy Taylor in the 1650s.[86] Such evidence also survives for parliamentarian works during the 1640s. The intention behind considering the text of Herbert of Cherbury's book in 1648, according to royalist commentators, was to ensure that 'the copy ought to be pat for their purpose', and North was allegedly instructed,

> to take special care there pass nothing that may anyways intrench on the members copyhold and where he sees a fit occasion, to insert such things as may approve the wickedness of that king in robbing the church of her rights, and by abolishing the abbeys and other religious houses: the better to justify their own sacrilegious acts, now against the honest bishops and their revenues.[87]

---

[81] Clarendon, *Life*, i. 145.

[82] Peck, *Northampton*, pp. 111–12; *CSPD 1648–9*, p. 416; PRO, SP 16/520, fos. 50–51v.

[83] *CCSP* iv. 321, 373, 391; Bodl. MS Clarendon 63, fos. 194–5; MS Clarendon 64, fos. 284–5; MS Clarendon 65, fos. 84–5; *Clarendon State Papers*, iii. 567–8.

[84] *CSPD 1639–40*, pp. 186–7, 349–50; PRO, SP 16/436, fos. 107–9v; SP 16/442, fos. 98–9v.

[85] Heylyn, *Cyprianus*, p. 381.

[86] *CSPD 1639–40*, pp. 212–13; PRO, SP 16/437, fos. 87–8; *TSP* iii. 592.

[87] *Mercurius Elencticus* 48 (18–25 Oct. 1648), p. 391; *LJ* x. 552.

Though probably without substance, such claims may accurately have reflected the treatment of other works, such as the unnamed work on law and history which received detailed comment in 1648.[88] Likewise, covenanter propaganda also underwent such criticial scrutiny, and Robert Baillie's papers contain a series of detailed points made regarding a work by David Buchanan from 1645, reflecting 'sundry passages which I conceive would much prejudice our cause, if the writing went abroad without some alteration'.[89] Later, the Edinburgh ministers' consideration of the reply to *Protesters No Subverters* in October 1658 involved detailed corrections and additions, including the suggestion that parallels be made with the experience of European churches.[90]

Of course, the danger inherent in detailed assessment and editing, particularly when such tasks fell to grandees such as Lord Hatton and Sir Edward Hyde, was that the pressure of time would prove damaging. This clearly proved to be a problem for the royalist propaganda machine. In September 1648, for example, Hatton told Sir Richard Browne to refuse all queries proposed by Robert Menteith, having 'seriously considered the work', and having found that it would 'do much disservice to the king and his affairs, and might much reflect to your disadvantage and mine if notice should be taken that we promote or assist him in such a work as this will prove'. Hatton, whose appreciation of the book clearly differed from that of Hyde, complained that the process of scrutiny had taken place at too late a stage in the proceedings, and that,

> the tender of it to my correction now when a great part is already printed and the rest drawn up … would require as much time to correct as would prepare and perfect a new history … It were unreasonable for me in scarce so much time as is allowed a corrector of the press, to undertake to averr all matters of fact.[91]

In June 1653, Ormond recommended to Massey that certain sections of the manuscript which had been submitted for consideration by one Halsall, and which had been sent to him to read, might require more strict survey and correction than he had time or authority to bestow.[92] On occasions, Hyde too felt disinclined to devote as much attention to such tasks as they required. In August 1652, he wrote to Hatton in the hope of being excused from involvement in supervising the work of a Venetian author who had written an account of the civil war. Hyde claimed that the task would require an interpreter, which would cause many errors, as had apparently been the case with Salmasius, and would also take up unacceptable amounts of time. He wondered, 'how patiently he will attend my leisure I know not, men of those faculties being often times supercilious enough'. Hyde concluded by attempting to offload to Hatton the task of making initial contact

[88] *CSPD 1648–9*, p. 412; PRO, SP 16/520, fos. 50–51v.

[89] *Letters and Journals of Robert Baillie*, ii. 252.

[90] Stephens, ed., *Registers of the Consultations*, ii. 141, 142.

[91] BL, Evelyn Papers, RB 2, vol. 10, unfol.

[92] Gloucestershire RO, D678, Barwick Papers, No. 25; *Sherborne Muniments*, pp. 135–6.

with the author, promising that he would involve himself later, 'if he be a man of weight'.[93]

Ultimately, evidence relating to the scrutiny, amendment and editing of manuscripts supports the impression that polemical writing could not only be supervised extremely closely, but also that it could be a collaborative process.[94] Contemporaries frequently alleged that certain authors were monitored rigorously during the writing process, in order to ensure that their works were acceptable to patrons and political superiors.[95] Writing of the draft version of Chillingworth's *Religion of Protestants* in 1637, therefore, Laud expressed his sorrow that 'the young man hath given cause why a more watchful eye should be held over him and his writings', but this comment, and subsequent evidence, reveals the lengths to which he and other grandees were prepared to go.[96] When Viscount Saye complained about the books written against his son, Nathaniel Fiennes, over the fall of Bristol to the royalists in 1643, he singled out Thomas May's *History* for particular criticism; suggesting not just that May was biased, and that he was the victim of 'false reports and ill-information', but also that he appeared to have been 'jogged on the elbow by him that set him on work, or some of his party ... to let his pen drop a blot upon the reputation of this gentleman'. Saye went on to suggest that Essex, or members of his faction, had 'plucked him by the sleeve, while he was writing ... as many that reads it may easily perceive'.[97]

Whatever the truth about May's relationship with Essex, and Laud's with Chillingworth, it is possible that an overly hierarchical model of author–patron relations, as they concern editorial processes, ought on occasions to be shelved in favour of one which recognises the possibility of collusion and collaboration. The manner in which the covenanters produced polemical treatises during the early 1640s indicates that they were circulated voluntarily, amended willingly, and published cooperatively. In March 1640, therefore, Robert Baillie sent a draft tract to a colleague and fellow-traveller, David Dickson, for comments before sending it to Archibald Johnston and Alexander Henderson. In May 1642, he sent another work to Robert Blair, after having sent it for consideration to Henderson and Dickson.[98] Baillie later recorded that though he was responsible for drafting a work

---

[93] *CCSP* ii. 143; Bodl. MS Clarendon 43, fo. 237r–v. Hyde continued to fulfil this role after the Restoration, when a tract by James Howell was sent to him: P. Seaward, 'A restoration publicist: James Howell and the Earl of Clarendon, 1661–6', *HR* 61 (1988), pp. 128–9; Bodl. MS Clarendon 78, fos. 120–34v (J. Howell, 'Touching the late rendition of Dunkirk'), which was published in 1664 as: [J. Howell], *A Discours of Dunkirk* (London, 1664).

[94] R. Rex, 'The English campaign against Luther in the 1520s', *TRHS*, 5th series 39 (1989), pp. 87–9; Willson, 'James I and his literary assistants', pp. 43, 55–6.

[95] J. Klaits, *Printed Propaganda Under Louis XIV* (Princeton, 1976), p. 122; Sanders, 'Household of Archbishop Parker', pp. 540, 542; Bruce and Perowne, eds, *Correspondence of Matthew Parker*, pp. 409–15, 474–7.

[96] Maizeaux, *Life of Chillingworth*, pp. 148–9.

[97] W. Fiennes, Viscount Saye, *Vindicaie Veritatis* (London, 1654), pp. 53–5.

[98] *Letters and Journals of Robert Baillie*, i. 244; *Letters and Journals of Robert Baillie*, ii. 27.

commissioned from his pen in 1641, nevertheless 'the last form, as of all our writings, was Mr Henderson's'.[99] During the mid-1640s, indeed, this collaborative approach probably incorporated English Presbyterian authors such as Thomas Edwards. The response to the *Apologetical Relation* of the 'dissenting brethren' of English Independents, the need for which had been discussed by the Scottish commissioners, was produced by Edwards with the knowledge of Baillie, who clearly surveyed the text prior to publication.[100] Such evidence suggests a division of labour and an interchange of ideas between a group of leading covenanter ministers and scholars, and later allegations point to the possibility of authors collaborating closely on the composition of tracts with leading grandees. More than one contemporary, therefore, claimed to be able to reveal the process by which Marchamont Nedham composed *News from Brussells*, which purported to have been written by a courtier with the exiled Charles II in 1660. One opponent wrote, sarcastically, of 'a special act of providence' which had 'made a near attendant on His Majesties person write so perfectly the sense of Sir Arthur Hesilrige and Mr [Thomas] Scot, that ... one would almost swear that, whilst the poor cavalier wrote, they guided his pen'.[101] Anthony Wood, meanwhile, recorded on his copy of the tract that it was written by Nedham in association with Sir Henry Vane junior, Scot and Major Richard Salway, and that it had been conveyed to the printer (Livewell Chapman) by Praisegod Barbon.[102]

Furthermore, such collaboration clearly extended to final editing, proofreading, and publication. When Baillie sent his book to David Dickson for comments in 1640, he said that he considered that it might prove necessary for the work to be seen through the press by Johnston and Henderson as well.[103] Other partnerships existed between like-minded men of rather different persuasions, and much editorial business was undertaken while books were 'in press', with political grandees sometimes remaining involved in making amendments to texts up to the point of publication. The process of drafting *Ormond's Curtain Drawn* – part of the attempt by the parliamentarian Independents to demonise Ormond in the autumn of 1646 – appears to have been produced in just this way, for although Adam Meredith drafted the tract, Sir John Temple made alterations while it was at the printers.[104] When John Jones wrote to Morgan Llwyd in 1653, he affirmed that the latter's 'little book is in the press', but noted that even at this late stage he was

---

[99] *Letters and Journals of Robert Baillie*, ii. 39.

[100] *Letters and Journals of Robert Baillie*, ii. 130, 190, 202, 215. Edwards presented Baillie with a copy of his *Antapologia*, issued in response to the 'dissenting brethren': T. Edwards, *Antapologia* (London, 1644).

[101] Sir E. Peirce, *True and Good News from Brussels* (London, 1660), p. 6; J. Raymond, 'The cracking of the republican spokes', *Prose Studies* 19 (1996), pp. 265–6.

[102] Raymond, 'Cracking', p. 265.

[103] *Letters and Journals of Robert Baillie*, i. 244.

[104] *Ormond's Curtain Drawn* ([London, 1646], E513/14); Adamson, 'Strafforde's ghost', p. 140; BL, Add. 46931a, fo. 16. Thomason attributed the work to Temple.

overseeing the text and recommending changes.[105] This picture of collaboration, rather than censorial supervision, is reinforced by the comments made by a number of authors in their correspondence with the grandees with whom they worked, which indicate their willingness to accommodate criticisms, and even to let their work stand or fall on the recommendation of their critics.[106] Joseph Hall explained to Laud in late 1639 that he was submitting his work for the latter's 'free censure'; adding that he was 'well content with either the light or the fire'.[107] When Baillie submitted his thoughts on the sectarians to the London divines in 1653, he granted them permission to 'revise them, and let them go, or suppress them, as you and your orthodox brethren shall see fit'.[108]

Amid the political turmoil of the 1640s and 1650s, detailed consideration of political and religious texts involved a commitment of time and energy which evidently proved problematic for royalists, who delegated such tasks to grandees such as Hyde and Hatton, who were more or less disinclined and unable to devote the attention which was required. Nevertheless, the evidence from their papers, as well as those of parliamentarians and covenanters, indicates the extent to which close scrutiny and amendment of texts was undertaken during this period, and the extent to which this extended to matters of substance as well as style. However, it also offers a reminder that the production of propaganda was as much collaborative as hierarchical; that authors were often fellow-travellers and colleagues as much as they were clients.

The clearest way of exploring the involvement of politicians in the process of writing polemical literature is by examining civil war newspapers, whose editors clearly came under pressure regarding the content of their papers.[109] Although journals were subject to pre-publication licensing, the extent to which this involved detailed scrutiny of texts, editorial direction, or *ex post facto* attempts to keep editors 'on message', is unclear, and it is difficult to be precise even about the workings of 'official' newspapers. Nevertheless, certain trends emerge.

Firstly, editors appear to have been favoured, at least occasionally, with access to privileged information. This appears to have applied to newsletter writers such as Pory and Rossingham before the 1640s, as well as to favoured printers of news pamphlets such as John Thomas, who seems to have been granted access to the proceedings of Parliament's 'recess committee' in the autumn of 1641.[110] It also

---

[105] National Library of Wales, Plas Yolyn MS 11440d, fos. 137–9.

[106] Sanders, 'Household of Archbishop Parker', pp. 541–2; Strype, *Annals of the Reformation*, II. i. 275; Strype, *Life and Acts of Matthew Parker*, ii. 253–4, iii. 207–8.

[107] *CSPD 1639–40*, pp. 186–7; PRO, SP 16/436, fos. 107–9v.

[108] *Letters and Journals of Robert Baillie*, iii. 227.

[109] *A New Diurnall of Passages* (Oxford, 1643), sig. A3.

[110] B. Dooley, 'News and doubt in early modern culture', in B. Dooley and S. Baron, *The Politics of Information in Early Modern Europe* (London, 2001), p. 279; F. J. Levy, 'Staging the news', in A. F. Marotti and M. D. Bristol, eds, *Print, Manuscript and Performance* (Columbus, 2000), p. 264; S.

seems clear that later parliamentarian editors were given privileged access to information. This certainly seems to explain their ability to publish official letters during the civil wars, which appear to have been 'leaked' from within Westminster, and which may have been 'on tap to the laziest editor'.[111] More importantly, the editor of *Mercurius Britanicus* was allegedly allowed to attend committee meetings in order to obtain information for his paper, 200 copies of which were supposed to have been distributed among MPs.[112] Perhaps this also explains why John Dillingham hosted meetings between Viscount Saye, Lord Wharton and Oliver Cromwell in the summer of 1648.[113] Special treatment for individual editors also took the form of selective leaking of sensitive documents. It is tempting to believe, therefore, that John Pym leaked to John Thomas a copy of his letter to Sir Edward Dering in February 1642, which quickly appeared in print.[114] It is also tempting to conclude that the appearance of advance news of the terms of the Instrument of Government in late 1653 represented a deliberate attempt to leak details of England's new constitution.[115] The problem with leaks is that they were naturally undertaken in a secretive way, such that little evidence survives with which to make unequivocal statements regarding editors' sources, and the motivation of those who provided information.[116]

Nevertheless, it is possible to highlight allegations regarding the process by which information was supposed to have reached the royalist newspaper, *Mercurius Aulicus*, whose editor somehow secured material from within Westminster. In the first week of October 1643, *Mercurius Britanicus* said that *Aulicus* had 'news out of the house still', and the source was identified as the minister Daniel Featley, who apparently confessed that he would 'now and then peep into Henry the 7th chapel, to observe what passed, that he might inform his Irish grace [Ussher] of their proceedings'.[117] If Featley was involved in leaking

---

Lambert, 'The beginning of printing for the House of Commons, 1640–42', *The Library*, 6th series 3 (1981), p. 53; *The Heads of Severall Petitions* (London, for Thomas, 1641); *The True Copy of a Letter Sent from Thomas, Earle of Arundel* (London, for Thomas, 1641); *The Discovery of a Late and Bloody Conspiracie* (London, for Thomas, 1641); *The Copy of a Letter Sent by the Lords and Commons* (London, for Thomas, 1641).

111 *The Weekly Account* 17 (23–29 Apr. 1645), sigs. Rrrr3r–v; A. Cotton, 'London newsbooks in the civil war: their political attitudes and sources of information' (Oxford University DPhil, 1971), p. 19.

112 P. W. Thomas, *Sir John Berkenhead, 1617–1679* (Oxford, 1969), p. 48; W. M. Clyde, *The Struggle for the Freedom of the Press* (St. Andrews, 1934), p. 45; *Mercurius Aulicus* 13 (26 Mar.–2 Apr. 1643), pp. 166–7; *Mercurius Anti-Britanicus* 1 (4 Aug. 1643), pp. 3–4; J. Taylor, *General Complaint* ([Oxford, 1645]) p. 5. See: Cotton, 'London newsbooks', p. 21.

113 *Mercurius Pragmaticus* 17 (18–25 July 1648), sig. R4v; *Mercurius Pragmaticus* 18 (25 July–1 Aug. 1648), sig. S2v; A. N. B. Cotton, 'John Dillingham, journalist of the middle group', *EHR* 93 (1978), p. 826. For a discussion of news sources, see: J. Raymond, *The Invention of the Newspaper: English Newsbooks, 1641–1649* (Oxford, 1996), pp. 144–8.

114 J. P., *The Copy of a Letter Written Unto Sir Edward Deering* (London, for John Thomas, 1641).

115 P. Gaunt, 'Drafting the Instrument of Government, 1653–54: a reappraisal', *PH* 8 (1989), p. 33.

116 Cotton, 'London newsbooks', pp. 223–4.

117 *Mercurius Britanicus* 6 (26 Sept.–3 Oct. 1643), pp. 43, 45, 47; Thomas, *Sir John Berkenhead*,

sensitive material, then as editor of the royalist *Mercurius Pragmaticus* in the late 1640s, Marchamont Nedham relied upon a spy to secure news of parliamentary debates, about whose skill he regularly boasted.[118] On other occasions, however, editors came under political pressure to include material in their papers. It was alleged that the Earl of Rutland sent a letter to the *Moderate Intelligencer*, for example, 'desiring that he would insert it' in order to keep the editor in line over the Derbyshire miners, and in December 1648 one editor explained his inclusion of an address from Glamorgan regarding the army 'Remonstrance' by saying that it was inserted 'at the desire of some of the authors' against his better judgement, 'because the reader may loath twice-sod Coleworts, and of this kind near 100 have been printed'.[119] A rather bizarre incident from April 1660 demonstrates contemporary assumptions regarding the ability of monarchs and ministers to manipulate the press in this way, when a young man who professed to have important information regarding threats to the safety of Charles II promised to reveal his identity upon the king giving him a sign, in the form of the insertion of a specific phrase in the following week's newspaper.[120]

The issue of editors being influenced by outside forces can also be addressed through the adverts which appeared in official or semi-official newspapers.[121] William Prynne – or his political patrons – was one of the first civil war authors to recognise the advertising potential of the new medium, and he relied upon the newspapers to achieve maximum publicity for his books. Prynne's edition of Laud's diary was plugged by papers such as *The Kingdomes Weekly Intelligencer*, whose editor recommended the *Breviate*, which was 'now in print by that living martyr Mr Pryn', to 'any judicious man'. The same editor also helped Prynne in his attempt to discredit Laud by saying that 'this man, under his own hand, condemns himself to be a wicked instrument in church and commonwealth', before printing extracts of Prynne's edition.[122] Subsequently, the author of *Mercurius Civicus* had access to Prynne's *Hidden Workes of Darkness* in advance of publication, and was able to offer his readers a summary of the work.[123] Indeed, Prynne may even have operated a system of 'press releases', and in early September 1645 one newspaper

---

pp. 43–5; *LJ* vi. 254; J. Peacey, 'The struggle for *Mercurius Britanicus*: factional politics and the parliamentarian press, 1643–6' (forthcoming); Cotton, 'London newsbooks', p. 43.

[118] J. Peacey, '"The counterfeit silly curr": money, politics, and the forging of royalist newspapers in the English civil war' (paper delivered at NACBS conference, Baltimore, 2002).

[119] Cotton, 'Dillingham', p. 819; *The Moderate Intelligencer* 197 (21–28 Dec. 1648), sig. Nnnnnnnnn.

[120] *CSPD 1659–60*, pp. 414–15; PRO, SP 18/220, fos. 131–2.

[121] D. Hirst, 'That sober liberty: Marvell's Cromwell in 1654', in J. M. Wallace, ed., *The Golden and the Brazen World* (Berkeley, Ca., 1985).

[122] *The Kingdomes Weekly Intelligencer* 70 (27 Aug.–3 Sept. 1644), p. 566; *The Kingdomes Weekly Intelligencer* 71 (3–10 Sept. 1644), pp. 568–70.

[123] *Mercurius Civicus* 85 (2–9 Jan. 1645), pp. 777–8. Similarly, his attack upon Lilburne was noticed in the press on 7 October 1645, while it was still in the press: *The Kingdomes Weekly Intelligencer* 120 (30 Sept.–7 Oct. 1645), p. 966.

reported that 'there will shortly be published a treatise written by the learned and laborious patriot, William Prynne esquire, entitled *A Vindication of Several Serious Questions of Grand Importance*'.[124] While Prynne may have been engaging in self-promotion, it is possible that other adverts, such as the plug for Joshua Sprigge's *Anglia Rediviva* in the *Perfect Diurnall*, were inserted as a result of political influence by army grandees.[125] Moreover, the use of advertising by *Mercurius Politicus* suggests a more concerted political campaign to manipulate the content of newspapers, in order to promote works which themselves demonstrated political exploitation of the print medium. Nedham clearly advertised works whose appearance had been backed by the Council of State in the 1650s, such as Sir John Borough's account of *The Sovereignty of the Seas*, and Rushworth's *Historical Collections*, as well as Ephraim Elcock's Engagement tract, Morland's history, and legal works by William Sheppard.[126] He also advertised works by the regime's most trusted propagandists, such as John Hall, John Milton, Andrew Marvell and Cuthbert Sydenham, whose *False Brother* was recommended as 'an excellent piece'.[127] There are, however, serious methodological problems for interpreters of such adverts, the process for the appearance of which is not entirely clear. It is possible that they were inserted by the publisher in order to promote other items for which he was responsible, which might explain the inclusion of adverts for works such as John Canne's *Emanuel*, and John Hall's *The Honour of the English Soldiery*, as well as *Anglia Liberata*.[128] It is also possible that adverts were inserted for works with which Nedham was himself associated, including *The Case Stated Between England and the United Provinces*, and the translation of Selden's *Mare Clausum*.[129] More seriously, Nedham and his publisher had a financial interest in selling space in the paper, and can be shown to have advertised a series of other works which do not appear to have been connected to the regime's propaganda campaigns, and which may not even have reflected its interests, including a series of literary works by known royalists which were published by Humphrey Moseley.[130]

124 *The True Informer* 24 (4 Sept. 1645), p. 192.

125 *Perfect Diurnall* 183 (25 Jan.–1 Feb. 1647), p. 1470.

126 *Mercurius Politicus* 89 (12–19 Feb. 1652), p. 1424; *Mercurius Politicus* 553 (3–10 Feb. 1659), p. 221; *Mercurius Politicus* 57 (3–10 July 1651), p. 916; *Public Intelligencer* 126 (15–22 Mar. 1658), p. 394; *Public Intelligencer* 17, p. 280; *Mercurius Politicus* 310, p. 6976.

127 *Mercurius Politicus* 77 (20–27 Nov. 1651), p. 1236; *Mercurius Politicus* 208 (1–8 June 1654), p. 3540; *Mercurius Politicus* 554 (10–17 Feb. 1659), p. 237; *Mercurius Politicus* 240 (11–18 Jan. 1655), p. 5066; *Mercurius Politicus* 31 (2–9 Jan. 1651), p. 518. See: B. Worden, 'Milton and Marchamont Nedham', in D. Armitage, A. Himy, and Q. Skinner, eds, *Milton and Republicanism* (Cambridge, 1998).

128 *Mercurius Politicus* 19 (10–17 Oct. 1650), p. 324; *Mercurius Politicus* 60 (24–31 July 1651), sig. Eeeeee4v; *Mercurius Politicus* 70 (2–9 Oct. 1651), p. 1124.

129 *Mercurius Politicus* 4 (27 June–4 July 1650), p. 64; *Mercurius Politicus* 191 (2–9 Feb. 1654), p. 3262; *Mercurius Politicus* 112 (22–29 July 1652), p. 1768; *Mercurius Politicus* 130 (25 Nov.–2 Dec. 1652), p. 2056.

130 *Mercurius Politicus* 128 (11–18 Nov. 1652), p. 2024; *Mercurius Politicus* 130 (25 Nov.–2 Dec.

Whatever is to be made of the phenomenon of advertising in official journals, such material is valuable in drawing attention to the fact that political involvement in the substantive content of newspapers may have extended to systematic influence rather than merely piecemeal interference. One way in which this can be explored is through consideration of the role of official intelligence mechanisms. From their first emergence, newspapers not only came under official scrutiny, but were also brought under the control of men intimately connected with intelligence gathering as well as the control of seditious literature, such as Georg Weckherlin (secretary to Secretary of State Dorchester) and Robert Reade (secretary to Secretary of State Windebanke).[131] The involvement of such men made it possible for intelligence to be provided to the press from within the administration on a regular and formal basis, and for characters such as Sir Edward Nicholas to be perceived as '*Aulicus* his intelligencer' during the civil wars.[132] It is certainly clear that Parliament's intelligence system progressed greatly during the 1640s, under Henry Parker at the Committee of Safety, and subsequently under Walter Frost at the Committee of Both Kingdoms, both of whom were closely involved with propaganda.[133] After the execution of the king, control of intelligence passed to Thomas Scot, who was subsequently assisted by George Bishop. Scot's own account of his role, written after the Restoration, outlined his attempts to infiltrate Leveller meetings, and his employment of secretaries, scoutmasters, soldiers, diplomats and politicians, and even men inside the exiled court, to provide him with news, as well as individuals such as John Wallis to crack cyphers. Scot claimed to have spent around £2,000 *per annum* on his system, and the government's opponents were clearly frustrated by the efficiency of

---

1652), p. 2056; *Mercurius Politicus* 138 (27 Jan.–3 Feb. 1652), p. 2208; *Mercurius Politicus* 141 (17–24 Feb. 1653), p. 2260; *Mercurius Politicus* 255 (26 Apr.–3 May 1655), p. 5308; *Mercurius Politicus* 259 (24–31 May 1655), p. 5367; *Mercurius Politicus* 266 (12–19 July 1655), p. 5484; *Mercurius Politicus* 298 (21–28 Feb. 1656), p. 5996; D. Hirst, 'The politics of literature in the English republic', *Seventeenth Century* 5 (1990), p. 146. Moseley may have been personally close to Milton and Nedham: S. A. Baron, 'Licensing readers, licensing authorities in seventeenth century England', in J. Andersen and E. Sauer, eds, *Books and Readers in Early Modern England* (Philadelphia, 2002), p. 226.

[131] For Weckherlin: *The Trumbull Papers* (London, 1989), pp. 121–5; E. Arber, ed., *A Transcript of the Registers of the Company of Stationers of London 1554–1640* (4 vols, London, 1877), iv. 146, 148–52, 161, 165, 170, 176–7, 193, 234, 246–7, 266, 304, 324; W. W. Greg, *Licensers for the Press, &c to 1640* (Oxford, 1962), pp. 94–5; BL, Trumbull MS LXI Weckherlin diary, unfol.; PRO, PSO 5/5, unfol. For Reade: *CSPD 1635–6*, p. 223; Arber, ed., *Transcript*, iv. 422, 424, 473, 495; Greg, *Licensers*, pp. 79–80; *CSPD 1631–3*, p. 524; *CSPD 1638–9*, pp. 489, 497, 517–18; 555; *CSPD 1639*, pp. 89, 517, 523.

[132] *The Kingdomes Weekly Intelligencer* 83 (26 Nov.–3 Dec. 1644), p. 666; *Kingdomes Weekly Intelligencer* 47 (6–13 Mar. 1644), p. 383; *CSPV 1642–3*, pp. 306–7; Thomas, *Sir John Berkenhead*, pp. 40–41; Cotton, 'London newsbooks', p. 42.

[133] Above, pp. 104–5; BL, Add. MS 31116, p. 168; *CSPD 1649–50*, p. 334; PRO, SC 6/Chas.1/1661, m.6d–7r; SC 6/Chas.1/1662, m.7d; SC 6/Chas.1/1663, m.6d; SC 6/Chas.1/1664, m.11d; SC 6/Chas.1/1665, m.15d; SC 6/Chas.1/1666, m.12r.

his intelligencers.[134] Under Scot's successor, John Thurloe, intelligence gathering and press control combined to infiltrate groups such as the Fifth Monarchists, and to investigate their printing and circulation of seditious literature.[135]

Crucially, however, there is evidence that intelligence gathering became intimately linked with journalism. In June 1648, Frost clearly received orders to communicate intelligence to John Rushworth, who was closely associated with the army press, but the connection between press control, intelligence, and propaganda became much more pronounced with Thomas Scot. He assisted John Bradshaw in formulating the press legislation of 1649, and became involved not only in suppressing works by opponents of the regime, but also in tightening control over the newspapers in October 1649, in order to enhance the government's ability to control the flow of intelligence, not least to prevent the publication of news of the Drogheda massacre.[136] Scot's propaganda credentials included work on official declarations, and his own pamphleteering, and the 1649 press legislation ensured that each of four official mercuries fell under the supervision of a key commonwealth employee.[137] One royalist said that the newsbooks were 'all wafted away by the breath of Jack Bradshaw ... that so the people may be abused for the future *cum privilegio*, suitable to the mind of Bradshaw and Scot, who sway all'.[138] By 1650, indeed, the Rump had achieved 'vertical integration' of intelligence agents, central administrators and journalists, with coordination being undertaken by Scot, Frost and eventually Thurloe.[139] In February 1650, one commentator described the body which oversaw the interception of the posts in London as the 'committee for news', and the regime was quick to realise the potential of this system.[140] The Commons passed letters of

---

[134] *CSPD 1649–50*, p. 221; C. H. Firth, 'Thomas Scot's account of his activities as intelligencer during the commonwealth', *EHR* 12 (1897). For references to his activity regarding the post, see: *CJ* vi. 385, 459, 488, 530, 550, 568, 573, 591; *CJ* vii. 25, 49, 161, 270, 273. As treasurer of the Council of State's contingencies, Frost remained involved in intelligence work, and continued to receive hefty payments (such as £2999 in December 1659): *CJ* vii. 832; BL, Add. MS 32471, fos. 15v–17. For contemporary mention of Scot, and his £800 per year, see: BL, Add. 18738, fos. 82–82v; *HMC De L'isle VI*, pp. 474–6. For Wallis as decipherer: Bodl. MS Eng.misc.e.475. For Bishop: *CSPD 1650*, pp. 339, 400, 443, 461; *CSPD 1651*, pp. 11, 33, 36, 49, 113, 170, 197, 223, 231, 260, 317, 354, 364, 389, 424, 426, 502; *CSPD 1651–2*, p. 39, 374; *CSPD 1652–3*, pp. 143, 397; J. Nickolls, *Original Letters and Papers of State* (London, 1743), pp. 33–4, 39, 54, 49–51, 55–7, 66, 75; Bodl. MS Tanner 55, fos. 12, 23, 25, 37–8. For royalists' frustration, see: *NP* i. 238.
[135] *CSPD 1653–4*, p. 14; *TSP* iii. 149–51; *TSP* iv. 379.
[136] *CSPD 1648–9*, p. 92; *CSPD 1649–50*, pp. 340, 361–2, 385, 401, 455, 500; *CSPD 1652–3*, p. 78; *CJ* vi. 189, 292, 312, 354; *CJ* vii. 236; above, p. 158.
[137] *CJ* vi. 300, 459, 460; *CJ* vii. 12, 13, 15, 20–22, 266, 271; [T. Scot], *A Paire of Cristall Spectacles* ([London], 1648); above, p. 159; Peacey, 'Henry Parker', pp. 152–3, 164.
[138] Quoted in J. B. Williams, 'Fresh light on Cromwell at Drogheda', *The Nineteenth Century and After* 72 (1912), p. 478.
[139] BL, Stowe 185, fos. 183–4; BL, Sloane 1519, fo. 157.
[140] *CCSP* ii. 44–5.

intelligence to Scot, so that he could consider which were fit for publication, and in December 1650 letters of intelligence from Scotland were referred to the Council of State to consider how much of the information could safely be published.[141] George Bishop, meanwhile, was ordered to make extracts of intelligence for Rushworth in June 1652.[142] Scot himself clarified the connection between his intelligence system and the pamphleteers by saying that he spent much time 'in suppressing the swarming number of pamphleteers, which sooner or later I always got into my power', and by adding that his intelligencers 'did little but inform common news ... fit to help to fill the gazette'.[143] On more than one occasion during 1652, Thurloe prepared extracts of news relating to the Dutch war, which may have been intended to assist those managing the conflict, but which would certainly have been useful for inclusion in official newspapers.[144]

The most dramatic evidence relating to the provision of intelligence to newspaper editors is provided by Marchamont Nedham and *Mercurius Politicus*, which Clement Walker described as the 'interpreter to our new state puppet play'.[145] In his prospectus for the new paper, Nedham had desired 'supplies of the best intelligence of state', although little precise information survives regarding the procedures by which *Politicus* was produced. Nedham probably developed his own network of domestic and Continental correspondents, and may even have lifted information from foreign newspapers. Nevertheless, it seems that Thurloe supplied at least some of the paper's intelligence.[146] During the investigation of a conspiracy against the Cromwellian regime in February 1657, for example, Thurloe's account of the plot was sent not merely to Parliament, but also to *Politicus*.[147] Furthermore, numerous contemporary comments provide a sense of the close relationship between Thurloe and Nedham's paper. In September 1655, the agent in Hamburg, Richard Bradshaw, asked Thurloe to pass to Nedham a specific paper, and other agents may have been trained to prepare extracts of news for the press before sending their material to Thurloe.[148] Indeed, such was the importance of Thurloe's information for *Politicus* that he himself admitted that the paper contained all that there was to know. Writing to Henry Cromwell, for example, he said that 'for the news concerning Sweden and other foreign affairs I am bold to refer your lordship to the print, which contains

---

[141] *CJ* vi. 321, 451, 471; *CSPD 1650*, p. 465.

[142] *CSPD 1651–2*, p. 285.

[143] Firth, 'Thomas Scot's account', pp. 117–24.

[144] *CSPD 1651–2*, pp. 255, 258. See: P. Fraser, *The Intelligence of the Secretaries of State and their Monopoly of Licensed News, 1660–1688* (Cambridge, 1956).

[145] C. Walker, *The High Court of Justice* (London, 1651), p. 17. See also: J. Webster, *The Picture of Mercurius Politicus* (London, 1653).

[146] PRO, SP 46/95, fos. 281–2; E. Jenks, 'Some correspondence of Thurloe and Meadowe', *EHR* 7 (1892), p. 730; J. Raymond, 'A mercury with a winged conscience: Marchamont Nedham, monopoly and censorship', *Media History* 4 (1998), p. 9. See: Cotton, 'London newsbooks', p. 21.

[147] *CSPV 1657–9*, p. 11.

[148] *TSP* iv. 23; BL, Add. 4364, fos. 58–9.

as much as I can inform', and writing to John Pell in December 1655, Thurloe enclosed a copy of the paper, because it contained 'all the news that we have here at this time'.[149]

With the newspapers, however, as with other tracts and pamphlets, official involvement in the writing process extended beyond the provision of information, to proactive influence over content and even editorial comment. The willingness and ability of Nedham's superiors and licensers, such as Thurloe and Milton, to supervise the text of *Politicus* has long been subject to a debate which is hard to resolve.[150] However, evidence from contemporary commentators indicates that Thurloe was presumed to have had at least some degree of control over Nedham, albeit he was urged to exert greater influence. In March 1655, Bulstrode Whitelocke wrote to Thurloe from his diplomatic mission to Sweden to say that he was 'sorry so much of our letters from Upall are printed, especially of discourse between the Queen and me'; adding that 'they have here the weekly diurnalls, and are not well pleased with them'.[151] In the following month, John Dury expressed similar concerns to his friend Samuel Hartlib:

> I pray salute Mr Nedham from me, and entreat him in case any extract be communicated to him from Germany or any other parts which have any spiteful or contemptible expressions of any German princes that he would favour us so much who are abroad as not to insert them.[152]

In the following November, furthermore, Dury wrote to Thurloe expressing his 'desire that *Mercurius Politicus* may not characterise me when he makes extracts', and provided chapter and verse from recent issues 'where the circumstantial matters point me so out as that I may suffer thereby hereafter'.[153] This concern regarding the content of *Politicus* in the context of European diplomatic affairs was repeated in the correspondence of Pell, who expressed his concern regarding the publication of Morland's evidence regarding the sufferings of the Piedmontese Protestants. He implored Thurloe to 'let nothing be said of it by *Mercurius Politicus* ... whose numbers are weekly sent to the baron of Greisy, who reads them over to see whether there be any passages concerning the Waldenses'.[154] In August 1656, furthermore, Pell relayed to Thurloe the wishes of the chief secretary of Zurich, that no news regarding Piedmont 'might be put into the English courants and mercuries, as being not yet ripe for the public view'.[155] Ultimately,

---

[149] *TSP* iv. 443; Vaughan, *Protectorate*, i. 320.

[150] H. S. Anthony, '*Mercurius Politicus* under Milton', *JHI* 27 (1966); J. M. French, 'Milton, Needham and *Mercurius Politicus*', *Studies in Philology* 33 (1936); E. A. Beller, 'Milton and *Mercurius Politicus*', *HLQ* 5 (1951–52), p. 479; Raymond, 'Mercury with a winged conscience', p. 9; Baron, 'Licensing readers, licensing authorities', pp. 219, 234–5.

[151] Bodl. MS Rawlinson A.24, p. 61.

[152] Hartlib Papers, 50H/4/3/95A–B.

[153] BL, Add. 4365, fo. 339v.

[154] Vaughan, *Protectorate*, ii. 287.

[155] Vaughan, *Protectorate*, ii. 10.

Pell concluded that *Politicus* 'deserves to be thoroughly sifted, and well circumstantiated, before it be printed by public authority'.[156]

It was clearly expected, therefore, that Thurloe's role should involve, if it did not automatically, careful monitoring of Nedham's paper, in order to ensure that certain stories were not printed. Rather than merely censoring the press, however, political grandees, and functionaries such as Thurloe, were able to exert positive influence on newspaper content, by placing concerted and perhaps regular pressure upon editors to include specific pieces of information. Henry Walker admitted the pressures under which he was placed by his political masters during the early months of the republic, by telling readers why he had included material relating to Robert Spavin, who was accused of having forged Cromwell's signature:

> I received this day these two papers, with the instructions following, viz "Mr Walker, print this verbatim in your occurrences, for satisfying the people how the army and they have been abused by practices of a papist and some others, to render the army odious, as will appear by the following account thereof, Westminster, 25 June 1649".[157]

The ability to secure the inclusion of specific texts into official newspapers, of course, does not indicate complete political control over even the most pliant of editors. On most occasions it is difficult to reach conclusions regarding political control from the inclusion of specific news items, or even official documents, such as *The Humble Remonstrance of the General Council of Officers*, which indicated approval for the dissolution of the Rump in 1653, and which appeared in a number of contemporary papers.[158]

Beyond demonstrating that newspapers received information from political sources, and that they succumbed to pressure to include or exclude specific stories, it is necessary to address the management of newspapers at a more general level, in terms of the supervision of texts and management of editorial lines. Royalists alleged that parliamentarian journalists were closely supervised, and described the process whereby John Hall's work on *Mercurius Britanicus* was undertaken:

> Each Friday night for to inform his muse
> He meets quack-Lilly at the Flower de Luce
> Behind St Clements where they do advise
> What way he best may blind the people's eyes.[159]

This merely developed a picture of the collaboration between editor and journalist, however. Later, in the summer of 1649, another royalist author claimed to have discovered the process whereby Henry Walker wrote his newspaper:

---

[156] Vaughan, *Protectorate*, ii. 47–8.

[157] *Perfect Occurrences* 130 (22–29 June 1649), p. 1089.

[158] *The Humble Remonstrance of the General Council of Officers* (London, 1653); *Moderate Intelligencer* 2 (9–16 May 1653), pp. 12–13; *Moderate Occurrences* 7 (10–17 May 1653), pp. 52–3; *A Perfect Account* 123 (11–18 May 1653), pp. 979–80.

[159] *Mercurius Elencticus* 34 (12–19 July 1648), p. 264.

A whole fardle of lies were prepared by a committee, and presented to good Noll, as if they came from the North of Ireland, when indeed they came from the North-East of Lothbury from Black-Corbet's House, and so from Cromwell delivered to Yellow-Beard the newsmonger, to print and delude the people with and make them go for truth.[160]

This portrayal of Cromwell's committee as editor, and Walker as tame journalist, must be treated with scepticism, although Walker had petitioned Parliament in April 1647, 'that some persons may be deputed by this House to peruse his occurrences of news before he prints them'.[161] Whatever the precise nature of such 'perusal', Walker was clearly displaying a willingness to place his paper at the service of the authorities. Ultimately, editors not only proved willing to include or exclude specific stories and pieces of information at the request, or command, of their superiors, but also displayed awareness of an ongoing relationship with political factions and parties. Referring to the 'pensioner' pamphleteers, Thomas Edwards alleged that Presbyterian attempts to secure publication of their September 1645 London petition had failed because the newspapers were controlled by Independents. He said that 'one of them being lately tried to insert into his weekly news the petition presented at the choice of the new Common Council, confessed ingenuously [that] he could not, for he was engaged to the other side'.[162] Such voluntary association with political factions means that it would be a mistake to assume that the absence of extremely close supervision of texts prior to publication meant that newspapers were not the tools of political grandees.

Journalists, like other polemical authors, were politically motivated and well-connected members of patronage networks. The most important editors ought to be regarded as having collaborated with like-minded members of the political elite, rather than having slavishly followed political patrons and paymasters. In 1645, the editor of *Britanicus* strenuously denied royalist claims that Parliament gave him specific instructions; saying that '*Britanicus* (though a weak private man) needs no such intimations as thou hast at Oxford'.[163] Disingenuous though this profession to be a 'private' author might have been, *Britanicus* was probably being truthful to the extent that he claimed to be rather more than a hack, and that he was motivated by political rather than financial goals. This did not preclude a close association with Westminster, and while he mocked the process by which *Aulicus* was produced, *Britanicus* arguably conceded the basic comparability between the two authors. In September 1643, *Britanicus* addressed his opponent by saying 'Master *Aulicus*, I think the Lord Digby whispered you now in the ear',

---

[160] *The Man in the Moon* 12 (27 June–4 July 1649), sig. M2.

[161] *LJ* ix. 142.

[162] T. Edwards, *Gangraena* (London, 1646), i. 110. Some papers ignored the petition, while others attacked it: *Perfect Passages* 48 (17–23 Sept. 1645); *Moderate Intelligencer* 30 (18–25 Sept. 1645), sig. Gg4.

[163] *Mercurius Britanicus* 85 (26 May–2 June 1645), p. 771.

and he later outlined the nature of the operation by which *Aulicus* was written in ways which have proved acceptable to later scholars: 'Berkenhead the scribe, Secretary Nicholas the informer, George Digby the contriver, and an assessment of wits is laid upon every college and paid weekly for the continuation of this thing'.[164] 'Professional' though journalists such as Nedham and Berkenhead might have been, they were nevertheless 'card carrying' members of the political interests that they represented in print.

Political grandees and regimes, both royalist and parliamentarian, participated in the composition as well as the commissioning and printing of polemical literature, and they did so in a high-level and in-depth fashion. In addition to ensuring that tracts and pamphlets were written, and that they were successfully printed and distributed, they played a proactive role in all aspects of textual construction, in terms of being involved in decision making processes relating to form, length, structure and style, as well as in influencing substantive content by supporting research and providing intelligence. They could also be involved in supervisory oversight of texts at any stage from planning to proofs. The treatment of individual works, and the outcome of textual scrutiny, depended upon their origins and the nature of the relationship between the authors and those political figures with whom they worked, and by whom they were considered. Works which were offered to politicians were likely to be treated more censorially – like those submitted in the hope of securing an official licence – than those which were commissioned, or discussed at the planning stages, and those written by collaborators and colleagues. The process of scrutinising works towards the latter end of this spectrum was more likely to involve editorial supervision, just as it was more likely to involve assistance in the form of access to official material. What resulted from such criticism varied, of course, depending upon the seriousness of the objections, and the nature of the relationship between author and critic. Authors who submitted works to licensers obviously had less scope for discussion than authors who voluntarily submitted their efforts to the censure of friends and experts, and those who worked in a collaborative fashion with political colleagues. Furthermore, political influence over substantive content need not necessarily have been effected through hands-on involvement in planning, composition and editing. As scholars of early modern court sermons have demonstrated, absence of direct involvement in, and censorship of, texts before their delivery, does not represent absence of influence. While many sermons were not vetted before they were preached, many ministers, not least favourite court preachers, would have

---

[164] *Mercurius Britanicus* 5 (19–26 Sept. 1643), p. 35; *Mercurius Britanicus* 16 (7–14 Dec. 1643), p. 121; Thomas, *Sir John Berkenhead*, pp. 38, 40–41. In February 1644, he exposed the royalist newsbooks further, telling readers 'who has a finger or a toe in the business, and who gave pens and who brought ink and who contributed paper, and conceits, such as they are'. He claimed that contributors to *Aulicus* included Professor John Prideaux, Jasper Mayne and Barton Holliday: *Mercurius Britanicus* 23 (12–19 Feb. 1644), pp. 176–7.

known what was, and was not, required of them, and would have exercised self-censorship.[165] It is certainly possible that authors wrote only what pleased their masters, while not being controlled in any direct sense, and that the involvement of politicians need not always have been conscious and direct in order to be effective.[166]

The results of such analysis of political involvement in textual construction support conclusions reached elsewhere in this study. Firstly, they indicate that political grandees had a clear sense of the need to negotiate the central propaganda dilemma which centred upon the tension between promulgating an official orthodoxy and producing subtle polemic, the origins of which were not immediately transparent. Secondly, they lend further support to the idea that, through circumstance as well as inclination, royalists occasionally faced difficulties in the production of propaganda as a result of relying upon the participation of a small band of political grandees, rather than upon a professionalised, bureaucratised, and institutionalised civil service propaganda machine. Thirdly, and finally, they reinforce the need to consider the possibility that the production of propaganda was a collaborative process involving authors who were politically committed rather than merely opportunistic and subservient to the wishes of patrons and employers. The precise nature of their working relationships with those political figures with whom they associated is almost impossible to assess, although it emerges most clearly by observing them over the course of time, and in the face of changing circumstances. This is the subject of Chapter 8.

---

[165] McCullough, *Sermons at Court*, pp. 59, 141.
[166] *The Court and Times of Charles the First* (2 vols, London, 1848), i. 214–15.

PART THREE
THE DYNAMICS OF PROPAGANDA

CHAPTER 7

The Limits of Propaganda

The preceding analysis demonstrated that the nature of propaganda during the civil wars and Interregnum can be appreciated on a mechanical level, in terms of the ways in which it was produced, the men who by whom it was commissioned and written, the forms it took, and the logistical methodologies adopted relating to composition, financing, printing and publication. The sophistication of propaganda can also be appreciated, however, at a conceptual level, by demonstrating how contemporaries understood the power of print and appreciated its utility in order to attack, and respond to, opponents and factional rivals, and the ways in which it could be deployed to achieve tactical goals. The focus of this chapter will be upon four key themes. The first involves recognising the ways in which attempts were made to undertake 'news management', in terms of the manipulation of political intelligence, and the ways in which news was presented to the public in order to maximise the impact of certain events and to minimise the significance of others. The second theme concerns attempts to 'manufacture consent', and the ways in which sophisticated political management incorporated control of a broader agenda, by testing popular opinion, nudging it in certain directions, and manipulating evidence regarding the public mood and desires. Thirdly, it explores the way in which print was employed in order to undertake 'ventriloquy', in terms of giving voice to those with different views and ideas, in order to exploit the potential which they offered at key moments, as well as in terms of mimicking opponents in order to undermine factional rivals, and counterfeiting their texts in order to hijack their readers in the interests of a different agenda. A final theme concerns propaganda 'campaigns', and concerns the ways in which print became a weapon in political processes, and was manipulated in close coordination with political manoeuvres and initiatives, whether parliamentary, legislative or judicial, as well as the development of multi-media print initiatives at times of acute political, military and diplomatic significance.

One of the most obvious ways in which print was used in the mid-seventeenth century was to alter people's perceptions about prominent individuals and significant events, by submitting them to either negative or positive 'spin'.[1]

---

[1] It is possible, therefore, that Jacobean bishops sought to undermine perceptions of the success of the Hampton Court Conference by means of subtle insinuation: M. H. Curtis, 'Hampton Court conference and its aftermath', *History* 46 (1961), pp. 13–14.

Individuals could be subjected to attacks and redescriptions, as well as analysis of their characters, intentions and motivations. Royalist literature lionised Charles I, while commonwealth literature lauded Cromwell, and attempts were made to bolster the reputations of grandees such as the Earl of Essex and Viscount Saye.[2] Charles could be attacked, on the other hand, as a weak and manipulated monarch, who was overly susceptible to the influence of evil counsellors who were bent upon usurping the royal prerogative; of churchmen who sought to place church power higher than regal authority; and of a queen who sought to reintroduce Catholicism. The exploitation of captured correspondence was clearly used to discredit leading royalists, such as Lord Digby, and even the king and queen themselves.[3] Royalist policies, meanwhile, could be portrayed as threatening to English liberties (whether personal or parliamentary) and to the English church, while parliamentarians could be decried as innovatory and rebellious, and as being intent upon overthrowing divine royal power. They could also be accused of delegitimising the king, and the royalist George Bate claimed that, 'in the pulpits, clubs and public pamphlets the crime was charged upon King Charles ... hoping that whilst they continued so boldly to vent their calumnies and slanders against him, some of them at least would stick'.[4] During the second civil war, meanwhile, royalists claimed that parliamentarians deliberately set out to discredit their Scottish allies, and one royalist journalist attacked a range of parliamentarian works, 'which they peale out daily from their presses and pulpits to gain the hearts of the poor deluded multitude: and thus far have they gone on in order to their first design, which is to make the Scots army odious to the people'.[5] Later, commonwealth propagandists could redescribe radical opponents in order to exaggerate the threat which they posed, whether political extremists such as the Levellers, or the various religious sects.[6] Nedham was accused, for example, of telling lies about the Fifth Monarchists, in order to 'render them odious to the people, and as much as in him lay to cast dirt upon and make null and void their faithful testimony against the late apostacy'.[7] Such processes of redescription could also be employed for factional ends. During August 1645, therefore, *Mercurius Britanicus* did not merely use the Naseby letters in order to oppose a treaty with the king, but also sought to label parliamentarian moderates as 'hypocriticall gulls'.[8] Later, in 1648, the royalist editor of one incarnation of *Mercurius Pragmaticus* indulged in overt criticism of two royalist

---

[2] Above, pp. 81–2, 113–15, 171.

[3] J. Peacey, 'The exploitation of captured royal correspondence and Anglo-Scottish relations in the British civil wars, 1645–6', *SHR* 79 (2000).

[4] G. Bate, *Elenchus Motuum* (London, 1685), p. 47. See: T. Harris, 'Propaganda and public opinion in seventeenth century England', in J. D. Popkin, *Media and Revolution* (Lexington, 1995), p. 55.

[5] *Mercurius Elencticus* 38 (9–16 Aug. 1648), sigs. Oo2–Oo2v.

[6] J. Peacey, 'The hunting of the Leveller: the effectiveness of parliamentarian propaganda, 1647–53' (forthcoming).

[7] *A True Catalogue* ([London, 1659]), p. 14.

[8] *Mercurius Britanicus* 92 (28 Jul.–4 Aug. 1645); *Mercurius Britanicus* 93 (11–18 Aug. 1645); *Mercurius Britanicus* 94 (18–25 Aug. 1645), p. 848; *Mercurius Britanicus* 96 (1–8 Sep. 1645).

grandees, John Ashburnham and William Legge, who were evidently perceived to be too close to the Independents at Westminster.[9]

However, in addition to such more or less straightforward use of 'spin', it was also possible to manipulate public opinion in more subtle ways. These included attempts to play upon popular fears in order to shore up popular support; attempts to overplay threats and dangers; and attempts to underplay defeats and setbacks. Politicians may have sought to create a sense of crisis in order to win approval for measures which might otherwise have been unpopular or unacceptable. In order to secure widespread emergency powers, in other words, it was necessary to engender a sense of emergency. This had provided part of the justification for the imposition of Ship Money in the 1630s, and although many of those who opposed Ship Money did so in part because they were unconvinced that there was a crisis which required the raising of such money, exploitation of the concept of 'necessity' became a commonplace among parliamentarian writers. Since 'reason of state' provided grounds for extraordinary political action, it was possible to exploit events which could be portrayed as threatening national stability, in order to justify new policies and initiatives. The author of the *True Informer* said that 'false rumours produced one politick effect (*and it was the end indeed for which they were dispersed*); they did atemorize [intimidate], and fill the people's hearts with fears, and so dispose of them to uproars and to part with money'.[10] Writing the royalist *Mercurius Pragmaticus*, meanwhile, Marchamont Nedham stated that Parliament:

> produce letters written by William Lenthall (yet said to be intercepted from Scotland) discovering wondrous strange and uncouth matters, of evil intents towards the city, all which, if they trust them as their rock of refuge, they shall be sure to be protected from, and to remain rich and potent.[11]

Parliamentarians certainly made efforts to publicise atrocity stories collected by the army secretariat, in order to discredit the royalists and to appeal to the popular appetite for scandal.[12] Indeed, such accusations of news management became a great deal more common as the 1640s progressed. The royalist author of *Sober Sadnes*, for example, claimed that parliamentarians 'beguiled the people with false alarms', and spoke of the 'conjuration of plots and conspiracies' to secure opposition to peace.[13] It was the perception that such tactics were being employed by the proto-parliamentarians at Westminster in late 1641 which helped justify the king's decision to attempt the arrest of the 'five members'.[14]

---

[9] *Mercurius Pragmaticus* 23 (29 Aug.–5 Sept. 1648), sig. Ff2.

[10] *The True Informer* (Oxford, 1643), p. 30.

[11] *Mercurius Pragmaticus* 20 (8–15 Aug. 1648), sig. Y3. See: R. Clifton, 'The popular fear of Catholics during the English revolution', in P. Slack, ed., *Rebellion, Popular Protest and the Social Order in Early Modern England* (Cambridge, 1984), pp. 145–6.

[12] *An Exact and True Relation* (imp. Elsyng, London, for Husband and Frank, 1642).

[13] *Sober Sadnes* (Oxford, 1643), pp. 11, 18.

[14] R. Cust, 'Charles I and popularity', in T. Cogswell, R. Cust and P. Lake, *Politics, Religion and Popularity in Early Stuart Britain* (Cambridge, 2002), p. 254.

The most obvious example of the way in which fears were stoked in this way occurred before the outbreak of civil war, when those most zealous for 'further reformation', and who sought to place pressure on Charles I to make political concessions, sought to exploit fears regarding the existence of 'popish plots' and jesuitical stratagems.[15] Following the outbreak of the Irish rebellion it was possible to capitalise on such fears by encouraging popular beliefs regarding atrocities and massacres.[16] Historians have demonstrated how the rebellion fed into existing English attitudes and preconceptions regarding the Catholic threat, and analysed the impact of the rebellion in heightening tensions between king and Parliament, and they have also sought to suggest that events in Ireland constituted a destabilising external or 'exogenous' factor – one of Conrad Russell's famous 'billiard balls' – which undermined a projected settlement in England. Events in Ireland were exploited by Charles's critics, enabling the passing of measures which themselves provoked constitutional crisis, including the 'Grand Remonstrance', the attack upon bishops and Catholic peers, the demand for a parliamentary guard, and eventually for control of the militia.[17] Historians have also recognised the crucial role of print.[18] What has been lacking from such analysis of the impact of the Irish rebellion, however, has been an understanding of the possibility that it was a carefully stage-managed news event.

It is necessary to synthesise our knowledge of the attitudes of English politicians, the preconceptions and prejudices of English public opinion, and the importance of the print medium, in order to examine the forces behind the publication of tracts relating to Ireland in 1641–42, and to identify those who ensured that the material was made available to the public. Such analysis reveals that Irish news was manipulated by politicians so that atrocity stories stoked long-

---

[15] Earlier it had proved possible for Laudians to try and demonstrate the existence of a Puritan plot in order to justify harsh treatment of 'conspiratorial' members of the clergy and laity: J. Peacey, 'The paranoid prelate: Archbishop Laud and the Puritan plot', in B. Coward and J. Swann, eds, *Conspiracies and Conspiracy Theory in Early Modern Britain and Europe, 1500–1800* (forthcoming, Aldershot, 2003).

[16] J. Peacey, 'Contexts and causes, or, putting the English back into the British civil wars, 1637–42' (paper delivered at NACBS conference, Pasadena, 2000); E. Shagan, 'Constructing discord: ideology, propaganda, and English responses to the Irish rebellion of 1641', *JBS* 36 (1997). Propaganda regarding massacres committed by the rebels, aimed at creating picture of the involvement of all Catholics, was arguably used in order to justify land confiscation: P. J. Corish, 'The rising of 1641 and the Catholic Confederacy, 1641–5', in T. W. Moody et al., *A New History of Ireland III. Early Modern Ireland, 1534–1691* (Oxford, 1976), p. 292.

[17] J. Peacey, 'The outbreak of the civil wars in the three kingdoms', in B. Coward, ed., *Blackwell Companion to Stuart Britain* (Oxford, 2003); T. Harris, 'Critical perspectives: the anatomy of English history?', in G. Burgess, ed., *The New British History* (London, 1999), p. 281. See: R. Clifton, 'Fear of Popery', in C. Russell, ed., *The Origins of the English Civil War* (Basingstoke, 1973); P. Lake, 'Anti-Popery: the structure of a prejudice', in R. Cust and A. Hughes, eds, *Conflict in Early Stuart England* (London, 1989); K. Lindley, 'The impact of the 1641 rebellion upon England and Wales, 1641–5', *IHS* 18 (1972), pp. 153, 161–3.

[18] Lindley, 'Impact', p. 161.

standing fears of a popish plot sufficiently to prompt popular acquiescence to the passage of provocative political measures. Parliament had the power to ignore, postpone or promote petitions from distressed Protestants in Ireland and their sympathisers in England, and to do so in order to suit their own political purposes. By allowing them to be read, and by ordering them to be published alongside 'leaked' official depositions regarding the rebellion, Parliament played a proactive part in the process by which news was received and interpreted.[19] Moreover, a remarkably high proportion of the tracts and pamphlets providing news from Ireland in late 1641 and early 1642 were published by John Thomas, the favoured printer of those at Westminster most zealous for reform, and they were aimed at all sections of the reading public.[20] Other works were produced by another favoured printer, Joseph Hunscott.[21] Indeed, it is possible to demonstrate that some works designed to stoke paranoia regarding the popish threat appeared at crucial moments in the passage of 'emergency' powers. It was in the tense weeks after the introduction of the Militia Ordinance, as the rhetorical heat of the 'paper war' increased, that Parliament sanctioned the publication of Henry Jones's remonstrance concerning the state of the rebellion in Ireland.[22] The publication of the controversial 'Nineteen Propositions', in the first week of June 1642, coincided with the order to publish Audley Mervyn's relation of proceedings in Ulster.[23] Furthermore, in the tense weeks between the first bloodshed of the war and the raising of the royalist standard at Nottingham, Henry Jones's evidence was republished.[24] The Irish rebellion was, therefore, spun by Englishmen for a domestic audience, with domestic political objectives in mind, and the domestic

---

[19] Lindley, 'Impact', p. 156.

[20] *Irelands Complaint Against Sir George Ratcliffe* (London, 1641); T. Lancton, *Dublin, Febr. 7. 1641, or, The Last True Newes from Ireland* (London, 1641); *More Newes from Ireland* (London, 1641); *The Last Newes from Ireland* (London, 1641); T. Creamor, *A Gun-Powder-Plot in Ireland* (London, 1641); *The Coppy of a Letter Sent from the Rebells in Ireland* (London, 1641); *A Late and True Relation from Ireland* (London, 1641); Sir Thomas Lucas, *Admirable Good Newes Againe from Ireland* (London, 'by authority', 1641); W. Brocket, *Good Newes from Ireland* (London, 1642); L. Haward, *A Continuation of the Last Occurrences from Irland* (London, 1642); L. Haward, *A Continuation of the Diurnal Occurrences and Proceedings of the English Army Against the Rebels in Ireland* (London, 1642); *Irelands Amazement, or the Heavens Armado* (London, 1641); *A Great Conspiracy By the Papists in the Kingdome of Ireland* (London, 1641); *The Demands of the Rebels in Ireland* (London, 1641); *March 21th 1641. Continuation of the Good Newes from Ireland* (London, 1641/2). On the Popish plot in general: *A Discovery of a Horrible and Bloody Treason and Conspiracie* (London, 1641); *A Bloody Plot Practised by Some Papists* (London, 1641); *A Great Conspiracy of the Papists* (London, 1641).

[21] *The Copy of a letter from Master Tristram Whitecombe, Major of Kinsale* (imp. Elsyng, London, for Hunscott, 1642); *A Warning Peece for London* (London, for Hunscott, 1642); *The Particular Relation of the Present Estate and Condition of Ireland* ('published by authority', London, for Hunscott, 1642).

[22] *CJ* ii. 490a; see above, p. 173.

[23] *PJ* iii. 20; see above, p. 171.

[24] *A Remonstrance of the Beginnings and Proceedings of the Rebellion … Written, Set Forth and Presented to the Most Honourable the Houses of Parliament by Henry Jones* (London, 1642).

reading audience was given timely reminders of the popish threat at key moments in 1642. Secretary Nicholas clearly recognised the tactics employed by parliamentarians, by saying that alarms regarding popish plots 'amuse and afright the people here ... and therefore that is the drum that is so frequently beaten upon all occasions'.[25]

It may also have been the case, however, that attempts were made to exploit and even invent good news, and contemporaries clearly perceived that politicians not only exaggerated the importance of certain pieces of news, but also engaged in lies, inaccuracies and embellishment. Losses could be turned into victories in order to terrify the people, and false stories could be spread in order to divert attention from bad news from the field.[26] One royalist claimed that parliamentarians resorted to 'lies, palpable slanders, and abominable accusations, invented, printed and scattered over all parts of this kingdom'.[27] When the king's correspondence was seized after the battle of Naseby in 1645, certain royalist authors proclaimed that the letters were a forgery, although this was something that no leading royalist, let alone the king, had claimed.[28] Writing in 1648, however, the disgruntled former parliamentarian, Clement Walker, wrote that radicals in Parliament and the army 'commonly publish counterfeit news and letters of great victories and successes gotten by their party in parts so remote that they cannot in a short time be confuted'. He added that 'this serves to credit and animate their party to go on boldly with their work and to dishearten their opponents, and though the profit and reputation of a lie is seldom long-lived, yet if it last some few days, until they have carried on their present business, they care not'.[29] In September 1644, *Mercurius Aulicus* claimed that Parliament was running short of money, 'for the rebels begin to assume their old method of cheating the people of it'. Their tactic, *Aulicus* alleged, was to 'broach a fresh tale of a great victory a great way off (called a final overthrow given to the Irish Papists by the Scots in the Province of Ulster)', which was 'scattered by the faction in their letters and vented abroad in print all last week'. Noting that 'the Committee of Both Kingdoms gave order to take subscriptions for advance money for the poor Scots Protestants in Ireland', *Aulicus* felt able to conclude that 'the committee

---

[25] Quoted in Clifton, 'Popular fear of Catholics', p. 145.

[26] B. Dooley, 'News and doubt in early modern culture', in B. Dooley and S. Baron, *The Politics of Information in Early Modern Europe* (London, 2001) pp. 277, 281. Royalists reported that 'to divert people's thoughts' from Monck's defeat in Scotland in June 1654, 'Cromwell pretended the discovery of a great plot against himself which was not believed; but in consequence no person was permitted to stir out of London without special license': *CCSP* ii. 367.

[27] G. Williams, *The Discovery of Mysteries* (Oxford, 1643), pp. 48–9, 69.

[28] *Mercurius Aulicus* (13–20 July 1645), p. 1665; E. Symmons, *A Vindication of King Charles* (London, 1647), pp. 25–7, 30, 45–7, 60, 91, 96–7, 102, 111, 216–17; J. Taylor, *The Generall Complaint* (Oxford, 1645), p. 7; H. B. Wheatley, ed., *The Diary of John Evelyn* (4 vols, London, 1906), iv. 167. Indeed, the king went to some lengths to explain some of the most damaging evidence from the letters: Bodl. MS Clarendon 25, fo. 74.

[29] C. Walker, *The History of Independency* ([London], 1648), p. 146.

broached the news, that they might have some colour to demand subscriptions'.[30] In August 1648, meanwhile, *Pragmaticus* complained of a 'pretended letter from Cromwell' regarding military successes, which he styled a 'paper kite'. Nedham warned his readers that 'till this be confirmed from some better hands than those of their creatures and members, you may suppose it rather a piece of godly leiger-deumaine acted by the Derby House junto, to gull their fellow members and the world, the better to fright away a personal treaty'.[31] Whether or not Nedham knew better, the letter in question, containing news of the victory over the Scots at Preston, was almost certainly genuine.[32] Furthermore, the presence of incorrect news reports need not necessarily indicate that editors lied, so much as that they were mistaken. On 6 July 1644, *Mercurius Aulicus* reported 'great newes' from York, in the form of 'certain intelligence that the rebels are absolutely routed'. In the following week's edition, however, once it had become clear that Marston Moor had witnessed a crushing parliamentarian victory, the paper was forced to amend its story, albeit with excuses and accusations that details of the battle had been delayed by parliamentarian efforts to prevent messengers travelling south, and that early accounts were based upon 'the rebels own assertions'.[33] Whatever the plausibility of particular accusations and specific claims, it is probably possible to concur with the observer of the 'lean and miserable' sheets of news who suggested in 1649 that they contained 'some things true, among many mistakes, and lies but probably reported'.[34]

More importantly, allegations frequently surfaced that even in the absence of fraudulent news reports, politicians embellished stories in order to exaggerate their importance. During the Anglo-Dutch war, for example, the Venetian ambassador suggested that veracity was an inevitable victim of the control over the press achieved by the commonwealth regime, and that 'the truth cannot yet be ascertained', because 'an order has been issued prohibiting the publication of any statements concerning the present war, except by the privileged printer ordinary to the Parliament'. He reported to the ambassador in Paris that 'the public prints are constantly recording victories gained over the Dutch', but added:

---

[30] *Mercurius Aulicus* 36 (1–7 Sept. 1644), pp. 1145–6. See: *CSPD 1644*, pp. 447, 454; *CJ* iii. 605, 609.

[31] *Mercurius Pragmaticus* 21 (15–22 Aug. 1648), sib. Bb2v.

[32] Cromwell wrote two letters (17 and 20 August), both of which were read in Parliament and ordered to be printed officially: *Lieutenant General Cromwel's Letter* (London, for Husband, 1648); *Lieut. General Cromwel's Letter* (London, for Husband, 1648); *A Full Relation of the Great Victory* (London, for Wright, 1648). These bore the imprimatur of Henry Elsyng (clerk of the Commons) and John Brown (Clerk of Parliament). For the letters, see: Abbott, *Cromwell*, i. 632–8.

[33] *Mercurius Aulicus* 27 (6 July 1644), p. 1072; *Mercurius Aulicus* 28 (13 July 1644), p. 1082. The author of one royalist newsbook commented, therefore, that 'My brother *Prag.* was misinformed the last week concerning the Lord Byron and his forces, had the news been true, we should have heard Walker's cock crow all the city over': *Mercurius Melancholicus* 52 (14–21 Aug. 1648), p. 154.

[34] C. Sydenham], *An Anatomy of Lieut. Col. John Lilburn's Spirit and Pamphlets* (London, 1649), p. 2.

they have converted into a signal national triumph a trifling engagement between Plymouth and Falmouth ... It is true that some of the enemies ships were roughly handled and several of their men killed, but the English incurred similar loss and many of their dead and wounded have been landed at Plymouth, according to private accounts, although the fact is recorded otherwise.[35]

Attacking Speaker Lenthall and 'his news hound Mr [Walter] Frost' in August 1648, one royalist author claimed that they 'stretcheth the victory' at Preston, although 'somewhat of the relation may be probably true'.[36] That such reports were not without foundation is evident from the possibility of documenting an instance of the embellishment of reports of military manoeuvres in Herefordshire in late 1642. Comparison of pamphlet literature with official despatches submitted to Parliament reveals the extent to which the former attempted to discredit royalists with tales of the pillaging of the 'wilde Welsh-men' on the royalist side, and how minor skirmishes between royalist forces under the Marquess of Hertford and Lord Herbert of Ragland, and parliamentarian troops under the Earl of Stamford, were transformed into a major battle, and a significant success for Parliament. Although the provenance of such tracts is somewhat obscure, at least one claimed to have parliamentary approval, in the form of the *imprimatur* of John Brown, clerk of Parliament.[37]

Beyond claims regarding the peddling of outright lies, and evidence regarding embellishment of military reports, attempts can be shown to have been made to ensure selective presentation of evidence and events. It was alleged, for example, that parliamentarian journalists ignored royalist victories, and it is apparent that the Rump attempted to manipulate the licensing of newspapers in order to suppress stories upon which royalists would have been able to capitalise.[38] One of the most dramatic instances of the suppression of news occurred over the massacre by Cromwell's forces at Drogheda in Ireland in 1649, in the aftermath of which there was a deliberate campaign to silence the newspapers to prevent them publishing accounts of the massacres.[39] Suggestions were also made, however, that news reports were carefully edited prior to publication. One royalist said: 'lest the people's zeal should waste with their purses, they keep them warm by a continual breathing of reports upon them'. He continued: 'if letters come that speak but upon hear-say they first expunge so much

[35] *CSPV 1647–52*, pp. 266, 279. Such views regarding the reports of the war were echoed by voices at home as well, such as John Langley, who wrote to his employer in June 1653, mentioning 'the pamphlet (which few believe) speakes all the news of the late great sea-fight': Staffordshire RO, D593/P/8/2/2: John Langley to Sir Richard Leveson, 7 June 1653.

[36] *Mercurius Aulicus* 4 (21–28 Aug. 1648), p. 29.

[37] *LJ* v. 415, 425–6, 440–41, 444, 453, 475, 511, R. Hutton, *The Royalist War Effort* (London, 1982), p. 34; *True Newes out of Herefordshire* (London, 1642), pp. 3–6. See also *A True Relation of a Most Blessed Victory, Obtained Against the Marquess of Hertford* (London, 1642), sigs. A2–A4. The latter claimed to have the imprimatur of John Brown (A4v).

[38] *Mercurius Elencticus* 29 (7–14 June 1648, E447/11), p. 227.

[39] Peacey, 'Henry Parker', pp. 152–3; J. B. Williams, 'Fresh light on Cromwell at Drogheda', *The Nineteenth Century and After* 72 (1912), pp. 472–3, 476, 478–9; *SR* i. 326–7.

of the relation as might tend to the discouraging of their party and then publish them as the history of some great defeat'; adding that 'they have their observator to write commentaries upon them'.[40] The disgruntled parliamentarian diarist, Sir Simonds D'Ewes, provides evidence with which to verify such claims, by expressing his frustration at the way in which Parliament ordered such practices to be carried out. He claimed that a letter from Sir William Brereton regarding a victory at Nantwich was ordered to be printed only after its postscript, demonstrating the dire need for arms and powder, was expunged. D'Ewes expressed outrage that 'the very truth must not be published on either side'.[41] That such tactics were adopted in order to protect the interests of distinct factions, rather than the 'parliamentarian' cause, is evident from another instance of textual manipulation of correspondence directed to Westminster prior to publication. Oliver Cromwell's letter from Bristol, dated 14 September 1645, was ordered to be printed by the Commons, but it appeared without the final section, in which Cromwell wrote sympathetically of the possibility of tolerating and accommodating religious Independents. In response to what appears to have been a Presbyterian attempt to place factional spin on Cromwell's letter, the Independents published the concluding part in a broadside, which was scattered through the streets of London.[42] By suppressing news in this way, and by telling only part of the story, authors and politicians were engaging in disingenuous propaganda of a subtle kind. Little wonder, therefore, that Clement Walker later alleged that newsbooks were 'taught to speak no language but Cromwell and his party, and were mute in such actions as he and they could claim no share in, for which purposes the presses were narrowly watched'.[43]

Contemporary allegations also focused on the way in which selective use was made of material such as Laud's diary, and the king's letters taken at Naseby. Prynne's *Breviate*, an edition of Laud's diary, was accused of being 'interlaced' with 'several fictions', and was probably 'emended, glossed, and misinterpreted … in order to give a less favourable picture of its author', not least by imaginative reconstruction of passages which had been destroyed by fire.[44] Charles,

---

[40] *Sober Sadnes*, p. 22.

[41] BL, Harl. 166, fo. 6a; *CJ* iii. 386.

[42] Abbott, *Cromwell*, i. 374–8; *LJ* vii. 583–6; *CJ* iv. 277; BL, Add. 31116, p. 464; *The Conclusion of Lieuten. Generall Cromwells Letter to the House of Commons, Concerning the Taking of Bristoll: Which Was Contained in the Originall (Signed by Himself) but Omitted in the Printed Copy, Which was Authorised by the House of Commons (Though There was a Whole Page Left Blank in that Sheet* ([London, 1645], BL, 669.f.10/38). Thomason noted that 'this was printed by the Independent partie and scattered up and down the streets last night but expressly omitted by order of the House.'. See: J. S. A. Adamson, 'Oliver Cromwell and the Long Parliament', in J. Morrill, ed., *Oliver Cromwell and the English Revolution* (London, 1990), pp. 66–8. Cromwell's letter survives in Lenthall's papers, with the conclusion highlighted in a contemporary hand: Bodl. MS Nalson IV, fos. 168–9v.

[43] Walker, *History of Independency*, p. 4.

[44] *Mercurius Aulicus* [101] (5–12 Jan. 1644[–5]), pp. 1332–3; H. R. Trevor-Roper, *Archbishop Laud, 1573–1645* (3rd ed., London, 1988), p. 424; C. Carlton, *Archbishop William Laud* (London, 1987), p. 222; *HMC House of Lords XI*, pp. 457–64.

meanwhile, claimed that only those of his letters which were damaging to his personal reputation were printed in 1645, while others which portrayed his actions in a better light were suppressed.[45] Plans to publish the correspondence of both the king and Lord Digby provoked the Scots, meanwhile, to express concern that their Independent rivals planned to use the selection process in order to damage their political interests.[46] It was clearly perceived, in other words, that it was possible to manipulate evidence, and to publish selectively, in order to achieve political goals, although on this occasion Scottish fears were misplaced, even though the Independents clearly controlled the material and its management within Parliament and the press.[47] While undoubtedly aimed at discrediting royalist credibility, by demonstrating their willingness to employ foreign Catholic forces, the process of suppressing or omitting certain letters was actually aimed at preventing the emergence into the public domain of material regarding the Scots' duplicity, and evidence of crypto-royalism within their army.[48] Furthermore, this ability to detect factionalism in the treatment of evidence is also apparent during the Rump, when the authors of 'official' newspapers could engage not merely in editorial comment, but also in selective documentation of current affairs. The more conservative newspapers, such as the *Perfect Diurnal*, ignored the passage of the Toleration Act, while *Several Proceedings* publicised the calls made for action against religious radicals in May and June 1652 (to coincide with moves to revive the committee for propagating the gospel), as well as the religious projects of Richard Baxter in early 1653.[49] More radical papers, such as the *Perfect Account* and the *Faithful Scout*, which were closer to the army, tended to play up Cromwell's reforming streak, and to advocate social reform.[50] That these were not unique cases is evident from the different newspaper reports of events in October 1659, in which Marchamont Nedham (writing for the Rump) was pitched against John Canne (who wrote for the army). While Canne used *Occurrences from Foreign Parts and Particular Advice from the Office of Intelligence* to publicise the demands of those officers whose commissions were removed by Parliament on 12 October, Nedham took a different path, and refused to publicise their demands in *Mercurius Politicus*.[51]

'News management' can hardly be said to have been invented in the mid-seventeenth century, but the conditions of civil war, not least the explosion of the

---

[45] *OPH* xvii. 41.

[46] *Letters and Journals of Robert Baillie*, ii. 294.

[47] Peacey, 'Exploitation of captured royal correspondence'.

[48] Peacey, 'Exploitation of captured royal correspondence'.

[49] B. Worden, *The Rump Parliament* (Cambridge, 1974), pp. 296–7, 322–3.

[50] Worden, *Rump*, pp. 239, 243, 274–5, 279, 308, 315–16. The *Scout*'s open criticism of Parliament prompted a clampdown on newspapers in December 1652, when the *Scout* was singled out as one of the reasons for suppression: *CJ* vii. 236.

[51] *A Particular Advice from the Office of Intelligence* 27 (4–7 Oct. 1659), pp. 365–8; *A Particular Advice* 39 (11–18 Nov. 1659), p. 464; *Mercurius Politicus* 590 (6–13 Oct. 1659), pp. 792–3.

popular press, provided the impetus for the perfection of its black arts. The possibility of documenting not just contemporary accusations regarding the manipulation of news and political information, but also evidence regarding the publication and suppression of material, its selective presentation, embellishment and exaggeration, enables appreciation of the subtlety with which grandees of all persuasions appreciated the power of the press, and their ability to influence print media. Moreover, with the manipulation of news regarding events such as the Irish rebellion, it is possible to gain a sense of the part which it was perceived that pamphlets, news reports and newspapers could play in the political process, and in massaging the popular mood at moments of intense political sensitivity.

Aside from the possibility that material was manipulated and spun for political ends, attention must also be drawn to other attempts to manufacture and engineer consent, in order to secure support for radical policies and controversial initiatives. In part, this was a question of finding ways of saying things in order to advance a debate and raise political stakes, as well as of 'flying kites' for particular policies, and sowing seeds in the public mind about forthcoming policy initiatives. As such, it was about setting the tone and parameters of political and religious debate.

Print could be used, and works deployed, for example, in order to expound a message which could not be stated overtly. In this sense, propaganda could play a more or less conscious part in a process whereby political and religious grandees heightened tension while distancing themselves from those authors who were directly responsible for inflammatory tracts and pamphlets.[52] Henry Parker's treatment of Ship Money, published in 1640, represented not merely an attack upon an unpopular policy, from the pen of a close associate of one of those grandees who led the opposition to the imposition, both in the 1630s and in the Long Parliament, but also a means of expressing opinions regarding the case which were too risky for Hampden's defence attorney, Oliver St John, to express either in court or in his printed works.[53] Subsequently, during tense debates in Parliament over the 'disposal' of the king, Independent grandees may have sought to place themselves at arms' length from the expression of radical ideas, and to rely upon the pens of known radicals, from whom they could distance themselves if necessary. Thus, in publishing a provocative speech (delivered on 26 October), Thomas Chaloner not only provoked a notable pamphlet debate, but may also have served as a 'front' for others in the House; a supposition that is supported by evidence which indicates that Chaloner was not alone in making radical statements regarding the king on that particular occasion.[54] Furthermore, contemporaries also

---

[52] J. Klaits, *Printed Propaganda Under Louis XIV* (Princeton, 1976), p. 246; A. Milton, 'The creation of Laudianism: a new approach', in Cogswell, Cust and Lake, eds, *Politics, Religion and Popularity*, pp. 177–9.

[53] Peacey, 'Henry Parker', pp. 51–3.

[54] T. Chaloner, *An Answer to the Scotch Papers* (London, by F. Leach, 1646); National Library of Wales, Wynnstay 90/16 (xxxviii). I am grateful to Dr Lloyd Bowen for this reference, and to Dr David

reflected upon the way in which print was used to test the public mood. Much comment was generated, for example, by Calybute Downing's 1640 sermon before the Honourable Artillery Company in London, in which the former chaplain to the Earl of Salisbury defended the Scottish covenanters in their 'defensive war'. Such treasonable ideas were almost certainly too dangerous for pro-Scottish peers and grandees to utter, and Downing's sermon may thus have represented a 'trial balloon to discover what acceptance the dangerous idea of resistance to the king would find among Puritans'. The controversial nature of Downing's comments certainly necessitated his seeking sanctuary with the Earl of Warwick, and at least one royalist later reflected that Downing had been instructed to 'feel the pulse' of the city.[55] Years later, as attitudes towards Charles I hardened after the outbreak of the second civil war, it may have been radical members of the army, or even MPs, who sanctioned Henry Walker's publication of a notorious monarchomach treatise by Robert Parsons, as well as the first English edition of the *Vindicaie Contra Tyrannos*, in order either to place pressure upon Charles, or to soften the public for the possibility of trying, overthrowing, and even executing the king.[56]

Print may have been employed, therefore, in order to prepare the ground for highly controversial policies and ideas, and the language of 'paper-kites' became common in the press during the period.[57] Most commonly, papers and pamphlets were used in order to pave the way for particular policy changes and legislative initiatives, and in July 1641 William Davie recognised that certain tracts served to 'prepare your thoughts for that change which is like to be'.[58] This was hardly a new phenomenon. Peter Heylyn recorded how Queen Elizabeth was prepared to 'tune the pulpits', and to have preachers 'ready at command to cry up her design', and it has long been recognised that Charles issued instructions to preachers to promote support for the Forced Loan, in accordance with which Richard Sibthorpe preached his infamous assize sermons.[59] Heylyn himself was accused of having

---

Scott for discussions regarding its significance. Chaloner's speech involved an exposition of the theory of the king's two bodies. For the ensuing debate, see: *An Answer to a Speech Without Doores* (London, 1646); *The Moderator* (London, 1646); G. G., *A Reply to a Namelesse Pamphlet* (London, 1646); *An Answer to Severall Objections* (London, 1646); *The Justification of a Safe and Wel-Grounded Answer* (London, 1646); *A Corrector of the Answerer to the Speech Out of Dorres* (Edinburgh, 1646); *The Speech Without Doores Defended* (np, 1646).

[55] C. Downing, *A Sermon Preached to the Renowned Company of the Artillery* (London, 1641); B. Donagan, 'The clerical patronage of Robert Rich, second Earl of Warwick, 1619–1642', *Proceedings of the American Philosophical Society* 120 (1976), p. 409; *A Letter from Mercurius Civicus* (np, 1643), p. 8; *A Discourse Discovering Some Mysteries* (Oxford, 1645), pp. 7–9.

[56] *Several Speeches* (London, 1648); *Vindiciae Contra Tyrannos* (London, 1648); C. Walker, *Relations and Observations* ([London], 1648), p. 115.

[57] *Mercurius Melancholicus* 53 (21–28 Aug. 1648), p. 156.

[58] Sir W. C. Trevelyan, and Sir C. E. Trevelyan, eds, *Trevelyan Papers* (3 vols, Camden Society, 1857–72), iii. 211; G. R. Elton, *Policy and Police. The Enforcement of the Reformation in the Age of Thomas Cromwell* (Cambridge, 1972), p. 206; F. J. Levy, 'Staging the news', in A. F. Marotti and M. D. Bristol, eds, *Print, Manuscript and Performance* (Columbus, 2000), p. 262.

[59] P. Heylyn, *Cyprianus Anglicus* (London, 1671), pp. 153, 158; G. Davies, 'English political

used the pulpit in order to prepare the way for the judicial assault upon the Feoffees for the Purchase of Impropriations, although it is unclear whether his sermon on the issue, delivered from the pulpit of St Mary's Church in Oxford in July 1630, was orchestrated by Laud, or rather merely facilitated by the vice-chancellor of Oxford, Accepted Frewen, master of Heylyn's college.[60] However, it seems certain that parliamentarian grandees used 'fast' sermons for precisely this purpose, and that the reformers used sermons not merely to declare the party line, but also to prepare the way for dramatic initiatives, such as the impeachment of Strafford in April 1641.[61] Sir Edward Hyde may thus have been justified in his claim that, 'by the Sunday's sermon, or a lecture, they could learn, not only what was done the week before, but also what was to be done in Parliament the week following'.[62]

It was not necessary to rely upon sermons to perform such tasks, of course. Rather more mundanely, the law reformer and Cromwellian confidante, William Sheppard, appears to have published certain works prior to the opening of the 1656 Parliament in order to lay the ground for specific legislative measures planned by a faction at court, and he may be regarded as having set forth their programme in preparation for a parliamentary campaign.[63] More interesting is the possibility that the appearance of certain political texts was supported at key moments in the 1640s and 1650s in order to set the political tone for important constitutional change. This is true of Henry Parker's *A Question Answered*, which was timed to coincide with the debates on the militia bill in the spring of 1642, and it also appears true of the early phase of the protectorate, when the Council of State ordered the publication of *Curia Politiae*, collecting the thoughts of various princes on aspects of monarchical rule.[64] Furthermore, figures such as John

---

sermons, 1603–1640', *HLQ* (1939), pp. 8, 14, 16; A. Hunt, 'Tuning the pulpits: the religious context of the Essex revolt', in L. A. Ferrell and P. McCullough, eds, *The English Sermon Revised* (Manchester, 2000), p. 87; P. E. McCullough, *Sermons at Court. Politics and Religion in Elizabethan and Jacobean Preaching* (Cambridge, 1998), p. 60.

[60] This may have been an attempt by Heylyn to draw attention to himself and to advance his career. See: W. Prynne, *Canterburies Doome* (London, 1646), p. 386; G. E. Gorman, 'A Laudian attempt to 'tune the pulpit': Peter Heylyn and his sermon against the Feoffees for the Purchase of Impropriations', *Journal of Religious History* 8 (1975). Heylyn presented the text of his sermon to Laud after it was delivered.

[61] H. Trevor-Roper, 'The Fast sermons of the Long Parliament', in *Religion, the Reformation, and Social Change* (London, 1973); J. F. Wilson, *Pulpit in Parliament* (Princeton, 1969), pp. 44–6, 98; C. Hill, *The English Bible and the Seventeenth Century Revolution* (London, 1994), pp. 82, 88–9, 97.

[62] Clarendon, *History*, iv. 194: 'It was an observation in that time, that the first publishing of extraordinary news was from the pulpit, and by the preacher's text, and his manner of discourse upon it, the auditors might judge, and commonly foresaw what was like to be next done in the Parliament or Council of State'.

[63] N. L. Matthews, *William Sheppard, Cromwell's Law Reformer* (Cambridge, 1994), pp. 123–5, 187; W. Sheppard, *A Survey of the County Judicatures* (London, 1656); W. Sheppard, *Englands Balme* (London, 1656).

[64] Peacey, 'Henry Parker', pp. 63–4; *Curia Politiae* (London, 1654).

Lambert, who sought a hereditary sovereign, seem to have been behind the appearance of *A Copy of a Letter Concerning the Election of a Lord Protector*, which was printed by favoured stationer Thomas Newcomb in December 1654, shortly after Parliament had discussed such issues, and which defended a hereditary form of government.[65] The strength of Lambert's opponents, however, is suggested by the appearance of much more important works, such as Nedham's *True State of the Case of the Commonwealth*, which defended an elective protectorate, as well as Marvell's *First Anniversary*.[66] Later in the 1650s, however, a stream of works appeared which continued to argue for the establishment of an hereditary form of government, including another work published by Newcomb.[67]

In addition to being willing and able to exploit news and political information, and to subject it to spin in order to manipulate popular opinion, grandees thus demonstrated a willingness to utilise tracts and pamphlets in order to set the political agenda, and to 'fly kites' for particular policies, not least plans for constitutional change. Such evidence attests not merely to the way in which print became an increasingly important tool of political action, but also to the fact that analysis of print propaganda is sometimes crucial for a sophisticated understanding of the political beliefs, motives and aims of grandees whose inner thoughts and political purposes are not always apparent from other sources of evidence, particularly at moments of high tension, and regarding issues of acute sensitivity.[68]

Whatever the success of tactics which employed pamphlets in order to manipulate public opinion, another way of manufacturing consent was through the utilisation of print in order to create the impression of popular support, as well as to demonstrate popular demand for controversial policies, and perhaps even to suggest that certain political manoeuvres were undertaken in response to public opinion.

The most obvious way in which this could be done was through the publication

---

[65] M. J. Tibbetts, 'Parliamentary parties under Oliver Cromwell' (Bryn Mawr University PhD, 1944), p. 79; *A Copy of a Letter Concerning the Election of a Lord Protector* (London, by Newcomb, 1654).

[66] M. Nedham, *The True State of the Case of the Commonwealth* (London, 1654); H. M. Margoliouth, ed., *The Poems and Letters of Andrew Marvell* (2 vols, Oxford, 1971), i. 103–13; J. M. Wallace, *Destiny His Choice* (Cambridge, 1980), pp. 106–44; D. Hirst, 'That sober liberty: Marvell's Cromwell in 1654', in J. M. Wallace, ed., *The Golden and the Brazen World* (Berkeley, Ca., 1985).

[67] *A Copy of a Letter Written to an Officer of the Army by a True Commonwealthsman and No Courtier* (London, by Newcomb, 1656). See also: *The Unparalleld Monarch, or the Portraiture of a Matchless Prince*, which appeared in September 1656, and John Moore's *Protection Proclaimed*, which appeared in November 1655, and which claimed to show that the protectorate was 'of divine institution': *The Unparalleld Monarch* (London, 1656); J. Moore, *Protection Proclaimed* (London, 1656). See: J. T. Peacey, 'Nibbling at *Leviathan*: politics and theory in England in the 1650s', *HLQ* 61 (1998).

[68] See also below, p. 261.

of petitions presented to either the king or Parliament. Peter Heylyn, who was finely attuned to sophisticated ways in which print could be deployed tactically during this period, argued that this was a 'common stratagem' by which Parliament 'wrought so far on some weak spirits', and such comments necessitate evaluation of the extent to which there is more to printed petitions than meets the eye.[69] Petitions may well have represented genuine grievances and demands, and may well have originated in independently organised campaigns at more or less grass-roots level. They may also have been published by petitioners in order to advertise their grievances and garner public support. However, it is also possible that they were exploited by being ordered into print.[70] Moreover, apparently spontaneous petitions which offered expressions of support for either side may actually have been promoted and encouraged by men closely linked to Parliament or the king. Of course, all petitions needed a degree of organisation in order to secure signatures, and some of those involved in petitioning and lobbying Parliament freely admitted that copies of petitions were circulated for subscription, and that organisers 'set forth notes' in order to arrange a rendezvous in a prominent public place, where petitioners could gather before marching to Westminster.[71] Manuscript copies of petitions occasionally survive with notes arranging such meetings, and one copy of the May 1648 Kent petition includes a memorandum that all subscriptions were to be taken to Rochester on 29 May, and that all who intended to accompany the petition were to meet at Blackheath the following morning at 9 am.[72]

However, some such campaigns were clearly organised on a much bigger scale, and even at a nationwide level. This was something that religious reformers had been undertaking since the late sixteenth century, and in September 1603 the Archbishop of Canterbury had complained about the 'clamorous petitions' produced by the Puritans.[73] The following year saw the drafting of 'advice tending to reformation', which proposed a coordinated national petitioning campaign, and which stressed that supporters should ensure that texts differed 'for the avoiding of the suspicion of conspiracy'.[74] Interestingly, this organisational document reappeared in October 1640, as new pressure for religious reform was mobilised.[75]

---

[69] Heylyn, *Cyprianus*, p. 494.

[70] Above, pp. 170, 241; Heylyn, *Cyprianus*, pp. 470–71.

[71] *An Humble Declaration of the Apprentices* (London, 1642), pp. 4–5.

[72] *CSPD 1648–9*, p. 63; PRO, SP 16/516, fos. 65–6. See also the Kent petition of May 1648: Bodl. MS Nalson XXII, fos. 362r–v.

[73] PRO, SP 14/3, fo. 142. See P. Collinson, *The Elizabethan Puritan Movement* (London, 1967), pp. 452–5, 502–3.

[74] R. G. Usher, *The Reconstruction of the English Church* (2 vols, London, 1910), i. 294–6, ii. 358–62; BL, Sloane 271, fos. 20r–v.

[75] PRO, SP 16/470, fo. 180; *CSPD 1640–1*, p. 210. It may have been used as an example rather than a model for substantive reform. While reformers in 1640 might have moved further towards root and branch reform, they probably favoured the idea that 'lawyers, against the time of the Parliament, are to provide and make ready penned statutes tending to this purpose, and others are to write some learned treatises against that time'.

Laud's concern at the involvement of large sections of the population in such petitioning is evident, and in September 1640 he was informed that 300 citizens resorted by companies of twenty or thirty to consult and subscribe to a petition to be presented to the king.[76] Moreover, contemporary accusations and evidence both suggest that petitions were sanctioned, supported and organised centrally.[77] This can be detected most obviously in the organisation of petitions calling for religious reform in 1640, when the authorities detected evidence of a petitioning campaign orchestrated by Cornelius Burges and Calybute Downing, who were investigated for circulating a petition in opposition to the Laudian canons.[78] Meanwhile, the number and similarity of petitions calling for church reform in the months which followed suggest a national campaign, which may have been both centrally organised and reflective of authentic local attitudes.[79] The Warwickshire petition was instigated in London by Simeon Ashe, organised in the locality by Thomas Dugard, and presented to Parliament by their mutual friend and patron, Sir Robert Harley.[80] Contemporaries certainly recognised Harley's role in organising petitions, and in ensuring that such works were not identical in their wording.[81] Moreover, the involvement of grandees in soliciting petitions can be demonstrated from the example of the MP who sought to encourage local petitions in February 1647, by informing a friend in the country that 'if the ministers do anything, let it be to frame a petition for the establishment of church government'.[82] In 1655, meanwhile, it was suggested that Cromwell himself wanted to be petitioned regarding the crown, while at the same time seeking to dissociate himself from such campaigns.[83]

Royalists repeatedly alleged that petitions were fraudulently framed in the name of thousands of people, and that fake petitions appeared in print.[84] It was also alleged that petitions were framed at Westminster before being sent to the localities for subscription and presentation to Parliament. During the autumn of 1646, therefore, suspicion arose regarding petitions purporting to come from inhabitants of Northern towns, which complained about their 'miserable

---

[76] *CSPD 1640–1*, p. 40; PRO, SP 16/467, fo. 16.

[77] J. Walter, *Understanding Popular Violence in the English Revolution* (Cambridge, 1999), pp. 320–21.

[78] *CSPD 1640*, p. 564; *CSPD 1640–1*, pp. 73, 84; PRO, SP 16/463, fo. 200.

[79] A. Fletcher, *The Outbreak of the English Civil War* (London, 1981), pp. 92, 191–3, 196.

[80] A. Hughes, *Politics, Society and Civil War in Warwickshire, 1620–1660* (Cambridge, 1987), p. 134; BL, Add. 23146, fo. 91v; S. Clarke, *The Lives of Sundry Eminent Persons* (London, 1683), pp. 7–8.

[81] Staffordshire RO, D868/2/32. Evidence also survives relating to the circulation of the petition for church reform in Rutland and Lincolnshire, and the negotiations which took place among the gentry regarding its text: Shakespeare Birthplace Trust, DR 98/1652/14–17.

[82] Somerset RO, DD/HI466, unfol.: Letter from 'Temple', 23 Feb. 1647. Internal evidence indicates that this was from an MP.

[83] *NP* iii. 36.

[84] Williams, *Discovery of Mysteries*, p. 21; Nalson, *Impartial Collection*, i. 795, 799; *A Letter from a Grave Gentleman* (Oxford, 1643), p. 5; *Mercurius Pragmaticus* 19 (1–8 Aug. 1648), sig. T3.

sufferings' at the hands of Scottish troops quartered in the region, and which may have been orchestrated by Thomas Westrop, a friend of the radical MP, Henry Marten. George Thomason certainly believed that these petitions were 'made at London by ye Indep[endents]', and he probably feared that this was but one in a range of propaganda ploys by the Scots' opponents during the period after the end of the first civil war. The Scots certainly issued a complaint about the matter.[85] Later, allegations were also made regarding the provenance of the many loyal addresses upon the succession of Richard Cromwell to the protectorate in 1658. One contemporary critic claimed that these 'blasphemous, lying, flattering addresses', which were printed in the government's newspapers, were hatched at court by Thurloe and Nedham, 'the old malignant pamphleteer, that lying railing Rabshekah, the defamer of the friends of the cause'.[86] Difficult though it is to substantiate such claims, it is possible that something very similar can be demonstrated. During the tense weeks before Pride's Purge and the trial of Charles I, evidence permits assessment of the extent to which petitions were organised, and the response which was elicited. On 25 November 1648, army headquarters sent a circular letter to commanders in the field and at sea, seeking support for the army's *Remonstrance*, and in the weeks which followed a number of regiments issued declarations which echoed its demands, many of them in printed form.[87] In October 1659, furthermore, the army council drafted another petition for circulation within the army, although its exposure by John Okey led to the revocation of the officers' commissions, and thus the army's interruption of the

---

[85] *A Declaration Concerning the Miserable Sufferings of the Countrie* (London, 1646, E358/18); *A Remonstrance Concerning the Misdemeanours of Some of the Scots Souldiers* (London, 1646, E365/9); *CJ* iv. 709; S. Barber, *Regicide and Republicanism* (Edinburgh, 1998), p. 21.

[86] *A True Catalogue* (London, 1659), pp. 3–5, 75–6; G. Davies, *The Restoration of Charles II, 1658–1660* (Oxford, 1955), p. 11; A. Woolrych, 'Introduction', *The Complete Prose Works of John Milton VII* (New Haven, 1980), p. 97.

[87] Worcester College, Clarke MS CXIV, fo. 104; Clarke MS XVI, fo. 19v; *A Moderate and Cleer Relation of the Private Soldierie of Colonell Scroops and Col. Sanders Regiments* (London, for William Larnar, 1648); *The Declaration and Engagement of the Commanders, Officers, and Seamen in the Shipps, Under the Command of the Right Honourable the Earle of Warwick* (London, for John Playford, 1648); *Severall Petitions Presented to His Excellency the Lord Fairfax by the Lieut. Generals, Colonel Harrison's, Coll. Prides, Coll. Deanes Regiment* (London, 1648); *A True Copie of the Berkshire Petition* (London, 1648); *To His Excellency Thomas Lord Fairfax ... the Humble Representation of the Desires of the Officers and Souldiers in the Regiment of Horse, for the County of Northumberland* (London, 1648); *The Declaration and Humble Representation of the Officers and Souldiers in Colonel Scroops, Colonel Sanders, Colonel Wautons Regiment* (London, for John Partridge, 1648); *A Declaration of Three Deputy Governors of the Isle of Wight* (London, 1648); *A Petition Presented by the Inhabitants of Newport Pagnell* (London, 1648); *The Kentish Petition* (London, for Hanna Allen, 1648); *The Humble Petition of Divers Gentlemen, Ministers and Well-Affected Inhabitants in the County of Somerset* (London, for Husband, 1648); *The Humble Petition and Representation of the Officers and Souldiers of the Garrisons of Portsmouth, Southsea Castle, Hurst Castle, Poole and Brownsea Castle* (np, 1648). Royalists certainly claimed that such petitions were centrally written. See: N. Carlin, 'Pragmatical petitions' (paper delivered at the IHR, London, Oct. 2002).

Rump.[88] Despite their willingness to complain about such tactics, royalists too appear to have been willing to undertake such manipulation of petitions and print in early 1660, for which period Hyde's papers contain a blank draft of, or heads for, county petitions calling for a 'free parliament', the return of the secluded members, an act of oblivion, confirmation of acts of sale, and the payment of army arrears. The implication is that royalist grandees lay behind the raft of petitions making precisely these demands which appeared in print.[89] The petitions of 1648 and 1660 were published separately, and by distinct printers, which may have reflected a deliberate attempt to avoid suspicion that the campaign was as organised as it can be demonstrated to have been. On other occasions, the fact that petitions were printed by stationers closely associated with politicians whose interests such petitions served, may provide grounds for suspicion regarding the provenance of the petitions themselves. In early 1660, therefore, George Monck, having helped to effect the recall of the Rump, may have instigated a declaration for the readmission of the secluded members from crypto-royalists such as Sir Charles Coote in Ireland. This declaration, published on 16 February 1660, was printed by John Macock, one of Monck's favourite printers, and may have been designed to provide support for Monck's decision to allow the old Presbyterians into the House.[90]

In order to foster support and manufacture consent, and in order to secure approval for particular policies, it was necessary to demonstrate convincingly that political positions and proposals were credible, and that they had a constituency within the political nation. In this sense, methods by which consent was manufactured were conceptually linked with one of the key roles of propaganda, which was to establish and demonstrate orthodoxy, albeit to help engineer support for, and demonstrate acceptance of, new orthodoxies. The importance placed upon demonstrating popular support probably helped to ensure that independent and spontaneous petitions were regarded as being insufficiently reliable, and that it was necessary to encourage the appearance of such pieces, in order that they could be exploited in printed form.

---

[88] *TSP* vii. 755; Whitelocke, *Memorials*, iv. 364; *CJ* vii. 796a; Ludlow, *Memoirs*, ii. 136.

[89] Bodl. MS Clarendon 68, fo. 214; *CCSP* iv. 527; *A Letter from Divers of the Gentry of the County of Lincolne* (London, 1659); *The Declaration of the Gentlemen, Freeholders and Inhabitants of the County of Bedford* (London, 1659); *A Declaration of the Lords, Knight and Gentlemen in the Counties of Chester, Salop, Stafford* (London, 1659); *The Declaration of the Gentry of the County of Norfolk* (London, 1659); *A Letter and Declaration of the Nobility and Gentry of the County of York* (London, 1659); *The Humble Desires ... of the County and Borough of Leicester* (London, 1659); *The Humble Address and Hearty Desires of the Gentlemen, Ministers and Free-Holders of the County of Northampton* (London, 1660). The latter two are particularly similar.

[90] Woolrych, 'Introduction', p. 162; Davies, *Restoration*, pp. 250–51, 267; *A Declaration of Sir Charls Coot* (London, by Macock, 1660); *The Lord General Monck his Speech* (London, by Macock, 1660). Monck was clearly willing to respond to demands for the return of the secluded members in print: Woolrych, 'Introduction', p. 161; *A Letter of General George Monck's* (London, 1660).

A further way of approaching the conceptual deployment of propaganda is to observe the ways in which the print medium was used in order to 'ventriloquise'. Certain methods were developed, in other words, by which grandees could adopt unexpected voices and assist unpredictable authors. Attempts were made, for example, to orchestrate the appearance of words by people with whom it was impossible to associate openly. There is evidence, for example, that during the mid-1640s, political Independents such as Nedham made a tactical gesture of support for John Lilburne, at much the same time that Independent politicians such as Viscount Saye did so too, on the basis of Lilburne's value as a powerful voice against the Earl of Essex.[91] In addition to defending Lilburne on the pages of *Britanicus* in February 1646, Nedham was responsible for re-issuing Lilburne's anti-Presbyterian *Answer to Nine Arguments*, originally published in 1638, and he may also have had a hand in another pro-Leveller work, *Vox Plebis*. Since Nedham was effectively on probation at the time, after his release from prison earlier in the year, such support for Lilburne may be presumed to have been sanctioned by the Independent grandees with whom he was so familiar.[92] On other occasions, attempts were made to assist in the publication of works by enemies, in order to foment divisions between opponents, and to play off their factions.[93] Saye allegedly sought to promote the publication of inferior Anglican works in order to discredit the episcopalian cause, while during the 1650s the Marquess of Ormond and William Rumbold discussed deploying a Levelleresque petition in order to 'distract Cromwell', and upon the split between the Resolutioners and Remonstrants in 1650s Scotland, the commonwealth authorities in England apparently sought to assist in the publication of Remonstrant literature.[94]

More importantly, ventriloquy took the form of impersonating opponents in order to discredit them. It was clearly considered perfectly acceptable to employ artifice in polemical literature to some degree, and there are many pamphlets which purport to be dialogues, or letters to 'friends', which were clearly nothing

---

[91] *Mercurius Britanicus* 95 (25 Aug.–1 Sept. 1645), p. 95; *Mercurius Britanicus* 101 (13–20 Oct. 1645), p. 902; *Mercurius Britanicus* 105 (10–17 Nov. 1645), p. 923; J. T. Peacey, 'John Lilburne and the Long Parliament', *HJ* 43 (2000).

[92] *Mercurius Britanicus* 116 (26 Jan.–2 Feb. 1646), p. 1021; J. Lilburne, *An Answer to Nine Arguments* (London, 1645), epistle by 'M. N'; [M. Nedham], *Vox Plebis* (London, 1646); B. Worden, '"Wit in a Roundhead": the dilemma of Marchamont Nedham', in S. D. Amussen and M. A. Kishlansky, eds, *Political Culture and Cultural Politics in Early Modern England* (Manchester, 1995), pp. 320–21; J. S. A. Adamson, 'The peerage in politics, 1645–49' (Cambridge University PhD, 1986), p. 159.

[93] PRO, SP 16/167, fo. 86; G. Jenkins, 'The archpriest controversy and the printers 1601–1603', *The Library*, 5th series 2 (1947–48), pp. 180–86; M. Curtis, 'William Jones: Puritan printer and propagandist', *The Library*, 5th series 19 (1964).

[94] G. Aylmer, 'Collective mentalities in mid-seventeenth century England II: royalist attitudes', *TRHS*, 5th series 37 (1987), pp. 19–20; S. R. Gardiner, 'Collections by Isaack Walton for the life of John Hales of Eton', *EHR* 2 (1887), p. 751; *Letters and Journals of Robert Baillie*, ii. 373, 377; Bodl. MS Clarendon 52, fos. 38, 70–75v; *NP* iii. 22–3; *The Remonstrance of the Presbyterie of Sterling* (Edinburgh, by Evan Tyler, 1651).

of the sort, although some were executed with more subtlety and guile than others. Little complaint was ever made about such works, and such disingenuousness was probably an accepted literary device and rhetorical form. The deceitfulness of such works was ultimately transparent; a fact which may or may not have been intentional. There are other examples, however, which fooled contemporaries and later historians, and which may have been more serious in intent. Nedham, for example, may have sought to discredit royalists in early 1660 by adopting a royalist voice in order to inculcate into the public a sense of the vindictiveness and likely retribution which would result from a restoration of the royalist cause, although his intention may have been to use such a work in order to dissuade the king, whose return seemed increasingly inevitable, from considering such policies.[95] Among royalists themselves, Sir Edward Hyde was responsible for *Two Speeches in the House of Peers*, which purported to publish copies of speeches by Lords Brooke and Pembroke, in which Pembroke was supposed to have advocated peace, while Brooke dissented.[96] This effort was, in part, the result of a wager between Charles and Viscount Falkland, after the king boasted that he could recognise anything written by Hyde. However, the latter, who claimed to have been unaware of this bet, recorded that the king failed to spot the deceit when shown the work, although he was 'very much pleased with reading the speeches and said he did not think that Pembroke could speak so long together'. The work was quickly exposed as a forgery by Parliament, and Brooke apparently wanted copies of the work to be burnt. However, it was not possible to burn Brooke's 'speech' without also burning Pembroke's, and the latter did not consent to consigning the book to the flames.[97] Another royalist who engaged in such forgeries was William Chillingworth, who penned *A Petition of the Most Substantial Inhabitants of the City of London*, although his handiwork was soon detected, not least by the bookseller George Thomason.[98] Thomas Swadlin, meanwhile, was responsible for inventing *A Letter of an Independent to his Honoured Friend Mr Glyn*, which pretended that the Independents would seriously consider an accommodation with the king if the latter would grant religious toleration.[99] Perhaps the most impressive forgery, however, was a 1656 tract produced to order by Hyde, which was intended to 'awaken the people', and which claimed to be *A Letter from a True and Lawful Member of Parliament*. This work 'was made great use of to inflame the people, and make them sensible of the destruction that attended them, and was thought then to produce many good

---

[95] [M. Nedham], *News from Brussells* ([London], 1660). I am grateful to Dr Sean Kelsey for a very stimulating conversation on this point.

[96] *Two Speeches in the House of Peers* (London, 1642).

[97] Clarendon, *Life*, i. 161–3; *CJ* ii. 925.

[98] [W. Chillingworth], *A Petition of the Most Substantial Inhabitants of the City of London* (Oxford, 1642, E244/39); Peacey, 'Henry Parker', pp. 88–9.

[99] T. Swadlin, *A Letter of an Independent to his Honoured Friend Mr Glyn* ([Oxford], 1645); Madan, *Oxford Books*, ii. 411.

effects'. Nevertheless, Hyde may not have dreamed that it would be taken seriously as the work of the republican, Sir Henry Vane junior, nor that it would not be exposed until the late nineteenth century, upon the discovery of the manuscript in Hyde's hand.[100]

More intriguing still are instances when enemies were impersonated in order to discredit factional rivals. Having lost control of *Mercurius Britanicus* in 1645, for example, the Presbyterian faction evidently undertook to attack the paper through a work entitled *Aulicus His Hue and Cry Sent Forth After Britanicus*, which was clearly intended to be passed off as a predictable and self-satisfied response to the disappearance of *Britanicus* by the Oxford propagandists. Things are not always what they seem, however, and this work was evidently licensed and entered into the Stationers' Register.[101] While it was possible for works to be licensed under false pretences, it seems highly unlikely that a tract so clearly masquerading as a royalist work would have managed to fool anybody. More importantly, it is known to have been the work of Francis Cheynell, which provides us with enough clues to offer an explanation of its provenance and purpose.[102] Cheynell was a prominent Presbyterian member of the Westminster Assembly, but more significantly he was a chaplain to the Earl of Essex, and was a leading spokesman for his 'high Presbyterian' policy.[103] It seems likely, therefore, that Cheynell impersonated a royalist pen-man at the behest of Essex in order to attack *Britanicus*, in response to the way in which the earl was removed from his position of influence over the paper, and as an attempt to discredit (in advance) a new and anti-Essex incarnation of the newsbook. Although it appears strange that Gilbert Mabbott, no friend of the moderates or Presbyterians, should have licensed Cheynell's tract, it seems perfectly plausible that he saw an opportunity to discredit Thomas Audley, and to supplant him as deputy licenser. Cheynell got his work approved, and Mabbott got the job he wanted.[104] As if guided by an 'invisible hand', conflicting interests came to work for the same result very effectively. From what we know of the affairs of the mid-

---

[100] *A Letter from a True and Lawful Member of Parliament* (London, 1656); *CCSP* iii. 79; Bodl. MS Clarendon 50, fos. 256–89; Clarendon, *Life*, i. 308.

[101] *Aulicus His Hue and Cry* (London, 1645); *SR* i. 187; W. M. Clyde, 'Parliament and the press, 1643–7', *The Library*, 4th series 13 (1933), p. 417.

[102] Nedham did not attribute the *Hue and Cry to Aulicus: Mercurius Britanicus* 86 (9–16 Jun. 1645), p. 777. Wing attributed it to Cheynell, who was also responsible for at least one of two variant editions of *Aulicus His Dream of the King's Sudden Comming to London* (London, 1644), which appeared in May 1644. Thomason noted the difference between two versions of the tract – E47(22) and E47(23) – on the latter of which he wrote 'written by Mr Ffran: Chenell much different from the former'. Neither seems to have been the work of *Aulicus*, and Cheynell seems to have made changes to this tract in order to attack the Lords (then moving to eclipse Essex) and radicals like Marten, and to lessen the impact of the opposition to peace.

[103] *DNB*; A. Laurence, *Parliamentary Army Chaplains, 1642–1651* (Woodbridge, 1990), pp. 111–12; Adamson, 'Peerage in politics', pp. 104–5.

[104] Above, p. 152; *DNB Missing Persons* (Oxford, 1993).

1640s, we should not be surprised at the possibility of such tactics, nor of the ability of the leaders to tear themselves apart in such dramatic fashion.

However, it was also possible to impersonate factional rivals in order to usurp their position, and to undermine both their credibility and their ability to promulgate unwelcome views. This seems to have been a particularly important way in which royalist factionalism was manifested during the late 1640s. This can be demonstrated through the differences between individual newspapers, and by the rival versions of specific papers such as *Mercurius Pragmaticus*. A paper such as *Pragmaticus* can be shown to have existed in seventeen more or less well-established permutations, and while some of these may have emerged as a result of the financial incentive of capitalising upon a popular and well-respected journal, others emerged because of the need to reflect divergent attitudes within both the domestic and exiled royalist communities. This was most apparent over the viability and advisability of forging an alliance with the Scots, a policy not universally popular among royalist grandees. It seems evident that *Mercurius Elencticus* was made to speak for the faction which was most eager to support the king's Scottish alliance, while Marchamont Nedham's version of *Pragmaticus* expressed the views of those who distrusted the Scots and opposed a Presbyterian church settlement, and who favoured instead an alliance with the Westminster Independents. This picture was further complicated, however, by the way in which 'counterfeit' editions of *Pragmaticus* emerged on a regular basis, the more important of which represented an attempt to hijack the name of *Pragmaticus* in the interests of the pro-Scots lobby.[105] Furthermore, and as a consequence, *Elencticus* and *Pragmaticus*, as well as the various competing versions of *Pragmaticus*, adopted different positions on the likely fate of Charles I in late 1648 and early 1649, with Nedham and the pro-Independent strand of royalist commentators more inclined than their rivals to expect the king to survive, even if his power was removed, and to regard the legal proceedings against him as a form of negotiation with menaces, rather than as reflecting a bloodthirsty desire for his death.[106]

The various forms of ventriloquy confirm the subtlety with which grandees of all persuasions exploited the print medium in order to support the appearance of works which not only bore little evidence of official or political involvement, but which did not even appear to represent the ideas and interests of those by whom they were orchestrated. They also reveal the extent to which the subtlety with which propaganda was organised and deployed extended into factional politics within parliamentarian and royalist ranks, particularly in terms of discrediting and hijacking semi-official newspapers, which were sufficiently valued as political mouthpieces to be the targets for underhand political machinations in order to ensure the purity of their editorial lines.

---

[105] J. Peacey, '"The counterfeit silly curr": money, politics, and the forging of royalist newspapers in the English civil war' (paper delivered at NACBS conference, Baltimore, 2002).

[106] Peacey, '"The counterfeit silly curr"'.

Propaganda could be deployed, therefore, in a number of extremely subtle ways, and individual tracts could be produced and deployed in order to place a positive or negative spin on current events; to manipulate public opinion; to create the impression of popular support; and to give voice to opinions which were perceived to be useful but which could not be espoused openly, and to those which could be espoused in such a way as to discredit rivals and opponents. Recognising such tactical deployment of the printed word, and of polemical literature, necessitates adopting a sceptical and closely analytical approach to vast swathes of civil war literature, and the need for re-evaluation of a great number of apparently independent tracts. However, while the preceding analysis has revealed the most subtle conceptual uses of print and pamphleteering, the most dramatic way in which propaganda was utilised was in order to undertake not simply the production of pieces of polemic, but rather the deployment of tracts at key political moments, and the formulation of literary campaigns to support and coincide with military offensives and political projects.[107] There were many circumstances, in other words, in which it was necessary not merely to produce propaganda, but also to try and maximise its likely impact.

The press could clearly be manipulated, for example, as part of political machinations surrounding peace negotiations during the 1640s. It was employed, therefore, by those who were disinclined to make peace with the king during the Oxford treaty in the spring of 1643, but who nevertheless had to pay lip-service to the search for a negotiated settlement, and who could not afford the implications of being seen to oppose peace openly. Contemporaries certainly alleged that peace was supported in public while being undermined surreptitiously through the use of printed pamphlets. One royalist wrote that 'when they have done sweating in the persecution of peace in the pulpit, they assault her in the press'.[108] Furthermore, Sir Edward Hyde later reflected upon those at Westminster who, in December 1642, 'resumed all professions of a desire of peace', and who sought to 'stay the appetite of those who were importunate to have any advance made towards peace', and who probably intended to wrong-foot the king with petitions which expressed 'specious and popular professions of great piety and zeal to his service'. While talks progressed, however, Hyde alleged that 'the license of seditious and treasonable discourses daily increased'.[109] Such works included the 'fast' sermon delivered by John Arrowsmith on 25 January, published as *The Covenant-Avenging Sword Brandished*, which argued that war was a manifestation of God's will, and that the sword of vengeance was drawn by God, and by him would be sheathed.

---

107 V. M. Murphy, 'The debate over Henry VIII's first divorce. An analysis of the contemporary treatises' (Cambridge University PhD, 1984), p. 261; V. Murphy, 'The literature and propaganda of Henry VIII's first divorce', in D. MacCulloch, ed., *The Reign of Henry VIII* (Basingstoke, 1995); J. Black, 'The rhetoric of reaction: the Martin Marprelate tracts (1588–89), anti-martinism and the uses of print in early modern England', *The Sixteenth Century Journal*, 28 (1994).

108 *Sober Sadnes*, p. 20. See also: *A New Diurnall of Passages* (Oxford, 1643), sig. Av.

109 Clarendon, *History*, ii. 430, 432, 438.

Arrowsmith effectively implored readers to ignore those responsible for 'daily supplications for peace'.[110] More important was *Plaine English*, written by the army chaplain, Edward Bowles, who appeared to hint at the emergence of a more radical strand of parliamentarian thought. He justified war as 'the unhappy, yet not always, yet not now the unjust means' to procure peace, and expressed doubts about the likelihood of securing accommodation with the king, and he suggested that unless the Parliament dropped plans for peace, the people might withdraw their support. In doing so, his tract may represent a classic instance of 'functional radicalism', in which the political stakes were raised, and novel political arguments were developed, in the course of an attempt to achieve precise political goals on behalf of his friends in Parliament who sought a vigorous pursuit of the war effort.[111] Later, in preparation for the Uxbridge peace treaty in 1645, those who sought to ensure the success of the treaty deployed a number of tactics to ensure that the press echoed their views. *Mercurius Britanicus*, which had been spinning against peace in the weeks and months before the opening of talks, was hijacked by the Earl of Essex immediately before the talks began, and was quickly made to alter its editorial line regarding the prospects for negotiations. Another journalist, John Dillingham, editor of the *Parliament Scout*, was actually arrested, having been nominated as Oliver St John's assistant at the talks, because he was evidently expected to give voice to those who were hostile to peace.[112] One of the chaplains to the commissioners, however, Christopher Love, may have been encouraged to preach the provocative sermon in which he called Charles a 'man of blood', and although Love was imprisoned for such words, he was quickly released.[113]

Particularly vital to the success of such propaganda episodes was the timing of a particular work's publication. It is clear, for example, that the appearance of individual tracts could be timed to coincide with particular debates, in order to influence the opinions of MPs as well as the public. Henry Parker's *Altar Dispute*, therefore, appeared on the day of the second reading of the bill on church reform.[114] Furthermore, the presentation of petitions could also be timed to achieve maximum impact, and the London publisher and Presbyterian activist, John Bellamy, who was close to the Earl of Essex, is known on at least one occasion in

---

[110] J. Arrowsmith, *The Covenant-Avenging Sword Brandished* (London, 1643), pp. 5, 12; Trevor-Roper, 'Fast sermons', pp. 310–11.

[111] E. Bowles, *Plaine English* (np, 1643), pp. 2, 9–13, 21–2; D. Wootton, 'From rebellion to revolution: the crisis of the winter of 1642/3 and the origins of civil war radicalism', *EHR* 105 (1990); Laurence, *Chaplains*, pp. 101–2. For 'functional radicalism', see: Milton, 'Creation of Laudianism', pp. 177–9.

[112] J. Peacey, 'The struggle for *Mercurius Britanicus*: factional politics and the parliamentarian press, 1643–6' (forthcoming); A. N. B. Cotton, 'John Dillingham, journalist of the middle group', *EHR* 93 (1978), pp. 821, 824–5; *LJ* vii. 164. Dillingham would wait until the talks collapsed before successfully petitioning for his release: *HMC 6th Report*, p. 48; HLRO, MP 22/2/45.

[113] *CJ* iv. 40; Laurence, *Chaplains*, p. 149.

[114] [H. P]arker, *The Altar Dispute* (London, 1641); *LJ* iv. 296, 298; Gardiner, *Constitutional Documents*, p. 167.

May 1646 to have asked his political superiors to name the day that they required him to deliver the Presbyterian petition to Parliament.[115] The petition, complaining about sectarians, and calling for a settlement with the king, was presented on 26 May, when the Lords nominated a committee to prepare a response, which was eventually printed by Bellamy.[116] However, questions of timing could also cause works to be abandoned. Having planned pamphlet attacks upon the Marquess of Ormond in the autumn of 1646, for example, Parliament's decision to re-open negotiations with Ormond caused publication plans to be altered. In particular, Adam Meredith's *Ormond's Curtain Drawn*, written upon the advice of Sir John Temple, was aborted in the press.[117]

The most obvious way in which propaganda was used in coordination with other political measures during specific campaigns was through prominent political trials. In 1637, the publication of Heylyn's commissioned reply to Henry Burton was apparently 'kept in readiness' until the execution of the Star Chamber sentence against Burton, Bastwick and Prynne, 'that so people might be satisfied as well in the greatness of the crimes, as the necessity and justice of the punishment inflicted upon those offenders'.[118] During the Long Parliament, it has been demonstrated that publication of the charges against Strafford, and the speeches of his prosecutors, which were effected against the wishes of the House of Lords, helped foment debate and polarise opinion, and served not only to pressurise the Lords, but also to talk to a broad section of the political nation.[119] The most accomplished exponent of such trial-propaganda, however, was its former victim, William Prynne. In the years between 1643 and 1645, Prynne acted as witch-hunter general for the Commons; prosecuting through both the courts and the booksellers those enemies of Parliament who were brought to trial. The first evidence of Prynne's ability to coordinate his legal and propaganda work was in

---

[115] Dr Williams Library, MS 24.50 (diary of Thomas Juxon), fo. 79. For the timing of petitions, see: Cust, 'Charles I and popularity', p. 279.

[116] *LJ* viii. 331–4. This committee was evenly divided between the friends and enemies of Essex, and when Manchester delivered the committee's answer to the Lords, Essex's opponents (Northumberland, Pembroke, Saye, Denbigh, Salisbury, Kent, Wharton, Grey, Howard and Montague) made a formal registration of their dissent. Their protest was of no avail, however, and the petition, together with the answer read by Manchester, was ordered to be printed: *LJ* viii. 332. See: V. Pearl, 'London's counter-revolution', in G. E. Aylmer, ed., *The Interregnum* (London, 1972).

[117] [Sir. Temple and A. Meredith], *Ormonds Curtain Drawn* ([London, S. Gellibrand, 1646], E513/14). Thomason possessed the only known copy of this book, which breaks off at page 32, and he noted that it was written by Temple 'but not finished'. He appears to have obtained his copy from Gellibrand. See: J. S. A. Adamson, 'Strafforde's ghost: the British context of Viscount Lisle's lieutenancy of Ireland', in J. H. Ohlmeyer, ed., *Ireland From Independence to Occupation, 1641–1660* (Cambridge, 1995), p. 140; P. Little, 'The Irish Independents and Viscount Lisle's lieutenancy of Ireland', *HJ* 44 (2001), pp. 953–4; Peacey, 'Henry Parker', pp. 119–20.

[118] G. Vernon, *The Life of the Learned and Reverend Dr Peter Heylyn* (London, 1682), p. 91.

[119] T. Kilburn and A. Milton, 'The public context of the trial and execution of Strafford', in J. F. Merritt, ed., *The Political World of Thomas Wentworth, Earl of Strafford, 1621–1641* (Cambridge, 1996), pp. 232–5, 237.

the 1643 prosecution of the parliamentarian MP and military commander, Nathaniel Fiennes, for his part in the capitulation of Bristol. Fiennes sought to defend himself in print, but Prynne and his friend Clement Walker, a member of Fiennes' council of war at Bristol, responded with *An Answer to Col: Nathaniel Fiennes Relation*. Fiennes countered not merely in print, but also with a plot to silence Walker, which alleged that he had spoken slanderous words against Viscount Saye. Upon Walker's committal in October, Fiennes orchestrated the appearance of *The True Causes of the Commitment of Mr C. Walker*; a fraudulent piece purporting to have been written by Walker himself.[120] Walker was released after presenting a succession of petitions, while Prynne, who was chosen to lead the prosecution, prepared the ground with his account of *The Doome of Cowardize and Treachery*, which appeared in the first week of November 1643, shortly before presentation of the 'articles of impeachment'.[121] Although successful in the prosecution of Fiennes at his trial before the general council of the army in December 1643, the death sentence was commuted by the Lord General, against the wishes of Prynne and Walker, who subsequently ventured into print with a detailed account of the trial in August 1644.[122] To this, furthermore, they added allegations regarding Fiennes' manipulation of the press; his forgery of the Walker pamphlet; his bribery of *Mercurius Britanicus*; and his plot to silence one of the prosecutors.[123]

Far more dramatic, however, was Prynne's propaganda in support of the proceedings against Archbishop Laud. In time for the *scheduled* opening of Laud's trial, Prynne published a chunk of the papers which he himself had helped seize from the archbishop's chamber in the Tower, as *The Popish Royal Favourite*.[124] Later, when Parliament granted Laud permission to present a recapitulation of his defence, Prynne was presented with an opportunity to pull off one of the most impressive propaganda coups of the period, and one of the most cynical and calculated uses of the press. The archbishop appeared before Parliament on 2 September, the very day that Prynne's *Breviate of the Life of William Laud* appeared in print. The appearance of this edition of Laud's diary was intended, therefore, to influence not merely the public's perception of Laud, but also the

---

[120] N. Fiennes, *A Relation Made in the House of Commons* (London, nd); *Colonell Fiennes Letter to my Lord General Concerning Bristol* (London, 1643); C. Walker and W. Prynne, *An Answer to Col: Nathaniel Fiennes Relation* (London, 1643); *Colonell Fiennes his Reply* (London, 1643); *The True Causes of the Commitment of Mr C. Walker* (np, nd); T. May, *The History of the Parliament of England* (London, 1647, reprinted Oxford, 1854), pp. 282–3; *HMC 6th Report*, p. 196. Prynne and Walker made the allegation that Fiennes was responsible for trying to silence Walker and for publishing the forgery: *A True and Full Relation of the Prosecution* (London, 1644), pp. 3–4.

[121] *HMC 5th Report*, pp. 108, 110, 111, 112; *LJ* vi. 241, 247, 265, 273, 278, 282; *CJ* iii. 280, 311; W. Prynne, *The Doome of Cowardize* (London, 1643); *SR* i. 81; Bodl. MS Tanner 62, fo. 363; *HMC 6th Report*, p. 1.

[122] *State Trials*, iv. 186–315; *The Humble Petition of Clement Walker and Will. Prynne* (np, nd).

[123] Walker and Prynne, *True and Full Relation*, pp. 2–4, 114.

[124] W. Prynne, *The Popish Royal Favourite* (London, 1643), pp. 34–5.

very members of Parliament he was about to address. Laud himself commented that, as he entered Parliament, 'so soon as I came to the bar I saw every lord present with a new thin book in folio, in a blue cover. I heard that morning that Mr Prynne had printed my diary, and published it to the world to disgrace me'.[125] The *Breviate*, however, formed merely the 'necessary prologue', as Prynne put it, to the story of Laud's trial. The 'necessary introduction' took the form of *Hidden Workes of Darkenes*, which appeared in December 1644, and which paved the way for *Canterburies Doom*, published following a Commons order that Prynne should print proceedings of Laud's trial. Although the legal case against Laud had proved no more successful than that against Strafford, the publication of *Hidden Workes* was probably intended to assist the process of convincing the Lords to agree to pass an ordinance of attainder, which they finally did on 4 January, clearing the way for the archbishop's execution on Tower Hill six days later.[126]

Later trials witnessed similar tactics. During the trial of Charles I in January 1649, two leading journalists, Henry Walker and Gilbert Mabbott, were granted access to the proceedings, and produced piecemeal accounts of the trial which gave Englishmen the most frequent news service they had ever witnessed, as well as collected editions of the proceedings. That two men were granted such privileges reflected factional tension within Westminster, between army radicals and Independent grandees, and each man gave his coverage subtle political spin, and reflected different attitudes towards the trial and the defendant.[127] A similar campaign was undertaken against the convicted Presbyterian plotter, Christopher Love. A huge number of works appeared in favour of Love both before and after his execution in the summer of 1651, including copies of his petitions and correspondence, as well as his scaffold speech and funeral sermon, and his vindicatory pieces written in prison. In addition, there appeared an account of the trial, and a substantial work called *Love's Advocate*. This literary barrage forced the Rump to issue a reply, which came in the form of John Hall's *A Gagg to Love's Advocate*. The speed with which this was produced, and the fact that it was printed by the Council's official printer, indicates the importance placed on countering Love's supporters.[128] Another enemy of the republican regime received similar

[125] W. Prynne, *A Breviate* (London, 1644); *SR* i. 130; *HMC House of Lords XI*, p. 457; Laud, *Works*, iv. 369; *Kingdomes Weekly Intelligencer* 70 (27 Aug.–3 Sept. 1644), p. 566; H. Trevor-Roper, *Archbishop Laud* (London, 1963), pp. 418–23.

[126] W. Prynne, *Hidden Workes* (London, 1645), epistle to the reader; *SR* i. 141; Trevor-Roper, *Laud*, pp. 427–8; Prynne, *Canterburies Doom*; *CJ* iv. 16, 68; W. G. Palmer, 'Invitation to a beheading: factions in Parliament, the Scots, and the execution of Archbishop Laud in 1645', *Historical Magazine of the Protestant Episcopal Church* 52 (1983).

[127] J. Peacey, 'Reporting a revolution: a failed propaganda campaign', in Peacey, ed., *The Regicides and the Execution of Charles I* (Basingstoke, 2001), pp. 161–9.

[128] J. H[all], *A Gagg to Love's Advocate* (London, for Dugard, 1652); J. Davies, 'An account of the author', in J. Hall, *Hierocles Upon the Golden Verses* (London, 1657), sig. b4v. For the volume of works concerning Love, see: *Catalogue of the Pamphlets, Books, Newspapers and Manuscripts Collected by George Thomason, 1640–1661* (2 vols, London, 1908), i. 841–4.

treatment. Before John Lilburne's 1649 trial, therefore, there appeared Cuthbert Sydenham's *An Anatomy of Lievt. Col. John Lilburn's Spirit and Pamphlets*, which, if it was not commissioned, was certainly rewarded handsomely.[129] Later, on the day that Lilburne's 1653 trial began, there appeared *Several Informations and Examinations*, which had been printed by the official publishers, read in the House of Commons, and dispersed through the army, and which was based upon official intelligence.[130] Following the trial, furthermore, official hacks such as John Hall and John Canne responded to the Levellers in works which were printed officially, and advertised in the official newspapers. Hall issued *Sedition Scourg'd* in reply to the *Charge of High Treason* which had been levelled against Cromwell, and which was distributed through London streets on 14 September 1653, while Canne produced *Lieut. Colonel John Lilb. Tryed and Cast*.[131]

It was not merely in relation to trials, however, that propaganda was deployed in order to contribute to politically driven campaigns. Prynne, for example, was able to exploit his literary talents in order to support his campaigning work as chairman of the Committee of Accounts, which he had helped fashion into a powerful tool of the Presbyterian faction.[132] One pamphlet which appeared in early 1647, and which may have been Prynne's handiwork, was *London's Account*; an attack upon the 'arbitrary and tyrannical exactions, taxations, impositions, excises, contributions, subsidies, twentieth parts, and other assessments', and an accusation against that money 'which your sharking committee-men resolve to give no good account of'.[133] That the appearance of this tract was unwelcome to the Independents, at whom the accusations were doubtless levelled, is clear from the fact that the Commons labelled it an 'obnoxious' pamphlet within a day of its publication, and from the unfriendly comments which it occasioned from the Independent author of *The Moderate Intelligencer*, who claimed that the account was 'most false'.[134] Later, Prynne was able to undertake both the literary and legal defence of the impeached 'eleven members', who had been targeted by the Independents in response to the Presbyterian counter-revolution in the first half of 1647. Prynne's involvement in their defence was particularly apposite, given that more than one of the individuals had been accused of financial impropriety. Sir John Clotworthy's defence, therefore, was undertaken by Prynne not merely in the Committee of Accounts, but also as counsel for the eleven members, and in the

---

[129] [C. Sydenham], *An Anatomy of Lievt. Col. John Lilburn's Spirit and Pamphlets* (London, 1649); see above p. 196.

[130] *Several Information and Examinations* (London, 1653).

[131] J. Hall, *Sedition Scourg'd* (London, 1653); *CSPD 1653–4*, pp. 151, 180, 187, 200; *CJ* vii. 333; [J. Canne], *Lieut. Colonel John Lilb. Tryed and Cast* (London, 1653); *Mercurius Politicus* 181 (24 Nov.–2 Dec. 1653), p. 3006.

[132] J. Peacey, 'Politics, accounts and propaganda in the Long Parliament', in C. R. Kyle and J. Peacey, eds, *Parliament at Work* (Woodbridge, 2002).

[133] *London's Account* ([London], 1647), p. 7.

[134] *CJ* v. 72–3; *The Moderate Intelligencer* 100 (28 Jan.–4 Feb. 1647), p. 890.

press. Prynne insisted in one pamphlet that 'the sums pretended that Sir John Clotworthy hath defrauded the state of, some are false, the rest expressed in his account'.[135] Prynne's use of the committee and the press in tandem in this way also served to defend another of the impeached MPs, Sir William Lewis, regarding his accounts as governor of Portsmouth. Prynne's anonymous pamphlet defence of the eleven members referred to 'an unanswerable certificate of the committee for taking the accounts of the whole kingdom', which had 'found it a very fair and frugal account'. Prynne supplemented this by producing another anonymous pamphlet specifically in defence of Lewis, which consisted of nothing more than a reprint of the certificate issued by the Committee of Accounts in 1645.[136] Prynne's defence of the eleven members also took the form of a counter-offensive against Independent enemies, on the grounds of their financial corruption. He attacked 'divers great officers in the army who ... have hitherto given in no accounts, and profess ingeniously they cannot do it, and thereupon cavil against the ordinances and committee of accounts and slander them in their declarations'.[137] In *The Hypocrites Unmasking*, meanwhile, Prynne launched an attack upon the Independent grandee, Viscount Lisle, who had allegedly received over £230,000 of public money for Irish service. Prynne claimed that Lisle had:

> obstructed the relief of Ireland, of purpose to gain a new commission for himself to be governor there; rather to promote his own ends, and the Independents interests and designs, than the welfare of the bleeding kingdom, which hath already suffered too much by his service (bought at an over dear rate) as will appear by his accounts when they come to be examined.

Another Independent grandee, Sir Hardress Waller – 'a great stickler against the accused members' – allegedly failed to go to Ireland despite having received over £5,000 from Parliament.[138] Furthermore, having been enlisted as counsel by the impeached Presbyterians, Prynne produced their 'official' defence, in *A Full Vindication and Answer of the XI Accused Members*, which was presented to Parliament on 19 July.[139]

The clearest way, therefore, in which print proved to be a weapon in political manoeuvres as well as in manipulating popular opinion, was by being deployed in coordination with political events and actions. Press campaigns were undertaken, in other words, alongside peace treaties, in order to give voice to agendas which could not be owned publicly, and in association with high profile political trials, in order to influence juries and judges. They were used in order to affect public opinion regarding individuals who were perceived to hold sway over the popular

---

135 [W. Prynne], *A Brief Justification of the XI Accused Members* (London, 1647), pp. 6–7; *A Full Vindication and Answer of the XI Accused Members* (London, 1647), pp. 20–23, 29–33.

136 [W. Prynne], *A Vindication of Sir William Lewis* (London, 1647); PRO, SP 28/255, unfol.: certificate of committee of accounts, 15 Mar. 1645.

137 [Prynne], *Brief Justification*, p. 9.

138 [W. Prynne], *The Hypocrites Unmasking* (London, 1647), pp. 5–8.

139 D. Underdown, *Pride's Purge* (Oxford, 1971), p. 82.

imagination, and whose judicial treatment was likely to provoke political unrest and civil disorder, as well as in support of everyday political activity, and the work of key parliamentary committees.

Demonstrating the sophistication of political propaganda requires, however, not merely the exploration of the conceptual uses of print, and the variety of ways in which polemic was deployed during the civil wars. It also requires consideration of the occasions on which political grandees demonstrated awareness of the need to deploy the full force of the literary skills at their disposal, and of the fact that certain political situations were sufficiently important to merit 'multi-media' campaigns, involving the exploitation of a wide range of individual works, and a variety of techniques.

The military campaign against the Scots during the early stages of the Rump, for example, was accompanied by a polemical campaign which drew together many different aspects of the regime's propaganda machinery. In part, the Rump needed official statements of its policy, which could be directed at the English, the Scots and the Continent, and John Milton was ordered to translate at least one of the declarations justifying the Scottish campaign into Latin, although Thomas May eventually undertook the task, before sending it to William Dugard to be printed.[140] The Council of State even went so far as to sanction Dugard's production of a new edition of Henry VIII's declaration against the Scots from 1542.[141] It was also necessary, of course, for the government to respond to declarations by the Scots, and Walter Frost was responsible for licensing an annotated edition of one of the statements issued by Montrose.[142] Much more weighty polemical works were also required, of course, and the importance of the anti-Scottish propaganda campaign is evident from the number of works produced in relation to Cromwell's military campaign, and from comments by men such as Robert Lilburne, who wrote to Cromwell from Scotland in early 1651 expressing his desire 'that some able minister were here to speak in public, and that I had some of Mr Owen's sermons, and other books to disperse amongst them'.[143] Some such literature may have catered for a domestic market, such as the sermon preached at Somerset House by the official journalist, Henry Walker, on the day that the troops marched out of London, which was printed at the cost of the Council of State (£20).[144] The English

---

[140] *A Declaration of the Parliament of England Upon the Marching of the Army into Scotland* (London, 1650); *Declaratio Parlamenti Angliae* (London, 1650); J. M. French, *The Life Records of John Milton* (5 vols, New Brunswick, 1949–58), ii. 317–18; *CSPD 1650*, p. 228.

[141] *A Declaration Conteyning the Just Causes and Considerations of this Present War with the Scots* (London, by Dugard, 1651).

[142] *A Short Reply Unto a Declaration Entitled the Declaration of the Army of England ... Together with a Vindication of the Declaration* (London, 1650); *The Declaration of ... Montrose* (London, 1650), p. 22.

[143] J. Nickolls, *Original Letters and Papers of State* (London, 1743), p. 48.

[144] H. Walker, *The Creation of the World* (London, 1649); *SR* i. 334; H. Walker, *A Sermon Preached in the Chapell at Sommerset House* (London, 1650); *CSPD 1650*, p. 345; J. B. Williams,

public also needed to be presented with regular supplies of news from the North, which explains why John Hall was ordered to accompany Cromwell to Scotland, and why Walter Frost worked with Dugard to produce narratives of military successes, including the relation sent from George Downing, scoutmaster of the army in Scotland, and reports sent from ministers such as Robert Stapylton, which were eagerly printed at official request.[145]

Among the more polemical tracts which the regime sanctioned for print, Dugard was clearly set to work to print an attack upon the Scottish Kirk written by James Rew, as well as an exposé of Charles II's relations with Rome, while Frost was commissioned to compile a historical account of relations between England and Scotland.[146] However, the most important propaganda against the Scots was provided by the leading authors in the pay of the Council. Cuthbert Sydenham produced *An English Translation of the Scottish Declaration*, as well as *The False Brother*; Marchamont Nedham devoted a chapter of *The Case of the Commonwealth* to a justification of the Scottish campaign; Thomas May published *The Changeable Covenant*; and John Hall provided tracts to add historical weight to the campaign.[147] Such works could not only be printed by men such as Newcomb, but could also be advertised in *Politicus*.[148] However, the case of Peter English demonstrates the willingness of the regime to co-opt the services of writers on an *ad hoc* basis as well, and to target specific audiences. English's attack upon the ideas of Salmasius, printed in *The Survey of Policy* in early 1654, was orchestrated by the leading agents of the commonwealth in Scotland, supervised by the commissioners at Dalkeith, and printed at Leith. The aim of the episode clearly appears to have been to mobilise Scottish authors and presses against the Scottish royalists.[149]

'Henry Walker, journalist of the commonwealth', *Nineteenth Century and After* 65 (1908), p. 462; J. B. Williams, *A History of English Journalism* (London, 1908), pp. 139–41; *Mercurius Pragmaticus* 14 (17–24 July 1649), sig. O3.

[145] *A Brief Narrative* (London, 1650); *SR* i. 350. See also: *A Declaration of the Army of England Upon their March into Scotland* (London, 1650); *A Declaration of the Army of the Commonwealth of England to the People of Scotland* (London, 1650); *A True Relation of the Proceedings of the English Army Now in Scotland* (London, 1650); *A Declaration of the English Army Now in Scotland* (London, 1650); G. Downing, *A True Relation* (London, 1651); *CSPD 1651*, p. 312; *CJ* vi. 535; R. Stapylton, *A More Full Relation of the Great Victory* (London, 1651); Laurence, *Chaplains*, pp. 177–8. For Hall, see above pp. 199–200; *CSPD 1650*, p. 325; Chequers, MS 782, fos. 6–13v; Davies, 'Account', sigs. b4–b4v; Abbott, *Cromwell*, ii. 584–5.

[146] J. Rew, *The Wounds of the Kirk of Scotland* (London, by Dugard, 1650); *SR* i. 351; *The King of Scotland's Negotiations at Rome* (London, 1650); *Collonel Grey's Portmanteau Opened* (London, 1650); *CSPD 1650*, pp. 221, 228, 550; *CJ* vi. 434–5; [W. Frost], *Remarkable Observations* (London, 1651); D. Masson, *The Life of John Milton* (7 vols, London, 1871–80), iv. 323; *CSPD 1651*, p. 388.

[147] Above, pp. 193–200; M. Nedham, *The Case of the Commonwealth of England Stated* (London, 1650, ed. P. A. Knachel, Charlottesville, Va., 1969), pp. 73–9; *CSPD 1650*, p. 228; T. May, *The Changeable Covenant* (London, 1650).

[148] *Mercurius Politicus* 31 (2–9 Jan. 1651), p. 518; *Mercurius Politicus* 60 (24–31 July 1651), sig. Eeeeee4v.

[149] P. English, *The Survey of Policy* (Leith, 1653); Worcester College, Clarke MS XLIV, p. 1.

Another broad press campaign which demonstrates the weight and variety of English propaganda which could be produced by the 1650s, centred on relations with the Dutch. Tension between the two nations, fuelled by the murder of the English agent Isaac Dorislaus, and the Dutch treaty with Spain, was exacerbated by the failure of Oliver St John's diplomatic mission in 1651, and eventually led to war (May 1652). In part, the Rump's propaganda effort involved advocacy of English trade policies in a general sense, through the works of advisers and administrators such as William Potter and Henry Robinson, at least some of which were officially encouraged and officially printed, and discussed Anglo-Dutch relations more or less explicitly.[150] More importantly, print was also deployed in a more focused way, in order to support specific pieces of legislation, in the form of the Navigation Act, which was defended in works that bore the hallmark of official instigation from the pen of Benjamin Worsley.[151] Moreover, the Council also orchestrated more scholarly works that supported such policies, by securing the republication of Sir John Borough's *The Sovereignty of the Seas*, to which the public's attention was drawn in the pages of *Politicus*.[152] Other works, meanwhile, addressed the need to respond to the propaganda produced by opponents, not least that which narrated the attempts by exiled royalists to scupper Oliver St John's diplomatic mission. The council seized imported copies of a book called *An Answer to the Propositions Made by the English Ambassadors*, written by Sir William MacDowal, Charles Stuart's resident at the Hague, and commissioned a response, which appeared as *Anglia Liberata*, again advertised by Nedham.[153] Moreover, tracts were deployed as part of diplomatic tactics, in the shape of a work by John Hall which revived allegations regarding the Amboyna massacre of 1624. Hall's work was not only advertised by Nedham, but was also published to coincide with the arrival of the Dutch ambassadors, in what may have been an attempt to undermine the talks or at least influence their outcome.[154]

Following the outbreak of hostilities with the Dutch, the commonwealth obviously needed to explain and justify its war against another Protestant country

---

[150] Above, pp. 105–6; W. Potter, *The Key of Wealth* (London, 1650); *SR* i. 350; *DNB*; W. Potter, *The Tradesman's Jewel* (London, for Husband and Field, 1650); H. Robinson, *Briefe Considerations Concerning the Advancement of Trade and Navigation* (London, 1649); *CSPD 1649–40*, p. 475; *CSPD 1650*, pp. 120, 182–3; PRO, SP 18/9, fos. 103–6; H. Robinson, *Certain Considerations* (London, 1651); H. Robinson, *Certain Proposals* (London, 1652).

[151] B. W[orsley], *The Advocate* (London, by Dugard, 1650); B. W[orsley], *Free Ports* (London, by Dugard, 1652).

[152] Sir J. Borough, *The Sovereignty* (London, 1651); *SR* i. 366; Rushworth, *Collections*, ii. 320; *Mercurius Politicus* 89 (12–19 Feb. 1652), p. 1424.

[153] *CSPD 1651*, p. 389; Sir W. MacDowal, *An Answer* (Hague, 1651); *DNB; Anglia Liberata* (London, 1651). Theodore Haak appears to have been involved in translating this last work, and was paid £100 for doing so: *CSPD 1651–2*, p. 619; Nickolls, *Original Letters and Papers*, pp. 55, 161; *Mercurius Politicus* 70 (2–9 Oct. 1651), p. 1124.

[154] [J. Hall], *A True Relation* (London, 1651); above, pp. 165, 200; S. Pincus, *Protestantism and Patriotism. Ideologies and the Making of English Foreign Policy, 1650–1668* (Cambridge, 1996), p. 59; *Mercurius Politicus* 77 (20–27 Nov. 1651), p. 1236.

to a domestic audience, and it thus orchestrated the publication of official statements which were printed by William Dugard. However, they also sought to secure translations of such pieces into Latin and French for export purposes, with the help of the Latin secretary, John Milton.[155] Among other works which justified the war to a domestic audience, Nedham's translation of Selden's *Mare Clausum*, the preface to which made explicit its pertinence to Anglo-Dutch relations, was obviously official in nature, although it was evidently valued on account of the reputation of its author, and of the sense of connection which it offered to an earlier age. Selden's work is also interesting for the light it sheds upon the eagerness of the regime to orchestrate propaganda, which is apparent not merely from the fact that it was plugged by Nedham's newspaper, but also from the extent to which logistical resources were deployed in order to ensure its publication. The authorities arranged and paid for its translation, organised its frontispiece, and orchestrated its printing, all of which appears to have been undertaken by the Council's committee for foreign affairs.[156] Aware of the need to supplement both official declarations and tracts which were transparently official in origin, however, the commonwealth regime may also have drawn upon the services of old friends, such as Francis Osborne, a longtime associate of the Earl of Pembroke, who produced *A Seasonable Expostulation with the Netherlands* in June 1652.[157] The council certainly relied upon official writers such as Nedham, who produced *The Case Stated Between England and the United Provinces* a month later.[158] Thurloe, meanwhile, exploited the intelligence-gathering network under his control, not least by digesting letters regarding the Dutch fleet, which appeared in *A True Relation of the Late Engagement* in June 1652, and by using official printers to publish relations of military manoeuvres sent to Whitehall from Robert Blake and George Monck.[159] Thurloe's diplomatic and intelligence roles, and his access to official papers, also assisted in the process of educating the public regarding the nature of Dutch internal political affairs. This had been undertaken since late 1650 in works produced by the Council's official printer, but was extended with Dugard's publication of the chronicle of the *Notable Revolutions* in

---

[155] *A Declaration of the Parliament of the Commonwealth* (London, 1652); *Scriptum Parlamenti Angliae* (London, Dugard, 1652); *La Declaration du Parlement de la Republique d'Angleterre* (London, Dugard, 1652); French, *Life Records*, iii. 229–33; *CSPD 1651–2*, p. 338; L. Miller, *John Milton's Writings in the Anglo-Dutch Negotiations, 1651–1654* (Pittsburgh, 1992), pp. 197–269.

[156] *Mercurius Politicus* 130 (25 Nov.–2 Dec. 1652), p. 2056; J. Selden, *Of the Dominion, or Ownership of the Sea* (London, 1652); *CSPD 1651–2*, pp. 303, 358, 483.

[157] F. Osborne, *A Seasonable Expostulation* (Oxford, 1652); *DNB*.

[158] *The Case Stated Between England and the United Provinces* (London, by Newcomb, 1652); *Mercurius Politicus* 112 (22–29 July 1652), p. 1768.

[159] PRO, SP 25/67, pp. 121, 134; Miller, *Milton's Writings*, pp. 47–8, 56; Nickolls, *Original Letters and Papers*, p. 87; R. Blake and G. Monck, *A True Relation of the Late Great Sea Fight* (London, Hills and Brewster, 1653); G. Monck, *A True Relation* (London, Calvert, Hills, and Brewster, 1653); *A Declaration from the General and Council of State* (London, Calvert, Hills, and Brewster, 1653); *SR* i. 420.

Holland of 1650–51, which was the work of Lieuwe van Aitzema, and which was based upon official documents. Aitzema clearly met Thurloe shortly before the Dutch hostilities began, and was also responsible for supplying the secretary with intelligence from the Continent.[160]

The multi-media approach to the task of deploying propaganda in support of political activity provides an expression of the seriousness with which grandees took the task of encouraging support within the political elite, the broader political nation, and the wider world of European affairs. Moreover, it reflects not just their appreciation of the extent to which resources needed to be mobilised, but also their understanding that specific political campaigns involved tasks and audiences which required different kinds of works, and different propaganda techniques. Nevertheless, the ability to combine conceptual understanding of propaganda with the political and administrative resources with which to undertake complex and multi-faceted literary campaigns was probably restricted to the commonwealth regime of the 1650s, and was most clearly evident from the propaganda orchestrated by the Council of State during the politico-military campaigns within the three kingdoms, and the geo-political conflict with the Dutch in the early years of the decade.

Subtle conceptual understanding of the power of print was possessed by individuals on all sides during the 1640s and 1650s. Print could be used in order to undertake news management, and in order to place political spin on current events, as well as to manipulate bodies of evidence with which the public were presented. It could also be used in an attempt to manufacture consent, and to convince the public that such consent already existed. And it could be used in order to give voice to those with whom it was impossible to associate openly, and to orchestrate the undermining of factional rivals in the world of newspapers. Moreover, print could be deployed in more or less close coordination with political machinations, legislative initiatives and judicial proceedings, and the gamut of propaganda techniques could be deployed simultaneously in order to create a campaign which was as complex and conceptually sophisticated as the audience for print, and as the task of political communication in a period of domestic and international conflict. Print was, in other words, a political weapon, and propaganda was part of the political process, rather than merely a commentary upon it and a means of securing support. Its power was understood by royalists and parliamentarians alike, who displayed conceptual subtlety not merely against each other, but also in their respective factional battles. Recognition of the fact that

---

[160] *A Faithful Advertisement* (London, by Dugard, 1650); L. W., *The Troubles of Amsterdam* (London, by Dugard, 1650); *SR* i. 352; *CSPD 1650*, p. 463; L. van Aitzema, *Notable Revolutions* (London, by Dugard, 1653); *TSP* i. 649; *TSP* ii. 480; *TSP* iii. 747; H. H. Rowen, 'Lieuwe van Aitzema: a soured but knowing eye', in P. Mack and M. C. Jacob, eds, *Politics and Culture in Early Modern Europe* (Cambridge, 1987), pp. 169–72, 176.

propaganda was a tool of the political process must influence our appreciation of the subtlety of those processes, and the nature and complexity of particular political situations. The ability to demonstrate political involvement in manipulation of print alters our perceptions regarding the beliefs and attitudes of contemporary grandees. It also provides a means of overcoming the absence of information regarding their motivations, aims and intentions at key moments during England's troubles, whether in terms of the attitude of opponents of Caroline policies before the outbreak of war, or in terms of the desires of key political players regarding specific constitutional proposals and reforms, from the militia bill to the nature of the protectorate.

CHAPTER 8

The Propagandist and the Politician

Understanding the 'dynamic' of propaganda consists not just in appreciating the tactics with which print was deployed and the uses to which it was put. Another avenue for analysis relates to examination of the relationships between propagandists and politicians. This can be explored both statically and dynamically, by investigating the various types of relationship which can be detected, as well as the ways in which those relationships developed over time. Such analysis is vital for understanding particular works, individual authors, and the nature of early modern propaganda in general. In part, this relates to the proximity of authors to their patrons, and the depth of their attachment, as well as the extent to which authors were selling their services, and the degree to which they were expressing personal beliefs. It involves questions of the exclusivity of literary service, and the degree of personal commitment to the interests which authors were willing to represent in print, not to mention the possibility that authors had other roles, purposes and goals – whether in terms of their careers or their financial needs – and the potential difficulties they faced in having to compromise personal ideals and beliefs in order to fulfil the requirements placed upon them by their patrons. Moreover, assessing author–grandee relations requires gaining an appreciation of the role and influence of money, and reaching conclusions relating to the extent to which the desire to acquire, or not to lose, a particular source of income affected authors' decisions, as well as the extent to which political principles existed in balance with financial necessity, both at particular moments and over the course of time, as personal and political circumstances changed. Indeed, given the nature of the conclusions in preceding chapters, it is impossible to avoid meditating upon the impact of the gradual professionalisation of propaganda. Understanding the dynamic of author–patron relations also requires exploration, however, of the circumstances in which authors became, and ceased to be, propagandists, and the cases of authors shifting their allegiance between patrons and even political sides, as well as those cases where authors found themselves in hot water with their patrons and employers as a result of their literary activity. In large part, therefore, an appreciation of author–patron relations rests upon an examination of the 'loyalty' and 'reliability' of authors. There are many opportunities to explore instances where authors, printers and licensers were accused by contemporaries, or subsequent scholars, of having been unreliable, in terms of having failed to undertake what was required of them, of having overstepped the mark of acceptability, or of having changed sides in an opportunistic and self-serving manner.

The place to commence analysis of author–patron relations is by outlining the different kinds of relationships which can be observed, and which have been noted in the preceding chapters. Not all authors (or indeed printers and publishers) can be contextualised in terms of relations with politicians and patrons. Polemicists such as Philip Hunton, author of some of the most important parliamentarian theory of the early 1640s, may have been driven merely by personal frustration with the work of royalist and parliamentarian contemporaries.[1] At the other extreme are authors such as Cuthbert Sydenham and Marchamont Nedham, the bulk of whose works can be understood as having been produced at the behest of, or on behalf of, political patrons. Between these two extremes are to be found the majority of authors considered in this volume. Having identified characters who can be labelled 'propagandists', for having worked closely with politicians, it is necessary to recognise the ways in which the relationships forged by individual polemicists differed. Individuals could occupy a range of positions along a spectrum that stretched from the *ad hoc* hack to the full-time propaganda partner, and a range of positions along a second spectrum which extended from those who worked on the basis of debts of honour, obedience and personal attachment, to those who wrote on the basis of contractual ties and the cash-nexus. Some propagandists, therefore, worked on an *ad hoc* basis and for money, and ought to be considered as little more than hacks and hired-pens. One such case was the scrivener, Alexander Aspinwall, whose interrogation by officials of the restored Rump in July 1659 revealed that he had been hired in order to write two tracts in accordance with outlines delivered to him by John Dunch, for which he was paid (or promised) 20*s.* and 40*s.* respectively.[2] Other part-time propagandists, however, had much closer relationships with politicians and patrons, whether as principled partners or 'clients'. Perhaps we ought to include among their number writers such as William Prynne and John Sadler during the 1640s. A third extreme involved the full-time, salaried writer, examples of which include John Dury and Cuthbert Sydenham in the 1650s. A fourth 'ideal type' is provided by the loyal client, of which the early careers of Henry Parker and John Dillingham provided instances. Of course, few civil war propagandists fit such ideal types in a precise fashion, and few can be characterised in one way throughout their literary careers. Furthermore, this categorisation makes little allowance for the role of authors' own political principles.

Despite its limitations, however, this schematic representation of propaganda

---

[1] P. Hunton, *A Treatise of Monarchy* (London, 1643); P. Hunton, *A Vindication of the Treatise of Monarchy* (London, 1644); J. Peacey, 'Philip Hunton', *New DNB* (forthcoming).

[2] *CCSP* iv. 271–2, 282; Bodl. MS Clarendon 62, fos. 76, 141–2; *CSPD 1659–60*, p. 14; See: J. Peacey, 'Glimpses of Grub Street' (forthcoming).

relationships reinforces the need to consider the role of money, and offers a reminder that not all works by 'propagandists' ought to be considered as propaganda. Many writers and printers worked only intermittently as propagandists, and retained independent literary and publishing lives, and not all of their works need be contextualised in ways which suggest that they were produced at the behest of patrons and grandees. John Hall, for example, who was retained as a writer by the Rump from May 1649, continued to produce works for his own purposes.[3] Slightly more difficult to contextualise are writers such as John Sadler, who can be shown to have been writing works such as *The King's Cabinet Opened* for Parliament, while also working on pamphlets which may or may not have been produced independently, and which may or may not have been written in collaboration with MPs such as Francis Rous.[4] It is also difficult to assess the degree of independence which editors of newspapers retained, and the extent to which the content of official journals – such as *Mercurius Politicus* – represented the voice of the editor or his paymasters.[5] However, 'independence' was not necessarily a condition to which authors aspired or strived to maintain, nor merely one which was granted to them by patrons and employers. It was sometimes a position into which authors found themselves thrust as a result of contradictions between their personal beliefs and prevailing factional divisions and alignments. Pre-eminent amongst these was William Prynne, whose vehemence against William Laud, and in support of aggressive claims for parliamentary sovereignty, was combined with hostility to religious Independency. His religious Presbyterianism, on the other hand, was combined with profound opposition to a church settlement along Scottish lines. Thus, he could be vilified by Viscount Saye as a 'malicious blood-thirsty man', while also being berated by Robert Baillie as one of the 'Erastian lawyers [who] are now our remora'.[6]

Confronted by the need to recognise that even the most important propagandists of the mid-seventeenth century could retain a degree of authorial independence, it is also vital to address the possibility of their having sold their

---

[3] Dionysius Longinus, *Of the Height of Eloquence* (London, 1652); M. Maier, *Lusus Serius* (London, 1654); J. Hall, *Paradoxes* (London, 1655).

[4] Above, pp. 54–5, 101; J. S[adler], *The Ancient Bounds* (London, 1645); J. S[adler], *Flagellum Flagelli* (London, 1645).

[5] J. Raymond, 'A mercury with a winged conscience: Marchamont Nedham, monopoly and censorship', *Media History* 4 (1998), pp. 7–18.

[6] W. Fiennes, Viscount Saye, *Vindiciae Veritatis* (London, 1654), p. 47; *Letters and Journals of Robert Baillie*, ii. 315; W. Prynne, *Faces About* (London, 1644); W. Prynne, *A Full Reply* (London, 1644); W. Prynne, *Independency Examined* (London, 1644); W. Prynne, *The Antidote Animadverted* (np, nd); W. Prynne, *A Fresh Discovery of Some Prodigious New Wandring Blasing Stars* (London, 1645); W. Prynne, *The Antidote* (London, 1645); W. Prynne, *Truth Triumphing* (London, 1645); [W. Prynne], *Foure Serious Questions* (np, nd); W. Prynne, *A Vidication of Foure Serious Questions* (London, 1645); W. Prynne, *Suspention Suspended* (London, 1646); W. Prynne, *The Sword of Christian Magistracie* (London, 1647); [W. Prynne], *Scotland's Ancient Obligation* (London, 1646); *SR* i. 132, 134, 141, 181, 190, 193, 232, 257.

pens to other causes and interests. Issues relating to the extent to which financial interests rather than political conviction guided the work of printers and stationers have yet to receive rigorous attention.[7] Indeed, detection of mercenary tendencies among authors is clearly fraught with methodological and evidential difficulties which are best explored through the work of Henry Parker, who appears to have sold his pen on a number of occasions in the 1640s. Recent scholarship has suggested, for example, that Parker's *Generall Junto* (1642) was a 'sponsored' publication which reflected the private agenda of the man who paid for its publication (Sir John Danvers), and that Parker cannot be presumed to have been committed to the views expressed therein.[8] This conclusion reflects, however, a failure of contextualisation, a misplaced notion of the role of an author such as Parker, and a rather limited conception of the art of pamphleteering. Parker's work can best be understood in the light of the process of drafting controversial official declarations, and of the need for 'paper kites' to float radical constitutional ideas.[9] It is also necessary to consider closely the circumstantial background to Parker's *Vintners Answer* (March 1642), which appears to have been penned on behalf of commercial interests and corporate 'clients'.[10] This attack upon the behaviour of Richard Kilvert and William Abell, for having masterminded a financial imposition on wine in return for a monopoly, may actually have been undertaken in the interests of Parker's grandee-allies, who were eager to target the two men, and to build bridges with the Vintners' Company. There is certainly no evidence that the latter paid for Parker's services.[11] Such considerations also apply to Parker's *Humble Remonstrance of the Company of Stationers* (April 1643), which may have involved him acting as a paid advocate for the company, but which clearly reflected the views of parliamentarians who sought tighter press control.[12]

---

[7] M. H. Curtis, 'William Jones: Puritan printer and propagandist', *The Library*, 5th series 19 (1964); J. N. King, 'John Day, master printer of the English reformation', in P. Marshall and A. Ryrie, eds, *The Beginnings of English Protestantism* (Cambridge, 2002). The army printer, Henry Hills, published editions of the *Eikon Basilike* in 1649: *The Life of H. H.* (London, 1688), p. 48; F. F. Madan, *A New Bibliography of the Eikon Basilike* (Oxford Bibliographical Society Publications, new series 3, 1949), pp. 28, 39–40. For a fascinating recent analysis, see: P. Lindenbaum, 'John Playford: music and politics in the Interregnum', *HLQ* 64 (2001). I am grateful to Peter Lindenbaum for sending me a copy of this article, and for a number of discussions on such issues.

[8] M. Mendle, *Henry Parker and the English Civil War* (Cambridge, 1995), pp. 134–5, 180.

[9] Above, pp. 51–62, 247–50; J. Peacey, 'Junto practices: printing and publishing and the meaning of texts in the English civil war' (paper delivered at SHARP conference, London, 2002).

[10] Mendle, *Henry Parker*, pp. 141–4.

[11] [H. Parker], *The Vintners Answer* (London, 1642); Mendle, *Henry Parker*, p. 15; Peacey, 'Henry Parker', p. 63; *D'Ewes Diary*, ed. Notestein, pp. 24, 42, 73, 100, 187, 194, 262, 345, 351, 546–7; *D'Ewes Diary*, ed. Coates, p. 217; *CJ* ii. 26, 31, 33, 37, 44, 58, 63, 70, 156–7, 162, 218, 279; *CSPD 1641*, pp. 289–90, 325, *CSPD 1641–3*, pp. 32, 56–7; *PJ* i. 280–81, 283–4; *PJ* ii. 148, 173; GL, MS 15201/4; GL, MS 15333/4.

[12] [H. Parker], *To the High Court of Parliament. The Humble Remonstrance of the Company of Stationers*, (London, 1643); W. Greg, *A Companion to Arber* (Oxford, 1967), p. 109; Mendle, *Henry Parker*, pp. 144–8; Peacey, 'Henry Parker', pp. 98–9; above, p. 144.

Parker had friends among prominent stationers – such as George Thomason, Richard Whitaker and Joseph Hunscott[13] – but unlike in later years, when Marchamont Nedham was hired by the Stationers as an advocate with connections at Whitehall, there is no evidence that Parker was hired by the company, and it may well have been the case that this petition was framed at Westminster and given the appearance of having been prompted by the Stationers themselves.[14]

More plausible evidence for Parker having sold his pen concerns *Mr William Wheeler's Case* (January 1645), which appears to have been a lobbying device drafted for an English engineer in the Netherlands, who had suffered at the hands of the king's ambassador, Sir William Boswell.[15] Nevertheless, Parker was not simply selling his services, since Wheeler's ill-treatment was exploited by Parliament, which commissioned an account of the claims of such individuals, to be used in negotiations with the Dutch ambassadors.[16] The work which seems most likely to have involved Parker selling his pen was *Of a Free Trade*, written for his employers in Hamburg in December 1647. Nevertheless, Parker was once again representing interests broader than those of the Merchant Adventurers and, in responding to critics of the company such as Thomas Johnson, he set his sights upon the ideas of the Levellers and can certainly not be said to have violated his own principles.[17] Parker's *oeuvre* includes, therefore, a number of tracts which appear to have involved him selling his services to individuals and corporate interests, but upon closer examination it seems that such appearances are deceptive, in the sense that these works also represented the interests of known patrons and allies, were rarely funded by supposed clients, and scarcely involved abnegation of his own principles. That Parker was not unique in this regard is evident from other prominent writers of the period, such as William Prynne, who

---

13 Stationers Company, Court Book C, fos. 187–9v; HLRO, MP 12/5/43.

14 Stationers Company, Liber A, fos. 136v–38; R. Myers, *The Stationers Company Archive* (London, 1990), pp. 47, 336–8; Mendle, *Henry Parker*, p. 15. This possibility is enhanced by our knowledge that William Prynne attended committees to discuss the printing industry at precisely this time: J. Raymond, *Making the News. An Anthology of the Newsbooks of Revolutionary England 1641–1660* (Moreton-in-Marsh, 1993), pp. 46–7; BL, Harl. 5909, fos. 26–57; BL, Hargrave 98, fos. 57–66.

15 [H. Parker], *Mr William Wheeler's Case From His Own Relation* ([London, 1645]); Mendle, *Henry Parker*, pp. 16, 180; Hartlib Papers, 50H/67/6/1A–2B: William Wheeler to Sir William Boswell, 2 Jan. 1641; Hartlib Papers, 50H/34/3/3A–B: William Wheeler to Samuel Hartlib, 29 Oct. 1644. For Wheeler, see: W. Wheeler, *A List of Some Chief Workes* (Amsterdam, 1651); C. Webster, *The Great Instauration* (London, 1975), pp. 372–4; Hartlib Papers, 50H/67/6/3A–10B; Hartlib Papers, 50H/34/3/1A–2B, 4A–10B; PRO, SO 3/12, fo. 204; PRO, C 66/2903/19.

16 L. Miller, *John Milton's Writings in the Anglo-Dutch Negotiations, 1651–1654* (Pittsburgh, 1992), pp. 142–53; *CJ* iv. 26; *A Collection of all the Publicke Orders, Ordinances, and Declarations* (London, 1646), pp. 726–33.

17 H. Parker, *Of a Free Trade* (London, 1648); H. N. Brailsford, *The Levellers and the English Revolution* (London, 1961), pp. 44, 59, 76, 80, 100, 105–6, 116, 121, 123, 132, 532; [T. Johnson], *A Discourse Consisting of Motives for the Enlargement and Freedom of Trade* (London, 1645); T. Johnson, *A Plea for Free-mens Liberties* (London, 1646); Peacey, 'Henry Parker', pp. 127–9; Mendle, *Henry Parker*, p. 181.

was engaged by the London watermen in 1659 in order to defend a constitution which included a king and House of Lords. Though he 'sold' his pen to a private interest group, Prynne only appears to have done so in order to represent ideas with which he was both in agreement and actively engaged in defending.[18]

Considered statically, therefore, author–patron relations which involved the production of propaganda took a number of forms. Authors could be motivated by money, loyalty or personal conviction, and they could work on a more or less full-time basis. But important though it is to recognise that authors could retain a degree of independence while acting as propagandists, the processes of interpreting the forces which lay behind particular works, and of establishing the precise interrelation of money, personal opinion and political patronage among authorial motives are highly complex. At times authors may have been able to sell their pen, express their own beliefs and represent the interests of patrons at the same time.

The complexity of the ties between politicians and pamphleteers, and of the factors which determined the nature of individual works, emerges equally clearly once attention is turned to the dynamic of individual relationships; the ways in which they changed and developed, and the reasons for such alterations. Mapping author–patron interaction over time requires addressing the importance of authorial ambition, and the role of principle and pecuniary concerns in the lives of polemical writers, as well as the impact of political changes and factional balances.

Although it is stating the obvious to say that, over the course of time, certain independent authors became propagandists, while certain propagandists became independent authors, it is necessary to reinforce the point that particular authors did not always serve the interests of political grandees and interest groups. Naturally, the precise timing of such changes in personal circumstances are difficult to determine, and attempts to map the relationships which characterised the career of writers, such as Henry Walker, who moved from being more or less 'independent' to more or less 'employed', are deeply problematic.[19] With authors whose status as 'propagandists' was reflected in formal contracts and salaries it is somewhat easier. John Milton's works prior to 1649 almost certainly appeared without official involvement, or even approval, and it was not until his employment as Latin Secretary in March 1649, after the appearance of the *Tenure of Kings and Magistrates*, that he should be considered as a propagandist in the sense employed in this book.[20] The difficulty of maintaining favour and

---

[18] *CJ* vii. 828; *To the Right Honourable the Lord Mayor … The Humble Petition and Address of the Sea-men and Watermen* (London, 1659); *CCSP* iv. 543; Pepys, *Diary*, i. 37.

[19] E. Sirluck, 'To Your Tents, O Israel: alost pamphlet', *HLQ* 19 (1956); J. B. Williams, 'Henry Walker, journalist of the commonwealth', *Nineteenth Century and After* 65 (1908).

[20] Above, pp. 193–4.

employment, on the other hand, can be demonstrated through the career of writers such as John Hall, whose salary was suspended in April 1655. This represents the terminal date of his employment by the Council of State, although his status in the preceding year is probably uncertain, since he felt sufficiently insecure in his position as a salaried propagandist to issue a petition, on 10 May 1654, in the hope of ensuring continued payment of his pension, and to secure his arrears. While Cromwell ordered the payment of £50 days later, this would be the last payment Hall received.[21]

Such obvious changes in authors' circumstances fail to reflect, however, the complexity of the literary careers of a great many of the individuals with which this work is concerned. Anthony Cotton argued that Walker could not be described as a 'publisher's hack', a 'politician's pawn', or a 'noble family's retainer'.[22] Yet he may have been all of these things at different times. Henry Parker's writing was certainly undertaken in a number of different situations and relationships. He moved from working as a propagandist within the patronage network around Viscount Saye, to employment with the Committee of Safety and the Earl of Essex in the summer of 1642. He later failed to secure employment under the Committee of Both Kingdoms, and may have been 'semi-independent' during 1644–45, until securing employment as a special secretary to Parliament in the summer of 1645. The explicit mention of his salary being withdrawn in January 1646 offers a terminal date for his 'employment' at Westminster, with the propaganda duties which that entailed, but this did not necessarily prevent him from reverting to his previous role as a writer with close links to specific grandees.[23] Later still, Parker's circumstances shifted again, as he was once more employed in an administrative-propagandist capacity after his return from Hamburg in 1649.[24] Other writers can likewise be shown to have shifted between different types of relationship in this fashion. John Sadler, for example, moved from the network of the Puritan grandee, Lord Brooke, to join Parker as a special secretary in 1645.[25]

Needless to say, the reasons for such changes in personal circumstances are also more or less complex. Sadler's resulted from the death of his aristocratic patron, for although he was able to remain living at Brooke House in Holborn after 1643, he needed the assistance of other members of Brooke's circle, such as Oliver St John, in order to secure further advancement.[26] More important are shifts which resulted

---

[21] Above, pp. 199–200; *CSPD 1654*, p. 163; Abbott, *Cromwell*, iii. 41; PRO, SP 18/71, fo. 127; Bodl. MS Rawl. A.328, fo. 107; *CSPD 1655*, p. 127.

[22] A. Cotton, 'London newsbooks in the civil war: their political attitudes and sources of information' (Oxford University DPhil, 1971), p. 215.

[23] Peacey, 'Henry Parker', chaps. 2–3; above, pp. 53–5, 104, 115, 126, 129–30.

[24] Above, p. 79; Peacey, 'Henry Parker', pp. 134–6.

[25] Above, pp. 54–5, 99, 101; J. T. Peacey, 'Led by the hand: manucaptors and patronage at Lincoln's Inn in the seventeenth century', *Journal of Legal History* 18 (1997), pp. 36–7.

[26] Peacey, 'Led by the hand', pp. 36–7. Earlier, William Barlow wrote on behalf of the Earl of Essex in 1596 regarding Cadiz, on the orders of Whitgift, Archbishop of Canterbury, but by 1601 was writing against Essex on the orders of Cecil: T. S. Nowack, 'Propaganda and the pulpit. Robert Cecil,

from the complexities of factional politics, and shifts in the balance of power between particular groups. Parker's career was probably affected by his attachment to the Earl of Essex, both in person and in print, as well as by his service for the Committee of Safety, which increasingly became perceived as being a bastion for moderate or even lukewarm parliamentarians. This probably explains Parker's failure to secure the positions of employment which he sought; whether sinecures such as the registrarship of the Prerogative Court, or positions which would have reflected his importance as a writer, such as the secretaryship of the Committee of Both Kingdoms, which was established in early 1644 as part of a campaign to undermine the Lord General.[27] Parker's alignment with Essex may have been based upon the need for a strong leader in a time of civil war, and his attachment to a negotiated settlement in the autumn of 1643 probably reflected a tactical decision regarding the prospects of securing the demands set out in the spring and summer of 1642. Parker's drift towards the Independents during 1645, and towards renewed employment as a special secretary – to work on the king's letters and on tracts such as *Jus Regum* – may have reflected scepticism regarding the possibility of negotiating with Charles I, and the emergence of principled debates regarding the nature of a projected settlement of the church, as well as the importance of negotiating Scottish demands. This, in turn, provides the context for Parker's removal from his special secretarial position with Parliament in early 1646. Parker was probably ousted as part of a Presbyterian manoeuvre aimed at undermining the Independents, just as his subsequent departure for Hamburg in 1646 may have been connected to possible repercussions for having written anti-Presbyterian works such as *The Trojan Horse*.[28] John Hall's difficulties in 1654–55, meanwhile, probably stemmed from tensions over the future direction of the protectoral regime, and he probably ceased to work for the government because of the nature of his support for the regime, and because of his being averse to the monarchical tendencies within the court, which are revealed in the way that official favour was shown to another writer with the same name but with somewhat different ideas.[29] The 'careers' of Parker and Hall were profoundly affected, in other words, by their inability or unwillingess to accommodate changes of political mood, in terms of either tactics or political theory, and by factional jealousies which sometimes saw authors penalised for their perceived attachment to particular political groupings.

William Barlow and the Essex and Gunpowder plots', in K. Z. Keller and G. J. Schiffhorst, eds, *The Witness of Times* (Pittsburgh, 1992). Some preachers remain close to Warwick, others move on: B. Donagan, 'The clerical patronage of Robert Rich, second Earl of Warwick, 1619–1642', *Proceedings of the American Philosophical Society* 120 (1976), pp. 408–10.

[27] Above, pp. 129–30; Peacey, 'Henry Parker', pp. 94–101; J. Adamson, 'The triumph of oligarchy: the management of war and the Committee of Both Kingdoms, 1644–1645', in C. R. Kyle and J. Peacey, eds, *Parliament at Work* (Woodbridge, 2002).

[28] Above, pp. 53–5, 79; H. Parker, *Jus Regum* (London, 1645); H. Parker, *Trojan Horse* (London, 1646); Peacey, 'Henry Parker', pp. 102–21.

[29] J. T. Peacey, 'Nibbling at *Leviathan*: politics and intellect in 1650s England', *HLQ* 61 (1998).

More challenging are cases of authors who appear to have 'changed sides' during the 1640s. Thomas May, for example, shifted from an attachment to, and reliance upon, the court in the 1630s, to support Parliament and the commonwealth, which he served as an official propagandist until his death.[30] Later, after the fall of Oxford in 1646, the leading royalist propagandist, Sir John Berkenhead, travelled to London and briefly wrote parliamentarian works, including responses to anti-Scottish works by the radical MP, Thomas Chaloner. This was obviously commented upon by other parliamentarians, one of whom wrote that Berkenhead had recently arrived in London – 'the trade of writing *Aulicus* at court failing' – and had become 'journeyman to the *Kingdomes Intelligencer*'.[31] The most famous 'turncoat' of the mid-seventeenth century, of course, was Marchamont Nedham, editor of the parliamentarian newspaper *Mercurius Britanicus* (1643–46) and subsequently the author of pro-Independent tracts during 1646–47.[32] Sometime between the beginning of July and the middle of September 1647, Nedham underwent the change of allegiance which saw him journey to Hampton Court to beg the forgiveness of King Charles. Upon this being 'readily granted', Nedham commenced literary activities on behalf of the royalists, most notably as editor of *Mercurius Pragmaticus*.[33]

Such career changes seem to suggest a willingness to sacrifice personal beliefs on the altar of personal success, to act as turncoats, and to betray a cause for apparently base motives. This was certainly the accusation made against Thomas May, of whom Sir Edward Hyde commented:

> though he had received much countenance and a very considerable donative from the king, upon His Majesty's refusing to give him a small pension, which he had designed and promised to another very ingenious person, whose qualities he thought inferior to his own, he fell from his duty and all his former friends, and prostituted himself to the vile office of celebrating the infamous acts of those who were in rebellion against the king, which he did so meanly, that he seemed to all men to have lost his wits, when he left his honesty, and so shortly after died miserable and neglected, and deserves to be forgotten.[34]

Such comments need to be handled with care, however, in the light of scholarship which has challenged simplistic notions regarding the predictive power of pre-1640s careers in terms of civil war allegiances.[35] This seems particularly true when

---

[30] Above, pp. 11, 55, 186.

[31] *A Perfect Diurnall* 169 (19–26 Oct. 1646), p. 1356; *Kingdomes Weekly Intelligencer* 170 (13–20 Oct. 1646), p. 272; P. W. Thomas, *Sir John Berkenhead, 1617–1679* (Oxford, 1969), pp. 130–32.

[32] Above, pp. 116–17, 151–2, 180.

[33] Wood, *Athenae*, iii. 1180–90; *Mercurius Pragmaticus* 1 (14–21 Sept. 1647); B. Worden, 'Wit in a Roundhead: the dilemma of Marchamont Nedham', in S. D. Amussen and M. A. Kishlansky, eds, *Political Culture and Cultural Politics in Early Modern England* (Manchester, 1995); J. Peacey, '"The counterfeit silly curr": money, politics and the forging of royalist newspapers in the English civil war', *HLQ* (forthcoming).

[34] Clarendon, *Life*, i. 39–40.

[35] C. Russell, *Parliaments and English Politics, 1621–1629* (Oxford, 1979), pp. 434–6.

considering May's transformation from an exponent of 'high-literature' into a pamphleteer and contemporary historian, and when considering recent claims regarding May's consistent interest in 'republicanism'.[36] Furthermore, while the behaviour of Berkenhead and Nedham seems to imply the triumph of ambition over loyalty, their having changed sides actually reflected a response to changing circumstances rather than authorial opportunism. The nature of both parliamentarianism and royalism shifted profoundly in the period between the fall of Oxford and the trial of the king, with the rise of the army and of radical impulses, and with royalists' need to find new allies, whether among the radicals, the Independents or the Scots. Nedham's shift occurred during a period when royalists found common ground with radical parliamentarians in the army and the Levellers, and it may have been the case that Nedham was shocked by violence in London, and by the army's action in marching towards the capital.[37] Furthermore, in assessing Nedham's motivation, it should be remembered that he had already professed himself supportive of a negotiated settlement between the king and the Independents at Westminster, in *The Case of the Kingdom Stated*. His consistent opposition to political change imposed by the military, together with his enmity towards the Presbyterian Scots – which characterised his royalist writing even after the invasion aimed at assisting Charles – indicates that after 1647 he sang the same song from a different hymnal. Indeed, Nedham was able to reprint *The Case of the Kingdom Stated* in late 1647 as a royalist text.[38] As the radicals were emerging in the army and at Westminster, in other words, the potential for the king's adoption of Presbyterianism left men like Saye and Nedham in a bind, and Nedham may have felt that he had more in common with the king than with the radicals, particularly if he calculated that Charles was merely exploiting the Scots. Furthermore, those who regard Nedham as a mercenary without scruple must also confront the risk he took in going over to the king, and the uncertainty as to royalists' willingness to forgive him, as well as the ruthlessness of those around the king who employed his services.[39]

Another interpretative challenge is posed by evidence relating to the ways in which writers negotiated regime change. That some authors did so unsuccessfully provides testimony to their political principles. The Presbyterian licensers who sought to inflict damage upon the commonwealth regime after the execution of the king probably did so in the expectation that their days as republican employees

[36] Peacey, 'Henry Parker', pp. 228–30; D. Norbrook, 'Lucan, Thomas May, and the creation of a republican literary culture', in K. Sharpe and P. Lake, eds, *Culture and Politics in Early Stuart England* (London, 1994).

[37] Peacey, 'Henry Parker', pp. 122–4, 161–2, 243–4; M. Mendle, 'Putney's pronouns: identity and indemnity in the great debate', in M. Mendle, ed., *The Putney Debates of 1647* (Cambridge, 2001).

[38] M. Nedham, *The Case of the Kingdom Stated* (London, 1647); M. N[edham], *The Case of the Kingdom Stated* (3rd edn, London, 1647). For Nedham's consistent opposition to the Scots, see: Peacey, '"Counterfeit silly curr"'.

[39] Cotton, 'London newsbooks', p. 303.

were numbered. They certainly did so in the name of religious policies which were no longer in favour, and of a constitution which was being unravelled, having been turned into opponents of the regime by the turn of political events at Westminster.[40] Similarly, it is less evident that Gilbert Mabbott, who was sacked as a licenser in 1649, became more radical during the period after Pride's Purge, than that the regime sought to distance itself from the radicalism with which he was associated, and no longer found the views which he licensed acceptable.[41] Likewise, the republican propagandist, John Canne, refused to cut his cloth to remain employed by the protectorate after December 1653, and suffered imprisonment in April 1658 for 'continuing to preach scandalously against his Highness'. He returned to regular employment only after the return of the Rump in 1659, upon publication of *A Seasonable Word to the Parliament Men*, and he was appointed editor of *Politicus* upon the interests of those supporters of the 'good old cause' which he represented in the weeks which followed.[42] Another republican propagandist who can be credited with having adopted a principled stance was John Streater, who was hounded by the Cromwellian government, but who secured employment alongside John Macock as official printer to the restored Rump from December 1659 until March 1660.[43]

In apparent contrast to Cranford, Canne, and Mabbott were those authors who negotiated regime-change more successfully, such as the Leveller printer, Thomas Newcomb, and the royalist printer, William Dugard, who turned their coats in order to work for Parliament and the Council of State after the execution of the king in 1649.[44] Attention might also be drawn to Payne Fisher, the former royalist officer who became a propagandist under the commonwealth.[45] More important, however, was Nedham, who was arrested by the republican authorities on 18 June 1649 and committed to Newgate, albeit royalists alleged that he was apprehended by his own consent.[46] Whether or not this was true, Nedham clearly intimated to the Council of State that he was prepared to 'serve the commonwealth, if I may yet be thought worthy of such service'. Nedham escaped from prison in August 1649, and managed to secure the publication of *Certain Considerations Tendered*

---

[40] Above, pp. 156–7.

[41] Above, pp. 156–8.

[42] *CP* iii. 146; *CJ* vii. 652; *The Weekly Intelligencer* 2 (10–17 May 1659), p. 15; J. Canne, *A Seasonable Word* (London, 1659); J. B. Williams, 'The newsbooks and letters of news of the Restoration', *EHR* 23 (1908), pp. 252–5; *Mercurius Politicus* 567 (12–19 May 1659), pp. 437, 447; *Mercurius Politicus* 568 (19–26 May 1659), pp. 449–64; *Mercurius Politicus* 569 (26 May–2 Jun. 1659), pp. 471–3; *Mercurius Politicus* 572 (16–23 Jun. 1659), pp. 516. For criticism of Canne, see: *The Acts and Monuments of Our Late Parliament* (London, 1659), p. 2.

[43] For example: *An Act for Further Continuation of the Customs* (London, 1659); *An Act for Taking the Accounts* (London, 1660). For payments to them, see: *CSPD 1659–60*, p. 596; PRO, SO 3/14, unfol.

[44] Above, pp. 45, 118, 119.

[45] BL, Add. 19863, fos. 2v, 7v, 10, 15, 27, 36v, 38v; PRO, SP 28/253Bi; above, pp. 109, 129, 197.

[46] *The Moderate* 50 (19–26 June 1649), sig. Dddv; *HMC Pepys*, pp. 286, 298; *CSPD 1649–50*, p. 537.

in all Humility to an Honourable Member of the Council of State, in which he affirmed his willingness to shift allegiance once more, and included his thoughts on the means of controlling 'idle pasquils and scandalous pamphlets'.[47] Nedham was recaptured shortly after the appearance of this pamphlet, but his veiled offer to work for the republic had evidently not gone unnoticed, and his career soon took a new turn.[48] That the new regime was interested in Nedham's literary talents is clear from the order for John Milton to examine copies of *Pragmaticus*, and it was probably the Latin Secretary who, along with William Lenthall and John Bradshaw, secured Nedham's release in November 1649. Indeed, it is interesting that eleven days before his release, Nedham wrote to Thomas Scot, one of the prime movers in the republic's propaganda machine, seeking 'both pity and pardon' for having 'left the prison without your leave'. Nedham told Scot that he had petitioned Lord President Bradshaw, and claimed that his ruin would 'no way advantage the commonwealth, but my preservation may; wherein if you will be so noble as to assist me, I dare be valiant and active, or remain innocent and silent, in prosecuting my own particular, under your protection'. Five days after gaining his freedom, Nedham explained to a friend that 'my Lord President's favour hath once more turned the wheele of my fortune'.[49] The final seal upon, and guarantee of, Nedham's rehabilitation was the salary of £100 *per annum* voted to him in May 1650, which was prompted by 'services already done', in the form of *The Case of the Commonwealth of England*.[50]

In seeking explanations for the willingness with which Newcomb, Dugard and Nedham accommodated the commonwealth, it is possible to do more than impugn their integrity. Writing in 1661, Dugard claimed to have been imprisoned for printing royalist tracts such as the *Eikon Basilike* and *Defensio Regia*, and that he would have been tried for his life had he not been saved by Sir James Harrington. He was evidently released upon condition that he placed his presses at the disposal of the Rump. An overwhelming, and perfectly natural, concern for his personal welfare probably drove Dugard to consent to such terms, and to decline Sir Edward Nicholas's request that he print further royalist works in April 1649.[51]

---

47 PRO, SP 46/95, fo. 151; D. Masson, *The Life of John Milton* (7 vols, London, 1871–80), iv. 146; M. Nedham, *Certain Considerations* (London, 1649), p. 9.

48 BL, Add. 28002, fo. 170.

49 *CSPD 1649–50*, pp. 537, 554; D. Gardiner, ed., *The Oxinden and Peyton Letters, 1642–1670* (London, 1937), p. 161; BL, Add. 28002, fo. 172; PRO, SP 46/95, fo. 190; Masson, *Milton*, iv. 149–50, 156. It seems that Milton and Nedham might have known each other already, since Hartlib seems to have known both men as early as 1647: W. R. Parker, *Milton; A Biography* (2 vols, Oxford, 1968), i. 312.

50 *CSPD 1650*, p. 174; Masson, *Milton*, iv. 226–7; M. Nedham, *The Case of the Commonwealth of England Stated* (London, 1650, ed. P. A. Knachel, Charlottesville, 1969).

51 *CSPD 1661–2*, p. 132. See: L. Rostenberg, 'Republican credo: William Dugard, pedagogue and political apostate', in *Literary, Scientific, Religious and Legal Publishing, Printing and Bookselling in England 1551–1700* (2 vols, New York, 1965), ii. 130–60; Merchant Taylors Company, Court Minute Book 9, fos. 338r–v, 346, 355, 357v, 361.

Likewise, Newcomb was released from prison in 1649 on condition that he assist the new regime, not least by giving evidence against John Lilburne. He subsequently became, of course, one of the leading printers of commonwealth propaganda.[52] Nedham too must have been motivated by the desire to secure release from prison. In the summer of 1649, therefore, his willingness to serve the republican regime reflected the fact that he was a 'distressed prisoner'.[53] During his spell on the run in the summer of 1649, he claimed to have been 'constrained to associate with rats, old books, and cobwebs, in the suburbs of hell', and his flight was evidently marred by profound poverty.[54] Later, he told Thomas Scot that if he could not obtain his freedom, 'I reckon myself undone, having no open way of subsistence'.[55] Nevertheless, Nedham can also be shown to have had other motives, and his desertion of the royalist cause can be contextualised in terms of frustration at Charles II's alliance with, and reliance upon, the Scots. This may have been more significant than his republicanism – which could accommodate different constitutional forms – in encouraging Nedham's apparent apostasy, and it suggests that, however much he was a mercenary publicist, there were clear limits to what he would write, and that even Nedham's career was not without principles.[56]

Although Nedham can no longer be regarded simply as an unprincipled 'Jack of all sides', there is certainly evidence of his willingness to trim his sails in certain ways in order to maintain favour in later years. Nedham's career was significantly more complex than has generally been recognised, and it was filled with many more changes of direction than has been suggested hitherto. More interesting than his tergiversations in 1647 and 1649 are his relations with the political regimes of the 1650s. Like so many public figures, he evidently found little difficulty in accommodating the protectorate, and felt able to produce *The True State of the Case of the Commonwealth* to justify the establishment of the new regime, just as his colleague, John Hall, did with *Confusion Confounded*.[57] Given Nedham's willingness to represent the interests of Oliver Cromwell, it probably came as no surprise that he transferred his loyalties seamlessly to the new protector, Richard Cromwell, in September 1658.[58] More complex, however, is his subsequent career. Nedham probably had little say over whether or not to accommodate the restored Rump in May 1659, when he was removed from his privileged position as editor of *Mercurius Politicus* (13 May). This was almost certainly engineered by the

---

[52] Above, pp. 118, 250, 267; *CSPD 1649–50*, pp. 296, 314, 316, 522.

[53] PRO, SP 46/95, fo. 151.

[54] BL, Add. 28002, fo. 170.

[55] PRO, SP 46/95, fo. 190.

[56] D. Norbrook, *Writing the English Republic* (Cambridge, 1999), p. 222; Worden, 'Wit in a Roundhead', pp. 301–37.

[57] [M. Nedham], *The True State of the Case of the Commonwealth* (London, 1654); [J. Hall], *Confusion Confounded* (London, Hills, 1654).

[58] *Mercurius Politicus* 432 (2–9 Sep. 1658), pp. 802–8.

army republicans, and was motivated by a desire to remove all protectoral hirelings, and particularly the man they regarded as the pre-eminent 'court pamphleteer'.[59] Within weeks, however, Nedham was able to return to *Politicus*; capitalising upon the re-emergence of the civilian republicans in the wake of Sir George Booth's royalist rising, and on the back of the reaction to the initial radicalism of the restored Rump. Nedham's appointment (15 August) was made in the wake of his having instituted a short-lived newspaper (*The Moderate Informer*), and came three days after he penned a tract in defence of the commonwealth, called *Interest Will Not Lie*, which was published immediately after his return to office.[60] Nedham's appointment reflected the shifting balance of power between civilian and army republicans, which also saw Canne emerge more clearly as the spokesman for the army, while another old servant of the Rump, William Dugard, who had petitioned the government in May 1659, resurfaced as printer to the Council from the last week of September.[61] Nedham used *Politicus* to advertise works such as Milton's *Considerations Touching the Likliest Means to Remove Hirelings Out of the Church*, as well as the *Modest Plea for an Equal Common-Wealth* by William Sprigge, an associate of Sir Henry Vane junior.[62] That Nedham was aligned with his old friends among the civilian republicans is also evident from the way in which he ignored the demands of the officers whose commissions were removed by Parliament (12 Oct.), which were publicised in the army's newspapers.[63]

Perhaps the most interesting phase of Nedham's career, however, was that which followed the army's interruption of the Rump's proceedings in October 1659. Nedham once more managed to align himself and his pen with the prevailing political power, and in the following weeks he became the most important spokesman for the Committee of Ten and the Committee of Safety – in support of men such as Charles Fleetwood, and in opposition to the supporters of the Rump such as Harbert Morley, Sir Arthur Hesilrige and

---

[59] *CJ* vii. 652; *Mercurius Politicus* 567 (12–19 May 1659), p. 437; *The Weekly Intelligencer* 2 (10–17 May 1659), p. 15; A. Woolrych, 'Introduction', *The Complete Prose Works of John Milton VII* (New Haven, 1980), p. 107; Williams, 'Newsbooks and letters of news', pp. 252–5; *Eighteen New Court-Quaeries* (London, 1659), p. 4.

[60] *CJ* vii. 758; *CP* iv. 43; M. Nedham, *Interest Will Not Lie* (London, by Newcomb, 1659); *Occurrences from Foreign Parts* 14 (12–16 August 1659), p. 183; *A True Catalogue* (London, 1659), p. 14.

[61] *CSPD 1658–9*, p. 358; *CSPD 1659–60*, p. 223. Canne was considered for other employment or a pension, and in September was ordered to receive 20s. per week until employment was found for him: *CJ* vii. 758; *CSPD 1659–60*, pp. 110, 163.

[62] *Mercurius Politicus* 585 (1–8 Sep. 1659), p. 713; *Mercurius Politicus* 591 (13–20 Oct. 1659), p. 809; J. Milton, *Considerations Touching the Likliest Means to Remove Hirelings out of the Church* (London, by Newombe, 1659); *Mercurius Politicus* 586 (8–15 Sep. 1659), p. 728; [W. Sprigge], *A Modest Plea for an Equal Common-Wealth* (London, 1659); PRO, SP 9/26, fo. 139; R. L. Greaves, 'William Sprigg and the Cromwellian revolution', *HLQ* 34 (1971).

[63] Canne published these demands, though Nedham did not: *A Particular Advice from the Office of Intelligence* 27 (4–7 Oct. 1659), pp. 365–8; *Mercurius Politicus* 590 (6–13 Oct. 1659), pp. 792–3.

George Monck.[64] Nedham led a vigorous campaign against the latter, by reprinting the hostile letter from the London militia commissioners in November, and by gloating at his failures. In late November and December 1659, furthermore, Nedham repeatedly informed his readers of Monck's lack of support, and produced lists of officers who had deserted him.[65] He also opposed Morley and Hesilrige, and in the second week of December went to great lengths to inform his readers of the problems which they too faced.[66] On the other hand, Nedham faithfully reported army council propaganda, such as the 'seven fundamentals' which were issued on 13 December, and when the Common Council drafted a declaration against the 'fundamentals', and against the way in which Nedham's papers had been used to publicise them (20 December), he endeavoured to reply to the Common Council's statement.[67] However, Nedham subsequently made another tactical switch once it became clear that fortune was favouring the civilians, and in the last week of December 1659 he printed the declaration which had been issued by Vice-Admiral John Lawson, calling for the return of the Rump, and also reported news from Portsmouth which now took Morley's side. Having previously reported the way in which troops had abandoned Monck, Nedham now reported how troops were abandoning the Wallingford House party, and publicised the declaration of those Irish officers who supported Parliament.[68] In the second week of January, he printed letters from Monck and Lord Fairfax, and reprinted the declaration issued by Parliament on 23 January.[69] Ultimately, of course, Nedham's past and present activities ensured that he was not able – at least immediately – to negotiate the Restoration of the Stuarts with notable success. Hostility towards him was evident in the demands of the London citizens for his removal from office, which eventually occurred on 9 April 1660, when he was succeeded as official newswriter by Monck's agents and allies, Giles Dury and Henry

---

[64] *Mercurius Politicus* 593 (3–10 Nov. 1659), pp. 850–53; *Mercurius Politicus* 594 (10–17 Nov. 1659), p. 876; *The Publick Intelligencer* 202 (7–14 Nov. 1659), pp. 845–7.

[65] *Mercurius Politicus* 593 (3–10 Nov. 1659), pp. 850–51; *Mercurius Politicus* 595 (17–24 Nov. 1659), pp. 907–8; *Mercurius Politicus* 596 (24 Nov.–1 Dec. 1659), pp. 922–3; *Mercurius Politicus* 597 (1–8 Dec. 1659), p. 938.

[66] *Mercurius Politicus* 597 (1–8 Dec. 1659), p. 939; *Mercurius Politicus* 598 (8–15 Dec. 1659), pp. 945–6.

[67] *Mercurius Politicus* 598 (8–15 Dec. 1659), pp. 955–6; Woolrych, 'Introduction', pp. 149, 152; *At a Common Council ... 20th of December 1659* (London, by James Flesher, printer to the City of London, 1659); *Mercurius Politicus* 599 (15–22 Dec. 1659), pp. 967-8. The Common Council found support from the new paper instigated by George Monck and Thomas Clarges, and written by Muddiman: *The Parliamentary Intelligencer* 1 (19–26 Dec. 1659), pp. 3, 4–5.

[68] *Mercurius Politicus* 600 (22–29 Dec. 1659), pp. 975–6, 977, 987–8; *The Publicke Intelligencer* 208 (19–26 Dec. 1659), pp. 957–8, 970, 972.

[69] *Mercurius Politicus* 602 (5–12 Jan. 1660), pp. 1009–11; *Mercurius Politicus* 604 (19–26 Jan. 1660), pp. 1037–40. Nedham's support for the Rump was mocked in contemporary pamphlets: *The Proceedings, Votes, Resolves, and Acts of the Late Half-Quarter Parliament Called the Rump* (London, 1660), p. 11.

Muddiman.[70] Unable and unwilling to trim once again, Nedham fled to exile in Holland.[71]

It is hard not to appreciate the derogatory comments to which Nedham was subjected by contemporaries, who made him synonymous with those cynical hacks who were prepared to change sides for money and favour.[72] His opponents claimed that he was 'a mercury with a winged conscience, the skip-Jack of all fortunes, that like a shuttle-cock, drive him which way you will, falls still with the cork end forwards'.[73] Another critic, writing in September 1659, claimed that Nedham was 'a man so infamous and scandalous everywhere', who 'stinks in the nostrils of all men', because he 'formerly writ *Pragmaticus* and told lies for the king, afterward writ intelligence for the Parliament, and in that day told lies for the protector', before being 'lately received again to write intelligence for the Parliament'. Moreover, it was claimed that Nedham would 'tell lies and maintain a wicked cause for any that will best reward him for so doing', and he was accused of having prostrated 'learning, conscience, credit, and pen, to serve the interests and lusts of a few corrupt men'.[74] However, it is important to recognise that contemporary unease regarding Nedham's behaviour reflected nervousness regarding the emergence of professional polemicists, who had to survive by their pens during a period of civil war, and who had 'livings to make as well as axes to grind'.[75] Nedham was not the last popular journalist to behave in such a fashion – his career mirrors that of William Cobbett – and his contemporary reputation sprang in large part from the fact that he was among the first to behave in such a way.[76] Moreover, there is something disingenuous about comment on such a phenomenon which concentrates on authors rather than politicians, and it ought to be remembered that Nedham's services were consistently in demand, and that those who employed him were equally cynical. Moreover, while Nedham certainly trimmed his sails during the commonwealth in order to maintain favour and employment with particular regimes, his ability to negotiate more profound changes of regime can be understood in terms of a republicanism which was more important than attachment to particular forms of government, and it can be

---

[70] W. L. Sachse, ed., *The Diurnal of Thomas Rugg, 1659–1661* (Camden Society, 3rd series 91, 1961), pp. 66–7; Whitelocke, *Memorials*, iv. 406; Williams, 'Newsbooks and letters of news', p. 257; J. Frank, *The Beginnings of the English Newspaper, 1620–1660* (Cambridge, Mass., 1961), p. 263; J. G. Muddiman, *The King's Journalist* (London, 1923), pp. 110–11; *Mercurius Publicus* 16 (22–29 Apr. 1660), p. 241; *Mercurius Publicus* 18 (26 Apr.–3 May 1660), p. 280; *Parliamentary Intelligencer* 14 (26 Feb–2 Apr. 1660), p. 209.

[71] *CJ* vii. 652, 758; *DNB*; Masson, *Milton*, v. 702.

[72] Sir F. Wortley, *Characters and Elegies* (London, 1646), pp. 26–7; *The Great Assizes Holden in Parnassus* (London, 1645); J. B. Williams, *The History of English Journalism* (London, 1908), pp. 60, 114; *The Poore Committee-Mans Accompt* (London, 1647).

[73] *The Character of the Rump* (London, 1660), p. 3.

[74] *True Catalogue*, pp. 14, 75, 76.

[75] Thomas, *Sir John Berkenhead*, p. 163.

[76] D. Green, *Great Cobbett. The Noblest Agitator* (Oxford, 1985), p. 454.

attributed, paradoxically, to his refusal to compromise over certain political and religious principles.

Turning from a static to a dynamic analysis of author–patron relations, therefore, requires contextualising the career trajectories of individual authors, and the apparent changes in their circumstances and fortunes. It involves confronting cases of writers who emerged into, and disappeared from, the world of propaganda, and recognising not merely that writers were 'hired and fired', but also that they shifted between patrons, and between different types of propaganda relationship. They did so, moreover, as a result of changes in personal circumstances, as well as shifts in factional politics, and in terms of both tactics and political philosophies, which meant that authors sometimes struggled to maintain favour, and endured periodic falls from, and returns into, grace. While Nedham's colourful and varied career draws attention to the phenomenon of writers who 'changed sides', it seems clear that it is unsatisfactory to characterise such individuals as opportunists, who were eager to work for whichever side offered most for their services. They generally reacted to changed political circumstances and the fluidity of 'royalism' and 'parliamentarianism' during the course of the 1640s, rather than demonstrating vaulting ambition, lack of principle and absence of loyalty. Finally, rather than merely dismissing propagandists – whether authors or stationers – as turncoats who were willing to accommodate changes of regime, it is important to recognise examples of individuals who took principled stands and fell from favour as a result, and to acknowledge that there was sometimes more to successful negotiation of regime-change than mere opportunism. In addition to the instinct for self-preservation, 'turncoats' may sometimes have been frustrated by the policies of their paymasters and patrons, and may also have been demonstrating attachments to political and religious principles which were more profound than loyalty to particular political structures.

The dynamic of relations between propagandists and politicians involves a great deal more, however, than the emergence and breakdown of particular relationships, and authorial negotiation of shifting political sands. It is also important to question the 'reliability' of propagandists at a more subtle level, during the course of given 'relationships'. This was something which infused contemporary rhetoric of both grandees and authors. Testimonials of service were written by the Earl of Essex for Henry Parker in 1643, as the latter sought administrative preferment, and during the Rump, propagandists such as John Milton and Cuthbert Sydenham were thanked for their 'good services'.[77] When William Dugard sought support for a petition to the Common Council for employment in early 1652, however, the Council of State appears to have given him a less than wholehearted endorsement, by explaining that they could not

---

[77] Above, pp. 129–30; H. Parker, *Memorial* ([London, 1647]); *CSPD 1649–50*, p. 476; *CSPD 1651*, p. 42.

directly recommend him, but rather that they had good proofs of Dugard's abilities as a printer for the state, and that they did not conceive there to be any impediment in his intended suit.[78] In seeking money and preferment, of course, authors could profess their own reliability and literary services. When John Hall petitioned for the payment of his salary in May 1654, for example, he reminded Cromwell of his having been 'a constant of the several Councils of State ever since the change of government'; of his 'several times' discharging his duty, including 'his attendance on your highness in Scotland'; and of his defence of the protectorate 'by his book called *Confusion Confounded*'.[79]

Nevertheless, reliability is a problematic concept, and can be defined and assessed in various ways. It can be related, therefore, to the rate at which authors wrote, and instances can clearly be found of individuals who were unable to write with sufficient speed, such as John Milton, who appears to have failed to produce the reply to the Levellers which was required of him, and who made slow progress with some later works.[80] It can also be related to the ability of writers to produce works which required little editorial work, and little managerial oversight, unlike Joseph Hall and Robert Creighton.[81] Moreover, reliability does not necessarily involve political consistency, and might involve writers cutting their cloth in order to fit the requirements of a particular benefactor, patron or employer with whom they were associated.[82] John Dillingham's parliamentarian newspaper vacillated wildly over the siege of Oxford, but in this it can be shown to have mirrored the attitude of the Committee of Both Kingdoms 'so exactly, that it may be assumed that he was simply writing what he was told'.[83] Furthermore, reliability did not always entail principled support. Individuals could be motivated by personal fealty to aristocratic patrons, or by loyalty to patronage networks, as well as by ties of kinship and friendship, and debts of gratitude. Those writers who were hired and contracted, and whose terms of service were expressed financially, meanwhile, were obviously motivated by monetary carrots and sticks. For the latter, reliability need not involve 'loyalty' in any meaningful sense. Some authors hired by the Rump regime, such as Nedham, were employed on probationary terms, and recognisances had long been used in order to ensure the good behaviour of printers.[84]

Moreover, the loyalty of writers who were hired and retained in the 1650s may

---

[78] *CSPD 1651–2*, p. 99.

[79] *CSPD 1654*, p. 163; PRO, SP 18/71, fo. 127.

[80] Above, p. 194.

[81] Above, pp. 204, 217–18, 222.

[82] J. S. A. Adamson, 'Parliamentary management, men of business, and the House of Lords, 1640–49', in C. Jones, ed., *A Pillar of the Constitution* (London, 1989), p. 30.

[83] A. N. B. Cotton, 'John Dillingham, journalist of the middle group', *EHR* 93 (1978), p. 825.

[84] *CSPD 1650*, pp. 174, 514–19. For earlier use of recognisances, see: *CSPD 1637*, pp. 344, 573; *CSPD 1625–49*, pp. 567–8; H. R. Plomer, 'Some petitions for appointment as master printers called forth by the Star Chamber decree of 1637', *The Library*, 3rd series 10 (1919).

only have been maintained by financial means. Continued employment and monetary rewards were tied closely to the production of polemical tracts, and could easily dry up along with an author's inkwell, although the correlation is often easier to observe than the causality is to discern. John Hall, therefore, appears to have played no part in commonwealth propaganda for over a year after the appearance of his *True Relation* of the Amboyna massacre (November 1651), and in this period he received no pay. The resumption of his quarterly payments of £25 coincided with the appearance of his defence of the dissolution of the Rump in May 1653, with a *Letter Written to a Gentleman*. Royalists, who recognised that the latter was written 'at Cromwell's order', also alleged that Hall was 'wholly mercenary', and that having published the book, he 'waited on his excellency for his reward'.[85] It may have been true that Hall would not write without the promise of money, but this does not explain why the payments dried up during 1652, although it is clear that, having secured his salary, Hall produced further works during 1653.[86] The 'mercenary' nature of John Dury's literary work for the regime, meanwhile, is evident from his intimation that his services could be hired for the £200 *per annum* which he had lost upon his return to England during the wars.[87] Finally, negotiations between Payne Fisher and the republican authorities in 1652 suggest that he too was willing to write on behalf of the regime only if suitable financial remuneration proved forthcoming.[88] Reliability, in other words, could be assessed in terms of a number of different criteria; need not have involved consistency; and may actually have involved loyalty on the part of authors which was more or less based upon principle, and more or less guaranteed by financial means.

Such caveats regarding the possibility of defining 'reliability' in the world of propaganda are extremely powerful. Nevertheless, a possible way to make progress involves approaching the issue in a negative fashion, by addressing cases of writers who were perceived to have stepped out of line with those whose interests they were supposed to be representing, and to have overstepped the mark of acceptable behaviour. There had always been instances of errant licensers, perhaps as a result of the laziness which appears to have enabled Prynne to secure approval for *Histriomastix*.[89] During the 1640s, however, licensers more often proved untrustworthy because of a willingness to approve works which their political masters found unacceptable, especially those seditious, sectarian and even blasphemous books which were approved by licensers who came close to approving toleration and a free press.[90] Overstepping the bounds of acceptable

---

[85] [Joh]N [Ha]ll, *A Letter Written to a Gentleman* (London, 1653); *CCSP* ii. 212; Bodl. MS Clarendon 45, fo. 438v; *CSPD 1653–4*, p. 173.

[86] Above, pp. 199–200.

[87] Above, pp. 90, 198–9.

[88] *CSPD 1651–2*, pp. 152, 366–7.

[89] Magdalen College Oxford, Ferrar Papers, unfol.; Greg, *Companion*, pp. 85–6, 277–82.

[90] Above, pp. 148–58.

behaviour was something of which writers and printers too could be guilty. Writing in April 1645, the royalist Joseph Jane commented that parliamentarian newsbooks were 'careful ... not to displease', but there is plenty of evidence that authors and stationers proved unwilling or incapable of keeping to the required path.[91] Peter Heylyn, therefore, alleged that William Prynne proved difficult to control, and that 'being once put into the road, it was not possible to get him out of it again by threats or punishments'.[92] And in February 1652, the Council of State was forced to examine the behaviour of its printer, William Dugard, for his role in printing the *Racovian Catechism*.[93]

Moreover, attention can certainly be drawn to key civil war propagandists who strained relationships with their 'employers'.[94] During the mid-1650s, therefore, both Nedham and Milton grew restless and impatient with the Cromwellian regime, and neither appears to have been wholly loyal to the government. Indeed, the two men seem to have been much in sympathy, and probably worked together, and the appearance of their works reflected the growing disillusionment with Cromwell from within the court, and the strength of the protector's detractors in Whitehall and Westminster. Milton's *Defensio Secundo* (1654) displayed an ambiguous attitude to Cromwell, and his radicalism was increasingly out of step with the conciliatory and even Presbyterian religious policy of the protectorate.[95] Nedham, too, was increasingly unreliable. On one level, he appears to have been susceptible, as editor of *Politicus*, to the influence of individual friends and politicians.[96] More importantly, his continual development of republican ideas may have caused sufficient tension to prompt the suspension of his salary in April 1655.[97] This opposition to Cromwell became most evident, however, from Nedham's *Excellencie of a Free State*, which was entered into the Stationers' register in November 1655 and published in June 1656, and which recycled his republican newspaper editorials from late 1651 and early 1652. The work was expressly stated to be a response to 'those high and ranting discourses of personal prerogative and unbounded monarchy' then circulating, and it was produced for Thomas Brewster, a publisher with close links to republicans such as Thomas May and Sir Henry Vane. Nedham was aligning himself, in other words, with Vane,

[91] *NP* ii. 243–4.

[92] P. Heylyn, *Cyprianus Anglicus* (London, 1671), p. 149.

[93] *CSPD 1651–2*, pp. 132, 550.

[94] Norbrook, *Writing the English Republic*, p. 328.

[95] B. Worden, 'Milton and Marchamont Nedham', in D. Armitage, A. Himy, and Q. Skinner, eds, *Milton and Republicanism* (Cambridge, 1998), pp. 176–7; B. Worden, 'John Milton and Oliver Cromwell', in I. Gentles, J. Morrill and B. Worden, eds, *Soldiers, Writers and Statesmen of the English Revolution* (Cambridge, 1998); A. Woolrych, 'Milton and Cromwell: "a short but scandalous night of interruption"?', in M. Lieb and J. T. Shawcross, eds, *Achievements of the Left Hand: Essays on the Prose of John Milton* (Amherst, 1974), pp. 185–218; J. Milton, *Pro Se Defensio* (London, by Newcomb, 1655).

[96] Hartlib Papers, 50H/4/3/94A–B: John Dury to Samuel Hartlib, 28 Apr. 1655.

[97] *CSPD 1655*, p. 127.

James Harrington and the 'good old cause', and the book appeared at the same Machiavellian moment as both Harrington's *Oceana* and Vane's *Healing Question*. These three men were expressing frustration with Cromwell and voicing disillusionment with his regime, and their works were published in advance of the elections for the second protectorate Parliament. Nedham, like Milton, was developing opposition to Cromwell from within the 'court', and representing the interests of old friends such as John Bradshaw, who had broken with Cromwell.[98]

However, such activity does not appear to have seriously imperilled Nedham's salary. His pension was suspended for only a few weeks in 1655, and was secured by Nedham's submission of a positional paper regarding the printing industry, and it was paid thereafter until at least October 1658.[99] That this should have been the case reflected Nedham's willingness to step back from the brink of outright opposition to Cromwell after the publication of *The Excellencie*. This may have been motivated by fear for his safety, particularly after Vane's arrest, and his subsequent actions clearly frustrated the republicans. One enemy claimed that Nedham 'was one of the spokes of Harrington's Rota till he was turned out for cracking'.[100] During the spring of 1657, indeed, Nedham tilted towards a monarchical constitution, by defending proposals encapsulated in the 'Humble Petition and Advice', which called for the adoption of hereditary monarchy, and for the crowning of Cromwell.[101] In March, therefore, Nedham penned four editorials for *Politicus* which, though ambiguous in tone, nevertheless suggest that he was distancing himself from Harrington, Vane ('the High-Notional Knight'), and 'that wondrous wise republican called *Mercurius Politicus*'. Instead, Nedham wrote respectfully of leading royalist authors, such as Henry Ferne, Thomas Hobbes, Thomas White and John Hall of Richmond; advocated pragmatism rather than utopianism regarding governmental forms; and concluded that 'men are as free, every jot, under a right principality, as under a popular form'.[102] Such lines clearly bemused contemporaries such as John Pell, who commented that *Politicus* 'spoke so darkly that no man can possibly have found out what it was'.[103]

---

[98] J. G. A. Pocock, 'James Harrington and the good old cause: a study of the ideological context of his writings', *JBS* 10 (1970), pp. 36–8; J. G. A. Pocock, *The Machiavellian Moment* (Princeton, 1975), pp. 381–4; [M. Nedham], *The Excellencie of a Free State* (London, for Brewster, 1656), sig. A2; *SR* ii. 20; B. Worden, 'Marchamont Nedham and the beginnings of English republicanism, 1649–1656', in D. Wootton, ed., *Republicanism, Liberty, and Commercial Society, 1649–1776* (Stanford, 1994); Worden, 'Milton and Marchamont Nedham', p. 175. For Vane, see: R. E. Mayers, 'Real and practicable, not imaginary and notional: Sir Henry Vane, *A Healing Question*, and the problems of the protectorate', *Albion* 28 (1996).

[99] *CSPD 1655–6*, p. 588; *CSPD 1656–7*, pp. 591–2; *CSPD 1657–8*, pp. 556–7; *CSPD 1658–9*, p. 584; Raymond, 'Mercury', p. 8.

[100] *Character of the Rump*, p. 3.

[101] Gardiner, *Constitutional Documents*, pp. 447–64.

[102] *Mercurius Politicus* 352 (5–12 Mar. 1657), pp. 7641–4; *Mercurius Politicus* 353 (12–19 Mar. 1657), pp. 7657–9; *Mercurius Politicus* 354 (19–26 Mar. 1657), pp. 7673–5; *Mercurius Politicus* 355 (26 Mar.–2 Apr. 1657), pp. 7689–92; Pocock, 'Harrington', pp. 38–9.

[103] R. Vaughan, *The Protectorate of Oliver Cromwell* (2 vols, London, 1839), ii. 126.

However, Nedham's 'shuttle-cock' mind, and his importance as a means of gauging the strength of various competing factions within the court, is made evident once again in the aftermath of the kingship debates, when he not only reported Cromwell's speech rejecting the crown, but turned his newspaper against the monarchical plans which he had so recently championed.[104] Thereafter, Nedham returned to his old habit of documenting Cromwell's statements faithfully, and he reported eagerly the arrest of the republican, Edward Sexby, whom he later claimed had been 'distracted in mind'.[105] During 1658, Nedham was clearly more circumspect in expressing his opposition to Cromwell, which indicates the way in which the forces seeking to reform the government, whether towards a monarchy or a republic, became far more muted. Nedham's proximity to the court is evident from his personal correspondence with John Fitzjames, which indicates that the place where he could most readily be found in 1658 was in Thurloe's office.[106] Nedham reported the renewed vigour against scandalous pamphleteers, and attacked the royalist plots involving the likes of John Hewitt, Sir Henry Slingsby and John Stapley.[107] Nedham did advertise the re-publication of Milton's *Defensio*, which offered a warning against backsliding into a monarchical regime, but he offered a concerted defence of the government in two works narrating the plot against Cromwell by the old Leveller, Miles Sindercombe, which were printed by Thomas Newcomb, and which included material from Nedham's editorials, as well as evidence presented to Parliament on 21 January 1657.[108] Nedham also issued a defence of the Cromwellian church settlement in July 1657, which he dedicated to Cromwell, and also advertised in the press.[109] This work clearly angered Nedham's enemies, and confirmed their impression that he was 'that state porter, that *venalis anima*, that mercenary soul

---

[104] *Mercurius Politicus* 355 (26 Mar.–2 Apr. 1657), pp. 7702–4; *Mercurius Politicus* 356 (2–9 Apr. 1657), pp. 7705–6, 7719–20.

[105] *Mercurius Politicus* 363 (21–28 May 1657), pp. 7810–11; *Mercurius Politicus* 369 (25 June–2 July 1657), pp. 7877–8; *Mercurius Politicus* 373 (23–30 July 1657), p. 9741 (error for p. 7941); *Mercurius Politicus* 398 (7–14 Jan. 1658), p. 240; *Mercurius Politicus* 399 (14–21 Jan. 1658), pp. 251–5.

[106] Alnwick Castle, Northumberland Papers 552, fos. 4–70v.

[107] *Mercurius Politicus* 403 (11–18 Feb. 1658), pp. 307–8; *Mercurius Politicus* 417 (20–27 May 1658), pp. 555–8; *Mercurius Politicus* 418 (27 May–3 June 1658), pp. 565–74; *Mercurius Politicus* 419 (3–10 June 1658), pp. 577, 582–6; *Mercurius Politicus* 420 (10–17 June 1658), pp. 589–94, 600–602.

[108] J. Milton, *Pro Populo Anglicano Defensio* (London, by Newcomb, 1658); *Mercurius Politicus* (18–25 Nov. 1658), p. 29; M. Dzelzainis, 'Milton and the protectorate in 1658', in Armitage, Himy and Skinner, eds, *Milton and Republicanism*; [M. Nedham], *A True Narrative of the Late Trayterous Plot* (London, by Newcomb, 1656); [M. Nedham], *The Whole Business of Sindercome* (London, by Newcomb, 1657); E. A. Beller, 'Milton and *Mercurius Politicus*', *HLQ* 5 (1951–52), pp. 479–87; *Mercurius Politicus* 345 (15–22 Jan. 1657), pp. 7541–3; *Mercurius Politicus* 348 (5–12 Feb. 1657), pp. 7588–92; *Mercurius Politicus* 349 (12–19 Feb. 1657), pp. 7604–8; *CJ* vii. 481; *CSPV 1657–9*, pp. 11, 18, 20.

[109] M. Nedham, *The Great Accuser Cast Down* (London, by Newcomb, 1657), sig. A2; *The Publick Intelligencer* 110 (23–30 Nov. 1657), p. 125.

that for a handful of earth shall be hired to assassinate the greatest fame and reputation'.[110]

Nedham's career under Oliver Cromwell indicates a tendency to drift between loyal reflection of the political mood among his paymasters, and his personal republicanism, not least when the stars of Vane and Harrington seemed to be in the ascendancy. Though he sailed close to the wind, Nedham managed to avoid losing his way. His behaviour under Richard Cromwell, however, suggests that republican inclinations led him to push his employer's tolerance to the limit. Richard's regime witnessed the resurgence of republican demands regarding the 'good old cause', and Nedham may once again have trimmed his sails to match the prevailing wind; a mood which was republican rather than Cromwellian. Nedham tentatively indicated his support for the republicans by advertising Milton's 1659 writings, such as the *Treatise of Civil Power*.[111] Similarly, he later tested the patience of his employers during the restored Long Parliament in early 1660. Having accommodated the return of the Rump in December 1659, Nedham set out his stall against the readmission of those MPs who had been secluded at Pride's Purge in 1648, by commenting that the petitions for their recall could have been 'penned at Brussells'.[112] Nedham confidently expected new elections, and reprinted the form of the new writs, but nevertheless had to report meetings which took place between Harbert Morley and Sir Arthur Hesilrige and the secluded members, as well as the letter by which George Monck announced their readmission. When the old Presbyterians were readmitted in February 1660, Nedham remained in his post and was nominally loyal, although his reports of the actions of the reconstituted Commons were mechanical and unenthusiastic, and devoid of comment.[113] Indeed, Nedham expressed his dissent from political developments by advertising the appearance of Milton's *Ready and Easie Way*, and alongside Milton was probably responsible for *Plain English to his Excellencie the Lord General Monck* (March 1660), which consisted of a provocative reprinting of the declaration of 'no further addresses' from 1648.[114] More famously, of course, Nedham produced *Newes from Brussells*, which some contemporaries attributed to Henry Neville, and which purported to be a letter from an attendant at the court of Charles II, while actually representing a cunning attack upon the exiled

---

[110] D. F., *A Letter of Addresse to the Protector Occasioned by Mr Needhams Reply to Mr Goodwins Book Against the Triers* (London, 1657), p. 2.

[111] Woolrych, 'Introduction', pp. 4–26; *Mercurius Politicus* 554 (10–17 Feb. 1659), p. 237.

[112] *Mercurius Politicus* 606 (2–9 Feb. 1660), pp. 1069–70; *The Publicke Intelligencer* 214 (30 Jan.–6 Feb. 1660), p. 1066; *The Publicke Intelligencer* 215 (6–13 Feb. 1660), p. 1079.

[113] *Mercurius Politicus* 608 (16–23 Feb. 1660), pp. 1114–15, 1117, 1119–23.

[114] *Mercurius Politicus* 610 (1–8 Mar. 1660), p. 1151; J. M[ilton], *The Readie and Easie Way to Establish a Free Commonwealth* (London, by Newcomb for Chapman, 1660); *Plain English to his Excellencie the Lord General Monck* (London, 1660); R. L'Estrange, *L'Estrange his Apology* (London, 1660), pp. 114–18; R. L'Estrange, *No Blinde Guides* (London, 1660); *Treason Arraigned* (London, 1660), pp. 3, 5.

king.[115] That the appearance of this work displeased Nedham's employers is evident from the order passed for the arrest of its publisher, Livewell Chapman, and from the reward of £20 offered for information leading to the discovery of its author.[116]

While study of the nature of the interaction between authors and politicians requires, therefore, scrutiny of the weaknesses as well as the strengths of such relationships, there is no straightforward way in which to assess the reliability of authors and printers, given the absence of clear criteria with which to make such judgements. Moreover, reliability is not only subject to a variety of definitions, but was clearly subjective in nature, and was probably assessed on an individual basis, and in ways which differed according to specific authors and particular relationships. To the extent that propagandists led independent print lives, and needed to make a living from the pen and the printing press, political consistency may not merely have been an unaffordable luxury, but also something which patrons treated as a virtue rather than a necessity. Reliability must be assessed in terms of contemporary perceptions, and through contemporary reactions to those who were considered to have been wayward. This is particularly clear from the example of Nedham, whose value to the regimes of the 1650s was such that he was able to drift away from the 'party line', without incurring the wrath of the Cromwellian and republican authorities. Nedham appears to have been given, in other words, a hefty degree of latitude, and his tendency to waywardness seems to have been accommodated, and corrected by means of control of his pension.

In assessing the reliability of authors and the instances where they stepped out of line, however, it is, once again, necessary to consider more than just the perspective of writers and their motivations. It is also possible to question the extent to which attempts to interrogate and punish authors for slips of the pen were entirely transparent, as well as to demonstrate that a number of such incidents resulted from factional manipulation of the parliamentary and judicial process. Punishment was not necessarily indicative of unreliability, particularly when such punishments were imposed by members of rival factions, and for saying things which were only unacceptable to some, but by no means all, within Westminster. It is necessary, in fact, to contextualise punishment in terms of precise circumstances and contemporary perceptions, as well as the identity of those responsible, and the outcome for all concerned.

Caution certainly needs to be used in the examination of instances where

---

[115] [M. Nedham], *News from Brussels* (np, 1660). The threat posed to Charles II by Nedham's forgery was clearly evident from the number of replies which it provoked: C. A. Edie, 'Reading popular political pamphlets: a question of meaning', in G. J. Schochet, ed., *Restoration, Ideology, and Revolution* (Washington, 1990), pp. 291–2, 302; N. P., *A Reply to that Malicious Letter* (London, 1660); Sir R. Baker, *A Chronicle of the Kings of England* (London, 1665), p. 762.

[116] *CCSP* iv. 629–30; Bodl. MS Clarendon 71, fos. 107, 112.

favoured writers were punished for overstepping the limits of acceptability. The parliamentarian author Henry Walker, for example, was imprisoned on a number of occasions in the early 1640s for producing scandalous pamphlets. However, the problem with such apparently unreliable behaviour is the contestable nature of the surviving evidence. It ought to be apparent by this stage that politicians could use print in order to manipulate political situations, and that the print medium could be used in order to express opinions which could not be stated openly. In the early 1640s, therefore, the speed with which Walker was released from prison – which prompted allegations that he received nothing more than 'slender punishment' – may indicate that he was regarded as a useful polemicist, at least by certain individuals within Westminster, who sought to use him in order to raise the political temperature with inflammatory statements and tracts, but who nevertheless needed to keep him at arm's length. Parliamentarian grandees could not avoid taking action against him, but they arguably sought to inflict the minimum possible punishment before releasing him and his pen until the next inflammatory incident.[117] Walker's punishment may be regarded, therefore, as having masked protection of his talents, albeit in a surreptitious manner, and albeit only by a faction within Parliament.

Factionalism also underpinned a number of well-known incidents where ministers and pamphleteers were punished for what were apparently loose words from the pulpit, in printed sermons, and in polemical pamphlets. Thus, when Christopher Love delivered a sermon before the commissioners gathered for the Uxbridge peace negotiations in early 1645, he declared that 'men who lie under the guilt of much innocent blood are not meet persons to be at peace with, till all the guilt of blood be expiated and avenged, either by the sword of the law, or law of the sword, else a peace can neither be saife nor just'.[118] Parliament quickly imprisoned him, and the future secretary of state, John Thurloe, who formed part of Oliver St John's coterie at Uxbridge, disowned the preacher as being 'none of our retinue, nor came hither by any privitie of ours'.[119] However, Love was released after the conclusion of the Uxbridge negotiations, and it is perfectly possible that he was representing the views of certain Independents who had little inclination to make the negotiations work, and that his arrest and imprisonment reflected the influence of the Presbyterians at Westminster, just as they sought to

---

[117] *LJ* iv. 182, 186, 204–5, 210; Nalson, *Impartial Collections*, i. 795; Williams, *History*, p. 74; Bodl. MS Tanner 63, fo. 10; HLRO, MP 9/5/42; *HMC 5th Report*, p. 22; HLRO, MP 25/6/42; J. Taylor, *The Whole Life and Progress of Henry Walker* (London, 1642), sig. A2v; *LJ* v. 647, 651. Anthony Milton has reached similar conclusions about the relationship between Laud and Peter Heylyn: A. Milton, 'The creation of Laudianism: a new approach', in T. Cogswell, R. Cust and P. Lake, eds, *Politics, Religion and Popularity in Early Stuart Britain* (Cambridge, 2002), pp. 178–9.

[118] C. Love, *England's Distemper* (London, 1645), p. 37.

[119] *CJ* iv. 40; CUL, Mm.1.46, p. 85; P. Crawford, 'Charles Stuart, that man of blood', in P. Gaunt, ed., *The English Civil War* (Oxford, 2000), pp. 311–12.

prevent *Britanicus* from voicing Independent views during the course of the talks.[120] Similar factors may have caused the questioning of Henry Walker in April 1646, for an edition of *Perfect Occurrences*, 'wherein divers questions are falsely and scandalously printed as questions from this house, to be propounded to the assembly concerning Jus Divinum'. They may also have underpinned the measures taken against him in November 1646, for publishing letters of the Scots' commissioners.[121] The same may also provide an explanation for the difficulty faced by the Independent preacher, William Dell, who was called before the Lords in May 1646, upon charges drawn up by Presbyterians such as John Bastwick, Thomas Edwards, and William Prynne, and who caused further offence in November 1646, by printing a fast sermon which had failed to receive the thanks of the Commons, or a request for its publication. However, once again it was probably the Presbyterians who objected to Dell, not least because of the inclusion of an aggressive polemical dedication to the Commons, in which he referred to the 'clergy-Antichristian power' which was sitting 'upon the power of the nation', and in which he hinted that the Westminster Assembly was the 'last prop of Antichrist in the kingdom'.[122] Finally, Henry Walker appears to have offended his patrons with the published version of a high-profile sermon before Cromwell on the eve of the Scottish campaign in 1650. On this occasion the printed edition was commissioned by the Council, who contributed £20 towards the costs, but in it Walker added passages against Sir Thomas Fairfax, which resulted in the work being publicly burnt.[123] However, it may be considered unlikely that Walker would have risked inserting such comments unless he had been sanctioned to do so by someone in authority.

Factional politics can also be shown to have provoked incidents whereby newspaper editors were questioned, and even imprisoned, for passages and phrases which were deemed unacceptable. In order to seize control of the press in preparation for the Uxbridge treaty in early 1645, therefore, the Earl of Essex and his allies orchestrated the arrest of John Dillingham, who as editor of *Parliament Scout* and an attendant of Oliver St John could be expected to give vent to the views of those opposed to the talks. They did so, however, by means of the rather weak allegation that Dillingham was responsible for 'defamation to the honour of

---

[120] *CJ* iv. 49; above, p. 260; J. Peacey, 'The struggle for *Mercurius Britanicus*: factional politics and the parliamentarian press, 1643–6' (forthcoming).

[121] *CJ* iv. 521; Williams, *History*, p. 68.

[122] W. Dell, *Right Reformation* (London, 1646); *CJ* iv. 707; *CJ* v. 10; C. Hill, *The English Bible and the Seventeenth Century Revolution* (London, 1994), p. 83; L. F. Solt, 'William Dell: New Model Army chaplain', *Church Quarterly Review* 155 (1954), pp. 44–5; E. C. Walker, *William Dell, Master Puritan* (Cambridge, 1970), pp. 66–71, 74, 76, 82, 85.

[123] H. Walker, *A Sermon Preached in the Chapell at Sommerset House* (London, 1650), sig. A3; *CSPD 1650*, p. 345; Williams, *History*, pp. 139–41; *Perfect Diurnall* 33 (22–29 July 1650), p. 391. In July 1650, Walker and Ibbitson were ordered to forbear printing the late declaration of Parliament upon marching the army into Scotland, and to search Ibbitson's house for copies of the same: *CSPD 1650*, p. 551.

the Lord General'. That this represented a mere tactical device, rather than genuine distaste at the tone of Dillingham's paper, is evident from the fact that he was detained on the day that peace talks began, and that he was able to secure his release upon their collapse, in late February 1645.[124] Likewise, the trouble in which Nedham found himself during 1645–46 can also be contextualised in terms of factional politics at Westminster. It was almost certainly pro-Essex editorialising in *Britanicus* which resulted in the order, engineered by the Independents, to question Nedham in the second week of March 1645. On 13 March, Edmund Reeve and Ralph Whitfield reported to the Lords, having perused the paper, that they had found one passage 'very derogatory and scandalous'. As a result of their findings, the general editor, Thomas Audley, was ordered to be arrested, while the chief journalist, Nedham, appears to have escaped the unwelcome attention of the House.[125] The aim appears, in other words, to have been to place factional pressure upon the paper, rather than to silence Nedham.

Later, a more convoluted episode involving the punishment of those responsible for *Britanicus* reflected renewed factional struggle for control of the press. In August 1645, the authorities arrested Audley and Nedham, as well as their printer, Robert White, for what Sir Roger Burgoyne called 'being so saucy and uncivil with the king in his pamphlets'. Although Burgoyne claimed that 'the parliament did very much resent the impudency of his style', the reality is somewhat different.[126] The Earl of Essex's enemies evidently orchestrated the infamous 'Hue and Cry' issue of *Britanicus* (4 Aug. 1645), in order to justify the removal of the Lord General from the position as licenser of this invaluable newspaper. It is unlikely that Essex would have sanctioned the comments contained in that issue, and it was clearly the last which he licensed.[127] Nedham opened by asking: 'where is King Charles? What's become of him?', and he went on to comment on the monarch's famous speech impediment. Nedham's comments were regarded as a means of 'feeding the hatred of the vulgar', and he was considered to have overstepped the boundary of acceptability.[128] Robert White was questioned at the bar of the Lords (5 August), where he claimed that he was directed by Audley, with the authority of John Rushworth. White was duly despatched to the Fleet, and Audley, who appeared on the following day, 'confessed he allowed it, but found fault to the author of the clause concerning the king's person, and he and the printer promised to put it out'. Despite such protestations of innocence, Audley was sent to the Gatehouse for a couple of

---

[124] Cotton, 'John Dillingham', pp. 821, 824–5; *LJ* vii. 164; *HMC 6th Report*, p. 48; HLRO, MP 22/2/45.

[125] *LJ* vii. 267, 272. In this, I perceive rather different factional politics than was detected by others: Cotton, 'London newsbooks', p. 101.

[126] Claydon House, Verney Papers, Reel 6, unfol.

[127] *SR* i. 146–185 (1 Feb.–4 Aug. 1645).

[128] *Mercurius Britanicus* 92 (28 July–4 Aug. 1645), p. 825; *CSPV 1643–7*, pp. 207–8; Claydon House, Verney Papers, Reel 6, unfol.: Sir Roger Burgoyne to Sir Ralph Verney, 7 Aug. 1645.

weeks, while Nedham once again escaped unscathed, and *Britanicus* disappeared for only one week before returning to the presses.[129] Once again, an episode which appears at first glance to have involved an attempt by Parliament to punish a favoured writer for a slip of the pen turns out to represent complex political intrigue centred on a factional battle for control of a valuable propaganda organ. Indeed, Nedham may have been cajoled by the Independents – working through Rushworth – into inserting the offending passages, in order to enable the removal of Essex from the paper's helm, and with the promise that he would escape punishment.

Similar recontextualisation can be undertaken regarding the eventual closure of *Britanicus* in late May 1646, after Nedham had been called to the bar of the Lords (23 May), and despatched to the Fleet. It is generally assumed that he was silenced because of his 'fierce tirades against the king', but it appears upon scrutiny that it was the peers who gave the order for his arrest, upon complaint of his having printed passages *between the two Houses*.[130] Examination of the final issue of *Britanicus* reveals the passage which caused offence:

> will the Scots send the king to his Parliament, or not? Ye shall know more, when 'tis determined in the upper House what to do, how we shall be demanded, and how received. Have we been all this while in earnest, and now stand we upon ceremony? Be resolved, O ye Commons of the kingdom, you have paid deare for your liberties, and whosoever he was that endeavoured to rob you of them, is *ipso facto* a tyrant.

It was not calling Charles a tyrant which brought Nedham to grief, but rather his report of the conference between the Lords and Commons in which the latter made their demands regarding the king. Nedham had nailed his colours to the cause of the Commons and their opposition to the prevaricating, and ultimately pro-Scottish, policy of the Lords.[131] *Britanicus* was closed down by the Earl of Essex and his allies, rather than by the likes of Viscount Saye, who were unlikely to have worried about this report of the dispute between the two Houses, since Nedham was espousing views with which they agreed. The pressure came from a House of Lords recently strengthened by the resurgent Essex – who had secured control of the Speaker's chair earlier in the year – and Nedham was silenced because he was attacking Essex, and not for anything he said about the king.[132] This reading is supported by events after Nedham's arrest. On 28 May, Nedham wrote a grovelling letter to the Earl of Denbigh from the Fleet prison, which was facilitated by Sir Henry Mildmay and William Lenthall, and which asked that his petition 'may be presented and read this Thursday, and that when it shall be taken into

---

129 *LJ* vii. 525, 528, 539; Worden, 'Wit in a Roundhead', p. 315; *HMC 6th Report*, p. 74; *The Scotish Dove* 94 (1–8 Aug. 1645), p. 744.

130 *LJ* viii. 321; Worden, 'Wit in a Roundhead', p. 316.

131 *Mercurius Britanicus* 130 (11–18 May 1646), pp. 1111, 1117. See: Cotton, 'London newsbooks', p. 102.

132 J. S. A. Adamson, 'The peerage in politics, 1645–49' (Cambridge University PhD, 1986), pp. 115–68.

debate you would be pleased to assure that right honourable house in my behalf'. Nedham sought to demonstrate to Parliament that 'whatever errors have fallen from my pen to their displeasure, my intents were ever fixed on their and the kingdom's service, from which end the desires of all my friends and the temptations of others, could never make me swerve'. Recognising that his troubles had been occasioned by the displeasure which he had caused 'their lordships', Nedham promised to continue his:

> endeavours with so much innocence, so much observance toward the House of peers, that they shall never have the least cause to repent of their favour towards me, nor your lordship that you have mediated (should God reserve so great an honour) for my present enlargement; without which I am undone, having a family to provide for, and besides the performance of my public profession to the House, I will frame the whole course of my life (in particular) to render myself worthy of that happy relation of (my lord) your lordship's most humbly devoted servant.[133]

That Nedham was quickly released, and able to resume writing works which represented the interests of Denbigh and his allies, indicates the attitude of the Independent grandees towards him.[134]

Detailed contextualisation of some of the most notorious incidents where authors who worked in close proximity to political grandees appear to have been punished for stepping out of line reveals the extent to which propagandists could find themselves as little more than pawns in bitter factional struggles within Parliament, and perhaps within the royalist court as well. Given the existence of factional politics, and given also the tendency for political factions to seek writers through whom to speak in public, prosecutions for 'unreliable' passages in tracts, pamphlets and newspapers tended to be determined less by the nature of such texts, than by the contingent balance of sectional interests.

Authors of polemical literature could be moved by a variety of considerations, including private concerns – in terms of pecuniary profit and personal safety – and political principles. This variety of motives, and the manifold ways in which they could be combined, ensured a wide range of different kinds of relationships between authors and patrons which involved the production of propaganda. Some of these involved propagandists retaining independent literary and publishing lives, and in studying polemical writers of the period it is crucial to remain alive to the possibility that works by authors who were known to have associated with political grandees need not be assumed to have been encouraged or commissioned. It would be a mistake, however, to conclude that such independence, together with the growing importance of money in the world of political print culture, and the ability to survive by the pen, denotes a tendency for authors to sacrifice principle on the altar of personal advantage. Examples can be found of authors who were

---

[133] Warwickshire RO, CR 2017/C10/115.
[134] Above, p. 116.

little more than hacks, and who were willing to sell their polemical talents to those who were willing to pay, although they probably eked out a meagre living. More common were authors who wrote in order to express personal convictions and opinions, and who were able to act as propagandists when such views were shared with prominent political figures. That such characters wrote from conviction and principle is evident from the fact that they sometimes found themselves sitting awkwardly alongside specific grandees, and among the factional configurations and political groupings at both Oxford and Westminster. Evidence suggests that such authors, while prepared to write on behalf of politicians, were not willing to do so on any terms, and in situations where their own beliefs clashed with those of potential or actual patrons.

This variety of author–patron relationships, and of authorial attitudes to money, personal security and political principle, also proves important for understanding the changing fortunes of polemical writers. It was not always easy to retain favour or patronage, and many writers experienced changing fortunes. It is possible to demonstrate that writers rose to favour and fell from grace, secured and lost employment, and won and lost substantial amounts of money, sometimes in spectacular circumstances. Some can be shown to have changed sides, sometimes on more than one occasion, and others occasionally proved 'unreliable'. Such cases, together with the plethora of contemporary comments, suggest that behaviour over time was driven by financial concerns, and that particular individuals were willing to act in unprincipled ways by trimming their sails to catch shifting political winds. Indeed, it is certainly true that, in an age which saw the emergence of the professional writer, authors could not afford to ignore matters of personal fortune in order to adhere rigidly to personal principles, although they tended to be motivated by personal security and a desire to avoid poverty and prison, rather than by the search for wealth. And it is clearly important to recognise the significance of new types of relationship, and the extent to which a professionalised machinery for producing propaganda resulted in authors being less willing to serve their paymasters unless money was forthcoming. However, this need not necessarily have made them less reliable, given that financial incentives could be used to control them and keep them in check. Furthermore, it is possible to explore alternative explanations of authorial actions. Instead of portraying civil war propagandists as being driven solely by money, the picture which emerges is one in which authors rarely betrayed their principles or trimmed their sails entirely, and it is necessary to contextualise such changes of fortune and relationships in terms of the precise political circumstances in which they operated.

It is undeniably true that certain authors retained an independency of spirit which caused them to write and publish things which provoked tensions with those alongside whom they worked, and by whom they were employed. Such tensions often reflected authors' willingess to place personal principles before personal success, and few writers shifted between factions and political sides for pecuniary benefit. While they could not be expected to be martyrs, and while they may have maintained a care for their own success, their career shifts often had as much to do with the shifts of political factions, and the changing nature of royalism, parliamentarianism and the political culture of the commonwealth. Evidence relating to instances where writers were punished for overstepping the mark of acceptability, and where they can be shown to have 'changed sides', needs to be handled with great care. While money had become a factor of much greater significance in the print culture of the mid-seventeenth century, and in the world of propaganda in particular, there is little evidence that the writers with whom this book is interested acted in entirely unprincipled ways. Furthermore, once the focus is shifted away from authors, in order to explore their context, and the attitudes of those political figures with whom they worked, it is possible to demonstrate that tensions between propagandists and politicians could be caused not just by truculent authors, but also by changes in political circumstances. Instances where writers fell from favour, changed sides, and proved wayward, can often be recontextualised in the light of evidence regarding the difficulties which resulted from changing political circumstances, factional positions, and regimes. As events unfolded and new issues came to the fore, the nature of particular factions, and the factional balance of power, tended to alter, and in such situations writers were forced to negotiate the shifting sands of political life, and often found it hard to remain associated with particular individuals and groups. Indeed, some changes of side were less dramatic than they appear from an overly schematic and decontextualised approach to political alignments and allegiance. Finally, it is possible to observe more or less overt attempts to push and pull authors in different directions by powerful political forces, and to recognise that the vagaries of their fortunes need to be understood in the light of factional manipulation of the press.

Relationships between authors and politicians can only be understood, therefore, through detailed contextualisation, which reveals that their nature, and their susceptibility to mutation, were conditioned by political manipulation and political change. By analysing them in this way it is possible to demonstrate that while there could be close interaction between writers and grandees, it would be mistaken to assume that propagandists – even those whose services were purchased – were merely hired pens who were prepared to write what was profitable. There were limits to individuals' willingness to compromise personal beliefs, and we ought perhaps to conclude that polemical writers could be hired but not bought; borrowed but not browbeaten.

Propaganda, the State, and the Public Sphere

This book has presented a fundamental reinterpretation of the political culture of print during the civil wars and Interregnum. It has revealed the extent and scope of propaganda during the mid-seventeenth century, and the growing importance of print not just in the lives of the political nation, but also in the minds of the political elite. Seventeenth-century politicians have been shown to have understood the developing importance of public opinion, and to have displayed an awareness of the growing interest which the public at large took in following, and participating in, the political events of the time. From the late 1630s, the press was exploited to an unprecedented degree, in order to mobilise public opinion, and to justify political actions. This book has explored the reasons for politicians and writers working together in order to produce political and religious polemic; demonstrated the methods that they used and techniques that they developed; and explored the uses to which propaganda was put, and the complex nature of relations between authors and patrons during a period of conflict and political upheaval.

The process of understanding early modern propaganda began, in the first section of the book, with the motivation of those who were responsible for its production: politicians and pamphleteers. For the former, propaganda reflected the need to communicate with the people. It was recognised as being vital in order to explain policies, and to generate and sustain support. It could be used in more or less official ways in order to create an orthodoxy, and in more or less subtle ways in order to conceal its origins. It could be used in order to fulfil polemical purposes, and to enable key political grandees to sideline awkward and time-consuming political processes, and it could be used in order to reach out to a broad cross-section of the political nation. Among civil war pamphleteers, on the other hand, engagement in the production of polemical literature reflected a desire to serve the interests of their friends and patrons; to display their personal support for religious and political causes; and to place their services at the disposal of political grandees.

The second part of the book sought to explore the mechanics of propaganda. This involved demonstrating the ways in which it is possible to decode polemical literature of the period in order to detect possible political influence and involvement. This was undertaken by exploring patronage networks and the employments of writers; by exploring the timing of particular works and the congruity of their message with the ideas of political grandees; by exploring bibliographical evidence and printing practices; and by being alive to the possibility of connecting various forms of 'reward' with literary effort. Beyond this, the analysis of the 'mechanics' of propaganda demonstrated the importance of licensing as a means of exerting positive as well as negative influence over the press, and explored evidence of proactive involvement in the production of political and religious texts, through commissions, payments and the hiring of writers, and through participation in the writing process. It also demonstrated how politicians were able to coordinate various elements of the propaganda machine, in terms of intelligencers, authors, licensers, printers, publishers and distributors, whose activities were integrated through the efforts of dedicated and specialised agents. This enabled effective control over particular works of propaganda from conception to consumption. Having demonstrated how the presses were turned to political advantage during the civil wars, in terms of the licensing system, the commissioning of specific works, and the retaining of certain writers, and the professionalisation of polemic, the third part of the book explored the 'dynamic' of propaganda, in terms of the uses to which polemic was put, and the techniques by which it was deployed. This involved analysis of the conceptual sophistication of propaganda to match its mechanical development. Thereafter, analysis of the 'dynamic' of propaganda demonstrated the complex nature of the relationships between propagandists and politicians, in terms of their longevity, the ways in which they developed over time, and the ways in which to interpret loyalty and reliability on the part of polemicists and pamphleteers, who can too easily be labelled as having been pragmatic and unprincipled, because they fell from grace and changed sides.

Such examination of the motives, mechanics and dynamics of propaganda in the mid-seventeenth century reveals the extent to which tracts, pamphlets and newspapers are not always what they seem, at first glance, to be, and the necessity of adopting a critical attitude towards them as texts and sources, and a thoroughly contextual approach to their study. It has been possible to demonstrate the extent to which political influences lay behind works which appear to have been produced independently; the possibility that political grandees can be connected with works which appear to convey messages contrary to, or more extreme than, their public utterances and declarations; and the probability that public figures supported the appearance of works which flatly contradicted their political and religious beliefs and opinions. It is also possible to demonstrate that judicial questioning of authors, and the prosecution of their works, need not always indicate 'official' disapproval, nor even represent punishment in any meaningful sense. Once books are recognised as weapons which could be deployed in the course of political processes, and as part of political campaigns, and that authors could become pawns – sometimes willingly – in such political machinations, it is necessary to approach all such works with caution, and armed with a methodology with which to try and recover the political relationships and expressions of power embedded within them. It is this methodology which this book has sought to develop and demonstrate.

The purpose of this epilogue is partly to draw out the key themes which have emerged throughout the preceding analysis, and to explore the implications of civil war propaganda for our understanding of early modern politics and political culture. Thereafter, however, the aim is to suggest how such findings can be used in order to influence assessments of the nature of the early modern 'public sphere', to which scholars have recently drawn attention.

A number of important themes emerge from the analysis of the preceding chapters. The first concerns the tension between two of the key aims of propaganda, namely the need to establish orthodoxy, on the one hand, while also avoiding making official involvement in propaganda transparent, on the other. Such purposes were mutually incompatible, and resulted in the production of works which aimed to fulfil either, but not both, goals. Some works, therefore, bore almost no evidence of the involvement of political grandees, and could be used in the most subtle conceptual ways. Other forms of propaganda were self-evidently official in their origins, as a result of bearing an official licence or *imprimatur*, or as a result of containing overt statements regarding the circumstances of their composition, and the involvement of official printers. Some were also known to have been produced with official backing and by leading propagandists. Some works bore a number of such visual clues, such as the translation of John Selden's *Mare Clausum*, which was undertaken 'by special command', by someone well known to have been an official propagandist (Marchamont Nedham), and which was printed by William Dugard, who was styled official printer to the Council of State, and who deployed the arms of the commonwealth on the title page.[1] Such works may have been used in order to make known 'official' lines, and to develop new orthodoxies. Some works, including newspapers such as *Mercurius Politicus*, may also have been intended to serve diplomatic as much as domestic propaganda purposes.[2]

A second key theme concerns the emergence of increasingly bureaucratised, centralised and professionalised methods of producing propaganda, and new kinds of relationship between propagandists and politicians. From the formulation of official declarations to the manner of their distribution, and from the development of the licensing system to the means by which the services of writers were employed, and the manner in which their projects were scrutinised, assisted and supervised, this study has revealed that the mid-seventeenth century witnessed the growing sophistication of print propaganda, indeed its complete transformation,

---

[1] J. Selden, *Of the Dominion, or Ownership of the Sea* (trans. M. Nedham, London, 1652).

[2] J. Klaits, *Printed Propaganda under Louis XIV: Absolute Monarchy and Public Opinion* (Princeton, 1976), pp. 67, 74–7; D. Hirst, '"That sober liberty": Marvell's Cromwell in 1654', in J. M. Wallace, ed., *The Golden and the Brazen World* (Berkeley, Ca., 1985), p. 43.

particularly after the execution of Charles I in 1649. It witnessed, in essence, the decline of propaganda and polemic which emerged as a result of personal loyalty to patrons, and the emergence of writers whose literary activities, if not the message of their texts, were generated by the prospect of financial remuneration. Writers were brought into political life and into bureaucratic administrations, and some fulfilled a range of duties – from intelligence gathering to the logistical management of propaganda, and from the composition of official statements to subtle polemic – which formed key elements of the machinery of propaganda. This is evident from the careers of Henry Parker, John Sadler and Walter Frost, and most particularly from the career of clerics such as Cornelius Burges. Well known in his own time and ours as a Puritan activist, who was involved in organising petitions in London in the 1640s, and who had his house searched by the authorities, it is less widely appreciated that his involvement with godly grandees may have extended to secretive missions to Scotland before the calling of the Long Parliament, and certainly took him to York in October 1640, perhaps in connection with the assembling of the Great Council of Peers.[3] Although well known as a preacher before Parliament, less well known is his involvement in the work of important committees dealing with religious affairs in the opening months of the Long Parliament, and the fact that this appears to have resulted in his having penned at least one work which had official sanction, and which represented an attempt to sideline the tricky process of drafting official declarations.[4]

From being essentially a renaissance operation – the product of individual patrons and authors – propaganda became centred on the early modern government, wherein the resources of the executive and its bureaucracy were brought to bear on the world of publishing. As such, it reflects directly upon the formation of the state in seventeenth-century England. The trends in the world of print with which this book is concerned reflect the transition from the renaissance monarchy to the modern state, and from aristocratic patronage to state's servants, which has been recognised by scholars as an important, if not necessarily permanent, development of the period covered by this work.[5] Indeed, as Michael Braddick and Steve Hindle have indicated, processes of state formation must be

---

[3] *CSPD 1640*, pp. 563–4; PRO, SP 16/463, fo. 200; *CSPD 1640–1*, p. 73; R. Chestlin, *Persecutio Undecima* ([London], 1648), pp. 57, 58, 62; A. Laurence, *Parliamentary Army Chaplains, 1642–1651* (Woodbridge, 1990), pp. 106–7; V. Pearl, *London and the Outbreak of the Puritan Revolution* (Oxford, 1961), pp. 109, 195, 280; C. Russell, *The Fall of the British Monarchies, 1637–1642* (Oxford, 1991), pp. 139, 140, 152, 166; BL, Add. 70002, fo. 310.

[4] *CJ* ii. 144; J. Bruce, ed., *Letters and Papers of the Verney Family* (Camden Society, 56, 1853), pp. 9, 10, 12, 75–7; *An Humble Examination of a Printed Abstract of the Answers to Nine Reasons of the House of Commons Against the Votes of Bishops in Parliament* (printed by order of a committee of the House of Commons, London, 1641); *SR* i. 26.

[5] Klaits, *Printed Propaganda*, pp. 6–7; P. Corrigan and D. Sayer, *The Great Arch. English State Formation as Cultural Revolution* (Oxford, 1985), pp. 55, 78–83; G. Aylmer, 'Bureaucracy', in *New Cambridge Modern History* (14 vols, Cambridge, 1951–79), vol. 13; G. Aylmer, 'From office-holding to civil service: the genesis of modern bureaucracy', *TRHS*, 5th series 30 (1980).

considered as being intimately connected with broader cultural trends during this period, of which the development of propaganda was a key element. State formation was directly linked, in other words, to exploitation of the means of legitimation. They have also indicated, as this study has found, that such processes need not be considered to have been deliberate, so much as the result of political and social dynamics, and that they must be recognised as having resulted from multilateral initiatives, rather than merely government action.[6] However, as with the tension between using propaganda to develop orthodoxy and to operate in subtle and invisible ways, so there existed a tension between 'traditional' and 'modern' methods of producing propaganda. The advantages of hired writers and civil service employees – most obviously in terms of the convenience of having expert polemical services 'on tap' – had to be played off against possible drawbacks relating to the 'reliability' of hired pens, whose loyalty was at least partly driven by financial incentives, and whose status may all too easily have been recognised by the public.

The third theme concerns the possibility of detecting evidence of differences in attitude towards the press and propaganda between royalists and parliamentarians. Stated crudely, royalists proved less willing (and less able) to engage with the public through the medium of print. Having said that, both parliamentarians and royalists turned to print to an unprecedented degree during the 1640s and 1650s; therefore, it is important to recognise that the majority of the most significant developments in the evolution of propaganda during this period were undertaken by Parliament and the commonwealth, rather than by the king and his court. This is as true of the print-runs of official statements as it is to the bureaucratisation of propaganda production, and the professionalisation of the polemicist's art. However, while it is tempting to conclude that the civil war led to profound changes in the nature of relations between politicians and the people, and profound changes in the nature of governmental practices, and that parliamentarians were in the vanguard of such developments, it is necessary to remain cautious. In many ways, such a picture represents an oversimplification, which masks differences in attitude within royalist and parliamentarian ranks. It is not clear how sensible it is to talk about 'royalists' and 'parliamentarians', at least in terms of their attitudes to print and propaganda, since both were to some degree internally divided over their attitude towards print and the public. The attitude of Sir Edward Hyde may have differed from that of Lord Digby, and the views of Viscount Saye may have differed from those of Sir Simonds D'Ewes. Furthermore, it is also possible that attitudes on either side were determined in part by changing events, and by the extent to which either side held a dominant political position. Attitudes to the press

---

[6] M. J. Braddick, *State Formation in Early Modern England, c.1550–1700* (Cambridge, 2000), pp. 432–5; S. Hindle, *The State and Social Change in Early Modern England, 1550–1640* (Basingstoke, 2002), pp. 2, 16, 23. See also: M. J. Braddick, 'State formation and social change in early modern England: a problem stated and approaches suggested', *Social History* 16 (1991), p. 2.

– in terms of the strictness of censorship, and the willingness to foment debate and discussion – could be altered, therefore, during the conditions of civil war, and by the winning and losing of power. It seems likely that the attitude of those Puritans who sought in the 1620s and 1630s to effect political and religious change, or to resist Caroline and Laudian innovation, changed somewhat during the 1640s, and that the possession of power in the 1650s altered perceptions once again. It is also possible that the attitude of the king and his courtiers during the period before the civil war was altered by the challenge posed by Parliament and the army in the 1640s, and that royalist attitudes too changed during a period of defeat and exile in the 1650s.

Recognising that neither royalists nor parliamentarians were united over the exploitation of print also provides the key to a fourth major theme of this book, namely the importance of factional tension – within either side – as a motor for change in the realm of propaganda, and for the development of new techniques, including centralisation, bureaucratisation and professionalisation. As factions emerged, so did the voices who were prepared to speak for them, and to publicise their views in print. Battle lines were drawn in the literary and publishing world, and the ability to influence the press assumed vital importance. During the 1640s, print propaganda was used by rival factions in order to undermine each other, and as factional divisions hardened, the press became a weapon not just for expounding a particular message, but also to criticise rivals. During the second half of the 1640s, factional tension at Westminster focused on the division between Presbyterians and Independents, and upon strategies regarding peace, and the demands to be made of the king, whether in terms of Parliament's power, the control of the militia or the shape of the church settlement. It became most evident in the press, however, in terms of tension between Independents and the Scots, allies of Parliament following the signing of the Solemn League and Covenant, but controversial partners because of the pressure which they exerted for the establishment of a Presbyterian church system. Although the Scots were reluctant to split with the English Independents, they became increasingly fearful of the outcome of discussions, and were clearly willing to use print in order to win the battle of ideas over the church, not least with books by Robert Baillie and Alexander Henderson against the Independents. The polemical skill displayed by the Scots was matched by their organisational innovation, and their ability to integrate different aspects of the propaganda process, and it was arguably their management of the licensing system, and their close relationship with key London ministers and stationers, which eventually provoked a response from the Independents, who not only began to produce propaganda against their putative allies but also strove to reform the licensing system in such a way as to centralise power. However, factionalism prompted not just a tussle for the means of effecting press control, but also the development of increasingly subtle conceptual tactics for the underhand manipulation of the press, in order to achieve political goals which could not be pursued openly. Later, another key factional battle emerged following the fracturing of the 'Independent alliance' and the rise of the army interest. This situation, which represented a jockeying for position between moderate and radical Independents over issues such as the chances for, and terms of, a possible settlement with the king, was also played out in the press, and likewise prompted changes which led to the centralisation and bureaucratisation of the means for producing propaganda.

Turning from the themes of this study to its implications, it is possible to highlight a number of ways in which the conclusions of the preceding analysis, and the study of propaganda in general, are of importance to students and scholars of early modern society, culture and politics. The first, rather negative, point to make, is that although this book has sought to demonstrate the extent to which the period from 1640 to 1660 witnessed profound and important innovations in the realm of propaganda and print culture, it does not necessarily seek to suggest that the 1640s and 1650s marked a 'turning point' in the history of governmental relations with the press. It does not seek to suggest that the civil wars and Interregnum marked a staging post in the historical development of ever more sophisticated management of the press and exploitation of print, in the sense that subsequent regimes built upon the developments made under Parliament and the Cromwells, or in the sense that the changes witnessed during the 1640s and 1650s proved longlasting, let alone permanent. The desire to control and restrain the press certainly continued after the political upheavals and constitutional experiments of the 1640s and 1650s, but this was something which also pre-dated the period under scrutiny in this book. The desire to exploit the press, developed so much in the period under consideration here, was not necessarily evident in the same way in later generations, whether in the late seventeenth century[7] or the early eighteenth century.[8] Nevertheless, it is possible to argue that the experiments and experiences of the 1640s in the world of print and propaganda, as in so much else, informed the minds and actions of subsequent generations. Never again would politicians be unaware of, or perhaps able to ignore, the powerful role which print and propaganda could play in the political life of the nation.

On a more positive note, the study of propaganda in the early modern period is

---

[7] P. Seaward, 'A Restoration publicist: James Howell and the Earl of Clarendon, 1661–6', *HR* 61 (1988), p. 123; P. Harth, *Pen for a Party. Dryden's Tory Propaganda in its Contexts* (Princeton, 1993); J. Sutherland, *The Restoration Newspaper and its Development* (Cambridge, 1986); J. S. T. Hetet, 'A literary underground in Restoration England. Printers and dissenters in the context of constraints 1660–1689' (Cambridge University PhD, 1987); T. J. Crist, 'Francis Smith and the opposition press in England, 1660–1688' (Cambridge University PhD, 1977).

[8] J. Downie, *Robert Harley and the Press* (Cambridge, 1979); J. Black, *The English Press in the Eighteenth Century* (London, 1987); M. Harris, *London Newspapers in the Age of Walpole* (London, 1987); W. Speck, 'Politics and the press', in M. Harris and A. Lee, eds, *The Press in English Society from the Seventeenth to Nineteenth Centuries* (London, 1986); M. Schonhorn, *Defoe's Politics. Parliament, Power, Kingship and Robinson Crusoe* (Cambridge, 1991); R. R. Rea, *The English Press in Politics, 1760–1774* (Lincoln, Nebraska, 1963).

important for our understanding of the highly contested nature of the degree of consensus and conflict in early Stuart society, and for our appreciation of the nature of political debate and polarisation in the months and years before the outbreak of civil war. Firstly, therefore, appreciation of the extent to which public print culture reflected the involvement of political grandees suggests that the press may have been used by men who wanted confrontation, and who used print in order to create conspiracy theories. Understanding this may help answer one of the questions posed by revisionist scholars of the civil war; namely how war broke out given conservatism and limited reformist aims, which appeared to have been achieved by 1641. It is possible, in other words, that there existed a small group of advanced parliamentarians who were dissatisfied with the achievements made by 1641, on the one hand, and a group of royalists who were concerned to limit further changes, if not roll back the political clock, on the other. It is possible, in fact, that both groups used propaganda in order to maintain and even heighten political tension. At the same time, of course, it was obviously necessary to be seen to be acting according to precedent and within the law. Parliament was accused in May 1641 of printing statutes 'to make it clear that their actions are warranted by precedent and law'.[9] This explains why, as scholars of early modern political thought have demonstrated, so much of the political theory regarding, and debates upon, the ancient constitution of the period, employed history, legal precedent and tradition. Contemporaries clearly feared that such determination to appear to be seen to be 'conservative' might have been a device which masked increasing aggression. In May 1642, therefore, William Davie said: 'I hope, under colour of preserving the king's prerogative, we shall not destroy one another, whilst we all protest on all sides to make the king glorious and the kingdom happy'.[10] 'Rebels' were forced to justify their actions in order to win support, while regimes in power, whether royalist or republican, needed to defend obedience. As regimes changed, meanwhile, it was crucial to justify positions and actions, not least in executing the king. Furthermore, given the prevalence of propaganda, it is important to understand the way in which print was manipulated and exploited in order to understand contemporary events, the appreciation of which may still be influenced by the propaganda produced in the early modern period.[11]

Secondly, the perceived need to rouse the public naturally involved putting forward arguments, and highlighting issues, which were thought likely to prove popular. It also involved defining a position which was different from that of one's opponents. In this sense, understanding propaganda, and the ways in which propaganda was perceived to be useful to politicians, is crucial for understanding the

---

9 Sir W. C. Trevelyan and Sir C. E. Trevelyan, eds, *Trevelyan Papers III* (Camden Society, 105, 1872), pp. 209–10.

10 Trevelyan and Trevelyan, eds, *Trevelyan Papers III*, pp. 209–10. See: D. Cressy, 'The Protestation protested, 1641 and 1642', *HJ* 45 (2002), pp. 268–9.

11 M. H. Curtis, 'Hampton Court conference and its aftermath', *History* 46 (1961); J. Davies, *The Caroline Captivity of the Church* (Oxford, 1992).

issues around which political polarisation took place, and the mechanisms by which sides were created. Exploration of the phenomenon of propaganda during the mid-seventeenth century illuminates our appreciation of the nature of political debate in the period, regarding the attitude of leading political figures towards the political process, and our understanding of consensus and conflict during the first half of the seventeenth century. By focusing upon the political use to which print was put, and by drawing attention to the involvement of politicians in its production, it is possible to postulate that the issues and arguments deployed in the press were selected in order to maximise the chances of securing popular support, and that certain politicians sought to control the issues around which parties coalesced. Propaganda needed to be tailored to political circumstances, and issues – whether political or religious – needed to be highlighted which were likely to prove popular. That the press was dominated by religious issues in the period 1640–42, therefore, may indicate as much about the sense which political grandees had of the opinions of taxpayers and potential soldiers, as it does about the motivations of the leaders of either side in the war. Addressing religious concerns, in other words, may have provided a means of securing support from the people for whom religion was the key issue in dispute. Propaganda provided a means of connecting with the wider political nation, and politicians may have recognised that gaining political support required addressing the concerns of the political nation at large.

Finally, analysis of propaganda in early modern Britain prompts reappraisal of the nature of 'public' texts of a polemical nature; namely works which were placed in the public domain by private authors as a result of an ingenuous desire to assist a public debate. Crude analyses of early modern books and pamphlets, which rely upon distinctions between 'public texts' on the one hand, and works which represented the deployment of 'patronage' on the other, misrepresent the reality of political literature in the seventeenth century. Works may have been produced by writers who were self-motivated, and who sought to use the print medium in order to convey to the public a personal message, whether it involved self-advancement and self-defence, or a more selfless and altruistic promotion of some variety of 'truth'. However, books could serve more than one purpose, and could embody a multiplicity of aims and influences. Privately inspired texts, whether selfish or selfless, could be used in order to defend 'causes' and 'interests', at the same time as they satisfied the author's desire for self-expression, self-defence and self-promotion. Furthermore, self-motivated authors often sought to use books in order to forge connections with 'patrons', and this could be done in order to achieve short-term financial benefits, protection and marketability, or in order to secure more substantial assistance in the form of employment, preferment and promotion. Moreover, the attempt by authors to forge links with prominent members of the gentry or aristocracy could be used in order to secure political protection, and to demonstrate shared political and religious visions. Authors, in other words, sometimes sought to use print in order to establish and demonstrate political allegiances and alliances.

Beyond this, there were a multiplicity of authors who used print in order to demonstrate to the world the strength of existing ties of friendship, employment and allegiance, and to express the bonds of gratitude that linked members of patronage networks. Such ties evidently included shared interest in literary projects, and many authors explained to the public the reasons for indulging in publication, and the circumstances in which their efforts appeared in print. Writers freely admitted, therefore, having been encouraged to publish, having been assisted in the publication process, and having being asked to compose works which included controversial polemical books, tracts and pamphlets. Ultimately, a few authors were prepared to admit that such works had been written at the behest of employers and members of the political elite, and a few works which were explicitly and overtly aimed at defending key political players and their causes were written by men who felt little need to conceal their status as long-term friends, employees and political associates. Authors could be motivated, in other words, by more than just the desire to write and publish, and by more than private and personal goals. While such factors may always have formed part of the creative process of writing, and of the logistical process of publication, other factors and motivations included the desire to represent causes and interests, and the desire to express and give thanks for ties of friendship and patronage. If polemical works betrayed patronage, they tended to do so in ways which reflected not simple or one-dimensional patron–client relationships, but rather the reciprocal and mutually beneficial nature of patronage networks. Ultimately, they could betray shared political and religious visions, and the motivation for the production of polemical tracts and pamphlets could be a desire not just to repay debts of gratitude, but also to demonstrate political allegiance, to advance a shared political goal, and to serve the political interests of associates. Authors, in other words, were willing to act as propagandists.

The importance of such conclusions regarding the mixed and multiple motives for the production of polemical literature lies in the fact that it is possible to demonstrate that many works which appear at first sight to have been 'public' texts, can be shown to have been produced with at least some degree of political and/or official sanction. Without detailed contextualisation, and the benefit of the fortunate survival of archival evidence, in other words, it is too easy, and profoundly dangerous, to label texts as 'public'. This is evident from a work such as *The Historie of Episcopacie*, published in 1642, whose author claimed to be 'offering my poor endeavours for the public service', but who was actually the leading propagandist employed by Laud and Charles: Peter Heylyn.[12] This phenomenon is similarly clear from books and pamphlets which informed readers that they were the work of 'private' men seeking to serve the public interest. When Henry Parker issued an anonymous annotated edition of the speech of the Dutch ambassadors in 1645, he professed to be a 'private gentleman'. This statement may have convinced

---

[12] Theophilus Churchman (aka P. Heylyn), *The Historie of Episcopacie* (London, 1642), sig. a2.

contemporaries that this was a public text, but it hardly bears up to historical scrutiny.[13] In August 1648, meanwhile, there appeared a work called *The Designs and Correspondence of the Present Committee of Estates*, which took the form of a printed edition of intercepted Scottish letters, together with 'some marginal notes and animadversions', which purported to be the work of 'a private pen'. However, this tract contained letters from an official source, bore the imprint of the 'printer to the honourable House of Commons', and the *imprimatur* of the clerk of Parliament.[14] Nedham's anonymous statement of *The Case Stated Between England*, meanwhile, professed to have been the work of 'a friend to this commonwealth'.[15] Another work which was produced officially, *Anglia Liberata*, informed readers that it was written 'by a private pen', and 'presented to the public'.[16] The use of such terminology appears to have been a propaganda tactic deployed in order to blur the distinction between 'public' and official polemic, and although such attempts tended to be somewhat transparent, and while the appearance of independent origins tended only to be superficial, they nevertheless serve to highlight the problematic and complex nature of private and public texts in the civil wars.[17] Another similar example concerns a tract called *A Just Apologie for an Abused Army*, which informed readers that it was written by 'an impartial observer of the army', but which was, in reality, the work of a prominent officer, William Goffe.[18] Beyond such cases, of course, lie the large number of tracts and pamphlets which can be shown to have been produced to serve the interests of, and at the behest of, a variety of political grandees, even though their appearance suggests otherwise. The title pages of the works which were produced by Alexander Aspinwall at the behest of the circle around Richard Cromwell, therefore, can be shown to be misleading regarding their authors and publishers, and even regarding their having been published for sale, rather than free distribution.[19]

Finally, it is necessary to turn our attention to how the findings of this book, and the implications outlined above, inform our understanding of the role of the 'public' in political life, and of the emergence of a 'public sphere' in the seventeenth century. Francis Bacon was quick to recognise that printing 'changed the face and condition of things all over the globe', and it is clearly possible to argue that print propaganda fundamentally altered the nature of political society in

---

[13] Peacey, 'Henry Parker', pp. 105–6.

[14] *The Designs and Correspondence of the Present Committee of Estates* (imp. Elsyng, London, for Husband, [16 Aug.] 1648).

[15] [M. Nedham], *The Case Stated Between England and the United Provinces* (London, 1652).

[16] *Anglia Liberata* (London, by Newcomb, 1651), above, pp. 214, 225.

[17] Much less transparent was a tract produced in 1645 called *The Speech of their Excellencies*, which republished a printed speech of the Dutch ambassadors, with the addition of 'a moderate answer by a private gentleman'. In fact it was the work of Henry Parker, and was probably officially sanctioned [H. Parker], *The Speech of their Excellencies* (London, 1645); Peacey, 'Henry Parker', p. 106.

[18] W. G[offe], *A Just Apologie for an Abused Army* (London, 1646).

[19] Above, pp. 206–7.

the 1640s and 1650s, and that it had a dramatic effect upon the conduct and activities of successive regimes.[20] However, in recent years, a number of scholars have also begun to detect evidence of a 'semi-public sphere' and of a 'nascent public sphere' in the period before the Restoration.[21] Peter Lake and David Como, for example, have sought to turn attention away from notions of a Puritan 'underground' in order to develop a picture of a Puritan 'public sphere', characterised by more or less internal – and consciously public – debate within the Calvinist community, 'within which, in the pulpit, in private conferences, through correspondence and the circulation of position papers, rumours and anecdotes, rival claims to orthodoxy were canvassed and derided, attacked and defended'.[22] Others too have drawn attention to the implications of Puritan lecturing.[23] David Zaret, meanwhile, has detected the public sphere (and the origins of democratic culture) in the rise of print and the growth of petitioning, as well as in the way in which politicians appealed to, and invoked, public opinion.[24] Others have detected the fleeting and episodic emergence of a public sphere in the late Elizabethan and early Stuart period, not least at times when Parliament was assembled.[25]

Habermas famously defined the 'public sphere' as 'a sphere which mediates between society and the state, in which the public organises itself as the bearer of public opinion'. While he detected its emergence in the eighteenth century, recent attempts have been made to suggest that it came into existence much earlier, and that the 'marketplace of print' which developed in the mid-seventeenth century, and particularly during the 1640s, provides the key to the creation of an 'arena' in which public opinion emerged as a force for the first time.[26] In order to detect the reality of Habermas' historico-philosophical construct, it would be necessary to demonstrate a number of things: access to the public sphere – through the medium of print – being guaranteed to all; a growing popular interest in political and public affairs; developing literacy and consumption of print; increased involvement of members of the public in production of print and polemic; and rational scrutiny of public issues, contributions to debates on which were capable of being assessed on

---

[20] F. Bacon, *The New Organon*, ed. L. Jardine and M. Silverthorne (Cambridge, 2000), p. 100.

[21] K. Fincham and P. Lake, 'Popularity, prelacy and Puritanism in the 1630s: Joseph Hall explains himself', *EHR* 111 (1996), pp. 858, 860; T. Claydon, 'The sermon, the 'public sphere' and the political culture of late seventeenth century England', in L. A. Ferrell and P. McCullough, eds, *The English Sermon Revised* (Manchester, 2000); D. Norbrook, '*Areopagitica*, censorship and the early modern public sphere', in R. Burt, ed., *The Administration of Aesthetics* (London, 1994); J. Raymond, 'The newspapers, public opinion, and the public sphere in the seventeenth century', in J. Raymond, ed., *News, Newspapers, and Society in Early Modern Britain* (London, 1999).

[22] P. Lake and D. Como, 'Orthodoxy and its discontents: dispute settlement and the production of consensus in the London (Puritan) underground', *JBS* 39 (2000), p. 63.

[23] S. Achinstein, *Milton and the Revolutionary Reader* (Princeton, 1994), p. 38.

[24] D. Zaret, *Origins of Democratic Culture* (Princeton, 2000).

[25] M. O'Callaghan, 'Literary commonwealths: a 1614 print community, *The Shepheards Pipe* and *The Shepherds Hunting*', *Seventeenth Century* 13 (1998).

[26] Habermas, quoted in A. Halasz, *The Marketplace of Print: Pamphlets and the Public Sphere in Early Modern England* (Cambridge, 1997), p. 42.

the basis of inherent cogency, rather than upon the status of their authors. A 'public sphere' would be distinguished by the quantity and quality of discourse, the extent of public participation, and by freedom from state interference. Although it certainly did not preclude the participation of agents of the impersonal state, and may actually have involved the space in which private individuals and the state met, it nevertheless required the absence of strict censorship. In the public sphere, men would 'think what they list, and write what they think', and reason would be individual, rather than communal.[27]

To what extent were these conditions fulfilled in the mid-seventeenth century? There is clearly evidence of growing literacy in the early modern period, as well as of popular reading, and of engagement with political and religious literature.[28] The spread of the vernacular Bible indicated the extent to which clerical monopoly on religious discourse had been broken, and to which individual scholarship and understanding had been fostered, and this was replicated in the civic discourse.[29] This 'engagement' may not always have been undertaken in an entirely critical and rational way. One contemporary commentator said that 'little books, widely disseminated, are like bait for the masses. The average person being attracted to whatever is new, takes them so much to heart that it is thereafter impossible to eradicate the impression they make'.[30] However, it is also possible to detect evidence of more rational popular debate. As early as 1641, therefore, proto-royalist literature complained that England had become too much 'Amsterdamnified by several opinions; religion is now become the common discourse and table talk in every tavern and alehouse, where a man shall hardly find five together in one mind, and yet every one presumes he is in the right'.[31] Furthermore, contemporaries also claimed that members of the public were increasingly guided in their beliefs by rational understanding, and by political and religious principles. In January 1648, therefore, one newspaper editor boasted that, in the Tudor period men were

---

[27] C. Calhoun, 'Introduction: Habermas and the public sphere', in C. Calhoun, ed., *Habermas and the Public Sphere* (London, 1997); P. Lake and M. Questier, 'Agency and appropriation at the foot of the gallows: Catholics (and Puritans) confront (and constitute) the English state', in *The Antichrist's Lewd Hat* (New Haven, 2002); D. Zaret, 'Religion, science and printing in the public spheres in seventeenth century England', ibid., pp. 218, 221.

[28] D. Cressy, *Literacy and the Social Order* (Cambridge, 1980); T. Laqueur, 'The cultural origins of popular literacy in England, 1500–1850', *Oxford Review of Education* 2 (1976); K. Thomas, 'The meaning of literacy in early modern England', in G. Baumann, ed., *The Written Word. Literacy in Transition* (Oxford, 1986); W. Ford, 'The problem of literacy in early modern England', *History* 78 (1993); P. Clark, 'The ownership of books in England, 1560–1640: the example of some Kentish townsfolk', in L. Stone, ed., *Schooling and Society* (Baltimore, 1976); M. Spufford, 'First steps in literacy: the reading and writing experiences of the humblest seventeenth century spiritual autobiographies', *Social History* 4 (1979).

[29] Zaret, 'Religion, science and printing', p. 221.

[30] A. Soman, 'Press, pulpit and censorship in France before Richelieu', *Proceedings of the American Philosophical Society* 120 (1976), p. 442.

[31] *Religions Enemies* (London, 1641), p. 6.

'guided by the tradition of their fathers' rather than by 'acting principles in reason and knowledge'. However:

> in these our days, the meannest sort of people are not only able to write etc., but to argue and discourse on matters of highest concernment and thereupon do desire, that such things which are most remarkable, may be truly committed to writing and made public, expecting to receive such satisfaction out of the variety of the present several actings, as may content all indifferent men and stop the mouths of wilful opposers.[32]

The issue of 'free access' to the public sphere, meanwhile, requires the breakdown of effective censorship, which was obviously a more or less important feature of at least portions of the civil war period. This is clear, of course, from the evidence which indicates an explosion of print in the mid-seventeenth century, including the emergence of new popular forms. Indeed, there is plentiful evidence of popular involvement not merely in reading, but also in producing popular literature. The extensive recent scholarship on political libels in the early modern period, for example, has tended to conclude that they represented 'spontaneous expressions of popular culture', as well as appeals to, and embodiments of, public opinion.[33] The growth of libels, furthermore, 'indicates an increasingly literate society, even at the fairly low social levels', and testifies to 'the interest and involvement of the literate and semi-literate classes in the behaviour and policies of their political leaders'.[34] Indeed, contemporaries regularly commented that they were living in a 'talkative' and 'scribbling' age.[35] Furthermore, it has proved possible to detect evidence of the emergence of 'Grub Street', and of the professionalisation of literature; of authors being paid for their books by publishers, and of the emergence of publishing contracts and the sale of manuscripts to stationers.[36] It has even been suggested that Milton's having worked his way free from traditional forms of aristocratic patronage, and towards a 'republican mode' of literary production, encapsulated notions of the virtue of civic humanism, and of the direct participation of intellectuals in public affairs.[37] Scholars are now familiar with the most important hacks and professional authors of the period, such as William Lilly and George Wharton, John Taylor and Henry Walker, who lived by their pens, and who engaged in volatile public debates.[38] They have also drawn attention to the growing

---

[32] *Perfect Weekly Account* (17–28 Jan. 1648), p. 358.

[33] P. Croft, 'The reputation of Robert Cecil: libels, political opinion and popular awareness in the early seventeenth century', *TRHS*, 6th series 1 (1991), pp. 62–3; P. Croft, 'Libels, popular literacy and public opinion in early modern England', *HR* 68 (1995), p. 266.

[34] Croft, 'Libels', p. 284.

[35] Folger Shakespeare Library, V.a.454, p. 69; Bodl. MS Clarendon 138, p. 1.

[36] D. T. Pottinger, *The French Book Trade in the Ancien Regime 1500–1791* (Cambridge, Mass. 1958), pp. 95–103.

[37] P. Lindenbaum, 'John Milton and the republican mode of literary production', *Yearbook of English Studies* 2 (1991), pp. 121, 135.

[38] H. Rusche, '*Merlini Anglici*: astrology and propaganda from 1644 to 1651', *EHR* 80 (1965); J. Loewenstein, 'Wither and professional work', in A. F. Marotti and M. D. Bristol, eds, *Print, Manuscript and Performance. The Changing Relations of the Media in Early Modern England*

importance of subscription publication.[39] There is also evidence, of course, that individuals such as John Lilburne increasingly turned to print in order to place their ideas and interests in the public domain, and to assist in their lobbying efforts, by placing such matters before a public 'tribunal'.[40]

There is certainly evidence, therefore, with which to support suggestions that the mid-seventeenth century witnessed the emergence of something approaching a 'public sphere'. In order to make a more thorough assessment of this issue, however, it is crucial to understand the attitude of contemporary politicians and governments towards print and the people, and ultimately towards such a public sphere. By participating in the explosion of print and the mass media in 1642, politicians were clearly being forced to come to terms with a new audience, and to adopt new tactics and techniques with which to win hearts and minds. Reticence about meddling in propaganda had traditionally sprung from a desire to avoid engaging with the people, and was related to a reluctance to inspire their 'participation' in matters of state and governance, as well as to a fear of provoking the opprobrium which was associated with the subtle political art of media exploitation, and the manipulation of public opinion. The former represented hostility to the idea of propaganda, while the latter involved concern about being seen to be involved in its production. It is possible that both fears were less powerful during the 1640s. However, assessing attitudes towards the 'public' requires teasing out from the practice of propaganda the nature of the audience(s) to whom print was addressed, and to whom politicians sought to speak, and the manner and tone which they adopted in so doing. It also means assessing the extent to which print was intended to foster political participation and engagement with political processes, as well as attitudes towards allegiance based upon rationality and political issues, as opposed to loyalty and duty. Furthermore, it requires examining conceptions of the impact of print, and contemporary attitudes to popular debate on political and religious issues. Only having undertaken such tasks will it be possible to assess the extent to which the mid-seventeenth century witnessed the emergence of anything approaching a Habermasian 'public sphere', and the extent to which civil war propaganda reflected upon the development of the state, and the extent to which the latter impacted upon the former.

Firstly, propaganda needs to be understood not merely in terms of the policies and initiatives which it was aimed at supporting or attacking, but also in terms of those people to whom it was addressed; the forms which propaganda took, and the tone with which it was written. It has been argued, therefore, that royalist works

---

(Columbus, 2000); S. Clark, *The Elizabethan Pamphleteers. Popular Moralistic Pamphlets 1580–1640* (London, 1983); E. H. Miller, *The Professional Writer in Elizabethan England* (Cambridge, Mass., 1959).

[39] A. Halasz, 'Pamphlet surplus: John Taylor and subscription publication', in Marotti and Bristol, eds, *Print, Manuscript and Performance*.

[40] Achinstein, *Milton*, pp. 28, 42, 55, 57. To the extent that this related to Lilburne's private case, of course, it contravened the essence of the public sphere, which was restricted to 'public' business.

were predominantly aimed at an elite audience, not least because they were very expensive to purchase, and because of their 'mocking aristocratic tone'.[41] However, it is also true that certain parliamentarian works were addressed to an elite audience, even to the extent that some printed tracts can be shown to have been produced in extremely small editions, for circulation to specific grandees, and in order to attempt to secure their support.[42] In reality, all sides and factions managed, with more or less reluctance, to move beyond official declarations, proclamations and speeches, and recognised that one type of propaganda did not fit all sections of the public. One motivation for using non-official media, in other words, was the need to convey a particular message to different audiences.[43] Politicians were aware, therefore, that a period of domestic strife and civil war necessitated talking to a variety of people, and they were motivated by the need to talk to a broad cross-section of the population. Since there were competing demands made upon the entire country, not least in order to provide money and men for the rival war machines, it was essential to talk to everyone, not least to those from the lower echelons of society who provided the backbone of both the military effort and the financial coffers of either side. The need to address the entire population explains the use of days of humiliation, thanksgiving and fasting, as well as the larger print-runs of official statements.[44] However, talking to the entire population required more than just a national curriculum of edification. Part of the essence of propaganda in the 1640s, as discussed at the outset of this work, was the need to 'appeal' to the people, and this became manifest in the ways in which political grandees adopted a variety of literary styles. One anonymous royalist author in late 1643 sought to prove his case,

> so clearly, that everyone which runs may read it, and everyone which reads may understand it, and everyone which understands may discern most evidently that all the miseries of war, blood and rapine which do now overflow this kingdom, come from no other fountain than the city of London.[45]

In September 1644, meanwhile, the editor of the parliamentarian *Mercurius*

---

[41] J. L. Malcolm, *Caesar's Due* (London, 1983), pp. 143, 145–8.

[42] J. Peacey, 'Junto practices: printing and publishing and the meaning of texts in the English civil war' (paper delivered at SHARP conference, London, 2002). Although evidence of such tactics is scarce, it is known that on certain occasions attempts were made to place pressure on the Lords by the Commons, as with private fast sermons, which were not ordered to be printed, not least when the Commons were seeking to secure approval for the Self Denying Ordinance in December 1644: H. Trevor-Roper, 'The Fast sermons of the Long Parliament', in *Religion, the Reformation and Social Change* (London, 1973), pp. 320–21; J. F. Wilson, *Pulpit in Parliament, Puritanism During the English Civil Wars 1640–1648* (Princeton, 1969), pp. 81–2.

[43] Above, chap. 7; C. E. Harline, *Pamphlets, Printing, and Political Culture in the Early Dutch Republic* (Dordrecht, 1987), p. 111; A. Walsham, '"Domme preachers": post-reformation English Catholicism and the culture of print', *P&P* 168 (2000), p. 114.

[44] C. Durston, 'For the better humiliation of the people: public days of fasting and thanksgiving during the English revolution', *Seventeenth Century* 7 (1992).

[45] *Lord Have Mercie Upon Us* ([Oxford], 1643), p. 4.

Britanicus claimed that, as a result of his efforts, 'there is not now so much as a young apprentice that keeps shop, or a labourer that holds the plough, not only from the city to the country, but he can tell you that *Aulicus* is a juggling lying piece of paper'.[46] Most importantly, it was necessary to supplement dry, theoretical and intellectual discourse with that which was more light-hearted and witty. With parliamentarians, and to a lesser extent royalists, the aim was to 'amuse the simple' as much as it was to appeal to the intellectual elite.[47] This was clearly appreciated by Marchamont Nedham, who issued a number of statements regarding his purpose and tactics as a propagandist. As editor of *Mercurius Britanicus*, Nedham had claimed to be 'serious with the sadder judgements and more pleasant with the sanguine'.[48] In *Mercurius Pragmaticus*, meanwhile, Nedham wrote of his desire to 'tickle and charm the more vulgar phancies, who little regard truths in a grave and serious garb'.[49] Later, in his prospectus for *Mercurius Politicus*, Nedham explained:

> the design of this pamphlet being to undeceive the people, it must be written in a jocular way, or else it will never be cried up, for those truths which the multitude regard not in a serious dress, being represented in pleasing popular aires, make music to the common sense, and charm the fancy, which ever sways the sceptre in vulgar judgement, much more than reason.[50]

However, if propaganda was to be conveyed to a broad cross-section of the public, then different kinds of text were required.[51] Historically, of course, this meant the exploitation of the stage for political purposes, and although this tactic was less apparent during the civil wars, the dramatic literary form clearly survived in both royalist and parliamentarian works, even if it is not easy to document political involvement in such texts.[52] Other attempts to reach wider audiences involved visual propaganda, and there was widespread appreciation of the power of visual grandeur, imagery and spectacle, as well as of pictorial representations of

---

[46] *Mercurius Britanicus* 51 (23–30 Sept. 1644), p. 399.

[47] J. G. Fotheringham, ed., *The Diplomatic Correspondence of Jean de Montereul* (2 vols, Edinburgh, 1898), ii. 243.

[48] *A Check to the Checker of Britannicus* (London, 1644), sig. E2.

[49] *Mercurius Pragmaticus* 1 (28 Mar.–4 Apr. 1648), sig. A.

[50] PRO, SP 46/95, p. 409.

[51] G. Elton, *Policy and Police: the Enforcement of the Reformation in the Age of Thomas Cromwell* (Cambridge, 1972), p. 190; V. Sanders, 'John Whitgift: primate, privy councillor and propagandist', *Anglican and Episcopal History* 56 (1987), p. 393.

[52] C. Read, 'William Cecil and Elizabethan public relations', in S. T. Bindoff, J. Hurstfield, and C. H. Williams, eds, *Elizabethan Government and Society* (London, 1961), pp. 27, 29; W. Ingram, *The Business of Playing* (Ithaca, 1992), p. 86; J. Guy, *Tudor England* (Oxford, 1988), pp. 447–9; B. T. Whitehead, *Brags and Boasts. Propaganda in the Year of the Armada* (Stroud, 1994), p. 195; P. W. White, 'Patronage, Protestantism and stage propaganda in early Elizabethan England', in C. C. Brown, ed., *Patronage, Politics and Literary Traditions in England, 1558–1658* (Detroit, 1991), p. 113; J. Limon, *Dangerous Matter. English Drama and Politics in 1623/4* (Cambridge, 1986), p. 4; T. Cogswell, 'Thomas Middleton and the court, 1624: *A Game at Chess* in context', *HLQ* 47 (1984), p. 284. See: S. Wiseman, *Drama and Politics in the English Civil War* (Cambridge, 1998).

individuals, and of crude 'cartoon' imagery.[53] Furthermore, contemporaries also appreciated that certain messages needed to be packaged in different forms for different audiences. Pym's high-profile speeches, for example, were certainly produced in more than one format, the unabridged edition being supplemented by edited versions for a less well-educated audience, although once again the provenance is uncertain.[54]

Furthermore, the desire to talk to the people is also evident from the exploitation of a wide variety of literary forms. This meant the use of ballads and broadsides, and the kind of street literature whose power had been recognised since the sixteenth century.[55] Sponsorship of ballads was certainly a royalist tactic, although it has been suggested that, even when popular forms were adopted by the king's supporters, the aristocratic tone remained the same.[56] However, parliamentarians too involved themselves in the production of ballads, at least to the extent of granting such works official licenses.[57] Broadsides, meanwhile, were also devised by well-connected parliamentarian propagandists, not least in the form of poster histories designed to create a pantheon of (Presbyterian) military heroes.[58] Furthermore, Parliament also exploited popular providentialism in cheap literature, and evidence of 'signs and wonders', and there is certainly evidence of support for, and exploitation of, the astrological literature of William Lilly and John Booker by parliamentarians, and of George Wharton by royalists.[59] There is even evidence of politicians having dabbled in the more sensationalist end of the

---

[53] Guy, *Tudor England*, p. 425; R. W. Scribner, *For the Sake of Simple Folk. Popular Propaganda for the German Reformation* (Oxford, 1994); G. Bak, 'Woodcut, text, font and ornament: the construction of an early seventeenth century news pamphlet' (paper delivered at SHARP conference, London, 2002).

[54] See: Pym's speech on the fate of Strafford, delivered on 12 April. For the long versions, at least one of which was probably official: *The Speech or Declaration of John Pym* (London, for John Bartlet, 1641); *The Declaration of John Pym Esquire* (London, 1641); *The Declaration of John Pym* (London, for John Bartlet, 1641). For the shorter version: *Mr Pymmes Speech to the Lords in Parliament* (London, 1641). See: T. Kilburn and A. Milton, 'The public context of the trial and execution of Strafford', in J. F. Merritt, ed., *The Political World of Thomas Wentworth, Earl of Strafford, 1621–1641* (Cambridge, 1996), p. 237.

[55] C. Ross, 'Rumour, propaganda and popular opinion during the Wars of the Roses', in R. A. Griffiths, ed., *Patronage, the Crown and the Provinces* (Gloucester, 1981), p. 23; P. M. Took, 'Government and the printing trade, 1540–1560' (London University PhD, 1979), pp. 121–2, 158.

[56] Malcolm, *Caesar's Due*, pp. 145–8.

[57] *Verses on the Siege of Glocester* ('printed according to order', London, for Husband, 1644). See the licensing of *Heaven is Angry* in August 1643: *SR* i. 67. See also: *The Kings Last Farewell to the World* (London, for Robert Ibbitson, 1649); *SR* i. 309; H. E. Rollins, ed., *Cavalier and Puritan. Ballads and Broadsides Illustrating the Period of the Great Rebellion 1640–1660* (New York, 1923), pp. 227–31.

[58] J. Ricraft, *A Perfect List of the Many Victories Obtained by Gods Blessing* (London, [2 Apr.] 1646); J. Ricraft, *A Perfect List of the Many Victories Obtained (Through the Blessing of God)* (London, [9 June] 1646); J. Ricraft, *A Perfect List of all the Victories* (London, [26 Aug.] 1646).

[59] C. Durston, 'Signs and wonders and the English civil war', *History Today* (October, 1987), p. 25; Bodl. MS Eng.misc.f.177; above, pp. 126, 166, 172.

literary spectrum, as with the murder pamphlets which have recently received scholarly attention.[60] One work, entitled *An Exact and True Relation of a Most Cruel and Horrid Murther Committed by One of the Cavaliers*, represented a blatant attempt to appeal to the popular end of the market for scandalous news, and was based upon examinations taken by one of the secretaries to the parliamentarian army, and was published officially by Parliament.[61] Similarly, there is evidence of the political exploitation of 'gallows literature', in terms of scaffold prayers and speeches by the likes of William Laud, the Marquess of Hamilton and Charles I.[62] Royalists, meanwhile, may have been more comfortable with the use of imaginative literature, albeit of an elitist nature, which was exploited in order to evade censorship, having been suitably, if subtly, politicised.[63]

Moreover, it is also possible to show how specific groups within society were targeted by specific texts. In part, of course, this meant the troops, and while it may always have been possible to subject them to harangues before battles in order to raise morale at crucial moments, the civil war period saw not just battlefield sermons from leading preachers but also specially devised texts, such as pocket bibles and catechisms, and other works designed specifically for the military audience.[64] Whatever the failings of the royalists in the field of popular literature, there are hints that at least certain activists adopted a more sophisticated approach, and in 1656 Charles Stuart was informed of a paper, the printing of which was arranged by Sir Thomas Peyton, which was targeted at members of Cromwell's navy, among whom it was apparently dispersed in the hope of fomenting mutiny.[65] Other works may have been targeted at children, the most obvious precedent having been set by Mocket's *God and the King*, which had been deemed 'fit for the capacity of youth, whereby in their tender years, the truth of that doctrine may be bred and settled in them, and thereby they the better armed and prepared to withstand any persuasions which in their riper years may be offered and used towards them'.[66]

It is also clear, however, that the 'public' which politicians of all persuasions

---

[60] P. Lake, 'Popular form, Puritan content? Two Puritan appropriations of the murder pamphlet from mid-seventeenth century London', in A. Fletcher and P. Roberts, eds, *Religion, Culture and Society in Early Modern Britain* (Cambridge, 1994).

[61] *An Exact and True Relation* (London, for E. Husband and J. Frank, 1642).

[62] *The Archbishop of Canterburys Speech* (London, 1644); *The Several Speeches of Duke Hamilton* (London, published by special authority, 1649). See: J. Sharpe, '"Last dying speeches": religion, ideology and public execution in seventeenth century England', *P&P* 107 (1985); Kilburn and Milton, 'Public context', p. 245; Lake and Questier, 'Agency and appropriation at the foot of the gallows'.

[63] D. Hirst, 'The politics of literature in the English republic', *Seventeenth Century* 5 (1990).

[64] J. Hale, 'War and public opinion in the fifteenth and sixteenth centuries', *P&P* 22 (1962), p. 27; above pp. 108, 110.

[65] *CCSP* iii. 192.

[66] *A Proclamation for the Confirmation of all Authorised Orders Tending to the Universal Publishing and Teaching of... God and the King* (London, 1615), above, p. 167.

sought to address was an international as much as a domestic one.[67] Attempts were made, therefore, to convince foreign powers and foreign audiences not just to suppress offending works which appeared on the Continent, but also to promulgate alternative views; and while this may always have been pertinent, it arguably only became truly vital in times of civil tension.[68] In January 1648, for example, Sir Edward Nicholas informed the royalist ambassador in Paris, Sir Richard Browne, of his hopes to 'rectify the understanding' of Europe's Protestant ministers regarding 'the goodness of the king's cause'.[69] The concern with foreign audiences also lay behind the plan to translate the *Eikon Basilike* into 'a language common to the most part of the world', there having long been recognition of the need to exploit Latin texts in order to target a foreign readership.[70] There were also attempts to ensure that royalist ambassadors used 'all fitting occasions and opportunities' to undermine negative images of Charles I which were being circulated on the Continent.[71] In January 1653, furthermore, Sir Edward Hyde sought to organise a manifesto by Charles II by writing: 'as soon as I hear that you have received it and resolve to publish it, I will give order for the printing it, here and in Holland, translating it into other languages'.[72] Likewise, for Parliament, Walter Strickland expressed anxieties regarding the false perception of English affairs, and the deliberate attempts to mislead Europeans, and proposed replying to Laud's scaffold speech with works which could be distributed abroad. In May 1645, indeed, he spoke of the need to 'justify the Parliament's proceedings' in order to 'wash off that dirt they cast in the Parliament's face'.[73] Diplomatic agents such as Theodore Haak, furthermore, were involved in translating key parliamentarian documents and tracts in the 1640s, and their official instructions made explicit the need to distribute such works abroad.[74] Indeed, under the Rump there appears to have been something of a division of labour between retained writers, with John Milton being specifically involved in targeting the foreign market with his major Latin works.[75] Ultimately, as was suggested above, it is possible to regard some overtly official newspapers as being intended as diplomatic tools, rather than as weapons of domestic propaganda, where their status and origins were widely

---

[67] Above, pp. 196–7, 228–30; S. Murdoch, 'The search for Northern allies: Stuart and Cromwellian propagandists and protagonists in Scandinavia, 1649–60', in B. Taithe and T. Thornton, eds, *Propaganda* (Stroud, 1999).

[68] R. Vaughan, *The Protectorate of Oliver Cromwell* (2 vols, London, 1839), i, *passim*; Bodl. MS Clarendon 51, fo. 204.

[69] BL, Add. 28104, fo. 5.

[70] BL, Eg. 2547, fo. 1; R. Rex, 'The English campaign against Luther in the 1520s', *TRHS*, 5th series 39 (1989), p. 98.

[71] BL, Eg. 2547, fo. 13.

[72] Bodl. MS Clarendon 45, fo. 16.

[73] BL, Add. 72435, fos. 57, 62, 74v.

[74] P. R. Barnett, *Theodore Haak* (Hague, 1962), pp. 55–6, 91, 95.

[75] Above, pp. 193–4, 196–7.

understood.[76] Although much more work needs to be done in order to explore the ways in which *Mercurius Politicus* was deployed in this way through its selection of both British and European news, and the spin which it placed on such events, there is clearly evidence that some of Nedham's contributors and intelligencers sought to offer advice on how evidence ought to be reported in order to manage relations with European powers.[77] In this light, it is interesting that Milton, the Latin secretary and chief foreign propagandist, was the paper's sometime licenser.[78]

Beyond considering the audiences to whom political propaganda was addressed during the mid-seventeenth century, it is also possible to question the extent to which it was aimed at fostering political action and political participation. Propaganda was clearly aimed at mobilising support for, and the definition of, factions, parties and political interest groups; for securing allegiance and maintaining support. It was used to explain and justify events, policies and actions, and it was described in terms of being educative and informative, while news was described as being 'true', 'perfect' and 'impartial'. However, it was also intended to arouse and awaken people, and to secure compliance, participation and financial contribution. It was also used in order to reply to opponents, and to undo the effects of their propaganda, and to this extent it was intended to 'undeceive', and to provide 'spectacles' for those who were viewing the events and personalities of the civil wars insufficiently well.[79] Moreover, in seeking to appeal to the people, it involved encouraging widespread political engagement, and it fostered an informed and knowledgeable public. However, it is possible to go beyond such generalities, in order to demonstrate that propaganda was about more than just rhetorical force, and attempts to persuade the public of particular ideas and truths. Print was used in more specific ways, in order to mobilise support for particular purposes. There were certainly allegations, therefore, that print was used in order to rouse crowds to pressurise parliament.[80] Moreover, the civil war was also the first age of electoral literature, and commentators such as Edmund Ludlow clearly felt that courtly and Cromwellian preachers were engaged in producing election propaganda in 1654.[81] Print was also used in order to secure outward conformity and displays of loyalty, by encouraging people to sign various convenants and oaths, whether through licensed pamphlets, or polemics produced by friends, colleagues and clients, or by means of propaganda penned by hired hacks, civil servants, and professional pen-men.[82]

---

[76] Klaits, *Printed Propaganda*, pp. 67, 74–7.

[77] Above, pp. 228–30.

[78] Above, pp. 196–7.

[79] Above, pp. 39–42.

[80] BL, Harl. 165, fos. 146, 147.

[81] *The Copy of a Letter Sent Out of Wiltshire* (London, 1654); H. Chambers et al., *An Apology for the Ministers of the County of Wilts* (London, 1654).

[82] See above, pp. 106, 112, 128, 147, 171, 173, 176, 198–9, 225.

Moreover, it is also necessary to establish the ways in which propaganda could achieve its desired aims of winning and securing support, and the tactics according to which such a potent weapon was deployed. There is little space here to discuss the rhetorical and ideological aspects of propaganda, or to enter the debate over the tone of the arguments used by either side.[83] However, it is certainly necessary to address claims that, while both sides recognised the need to engage with the public through the medium of print, they did so in very different ways. The notion of a 'public sphere' requires conditions wherein contributions to political and religious debates could be judged on their merits and their cogency, rather than on the status of the speaker or writer. It is possible to argue, therefore, that while parliamentarians sought to establish support on the basis of issues, royalists preferred to 'lecture' the people. The most perceptive analyst of royalist propaganda during the 1640s has argued that 'the material and arguments presented ... were not selected from the point of view of convincing the English commoner of the wisdom of supporting the crown'. Charles, it is suggested, did little to reassure the people that the king would preserve law, government and the church, but rather lectured them on obedience, and royalists only appealed to the people to the extent of seeking to convince them to trust their monarch.[84] The 'outlook and even arrogance of its writers, aristocrats or their sycophants', it is suggested, was 'ill-suited to win the allegiance of commoners'.[85] This can be taken to reflect opposition to the notion of a politically engaged public, though not to the importance of propaganda, which was needed to counter the polemic of the king's opponents. If royalists sought to secure allegiance upon the foundation of duty, recent scholars have argued that parliamentarians' notions of allegiance were grounded upon issues, and upon the idea that leaders needed to convince the public of their legitimacy through public appeals.[86] Writing in June 1642, the Venetian ambassador claimed that Parliament's statements 'sound very plausible in the ears of the people here, and they do not faile to arouse feelings prejudicial to the interests of His Majesty'.[87] Nevertheless, it is worth recalling that royalist polemic tended to be far more anonymous than that produced by parliamentarians, both in terms of identifying authors and in terms of indicating the origins of particular texts, in terms of the circumstances in which they were written, and the degree of their official sanction and support. Insomuch as this was true, it could be argued

---

[83] B. Donagan, 'Casuistry and allegiance in the English civil war', in D. Hirst and R. Strier, eds, *Writing and Political Engagement in Seventeenth Century England* (Cambridge, 1999); T. Harris, 'Propaganda and public opinion in seventeenth century England', in J. D. Popkin, ed., *Media and Revolution* (Lexington, 1995), p. 49; E. Skerpan, *The Rhetoric of Politics in the English Revolution, 1642–1660* (London, 1992).

[84] Malcolm, *Caesar's Due*, pp. 131, 133–40.

[85] Malcolm, *Caesar's Due*, p. 128.

[86] S. Achinstein, 'The uses of deception from Cromwell to Milton', in K. Z. Keller and G. J. Schiffhorst, eds, *The Witness of Time* (Pittsburgh, 1993).

[87] *CSPV 1642–3*, p. 72.

that royalist propaganda was open to being judged on its merits, rather than upon the status of its authors. Moreover, it must also be remembered that royalists did not have a monopoly on notions about the 'silly multitude', who were beyond rational discourse. Similar comments can be found in parliamentarian authors such as John Hall, who repeatedly mocked the ability of the 'credulous' and 'giddy multitude'.[88]

Such issues can also be explored by monitoring contemporary reflections upon the value of mass media, and upon the impact of civil war pamphlets.[89] Comments regarding the danger of print can be traced back as far as the late fifteenth century, when one early critic claimed that printed books 'crammed with the foolishness of common folk' had 'driven reputable writers from their homes', and that they contained material which could 'inflame impressionable youths', and 'at such a low price that anyone and everyone procures it for himself in abundance'.[90] Others complained that things were better 'when most was unlettered', and fear of popular access to the Bible persisted into the seventeenth century.[91] Elizabeth I feared that seditious books and libels would 'breed some schism among Her Majesties subjects, being persons unlearned and unable to discern the errors therein contained'.[92] In 1608, a Papal nuncio worried that books 'will be read by people who will be befogged in them, will search for the truth and will not find it, and so be tripped up'.[93] During the civil wars, it was generally royalists who bemoaned the deleterious effects of print as a political weapon, and they did so even before they had been defeated in the civil war.[94] In July 1642, therefore, Lord Montagu claimed that 'so much printing hath stirred up too much heat'.[95] Indeed, royalist commentators detected a deliberate ploy on the part of their parliamentarian enemies, who sought to use the press in order to foment divisions within the country. The royalist author of *The True Informer* suggested that the press had helped to 'kindle this fire' of civil war; asking: 'what base scurrilous pamphlets were cried up and down the street and dispersed in the country? What palpable and horrid lies were daily printed? How they multiplied in every corner in such plenty, that one might say there was a supersaetation of lies'.[96] *Mercurius*

---

[88] Surrey RO, G52/2/19/10. For Hall, see: J. Hall, *A Stop to the Mad Multitude* (London, 1653), pp. 7, 24; J. Hall, *Confusion Confounded* (London, 1654), p. 3.

[89] I. Green, *Print and Protestantism in Early Modern England* (Oxford, 2000), p. 1; J. Rigney, '"To lye upon a stationer's stall, like a piece of coarse flesh in a shambles": the sermon, print and the English civil war', in Ferrell and McCullough, eds, *English Sermon Revised*, pp. 188–9.

[90] F. de Strata, *Polemic Against Printing*, ed. M. Lowry (London, 1986).

[91] A. Wood, *Riot, Rebellion and Popular Politics in Early Modern England* (Basingstoke, 2002), pp. 28, 35; C. Hill, *The English Bible and the Seventeenth Century Revolution* (London, 1994), pp. 14–16.

[92] Soman, 'Press, pulpit and censorship', p. 442.

[93] *CSPV 1607–10*, p. 121.

[94] See for example: G. Williams, *The Discovery of Mysteries* (Oxford, 1643), pp. 48–9, 69, 77.

[95] *HMC Buccleuch III*, p. 417.

[96] *The True Informer* (Oxford, 1643), p. 30.

Pragmaticus wrote of 'a Parliament paper plot'.[97] In the 1650s, Thomas Fuller wrote of 'the epidemicall disease of the books in our age'.[98] Later, John Nalson reflected that the popular press 'wrought upon the inferior sorts of people', and 'did strangely exasperate them', by drawing them into the world of public affairs. He also demonstrated his belief that tracts and pamphlets 'are of such dangerous influence upon the lower ranks of people', and claimed to 'know not any one thing that more hurt the late king than the paper bullets of the press'.[99] However, this did not necessarily provoke royalists to spurn the press themselves. Rather, as Paul Knell explained, 'as the pulpit and press have both helped to heighten this rebellion, so it is fit they should both endeavour the dethroning of it'.[100] This line of reasoning was echoed by Sir Roger L'Estrange, who claimed: 'tis the press that is made 'em mad, and the press must set 'em right again'. Although hostile to popular literature, therefore, royalists used propaganda in order to 'redeem the vulgar from their former mistakes and delusions'.[101] Once again, however, it is important to highlight evidence which demonstrates that certain parliamentarians expressed similar hostility to the popular press. The Presbyterian minister, Richard Vines, therefore, complained of the 'poison' which was 'carried up and down in books and cried at mens doors every day, in which there are many strange doctrines going abroad open-faced, and some more strange and go veiled and dropped to the reader by insinuation'.[102] Another parliamentarian complained that *Aulicus* did Parliament 'more hurt than 2,000 of the king's soldiers'.[103] Later, the Cromwellian propagandist, John Hall, alleged that printing had become the 'pestilent midwife' to error and sedition.[104]

Most importantly, fears of print were conceptualised in terms of the attitude towards popular debate, and towards the idea that a critical and open press provided a 'vehicle for generating and propelling public debate'.[105] The use of print by public authorities in order to enter into debate was controversial in the period before the civil wars, when there was more or less widespread reluctance to engage with the public in such an obvious manner. Such reticence was overcome to a greater or lesser extent by different monarchs and ministers. Henry VIII complained that the bible was 'disputed, rhymed, sung and jangled in every

---

[97] *Mercurius Pragmaticus* 53 (7–14 May 1650), sig. Ggg2.

[98] T. Fuller, *Ephemeris Parliamentaria* (London, 1654), sig. ¶3.

[99] Nalson, ii. 806–7, 809.

[100] P. Knell, *Israel and England Paralelled* (London, 1648), sig. A2.

[101] Quoted in Wood, *Riot*, p. 181. See: C. J. Sommerville, *The News Revolution in England* (Oxford, 1996), p. 61; H. Weber, *Paper Bullets. Print and Kingship under Charles II* (Lexington, 1996), pp. 156–7; P. Hinds, 'Roger L'Estrange, the Rye House Plot and the regulation of political discourse in late seventeenth century London', *The Library*, 7th series 3 (2002).

[102] Quoted in Rigney, 'To lye upon a stationers stall', p. 197.

[103] *The True Character of Mercurius Aulicus* (London, 1645), p. 4.

[104] J. Hall, *Sedition Scourg'd* (London, 1653), p. 2.

[105] G. Leth, 'A Protestant public sphere: the early European newspaper press', in *Studies in Newspaper and Periodical History* (1993), p. 85.

alehouse and tavern', while Thomas Norton occasionally expressed his fear about fanning the flames of controversy with printed propaganda, and the authorities consciously sought to prevent the emergence of a public arena of debate which was in danger of being carved out during the Marprelate controversy.[106] Likewise, Charles I and his advisers can be shown to have been concerned about encouraging public debate.[107] In 1620, therefore, a royal proclamation was published against 'excess of lavish and licentious speech of matters of state', and against 'greater openness and liberty of discourse, even concerning matters of state, which are no themes or subjects fit for vulgar persons or common meetings', and which warned men to 'take heed not to intermeddle by pen or speech with secrets of empire, either at home or abroad'. The Caroline regime sought to prevent open debate in order to preserve national unity and public order, decorum and hierarchy.[108] Both James and Charles appear to have been more concerned to stifle the debate which could be fostered by newspapers than to exploit the possible monopoly potential of the new medium. News was perceived as threatening, rather than beneficial.[109] Censorship may always have been the policy of choice in order to shape the news that was available, although there is evidence that, by 1624, the government was prepared, occasionally, to achieve this by issuing its own versions of events. However, exploitation of the news, in the eyes of men such as John Pory, was a means not of fostering debate, but rather of instilling obedience.[110] In 1628, Dorchester sought to enforce control over the publication of newspapers which contained 'matters of state', and in 1631, the king himself complained of books which contained matter which was considered 'unfit for popular view and discourse'.[111] In addition to what appears to have been a principled objection to public discussion of political subjects, Charles also expressed practical concerns about the need to avoid inflaming controversies.[112] Charles, indeed, construed matters of state very broadly, and was 'serious in his belief that almost any discussion of politics or international news led to "scandal of government and disadvantage of our service"'.[113] Thus, when the covenanters

---

[106] Quoted in Hill, *Bible*, p. 15; M. A. R. Graves, *Thomas Norton* (Oxford, 1994); pp. 301–2; J. Black, 'The rhetoric of reaction: the Martin Marprelate tracts (1588–9), anti-Martinism and the uses of print in early modern England', *Sixteenth Century Journal* 28 (1994), p. 709.

[107] Lambeth Palace Library, MS 943, p. 97; Bodl. MS Clarendon 7, fo. 45; P. A. Welsby, *George Abbot. The Unwanted Archbishop, 1562–1633* (London, 1962), p. 138.

[108] J. F. Larkin and P. L. Hughes, eds, *Stuart Royal Proclamations* (2 vols, Oxford, 1973–83), i. 495–6; G. Davies, 'English political sermons, 1603–1640', *HLQ* (1939), p. 5; F. J. Levy, 'Staging the news', in Marotti and Bristol, eds, *Print, Manuscript and Performance*, pp. 252, 255, 257.

[109] R. Cust, 'News and politics in early seventeenth century England', *P&P* 112 (1986), p. 81; F. Levy, 'The decorum of news', in Raymond, ed., *News, Newspapers and Society*; *CSPD 1619–23*, p. 330.

[110] Levy, 'Staging the news', p. 273; Levy, 'Decorum of news', p. 28.

[111] BL, Add. 72439, fos. 4, 6.

[112] *CSPD 1629–31*, pp. 4, 411. See also: Bodl. MS Clarendon 7, fo. 45.

[113] A. B. Thompson, 'Licensing the press: the career of G. R. Weckherlin during the personal rule of Charles I', *HJ* 41 (1998), p. 669.

fostered debate on the sources and boundaries of royal authority through print in the 1630s, the king responded with the claim that 'print is the king's in all kingdoms'. He sought to assert, in other words, prerogative rights to the public domain.[114]

For many royalists during the civil wars, the reluctance to inflame public opinion was suppressed rather than extinguished. It was royalists who most often expressed hostility to 'itching in the tongues and pens' and to the 'meddling in mysteries of state'.[115] This emerges clearly from the 1641 comment, quoted above, which complained about the way in which religion had become the 'common discourse and table talk in every tavern and alehouse'.[116] In complaining about the popular pamphlets in December of that year, Charles himself expressed horror and amazement 'by what eyes these are seen'.[117] Royalists also deployed the metaphor of the Tower of Babel in order to 'register horror at the fact of political disagreement', and at the fracturing of debate which the press brought about.[118] They feared that the existence of a variety of opinions – rather than the king's single voice – signalled political chaos, and that the participation of the lower and middling sorts in public debates would lead to anarchy.[119] Such attitudes underpinned comments by even the most enthusiastic proponents of royalist propaganda, to the effect that though it was important to foster a 'good understanding with the people', nevertheless public declarations might prove damaging by inflaming debate.[120] Charles's reluctance to employ print is evident from his comment that he was 'sorry there should be such a necessity of publishing so many particulars'. He also said that 'it is below the high and royal authority ... to trouble ourself with answering those many scandalous, seditious pamphlets and printed papers', but he nevertheless explained that he now had to 'take more pains this way by our own pen than ever king hath done'.[121] This hostility became more marked after the mid-1640s, and reached its peak in the advice presented to Charles II in 1660, in which the protection of the *arcana imperii* once again became a guiding principle, and in which the recommendation was made to prevent public debate outside of the universities.[122] Sir Roger L'Estrange expressed

---

[114] Larkin, *Proclamations*, ii. 663–4; J. Black, 'Pikes and protestations: Scottish texts in England, 1639–40', *Publishing History* 62 (1997), 7–9; K. Sharpe, 'The king's writ: royal authors and royal authority in early modern England', in K. Sharpe and P. Lake, eds, *Culture and Politics in Early Stuart England* (Basingstoke, 1994), p. 134.

[115] Malcolm, *Caesar's Due*, p. 128.

[116] *Religions Enemies*, p. 6.

[117] Nalson, ii. 747–8.

[118] S. Achinstein, 'The politics of Babel in the English revolution', in J. Holstun, ed., *Pamphlet Wars* (London, 1992), pp. 17–18.

[119] Nalson, ii. 747–8; Achinstein, 'Politics of Babel', p. 22; Achinstein, *Milton*, pp. 83–8.

[120] *NP* iii. 22–3. See also: *NP* ii. 350; *CCSP* iv. 236; Bodl. MS Clarendon 45, fo. 30.

[121] Sharpe, 'King's writ', pp. 134–5. See also: K. Sharpe, 'Crown, Parliament and locality: government and communication in early Stuart England', *EHR* 101 (1986), p. 345.

[122] T. P. Slaughter, ed., *Ideology and Politics on the Eve of the Restoration. Newcastle's Advice to Charles II* (Philadelphia, 1984), pp. 21, 54.

his opposition to newspapers on the grounds that they made 'the multitude too familiar with the actions and counsels of their superiors', and others agreed in bemoaning how they had ensured that 'every man is becomed a state man'.[123] Thomas Hobbes, of course, placed great emphasis upon the danger of private judgements being made public, and of public discourse in general.[124] Indeed, it has been suggested that, after the Restoration, the government had 'only an occasional interest in the guidance of public opinion, and the handling of information in the newsbooks often suggests a desire to suppress news rather than to disseminate it'.[125]

Among parliamentarians, attitudes to debate were somewhat different. From the early 1640s, Hartlibians declared that 'the art of printing will so spread knowledge that the common people, knowing their own rights and liberties, will not be governed by way of oppression'.[126] Hartlib's circle consciously fostered the uncensored flow of ideas, not least through the 'office of address' and the 'invisible college', and the sometime Rump propagandist, John Dury, argued that 'mutual communication in good things is the chief fruit of all society'. Such views involved a rewriting of notions of the state in which information was hierarchically distributed and controlled.[127] Another key propagandist, Marchamont Nedham, recommended treating dissent modestly, and with 'neglect and scorn, as unworthy their revenge or notice'. He also claimed that the 'opinions and tongues of men ought to be free', and wrote of an 'itch of scribbling', and argued that attacking pamphlets gave them a reputation and made them more sought after. Ultimately, he advocated 'so great a liberty of writing and speaking'.[128] Milton, of course, advocated freedom of the press, and may even be regarded as having conceptualised the early modern public sphere, by arguing that people should be 'disputing, reasoning, reading, inventing, [and] discoursing', and by suggesting that 'true liberty' existed when 'free born men, having to advise the public may speak free'. Milton's 'good readers' surveyed all evidence rationally, and made reasoned judgements on what they read.[129] It has also been suggested that the explosion of popular political prints which adopted a dialogic form turned

---

[123] C. Hill, 'Censorship and English literature', in *The Collected Essays of Christopher Hill* (3 vols, Brighton, 1985–6), i. 51; Slaughter, ed., *Ideology and Politics*, p. 56. See also: Nalson, ii. 809.

[124] Achinstein, 'Politics of Babel', p. 36.

[125] Seaward, 'Restoration publicist', p. 123. See also: T. Harris, '"Venerating the honesty of a tinker": the king's friends and the battle for the allegiance of the common people in Restoration England', in T. Harris, ed., *The Politics of the Excluded, c.1500–1850* (Basingstoke, 2001), pp. 208–9.

[126] Achinstein, 'Politics of Babel', p. 26.

[127] K. Dunn, 'Milton among the monopolists: *Areopagitica*, intellectual property and the Hartlib circle', in M. Greengrass, M. Leslie and T. Raylor, eds, *Samuel Hartlib and Universal Reformation* (Cambridge, 1994), pp. 181, 182; C. Webster, 'Benjamin Worsley: engineering for universal reform from the Invisible College to the Navigation Act', ibid.

[128] M. Nedham, *Certain Considerations* (London, 1649), pp. 7, 8, 9.

[129] Norbrook, '*Areopagitica*'; Achinstein, 'Politics of Babel', pp. 18–19; Achinstein, *Milton*, pp. 58–9, 65–6. See: A. Patterson, 'The civic hero in Milton's prose', *Milton Studies* 8 (1975).

readers into a 'jury', and relied upon the idea that the reading public was fit to take part in public debate.[130]

Whether or not the superiors, and sometime employers, of Dury, Milton and Nedham consciously sought to foster debate is difficult to discern. It is certainly possible to argue that, while measures such as the Protestation were intended to produce concurrence rather than discussion, the result was to trigger debate, and to legitimate a questioning attitude.[131] However, it may only have been on the radical fringes of parliamentarian circles that the press was thought to define an arena which was the only legitimate space for the conduct of politics.[132] Reflecting upon the history of England's troubles, writers such as Peter Heylyn alleged that, since the mid-1620s, Puritans had relished the idea of fostering debate, and that they had been intent 'not to lose the opportunity of a parliament-time (when the press is open to allcomers) for publishing their books'.[133] Subsequently, however, parliamentarians can only occasionally be regarded as having sought to foster debate, and it is probable that while they recognised the importance of public opinion, they quickly realised that public discussion of key political issues rapidly 'developed its own momentum', and a spontaneous life of its own.[134] Whatever the extent to which parliamentarians engaged with the public through the medium of popular print during the civil wars and Interregnum, this needs to be considered in the light of the fact that the story of the 1640s and 1650s, as discussed in Chapter 4, was one which involved ever greater press control. Press control was far from oppressive in the 1650s, and there was clearly a 'space' for royalist texts, particularly those of a high-brow and elitist nature, and strict censorship may have focused only upon treason and blasphemy. But this was combined with fairly strict control over one of the most important forms of popular literature, namely the news press.[135] In 1654, it was claimed that Cromwell expressed concern that publication of his speech at the dissolution of the first protectoral Parliament would provoke printed responses, and thus a public debate.[136] And one of Cromwell's leading propagandists, John Hall, claimed that printing was 'ever accounted among the regalia of every government ... it should be looked on with such a jealous and strict eye'. Like Charles before them, Cromwellians in power claimed a prerogative over the public domain.[137] This combination of censorship

---

130 Achinstein, *Milton*, pp. 102–3.

131 Cressy, 'Protestation protested', pp. 252, 262.

132 Achinstein, *Milton*, p. 37.

133 P. Heylyn, *Cyprianus Anglicus* (London, 1671), p. 148.

134 Kilburn and Milton, 'Public context', pp. 244, 249.

135 A. Mann '"Triumphs, trials and tribulations": patterns of censorship in early modern Scotland' (paper delivered at SHARP conference, London, 2002); F. Levy, 'The tribulations of Christopher Love and the problems of censorship' (paper delivered at SHARP conference, London, 2002). See also: A. J. Mann, *The Scottish Book Trade, 1500 to 1720* (East Linton, 2000); Sommerville, *News Revolution*, p. 42.

136 *TSP* iii. 134; BL, Add. 4156, fo. 142v.

137 Hall, *Sedition Scourg'd* (London, 1653), p. 2.

and propaganda, together with evidence of reticence about fostering debate – a cocktail which may have been learnt from the covenanters – indicates that public discussion was welcomed, by all but a minority, only to the extent that it could be controlled by a state apparatus.[138]

The early modern period clearly witnessed the growth of public debate, undertaken through the medium of print, and the growth of a realm of contestation which, at brief moments, approached something which was more or less autonomous. However, while it is clearly of interest to note the development of the rise of a public print culture, and of a growing tendency for politicians to talk to, and to even appeal to, and invoke the support of, the people, it would be a mistake to confuse this with the emergence of a public sphere. Press control and press manipulation were inversely proportional to the existence of the public sphere. Royalists fairly clearly opposed the idea of public debate, and sought to use strict press control as their primary means of clamping down on discussion, with propaganda as a reserve option. Parliamentarians, on the other hand, adopted a somewhat different approach to the emergence of a mass political audience. Although they clearly did not neglect censorship, they combined this with active engagement with the public through the medium of print. They experimented with different literary forms, and addressed a variety of audiences, and may briefly have recognised the value of press freedom and public debate.[139] However, their more settled and consistent approach involved the attempt to impose censorship, and to harness popular forms of print, and the 'distortions of propaganda' undermined a nascent public sphere. Perhaps recognising the growing difficulty of imposing control through censorship, they sought to do so through the printing press, which may have provided a more subtle means of undermining opponents, and one which did not necessarily have the appearance of stifling debate. Whether or not scholars agree on the extent of press freedom in the middle of the seventeenth century, it seems hard to neglect the importance of 'the startling arrival and widespread deployment of propaganda'.[140] Propaganda, and the engagement with the public through a broad range of literary forms, represents an attempt to restrict the boundaries of discussion and to control the terms of debate. Sometimes this was transparent, and those works – whether sermons, tracts or newspapers – which clearly betrayed official involvement could certainly not be judged 'rationally', in the sense of being susceptible to public judgement merely on the basis of ideas and issues, rather than on the status of the 'author'.[141] Propaganda involved not so much rational

---

[138] D. Stevenson, 'A revolutionary regime and the press: the Scottish covenanters and their printers', *The Library*, 6th series 7 (1985), p. 322.

[139] M. Mendle, 'De facto freedom, de facto authority: press and parliament, 1640–1643', *HJ* 38 (1995), p. 323; M. Mendle, 'Grub Street and Parliament at the beginning of the English revolution', in Popkin, ed., *Media and Revolution*.

[140] Achinstein, 'Uses of deception', pp. 178, 199; Levy, 'Decorum of news', p. 34. On the harnessing of popular forms of culture, see: A. Duffy, 'The godly and the multitude in Stuart England', *Seventeenth Century* 1 (1986), pp. 41–9.

[141] See: Claydon, 'The sermon'; Sommerville, *News Revolution*, p. 59.

evaluation of political issues, or a search for truth, but rather the presentation of an exclusive viewpoint, and to the extent that civil war politicians lacked a monopoly over the public domain of print, they arguably sought to use propaganda in order to ensure their dominant position within it.[142] To the extent that the aim was to control the terms of debate, propaganda was to censorship as the velvet glove is to the iron fist. Furthermore, to the extent that the ability to produce propaganda became associated with state formation, it is possible to argue that the early modern public sphere was seriously distorted by the state apparatus.[143]

As scholars since Francis Bacon have recognised, the arrival of print created the possibility for a democratisation of learning, with more people receiving education, and having the means with which to join the political nation. However, it also provided new possibilities for the manipulation and control of public opinion.[144] In assessing the impact of moveable type in *The Gutenberg Galaxy*, Marshall McLuhan claimed that the printing press both increased individualism on the one hand, and national uniformity and government centralisation on the other. The emergence of print created both the necessity of, and possibility for, government propaganda.[145] Furthermore, the determination to use print in order to constrain debate and impose 'orthodoxy' may not have changed until much later in the seventeenth century, when there appears to have emerged a more widespread tolerance of public debate, and a recognition that public discussion did not necessarily lead to rebellion, but may actually have fostered civility.[146] Until then, all sides used print, albeit in different ways. Royalists 'often cursed the press', although they 'published in droves' in an attempt to reimpose order, and although they clearly sought to avoid politicising the people by fostering rational debate. Many, though not all, parliamentarians appear to have been willing to see the emergence of a broad and inclusive political nation, but sought to use print in order to constrain the terms of debate within it. Perhaps only the Levellers, and a few prominent parliamentarian propagandists such as Nedham and Milton, genuinely seem to have sought to create anything approaching a Habermasian public sphere which was free from state control, and into which a politicised, literate and educated people could enter.[147]

---

[142] Achinstein, *Milton*, pp. 145–6; Sommerville, *News Revolution*, p. 61.

[143] H. M. Solomon, 'The *Gazette* and antistatist propaganda: the medium of print in the first half of the seventeenth century', *CJH* 9 (1974), pp. 7–9.

[144] Hill, *Bible*, p. 19; H. Love, *Scribal Publication in Seventeenth Century England* (Oxford, 1993); N. Z. Davis, 'Printing and the people', in *Society and Culture in Early Modern France* (London, 1987), pp. 190, 224–5.

[145] M. McLuhan, *The Gutenberg Galaxy* (London, 1962), pp. 146–8, 176, 206, 235.

[146] S. Pincus, 'Coffee politicians does create: coffeehouses and restoration political culture', *JMH* 67 (1995), p. 832; Sommerville, *News Revolution*, pp. 76–9.

[147] Achinstein, *Milton*, pp. 32, 70, 72.

Bibliography

Manuscripts

Alnwick Castle, Northumberland
  Northumberland MSS

Beinecke Library, Yale University
  Osborn MSS

British Library
Add. 4156	Thurloe Papers
Add. 4165	Fleetwood Papers
Add. 4184	Privy Seal Warrants
Add. 4364–5	Collections Regarding Swiss Cantons
Add. 4777	Milles Collection
Add. 4819	Pococke Collection
Add. 5501	Civil War Financial Papers
Add. 5755	Miscellaneous Financial Papers
Add. 5756	Miscellaneous Political Papers
Add. 5851	Papers Relating to Cambridge University
Add. 10114	John Harington Diary
Add. 18738	Original Letters
Add. 18777–9	Walter Yonge Diary
Add. 19863	Payne Fisher Verses
Add. 21417	Adam Baynes Correspondence
Add. 22546	Naval Papers
Add. 23146	Thomas Dugard Diary
Add. 24863	Miscellaneous Political Papers
Add. 25278	Tract Presented to Oliver St John
Add. 26785	Kent Papers, 1639–41
Add. 28002–4	Oxinden Papers
Add. 28104	Original Letters
Add. 31116	Lawrence Whitaker Diary
Add. 32093	Malet State Papers
Add. 32426	Admiralty Papers
Add. 32471	Cromwellian Papers
Add. 33145	Sir Thomas Pelham Accounts

Add. 33223–4	Sir Edward Walker Papers
Add. 33374	John Jones Papers
Add. 34164	Twysden Papers
Add. 34253	Manchester Papers
Add. 34312	Tracts
Add. 36913	Aston Papers
Add. 37047	Robert Long Correspondence
Add. 39477	Dunkin Collection
Add. 42081	Hamilton and Greville Papers
Add. 44846	Capel Cure Papers
Add. 46189	Jessop Papers
Add. 46931	Egmont Papers
Add. 63788	Civil War Papers
Add. 70001–2	Harley Papers
Add. 71534	Henry Marten Papers
Add. 72435	Trumbull Papers
Add. 72439	Trumbull Papers
Cotton MS Titus C.I	Tracts
Eg. 2542	Sir Edward Nicholas Papers
Eg. 2547	*Eikon Basilike* Papers
Evelyn Papers, RB 2	Sir Richard Browne Correspondence
Hargrave 98	Tracts
Harl. 163–6	Sir Simonds D'Ewes Diary
Harl. 479	John Moore Diary
Harl. 581	Declarations and Ordinances
Harl. 5909	Papers Regarding Bible Printing
Harl. 6034	Thomas Violet Papers
Harl. 6802	Sir Edward Walker Papers
Lans. 823	Henry Cromwell Correspondence
Sloane 271	Puritan Papers
Sloane 1519	Miscellaneous Letters and Papers
Sloane 2035b	George Willingham Papers
Stowe 107	Thomas Hearding Tract
Stowe 184–5	Sir Edward Dering Papers
Stowe 497	Cromwellian Letters Patent
Stowe 743	Sir Edward Dering Papers
Trumbull Papers	Georg Rudolph Weckherlin Diary
E286/16	Parker, H., 'Points of Consideration'
E358/1	Parker, H., 'An Elegie'
E693/5	Streater, J., 'Ten Queries'

Bodleian Library
MS Add. C.209	Civil War Tracts

MS Ballard 49	Oxford University Papers
MS Carte 64	Irish papers, 1634–66
MS Carte 77	Earls of Huntingdon Papers
MS Carte 130	Sir Robert Long Correspondence
MS Clarendon 7	Sir Edward Hyde Papers
MS Clarendon 21-78	Sir Edward Hyde Papers
MS Clarendon 92	Sir Edward Hyde Papers
MS Clarendon 132	Sir Edward Hyde Papers
MS Clarendon 136	Sir Edward Hyde Papers
MS Clarendon 138	Sir Edward Hyde Papers
MS Eng.misc.e.475	John Wallis Papers
MS Eng.misc.f.177	John Booker Alamanack
MS Nalson II–XXII	John Nalson Collections
MS Rawl. A.14	John Thurloe Papers
MS Rawl. A.24	John Thurloe Papers
MS Rawl. A.27	John Thurloe Papers
MS Rawl. A.60	John Thurloe Papers
MS Rawl. A.67	John Thurloe Papers
MS Rawl. A.246	Delinquents' Estates
MS Rawl. A.328	Cromwellian Warrants
MS Rawl. B.156	Speculum Chronologicon
MS Selden Supra 123–4	John Selden Legal Papers, 1642
MS Tanner 54–68	William Lenthall Papers
MS Tanner 88*	Inventory of Papers Seized, 1630s

Cambridge University Library
Add. 33	Arthur Wilson Papers
Mm.1.46	Baker MSS

Cambridgeshire Record Office, Cambridge
R.59.31	Adventurers for Drainage of the Fens

Centre for Kentish Studies, Maidstone
U350	Dering MSS

Chatsworth House
Lismore MS

Chequers, Buckinghamshire
MS 782	Army Accounts

Claydon House, Buckinghamshire
Verney Papers

Corporation of London Record Office
JOR 41X	Journal of the Common Council

Dr Williams Library
    MS 24.50   Diary of Thomas Juxon

East Sussex Record Office, Lewes
    AMS 1503   Thomas May Family
    Rye 48/1   Rye Corporation MSS
    SAS/M/691   Thomas May Family

Essex Record Office, Chelmsford
    D/Dba/A5   Barrington Papers

Flintshire Record Office
    D/DE271   Pennant Papers

Folger Shakespeare Library, Washington DC
    L.d.259   Bacon-Townshend Papers
    V.a.454   John Martin Letterbook, 1652–63
    X.d.154   Anthony Ascham Petition
    X.d.483   Robert Bennet Papers

Guildhall Library, London
    MS 12806   Christ's Hospital Court Minutes
    MS 15201   Vintners' Company Records
    MS 15333   Vintners' Company Records

Gloucestershire Record Office, Gloucester
    D678   Barwick MSS

House of Lords Record Office, Westminster
    Braye MSS
    Main Papers (MP)

Hull Record Office
    Hull Corporation Letterbook

Lambeth Palace Library, London
    MS 731   Peter Heylyn, 'A Briefe Survey' (1638)
    MS 943   Laud Papers
    MS 3516   Fairhurst MSS

Leicestershire Record Office, Leicester
    DG21   Sir Arthur Hesilrige Papers

Longleat House, Wiltshire
    Whitelocke Papers
    Coventry Papers

Magdalen College, Oxford
    Ferrar Papers

MS 312   Peter Heylyn Sermon

Merchant Taylors Company, London
   Court Minute Books

National Library of Scotland, Edinburgh
   Adv.MS 35.5.11   Army Papers, 1648

National Library of Wales, Aberystwyth
   Plas Yolyn MS 11440d   John Jones Letterbook
   Wynnstay 90/16   Notes on Parliamentary Debates, 1646

Northamptonshire Record Office, Northampton
   Finch Hatton (FH) 61   Civil War Pamphlet

Oxfordshire Record Office, Oxford
   Burford parish register
   Dashwood Family Papers
   Hyde Family Papers
   Fiennes Family Papers
   Willoughby Family Papers

Public Record Office, Kew
   C 54   Close Rolls
   C 66   Patent Rolls
   E 101   King's Remembrancer Accounts
   E 159   King's Remembrancer Memoranda Rolls
   E 403   Exchequer of Receipt Rolls
   E 404   Exchequer of Receipt Warrants
   LC 5   Lord Chancellor's Department
                                             Miscellaneous Records
   PC 2   Privy Council Registers
   PRO 30/5/6   Petitions to Crown, 1638-46
   PRO 31/17/33   Council of State Order Book, 1658-9
   PROB 11   Prerogative Court of Canterbury Will
                                             Registers
   PSO 5   Privy Seal Office Docquet Books
   SC 6   Special Collections Receivers Accounts
   SO 3   Signet Office Docquet Books
   SP 14   State Papers, James I
   SP 16   State Papers, Charles I
   SP 18   State Papers, Interregnum
   SP 21   State Papers, Committee of Both Kingdoms
   SP 23   State Papers, Commissioners for
                                             Compounding
   SP 24   State Papers, Committee of Indemnity

SP 25	State Papers, Council of State Order Books
SP 28	State Papers, Commonwealth Exchequer Papers
SP 29	State Papers, Charles II
SP 46	State Papers, Supplementary
SP 77	State Papers, Flanders
SP 9	Joseph Williamson Papers
T 56	Treasury Warrants
WARD 9	Court of Wards and Liveries Books

Scottish Record Office, Edinburgh

PA.11/6	Committee of Estates Register
PA.15/2	Inventory of Printing by Evan Tyler

Shakespeare Birthplace Trust, Stratford-upon-Avon

DR 98/1652	Heath Papers

Sheffield University Library
  Hartlib Papers

Somerset Record Office, Taunton

DD/GB/148	Walker Papers
DD/HI/466	Hippesley Papers
DD/WHb/140-2	Walker-Heneage Papers

Staffordshire Record Office, Stafford

D593/P/8/2/2	Leveson Correspondence
D868/2	Leveson Correspondence

Stationers Company, London
  Court Books C–D
  Liber A

Surrey Record Office, Woking

G52	Bray Family Papers
G85	Bray Family Papers

Warwickshire Record Office, Warwick

CR 1886	Warwick Castle Accounts
CR 2017	Feilding Papers

Worcester College, Oxford
  Clarke MSS

Printed Primary Sources

A Narrative by John Ashburnham (2 vols, London, 1830)

Abbott, W. C., *The Writings and Speeches of Oliver Cromwell* (4 vols, Oxford, 1988)

Arber, E., ed., *A Transcript of the Registers of the Company of Stationers of London 1554–1640* (4 vols, London, 1877)

Bell, R., ed., *Memorials of the Civil War* (2 vols, London, 1849)

Berwick, E., ed., *The Rawdon Papers* (London, 1819)

Birch, T., ed., *A Collection of the State Papers of John Thurloe* (7 vols, London, 1742)

———— *The Court and Times of Charles the First* (2 vols, London, 1848)

Bruce, J., and Perowne, T. T., eds, *The Correspondence of Matthew Parker* (Parker Society, Cambridge, 1853)

Bruce, J., ed., *Letters and Papers of the Verney Family* (Camden Society, 1853)

———— *Proceedings, Principally in the County of Kent* (Camden Society, 1862)

Burman, C., ed., *The Lives of Those Eminent Antiquaries* (London, 1774)

Burrows, M., ed., *The Register of the Visitors of the University of Oxford* (Camden Society, new series, 29, 1881)

Calder, I. M., ed., *Activities of the Puritan Faction of the Church of England, 1625–33* (Church History Society, 1957)

Calder, I. M., ed., *Letters of John Davenport* (London, 1937)

Calendar of Sherborne Muniments (1900)

Chester, J. L., and Armitage, G. J., *Allegations for Marriage Licences* (Harleian Society, 23, 1886)

Coates, W. H., ed., *The Journal of Sir Simonds D'Ewes* (New Haven, 1942)

Coates, W. H., Young, A. S., and Snow, V., eds, *Private Journals of the Long Parliament* (3 vols, New Haven, 1982–92)

Cobbett's Parliamentary History of England (36 vols, London, 1806–20)

Crossley, J., ed., *The Diary and Correspondence of Dr John Worthington* (2 vols, Chetham Society, 1847)

Calendar of State Papers Domestic

Calendar of State Papers Ireland

Calendar of State Papers Venetian

Darnell, W. N., ed., *The Correspondence of Isaac Basire* (London, 1831)

Firth, C. H., ed., *The Clarke Papers* (4 vols, Camden Society, 1891–1901)

———— *Memoirs of Edmund Ludlow* (2 vols, Oxford, 1894)

Firth, C. H., and Rait, R. S., eds, *Acts and Ordinances of the Interregnum, 1642–1660* (3 vols, London, 1911)

Foster, E. R., ed., *Proceedings in Parliament, 1610* (2 vols, New Haven, 1966)

Fotheringham, J. G., ed., *The Diplomatic Correspondence of Jean de Montereul* (2 vols, Edinburgh, 1898)

Galpin, F. W., ed., 'The household expenses of Sir Thomas Barrington', *Transactions of the Essex Archaeological Society* 12 (1913)

Gardiner, D., ed., *The Oxinden and Peyton Letters, 1642–1670* (London, 1937)

Gardiner, S. R., ed., *Constitutional Documents of the Puritan Revolution, 1625–1660* (Oxford, 1979)

—— *Reports of Cases in Star Chamber* (Camden Society, 1886)

Gretton, R. H., ed., *The Burford Records* (Oxford, 1920)

Groombridge, M. A., 'Calendar of Chester city council minutes 1603–42', *Lancashire and Cheshire Record Society* 106 (1956)

Heylyn, P., *Memorial of Bishop Waynflete*, ed. J. R. Bloxam (London, 1851)

Historical Manuscripts Commission

  3rd Report

  5th Report

  6th Report

  7th Report

  10th Report VI

  13th Report I

  Buccleuch I–III

  De L'isle VI

  Egmont I

  Hastings II

  House of Lords XI Addenda 1514–1714

  Leyborne-Popham

  Montagu

  Pepys

  Portland I

Howell, T. B., ed., *A Complete Collection of State Trials* (34 vols, London, 1809–26)

Hutchinson, L., *Memoirs of the Life of Colonel Hutchinson* (ed. J. Sutherland, London, 1973)

Hyde, E., Earl of Clarendon, *The History of the Rebellion and Civil Wars in England*, ed. W. D. Macray (6 vols, Oxford, 1888)

Jackson, W. A., ed., *Records of the Court of the Stationers' Company 1602–1640* (London, 1957)

Jenks, E., 'Some correspondence of Thurloe and Meadowe', *EHR* 7 (1892)

'The Life of Master John Shaw', in *Yorkshire Diaries and Autobiographies* (Surtees Society, 1875)

Keeble, N. H., and Nuttall, G. F., eds, *Calendar of the Correspondence of Richard Baxter* (2 vols, Oxford, 1991)

Kingsbury, S. M., ed., *The Records of the Virginia Company* (4 vols, Washington, 1906–35)

Kitson, E., and Clarke, E. K., 'Some civil war accounts, 1647–50', *Publications of the Thoresby Society* 11 (1904)

LaFantasie, G. W., ed., *The Correspondence of Roger Williams. Volume I, 1629–53* (London, 1988)

Laing, D., ed., *The Letters and Journals of Robert Baillie* (3 vols, Edinburgh, 1841–42)

Larkin, J. F., and Hughes, P. L., eds, *Stuart Royal Proclamations* (2 vols, Oxford, 1973–83)

Latham, R., and Matthews, W., eds, *The Diary of Samuel Pepys* (11 vols, London, 1970–83)

Macnamara, F. N., and Story-Maskelyne, A., eds, *The Parish Register of Kensington* (London, 1890)

Malcolm, N., ed., *The Correspondence of Thomas Hobbes* (2 vols, Oxford, 1994)

Mayor, J. E. B., ed., *Autobiography of Matthew Robinson* (Cambridge, 1856)

Nalson, J., ed., *An Impartial Collection* (2 vols, London, 1682)

Nickolls, J., ed., *Original Letters and Papers of State* (London, 1743)

Notestein, W., ed., *The Journal of Sir Simonds D'Ewes* (New Haven, 1923)

Ogle, O., Bliss, W. H., Macray, W. D., and Routledge, F. J., eds, *Calendar of the Clarendon State Papers* (5 vols, Oxford, 1872–1970)

Osborn, J. M., 'Thomas Stanley's lost "register of friends"', *Yale University Library Gazette* 32 (1958)

The Parliamentary or Constitutional History of England (24 vols, London, 1761–63)

Peck, F., *Desiderata Curiosa* (2 vols, London, 1732)

Phillips, W., ed., 'The Ottley papers relating to the civil war', *Transactions of the Shropshire Archaeological and Natural History Society*, 2nd series 6 (1894)

——— 'The Ottley papers relating to the civil war', *Transactions of the Shropshire Archeaological and Natural History Society*, 2nd series 7 (1895)

Plucknett, T. F. T., and Barton, J. L., eds, *St German's Doctor and Student* (Selden Society, 91, 1974)

Roberts, G., ed., *The Diary of Walter Yonge* (Camden Society, 41, 1847)

Rushworth, J., ed., *Historical Collections of Private Passages of State* (8 vols, London, 1721)

Rymer, T., *Foedera* (Hague, 1744)

Sachse, W. L., ed., *The Diurnal of Thomas Rugg, 1659–1661* (Camden Society, 3rd series 91, 1961)

Scrope, R., and Monkhouse, T., eds, *State Papers Collected by Edward, Earl of Clarendon* (3 vols, Oxford, 1767–86)

Searle, A., ed., *Barrington Family Letters, 1628–1632* (Camden Society, 1983)

Seddon, P. R., ed., *Letters of John Holles 1587–1637* (3 vols, Thoroton Society Records Series, 1975–86)

Slaughter, T., ed., *Ideology and Politics on the Eve of the Restoration. Newcastle's Advice to Charles II* (Philadelphia, 1984)

Spalding, R., ed., *The Diary of Bulstrode Whitelocke 1605–1675* (Oxford, 1990)

Steele, R., ed., *Tudor and Stuart Proclamations 1485–1714* (2 vols, Oxford, 1910)

Stephens, W., ed., *Registers of the Consultations of the Ministers of Edinburgh* (2 vols, Scottish Records Society, Edinburgh, 1921–30)

Strype, J., *Annals of the Reformation* (4 vols, Oxford, 1824)
——— *The Life and Acts of Matthew Parker* (3 vols, Oxford, 1821)
——— *The Life of Edward, Earl of Clarendon* (3 vols, Oxford, 1827)
The Trumbull Papers (London, 1989)
The Winthrop Papers III (Massachusetts Historical Society Collections, 5th series 1, 1871)
Toennies, F., 'Contributions a l'histoire de la pensee de Hobbes', *Archives de Philosophie* 12 (1936)
Toon, P., ed., *The Correspondence of John Owen (1616–1683)* (London, 1970)
A Transcript of the Registers of the Worshipful Company of Stationers (3 vols, London, 1913)
Trevelyan, Sir W. C., and Trevelyan, Sir C. E., eds, *Trevelyan Papers* (3 vols, Camden Society, 1857–72)
Vaughan, R., *The Protectorate of Oliver Cromwell* (2 vols, London, 1839)
Warner, G. F., ed., *The Nicholas Papers* (4 vols, Camden Society, 1886–1920)
Wheatley, H. B., ed., *The Diary of John Evelyn* (4 vols, London, 1906)
Whitelocke, B., *Memorials of the English Affairs* (4 vols, Oxford, 1853)
Winthrop Papers (5 vols, Massachusetts Historical Society, 1929–47)
Wood, A., *Athenae Oxonienses*, ed. P. Bliss (4 vols, London, 1813–20)

Newspapers

(numbers in brackets refer to C. Nelson and M. Seccombe, *British Newspapers and Periodicals, 1641–1700* (New York, 1987)

Briefe Relation (1649–50, 27)
Continuation of the Proceedings (1645, 565)
Continuation of the True Diurnall (1642, 68)
Country Foot Post (1644, 78)
Diurnall Occurrences (1642, 104)
England's Memorable Accidents (1642–43, 579)
Exact and Perfect Relation of the Proceedings of the Army (1645, 565)
Faithfull Intelligencer (1659–60, 146)
Kingdomes Faithfull and Impartiall Scout (1649, 210)
Kingdomes Weekly Intelligencer (1643–49, 214)
Kingdoms Weekly Post (1647–48, 215)
London Post (1646–47, 232)
London Post (1644–45, 233)
Man in the Moon (1649–50, 248)
Mercurius Academicus (1645–46, 260)
Mercurius Anti-Britanicus (1645, 267)
Mercurius Aulicus (1648, 274)

Mercurius Aulicus (1643–45, 275)
Mercurius Bellicus (1647–48, 279)
Mercurius Britanicus (1643–46, 286)
Mercurius Britanicus (1659–60, 146)
Mercurius Brittanicus (1649, 285)
Mercurius Civicus (1643–46, 298)
Mercurius Elencticus (1647–49, 312)
Mercurius Melancholicus (1647–48, 344)
Mercurius Militaris (1649, 349)
Mercurius Politicus (1650–60, 361)
Mercurius Pragmaticus (For King Charles II) (1649–50, 370)
Mercurius Pragmaticus (1647–49, 369)
Mercurius Publicus (1659–63, 378)
Moderate (1648–49, 413)
Moderate Intelligencer (1653, 418)
Moderate Intelligencer (1645–49, 419)
Moderate Occurrences (1653, 425)
Modest Narrative (1649, 433)
Occurrences from Foreign Parts (1659–60, 491)
Parliamentary Intelligencer (1659–63, 486)
Particular Advice from the Office of Intelligence (1659–60, 491)
Perfect Account (1651–55, 496)
Perfect Diurnall (1649–55, 503)
Perfect Diurnall (1643–49, 504)
Perfect Diurnall (1642–43, 511)
Perfect Occurrences (1644–49, 465)
Perfect Passages (1644–46, 523)
Perfect Proceedings of State Affaires (1649–55, 599)
Perfect Summary (1647, 528)
Perfect Summary (1649, 530)
Perfect Weekly Account (1648–49, 533)
Proceedings of the Army (1645, 565)
Publick Intelligencer (1655–60, 575)
Royall Diurnall (1648, 588)
Scotish Dove (1643–46, 594)
True Diurnal of the Passages (1642, 652)
True Informer (1643–45, 629)
Weekly Account (1643–48, 671)
Weekly Intelligencer (1659–60, 689)

Printed Pamphlets

An Act for Appointing Judges (London, 1659)

An Act for Further Continuation of the Customs (London, 1659)

An Act for Taking the Accounts (London, 1660)

The Acts and Monuments of Our Late Parliament (London, 1659)

After Debate About the Printing and Publishing of the Orders of the 16th of January Last (London, 1641)

The Agreement of the General Council of Officers (London, 1659)

Aitzema, L. van, *Notable Revolutions* (London, 1653)

The Anabaptists Catechisme (London, 1645)

Anglia Liberata (London, 1651)

Animadversions Upon a Declaration of the Proceedings Against the XI Members (Cambridge, 1647)

An Anniversary Ode upon the Kings Birthday (Hague, 1654)

Another Famous Victorie Obtained (London, 1642)

The Answer of the Commons to a Petition in the Name of Thousands of Wel-Affected Persons (London, 1648)

The Answer of the Parliament of the Commonwealth of England, to Three Papers Delivered into the Councel of State (London, 1652)

An Answer to a Speech Without Doores (London, 1646)

An Answer to Severall Objections (London, 1646)

Apophthegmata Aurea (London, 1649)

An Appeale to the World in These Times of Extreame Danger (London, 1642)

Arguments Proving that We Ought Not to Part with the Militia (London, 1646)

The Army's Plea for their Present Practice (London, 1659)

Arrowsmith, J., *The Covenant-Avenging Sword Brandished* (London, 1643)

Articles of Impeachment (London, 1642)

Articles of Peace Made and Concluded with the Irish Rebels and Papists by James Earle of Ormond (London, 1649)

Ascham, A., *A Combat Between Two Seconds* (London, 1649)

―――― *A Discourse* (London, 1648)

―――― *Of the Confusions and Revolutions of Governments* (London, 1649)

―――― *The Bounds and Bonds of Publique Obedience* (London, 1649)

Ashe, J., *A Perfect Relation* (London, 1642)

―――― *A Second Letter* (London, 1642)

Ashe, S., *The Doctrine of Zeal* (London, 1655)

―――― *Religious Covenants Directed* (London, 1646)

Atkyns, R., *Original and Growth of Printing* (London, 1664)

Aulicus His Hue and Cry (London, 1645)

B., T., *The Engagement Vindicated* (London, 1650)

Bacon, F., *The New Organon*, ed. L. Jardine and M. Silverthorne (Cambridge, 2000)

Bacon, R., *Christ Mighty in Himself and Members* (London, 1646)
—— *The Spirit of Prelacie Yet Working* (London, 1646)
—— *The Spirit of Prelacy* (London, 1646)
Baker, Sir R., *A Chronicle of the Kings of England* (London, 1665)
—— *Meditations and Disquisitions* (London, 1640)
Bakewell, T., *The Ordinance of Excommunication Rightly Stated* (London, 1646)
—— *A Short View of the Antinomian Errours* (London, 1643)
Ball, W., *A Briefe Treatise* (London, 1651)
—— *Tractatus de Jure Regnandi et Regni* (London, 1645)
Barton, T., *ΑΠΟΔΕΙΞΙΣ... or, a Tryall of the Counterscarfe* (London, 1643)
Barwick, J., *Certain Disquisitions* (Oxford, 1644)
—— *ΙΕΡΟΝΚΗΣ or the Fight, Victory and Triumph of St Paul* (London, 1660)
Basire, I., *Deo et Ecclesiae Sacrum. Sacriledge Arraigned* (Oxford, 1646)
Bastwick, J., *A Learned, Useful, and Seasonable Discourse* (London, 1643)
Bate, G., *Elenchus Motuum* (London, 1685)
Beadle, J., *The Journal or Diary of a Thankful Christian* (London, 1656)
Bedford, T., *A Treatise of the Sacraments* (London, 1639)
Bennet, R., *King Charle's Triall Justified* (London, 1649)
Bernard, N., *A Looking-Glasse for Rebellion* (Oxford, 1644)
Birkenhead, J., *A Sermon* (Oxford, 1644)
Blake, R., and Monck, G., *A True Relation of the Late Great Sea Fight* (London, 1653)
Blake, T., *Mr Blake's Answer to Mr Tombes* (London, 1646)
A Bloody Plot Practised by Some Papists (London, 1641)
Bolton, S., *A Tossed Ship* (London, 1644)
Borough, Sir J., *The Sovereignty* (London, 1651)
Boteler, E., *The Worthy of Ephratah* (London, 1659)
Boughen, E., *Mr Geree's Case of Conscience Sifted* (London, 1648)
—— *A Sermon of Confirmation* (London, 1620)
Bowles, E., *Manifest Truths* (London, 1646)
—— *Plaine English* (np, 1643)
Bramhall, J., *A Sermon Preached in the Cathedrall Church of York* (York, 1643)
—— *A Sermon Preached in York Minster* (York, 1643)
Bray, W., *A Sermon of the Blessed Sacrament* (London, 1641)
Bridge, W., *The Loyall Convert* (London, 1644)
—— *The Wounded Conscience Cured* (London, 1642)
A Brief Narrative (London, 1650)
A Brief Narrative of the Great Victory (London, 1650)
A Briefe Answer to a Late Pamphlett Entituled Unparralleld Reasons for Abolishing Episcopacy (Oxford, 1644)
Brocket, W., *Good Newes from Ireland* (London, 1642)
Brockett, J., *God's Statute for General Judgment* (London, 1642)
Brome, R., *Joviall Crew* (London, 1652)

———— *Lachrymae Musarum* (London, 1650)

Bryan, J., *The Virtuous Daughter* (London, 1636)

Buchanan, D., *L'Histoire Veritable de ces Derniers Troubles* (np, nd)

———— *A Short and True Relation* (London, 1645)

———— *Truth Its Manifest* (London, 1646)

Bulkley, P., *The Gospel Covenant* (London, 1646)

Burges, C., *Another Sermon* (London, 1641)

———— *The Fire of the Sanctuarie* (London, 1625)

———— *A Vindication* (London, 1648)

Burgess, A., *Vindiciae Legis* (London, 1646)

Burrell, A., *The Humble Remonstrance of Andrewes Burrell* (London, 1646)

Burroughes, J., *The Glorious Name of God* (London, 1643)

———— *Moses his Choice* (London, 1641)

———— *A Vindication* (London, 1646)

Byfield, A., *The Reasons Presented by the Dissenting Brethren* (London, 1648)

C., W., *A Manuall of Prayers Collected for the Use of Sir Ralph Hopton's Regiment* (Oxford, 1643)

C., B., *The Souldiers Alarum Bell* (Np, 1659)

Canne, J., *The Discoverer* (London, 1649)

———— *The Discoverer ... the Second Part* (London, 1649)

———— *Emanuel* (London, 1650)

———— *The Improvement of Mercy* (London, 1649)

———— *Lieut. Colonel John Lilb. Tryed and Cast* (London, 1653)

———— *A Seasonable Word to the Parliament Men* (London, 1659)

———— *A Voice from the Temple* (London, 1653)

Cary, M., *The Resurrection of the Witnesses* (London, 1653)

Casaubon, M., *The Original Cause* (London, 1645)

Case, T., *God's Rising* (London, 1644)

The Case of the Commission of Array Stated ([London, 1642])

The Case Stated Between England and the United Provinces (London, 1652)

Castle, W., *The Jesuit's Undermining of Parliaments and Protestants* (London, 1642)

Cavalier and Puritan. Ballads and Broadsides Illustrating the Period of the Great Rebellion 1640–1660, ed. H. E. Rollins (New York, 1923)

Cawdry, D., *The Inconsistencie* (London, 1651)

Certain Observations Touching the Two Great Offices of the Seneshalsey or High Stewardship and High Constableship of England (London, 1642)

Chaloner, T., *An Answer to the Scotch Papers* (London, 1646)

Chambers, H. et al., *An Apology for the Ministers of the County of Wilts* (London, 1654)

The Character of Mercurius Politicus (London, 1650)

The Character of the Rump (London, 1660)

Charles I, *His Majesties Answer to a Printed Book* (Oxford, 1642)

——— *His Majesties Declaration* (London, 1628)

——— *His Majesties Declaration to all his Loving Subjects* (London, 1641)

——— *His Majesties Declaration to Both Houses of Parliament* (London, 1641)

——— *His Majesties Letter to the Lord Keeper* (London, 1642)

——— *His Majesties Message to the House of Peers, April 22 1642* (London, 1642)

——— *His Majesties Proclamation and Declaration* (Oxford, 1642)

Cheshire, T., *A Sermon Preached at St Peters* (London, 1642)

Chestlin, R., *Persecutio Undecima* (London, 1648)

Cheynell, F., *Aulicus His Dream* (London, 1644)

——— *The Beacon Flameing* (London, 1652)

——— *Chillingworthi Novissima* (London, 1644)

——— *The Rise, Growth and Danger of Socinianism* (London, 1643)

Chillenden, E., *Preaching Without Ordination* (London, 1647)

Chillingworth, W., *A Petition of the Most Substantial Inhabitants of the City of London* (Oxford, 1642)

——— *A Sermon Preached at the Publike Fast* (Oxford, 1644)

Christus Dei (Oxford, 1643)

Church Levellers (London, 1649)

Church, J., *The Divine Warrant of Infant Baptism* (London, 1648)

Clarke, S., *The Lives of Sundry Eminent Persons* (London, 1683)

——— *The Second Part of the Marrow of Ecclesiastical History* (London, 1650)

The Cleere Sense: Or, a Just Vindication of the Late Ordinance (London, 1645)

Cobbet, T., *The Civil Magistrates Power in Matters of Religion* (London, 1653)

Coke, Sir E., *The Second Part of the Institutes* (London, 1642)

The Collection of all the Particular Papers (Oxford, 1643)

A Collection of all the Publicke Orders (London, 1646)

A Collection of Sundry Petitions (Np, 1642)

Collonel Grey's Portmanteau Opened (London, 1650)

By the Committee of Safety. A Proclamation (London, 1659)

At a Common Council … 20th of December 1659 (London, 1659)

A Continuation of Our Weekly Intelligence (London, 1642)

A Continuation of the True Intelligence (London, 1644)

Cook, J., *Monarchy no Creature of Gods Making* (London, 1652)

——— *Redintegratio Amoris* (London, 1647)

——— *Unum Necessarium* (London, 1648)

——— *Vindication of the Professors and Profession of the Law* (London, 1646)

——— *What the Independents Would Have* (London, 1647)

Coote, Sir C., *A Declaration of Sir Charls Coot* (London, 1660)

The Coppy of a Letter Sent from the Rebells in Ireland (London, 1641)

A Copy of a Letter Concerning the Election of a Lord Protector (London, 1654)

The Copy of a Letter Sent by the Lords and Commons (London, 1641)

The Copy of a Letter Sent Out of Wiltshire (London, 1654)

A Copy of a Letter Written to a Private Friend to Give Him Satisfaction in Some Things Touching the Lord Say (London, 1643)

A Copy of a Letter Written to an Officer of the Army by a True Commonwealthsman and No Courtier (London, 1656)

A Corrector of the Answerer to the Speech Out of Dorres (Edinburgh, 1646)

Cotton, J., *Way of the Churches* (London, 1645)

Cotton, Sir R., *A Briefe Discourse Concerning the Power of the Peeres and Commons of Parliament in Point of Judicature* (London, 1640)

The Covenant … Also Two Speeches … the One by Mr Nye (London, 1643)

Cranford, J., *Haereseo-Machia* (London, 1646)

Creamor, T., *A Gun-Powder-Plot in Ireland* (London, 1641)

Creighton, R., ed., *Sylvester Sgouropoulos, Vera Historia Unionis … sive Concilii Florentini* (Hague, 1660)

Cromwell, O., *The Conclusion of Lieuten. Generall Cromwells Letter* (London, 1645)

———— *Lieutenant General Cromwel's Letter* (London, 1648)

Curia Politiae (trans. E. Wolley, London, 1654)

The Danger to England Observed (London, 1642)

Davies, J., *A Scourge for Paper Persecutors* (London, 1625)

Declaratio Parlamenti Angliae (London, 1650)

The Declaration and Engagement of the Commanders, Officers, and Seamen (London, 1648)

The Declaration and Humble Representation of the Officers and Souldiers in Colonel Scroops, Colonel Sanders, Colonel Wautons Regiment (London, 1648)

A Declaration Concerning the Miserable Sufferings of the Countrie (London, 1646)

A Declaration Conteyning the Just Causes and Considerations of this Present War with the Scots (London, 1651)

A Declaration from the General and Council of State (London, 1653)

A Declaration of Parliament (London, 1659)

A Declaration of the Army of England Upon their March into Scotland (London, 1650)

A Declaration of the Army of the Commonwealth of England to the People of Scotland (London, 1650)

A Declaration of the Commons Against a Scandalous Book Entituled The Second Part of England's New Chains Discovered (London, 1649)

A Declaration of the English Army Now in Scotland (London, 1650)

A Declaration of the General Council (London, 1659)

The Declaration of the Gentlemen, Freeholders and Inhabitants of the County of Bedford (London, 1659)

The Declaration of the Gentry of the County of Norfolk (London, 1659)

A Declaration of the Iust Causes Moouing her Maiestie to Send a Nauie, and Armie to the Seas, and Toward Spaine (London, 1597)

A Declaration of the Lords and Commons … Concerning Irregular Printing and for the Suppressing of all False and Scandalous Pamphlets (London, 1642)

A Declaration of the Lords and Gentry ... of Lemster and Munster (London, 1644)

A Declaration of the Lords, Knight and Gentlemen in the Counties of Chester, Salop, Stafford (London, 1659)

A Declaration of the Officers (London 1659)

A Declaration of the Parliament of England Upon the Marching of the Army into Scotland (London, 1650)

A Declaration of the Parliament of the Commonwealth (London, 1652)

A Declaration of the State of the Colonie and Affaires in Virginia (London, 1620)

A Declaration of Three Deputy Governors of the Isle of Wight (London, 1648)

The Declaration or Remonstrance of the Lords and Commons ... with Divers Depositions and Letters (London, 1642)

A Declaration Wherein is Full Satisfaction Given Concerning Sir Edward Dering (London, 1644)

A Declaration, Conteynyng the Iust Causes of this Present Warre with the Scotts (London, 1542)

Dell, W., *The Building and Glory of the Truely Christian and Spiritual Church* (London, 1646)

———— *Power from on High* (London, 1645)

———— *Right Reformation* (London, 1646)

The Demands of the Rebels in Ireland (London, 1641)

Dering, E., *A Declaration by Sir Edward Dering* (London, 1644)

The Designs and Correspondence of the Present Committee of Estates (London, 1648)

Despagne, J., *New Observations upon the Decalogue* (London, 1652)

Devereux, R., Earl of Essex, *The Earle of Essex his Letter to Master Speaker* (Oxford, 1643)

Digby, Lord George, *The Lord George Digbies Apologie for Himselfe* (Oxford, 1642)

Digby, Sir K., *Two Treatises* (Paris, 1644, reprinted London, 1645)

Digges, D., *An Answer to a Printed Book* (Oxford, 1642)

———— *A Review of the Observations* (York, 1643)

Disbrowe, J., *A Letter Sent from Col. John Disbrowe* (London, 1659)

A Disclaimer of the Commons of England (London, 1643)

A Discourse Concerning the Engagement (London, 1650)

A Discourse Discovering Some Mysteries of Our New State (Oxford, 1645)

A Discovery of a Horrible and Bloody Treason and Conspiracie (London, 1641)

The Discovery of a Late and Bloody Conspiracie (London, 1641)

A Discovery to the Praises of God ... of a Late Intended Plot (London, 1641)

Divers Questions Upon His Majesties Last Answer (London, 1641)

Dobson, E., *XIV Articles of Treason* (Oxford, 1643)

Dominium Maris, or the Dominion of the Sea (London, 1652)

Downing, C., *A Sermon Preached to the Renowned Company of the Artillery* (London, 1641)

Downing, G., *A True Relation* (London, 1651)

Drayton, T., *The Proviso or Condition of the Promises* (London, 1657)

Dugdale, Sir W., *Considerations Touching the Late Treaty* (Oxford, 1645)

Duppa, B., *A Collection of Prayers* (Oxford, 1643)

Dury, J., *A Case of Conscience* (London, 1649)

———— *A Case of Conscience Concerning Ministers* (London, 1650)

———— *Conscience Eased* (London, nd)

———— *Considerations Concerning the Present Engagement* (London, 1649)

———— *A Disengag'd Survey* (London, 1650)

———— *Just Reproposals* (London, 1650)

———— *Objections Against the Taking of the Engagement Answered* (London, 1650)

———— *A Second Parcel of Objections Against the Taking of the Engagement Answered* (London, 1650)

———— *Two Treatises Concerning the Matter of the Engagement* (London, 1650)

———— *The Unchanged, Constant and Single Hearted Peacemaker* (London, 1650)

Dyve, Sir L., *A Letter from Sr Lewis Dyve to the Lord Marquis of Newcastle* (Hague, 1650)

E., R., *A Letter Written Out of the Country to Mr John Pym* (Oxford, 1642)

Edwards, T., *Antapologia* (London, 1644)

———— *Gangraena* (London, 1646)

Eighteen New Court-Quaeries (London, 1659)

Eikon Basilike (London, 1649)

Elcock, E., *Animadversions* (London, 1651)

English, P., *The Survey of Policy* (Leith, 1653)

The Essex Watchman's Watchword (London, 1649)

Evans, D., *Justa Honoraria* (London, 1646)

An Exact Accompt of the Receipts and Disbursements Expended by the Committee of Safety (London, 1660)

An Exact and True Relation (London, 1642)

An Exact Collection of all Remonstrances (London, 1643)

Exploits Discovered (London, 1643)

Extracts of Letters (London, 1644)

F., D., *A Letter of Addresse to the Protector Occasioned by Mr Needhams Reply to Mr Goodwins Book Against the Triers* (London, 1657)

Fairfax, Sir T., *A Declaration from his Excellencie Sir Thomas Fairfax* (London, 1647)

———— *A Declaration of his Excellency Sir Thomas Fairfax Disclaiming a Pamphlet* (London, 1647)

———— *A Declaration of the Engagements, Remonstrances, Representations* (London, 1647)

A Faithful Advertisement (London, 1650)

A Faithful Relation (London, 1644)

A Faithfull Discovery of a Treacherous Design (London, 1653)

The Fallacies of Mr William Prynne (Oxford, 1644)

A False Jew (Newcastle, 1653)

Farnworth, R., *The Generall-Good to All People* (London, 1653)

Fast Sermons to Parliament, ed. R. Jeffs (34 vols, London, 1970–71)

Fawne, L., *A Beacon Set on Fire* (London, 1652)

Featley, D., *Sacra Nemesis* (Oxford, 1644)

——— *Virtumnus Romanus* (London, 1642)

Fenwick, W., *An Exact Enquiry after Ancient Truths* (London, 1643)

——— *Zion's Rights* (London, 1642)

Ferne, H., *The Camp at Gilgal* (Oxford, 1643)

——— *Conscience Satisfied* (Oxford, 1643)

——— *Of the Division* (London, 1652)

——— *A Reply unto Severall Treatises* (Oxford, 1643)

——— *Resolving of Conscience* (Cambridge, 1642)

——— *A Sermon* (Oxford, 1644)

Fiennes, N., *Colonell Fiennes his Reply* (London, 1643)

——— *Colonell Fiennes Letter to my Lord General Concerning Bristol* (London, 1643)

——— *A Relation Made in the House of Commons* (London, nd)

Fiennes, W., Viscount Saye, *Vindiciae Veritatis* (London, 1654)

Filmer, Sir R., *Observations* (London, 1652)

Fisher, P., *Apobaterion* (London, 1655)

——— *Inauguratio Oliviariana* (London, 1654)

——— *Irenodia Gratulatoria* (London, 1652)

——— *Marston Moor* (London, 1650)

——— *Miscellania* (London, 1655)

——— *Oratio Anniversaria* (London, 1655)

——— *Panegyrici Cromwello* (Np, 1654)

——— *Pro Navali Anglorum* (London, 1653)

——— *Veni, Vidi, Vici* (London, 1652)

Fowler, C., *Daemonium Meridianum, Satan at Noon. The Second Part* (London, 1656)

Frost, W., *A Declaration of Some Proceedings* (London, 1648)

——— *Remarkable Observations* (London, 1651)

A Full Relation of the Great Defeat (London, 1643)

A Full Relation of the Great Victory (London, 1648)

A Full Relation of the Late Expedition of Lord Monroe in Ulster (London, 1644)

A Full Relation of the Passages Concerning the Late Treaty (Oxford, 1645)

Fuller, T., *The Appeal of Iniured Innocence* (London, 1659)

——— *The Cause and Cure of a Wounded Conscience* (London, 1647)

——— *Ephemeris Parliamentaria* (London, 1654)

—— *Good Thoughts in Bad Times* (Exeter, 1645)

—— *The Holy State* (Cambridge, 1642)

—— *The Holy State* (3rd ed., London, 1652)

—— *Jacobs Vow* (Oxford, 1644)

—— *A Sermon of Assurance* (London, 1647)

—— *A Sermon of Contentment* (London, 1648)

G, G., *A Reply to a Namelesse Pamphlet, Intituled an Answer to a Speech Without Doors* (London, 1646)

Gataker, T., *The Decease of Lazarus* (London, 1640)

Gatford, L., *An Exhortation to Peace* (London, 1643)

Geree, J., *A Catechisme* (Oxford, 1629)

—— *The Downfall of Antichrist* (London, 1641)

—— *Judah's Joy* (London, 1641)

—— *The Red Horse* (London, 1648)

—— *Touching the Subject of Supremacy* (London, 1647)

—— *Vindiciae Voti* (London, 1641)

God and the King (London, 1615)

God Appearing for the Parliament in Sundry Late Victories (London, 1644)

Goffe, W., *A Just Apologie for an Abused Army* (London, 1646)

The Good and Prosperous Success (London, 1642)

Good Newes from Sea, Being a True Relation of the Late Sea-Fight (London, 1643)

Goodwin, J., *Calumny Arraigned* (London, 1645)

—— *Grand Imprudence* (London, 1644)

—— *Innocency and Truth* (London, 1644)

—— *Sion- Colledg Visited* (London, 1648)

—— *Twelve Considerable Serious Cautions* (London, 1646)

Gosnold, P., *A Sermon* (Oxford, 1644)

Graham, J., Marquis of Montrose, *The Declaration of ... Montrose* (London, 1650)

The Grand Case of Conscience (London, 1650)

The Grave and Learned Speech of Serjeant Wilde (London, 1648)

Gre, G du, *Breveet Accuratum Grammaticiae* (Cambridge, 1636)

The Great Assizes Holden in Parnassus (London, 1645)

A Great Conspiracy By the Papists in the Kingdome of Ireland (London, 1641)

A Great Conspiracy of the Papists (London, 1641)

That Great Expedition for Ireland (London, 1642)

The Great Mysterie of God (London, 1645)

Grenvile, Sir R., *A Letter Written by Sir Richard Grenvile* (London, 1646)

Greville, R., Lord Brooke, *The Nature of Truth* (London, 1641)

Gumbleden, J., *Christ Tempted* (London, 1657)

Hall, John, *Catch that Catch Can* (London, 1652)

—— *Confusion Confounded* (London, 1654)

—— *A Gagg to Love's Advocate* (London, 1652)

———— *The Grounds and Reasons of Monarchy Considered* (Edinburgh, 1650)

———— *Hierocles Upon the Golden Verses* (London, 1657)

———— *The Honour of the English Soldiery* (London, 1651)

———— *A Letter Written to a Gentleman* (London, 1653)

———— *The Nonesuch Charles his Character* (London, 1651)

———— *Paradoxes* (London, 1655)

———— *Sedition Scourg'd* (London, 1653)

———— *A Serious Epistle to Mr William Prynne* (London, 1649)

———— *A Stop to the Mad Multitude* (London, 1653)

———— *A True Relation* (London, 1651)

Hall, Joseph, *Episcopacie by Divine Right Asserted* (London, 1640)

———— *The Lawfulnes and Unlawfulnes of an Oath or Covenant* (Oxford, 1643)

Hamilton, J., Duke of Hamilton, *The Several Speeches of Duke Hamilton* (London, 1649)

Hardy, N., *Justice Triumphing, or the Spoylers Spoyled* (London, 1647)

———— *Thankfulness in Grain* (London, 1654)

The Harmony of Our Oaths (London, 1643)

Harrison, E., *Plain Dealing* (London, 1649)

Hartlib, S., *A Discours of Husbandrie* (London, 1650)

Harwood, R., *The Loyall Subject's Retiring Room* (Oxford, 1645)

Haward, L., *A Continuation of the Diurnal Occurrences and Proceedings of the English Army Against the Rebels in Ireland* (London, 1642)

———— *A Continuation of the Last Occurrences from Irland* (London, 1642)

Hawke, M., *Killing is Murder* (London, 1657)

———— *The Right of Dominion* (London, 1655)

The Heads of Proposals (London, 1647)

The Heads of Severall Petitions (London, 1641)

Herbert, E., Baron Herbert of Cherbury, *The Life and Reign of King Henry the Eighth* (London, 1649)

Herring, F., *Mischeefes Mysterie* (trans. J. Vicars, London, 1617)

Heylyn, P., *A Brief and Moderate Answer to the Seditious and Scandalous Challenges of Henry Burton* (London, 1637)

———— *Cyprianus Anglicus* (London, 1671)

———— *The Historie of Episcopacie* (London, 1642)

———— *The Rebells Catechisme* (Oxford, 1644)

Holmes, N., *The Resurrection Revealed* (London, 1653)

———— *A Sermon Preached Before the Right Honourable Thomas Foote* (London, 1650)

———— *A Sermon Preached Before Thomas Andrews* (London, 1650)

Howard, T., Earl of Arundel, *The True Copy of a Letter Sent from Thomas, Earle of Arundel* (London, 1641)

Howard W. (pseud. Roger Widdrington), *A Pattern of Christian Loyaltie* (London, 1634)

Howell, J., *Bella Scot Anglica* (London, 1648)

―――― *A Discours of Dunkirk* (London, 1664)

―――― *Dodonas Grove* (Cambridge, 1645)

―――― *Epistolae Ho Elianae* (London, 1645)

―――― *Finetti Philoxenis* (London, 1656)

―――― *Som Sober Inspections* (London, 1655)

―――― *SPQV. A Survay of the Signorie of Venice* (London, 1651)

Huit, E., *The Whole Prophecie of Daniel* (London, 1644)

The Humble Address and Hearty Desires of the Gentlemen, Ministers and Free-Holders of the County of Northampton (London, 1660)

An Humble Declaration of the Apprentices (London, 1642)

The Humble Desires ... of the County and Borough of Leicester (London, 1659)

An Humble Examination of a Printed Abstract of the Answers to Nine Reasons (London, 1641)

The Humble Petition and Address of the Sea-men and Watermen (London, 1659)

The Humble Petition and Representation of the Officers and Souldiers of the Garrisons of Portsmouth, Southsea Castle, Hurst Castle, Poole and Brownsea Castle (np, 1648)

The Humble Petition of Divers Gentlemen, Ministers and Well-Affected Inhabitants in the County of Somerset (London, 1648)

The Humble Petition of Divers Poor Prisoners (London, 1642)

The Humble Petition of the County of Southampton (London, 1641)

The Humble Petition of the Inhabitants of the County of Essex (Oxford, 1642)

The Humble Petition of the Inhabitants of the County of Hertford (Oxford, 1642)

The Humble Petition of the Major, Aldermen and Commons of the Citty of London (Oxford, 1642)

The Humble Remonstrance of the General Council of Officers (London, 1653)

Humble Representation of the Committee ... Leicester (London, 1648)

The Humble Representation of the Desires of the Officers and Souldiers in the Regiment of Horse, for the County of Northumberland (London, 1648)

Hunton, P., *A Treatise of Monarchy* (London, 1643)

―――― *A Vindication of the Treatise of Monarchy* (London, 1644)

Hyde, E., *Transcendent and Multiplied Rebellion* (Oxford, 1645)

Hypocrites Unmasked, or, the Hypocrisie of the New Usurpers (London, 1659)

Independency to be Abandoned (London, 1647)

Insigma Civicas (Oxford, 1643)

Intelligence from the Scottish Army (London, 1644)

Intelligence from the South Borders (London, 1644)

Ionsonus Virbius, or, the Memorie of Ben: Johnson (London, 1638)

Irelands Amazement, or the Heavens Armado (London, 1641)

Irelands Complaint Against Sir George Ratcliffe (London, 1641)

Jane, J., *Eikon Aklastos* (Np, 1651)

Jennings, T., *The Right Way to Peace* (London, 1647)

——— *Truth's Return* (London, 1646)

Johnson, T., *A Discourse Consisting of Motives for the Enlargement and Freedom of Trade* (London, 1645)

——— *A Plea for Free-mens Liberties* (London, 1646)

Jones, H., *A Remonstrance of Divers Remarkable Passages* (London, 1642)

——— *A Remonstrance of the Beginnings and Proceedings of the Rebellion* (London, 1642)

Jones, M., *Lieut. General Jones's Letter to the Council of State* (London, 1649)

Joyce, G., *A True Impartiall Narration* (London, 1647)

——— *A Vindication of His Majesty and the Army* (London, 1647)

Joyfull Newes from Ireland (London, 1642)

The Justification of a Safe and Wel-Grounded Answer (London, 1646)

Kem, S., *The New Fort of True Honour* (London, 1640)

Kennett, W., *A Register and Chronicle* (London, 1728)

The Kentish Petition (London, 1648)

Keymor, J., *A Cleare and Evident Way for Enriching the Nations of England and Ireland* (London, 1650)

King Charles the First, No Man of Blood But a Martyr for his People (London, 1649)

The King of Scotland's Negotiations at Rome (London, 1650)

The Kingdomes Case (London, 1643)

The Kings Cabinet Opened (London, 1645)

The Kings Last Farewell to the World (London, 1649)

Knell, P., *Israel and England Paralelled* (London, 1648)

L'Estrange, H., *Gods Sabbath* (Cambridge, 1641)

L'Estrange, R., *L'Estrange his Apology* (London, 1660)

——— *No Blinde Guides* (London, 1660)

La Declaration du Parlement de la Republique d'Angleterre (London, 1652)

Lancton, T., *Dublin, Febr. 7. 1641, or, The Last True Newes from Ireland* (London, 1641)

The Last Newes from Ireland (London, 1641)

The Last Speeches and Confession (London, nd)

The Last Will and Testament of Tom Fairfax (Np, 1648)

The Late Proceedings of the Scottish Army (London, 1644)

A Late and True Relation from Ireland (London, 1641)

Laud, W., *The Archbishop of Canterburys Speech* (London, 1644)

——— *The History of the Troubles and Tryal* (London, 1695)

——— *The Works, ed. J. H. Parker* (8 vols, Oxford, 1847–60)

Lawrence, R., *The Wolf Stript of his Sheeps Clothing* (London, 1647)

Leslie, H., *The Blessing of Judah* (Oxford, 1644)

——— *The Martyrdome of King Charles* (Hague, 1649)

——— *A Speech Delivered at the Visitation* (London, 1639)

——— *A Treatise of the Authority of the Church* (Dublin, 1637)

A Letter … From an Eminent Officer in the Army at Edenburgh (np, 1659)

A Letter and Declaration of the Nobility and Gentry of the County of York (London, 1659)

A Letter from a Captain of the Army (London, 1660)

A Letter from a Grave Gentleman (Oxford, 1643)

A Letter from a True and Lawful Member of Parliament (London, 1656)

A Letter from Divers of the Gentry of the County of Lincolne (London, 1659)

A Letter from Mercurius Civicus (np, 1643)

A Letter Sent from Ireland (London, 1659)

Ley, J., *A Case of Conscience* (London, 1641)

———— *A Comparison of the Parliamentary Protestation* (London, 1641)

———— *Defensive Doubts* (London, 1641)

———— *Englands Doxologie* (London, 1641)

———— *A Letter (Against the Erection of an Altar)* (London, 1641)

———— *Sunday a Sabbath* (London, 1641)

The Life and Reign of King Charls (London, 1651)

The Life of H. H. (London, 1688)

Lilburne, J., *An Answer to Nine Arguments* (London, 1645)

———— *Innocency and Truth* (London, 1645)

———— *Jonah's Cry* (London, 1647)

Lilly, W., *An Astrologicall Prediction* (London, 1648)

———— *Merlinus Anglicus Junior* (London, 1644)

Lluelin, M., *Men Miracles* (Oxford, 1646)

A Logical Demonstration (London, 1650)

London's Account (London, 1647)

Lockhart, W., *A Letter Sent from Col. William Lockhart* (London, 1660)

Longinus, D., *Of the Height of Eloquence* (London, 1652)

Lord Have Mercie Upon Us (Oxford, 1643)

Love, C., *England's Distemper* (London, 1645)

———— *Heaven's Glory* (London, 1653)

———— *A Modest and Clear Vindication of the Serious Representation and Late Vindication of the Ministers of London* (London, 1649)

———— *A Treatise of Effectual Calling and Election* (London, 1653)

Lovelace, R., *Lucasta* (London, 1649)

Lucas, Sir T., *Admirable Good Newes Againe from Ireland* (London, 1641)

MacDowal, Sir W., *An Answer* (Hague, 1651)

Magnalia Dei (London, 1644)

Maier, M., *Lusus Serius* (London, 1654)

Maizeaux, P. des, *The Life of William Chillingworth* (London, 1683)

Making the News. An Anthology of the Newsbooks of Revolutionary England 1641–1660, ed. J. Raymond (Moreton-in-Marsh, 1993)

Malvezzi, V., *Discourses Upon Cornelius Tacitus* (London, 1642)

March 21th 1641. Continuation of the Good Newes from Ireland (London, 1641)

Marshall, S., *A Letter from Mr Marshall and Mr Nye* (London, 1643)
—— *Meroz Cursed* (London, 1642)
—— *A Sermon* (London, 1641)
Massey, E., *The Declaration and Speech of Colonel Massey Concerning* (London, 1650)
Maxwell, J., *Sacro-Sancta Regum Majestas* (Oxford, 1644)
May, T., *The Changeable Covenant* (London, 1650)
—— *The Character of a Right Malignant* (London, 1645)
—— *A Discourse Concerning the Successe of Former Parliaments* (London, 1642)
—— *The History of the Parliament of England* (London, 1647, reprinted Oxford, 1854)
—— *Observations Upon the Effects of Former Parliaments* (London, 1642)
Menteith, R., *Histoire des Troubles de la Grand Bretagne* (Paris, 1649)
Mercurius Elencticus, *The Anatomy of Westminster Juncto* (np, 1648)
Mervyn, A., *An Exact Relation* (London, 1642)
Milton, J., *Animadversions upon the Remonstrants Defence* (London, 1641)
—— *The Complete Prose Works of John Milton IV* (New Haven, 1966)
—— *Considerations Touching the Likeliest Means to Remove Hirelings* (London, 1659)
—— *Eikonoklastes* (London, 1652)
—— *Eikonoklastes, ou Response au Livre* (London, 1652)
—— *Pro Populo Anglicano* (London, 1652)
—— *Pro Populo Anglicano Defensio* (London, 1658)
—— *Pro Populo Defensio* (London, 1651)
—— *Pro Se Defensio* (London, 1655)
—— *The Readie and Easie Way to Establish a Free Commonwealth* (London, 1660)
—— *The Works of John Milton* (19 vols, New York, 1931–38)
A Miraculous Victory (London, 1643)
A Moderate and Cleer Relation of the Private Soldierie of Colonell Scroops and Col. Sanders Regiments (London, 1648)
The Moderator (London, 1646)
Monck, G., *A Letter of General George Monck's* (London, 1660)
—— *A Letter Sent from General Monck* (London, 1660)
—— *The Lord General Monck his Speech* (London, 1660)
—— *A True Relation* (London, 1653)
Moore, J., *Protection Proclaimed* (London, 1656)
More Newes from Ireland (London, 1641)
Morley, T., *A Remonstrance of the Cruelties Committed by the Irish Rebels* (London, 1644)
Mossom, R., *Anti-Paraeus* (York, 1642)
—— *The Preachers Tripartite* (London, 1657)

———— *Sion's Prospect in its First View* (London, 1651)

A Most Exact Relation of a Great Victory (London, 1642)

A Most Miraculous and Happy Victory (London, 1643)

A Most True and Exact Relation of Both the Battels (London, 1642)

Moulin, P. du, *Of Peace and Contentment of Minde* (London, 1657)

Nedham, M., *The Case of the Commonwealth of England Stated* (London, 1650, ed. P. A. Knachel, Charlottesville, Va, 1969)

———— *The Case of the Kingdom Stated* (London, 1647)

———— *The Case of the Kingdom Stated* (3rd edn, London, 1647)

———— *The Case Stated Between England and the United Provinces* (London, 1652)

———— *A Cat May Look at a King* (London, 1652)

———— *Certain Considerations* (London, 1649)

———— *A Check to the Checker of Britannicus* (London, 1644)

———— *The Excellencie of a Free State* (London, 1656)

———— *Good English* (London, 1648)

———— *The Great Accuser Cast Down* (London, 1657)

———— *Independencie* (London, 1646)

———— *Interest Will Not Lie* (London, 1659)

———— *The Lawyer of Lincolnes-Inn* (London, 1647)

———— *News from Brussells* (London, 1660)

———— *A Paralell of Governments* (London, 1647)

———— *A True Narrative of the Late Trayterous Plot* (London, 1656)

———— *The True State of the Case of the Commonwealth* (London, 1654)

———— *Vox Plebis* (London, 1646)

———— *The Whole Business of Sindercome* (London, 1657)

A New Diurnall of Passages (Oxford, 1643)

Norwood, A., *A Clear Optick Discovering to the Eye of Reason* (London, 1654)

———— *New Errors Made Palpable by an Old Light* (London, 1652)

Nye, P., *The Covenant* (London, 1643)

———— *The Excellency and Lawfulness* (London, 1646)

———— *An Exhortation* (London, 1644)

O'Brien, M., Lord Inchiquin, *The Desires and Propositions of the Lord Inchiquin* (London, 1648)

———— *A Manifestation Directed to the Honourable Houses of Parliament* (London, 1644)

Orders of his Highness the Lord Protector … for Putting in Speedy and Due Execution (London, 1655)

An Ordinance of the Lords and Commons … With Instructions for Taking of the League and Covenant … With an Exhortation for the Taking of the Covenant (London, 1643)

Ormond's Curtain Drawn (London, 1646)

Osborne, F, *A Seasonable Expostulation* (Oxford, 1652)

Owen, J., *The Labouring Saints Dismission to Rest* (London, 1652)

——— *Vindiciae Evangelicae* (Oxford, 1655)

Owen, L., *The Running Register* (London, 1626)

Oxinden, H., *Charls Triumphant* (London, 1660)

——— *Eikon Basilike* (London, 1660)

P., J., *The Copy of a Letter Written Unto Sir Edward Deering* (London, 1641)

P., N., *A Reply to that Malicious Letter* (London, 1660)

Palmer, G., *Sectaries Unmasked* (London, 1647)

Palmer, H., *Scripture and Reason Pleaded* (London, 1643)

The Papists Conspiracie (London, 1641)

Parker, H., *The Altar Dispute* (London, 1641)

——— *Answer to the Lord Digbies Speech* (London, 1641)

——— *The Case of Shipmony* (London, 1640)

——— *The Cheif Affairs of Ireland* (London, 1651)

——— *The Contrareplicant* (London, 1643)

——— *A Discourse Concerning Puritans* (London, 1641)

——— *Divine and Publike Observations* (Amsterdam, 1638)

——— *Of a Free Trade* (London, 1648)

——— *To the High Court of Parliament. The Humble Remonstrance of the Company of Stationers* (London, 1643)

——— *The Irish Massacre* (London, 1646)

——— *Jus Populi* (London, 1644)

——— *Jus Regum* (London, 1645)

——— *A Letter of Due Censure* (London, 1650)

——— *Memorial* (London, 1647)

——— *Mr William Wheeler's Case From His Own Relation* (London, 1645)

——— *The Oath of Pacification* (London, 1643)

——— *Observations* (London, 1642)

——— *Poincten van Consideration* (Rotterdam, 1645)

——— *A Question Answered* (London, 1642)

——— *The Question Concerning the Divine Right of Episcopacy* (London, 1641)

——— *Reformation in Courts* (London, 1650)

——— *A Remonstrance to Vindicate His Excellencie* (London, 1643)

——— *Scotland's Holy War* (London, 1650)

——— *Some Few Observations* (London, 1642)

——— *The Speech of their Excellencies* (London, 1645)

——— *Trojan Horse* (London, 1646)

——— *The True Grounds of Ecclesiastical Regiment* (London, 1641)

——— *The Vintners Answer* (London, 1642)

A Particular Relation of the Most Remarkable Occurrences (London, 1644)

The Particular Relation of the Present Estate and Condition of Ireland (London, 1642)

A Particular Relation of the Several Removes (London, 1644)

The Path Way to Peace (London, 1643)

Peirce, Sir E., *True and Good News from Brussels* (London, 1660)

A Perfect Relation of the Taking of ... Preston (London, 1642)

Peter, H., *Good Work for a Good Magistrate* (London, 1651)

―――― *Mr Peters Last Report of the English Wars* (London, 1646)

The Petition and Addresse of the Officers (London, 1659)

A Petition or Declaration (London, 1642)

A Petition Presented by the Inhabitants of Newport Pagnell (London, 1648)

Philips, J., *Joannis Philippi Angli Responsio* (London, 1652)

Pierson, T., *The Cure of Hurtfull Cares and Feares* (London, 1636)

Pinke, W., *The Tryall* (Oxford, 1631)

A Plaine Case (Oxford, 1643)

Plain English to his Excellencie the Lord General Monck (London, 1660)

Pocklington, J., *Altare Christianum* (London, 1637)

―――― *Sunday No Sabbath* (London, 1636)

The Poore Committee-Mans Accompt (London, 1647)

Potter, W., *The Key of Wealth* (London, 1650)

―――― *The Tradesman's Jewel* (London, 1650)

The Power of the Christian Magistrate (London, 1650),

Powers to be Resisted (London, 1643)

Prerogative Anatomised (London, 1644)

Preston, J., *The Breast-Plate of Faith and Love* (London, 1630)

―――― *The Golden Scepter* (London, 1638)

―――― *Sermons Preached Before His Majestie* (London, 1634)

Price, J., *Clerico Classicum* (London, 1649)

―――― *The Mystery and Method* (London, 1680, in F. Maseres, ed., *Select Tracts*, 2 vols, London, 1815)

Pricket, M., *An Appeale to the Reverend and Learned Synod of Divines* (Oxford 1644);

Pride, T., *The Beacons Quenched* (London, 1652)

The Proceedings, Votes, Resolves, and Acts of the Late Half-Quarter Parliament Called the Rump (London, 1660)

A Proclamation for the Confirmation of all Authorised Orders (London, 1615)

Proquiritatio (London, 1642)

Prynne, W., *The Antidote* (London, 1645)

―――― *The Antidote Animadverted* (Np, nd)

―――― *A Breviate* (London, 1644)

―――― *A Brief Justification of the XI Accused Members* (London, 1647)

―――― *A Briefe Survey and Censure of Mr Cozens* (London, 1628)

―――― *Canterburies Doome* (London, 1646)

―――― *A Checke to Brittanicus* (London, 1644)

―――― *The Doome of Cowardize and Treachery* (London, 1643)

―――― *Faces About* (London, 1644)

—————— *The Falsities and Forgeries* (London, 1644)

—————— *Foure Serious Questions* (np, nd)

—————— *A Fresh Discovery* (London, 1645)

—————— *A Full Reply* (London, 1644)

—————— *A Full Vindication and Answer of the XI Accused Members* (London, 1647)

—————— *Hidden Workes of Darkenes* (London, 1645)

—————— *The Hypocrites Unmasking* (London, 1647)

—————— *Independency Examined* (London, 1644)

—————— *A New Discovery of the Prelates Tyranny* (London, 1641)

—————— *The Popish Royal Favourite* (London, 1643)

—————— *Romes Masterpeece* (London, 1644)

—————— *Scotland's Ancient Obligation* (London, 1646)

—————— *The Soveraigne Power of Parliaments* (London, 1643)

—————— *The Subjection of all Traytors* (London, 1658)

—————— *Suspention Suspended* (London, 1646)

—————— *The Sword of Christian Magistracie* (London, 1647)

—————— *A True and Full Relation of the Prosecution, Arraignment, Tryall and Condemnation of Nathaniel Fiennes* (London, 1644)

—————— *Truth Triumphing* (London, 1645)

—————— *A Vindication of Foure Serious Questions* (London, 1645)

—————— *A Vindication of Sir William Lewis* (London, 1647)

—————— *The Whole Triall of Connor Lord Macquire* (London, 1645)

Pym, J., *The Declaration of John Pym* (London, 1641)

—————— *Mr Pymmes Speech to the Lords in Parliament* (London, 1641)

—————— *The Speech or Declaration of John Pym* (London, 1641)

Quarles, F., *A Plea for the King* (Oxford, 1642)

Ram, R., *Paedobaptism* (London, 1645)

—————— *A Sermon Preached at Balderton* (London, 1646)

—————— *The Souldier's Catechisme* (London, 1644)

Reading, J., *An Antidote* (London, 1654)

The Reasons Presented by the Dissenting Brethren (London, 1648)

Reasons Why This Kingdome Ought to Adhere to the Parliament (London, 1642)

The Recantation of Mercurius Aulicus, or Berkinheads Complaint (Oxford, 1644)

Rectifying Principles (London, 1648)

Religions Enemies (London, 1641)

Reliquae Sacrae Carolinae (Hague, 1650)

Remarkable Observations of Gods Mercies Towards England (London, 1651)

A Remonstrance Concerning the Misdemeanours of Some of the Scots Souldiers (London, 1646)

The Remonstrance of the Commons of England (London, 1643)

The Remonstrance of the Presbyterie of Sterling (Edinburgh, 1651)

A Reply to the House of Commons (London, 1648)

The Representation and Petition of the Officers of the Army (London, 1659)

Rew, J., *The Wounds of the Kirk of Scotland* (London, 1650)

Reynolds, E., *Animalis Homo* (London, 1650)

―――― *A Sermon Touching The Use of Humane Learning* (London, 1658)

Richardson, S., *An Apology for the Present Government* (London, 1654)

―――― *Plain Dealing* (London, 1656)

―――― *Of the Torments of Hell* (London, 1657)

Ricraft, J., *A Perfect List of all the Victories* (London, 1646)

―――― *A Perfect List of the Many Victories* (London, 1646)

―――― *A Survey of England's Champions* (London, 1647)

Ridley, J., *A Sermon of Humbly Walking with God* (London, 1649)

Robinson, H., *Briefe Considerations* (London, 1649)

―――― *Certain Considerations* (London, 1651)

―――― *Certain Proposals* (London, 1652)

―――― *The Falsehood of Mr William Pryn's Truth Triumphing* (London, 1645)

―――― *A Short Discourse* (London, 1649)

Robotham, J., *The Preciousness of Christ* (London, 1647)

Rosse, A., *Leviathan Drawn Out with a Hook* (London, 1653)

Rous, F., *The Lawfulness of Obeying the Present Government* (London, 1649)

Rr, *The Armies Remembrancer* (London, 1649)

Russell, J., *The Two Famous Pitcht Battels of Lypsich and Lutzen* (Cambridge 1634)

Sadler, J., *The Ancient Bounds* (London, 1645)

―――― *Flagellum Flagelli* (London, 1645)

―――― *Malignancy Un-masked* (London, 1642)

―――― *Masquarade du Ciel* (London, 1640)

―――― *A True Relation of the Lord Brooke's Setling of the Militia* (London, 1642)

St John, O., *An Argument of Law* (London, 1641)

Sales, W., *Theophania* (London, 1655)

Salmasius, C., *Claudii Salmasii Ad Johannem Miltonum Responsio* (London, 1660)

Salmon, J., *Heights in Depths* (London, 1651)

Saltmarsh, J., *The Opening of Master Prynnes New Book* (London, 1645)

―――― *A Peace But No Pacification* (London, 1643)

―――― *A Solemn Discourse* (London, 1643)

The Same Hand Again Against the Present Council of State's Bad Friends (London, 1649)

Sancroft, W., *Modern Policies* (London, 1652)

Scot, T., *A Paire of Cristall Spectacles* (London, 1648)

Scriptum Parlamenti Angliae (London, 1652)

The Second Character of Mercurius Politicus (London, 1650)

A Second Narrative of the Late Parliament (So Called) (np, 1659)

The Second Part of the Undeceiver (London, 1643)

Selden, J., *Of the Dominion, or Ownership of the Sea* (trans. M. Nedham, London, 1652)

A Serious and Faithfull Representation of the Judgments of Ministers (London, 1649)

Several Information and Examinations (London, 1653)

Several Speeches (London, 1648)

Severall Petitions Presented to His Excellency the Lord Fairfax (London, 1648)

Shaw, J., *Britannia Rediviva* (London, 1649)

Sheppard, W., *Englands Balme* (London, 1656)

—— *A Survey of the County Judicatures* (London, 1656)

Shirley, J., *The Cardinall* (London, 1652)

A Short Discourse Tending to the Pacification of all Unhappy Differences (London, 1642)

A Short Plea for the Commonwealth (London, 1651)

A Short Reply Unto a Declaration Entitled the Declaration of the Army of England (London, 1650)

Sibbes, R., *The Complete Works*, ed. A. B. Grosart (6 vols, Edinburgh, 1862–64)

Skippon, P., *The Christian Centurians Observations* (1645)

—— *A Salve for Every Sore* (London, 1643)

—— *True Treasure; or Thirtie Holy Vowes* (London, 1644)

Smart, P., *Canterburies Crueltie* (London, 1643)

—— *A Catalogue of Superstitious Innovations* (London, 1642)

—— *A Short Treatise* (London, 1643)

Smith, G., *The Three Kingdoms Healing Plaster* (London, 1643)

Sober Sadnes (London, 1643)

Some Considerations About the Nature of an Oath (London, 1649)

Some Considerations Tending to the Undeceiving (London, 1642)

Some Notable Observations Upon the Late Summons by the Earl of Newcastle (London, 1643)

Some Passages that Happened the 9th of March (London, 1642)

Sparke, M., *The Narrative History of King James* (London, 1651)

—— *A Second Beacon Fired by Scintilla* (London, 1652)

The Speech of Their Excellencies the Lords Ambassadors (London, 1645)

The Speech Without Doores Defended (np, 1646)

Spelman, H., *The Case of our Affaires* (Oxford, 1643)

—— *Certain Considerations* (Oxford, 1642)

—— *A Protestant's Account* (Cambridge, 1642)

—— *A View of a Printed Book* (Oxford, 1642)

Spittlehouse, J., *The Army Vindicated* (London, 1653)

Sprigge, J., *Anglia Rediviva* (London, 1647, reprinted Oxford, 1854)

Sprigge, W., *A Modest Plea for an Equal Common-Wealth* (London, 1659)

Stalham, J., *The Reviler Rebuked* (London, 1657)

Stampe, W., *A Sermon Preached Before His Maiestie* (Oxford, 1643)

———— *A Treatise of Spiritual Infatuation* (Hague, 1653)

Stanley, T. (trans.) *Aurora Ismenia* (London, 1650)

———— *Poems* (London, 1651)

Stapylton, R., *A More Full Relation of the Great Victory* (London, 1651)

Sterry, P., *England's Deliverance from the Northern Presbytery* (London, 1652)

Steward, R., *An Answer to a Letter Written at Oxford* (London, 1647)

Stipendariae Lacrymae (Hague, 1654)

Strata, F. de, *Polemic Against Printing*, ed. M. Lowry (London, 1986)

Streater, J., *Clavis as Aperiendum ... the Case of Mr John Streater* (London, 1654)

———— *A Further Continuance of the Grand Politick Informer* (np, nd)

———— *A Glimpse of that Jewel* (London, 1653)

———— *The Grand Informer* (np, 1647)

Strode, W., *A Sermon* (Oxford, 1644)

Stubbe, H., *Clamor, Rixa, Joci, Medacia* (London, 1657)

———— *The Common-Wealth of Oceana Put Into the Ballance* (London, 1660)

———— *The Commonwealth of Israel* (London, 1659)

———— *An Essay in Defence of the Good Old Cause* (London, 1659)

———— *A Letter to an Officer* (London, 1659)

———— *Malice Rebuked* (London, 1659)

Swadlin, T., *A Letter of an Independent to his Honoured Friend Mr Glyn* (Oxford, 1645)

———— *A Manuall of Devotions* (London, 1643)

———— *The Scriptures Vindicated* (np, 1643)

Sydenham, C., *An Anatomy of Lieut. Col. John Lilburn's Spirit* (London, 1649)

———— *A Christian, Sober, and Plain Exercitation* (London, 1653)

———— *An English Translation* (London, 1650)

———— *The False Brother* (London, 1651)

———— *A False Jew* (Newcastle, 1653)

———— *The Greatness and the Mystery of Godlines* (London, 1654)

———— *Hypocrisie Discovered* (London, 1654)

———— *The True Portraiture* (London, 1650)

Symmons, E., *A Military Sermon* (Oxford, 1644)

———— *A Vindication of King Charles* (London, 1647)

———— *A Vindication of King Charles* (London, 1648)

Tany, T., *Theauraujohn* (London, 1651)

Taylor, J., *General Complaint* (Oxford, 1644)

———— *General Complaint* (Oxford, 1645)

———— *John Taylor ... to John Booker* (Oxford, 1644)

———— *A Letter Sent to London from a Spie at Oxford* (1643)

———— *Mercurius Aquaticus* (Oxford, 1643)

———— *Mercurius Infernalis* (Oxford, 1644)

———— *A New Diurnall of Passages* (Oxford, 1643)

———— *A Reply as True as Steele* (London, 1641)

—————— *The Whole Life and Progress of Henry Walker* (London, 1642)

Taylor, Jeremy, *An Apology for Authorised and Set Forms of Liturgie* (London, 1649)

—————— *The Great Exemplar* (London, 1649)

—————— *The Rule and Exercises of Holy Dying* (London, 1651)

—————— *Of the Sacred Order and Offices of Episcopacy* (Oxford, 1642)

Temple, Sir J., *The Irish Rebellion* (London, 1646)

—————— *Ormonds Curtain Drawn* (London, 1646)

The Testimony of the Truth of Jesus Christ (London, 1648)

A Testimony to the Truth of Jesus Christ and to our Solemn League and Covenant (London, 1648)

Three Great Victories Obtained by the Parliament Forces (London, 1644)

Tillinghast, J., *Demetrius his Opposition to Reformation* (London, 1642)

Timely Advice From the Major Part of the Ould Souldiers in the Army (np, 1659)

Tombes, J., *Fermentum Pharisaeorum* (London, 1643)

—————— *Two Treatises* (London, 1645)

Torshell, S., *Case of Conscience* (London, 1643)

—————— *The Saints Humiliation* (London, 1633)

—————— *The Three Questions* (London, 1632)

Tracts on Liberty in the Puritan Revolution, 1638–47, ed. W. Haller (2 vols, New York, 1965)

Trapp, J., *A Brief Commentary or Exposition* (London, 1646)

—————— *A Commentary* (London, 1647)

Traytors Deciphered (Hague, 1650)

Treason Arraigned (London, 1660)

The Triall of Mr John Lilburn (London, 1653)

The Troubles of Amsterdam (London, 1650)

A True Catalogue (London, 1659)

The True Causes of the Commitment of Mr C. Walker (np, nd)

The True Character of Mercurius Aulicus (London, 1645)

A True Confutation (London, 1650)

A True Copie of the Berkshire Petition (London, 1648)

The True Copy of the Letter Which Was Sent from Divers Ministers (London, 1643)

A True Copy of the Relation of the Lord Major (London, 1642)

The True Informer (Oxford, 1643)

A True Narrative of the Examination, Tryall and Sufferings of James Nayler (London, 1657)

True Newes out of Herefordshire (London, 1642)

A True Relation Concerning the Late Fight at Torrington (London, 1645)

A True Relation from Hull (London, 1643)

A True Relation of a Late Victory Obtained by Sir Ralph Hopton (Oxford, 1642)

A True Relation of a Most Blessed Victory, Obtained Against the Marquess of Hertford (London, 1642)

A True Relation of the Last Great Fight at Sea (London, 1653)

A True Relation of the Late Expedition (London, 1643)

A True Relation of the Late Proceedings of the London Dragonners Sent to Oxford under Sir John Seaton (London, 1642)

A True Relation of the Most Chief Occurrences (London, 1644)

A True Relation of the Proceedings of Colonell Langharne (London, 1644)

A True Relation of the Proceedings of the English Army Now in Scotland (London, 1650)

True Relation of the Progress of the Parliamentary Force in Scotland (London, 1651)

The Tryall of Leiutenant Colonell John Lilburn (London, 1653)

Two Letters Sent from Amsterdam (London, 1642)

Two Speeches in the House of Peers (London, 1642)

The Unparalleld Monarch (London, 1656)

Vane, H., *A Light Shining Out of Darknes* (2nd edn, London, 1659)

Vaughan, H., *A Sermon* (Oxford, 1644)

Vere, Sir F., *The Commentaries of Sir Francis Vere*, ed. W. Dillingham (Cambridge, 1657)

Vernon, G., *The Life of the Learned and Reverend Dr Peter Heylyn* (London, 1682)

Verses on the Siege of Glocester (London, 1644)

Vicars, J., *Coleman-Street Conclave Visited* (London, 1648)

———— *Englands Hallelu-jah* (London, 1631)

———— *A Looking Glass for Malignants* (London, 1643)

———— *November the 5. 1605* (London, 1641)

———— *A Prospective Glasse* (London, 1618)

Vindicaie Contra Tyrannos (London, 1648)

A Vindication of the King (London, 1642)

A Vindication of the Presbyteriall Government and Ministry (London, 1650)

Vines, R., *The Hearse of the Renowned, the Right Honourable the Earle of Essex* (London, 1646)

———— *Obedience to Magistrates* (London, 1656)

Vinke, P., *The Reason of Faith* (London, 1659)

Violet, T., *The Advancement of Merchandize* (London, 1651)

———— *The Answer of the Corporation of Moniers* (London, 1653)

———— *Mysteries and Secrets* (London, 1653)

———— *Proposals Humbly Presented* (London, 1656)

———— *A True Discoverie* (London, 1651)

———— *A True Narrative of Some Remarkable Procedings* (London, 1653)

Vox Veritatis (Hague, 1650)

W., L., *The Troubles of Amsterdam* (London, 1650)

Walwyn, W., *The Writings*, eds J. R. McMichael and B. Taft (London, 1989)

Waring, T., *A Brief Narrative of the Plotting* (London, 1650)

Walker, C., *Anarchia Anglicana* (London, 1649)

—— *The High Court of Justice* (London, 1651)

—— *The History of Independency* (London, 1648)

—— *Relations and Observations* (London, 1648)

—— *The Triall of Lieut. Collonell John Lilburne* (London, 1649)

Walker, C., and Prynne, W., *An Answer to Col: Nathaniel Fiennes Relation* (London, 1643)

—— *The Humble Petition of Clement Walker and Will. Prynne* (np, nd)

—— *A True and Full Relation of the Prosecution, Arraignment, Tryall, and Condemnation of Nathaniel Fiennes* (London, 1644)

Walker, H., *The Creation of the World* (London, 1649)

—— *A Sermon Preached in the Chapell at Sommerset House* (London, 1650)

Walker, Sir E., *Historical Discourses* (London, 1705)

Wallis, J., *Truth Tried* (London, 1643)

Walsingham, E., *Britanicae Virtutis Imago* (Oxford, 1644)

Ward, N., *The Simple Cobbler* (London, 1647)

Ward, R., *The Analysis, Explication and Application of the Sacred Vow and Covenant* (London, 1643)

—— *The Analysis, Explication and Application of the Sacred and Solemn League and Covenant* (London, 1643)

—— *Theological Questions* (London, 1640)

—— *The Undeceiver* (London, 1643)

—— *A Vindication of the Late Vow and Covenant* (London, 1643)

Waring, T., *An Answer to Certain Seditious and Jesuitical Queries* (London, 1651)

A Warning Peece for London (London, 1642)

A Warrant of the Lord General (London, 1649)

Watson, R., *Regicidium Judaicum* (Hague, 1649)

—— *A Sermon Touching Schism* (Cambridge, 1642)

Webster, J., *The Picture of Mercurius Politicus* (London, 1653)

Wharton, G., *Naworth 1644. A New Almanack* (Oxford, 1644)

—— *Wharton 1645. An Almanack* (Oxford, 1645)

Wheeler, W., *A List of Some Chief Workes* (Amsterdam, 1651)

Whetcomb, T., *The Copy of a letter from Master Tristram Whitecombe* (London, 1642)

Whitby, D., *The Vindication of a True Protestant* (Oxford, 1644)

White, J., *The First Century of Scandalous Malignant Priests* (London, 1643)

The Whole Business of Sindercome (London, 1657)

The Whole Triall of Mr Love (London, 1651)

Wilbee, A., *Plain Truth Without Fear of Flattery* (London, 1647)

Wilkinson, H., *A Sermon Against Lukwarmenesse in Religion* (London, 1641)

Williams, G., *The Discovery of Mysteries* (Oxford, 1643)

—— *The Persecution and Oppression* (London, 1664)

—— *Vindicaie Regum* (Oxford, 1643)

Winslow, E., *The Danger of Tolerating Levellers* (London, 1649)
—— *Hypocrisie Unmasked* (London, 1646)
—— *New England's Salamander* (London, 1647)
Wither, G., *British Appeals* (London, 1651)
—— *Campo Musae* (London, 1643)
—— *A Cordial Confection* (London, 1659)
—— *Justitiarius Justificatus* (London, 1646)
—— *The Modern States-man* (London, 1654)
—— *The Protector* (London, 1655)
—— *Republica Anglicana* (London, 1650)
—— *Se Defedendo* (London, 1643)
—— *Vaticinium Causuale* (London, 1655)
—— *A View of the Marginal Notes* (London, 1588)
—— *Vox Pacifica* (London, 1645)
The Wolf Stript of his Sheeps Clothing (London, 1647)
Woodnote, T., *Hermes Theologus* (London, 1649)
Woodward, H., *The Life and Death of William Lawd* (London, 1645)
—— *Soft Answers Unto Hard Censures* (London, 1645)
—— *A Solemn Covenant* (London, 1643)
—— *The Solemn League and Covenant* (London, 1643)
Worse and Worse Newes from Ireland (London, 1641)
Worsley, B., *The Advocate* (London, 1650)
—— *Free Ports* (London, 1652)
Worth, E., *The Servant Doing and the Lord Blessing* (Dublin, 1659)
Wortley, Sir F., *Characters and Elegies* (London, 1646)
To Xeiphos Ton Marytron (Hague, 1651)

Secondary Literature

Achinstein, S., *Milton and the Revolutionary Reader* (Princeton, 1994)
—— 'The politics of Babel in the English revolution', in J. Holstun, ed., *Pamphlet Wars* (London, 1992)
—— 'The uses of deception from Cromwell to Milton' in K. Z. Keller and G. J. Schiffhorst, eds, *The Witness of Time* (Pittsburgh, 1993)
Adamson, J. S. A., 'The baronial context of the English civil wars', *TRHS*, 5th series 40 (1990)
—— 'The English nobility and the projected settlement of 1647', *HJ* 30 (1987)
—— 'The frighted junto: perceptions of Ireland, and the last attempts at settlement with Charles I', in J. Peacey, ed., *The Regicides and the Execution of Charles I* (Basingstoke, 2001)
—— 'Oliver Cromwell and the Long Parliament', in J. Morrill, ed., *Oliver Cromwell and the English Revolution* (London, 1990)

——— 'Parliamentary management, men of business and the House of Lords, 1640-49', in C. Jones, ed., *A Pillar of the Constitution* (London, 1989)

——— 'The peerage in politics 1645–49' (Cambridge University PhD, 1986)

——— 'Pym as draftsman: an unpublished declaration of March 1643', *PH* 6 (1987)

——— 'Strafford's ghost: the British context of Viscount Lisle's lieutenancy of Ireland', in J. H. Ohlmeyer, ed., *Ireland from Independence to Occupation, 1641–1660* (Cambridge, 1995)

——— 'The triumph of oligarchy: the management of war and the Committee of Both Kingdoms, 1644–1645', in C. R. Kyle and J. Peacey, eds, *Parliament at Work* (Woodbridge, 2002)

——— 'The *Vindicaie Veritatis* and the political creed of Viscount Saye and Sele', *HR* 60 (1987)

Allan, A., 'Royal propaganda and the proclamations of Edward IV', *BIHR* 59 (1986)

——— 'Yorkist propaganda: pedigree, prophecy and the 'British History' in the reign of Edward IV', in C. Ross, ed., *Patronage, Pedigree and Power in Later Medieval England* (Gloucester, 1979)

Allen, J. W., *English Political Thought, 1603–1644* (London, 1967)

Allis, F. S., 'Nathaniel Ward: constitutional draftsman', *Essex Institute Historical Collections* 120 (1984)

Allnutt, W. H., 'The king's printer at Shrewsbury, 1642–43', *The Library*, new series 1 (1900)

Andrews, C. M., *British Committees, Commissions, and Councils of Trade and Plantations 1622–1675* (Baltimore, 1908)

——— *The Colonial Period of American History* (4 vols, New Haven, 1934–38)

Anglo, S., *Images of Tudor Kingship* (London, 1992)

Anthony, H. S., '*Mercurius Politicus* under Milton', *JHI* 27 (1966)

Armitage, D., Himy, A., and Skinner, Q., eds, *Milton and Republicanism* (Cambridge, 1995)

Ashcraft, R., *Revolutionary Politics and John Locke's Two Treatises of Government* (Princeton, 1986)

Atherton, I., 'The itch grown a disease: manuscript transmission of news in the seventeenth century', in J. Raymond, ed., *News, Newspapers, and Society in Early Modern Britain* (London, 1999)

Aylmer, G., 'Bureaucracy', in *New Cambridge Modern History* (14 vols, Cambridge, 1951–79), vol. 13

——— 'Collective mentalities in mid-seventeenth century England II: royalist attitudes', *TRHS*, 5th series 37 (1987)

——— 'Collective mentalities in mid-seventeenth century England III: varities of radicalism', *TRHS*, 5th series 38 (1988)

——— 'From office-holding to civil service: the genesis of modern bureaucracy', *TRHS*, 5th series 30 (1980)

——— *The King's Servants* (London, 1961)

—— *The Levellers and the English Revolution* (London, 1975)

—— *The State's Servants* (London, 1973)

Bak, G., 'Woodcut, text, font and ornament: the construction of an early seventeenth century news pamphlet' (paper delivered at SHARP conference, London, 2002)

Barber, S., *Regicide and Republicanism* (Edinburgh, 1998)

Barker, F., 'In the wars of truth: violence, true knowledge and power in Milton and Hobbes', in T. Healy and J. Sawday, eds, *Literature and the English Civil War* (Cambridge, 1990)

Barnard, T., 'Crises of identity among Irish Protestants, 1641–1685', *P&P* 127 (1990)

—— *Cromwellian Ireland* (Oxford, 1975)

—— 'Planters and policies in Cromwellian Ireland', *P&P* 61 (1973)

Barnett, P. R., *Theodore Haak* (Hague, 1962)

Baron, S. A., 'Licensing readers, licensing authorities in seventeenth century England', in J. Andersen and E. Sauer, eds, *Books and Readers in Early Modern England* (Philadephia, 2002)

Barry, J., 'Literacy and literature in popular culture: reading and writing in historical perspective', in T. Harris, ed., *Popular Culture in England, c.1500–1850* (Basingstoke, 1995)

Baskerville, E. J., *A Chronological Bibliography of Propaganda and Polemic Published in English Between 1553 and 1558* (Philadelphia, 1979)

Batten, J. M., *John Dury* (Chicago, 1944)

Bawcutt, N. W., 'A crisis of Laudian censorship: Nicholas and John Okes and the publication of Sales's *An Introduction to a Devout Life* in 1637', *The Library*, 7th series 1 (2000)

Bell, H. E., *An Introduction to the History and Records of the Court of Wards* (Cambridge, 1953)

Bellany, A., 'Libels in action: ritual, subversion and the English literary underground, 1603–42', in T. Harris, ed., *The Politics of the Excluded, c.1500–1850* (Basingstoke, 2001)

—— *The Politics of Court Scandal in Early Modern England* (Cambridge, 2002)

—— 'Raylinge rymes and vaunting verse': libellous politics in early Stuart England, 1603–1628', in K. Sharpe and P. Lake, eds, *Culture and Politics in Early Stuart England* (Basingstoke, 1994)

Beller, E. A., 'Milton and *Mercurius Politicus*', *HLQ* 5 (1951–52)

Bennett, H. S., *English Books and Readers, 1603 to 1640* (Cambridge, 1970)

Berkowitz, D. S., *Humanist Scholarship and Public Order. Two Tracts Against the Pilgrimage of Grace by Sir Richard Morison* (Washington, 1984)

—— *John Selden's Formative Years* (Washington, 1988)

Bernard, G. W., 'Politics and government in Tudor England', *HJ* 31 (1988)

Bevington, D., *Tudor Drama and Politics* (Cambridge, Mass., 1968)

Black, J., *The English Press in the Eighteenth Century* (London, 1987)
—— 'Fresh light on ministerial patronage of eighteenth century pamphlets', *Publishing History* 19 (1986)
Black, J., 'Pikes and protestations: Scottish texts in England, 1639–40', *Publishing History* 62 (1997)
—— 'The rhetoric of reaction: the Martin Marprelate tracts (1588–89), anti-Martinism, and the uses of print in early modern England', *Sixteenth Century Journal* 28 (1994)
—— 'Thomas Cromwell's patronage of preaching', *Sixteenth Century Journal* 8 (1977)
Blagden, C., *The Stationers Company: A History, 1403–1959* (London, 1960)
—— 'The Stationers' Company in the civil war period', *The Library*, 5th series 13 (1958)
Bland, M., '"Invisible dangers": censorship and the subversion of authority in early modern England', *Papers of the Bibliographical Society of America* 90 (1996)
Blayney, P., 'William Cecil and the Stationers', in R. Myers and M. Harris, eds, *The Stationers' Company and the Book Trade, 1500–1900* (Winchester, 1997)
Bossy, J., 'The character of Elizabethan Catholicism', in T. Aston, ed., *Crisis in Europe 1560–1660* (London, 1965)
—— 'The English Catholic community, 1603–1625', in A. G. R. Smith, ed., *The Reign of James VI and I* (Basingstoke, 1973)
Bowler, G., 'Marian protestants and the idea of violent resistance to tyranny', in P. Lake and M. Dowling, eds, *Protestantism and the National Church in Sixteenth Century England* (London, 1987)
Braddick, M. J., 'State formation and social change in early modern England: a problem stated and approaches suggested', *Social History* 16 (1991)
—— *State Formation in Early Modern England, c.1550–1700* (Cambridge, 2000)
Brailsford, H. N., *The Levellers and the English Revolution* (London, 1961),
Brennan, M., *Literary Patronage in the English Renaissance: the Pembroke Family* (London, 1988).
Brook, C. W., *Pettyfoggers and Vipers of the Commonwealth* (Cambridge, 1986).
Brownly, M. W., *Clarendon and the Rhetoric of Historical Form* (Philadelphia, 1985)
Burgess, G., *Absolute Monarchy and the Stuart Constitution* (New Haven, 1996)
—— 'Contexts for the writing and publication of Hobbes's *Leviathan*', *HPT* 11 (1990)
—— *The Politics of the Ancient Constitution* (Basingstoke, 1992)
—— 'Usurpation, obligation and obedience in the thought of the Engagement controversy', *HJ* 29 (1986)
Burn, J. S., *The Star Chamber* (London, 1870)
Burnett, M. T., 'Apprentice literature and the "crisis" of the 1590s', in C. C. Brown, ed., *Patronage, Politics and Literary Traditions in England, 1558–1658* (Detroit, 1991)

Burns, J. H., and Goldie, M., eds, *The Cambridge History of Political Thought, 1450–1700* (Cambridge, 1991)

Butler, M., 'Politics and the masque: *Salmacida Spolia*', in Healy and Sawday, eds, *Literature and the English Civil War*

—— 'Politics and the masque: *The Triumph of Peace*', *Seventeenth Century* 2 (1987)

—— 'Reform or reverence? The politics of the Caroline masque', in J.R. Mulryne and M. Shewring, eds, *Theatre and Government under the Early Stuarts* (Cambridge, 1993)

Calder, I. M., 'The St Antholin's lecturers', *Church Quarterly Review* 160 (1959)

Calhoun, C., 'Introduction: Habermas and the public sphere', in C. Calhoun, ed., *Habermas and the Public Sphere* (London, 1997)

Candy, H. C. H., 'Milton, N.LL, and Sir Thomas Urquhart', *The Library*, 4th series 14 (1934)

Capp, B., *Astrology and the Popular Press* (London, 1979)

—— *The Fifth Monarchy Men* (London, 1972)

—— 'Popular literature', in B. Reay, ed., *Popular Culture in Seventeenth Century England* (London, 1985)

—— *The World of John Taylor the Water Poet, 1578–1653* (Oxford, 1994).

Carlin, N., 'Extreme or mainstream? The English Independents and the Cromwellian reconquest of Ireland, 1649–51', in B. Bradshaw, A. Hadfield and W. Maley, eds, *Representing Ireland* (Cambridge, 1993)

—— 'Pragmatical petitions' (paper delivered at the IHR, London, Oct. 2002)

Carlson, D. R., *English Humanist Books. Writers and Patrons, Manuscript and Print, 1475–1525* (Toronto, 1993)

—— 'Royal tutors in the reign of Henry VII', *Sixteenth Century Journal* 22 (1991)

Carlson, L. H., 'A history of the Presbyterian party from Pride's Purge to the dissolution of the commonwealth', *Church History* 11 (1942)

Carlton, C., *Archbishop William Laud* (London, 1987)

Censer, J. R., *The French Press in the Age of Enlightenment* (London, 1994)

Chartier, R., *The Cultural Uses of Print* (1987)

Chartier, R., *Frenchness in the History of the Book: From the History of Publishing to the History of Reading* (Worcester, Mass., American Antiquarian Society, 1988)

—— *The Order of Books* (trans. Lydia G. Cochrane, Cambridge, 1992)

Chester, A. G., *Thomas May, Man of Letters, 1595–1650* (Philadelphia, 1932)

Clare, J., *Art Made Tongue-Tied by Authority* (Manchester 1990)

Clark, P., 'The ownership of books in England, 1560–1640: the example of some Kentish townsfolk', in L. Stone, ed., *Schooling and Society* (Baltimore, 1976)

Clark, S., *The Elizabethan Pamphleteers. Popular Moralistic Pamphlets 1580–1640* (London, 1983)

Claydon, T., 'The sermon, the 'public sphere' and the political culture of late seventeenth century England', in L. A. Ferrell and P. McCullough, eds, *The English Sermon Revised* (Manchester, 2000)

————— *William III and the Godly Revolution* (Cambridge, 1996)

Clegg, C. S., *Press Censorship in Elizabethan England* (Cambridge, 1997)

————— *Press Censorship in Jacobean England* (Cambridge, 2001)

Clifton, R., 'Fear of Popery', in C. Russell, ed., *The Origins of the English Civil War* (Basingstoke, 1973)

————— 'The popular fear of Catholics during the English revolution', in P. Slack, ed., *Rebellion, Popular Protest and the Social Order in Early Modern England* (Cambridge, 1984)

Clough, C. H., 'Erasmus and the pursuit of English royal patronage in 1517 and 1518', *Erasmus of Rotterdam Society Yearbook* 1 (1981)

Clyde, W. M., 'Parliament and the press, 1643–7', *The Library*, 4th series 13 (1933)

————— 'Parliament and the press II', *The Library*, 4th series 14 (1933)

————— *The Struggle for the Freedom of the Press* (St Andrews, 1934)

Coates, W. H., 'Some observations on the Grand Remonstrance', *JMH* 4 (1932)

Coffey, J., *Politics, Religion, and the British Revolutions: the Mind of Samuel Rutherford* (Cambridge, 1997)

————— 'Samuel Rutherford and the political thought of the Scottish covenanters', in J. R. Young, ed., *Celtic Dimensions of the British Civil Wars* (Edinburgh, 1997)

Cogswell, T., *Home Divisions* (Manchester, 1998)

————— 'The people's love: the Duke of Buckingham and popularity', in T. Cogswell, R. Cust and P. Lake, eds, *Politics, Religion and Popularity in Early Stuart Britain* (Cambridge, 2002)

————— 'The politics of propaganda. Charles I and the people in the 1620s', *JBS* 29 (1990)

————— 'Thomas Middleton and the court, 1624: *A Game at Chess in context*', *HLQ* 47 (1984)

————— 'Underground verse and the transformation of early Stuart political culture', in S. D. Amussen and M. Kishlansky, eds, *Political Culture and Cultural Politics in Early Modern England* (Manchester, 1995)

Collinson, P., *Elizabethan Essays* (1994)

————— *The Elizabethan Puritan Movement* (London, 1967)

————— 'Lectures by combination. Structures and characteristics of church life in 17th century England', in *Godly People* (London, 1983)

————— 'The monarchical republic of Queen Elizabeth I', *BJRL* 69 (1986–87)

————— 'Puritans, men of business, and Elizabethan parliaments', *PH* 7 (1988)

Condick, F., 'The Life and Works of Dr John Bastwick' (London University PhD, 1982)

Condren, C., 'Andrew Marvell as polemicist: his account of the growth of popery and arbitrary government', in C. Condren and A. D. Cousins, eds, *The Political Identity of Andrew Marvell* (Aldershot, 1990)

Cope, E. S., 'The king's declaration concerning the dissolution of the Short

Parliament of 1640: an unsuccessful attempt at public relations', *HLQ* 40 (1976–77)

—— *The Life of a Public Man. Edward, First Baron Montagu* (Philadelphia, 1981)

Corish, P. J., 'The rising of 1641 and the Catholic Confederacy, 1641–5', in T. W. Moody et al., *A New History of Ireland III. Early Modern Ireland, 1534–1691* (Oxford, 1976)

Corns, T. N., 'Milton's *Observations Upon the Articles of Peace*: Ireland under English eyes', in D. Lowenstein and J. G. Turner, eds, *Politics, Poetics, and Hermeneutics in Milton's Prose* (Cambridge, 1990)

—— '"Some rousing motions": the plurality of Miltonic ideology', in T. Healy and J. Sawday, eds, *Literature and the English Civil War* (Cambridge, 1990)

De Groot, J., 'Space, patronage, procedure: the court at Oxford, 1642–46', *EHR* 117 (2002)

Dever, M., 'Richard Sibbes' (Cambridge University PhD, 1993)

Doig, J. A., 'Political propaganda and royal proclamations in late medieval England', *HR* 71 (1998)

Donagan, B., 'Casuistry and allegiance in the English civil war', in D. Hirst and R. Strier, eds, *Writing and Political Engagement in Seventeenth Century England* (Cambridge, 1999)

—— 'The clerical patronage of Robert Rich, second Earl of Warwick, 1619–1642', *Proceedings of the American Philosophical Society* 120 (1976)

Donald, P., *An Uncounselled King* (Cambridge, 1990)

Dooley, B., 'News and doubt in early modern culture', in B. Dooley and S. Baron, eds, *The Politics of Information in Early Modern Europe* (London, 2001)

Dorsten, J. A. van, *Poets, Patrons and Professors. Sir Philip Sidney, Daniel Rogers, and the Leiden Humanists* (London, 1962)

—— 'Sidney and Languet', *HLQ* 29 (1966)

Dow, F. D., *Radicalism in the English Revolution, 1640–1660* (Oxford, 1985)

Dowling, M., 'The gospel and court: reformation under Henry VIII', in P. Lake and M. Dowling, eds, *Protestantism and the National Church in Sixteenth Century England* (London, 1987)

Downie, J., *Robert Harley and the Press* (Cambridge, 1979)

Duffy, E., 'The godly and the multitude in Stuart England', *Seventeenth Century* 1 (1986)

Dunn, K., 'Milton among the monopolists: *Areopagitica*, intellectual property and the Hartlib circle', in M. Greengrass, M. Leslie, and T. Raylor, eds, *Samuel Hartlib and Universal Reformation* (Cambridge, 1994)

Dunn, T. A., *Philip Massinger* (London, 1957)

Durston, C., 'For the better humiliation of the people: public days of fasting and thanksgiving during the English revolution', *Seventeenth Century* 7 (1992)

—— 'Signs and wonders and the English civil war', *History Today* (October, 1987)

Dutton, R., *Mastering the Revels. The Regulation and Censorship of English Renaissance Drama* (Iowa City, 1990)

——— 'Patronage, politics, and the Master of the Revels, 1622–1640: The case of Sir John Astley', *English Literary Renaissance* 20 (1990)

Dzelzainis, M., 'Milton and the protectorate in 1658', in Armitage, Himy and Skinner, eds, *Milton and Republicanism*

Eales, J., 'Provincial preaching and allegiance in the first English civil war, 1640–6', in Cogswell, Cust and Lake, eds, *Politics, Religion and Popularity*

——— *Puritans and Roundheads. The Harleys of Brampton Bryan and the Outbreak of the English Civil War* (Cambridge, 1990)

Eccles, M., 'Thomas Gainsford, "Captain Pamphlet"', *HLQ* 45 (1982)

Eccleshall, R., *Order, Reason and Politics* (Oxford, 1978)

Edie, C. A., 'Reading popular political pamphlets: a question of meaning', in G. J. Schochet, ed., *Restoration, Ideology, and Revolution* (Washington, 1990)

Edwards, M. U., *Printing, Propaganda and Martin Luther* (London, 1994)

Eisenstein, E., *The Printing Revolution in Early Modern Europe* (Cambridge, 1983)

Elsky, M., *Authorizing Words* (London, 1989)

Elton, G. R., *Policy and Police. The Enforcement of the Reformation in the Age of Thomas Cromwell* (Cambridge, 1972)

Epstein, W., 'Judge David Jenkins and the great civil war', *Journal of Legal History* 3 (1982)

Everitt, A., *The Community of Kent in the Great Rebellion* (Leicester, 1973)

Fallon, R. T., 'Filling the gaps: new perspectives on Mr Secretary Milton', *Milton Studies* 12 (1978)

——— *Milton in Government* (Pennsylvania, 1993)

Farnell, J. E., 'The Navigation Act of 1651, the first Dutch war, and the London merchant community', *Journal of Economic History*, 2nd series 16 (1964)

Feather, J., 'Cross-channel currents: historical bibliography and *l'histoire du livre*', *The Library*, 6th series 2 (1980)

Febvre, L., and Martin, H. J., *The Coming of the Book* (London, 1976)

Ferrell, L. A., *Government by Polemic. James I, the King's Preachers and the Rhetoric of Conformity 1603–1625* (Stanford, 1998)

Ferrell, L. A., and McCullough, P., eds, *The English Sermon Revised* (Manchester, 2000)

Fincham, K., 'Prelacy and politics: Archbishop Abbot's defence of Protestant orthodoxy', *HR* 61 (1988)

Fincham, K., and Lake, P., 'Popularity, prelacy and Puritanism in the 1630s: Joseph Hall explains himself', *EHR* 111 (1996)

Fink, Z., *The Classical Republicans* (Chicago, 1962)

Firth, C. H., 'The battle of Dunbar', *TRHS*, new series 14 (1900)

——— 'George Wither', *Review of English Studies* 2 (1926)

——— 'Thomas Scot's account of his activities as intelligencer during the commonwealth', *EHR* 12 (1897)

Fitzmaurice, A., '"Every man, that prints, adventures": the rhetoric of the Virginia Company sermons', in Ferrell and McCullough, eds, *The English Sermon Revised*

Fletcher, A., *The Outbreak of the English Civil War* (London, 1981)

Ford, J. D., 'Lex, rex iusto posita: Samuel Rutherford on the origins of government', in R. A. Mason, ed., *Scots and Britons* (Cambridge, 1994)

Ford, W., 'The problem of literacy in early modern England', *History* 78 (1993)

Fortescue, G. K., *Catalogue of the Pamphlets, Books, Newspapers and Manuscripts Collected by George Thomason, 1640–1661* (2 vols, London, 1908)

Foster, A., 'The function of a bishop: the career of Richard Neile, 1562–1640', in R. O'Day and F. Heal, eds, *Continuity and Change. Personnel and Administration of the Church of England, 1500–1642* (Leicester, 1976)

Foster, E. R., 'Printing the Petition of Right', *HLQ* 38 (1974)

Foster, S., *Notes from the Caroline Underground* (Hamden, Ct., 1978)

Fox, A., 'Ballads, libels and popular ridicule in Jacobean England', *P&P* 145 (1994)

────── 'The complaint of poetry for the death of liberality: the decline of literary patronage in the 1590s', in J. Guy, ed., *The Reign of Elizabeth I* (Cambridge, 1995)

────── *Politics and Literature in the Reigns of Henry VII and Henry VIII* (Oxford, 1989)

────── 'Popular verses and their readership in the early seventeenth century', in J. Raven, N. Tadmor, and H. Small, eds, *The Practice and Representation of Reading in England* (Cambridge, 1996)

Frank, J., *The Beginnings of the English Newspaper, 1620–1660* (Cambridge, Mass., 1960)

────── *Cromwell's Press Agent* (Lanham, 1980)

Franklin, J. H., *John Locke and the Theory of Sovereignty* (Cambridge, 1981)

Fraser, P., *The Intelligence of the Secretaries of State and their Monopoly of Licensed News, 1660–1688* (Cambridge, 1956)

Frearson, M., 'The distribution and readership of London corantos in the 1620s', in R. Myers and M. Harris, eds, *Serials and their Readers, 1620–1914* (Winchester, 1993)

────── 'London corantos in the 1620s', *Studies in Newspaper and Periodical History* (1993)

Freeman, T., 'Nicholas Harpsfield and the genesis of anti-martyrology' (paper delivered at the IHR, London, 7 February 2000)

Freist, D., 'The world is ruled and governed by opinion. For formation of opinion and the communication network in London, 1637 to c.1645' (Cambridge University PhD, 1992)

French, J. M., 'George Wither in prison', *Publications of the Modern Language Association* 45 (1930)

—————— *The Life Records of John Milton* (5 vols, New Brunswick, 1949–58)

—————— 'Milton, Needham and *Mercurius Politicus*', *Studies in Philology* 33 (1936)

—————— 'Some notes on Milton', *N&Q* 188 (1945)

Friedman, J., *Miracles and the Pulp Press During the English Revolution* (London, 1993)

Furgol, E. M., 'The military and ministers as agents of Presbyterian imperialism in England and Ireland, 1640–1648', in J. Dwyer, R. A. Mason, and A. Murdoch, eds, *New Perspectives on the Politics and Culture of Early Modern Scotland* (Edinburgh, 1982)

Galloway, B., *The Union of England and Scotland, 1603–1608* (Edinburgh, 1986)

Gardiner, S. R., 'Collections by Isaack Walton for the life of John Hales of Eton', *EHR* 2 (1887)

—————— *History of the Great Civil War* (4 vols, Adlestrop, 1987)

—————— 'The political element in Massinger', *The Contemporary Review* 28 (1876)

Gaunt, P., 'Drafting the Instrument of Government, 1653–54: a reappraisal', *PH* 8 (1989)

—————— 'Interregnum governments and the reform of the post office, 1649–59', *HR* 60 (1987)

Gaunt, S., 'Visual propaganda in England in the later middle ages', in B. Taithe and T. Thornton, eds, *Propaganda* (Stroud, 1999)

Gebert, C., *An Anthology of Elizabethan Dedications and Prefaces* (Philadelphia, 1933)

Gentles, I., *The New Model Army* (Oxford, 1992)

—————— 'The struggle for London in the second civil war', *HJ* 26 (1983)

Gibbs, G. C., 'Press and public opinion: prospective', in Jones, ed., *Liberty Secured*

Gibson, W., *A Social History of the Domestic Chaplain, 1530–1840* (London, 1997)

Giesey, R. E., 'When and why Hotman wrote the Francogalia', *Biblioteque d'Humanisme et Renaissance* 29 (1967)

Gill, R., 'Necessitie of State: Massinger's *Believe as You List*', *English Studies* 46 (1965)

Goldberg, J., *James I and the Politics of Literature* (London, 1983)

Goldie, M., 'John Locke's circle and James II', *HJ* 35 (1992).

Gorman, G. E., 'A Laudian attempt to 'tune the pulpit': Peter Heylyn and his sermon against the Feoffees for the Purchase of Impropriations', *Journal of Religious History* 8 (1975)

Grafton, A., and Jardine, L., 'Studied for action: how Gabriel Harvey read his Livy', *P&P* 129 (1990)

Gransden, A., 'Propaganda in medieval English historiography', *Journal of Medieval History* 1 (1975)

Graves, M. A. R., 'The common lawyers and the Privy Council's parliamentary men of business, 1584–1601', *PH* 8 (1989)

——— 'The management of the Elizabethan House of Commons: the Council's 'men of business'', *PH* 2 (1983)

——— 'Patrons and clients: their role in sixteenth century parliamentary politicking and legislation', *The Turnbull Library Record* 18 (1985)

——— *Thomas Norton* (Oxford, 1994)

——— 'Thomas Norton the parliament man: an Elizabethan MP, 1559–1581', *HJ* 23 (1980)

Greaves, R. L., 'William Sprigg and the Cromwellian revolution', *HLQ* 34 (1971)

Green, D., *Great Cobbett. The Noblest Agitator* (Oxford, 1985)

Green, I. M., *Print and Protestantism in Early Modern England* (Oxford, 2000)

Greengrass, M., 'The financing of a seventeenth century intellectual: contributions for Comenius, 1637–1641', *Acta Comeniana* 11 (1995)

Greenleaf, W. H., *Order, Empiricism and Politics* (Oxford, 1964)

Greg, W. W., *A Companion to Arber* (Oxford, 1967)

——— *Licensers for the Press, &c to 1640* (Oxford, 1962)

Gross, A., 'Contemporary politics in Massinger', *Studies in English Literature* 6 (1966)

Gunn, J. A. W., *Politics and the Public Interest* (London, 1969)

Gurney, J., 'George Wither and Surrey politics, 1642–1649', *Southern History* 19 (1997)

Guy, J., *Tudor England* (Oxford, 1988)

Halasz, A., *The Marketplace of Print: Pamphlets and the Public Sphere in Early Modern England* (Cambridge, 1997)

——— 'Pamphlet surplus: John Taylor and subscription publication', in A. F. Marotti and M. D. Bristol, eds, *Print, Manuscript and Performance. The Changing Relations of the Media in Early Modern England* (Columbus, 2000)

Hale, J., 'War and public opinion in the fifteenth and sixteenth centuries', *P&P* 22 (1962)

Ham, R. G., 'Dryden as historiographer-royal: the authorship of *His Majesties Declaration Defended*, 1681', *Review of English Studies* 11 (1935)

Hammer, P., 'The Earl of Essex, Fulke Greville, and the employment of scholars', *Studies in Philology* 91 (1994)

——— 'Patronage at court, faction and the Earl of Essex', in J. Guy, ed., *The Reign of Elizabeth I. Court and Culture in the Last Decade* (Cambridge, 1985)

——— 'The uses of scholarship: the secretariat of Robert Devereux, 2nd Earl of Essex, c.1585–1601', *EHR* 109 (1994)

Hanson, L., 'English newsbooks, 1620–1641', *The Library*, 4th series 18 (1938)

Harline, C. E., *Pamphlets, Printing and Political Culture in the Early Dutch Republic* (Dordrecht, 1987)

Harris, B., *Politics and the Rise of the Press* (London, 1996)

Harris, M., *London Newspapers in the Age of Walpole* (London, 1987)
———— 'Print and politics in the age of Walpole', in J. Black, ed., *Britain in the Age of Walpole* (Basingstoke, 1984)
Harris, R., *A Patriot Press* (Oxford, 1993)
Harris, T., 'Critical perspectives: the anatomy of English history?', in G. Burgess, ed., *The New British History* (London, 1999)
———— *London Crowds in the Reign of Charles II* (Cambridge, 1987)
———— 'Propaganda and public opinion in seventeenth century England', in J. D. Popkin, ed., *Media and Revolution* (Lexington, 1995)
———— '"Venerating the honesty of a tinker": the king's friends and the battle for the allegiance of the common people in Restoration England', in T. Harris, ed., *The Politics of the Excluded, c.1500–1850* (Basingstoke, 2001)
Harth, P., *Pen for a Party. Dryden's Tory Propaganda in its Contexts* (Princeton, 1993)
Hasler, P. W., *The House of Commons 1558–1603* (3 vols, London, 1981)
Hay, D., *Polydore Vergil. Renaissance Historian and Man of Letters* (Oxford, 1952)
Hayden, J. M., 'The uses of political pamphlets: the example of 1614–15 in France', *CJH* 21 (1986)
Healy, T., '"Dark all without it knits": vision and authority in Marvell's *Upon Appleton House*', in T. Healy and J. Sawday, eds, *Literature and the English Civil War* (Cambridge, 1990)
Heinemann, M., 'Drama and opinion in the 1620s: Middleton and Massinger', in J. R. Mulryne and M. Shewring, eds, *Theatre and Government under the Early Stuarts* (Cambridge, 1993)
———— 'Rebel lords, popular playwrights and political culture: notes on the Jacobean patronage of the Earl of Southampton', in *Politics, Patronage and Literature in England, 1558–1685* (Yearbook of English Studies, 21, 1991)
Henderson, F., 'Posterity to judge – John Rushworth and his *Historical Collections*', *Bodleian Library Record* 15 (1996)
Hensley, C. S., *The Later Career of George Wither* (The Hague, 1969)
Hetet, J. S. T., 'A literary underground in Restoration England. Printers and dissenters in the context of constraints 1660–1689' (Cambridge University PhD, 1987)
Hill, C., 'Censorship and English literature', in *The Collected Essays of Christopher Hill* (3 vols, Brighton, 1985–86)
———— *The English Bible and the Seventeenth Century Revolution* (London, 1994)
———— *Milton and the English Revolution* (New York, 1977)
———— *The World Turned Upside Down. Radical Ideas During the English Revolution* (Harmondsworth, 1975)
Hindle, S., *The State and Social Change in Early Modern England, 1550–1640* (Basingstoke, 2002)

Hinds, P., 'Roger L'Estrange, the Rye House Plot and the regulation of political discourse in late seventeenth century London', *The Library*, 7th series 3 (2002)

Hirsch, R., *Printing, Selling and Reading 1450–1550* (Wiesbaden, 1967)

Hirst, D., 'The defection of Sir Edward Dering, 1640–1641', *HJ* 15 (1972)

—— 'The politics of literature in the English republic', *Seventeenth Century* 5 (1990)

—— 'That sober liberty: Marvell's Cromwell in 1654', in J. M. Wallace, ed., *The Golden and the Brazen World* (Berkeley, Ca., 1985)

Hirst, D., and Strier, R. 'Introduction', in *Writing and Political Engagement in Seventeenth Century England* (Cambridge, 1999)

Hirst, D., and Zwicker, S., 'High summer at Nun Appleton, 1651: Andrew Marvell and Lord Fairfax's occasions', *HJ* 36 (1993)

Historical Sketches of Nonconformity in the County Palatine of Chester (London, 1864)

Holmes, C., 'Colonel King and Lincolnshire politics, 1642–1646', *HJ* 16 (1973)

—— 'Drainers and fenmen: the problem of popular political consciousness in the seventeenth century', in A. Fletcher and J. Stevenson, eds, *Order and Disorder in Early Modern England* (Cambridge, 1985)

—— *The Eastern Association in the English Civil War* (Cambridge, 1974)

Howard-Hill, T. H., 'Political interpretations of Middleton's *Game at Chess* (1624)', *Yearbook of English Studies* 21 (1991)

Howarth, D., ed., *Art and Patronage in the Caroline Courts* (Cambridge, 1993)

Hughes, A., 'Approaches to Presbyterian print culture. Thomas Edwards's *Gangraena* as source and text', in J. Andersen and E. Sauer, eds, *Books and Readers in Early Modern England* (Philadelphia, 2002)

—— *Politics, Society and Civil War in Warwickshire, 1620–1660* (Cambridge, 1987)

—— 'Thomas Dugard and his circle in the 1630s', *HJ* 29 (1986)

Hume, R. D., 'Texts within contexts: notes towards a historical method', *Philological Quarterly* 71 (1992)

Hunt, A., 'Book trade patents, 1603–1640', in A. Hunt, G. Mandelbrote, and A. Shell, eds, *The Book Trade and its Customers 1450–1900* (Winchester, 1997)

—— 'Tuning the pulpits: the religious context of the Essex revolt', in L. A. Ferrell and P. McCullough, eds., *The English Sermon Revised* (Manchester, 2000)

Hunter, M., 'The impact of print', *Book Collector* 28 (1979)

Hutton, R., 'Clarendon's *History of the Rebellion*', *EHR* 97 (1982)

—— *The Royalist War Effort* (London, 1982)

Hyland, P. B. J., 'Liberty and libel: government and the press during the succession crisis in Britain, 1712–1716', *EHR* 101 (1986)

Ianziti, G., *Humanistic Historiography Under the Sforzas. Politics and Propaganda in Fifteenth Century Milan* (Oxford, 1988)

Infelise, M., 'The war, the news and the curious', in B. Dooley and S. Baron, eds,

The Politics of Information in Early Modern Europe (London, 2001)

Ingram, W., *The Business of Playing* (Ithaca, 1992)

Jacob, J. R., *Henry Stubbe* (Cambridge, 1983)

Jardine, L., and Sherman, W., 'Pragmatic readers: knowledge transactions and scholarly services in late Elizabethan England', in A. Fletcher and P. Roberts, eds., *Religion, Culture and Society in Early Modern Britain* (Cambridge, 1994)

Jenkins, G., 'The Archpriest controversy and the printers, 1601–1603', *The Library*, 5th series 2 (1947–48)

Johns, A., *The Nature of the Book* (Chicago, 1998)

Johnson, A. F., 'The exiled English church at Amsterdam and its press', *The Library*, 5th series 5 (1951)

———— 'J. F. Stam, Amsterdam and English Bibles', *The Library*, 5th series 9 (1954)

Johnson, G. D., 'The Stationers versus the Drapers: control of the press in the late sixteenth century', *The Library*, 6th series 10 (1988)

Jones, W. R., 'The English church and royal propaganda during the hundred years war', *JBS* 19 (1979)

Jordan, W. K., *The Development of Religious Toleration in England, 1640–1660* (London, 1938)

———— *Men of Substance* (Chicago, 1942)

Judson, M., *The Crisis of the Constitution* (London, 1988)

———— 'Henry Parker and the theory of parliamentary sovereignty', in *Essays in History and Political Theory in Honour of Charles Howard McIlwain* (Cambridge, Mass., 1936)

Kaiser, T., 'The Abbe de Saint-Pierre, Public opinion, and the reconstitution of the French Monarchy', *JMH* 55 (1983)

Kaplan, L., *Politics and Religion During the English Revolution* (New York, 1976)

Keeble, N. H., ed., *The Cambridge Companion to Writing of the English Revolution* (Cambridge, 2001)

Kelliher, H., *Andrew Marvell, Poet and Politician, 1621–78* (London, 1978)

Kelsey, S., 'The death of Charles I' (forthcoming)

———— *Inventing a Republic* (Manchester, 1997)

———— 'Legal aspects of the trial of Charles I' (forthcoming)

———— 'The trial of Charles I' (forthcoming)

Kendall, L. H.., 'An unrecorded prose pamphlet by George Wither', *HLQ* 20 (1957)

Ketton-Cremer, R. W., *Norfolk in the Civil War* (London, 1969)

Kiefer, B., 'The authorship of *Ancient Bounds*', *Church History* 22 (1953)

Kilburn, T., and Milton, A., 'The public context of the trial and execution of Strafford', in J. F. Merritt, ed., *The Political World of Thomas Wentworth, Earl of Strafford, 1621–1641* (Cambridge, 1996)

King, J. N., *English Reformation Literature* (Princeton, 1982)

—— 'Freedom of the press, Protestant propaganda and Protector Somerset', *HLQ* 40 (1976)

—— 'John Day, master printer of the English reformation', in P. Marshall and A. Ryrie, eds, *The Beginnings of English Protestantism* (Cambridge, 2002)

Kingdon, R. N., 'Patronage, piety and printing in sixteenth century Europe', in D. H. Pinkney and T. Ropp, eds, *A Festschrift for Frederick B. Artz* (Durham, NC, 1964)

Kirby, D. A., 'The parish of St Stephen's, Coleman Street' (Oxford University BLitt, 1968)

Kirby, E. W., 'The lay feoffees: a study in militant Puritanism', *JMH* 14 (1942)

—— *William Prynne* (Cambridge, Mass., 1931)

Kirwood, A. E. M., 'Richard Field, printer, 1589–1624', *The Library*, 4th series 12 (1931)

Kishlansky, M., *The Rise of the New Model Army* (Cambridge, 1979)

Klaits, J., *Printed Propaganda Under Louis XIV* (Princeton, 1976)

Knight, L. B., 'Crucifixion or apocalypse? Refiguring the *Eikon Basilike*', in D. B. Hamilton and R. Strier, eds, *Religion, Literature and Politics in Post Reformation England, 1540–1688* (Cambridge, 1996)

Knights, M., *Politics and Opinion in Crisis, 1678–81* (Cambridge, 1994)

Kuhl, E., 'The Stationers' Company and censorship, 1599–1601', *The Library*, 4th series 9 (1929)

Lake, P., 'Anti-Popery: the structure of a prejudice', in R. Cust and A. Hughes, eds, *Conflict in Early Stuart England* (London, 1989)

—— 'Constitutional consensus and Puritan opposition in the 1620s: Thomas Scott and the Spanish match', *HJ* 25 (1982)

—— 'Deeds against nature: cheap print, Protestantism and murder in early seventeenth century England', in Sharpe and Lake, eds, *Culture and Politics in Early Stuart England*

—— 'Popular form, Puritan content? Two Puritan appropriations of the murder pamphlet from mid-seventeenth century London', in A. Fletcher and P. Roberts, eds, *Religion, Culture and Society in Early Modern Britain* (Cambridge, 1994)

—— 'Puritanism, Arminianism and a Shropshire axe-murder', *Midland History* 15 (1990)

Lake, P., and Como, D., 'Orthodoxy and its discontents: dispute settlement and the production of consensus in the London (Puritan) underground', *JBS* 39 (2000)

Lake, P., and Questier, M., *The Antichrist's Lewd Hat* (New Haven, 2002)

Lambert, S., 'The beginning of printing for the House of Commons, 1640–42', *The Library*, 6th series 3 (1981)

—— 'Coranto printing in England: the first newsbooks', *Journal of Newspaper and Periodical History* 8 (1992)

—— 'The printers and the government, 1604–1637', in R. Myers and M. Harris, eds, *Aspects of Printing from 1600* (Oxford, 1987)

—— *Printing for Parliament 1641–1700* (London, 1984)

—— 'Richard Montague, Arminianism, and censorship', *P&P* 124 (1989)

————— 'State control of the press in theory and practice: the role of the Stationers' Company before 1640', in R. Myers and M. Harris, ed., *Censorship and the Control of Print in England and France, 1600–1910* (Winchester, 1992)

Lamont, W., *Marginal Prynne, 1600–69* (London, 1963)

————— 'Pamphleteering, the Protestant consensus and the English revolution', in R. C. Richardson and G. M. Ridden, eds, *Freedom and the English Revolution* (Manchester, 1986)

————— 'Prynne, Burton and the Puritan triumph', *HLQ* 27 (1963–64)

————— 'The religion of Andrew Marvell', in C. Condren and A. D. Cousins, eds, *The Political Identity of Andrew Marvell* (Aldershot, 1990)

Laqueur, T., 'The cultural origins of popular literacy in England, 1500–1850', *Oxford Review of Education* 2 (1976)

Laurence, A., *Parliamentary Army Chaplains, 1642–1651* (Woodbridge, 1990)

Leth, G., 'A Protestant public sphere: the early European newspaper press', in *Studies in Newspaper and Periodical History* (1993)

Levy, F., 'The decorum of news', in J. Raymond, ed., *News, Newspapers and Society in Early Modern Britain* (London, 1999)

————— 'Hayward, Daniel and the beginning of politic history in England', *HLQ* 50 (1987)

————— 'How information spread among the gentry, 1550–1640', *JBS* 21 (1982)

————— 'Staging the news', in A. F. Marotti and M. D. Bristol, eds, *Print, Manuscript and Performance* (Columbus, 2000)

————— 'The tribulations of Christopher Love and the problems of censorship' (paper delivered at SHARP conference, London, 2002)

Limon, J., *Dangerous Matter. English Drama and Politics in 1623/24* (Cambridge, 1986)

Lindenbaum, P., 'Authors and publishers in the late seventeenth century: new evidence on their relations', *The Library*, 6th series 17 (1995)

————— 'Authors and publishers in the late seventeenth century, II: Brabazon Aylmer and the mysteries of the trade', *The Library*, 7th series 3 (2002)

————— 'John Milton and the republican mode of literary production', *Yearbook of English Studies* 2 (1991)

————— 'John Playford: music and politics in the Interregnum', *HLQ* 64 (2001)

Lindley, K., *Fenland Riots and the English Revolution* (London, 1982)

————— 'The impact of the 1641 rebellion upon England and Wales, 1641–5', *IHS* 18 (1972)

————— 'London and popular freedom in the 1640s', in R. C. Richardson and G. M. Ridden, eds, *Freedom and the English Revolution* (Manchester, 1986)

Little, P., 'The Irish Independents and Viscount Lisle's lieutenancy of Ireland', *HJ* 44 (2001)

Liu, Tai, *Puritan London* (London, 1986)

Loach, J., 'The function of ceremonial in the reign of Henry VIII', *P&P* 142 (1994)

———— 'The Marian establishment and the printing press', *EHR* 101 (1986)

———— 'Pamphlets and politics 1553–9', *BIHR* 48 (1975)

Loades, D., 'Books and the English reformation prior to 1558', in J. F. Gilmont, ed., *The Reformation and the Book* (Aldershot, 1998)

———— 'Illicit presses and clandestine printing in England, 1520–1590', in A. C. Duke and C. A. Tamse, eds, *Too Might to be Free. Censorship and the Press in England and the Netherlands* (Zutphen, 1987)

———— 'The press under the early Tudors', *Transactions of the Cambridge Bibliographical Society* 4 (1964)

———— 'The theory and practice of censorship in sixteenth century England', in *Politics, Censorship and the English Reformation* (London, 1991)

Loewenstein, J., 'Wither and professional work', in A. F. Marotti and M. D. Bristol, eds., *Print, Manuscript and Performance. The Changing Relations of the Media in Early Modern England* (Columbus, 2000)

Love, H., *Attributing Authorship* (Cambridge, 2002)

———— 'Preacher and publisher: Oliver Heywood and Thomas Parkhurst', *Studies in Bibliography* 31 (1978)

———— *Scribal Publication in Seventeenth Century England* (Oxford, 1993)

Lucas, P. J., 'The growth and development of English literary patronage in the later Middle Ages and early Renaissance', *The Library*, 6th series 4 (1982)

MacGillivray, R., *Restoration Historians and the English Civil War* (The Hague, 1974)

Madan, F., 'Milton, Salmasius and Dugard', *The Library* 4 (1923)

———— *A New Bibliography of the Eikon Basilike* (Oxford Bibliographical Society Publications, new series 3, 1949).

———— *Oxford Books* (3 vols, Oxford, 1895–1931)

Mahoney, M., 'The Presbyterian party in the Long Parliament, 2 July 1644–3 June 1647' (Oxford University DPhil, 1973)

———— 'Presbyterianism in the City of London, 1645–1647', *HJ* 22 (1979)

———— 'The Savile affair and the politics of the Long Parliament', *PH* 7 (1988)

Malcolm, J, L., *Caesar's Due. Loyalty and King Charles, 1642–1646* (London, 1983)

Maltzahn, N. von, 'Henry Neville and the art of the possible: a republican *Letter Sent to General Monk* (1660)', *Seventeenth Century* 7 (1992)

Mann, A. J., *The Scottish Book Trade, 1500 to 1720* (East Linton, 2000)

———— '"Triumphs, trials and tribulations": patterns of censorship in early modern Scotland' (paper delivered at SHARP conference, London, 2002)

Marcus, L. S., 'From oral delivery to print in the speeches of Elizabeth I', in Marotti and Bristol, eds, *Print, Manuscript and Performance*

Margoliouth, H. M., ed., *The Poems and Letters of Andrew Marvell* (2 vols, Oxford, 1971)

Marotti, A. F., 'Patronage, poetry and print', in *Politics, Patronage and Literature in England, 1558–1658* (Yearbook of English Studies, 21, 1991)

Martin, H. J., *Print, Power and People in 17th-Century France* (trans. D. Gerard, London, 1993)

Martin, J. W., 'The Marian regime's failure to understand the importance of printing', *HLQ* 44 (1981)

Martinich, A. P., *Hobbes, A Biography* (Cambridge, 1999)

Maslen, K. I. D., 'Printing charges: inference and evidence', *Studies in Bibliography* 24 (1971)

Mason, W. G., 'The annual output of Wing-listed titles, 1649–1684', *The Library*, 5th series 29 (1978)

Masson, D., *The Life of John Milton* (7 vols, London, 1871–80)

Matthews, A. G., *Calamy Revised* (Oxford, 1934)

Matthews, N. L., *William Sheppard, Cromwell's Law Reformer* (Cambridge, 1984)

Mattingley, G., 'William Allen and Catholic propaganda in England', in *Aspects de la Propagande Religieuse* (Travaux d'Humanisme et Renaissance 28, 1957)

May, S. W., 'Tudor aristocrats and the mythical stigma of print', *Renaissance Papers* (1980)

Mayers, R. E., '"Real and practicable, not imaginary and notional": Sir Henry Vane, *A Healing Question* and the problems of the protectorate', *Albion* 27 (1995)

McCann, T. J., '"The known style of a dedication is flattery": Anthony Browne, 2nd Viscount Montague of Cowdray and his Sussex flatterers', *Recusant History* 19 (1989).

McConica, J. K., *English Humanists and Reformation Politics* (Oxford, 1965)

McCoog, T. M., 'The slightest suspicion of avarice: the finances of the English Jesuit mission', *Recusant History* 19 (1988)

McCullough, P., 'Making dead men speak: Laudianism, print, and the works of Lancelot Andrewes, 1626–1642', *HJ* 41 (1998)

——— *Sermons at Court. Politics and Religion in Elizabethan and Jacobean Preaching* (Cambridge, 1998)

McElligott, G. J., 'Propaganda and censorship: the underground royalist newsbooks, 1647–1650' (Cambridge University PhD, 2000)

McGregor, J. F., and Reay, B., eds, *Radical Religion in the English Revolution* (Oxford, 1984)

McHardy, A. K., 'Liturgy and propaganda in the diocese of Lincoln during the hundred years war', *SCH* 18 (1982)

McKenna, J. W., 'Henry VI of England and the dual monarchy: aspects of royal political propaganda 1422–1432', *Journal of the Warburg and Courtauld Institutes* 28 (1965)

——— 'Piety and propaganda: the cult of King Henry VI', in B. Rowland, ed., *Chaucer and Middle English Studies* (London, 1974)

McKenzie, D. F., *Bibliography and the Sociology of Texts* (London, 1986)

——— 'Printers of the mind: some notes on bibliographical theories and printing house practices', *Studies in Bibliography* 22 (1969)

McKitterick, D., *A History of Cambridge University Press* (2 vols, Cambridge, 1992–98)

McLuhan, M., *The Gutenberg Galaxy* (London, 1962)

McLure, M., *The Paul's Cross Sermons, 1534–1642* (Toronto, 1958)

McNeil, W., 'Milton and Salmasius, 1649', *EHR* 80 (1965)

Mendle, M., *Dangerous Positions* (Alabama, 1984)

―――― 'De facto freedom, de facto authority: press and parliament 1640–1643', *HJ* 38 (1995)

―――― 'The Great Council of Parliament and the first ordinances: the constitutional theory of the civil war', *JBS* 31 (1992)

―――― 'Grub Street and Parliament at the beginning of the English revolution', in J. D. Popkin, ed., *Media and Revolution* (Lexington, 1995)

―――― *Henry Parker and the English Civil War* (Cambridge, 1995)

―――― 'Henry Parker: the public's privado', in G. J. Schochet, ed., *Religion, Resistance and Civil War* (Washington, 1990)

―――― 'News and the pamphlet culture of mid-seventeenth century England', in B. Dooley and S. Baron eds, *The Politics of Information in Early Modern Europe* (London, 2001)

―――― 'Putney's pronouns: identity and indemnity in the great debate', in M. Mendle, ed., *The Putney Debates of 1647* (Cambridge, 2001)

―――― 'The ship money case, *The Case of Shipmony*, and the development of Henry Parker's parliamentary absolutism', *HJ* 32 (1989)

Merritt, J. F., 'The pastoral tight-rope: a Puritan pedagogue in Jacobean London', in T. Cogswell, R. Cust, and P. Lake, eds, *Politics, Religion and Popularity in Early Stuart Britain* (Cambridge, 2002)

Miller, A. C., 'Joseph Jane's account of Cornwall during the civil war', *EHR* 90 (1975)

Miller, E. H., *The Professional Writer in Elizabethan England* (Cambridge, Mass., 1959)

Miller, L., 'Before Milton was famous: January 8, 1649/50', *Milton Quarterly* 21 (1987)

―――― *John Milton and the Oldenburg Safeguard* (New York, 1985)

―――― *John Milton's Writings in the Anglo-Dutch Negotiations, 1651–1654* (Pittsburgh, 1992)

Milton, A., 'The creation of Laudianism: a new approach', in T. Cogswell, R. Cust and P. Lake, eds, *Politics, Religion and Popularity in Early Stuart Britain* (Cambridge, 2002)

―――― 'The Laudians and the Church of Rome, c.1625–1640' (Cambridge University PhD, 1989)

―――― 'Licensing, censorship and religious orthodoxy in early Stuart England', *HJ* 41 (1998)

―――― 'The unchanged peacemaker, John Dury, and the politics of irenicism in England, 1628–1643', in M. Greengrass, M. Leslie, and T. Raylor, eds, *Samuel Hartlib and Universal Reformation* (Cambridge, 1994)

Morgan, I., *Prince Charles' Puritan Chaplain* (London, 1957)

Morrill, J., *Cheshire 1630–1660* (Oxford, 1974)

Morrill, J., and Baker, P., 'The case of the armie truly re-stated', in Mendle, ed., *Putney Debates*

Morton, A. L., *The World of the Ranters* (London, 1970)

Mousley, A., 'Self, state and seventeenth century news', *Seventeenth Century* 6 (1991)

Muddiman, J. G., *The King's Journalist* (London, 1923)

Murdoch, S, 'The search for Northern allies: Stuart and Cromwellian propagandists and protagonists in Scandinavia, 1649–60', in B. Taithe and T. Thornton, eds, *Propaganda* (Stroud, 1999)

Murphy, V., 'The debate over Henry VIII's first divorce. An analysis of the comptemorary treatises' (Cambridge University PhD, 1984)

———— 'The literature and propaganda of Henry VIII's first divorce', in D. MacCulloch, ed., *The Reign of Henry VIII* (Basingstoke, 1995)

Myers, R., *The Stationers Company Archive* (London, 1990)

Nash, N. F., 'English licenses to print and grants of copyright in the 1640s', *The Library*, 6th series 4 (1982)

Nelson, C., and Seccombe, M., *British Newspapers and Periodicals 1641–1700* (New York, 1987)

Newton, A. P., *The Colonising Activities of the English Puritans* (New Haven, 1944)

Nicholl, C., *A Cup of News. The Life of Thomas Nashe* (London, 1984)

Nobbs, D., 'Philip Nye on church and state', *Cambridge Historical Journal* 5 (1935)

Norbrook, D., '*Areopagitica*, censorship and the early modern public sphere', in R. Burt, ed., *The Administration of Aesthetics* (London, 1994)

———— 'Levelling poetry: George Wither and the English revolution, 1642–1649', *English Literary Renaissance* 21 (1991)

———— 'Lucan, Thomas May, and the creation of a republican literary culture', in K. Sharpe and P. Lake, eds, *Culture and Politics in Early Stuart England* (London, 1994)

———— 'Marvell's 'Horatian Ode' and the politics of genre', in T. Healy and J. Sawday, eds, *Literature and the English Civil War* (Cambridge, 1990)

———— '*The Masque of Truth*: court entertainment and international Protestant politics in the early Stuart period', *Seventeenth Century* 1 (1986)

———— *Poetry, Rhetoric and Politics, 1627–1660* (Cambridge, 1999)

———— 'Safest in storms: George Wither in the 1650s', in D. Margolies and M. Joannou, eds, *Heart of the Heartless World* (London, 1995)

———— *Writing the English Republic* (Cambridge, 1999)

Nowack, T. S., 'Propaganda and the pulpit. Robert Cecil, William Barlow and the Essex and Gunpowder plots', in K. Z. Keller and G. J. Schiffhorst, eds, *The Witness of Times* (Pittsburgh, 1992)

Nutkiewicz, M., 'A rapporteur of the English civil war: the courtly politics of James Howell', *CJH* 25 (1990)

O'Callaghan, M., 'Literary commonwealths: a 1614 print community, *The Shepheards Pipe* and *The Shepherds Hunting*', *Seventeenth Century* 13 (1998)

O'Malley, T., 'Religion and the newspaper press, 1660–1685: a study of the *London Gazette*', in M. Harris and A. Lee, eds, *The Press in English Society from the Seventeenth to Nineteenth Centuries* (London, 1986)

Oastler, C. L., *John Day, the Elizabethan Printer* (Oxford Bibliographical Society, occasional publications, 10, 1975)

Ogilvie, J. D., 'Papers from an army press, 1650', *Edinburgh Bibliographical Society Transactions* 2 (1938–45)

Palmer, W. G., 'Invitation to a beheading: factions in Parliament, the Scots, and the execution of Archbishop Laud in 1645', *Historical Magazine of the Protestant Episcopal Church* 52 (1983)

Parker, H. A., 'The feoffees of impropriations', *Publications of the Colonial Society of Massachusetts* (1906–7)

Parker, W. R., *Milton: A Biography* (2 vols, Oxford, 1968)

Parmelee, L. F., *Good Newes from Fraunce* (Rochester, NY, 1996)

——— 'Printers, patrons, readers and spies: importation of French propaganda in late Elizabethan England', *Sixteenth Century Journal* 25 (1994)

Parry, G., 'The politics of the Jacobean masque', in J. R. Mulryne and M. Shewring, eds, *Theatre and Government under the Early Stuarts* (Cambridge, 1993)

Patterson, A., *Censorship and Interpretation. The Conditions of Writing and Reading in Early Modern England* (Madison, 1984)

——— 'The civic hero in Milton's prose', *Milton Studies* 8 (1975)

Paul, R. S., *The Assembly of the Lord* (Edinburgh, 1985)

Peacey, J., 'Contexts and causes, or, putting the English back into the British civil wars, 1637–42' (paper delivered at NACBS conference, Pasadena, 2000)

——— 'Cromwellian England: a propaganda state?' (forthcoming)

——— '"The counterfeit silly curr": money, politics and the forging of royalist newspapers in the English civil war', *HLQ* (forthcoming)

——— 'The exploitation of captured royal correspondence and Anglo-Scottish relations in the British civil wars, 1645–6', *SHR* 79 (2000)

——— 'Glimpses of Grub Street' (forthcoming)

——— 'Henry Parker and parliamentary propaganda in the English civil wars' (Cambridge University PhD, 1994)

——— 'The hunting of the Leveller: the effectiveness of parliamentarian propaganda, 1647–53' (forthcoming)

——— 'John Lilburne and the Long Parliament', *HJ* 43 (2000)

——— 'Junto practices: printing and publishing and the meaning of texts in the English civil war' (paper delivered at SHARP conference, London, 2002)

———— 'Led by the hand: manucaptors and patronage at Lincoln's Inn in the seventeenth century', *Journal of Legal History* 18 (1997)

———— 'Nibbling at *Leviathan*: politics and theory in England in the 1650s', *HLQ* 61 (1998)

———— 'Order and disorder in Europe: parliamentary agents and royalist thugs 1649–1650', *HJ* 40 (1997)

———— 'The outbreak of the civil wars in the three kingdoms', in B. Coward, ed., *Blackwell Companion to Stuart Britain* (Oxford, 2003)

———— 'The paranoid prelate: Archbishop Laud and the Puritan plot', in B. Coward and J. Swann, eds, *Conspiracies and Conspiracy Theory in Early Modern Britain and Europe, 1500–1800* (forthcoming, Aldershot, 2003)

———— 'Politics, accounts and propaganda in the Long Parliament', in C. R. Kyle and J. Peacey, eds, *Parliament at Work* (Woodbridge, 2002)

———— 'Print detection and political propaganda: a radical press in 1642' (paper delivered at IHR, 2002)

———— 'Reporting a revolution: a failed propaganda campaign', in Peacey, ed., *The Regicides and the Execution of Charles I* (Basingstoke, 2001)

———— 'Seasonable treatises: a godly project of the 1630s', *EHR* 113 (1998)

———— 'The struggle for *Mercurius Britanicus*: factional politics and the parliamentarian press, 1643–6' (forthcoming)

Peacock, E., *Army Lists* (London, 1874)

Pearl, V., *London and the Outbreak of the Puritan Revolution* (Oxford, 1961) 'London Puritans and Scotch fifth columnists: a mid-seventeenth century phenomenon', in A. Hollaender and W. Kellaway, eds, *Studies in London History* (London, 1969)

———— 'London's counter-revolution', in G. E. Aylmer, ed., *The Interregnum* (London, 1972)

———— 'Oliver St John and the middle group in the Long Parliament', *EHR* 81 (1966)

———— 'The royal Independents', *TRHS*, 5th series 18 (1968)

Peck, L. L., 'Benefits, brokers and beneficiaries: the culture of exchange in seventeenth century England', in B. Y. Kunze and D. D. Brautigam, eds, *Court, Country and Culture* (Rochester, 1992)

———— *Northampton. Patronage and Policy at the Court of James I* (London, 1982)

Peters, K., 'Quaker pamphleteering and the development of the Quaker movement, 1652–1656' (Cambridge University PhD, 1996)

———— 'The Quakers quaking: print and the spread of a movement', in S. Wabuda and C. Litzenberger, eds, *Belief and Practice in Reformation England* (Aldershot, 1998)

Pettegree, A., 'Printing and the reformation: the English exception', in P. Marshall and A. Ryrie, eds, The Beginnings of English Protestantism (Cambridge, 2002)

Philipson, J., 'The king's printer in Newcastle-upon-Tyne in 1639', *The Library*, 6th series 11 (1989)

Phillips, J. E., 'George Buchanan and the Sidney circle', *HLQ* 12 (1948)

Phillipson, N. and Skinner, Q., eds, *Political Discourse in Early Modern Britain* (Cambridge, 1993)

Pincus, S., 'Coffee politicians does create: coffeehouses and restoration political culture', *JMH* 67 (1995)

—— *Protestantism and Patriotism. Ideologies and the Making of English Foreign Policy, 1650–1668* (Cambridge, 1996)

Plant, M., *The English Book Trade* (London, 1939)

Plomer, H. R., 'An analysis of the civil war newspaper *Mercurius Civicus*', *The Library*, new series 6 (1905)

—— *A Dictionary of the Booksellers … 1641–1667* (London, 1907)

—— 'The king's printing house under the Stuarts', *The Library*, new series 2 (1901)

—— *A Short History of English Printing, 1476–1900* (London, 1915)

—— 'Some petitions for appointment as master printers called forth by the Star Chamber decree of 1637', *The Library*, 3rd series 10 (1919)

Pocock, J. G. A., 'The history of political thought: a methodological enquiry', in P. Laslett and W. G. Runciman, eds, *Philosophy, Politics and Society*, 2nd series (Oxford, 1962)

—— 'James Harrington and the good old cause: a study of the ideological context of his writings', *JBS* 10 (1970)

—— *The Machiavellian Moment* (Princeton, 1975)

—— 'Texts as events: reflections on the history of political thought', in Sharpe and Zwicker, eds, *Politics of Discourse*

—— 'Thomas May and the narrative of the civil war', in Hirst and Strier, eds, *Writing and Political Engagement*

Pollard, A. W., 'The regulation of the book trade in the sixteenth century', *The Library*, 3rd series 7 (1916)

Potter, L., 'Royal actor as royal martyr: the *Eikon Basilike* and the literary scene in 1649', in G. J. Schochet, ed., *Restoration, Ideology and Revolution* (Washington, 1990)

—— *Secret Rites and Secret Writing. Royalist Literature, 1641–1660* (Cambridge, 1989)

Pottinger, D. T., *The French Book Trade in the Ancien Regime* (Cambridge, Ma., 1958)

Pritchard, A., '*Abuses Stript and Whipt* and Wither's imprisonment', *Review of English Studies*, new series 14 (1963)

—— 'George Wither and the sale of the estate of Charles I', *Modern Philology* 77 (1980)

—— 'George Wither and the Somers Islands', *N&Q* 206 (1961)

—— 'George Wither: the poet as prophet', *Studies in Philology* 59 (1962)

────── 'George Wither's quarrel with the Stationers: an anonymous reply to *The Schollers Purgatory*', *Studies in Philology* 16 (1963)

Raven, J., 'New reading histories, print culture and the identification of change: the case of eighteenth century England', *Social History* 23 (1998)

Raymond, J., 'The cracking of the republican spokes', *Prose Studies* 19 (1996)

────── 'Framing liberty: Marvell's *First Anniversary* and the Instrument of Government', *HLQ* 62 (1999)

────── '*The Great Assises Holden in Parnassus*: the reputation and reality of seventeenth century newsbooks', *Studies in Newspaper and Periodical History* (1994)

────── *The Invention of the Newspaper. English Newsbooks, 1641–1649* (Oxford, 1996)

────── 'John Streater and The Grand Politick Informer', *HJ* 41 (1998)

────── '"A mercury with a winged conscience": Marchamont Nedham, monopoly and censorship', *Media History* 4 (1998)

────── ed., *News, Newspapers and Society in Early Modern Britain* (London, 1999)

────── 'The newspapers, public opinion, and the public sphere in the seventeenth century', in J. Raymond, ed., *News, Newspapers, and Society in Early Modern Britain*

Rea, R. R., *The English Press in Politics, 1760–1774* (Lincoln, Nebraska, 1963)

Read, C., 'William Cecil and Elizabethan public relations', in S. T. Bindoff, J. Hurstfield and C. H. Williams, eds, *Elizabethan Government and Society* (London, 1961)

Rex, R,. 'The English campaign against Luther in the 1520s', *TRHS*, 5th series 39 (1989)

Richards, J., 'His nowe majestie and the English monarchy: the kingship of Charles I before 1640', *P&P* 113 (1986)

Richards, J. O., *Party Propaganda Under Queen Anne* (Athens, Ga, 1972)

Richardson, B., *Printing, Writers and Readers in Renaissance Italy* (Cambridge, 1999)

Richardson, L., 'Tacitus, Sir John Hayward and the historiography of the 1590s' (paper delivered at the IHR, London, 5 June 2000)

Richardson, R. C., *Puritanism in North West England* (Manchester, 1972)

Rigney, J., 'To lye upon a stationers stall, like a piece of coarse flesh in a Shambles': the sermon, print and the English civil war', in L. A. Ferrell and P. McCullough, eds, *The English Sermon Revised*

Robertson, M. L., 'Thomas Cromwell's servants: the ministerial household in early Tudor government and society' (UCLA PhD, 1975)

Roebuck, G., *Clarendon and Cultural Continuity* (London, 1981)

Rose, J. 'The history of books: revised and enlarged', in H. T. Mason, ed., *The Darnton Debate* (Oxford, 1998)

Rosenberg, E., *Leicester, Patron of Letters* (New York, 1955)

Ross, C., 'Rumour, propaganda and popular opinion during the Wars of the Roses', in R. A. Griffiths, ed., *Patronage, the Crown and the Provinces* (Gloucester, 1981)

Rostenberg, L., *The Minority Press and the English Crown. A Study in Repression 1558–1625* (The Hague, 1971)

—— 'Nathaniel Butter and Nicholas Bourne. First "masters of the staple"', *The Library*, 5th series 12 (1957)

—— 'The new world: John Bellamy, "pilgrim" publisher of London', in *Literary, Scientific, Religious and Legal Publishing, Printing and Bookselling in England 1551–1700* (2 vols, New York, 1965)

—— 'Republican credo: William Dugard, pedagogue and political apostate', in *Literary, Political Scientific, Religious and Legal Publishing, Printing, and Bookselling in England, 1551–1700* (2 vols, New York, 1965)

—— 'The regeneration of man and trade: Michael Sparke, Puritan crusader', in *Literary, Political Scientific, Religious and Legal Publishing, Printing, and Bookselling in England, 1551–1700* (2 vols, New York, 1965)

—— 'William Dugard, pedagogue and printer to the commonwealth', *Papers of the Bibliographical Society of America* 52 (1958)

Rowen, H. H., 'Lieuwe van Aitzema: a soured but knowing eye', in P. Mack and M. C. Jacob, eds, *Politics and Culture in Early Modern Europe* (Cambridge, 1987)

Roy, I., 'The royalist council of war, 1642–6', *BIHR* 35 (1962)

Rusche, H., '*Merlini Anglici*: astrology and propaganda from 1644 to 1651', *EHR* 80 (1965)

—— 'Prophecies and propaganda, 1641 to 1651', *EHR* 84 (1969)

Russell, C., 'The Anglo-Scottish union, 1603–1643: a success?', in A. Fletcher and P. Roberts, eds, *Religion, Culture and Society in Early Modern Britain* (Cambridge, 1994)

—— *The Fall of the British Monarchies, 1637–1642* (Oxford, 1991)

—— *Parliaments and English Politics, 1621–1629* (Oxford, 1979)

Sachse, W. L., 'English pamphlet support for Charles I, November 1648-January 1649', in W. A. Aiken and B. D. Henning, eds, *Conflict in Stuart England* (London, 1960)

Sanders, V., 'The household of Archbishop Parker and the influencing of public opinion', *JEH* 34 (1983)

—— 'John Whitgift: primate, privy councillor and propagandist', *Anglican and Episcopal History* 56 (1987)

Sanderson, J., 'The *Answer to the Nineteen Propositions* revisited', *Political Studies* 32 (1984)

—— 'Phillip Hunton's appeasement', *HPT* 3 (1982)

—— 'Serpent Salve, 1643: the royalism of John Bramhall', *JEH* 25 (1974)

Saslow, E. L., 'Dryden as historiographer royal, and the authorship of *His Majesties Declaration Defended*', *Modern Philology* 75 (1978)

Saunders, J. W., 'The stigma of print. A note on the social bases of Tudor poetry', *Essays in Criticism* 1 (1951)

Sawyer, J. K., *Printed Poison. Pamphlet Propaganda, Faction Politics and the Public Sphere in Early Seventeenth Century France* (Berkeley, 1990)

Scattergood, V. J., *Politics and Poetry in the Fifteenth Century* (London, 1971)

Schochet, G., 'The English revolution in the history of political thought', in B. Y. Kunze and D. D. Brautigam, eds, *Court, Country and Culture* (Rochester, NY, 1992)

Schonhorn, M., *Defoe's Politics. Parliament, Power, Kingship and Robinson Crusoe* (Cambridge, 1991)

Schwoerer, L., *The Declaration of Rights, 1689* (London, 1981)

——— 'Liberty of the press and public opinion, 1660–1695', in J. R. Jones, ed., *Liberty Secured? Britain Before and After 1688* (Stanford, 1992)

——— 'Propaganda in the revolution of 1688–89', *AHR* 82 (1977)

Scott, D., 'The Barwis affair: political allegiance and the Scots during the British civil wars', *EHR* 115 (2000)

——— 'The 'Northern gentlemen', the parliamentary Independents and Anglo-Scottish relations in the Long Parliament', *HJ* 42 (1999)

Scott, J., *Algernon Sidney and the English Republic, 1623–1677* (Cambridge, 1988)
Algernon Sidney and the Restoration Crisis, 1677–1683 (Cambridge, 1991)

Scribner, R. W., *For the Sake of Simple Folk. Popular Propaganda for the German Reformation* (Oxford, 1994)

Seaver, P., *The Puritan Lectureships* (Stanford, 1970)

Seaward, P., 'A restoration publicist: James Howell and the Earl of Clarendon, 1661–6', *HR* 61 (1988)

Sessions, W. K., *The King's Printer at Newcastle upon Tyne in 1639, at Bristol in 1643–1645, at Exeter in 1645–1646* (York, 1982)

——— *The King's Printer at York in 1642, at Shrewsbury in 1642–3* (York, 1981)

Shaaber, M. A., 'The meaning of the imprint in early printed books', *The Library*, new series 24 (1943)

——— *Some Forerunners of the Newspaper in England, 1476–1622* (Philadelphia, 1929)

Shagan, E., 'Constructing discord: ideology, propaganda and English responses to the Irish rebellion of 1641', *JBS* 36 (1997)

Shapiro, B. J., *John Wilkins, 1614–1672* (Berkeley, Ca., 1969)

Sharp, A., 'John Lilburne and the Long Parliament's *Book of Declarations*: a radical's exploitation of the words of authorities', *HPT* 9 (1988)

Sharpe, J., '"Last dying speeches": religion, ideology and public execution in seventeenth century England', *P&P* 107 (1985)

Sharpe, K., 'Court and communication', *HJ* 25 (1982)

——— *Criticism and Compliment* (Cambridge, 1987)

——— 'Crown, parliament and locality: government and communication in early Stuart England', *EHR* 101 (1986)

———— 'The king's writ: royal authors and royal authority in early modern England', in K. Sharpe and P. Lake, eds, *Culture and Politics in Early Stuart England* (Basingstoke, 1994)

———— 'The politics of literature in renaissance England', in *idem, Politics and Ideas in Early Stuart England* (London, 1989)

———— 'Religion, rhetoric and revolution in seventeenth century England', *HLQ* 57 (1995)

Sharpe, K., and Zwicker, S., eds, *Politics of Discourse. The Literature and History of Seventeenth Century England* (Berkeley, 1987)

Shaw, H., *The Levellers* (London, 1968)

Shaw, W. A., *A History of the English Church During the Civil Wars and Under the Commonwealth* (2 vols, London, 1900)

Sheavyn, P., The *Literary Profession in the Elizabethan Age* (Manchester, 1967)

Sherman, W., *John Dee: The Politics of Reading and Writing in the Renaissance* (Amherst, Mass., 1994)

Shuffleton, F., *Thomas Hooker* (Princeton, 1977)

Siebert, F. S., *Freedom of the Press in England 1476–1776* (Urbana, 1965)

Silver, R., 'Financing the publication of early New England sermons', *Studies in Bibliography* 11 (1958)

Sippell, T., 'The testimony of Joshua Sprigge', *The Journal of the Friends Historical Society* 38 (1946)

Sirluck, E., 'To Your Tents, O Israel: a lost pamphlet', *HLQ* 19 (1956)

Skerpan, E., *The Rhetoric of Politics in the English Revolution, 1642–1660* (London, 1992)

Skinner, Q., 'Conquest and consent: Thomas Hobbes and the Engagement controversy', in G. Aylmer, ed., *The Interregnum* (Basingstoke, 1972)

———— 'The ideological context of Hobbes's political thought', *HJ* 9 (1966)

Slavin, A. J., 'Profitable Studies: Humanists and Government in Early Tudor England', *Viator* 1 (1970)

Smart, I. M., 'An interim period in royalist political writing, 1647–8', *Durham University Journal* 76 (1983)

Smith, D. B., 'Francois Hotman', *SHR* 13 (1916)

Smith, D., *Constitutional Royalism and the Search for Settlement, 1640–49* (Cambridge, 1994)

———— 'The political career of Edward Sackville, 4th Earl of Dorset' (Cambridge University PhD, 1990)

Smith, N., ed., *A Collection of Ranter Writings* (London, 1983)

———— *Literature and Revolution in England, 1640–1660* (New Haven, 1994)

———— 'Popular republicanism in the 1650s: John Streater's 'heroick mechanicks', in D. Armitage, A. Himy, Q. Skinner, eds, *Milton and Republicanism* (Cambridge, 1998)

Snapp, H. F., 'The impeachment of Roger Maynwaring', *HLQ* 30 (1967)

Snow, V,. *Essex the Rebel* (Lincoln, Nebraska, 1970)

———— 'An inventory of the Lord General's library, 1646', *The Library*, 5th series 21 (1966)

Soden, S., *Godfrey Goodman, Bishop of Gloucester, 1583–1656* (London, 1953)

Solomon, H. M., 'The *Gazette* and Antistatist propaganda: the medium of print in the first half of the seventeenth century', *CJH* 9 (1974)

———— *Public Welfare, Science and Propaganda in Seventeenth Century France* (Princeton, 1972)

Solt, L. F., 'John Saltmarsh, New Model Army chaplain', *JEH* 2 (1951)

———— 'William Dell: New Model Army chaplain', *Church Quarterly Review* 155 (1954)

Soman, A., 'Press, pulpit and censorship in France before Richelieu', *Proceedings of the American Philosophical Society* 120 (1976)

Sommerville, C. J., *The News Revolution in England* (Oxford, 1996)

Sommerville, J. P., 'History and theory: the Norman Conquest in early Stuart political thought', *Political Studies* 34 (1986)

———— 'John Selden, the law of nature, and the origins of government', *HJ* 27 (1984)

———— *Politics and Ideology in England, 1603–1640* (London, 1986)

———— *Thomas Hobbes: Political Ideas in Historical Context* (Basingstoke, 1992)

Speck, W., 'Politics and the press', in G. Holmes, ed., *After the Glorious Revolution* (London, 1969)

———— 'Politics and the press', in M. Harris and A. Lee, eds., *The Press in English Society from the Seventeenth to Nineteenth Centuries* (London, 1986)

Spencer, L., 'The politics of George Thomason', *The Library*, 5th series 14 (1959)

———— 'The professional and literary connexions of George Thomason', *The Library*, 5th series 13 (1958)

Sprunger, K. L., 'The Dutch career of Thomas Hooker', *New England Quarterly* 46 (1973)

———— *Dutch Puritanism* (Leiden, 1982)

———— *The Learned Doctor William Ames* (Urbana, 1972)

———— *Trumpets from the Tower. English Puritan Printing in the Netherlands, 1600–1640* (Leiden, 1994)

Spufford, M., 'First steps in literacy: the reading and writing experiences of the humblest seventeenth century spiritual autobiographies', *Social History* 4 (1979)

———— *Small Books and Pleasant Histories: Popular Fiction and its Readership in Seventeenth Century England* (London, 1981)

Squibb, G. D., *Founders' Kin* (Oxford, 1972)

Stearns, R. P., *The Strenuous Puritan. Hugh Peter, 1598–1660* (Urbana, 1954)

———— 'The Weld-Peter mission to England', *Publications of the Colonial Society of Massachusetts* 32 (1937)

Stern, V. F., *Gabriel Harvey* (Oxford, 1979)

Sterry-Cooper, W., *Edward Winslow* (Birmingham, 1953)

Stevenson, D., 'A revolutionary regime and the press: the Scottish covenanters and their printers 1638–51', *The Library*, 6th series 7 (1985)

———— 'Scotland's first newspaper, 1648', *The Bibliothek. A Scottish Journal of Bibliography and Allied Topics* 10 (1981)

Sutherland, J., *The Restoration Newspaper and its Development* (Cambridge, 1986)

Tanselle, G. T., 'Printing history and other history', *Studies in Bibliography* 48 (1995)

Targett, S., 'The premier scribbler himself: Sir Robert Walpole and the management of political opinion', *Studies in Newspaper and Periodical History* (1994)

Thomas, K., 'The meaning of literacy in early modern England', in G. Baumann, ed., *The Written Word. Literacy in Transition* (Oxford, 1986)

Thomas, P. W., *Sir John Berkenhead, 1617–1679* (Oxford, 1969)

Thompson, A. B., 'Licensing the press: the career of G. R. Weckherlin during the personal rule of Charles I', *HJ* 41 (1998)

Thomson, P., 'The literature of patronage, 1580–1630', *Essays in Criticism* 2 (1952)

Thornton, T., 'Propaganda, political communication and the problem of English responses to the introduction of printing', in B. Taithe and T. Thornton, eds, *Propaganda. Political Rhetoric and Identity, 1300–2000* (Stroud, 1999)

Tibbetts, M. J., 'Parliamentary parties under Oliver Cromwell' (Bryn Mawr University PhD, 1944)

Todd, C., *Political Bias, Censorship and the Dissolution of the 'Official' Press in Eighteenth Century France* (Lampeter, 1991)

Took, P. M., 'Government and the printing trade, 1540–1560' (London University PhD, 1979)

Toon, P., *God's Statesman* (Exeter, 1971)

Trevor-Roper, H., *Archbishop Laud, 1573–1645* (London, 1963, 3rd edn, London, 1988)

———— 'The Fast sermons of the Long Parliament', in *Religion, the Reformation and Social Change* (London, 1973)

———— 'The Great Tew circle', in *idem, Catholics, Anglicans and Puritans* (London, 1989)

———— 'Three foreigners: the philosophers of the Puritan revolution', in *idem, Religion, Reformation, and Social Change*

Tuck, R., '"The ancient law of freedom": John Selden and the civil war', in J. Morrill, ed., *Reactions to the English Civil War, 1642–1649* (Basingstoke, 1982)

———— *Hobbes* (Oxford, 1989)

———— *Natural Rights Theories* (Cambridge, 1979)

———— *Philosophy and Government, 1572–1651* (Cambridge, 1993)

Tully, J., ed., *Meaning and Context. Quentin Skinner and his Critics* (Oxford, 1988)

Turnbull, G. H., *Hartlib, Dury and Comenius* (London, 1947)

———— 'John Hall's letters to Samuel Hartlib', *Review of English Studies*, new series 4 (1953)

Underdown, D., 'The Man in the Moon: loyalty and libel in popular politics, 1640–1660', in *idem, A Freeborn People* (Oxford, 1996)

———— 'Party management in the recruiter elections, 1645–48', *EHR* 83 (1968)

———— *Pride's Purge* (Oxford, 1971)

———— *Royalist Conspiracy in England, 1649–1660* (New Haven, 1960)

Usher, R. G., *The Reconstruction of the English Church* (2 vols, London, 1910)

Vernon, E. C., 'The Sion College conclave and London Presbyterianism during the English Revolution' (Cambridge University PhD, 1999)

Voss, P. J., 'Books for sale: advertising and patronage in late Elizabethan England', *Sixteenth Century Journal* 29 (1998)

———— *Elizabethan News Pamphlets* (Pittsburgh, 2001)

Walker, E. C., *William Dell, Master Puritan* (Cambridge, 1970)

Walker, G., *John Skelton and the Politics of the 1520s* (Cambridge, 1988)

Walker, R. B., 'The newspaper press in the reign of William III', *HJ* 17 (1974)

Wall, J. N., 'The reformation in England and the typographical revolution', in G. P. Tyson and S. S. Wagonheim, eds, *Print and Culture in the Renaissance* (New York, 1986)

Wallace, J. M., *Destiny His Choice* (Cambridge, 1980)

———— 'The Engagement controversy, 1649–1652', *Bulletin of the New York Public Library* 68 (1964)

Wallis, P. J., *William Crashawe, The Sheffield Puritan* (Transactions of the Hunter Archaeological Society, 8, 1960–63)

Walsham, A., '"Domme preachers": post-reformation English Catholicism and the culture of print', *P&P* 168 (2000)

———— '"The fatall vesper": providentialism and anti-popery in late Jacobean London', *P&P* 144 (1994)

———— '"A glose of godlines": Philip Stubbes, Elizabethan Grub Street and the invention of Puritanism', in S. Wabuda and C. Litzenberger, eds, *Belief and Practice in Reformation England* (Aldershot, 1998)

———— *Providence in Early Modern England* (Oxford, 1999)

Walter, J., *Understanding Popular Violence in the English Revolution* (Cambridge, 1999)

Warner, J. C., *Henry VIII's Divorce. Literature and the Politics of the Printing Press* (Woodbridge, 1998)

Watt, T., *Cheap Print and Popular Piety, 1550–1640* (Cambridge, 1991)

Weber, H., *Paper Bullets. Print and Kingship under Charles II* (Lexington, 1996)

Weber, K., *Lucius Cary, Second Viscount Falkland* (New York, 1940)

Webster, C., 'Benjamin Worsley: engineering for universal reform from the invisible college to the Navigation Act', in M. Greengrass, M. Leslie, T. Raylor, eds, *Samuel Hartlib and Universal Reformation* (Cambridge, 1994)

————— *The Great Instauration* (London, 1975)

Webster, T., *Godly Clergy in Early Stuart England* (Cambridge, 1997)

Weinzierl, M. P., 'Parliament and the army in England, 1659: constitutional thought and the struggle for control', *PER* 2 (1982)

Welsby, P. A., *George Abbot. The Unwanted Archbishop, 1562–1633* (London, 1962)

Weston, C. C., and Greenberg, J. R., *Subjects and Sovereigns* (Cambridge, 1981)

Wheale, N., *Writing and Society. Literacy, Print and Politics in Britain, 1590–1660* (London, 1999)

White, B. R., 'Henry Jessey in the great rebellion', in R. Buick Knox, ed., *Reformation, Conformity and Dissent* (London, 1977)

White, P. W., 'Patronage, Protestantism and stage propaganda in early Elizabethan England', in C. C. Brown, ed., *Patronage, Politics and Literary Traditions in England, 1558–1658* (Detroit, 1991)

White, P., *Predestination, Policy, and Polemic* (Cambridge, 1992)

Whitehead, B. T., *Brags and Boasts. Propaganda in the Year of the Armada* (Stroud, 1994)

Wilcher, R., *The Writing of Royalism, 1628–1660* (Cambridge, 2001)

Wilding, M., *Dragons Teeth. Literature in the English Revolution* (Oxford, 1987)

Williams, C. M., 'Extremist tactics in the Long Parliament, 1642–1643', *Historical Studies* 57 (1971)

Williams, F. B., *Index of Dedications and Commendatory Verses in English Books Before 1641* (London, 1962)

————— 'The Laudian imprimatur', *The Library*, 5th series 15 (1960)

Williams, J. B., 'Fresh light on Cromwell at Drogheda', *The Nineteenth Century and After* 72 (1912)

————— 'Henry Walker, journalist of the commonwealth', *Nineteenth Century and After* 65 (1908)

————— *A History of English Journalism* (London, 1908)

————— 'The newsbooks and letters of news of the Restoration', *EHR* 23 (1908)

Willson, D. H., 'James I and his literary assistants', *HLQ* 8 (1944)

Wilson, C., *Profit and Power* (London, 1957)

Wilson, J. F., 'Another look at John Canne', *Church History* 33 (1964) *Pulpit in Parliament, Puritanism During the English Civil Wars 1640–1648* (Princeton, 1969)

Winger, H. W., 'Regulations relating to the book trade in London from 1357–1586' (Illinois University PhD, 1953)

Winn, J. A., *John Dryden and His World* (New Haven, 1987)

Wiseman, S., *Drama and Politics in the English Civil War* (Cambridge, 1998)

Wood, A., *Riot, Rebellion and Popular Politics in Early Modern England* (Basingstoke, 2002)

Woodfield, D. B., *Surreptitious Printing in England, 1550–1640* (New York, 1973)

Woolf, D., 'Conscience, consistency and ambition in the career and writings of James Howell', in J. Morrill, P. Slack and D. Woolf, eds, *Public Duty and Private Conscience in Seventeenth Century England* (Oxford, 1993)

—— 'News, history and the construction of the present in early modern England', in B. Dooley and S. Baron eds, *The Politics of Information in Early Modern Europe* (London, 2001)

Woolrych, A., *Commonwealth to Protectorate* (Oxford, 1982)

—— 'Introduction', in *The Complete Prose Works of John Milton VII* (New Haven, 1980)

—— 'Milton and Cromwell: "a short but scandalous night of interruption"?', in M. Lieb and J. T. Shawcross, eds, *Achievements of the Left Hand: Essays on the Prose of John Milton* (Amherst, 1974)

—— 'Yorkshire and the Restoration', *Yorkshire Archaeological Journal* 39 (1958)

Wootton, D., ed., *Divine Right and Democracy* (Harmondsworth, 1986)

—— 'From rebellion to revolution: the crisis of the winter of 1642/3 and the origins of civil war radicalism', *EHR* 105 (1990)

Worden, B., 'Classical republicanism and the Puritan revolution', in H. Lloyd Jones, V. Pearl, and B. Worden, eds, *History and Imagination* (London, 1981)

—— 'Harrington's 'Oceana': origins and aftermath, 1651–1660', in D. Wootton, ed., *Republicanism, Liberty and Commercial Society, 1649–1776* (Stanford, 1994)

—— 'James Harrington and the commonwealth of Oceana, 1656', in Wootton, ed., *Republicanism*

—— 'John Milton and Oliver Cromwell', in I. Gentles, J. Morrill and B. Worden, eds, *Soldiers, Writers and Statesmen of the English Revolution* (Cambridge, 1998)

—— 'Literature and political censorship in early modern England', in A. C. Duke and C. A. Tamse, eds, *Too Mighty to be Free* (Zutphen, 1987)

—— 'Marchamont Nedham and the beginnings of English republicanism, 1649–1656', in D. Wootton, ed., *Republicanism, Liberty, and Commercial Society, 1649–1776* (Stanford, 1994)

—— 'Milton and Marchamont Nedham', in D. Armitage, A. Himy, and Q. Skinner, eds, *Milton and Republicanism* (Cambridge, 1998)

—— 'Providence and politics in Cromwellian England', *P&P* 109 (1985)

—— *The Rump Parliament* (Cambridge, 1974)

—— '"Wit in a roundhead": the dilemma of Marchamont Nedham', in S. D. Amussen and M. A. Kishlansky, eds, *Political Culture and Cultural Politics in Early Modern England* (Manchester, 1995)

Woudhuysen, H. R., *Sir Philip Sidney and the Circulation of Manuscripts 1558–1640* (Oxford, 1996)

Wright, L. B., 'Propaganda against James I's "appeasement" of Spain', *HLQ* 6 (1943)

Zagorin, P., 'The authorship of *Mans Mortalitie*', *The Library*, 5th series 5 (1950)

——— *A History of Political Thought in the English Revolution* (New York, 1966)

Zaller, R., 'The figure of the tyrant in English revolutionary thought', *JHI* 54 (1993)

Zaret, D., *Origins of Democratic Culture* (Princeton, 2000)

——— 'Religion, science and printing in the public spheres in seventeenth century England', in C. Calhoun, ed., *Habermas and the Public Sphere* (London, 1997)

Zeeveld, W. G., 'Richard Morison, official apologist for Henry VIII', *Publications of the Modern Language Association* 55 (1940)

Zwicker, S., *Lines of Authority. Politics and English Literary Culture, 1649–1689* (London, 1993)

Index